# Company Law in Uganda

**David J. Bakibinga**



Fountain Publishers

Fountain Publishers
P.O. Box 488
Kampala


First published 2001



ISBN 9970 02 244 X

---

Cataloguing-in-publication Data

Bakibinga J. David
Company Law in Uganda – Kampala: Fountain Publishers, 2001
295 p. 25cm
Includes index

ISBN 9979 02 244 X
1. Laws - Uganda 2. Company law – Uganda 3. Commercial laws – Uganda
346.066'096761

# CONTENTS


| | |
|---|---|
| *Table of Cases* | v |
| *Table of Statutes* | xxiv |
| *Preface* | xxxiii |
| **1. INTRODUCTION** | **1** |
| Law applicable | 1 |
| General features of company law | 1 |
| The company and society | 2 |
| The need for reform | 3 |
| **2. NATURE AND CONSEQUENCES OF INCORPORATIONS** | **4** |
| Nature | 4 |
| Consequences | 6 |
| Lifting the veil of incorporation | 8 |
| Incorporated company distinguished from other associations | 15 |
| **3. PROMOTION AND FORMATION OF THE COMPANY** | **19** |
| Promotion | 19 |
| Formation of a company | 23 |
| **4. THE MEMORANDUM OF ASSOCIATION** | **27** |
| General | 27 |
| Contents of the memorandum | 27 |
| The rule and its purpose | 29 |
| Application of the doctrine | 30 |
| Extension of the rule? | 34 |
| Who may invoke the doctrine? | 35 |
| Reform of the rule | 36 |
| Conclusion | 37 |
| **5. ARTICLES OF ASSOCIATION** | **41** |
| Introduction | 41 |
| Contents of the articles | 42 |
| The contractual effect of the memorandum and articles | 43 |
| Effects of articles incorporated into or underlying contracts | 45 |
| Alteration of the articles | 47 |
| **6. COMPANY FINANCE** | **51** |
| Ways of raising capital | 51 |
| Underwriting | 51 |
| The principle of disclosure and the prospectus | 52 |
| Allotment | 55 |
| Return of allotments | 57 |

**7. LIABILITY IN RESPECT OF PROSPECTUS** 58
Civil liabilities 58
General remedies 58
Statutory remedies 61
Criminal liabilities 62

**8. SHARES** 64
Nature of shares 64
The mode of issue of shares and becoming a shareholder 64
The process of becoming a member 65
Transfer of shares 68
The register of members 75
Annual return 77

**9. CAPITAL** 78
Types of share capital 78
Classes of share capital 79
Variation of class rights 82
Alteration of share capital 83
Reduction of capital 84
Maintenance of capital 87

**10. DEBENTURES AND BORROWING** 92
Authority to borrow 92
Debentures 92
Charges 94
Remedies of debenture holders 100

**11. DIRECTORS AND OFFICERS OF THE COMPANY** 105
Introductory: Position of directors 105
Appointment 106
Publicity requirements of directors and secretaries 108
Termination of directorship 109
Remuneration of directors 111
Powers of directors 112
Proceedings of the directors 118
The managing director 119
The secretary 120
The auditors 123

**12. AUTHORITY OF CORPORATE INDIVIDUAL DIRECTORS AND OFFICERS** 124
Introduction 124
The indoor management rule 124
The application of agency principles 125
Some aspects of reform and trends on other jurisdictions 133
Liability under the organic theory 135

| | |
|---|---|
| **13. ACCOUNTS AND AUDIT OF THE COMPANY** | **139** |
| Introductory | 139 |
| Accounts | 139 |
| Directors' report | 141 |
| Auditors' report | 141 |
| Auditors | 141 |
| **14. DIRECTOR'S DUTIES** | **149** |
| Duty to a holding company or subsidiary | 149 |
| Duty to a person or body in a fiduciary position to the company | 150 |
| Duty to shareholders | 154 |
| The duty to act bona fide in the interest of the company | 159 |
| Duty to exercise powers for a proper purpose | 166 |
| The requirement upon a director to avoid conflict of duty | 174 |
| The duties of care and skill | 191 |
| Ratification: Reconciling Cook v. Deeks and Regal (Hastings) Ltd. v. Gulliver | 194 |
| **15. ENFORCEMENT OF CORPORATE DUTIES** | **198** |
| Litigation by the company | 198 |
| Litigation by a member | 201 |
| Corporate irregularities and personal shareholders' Rights | 203 |
| The "just and equitable" ground for winding up | 232 |
| Misfeasance summons | 237 |
| Investigations and inspections | 238 |
| **16. MEETING AND PROCEEDINGS** | **242** |
| Introduction | 242 |
| Statutory meeting | 242 |
| Annual general meeting | 243 |
| Extra-ordinary general meeting | 244 |
| Notices of meetings | 245 |
| Circulation of members' resolutions | 248 |
| Proceeding at meetings | 248 |
| Class meetings | 252 |
| Privilege and the press | 252 |
| **17. RECONSTRUCTION AND AMALGAMATION OF COMPANIES** | **254** |
| Introduction | 254 |
| Compromise and arrangement | 254 |
| Reconstruction and amalgamation | 256 |
| Take-overs through acquisition of shares | 258 |
| **18. LIQUIDATION** | **261** |
| Introduction | 261 |
| Bases for winding up by the court | 261 |
| Persons entitled to petition | 264 |
| Petition and procedure for winding-up | 266 |
| Company's property | 269 |

Contributories 272
Creditors 272
The liquidator 273
Completion of winding up by court 276
Defunct companies 277
Voluntary winding up 277
Winding up subject to supervision of court 281

*Index* 283

# TABLE OF CASES


**A**

A.B.C. Coupler & Engineering Co. Ltd., Re: [1970] 1 W.L.R. 1236 240
[1970] 1 All E.R. 650 271

A & B.C. Chewing Gum Ltd. Re: [1975] 1 W.L.R. 579 235, 237

A-G v Etukudo [1975] 1 N.M.L.R. 292 268

A-G v Great Eastern Railway (1880) App. Cas. 473 H.L. 29, 30

A-G, Lagos State v. Nigerian Oxygen & Allied Gases FRC/L/M/3/77 261

A.R. v. Commissioner Income Tax Case No. 44 (1956) 2 E.A.T.C. 11

Aaron's Reef's Ltd. v. Twiss [1896] A.C. 273 60

Abbey Glen Property Corp. v. Stamborg (1978) 85 D.L.R. (3rd) 35 182

Abbey Malvern Wells Ltd. v. Ministry of Local Government [1951] Ch. 728 9 - 10

Aberdeen Rly Co. v. Blaikie Bross (1854) 1 Macq. 461 178

Abina v. Tika-Tore Press Ltd. 1968 N.C.L.R. 424 56, 69, 171

Abraham V. Tait (1935) 2 EACA 51 9

Adebayo v. Official Receiver [1954] 1 W.L.R. 681 P.C. 266

Adebesin v. May & Baker (Nig.) Ltd. (1978) 4. F.R.C.R. 232 120, 122

Afolabi v. Polymera Industries (Nig.) Ltd. 1964(2) A.L.R. Comm.205 35-36, 126

African Continental Bank v. Registrar of Companies (1974) I.F.R.C.R.125 277

African Continent Seaways Ltd. 1977 3 F.R.C.R.363 55

African Development Corporation Ltd. v. L.E.D.B. 1966 N.C.L.R. 124

Agbaoye v. Chief Federal Land Officer 1976 2 F.R.C.R.33 274

Agbonmagbe Bank Ltd. v. General Manager, G.B.O. [1961] 1 All E.R. 116 6

Air Rep. International Ltd. Re [1984] HCB 63 244

Air Safaris (Tim Air) Ltd., Re: [1969] E.A. 265

Aircraft (B.C.) Propeller & Engine Ltd. Re: (1968) D.L.R. (2D) 628 226

Airlines Airspares Ltd. v. Handley Page Ltd. (1970) Ch. 193 10, 102

Ajayi v. Lagos City Council 1967(3) A.L.R. Comm. 212 130

Akerhielm v. De Marc (1959) A.C. 789 58

Akinbobola v. Fisko (Nig) Ltd. (1986) 4 N.W.L.R. 101

Alabama, New Orleans, Texas & Pacific Rly Co., Re: (1891) 1 Ch. Ch. 213 255

Albazero, The (1975) 3 W.L.R. 491 11

Alexander v. Automatic Telephone Co. (1900) 2 Ch. 56 73-74, 195-96, 218, 219

Alexander v. Simpson (1890) 43 Ch. d. 139 C.A. 206-7, 209-10, 247

Alexander Ward & Co. Ltd. v. Samyang Navigation Ltd. (1975) 1 W.L.R. 673 115, 201

Ali El Kadra v. International Metal Industries Ltd. (1972) 2 F.R.C.R.84 110

Alitalia Airlines Ltd. v. N.I.D.B. (1967) F.N.L.R. 134 273

Allen v. Gold Reefs of West Africa Co. Ltd. (1900) 1 Ch. 656 47, 48, 49

Allen v. Hyatt (1914) 30 T.L.R. 444 P.C. 157

Allied Produce Co. Ltd. Re: (1967) 1 W.L.R. 1469 240

Alma Spining Co., Bottomley Case Re: (1880) 16 Ch. D. 681 119

Aluminium Industries v. Romalpa (1976) 2 All E.R.553 96

Aluminium Industries A.G. v. F.B.I.R. 1981 (2) NCLR 15

Amalgamated Syndicates Ltd., Re: (1901) 2 Ch. 181 279

American Cyanamid Co. v. Ethicon (1975) A.C. 396 H.L. (E) 189

Ammonia Soda Co. v. Chamberlain (1918) 1 Ch. 266 90

Andrea v. Zinc Mines of Great Britain (1918) 2 K.B. 454 52

Andrew, Re Exp. Official Receiver (Trusts) [1937] Ch. 122269

Andrews v. Gas Meter Co. [1897] 1 Ch. 361 41-42, 79

Andrews v. Mockford [1896] 1 Q.B. 372 C.A. 58-59

Anglesea Colliery Co., Re: (1866) 1 Ch. App. 555 265

Anglo-Continent Supply Co. (1922) 2 Ch. 723 258

Angostura Bitters Ltd. v. Kerr (1933) A.C. 550 41

Anselt v. Butter Air Transport Ltd.
(No. 1) (1958) 75 W.N. (N.S.W.) 299 170
(No. 2) (1958) 75 W.N. (N.S.W.) 306 251

Apthorpe v. Peter Schoenfofen Brewing Co. (1899) 4 T.C. 41 C.A. 11
Archer v. Lavender Ir. Rep. 1 Eq. 220 150
Arenson v. Arenson [1977] A.C. 405 H.L. 148
Argentum Reductions Re: (1975) 1 All E.R. 608 267
Armstrong Whitworth Securities Co. Re: [1947] Ch. 673 272, 275
Arnison v. Smith (1889) 41 Ch. D. 348 60
Arthur (Insurance) Ltd. v. Sisson, [1966] 1 W.L.R. 1384 102
Asaboro (Joseph) Ltd. v. Western Finance Corpn. 1974 NCLR 266 108, 201
Ashbourne Investments Ltd. Re: [1978] 1. W.L.R. 1346 241
Ashbury Rlway Carriage Co. Ltd. v. Riche (1875) L.R. 7 H.L. 653 29-30, 35, 38, 42, 202
Assoc. Registered Eng. Contractors Ltd. v. Amaye [1986] 3 N.W.L.R. 653 110
Associated Tool Industries Ltd. Re: [1964] A.L.R. 73 226
Astoria Garage (Streatham) Ltd., Re: [1952] Ch. 637 46
Atewologun v. Metro Motors Ltd., (1978) 2 L.R.N. 46 F.R.C. 105, 113
Atwool v. Merry Weather (1867) L.R. Eq. 464 199, 202, 212, 214
Australian Auxiliary Steam Clipper Co. v. Mounsey (1858) 4 K & J 733 92
Australian Metropolitan Life Ass. Co. Ltd. v. Ure (1923) 33 167-68, 170 C.L.R. 199
Automatic Bottle Makers Re: [1926] Ch. 412 C.A. 96
Automatic Self-Cleansing Filter Syndicate Co. v. Cunninghame [1906] 2 Ch.34 106, 112-116, 200-201
Awoyemi v. Salomon (1976) 2 FR CR 165 (FHC Nigeria) 110, 247
Ayodeji v. Lagos City Council 1974 NCLR 123


## B


B.D. & Co, Ltd. c. Commissioner of Income Tax (1959) Case 10 - 11
Bahia & San Francisco Rly co. (1868) L.R. 3 Q.B. 584 67
Bailey, Hay & Co. Ltd. Re: [1971] 1 W.L.R. 1357 12
Baillie v. Oriental Telephone Co. [1915] Ch. 503 202, 207-08, 209, 246-47
Baily v. British Equitable Assurance Co., [1904] 1 Ch. 374 46
Bakare v. Bakado Line Ltd. Lagos H.C. NOM/ 144/68 of 9/4/69 Unreported 262
Balkis Consolidated Co. v. Tomkison [1893] A.C. 396 H.L. 67
Balogun v. Agbaoye (1977) F.R.C.R. 122 274
Bambi Restaurant Ltd., Re: [1965] W.L.R. 750 236
Bamford v. Bamford [1969] 1 All E.R. 969; [1970] Ch. 21256, 115, 116, 167, 170, 199, 202, 205, 242
Bank of America National Trust & Savings Assoc. v. Niger International Dev. Corp. Ltd. 1969 N.C.L.R. 268 10, 11
Bank of the North v. Registrar of Companies (1973 - 74) 1 FRCR 56 100
Bank of West Africa Ltd. v. Fadoul 1960 N.R.N.L.R. 15 72-73
Barnett Hoares & Co. v. South London Tramways Co. (1887) 1890 . B. 815 121, 132
Barron v. Potter [1914] 1 Ch. 894 242
Bath v. Standard Land Co. [1910] 2 Ch. 408 [1911] 1 Ch. 618 C.A. 136, 151
Bayswater Trading Co. Ltd. Re: [1970] 1 W.L.R. 343 225, 277
Beaton & Co. Re: [1913] 2 Ch. 279 273
Beattie v. Beattie [1938] Ch. 708 44
Bechuanaland Exploration Co. v. London Trading Bank [1898] 2 Q.B. 658 74, 94
Bedde Steam Shipping Co., Re: [1917] 1 Ch. 123 68, 69
Beddoe, Re: [7893] 1 Ch. 547, 567, C.A. 217
Bell v. Lever Bross Ltd. [1932] A.C. 161 H.L. 149, 187,
Bell Bross., Re: [1891] 65 L.T. 245 68
Bell Houses Ltd. v. City Wall Properties Ltd. [1966] 2 All E.R. 674 C.A. 32-34, 35, 160-161
Bellador Silk Ltd., Re: [1965] 1 All E.R. 669 226
Bellaglade, Re: [1977] 1 All E.R. 319267, 269
Bellerby v. Rowland & Marword's Steamship Co. Ltd. [1902] 2 Ch. 14 86
Bendel Line Co. Ltd., Rel: (1979) F.R.C.R. 19 256

Bentley Stevens v. Jones [1974] 1 W.L.R. 638 118, 211, 212
Berry & Steard v. Tottenham Hotspur [1935] 1 Ch. 318 69
Biba Ltd. v. Stratford Investments Ltd. [1973] ch. 281 138
Biney (W) & Co., Re: 1972 N.C.L.R. 282 236, 262-263
Birch v. Cropper (1880) 14 App. Cas. 525 H.L. 80
Birchin Lane Nominees Ltd. v. Nicholson [1969] 3 All E.R. 1352 274
Bisgood v. Hendersons' Transvaal Estates [1908] 1 Ch. 743 C.A. 257-58
Black v. Homersham (1878) Ex. D. 24 70
Blackburn Building Soc. v. Cuncliffe Brooks & Co. (1882) 22 Ch. D.61 35
Bleriot Aircraft Co., Re: (1916) 3 T.L.R. 253 236
Bletchley Boat Co. Re: [1974] 1 All E.R. 1225 269
Bloomenthal v. Ford 1897 A.C. 156 67
Bloomingdale v. Cushman 134 Minn. 445, 159 N.W. 1076 (1916) 135
Bolton (Engineering) Co. Ltd. v. Graham & Sons [1957] 1 Q.B. 159 136
Bonnelli's Telegraph Co., Re: (1871) LR. 12 Eq. 246 118
Boraxco, Re: [1901] 1 Ch. 326 95
Borland's Trustees v. Steel Bros. & co. Ltd. [1901] 1 Ch. 279 64
Bornu Holdings Co. Ltd. v. Dipcharima (1976) 1 S.C.63 (Nigeria) 214
Boschoek Proprietary Ltd. v. Fuke [1906] 1 Ch.148 210
Boston Deep Sea Fishing & Ice Co. v. Ansell (1888) 39 Ch. D. 339 C.A. 189
Boulting v. A.C.T.A.T. [1963] 2 Q.B. 606 164
Bowman v. Secular Society Ltd. [1917] A.C. 406 H.L. 26
Boxco Ltd. Re: [1970] ch. 442277
Bozak (Nig.) Ltd. v. Ziregbe (1978) 4 F.R.C.R. 83 6, 108, 238
Bradford Banking Co. v. Briggs (1886) 12 App. Cas. 29 H.L. 71
Bradley Egg Fram v. Clifford [1943] 2 All E.R. 378 15
Bread Ltd. v. Uganda Co. Ltd., [1975] H.C.B.218 68
Bretts & Co. v. Macnaghaten [1910] 1 Ch. 430 206, 208
Bridge Water Navigation Co., Re: [1891] 2 Ch. 317 81
Briess v. Wooley [1954] A.C. 333 H.L 157
Brinsmead & Sons, Re: [1897] 1 Ch. 406 C.A. 237
British American Nickel Corpon. Ltd. v. O'Brien [1927] A.C. 269 83, 202
British American Tobacco Co. V IRC [1942] AC 335 116
British Eagle Int. Airline Ltd. v. Compagnie Nationale Airline (1975) 2 All E.R. 390 280
British India Steam Navigation Co. v. IR.C. (1991) 7 92 - 93 Q.B.D. 165
British Medical & General Life Assoc. Re (1888) 39 Ch.D. 61 77
British Thomson - Houston Co. Ltd. v. Fed. European Bank Ltd. [1932] 2 K.B. 176 127-128, 131
Britton & Millard Ltd., Re: (1957) 107 L.J. 602 280
Broadcasting Station 2 G.B. Re: [1964-65] N.S.W.R. 1648226, 227
Brooks v. Buys 186 N.W. 47 (1921) 152
Brown v. British Abrasive Steel Co. [1919] 1 Ch. 290 48, 49
Browne v. La Trinidad (1887) 37 Ch. D. 1 211, 212
Bryanston, Finance Ltd. v. De Vries (No. 2) [1976] Ch. 63 C.A. 232
Bugle Press Ltd., Re [1961] Ch. 270 C.A. 259
Burland v. Earle [1902] A.C. 83 P.C. 175, 197, 202, 203, 212, 224
Burns v. Siemens Bros Dynamo Works [1919] 1 Ch. 225 76
Burston Finance Ltd. v. Speirway Ltd. [1974] 1. W.L.R. 1948 99
Burton & Deakin Ltd. Re: [1977] 1 All E.R. 631 267
Bushell v. Faith [1970] A.C. 1099 P.C. 25, 111
Business, Computers Ltd. v. Anglo African [1977] 2 All E.R. 741 97
Busoga Miller's & Industries Ltd. v. Patel (1955) 22 E.A.C.A. 548 76
Butt v. Kelson [1952] Ch. 197 C.A. 10

## C

C.L. Nye Ltd., Re: [1970] All E.R. 1061 99
Cadiz Waterworks v. Barnett (1974) L.R. 19 Q. 1821 263

Cakes v. Turquand & Harding (1867) L.R. 2 H.L. 325 60

Caledonian Community Credit Union Ltd. v. Halimand Feed Mill (1974) 4 D.LR. (3D) 376 35

Caligari v. Giovani Sartori & Co. [1961] All N.L.R. 534 21

Campbell v. Rofe [1933] A.C. 91 79

Campbell's Case (1973) L.R. 9 Ch. App. 1 84

Campbell Coverings Ltd., Re: [1943] Ch. D. 281

Camps, Re: [1962] E.A. 403 CA 107, 108

Canada Safeway Ltd. v. Thompson (1951) 3 D.L.R. 295 181, 182

Canadian Aero Services v. O'Malley (1974) 40 D.L.R. (3d) 371 119, 181-83, 187

Candler v. Crane & Christmas Co. [1961] 2 K.B. 164 60

Cane v. Jones [1981] 1 All E.R. (1980) 1 W.L.R. 1451 50, 246

Cape Bretton, Re: (1885) 29 Ch. D. 78 20

Capital Annuities Ltd. Re: [1978] 3 All E.R.704 262

Capital Finance Co. Ltd. v. Stokes [1968] 3 All E.R. 625 99

Capital Fire Insurance Association, Re: (1882) 21 Ch. D. 209 261

Carib Construction Co. Ltd. v. Lynch CCHCJ/12/73/29 118

Carlen v. Drury (1812) IV & B 154 173

Carlton Holdings Ltd. Re: [1971] W.LR. 918 259

Carribean Products, Re: [1966] Ch. 331 C.A. 269

Caruth v. Imperial Chemical Industries Ltd. [1937] 2 All E.R. 422 83, 84, 250

Castell & Brown Ltd. Re: [1898] 1 Ch. 315 96

Castiglione's Will Trusts, Re: [1958] Ch. 549; [1958] 1 All E.R. 480 87

Castle New Homes Ltd., Re: [1979] All E.R.775 269

Cowley & Co. Re: (1889) 402 Ch. D. 209 73

Central Masaka Coffee Co. v. Masaka Farmers [1991] ULSLR p.220 21

Central Rly Co. of Venezuela v. Kisch (1867) L.R. 2 H.L. 99 59

Champaany Jute Co. Ltd. Petitioners 1924 S.C.209 226

Chand v. Liquidator, Exchange Bank (1950) 17 EACA 270

Chapman's Case (1886) L.R. Eq. 346 267

Charitable Corporation v. Sutton (1742) 2 A.E.R. 400 105

Charles Forte Investments Ltd. v. Amanda [1964] 1 Ch. 240 C.A. 237

Charterbridge Corpn. Ltd. v. Lloyds Bank [1969] 2 All E.R. 1185 34, 35, 160

Charterland & Barrett Ltd., Re: (1909) 26 T.K.R. 132 279

Chatterley - Whitfield Collieries Ltd. Re: [1948] 2 All E.R. 593 85

Chesterfield Catering; Re: [1976] 3 All E.R.294 265

City & County Investment Co., Re: (1879) 13 Ch. D. 475 257

City Equitable Fire Insurance Co. Re: [1925] Ch. 407 105, 145, 190, 192-93

Clayton's Case (1816) 1 Mer. 572 97

Cleadon Trust Ltd., Re: (1939) Ch. 286 121

Clemens v. Clemens Bros. Ltd. [1976] 2 All E.R. 268 227-28, 235

Clifton Place Garage Ltd; Re: [1969] R.P.C. 41 189

Coker (Chief T.) v. Iro (1976) F.R.C.R. 136 68, 69

Cole v. R.C. Irving & Com. Ltd. 1970 N.C.L.R.472 201-203, 226, 232, 236, 237, 265

Coleman v. Meyers [1977] 2 NLR 225 154-159

Commissioner Income Tax v. Bjordal (1955) 22 EACA 156 9

Compania de Electricidad de Buenos Aires, Re: [1979] 2 W.L.R. 316 272

Conley, Re: Exp. Trustees v. Barclays Bank Ltd. [1937] 4 All E.R. 434 270

Consolidated South Land Mines Deep Ltd., Re: [1909] 1 Ch. 491 232, 257

Consort Deep Level Gold Mines Ltd. Re: [1897] 1 Ch. 575 52

Containers (Nig.) Ltd. v. Niglasco Ltd. (1979) 4-6 CCHCJ 29 129

Continental Chemists v. Ifeakandu [1966] 1 All N.L.R. 1, S.C.N. 33, 34

Conway v. Petronius Clothing Co. Ltd. [1978] 1 All E.R. 185 139

Cook v. Deeks [1916] A.C. 554 P.C. 174-75, 189-90, 194-97, 202, 218-219

Cornish Manures ltd. Re: [1967] 1 W.LR. 807
278
Cotman v. Brougham [1918] A.C. 514
28, 30-32, 38
Cotter v. National union of Seamen [1929] 2 Ch. 58 202, 203, 211
Cousins v. International Brick Co. [1931] 2 Ch. 90 C.A. 251
Craven-Ellis v. Canons Ltd. [1936] 2 K.B.103
111, 120
Crown Bank, Re: (1890) 44 Ch.D. 634
33, 34
Cuckmere Brick Co. Ltd. v. Mutual Finance Ltd. [1971] Ch. 949 102
Cumberland Holdings Ltd., Re: (1974-76) A.C.L.R. 361 227, 228
Cummings v. United Artists Theatre Circuit Inc. (1964) 204A (2d) 795 173
Cuthbert Cooper & Sons Ltd., Re: [1937] Ch.392 233, 234, 237
Cyclist Touring Club, Re: [1907] 1 Ch. 269 D.
39

**D**

D.H.N. Food Distributors Ltd. v. Tower Hamlets [1976] 1 W.LR. 852 10, 12
Daarnhouwer & Co. Ltd. v. Christian (J) & Co. 1967 N.C.L.R. 434 129
Dafen Tinplate Co. Ltd. v. Llanely Steel Co. [1920] Ch. 124 48
Daimler Co. Ltd. v. Continental Tyre Rubber Co. [1916] 2 A.C. 307
13-14, 121, 242
Daniels v. Daniels [1978] Ch. 406
194-197, 201, 202, 212, 217-221
Danish Mercantile Co. Ltd. v. Beaumont [1951] Ch. 680 115, 199
Daponte v. Schubert [1939] Ch. 958
72
David Payne & Co., Re: [1904] 2 Ch. 608
31-32, 35
Davis & Collet Ltd., Re: [1935] 1 Ch. 693
232, 235
Davis Investments (West Home) Ltd. Re: [1961] 2 W.LR. 1396 232
Dawson v. African Consolidated Land & Trading Co. [1898] 1 Ch. 6 73, 108
Day v. Tait (O.M.) (1900) 85 L.T.40 267
De Beers Consolidated Mines v. Howe [1966] A.C. 455 13
Destone Fabrics Ltd., Re: [1941] Ch. 319 C.A
97
Denham & Co. Re: (1883) 25 Ch. D. 752
192
Derry v. Peek (1889) 14 App. Cas. 339
58, 60
De Mare (Rolf) v. Akerhielm (1956) 23 E.A.C.A. 214 58
Development Finance Co. Ltd. v. Registrar of Companies 1973 N.C.L.R. 497
100
Diamond Fuel Co. Re: (1879) 13 ch. D. 400
267
Diamond Manufacturing Co. Ltd. v. Hamilton [1969] N.Z.L.R. 609 61
Dimbula Valley (Ceylon) Tea Co. Ltd. v. Laurie [1961] Ch. 353 81, 91
Dipcharima v. Ali (1914) 1 All N.L.R.
108
Dipcharima v. Bornu Holding Co. Ltd. 1965 (3) A.L.R. Comm. 112
65, 101, 198, 220
Director of Public Prosecutions v. Kent & Sussex Contractors Ltd. [1944] K.B. 146 137
Dixon v. Kennaway & Co. Ltd. [1900] 1 Ch. 833 67
Dodds v. Walker [1981] 2 All E.R. 609
242
Dominion Freeholders Ltd. v. Spargo Aird (Third Party) 1966 2 N.S.W.R. 293
142
Dorman Long & Co. Ltd., Re: [1934] Ch. 635
255
Dowse v. Marks (1913) S.R. (N.S.W.) 332
114
Drages, Re: [1942] 1 All E.R. 194 39
Duckett v. Gover (1977) 6 Ch. D. 82 199
Duncan Gilmour & Co. Ltd. Re: [1952] 2 All E.R. 871 41
Dunderland Irone-Ore Co. Ltd., Re: [1909] 1 Ch. 446 265
Dunlop Nig. Industries Ltd. v. Forward Nig. Enterprises Ltd. 1976 N.C.L.R. 243
5, 8
Dunlop Pneumatic Tyre Co. v. Motor Und A.G. (1900-3) All E.R. Ref. 197 14
Duomatic ltd., Re: [1969] 2 Ch. 365
12, 38, 193
Durfee v. Durfee & Canning Inc. 80 N.E. 2d 522 (Mass. 1948) 179
Dutton v. March LR.6 Q.B. 364 129

**E**

E.A. Tobacco Ltd. Re: (1921-52) 1 T.LR. (2) 389 235
East v. Bennett Bros [1911] 1 Ch. 162
248

East African Electric Co. Ltd. v. Registrar of Companies (1952) 25 (1) KLR 2 28
East Pant Du United Lead Mining Co. Ltd. v. Merryweather (1864) 2 H & M 254 199, 214
Eastmanco (Kilner House) Ltd. v. G.L.C. [1982] 1 all E.R. 437 202
Eastern National Bank v. American Brick & Tile co. C.A. 917 152
Ebbw Vale U.D.C. v. South Wales Traffic Area [1951] 2 K.B. 366 C.A. 5, 9, 11
Ebrahim v. Tait (1935) 2 E.A.C.A. 51 238, 271
Ebrahimi v. Westbourne Galleries [1973] A.C. 360 H.L. 116-226, 227, 229, 232-235, 238
Economic Exports Ltd. v. Kasumu 1966 N.C.L.R. 104 201, 274
Eddystone Marine Co., Re: [1893] 3 Ch.9 66
Edmunds v. Edmunds (1904) p.362 10
Edokpolor v. Sem-Edo Wire Ltd., (1984) 7 S.C.119 21, 40, 201, 202
Edwards v. Halliwell [1950] 2 All E.R. 1064 198-199, 201-203, 204-205
Edwards v. Standard Rolling Stock [1893] 1 Ch. 574 101
Eguekweh v. Barclays Bank of Nigeria Ltd. 1973 N.C.LR. 432 68
Einhorn v. West Mount Investment Ltd. (1969) 60 D.LR. (3d) 371 10
Ekweozor v. Building & Civil Construction Co. (1980) 7-9 CCHCJ 301 127, 132, 133
El Sombrero Re: [1958] Ch. 900 243, 244
Elder v. Elder & Watson 1952 S.C. 49 226-27
Elder's Trustee & Executor Co. Ltd. v. Commonwealth Home (1941) 65 C.L.R.603 59
Eley v. Positive Govt. Life Ass. Co. (1876) 1 Ex. D.88 44, 45
Ellis v. Bailey & Co. (E.A.) Ltd. [1962] E.A.626 118-20
Elkington's Case (1967) LR.2. Ch. 511 56
Emmadart, Re: [1979] 1 All E.R. 599 199
Empire Mining Co. Re: [1890] 4 Ch.40 254
English & Scottish Mercentile Co. v. Brunton [1898] 1 Ch. 315 96
Equity Corpn. v. Milton (1966) 221 A (2d) 427 179
Eric Holmes Re: [1965] Ch. 1052 97, 99, 270
Erlanger v. New Sombrero Phosphate Co. (1878) 3 App. Cas. 1218 19, 155
Ernest v. Ernest Loma Gold Mines [1897] Ch. 1 C.A. 250
Ernest v. Nicholls [1857] 6 H.L.C. 401 28, 125, 258
Eronin v. Harbor (1952) 2 F.S.C. 43 109
Eryeza Bwambale & Co. Ltd. Re: (1969) E.A.430 229, 235
Escott v. Barchris Construction Corp. 283 F Supp. 643 (SDNY 1968) 147
Esparto's Trading Co., Re: (1879) 12 Ch. D.191 86
Eternal Sacred Order of Cherubim & Seraphim v. Adewunmi 1969 N.C.L.R. 322 198
Evans v. Rival Granite Quarries Ltd. [1910] 2 K.B. 96
Evertite Locknuts Ltd., Re: [1945] Ch. 220 259
Exchange Banking Co. Flitcroft's Case (1882) 21 ch. D. 519 C.A. 89-90
Exeter & Credition Rlywy v. Butler (1947) 16 L.J. Ch. 449 199
Expo International Property Ltd. v. Chant (1979) 4 A.C.LR. 679 103
Express Engineering Works Ltd., Re: [1920] 1 Ch. 466 C.A. 12
Express Engineering Co. (1880) 16 Ch.D. 125 22
Ezebube v. Aplin & co. Ltd. 1966 N.C.L.R. 39 14
Ezeoke v. Registrar of Companies (1971) U.I.L.R. 351 277

**F**

F.G. (Films) Ltd., Re: [1953] 1 W.L.R. 483 9
F.L.E. Holding, Re: [1967] 1 W.L.R. 1409 97, 270
F & E Stanton, Re: [1927] 1 Ch. 180 96
Fadipe v. Manager, U.B.A. (1973) F.R.C.C. 154 8
Farmart Produce & Shipping Line Ltd. [1971] 1 All N.L.R. 247236
Farnham v. Fingold [1973] O.R. 132 C.A. 224
Farrer (T.N.) Ltd. Re: [1937] Ch. 352 [1937] 2 All E.R. 505 111
Fasteners (J.E.B.) v. Marks, Bloom & Co. [1981] 3 All E.R. 289 148
Ferguson v. Wilson (1866) LR. 2 Ch. 77 105

Ferris George & Sons v. Khoury [1965] 1 All N.L.R. 68
Fildes Bros. Ltd. Re: [1970] 1 W.L.R. 592 233
Fine Industrial Commodities v. Powling (1954) 71 R.P.C. 253 179, 182
Fireproof Doors, Re: [1916] 2 Ch. 142 252
Firestone, Tyre & Rubber Co. v. Llewellin [1957] 1 W.L.R. 464 H.L. 11
First National Re-Insurance Co. v. Grenfield [1921] 2 K.B. 260 74
Five Minute Car Wash Service Ltd. Re: [1966] 1 W.L.R. 745 229
Flagstaff Silver Mining Co. Re: (1875) LR. 20 Eq. 268 264
Folawiyo (Y) & Sons Ltd. v. Hammond Projects Ltd. FRC/C/M62/76 262
Fomento (Sterling Area) Ltd. v. Selsdon Fountain Pen Co. Ltd. [1958] 1 All E.R11 145-146
Foss v. Harbottle (1843) 2 Hare 461 V.C. 87, 148, 196-197, 198-224, 236
Foster v. New Trinidad Lake Asphalt Co. Ltd. [1901] 1 Ch. 208 91
Foster Clark's Indenture, Re: [1966] 1 W.L.R.125 102
Fowler v. Broads Patent Night Light Co. Ltd. [1983] 1 Ch. 724 267
Fowler v. Commercial Timber co. Ltd. [1930] 2 K.B. 1 C.A. 280
Freeman & Lockyer v. Buckhurst Part Properties (Mangal) Ltd. [1964] 2 W.B.480 126-131, 134, 135
Friedman v. Njoro (1954) 21 E.A.C.A. 172 58
Furs v. Tomkies (1936) 154 C.LR.C. 583 178, 194

## G

Galloway v. Halle Concerts Society [1915] 2 Ch. 233 202
Garden Gully United Quarry Mining Co. v. McLister (1875) 1 App. Cas. 39 86
Gasque v. C.I.R. [1940] 2 K.B. 80 14
General Auction Estate & Monetary Co. v. Smith [1891] 3 Ch. 432 92
General Rolling Stock Discount Co's Claim (1872) 7 Ch. App. 646275
Geo Baker v. Eynon [1974] 1 All E.R. 900 97
George Newman Ltd., Re: [1895] 1 Ch. 674 C.A. 12, 111
German Date Coffee Co., Re: (1882) 20 Ch. D. 169 237
Gibson v. Barton (1875) L.R. 10 Q.B. 329 243
Gilford Motor Co. v. Horne (1933) Ch. 935 10
Glaisden v. Benetto (1913) 9 D.L.R. 714 157
Globe New Patent Iron & Steel Co. Re: (1875) L.R. 20 Eq. 337 264
Glossop v. Glossop [1907] 2 Ch. 370 109
Gluckstein v. Barnes [1900] A.C. 240 H.L. 20
Glyncorrwg Co. Ltd. Re: [1926] ch. 951 103
Goldex Mines Ltd. v. Revill 1974 54 D.L.R. (3d) 672 (Ont. C.A.) 212, 223-224
Goldhill Mines Re: (1883) 23 Ch. D. 210 263
Gosling v. Gaskell [1897 A.C. 575 H.L. 101
Govt. of Midwestern State v. Mid Motors (Nig.) Ltd., (1977) 10 S.C. 436
Govt. Stock & Other Securities Investment Co. v. Christopher [1956] 1 All E.R. 490 53
Govt.. Stock & Other Securities Co. v. Manila Railway Co. [1897] A.C. 81 95
Goy & Co. Ltd. Re: [1900] 2 Ch. 149 94
Gramophone & Typewriter Ltd. v. Stanley [1908] 2 K.B. 89 112-113, 116
Grant v. John Grant & Sons Pty Ltd. (1950) 82 C.L.R.I 170, 209, 211
Gray v. Lewis (1873) LR. 8 Ch. App. 1035 201
Gray v. New Angurita Porcupine Mines Ltd. [1952] 3 D.L.R.1 PC 185
Great Eastern Rlwy v. Turner (1872) LR. 8 Ch.149 105
Greene, Re: [1949] Ch. 333 69
Greene v. Dunhill Int. Inc. (1968) 249 A 2d 427 179
Greenhalgh v. Ardenne Cinemas Ltd. [1951] Ch. 286 C.A. 2, 49, 83, 179, 228
Greenwood v. Algeciras (Gibraltar) Rail Co. [1894] 2 Ch. 205 103
Greenwood v. Leathershod Wheel Co. [1900] 1 Ch. 421 59
Gresham Life Assurance (Nig.) Ltd. Re: 1970 NCLR 78 14-15, 281-282
Greymouth Point Elizabeth Rlwy & Coal Ltd., [1904] 1 Ch. 32 118
Grierson Oldham & Adams Ltd. Re: [1968] Ch. 17 259

Griffith v. Paget (No. 1) (1877) 5 Ch. D. 894; No. 2 (1877) 6 Ch. D. 511 257
Griffith v. Social Services Secretary [1974] Q.B. 468 102
Grosvenor & West End Rlwy Terminus Total Co. Ltd. Re: (1897) 76 L.T. 367 239
Grundt v. Great Boulder Pty Goldmines Ltd. [1948] 1 All E.R. 21 109
Guardian Assurance Co. Re: (1917 1 Ch. 431 C.A. 258
Guinness v. Land Corpn. of Ireland (1882) 22 Ch. D. 349 27, 41
Guth v. Loft (1939) 5A 2d 503 (S.C. Del) 180

**H**

HMS Truculent [1952] 136
H.A. Logging Co. Ltd. v. Random Services Corpn (1967) 63 D.L.R. (3d) 6 32
H.A. Stephenson & sons Ltd. v. Gillanders Arbuthnot & Co. (1931) 45 C.LR. 476 33-34
Hackney Pavillion Ltd. Re: [1924] 1 Ch. 276 69
Hampson v. Price's Patent Candle 45 L.J. Ch. 437 159, 163
Hampstead Garden Suburbs Ltd. Re: [1962] Ch. 806 39
Hang (Suerre) v. Buhemba Mines Ltd. (1935) 20 EACA 28 137
Hannan's Empress Gold Mining & Div. Co. Re: [1896] 2 Ch. 643 52
Harlowee's Nomines Pty Ltd. v. Woodside Oil Co. (1968) 121 C.LR. 483 171, 173
Harmer, H.R. Re: [1959] 1 W.L.R. 62 C.A. 205, 224, 225, 228
Harold Holdsworth & Co. (Wakefield) ltd. v. Caddies [1955] 1 W.LR. 352 H.L. 120
Harris v. Beauchamp Bros [1894] 1 Q.B. 801 101
Hartley Baird Ltd. Re: [1955] Ch. 143; [1954] 3 All E.R. 695 242, 248
Haslir v. Zaird & Co. Ltd. (1973-4) 1 F.R.C. 235 66, 118
Hawks v. McCarthur [1951] 2 All E.R. 22 71, 72
Head v. Ropner Holdings Ltd. [1951] 2 All E.R. 994 66
Heald v. O'Connor [1971] 2 All E.R. 1105 88
Healey v. Societe Anonyme Francaise - Rubastic [1917] 1 KB 946 151
Heap (Samuel) & Sons Ltd.; Re: [1965] 1 W.L.R. 1458 259
Heaton & Duggard Ltd. v. Cutting Bros [1925] 1 K.B. 655 96
Hector Whaling, Re: [1936] Ch. 208 245
Hedley Byrne & Co. Ltd. v. Heller & Partners Ltd. [1964] A.C. 465 60, 61, 148
Hellenic & General Trust, Re: [1975] 1 All E.R. 382 83, 255
Hely Hutchinson v. Brayhead [1968 1 Q.B. 549 126, 128, 134, 185
Henderson v. Bank of Australasia (1890) 45 Ch.D. 330 159, 209
Henshall (John) (Quarries) Ltd. v. Harvey [1965] 2 Q.B. 233 121, 137
Herbert Morris Ltd. v. Saxelby [1916] 1 A.C.688 189
Heyting v. Dupont [1964] 1 W.L.R. 843 202
Hickman v. Kent [1915] 1 Ch. 881 44
Higgs v. West African Air Ways Corpn. (Nig.) Ltd. 1969 N.C.L.R. 304 105, 118
Highlands Commercial Union Ltd. v. Jamal [1957] E.A. 641 270
Hillman v. Crystal Bowl [1973] 1 All E.R.379 65, 251
Hills Waterfall Estate & Gold Mining Co. Re: [1896] 1 Ch. 947 275
Hindle v. John Cotton Ltd. [1919] 56 Sc. L.R. 625 173
Hindu Dispensary v. Patwa [1958] E.A. 74 C.A. 6
Hirsche v. Sims [1894] A.C. 654 169
Hirth, In Re: [1899] 1 Q.B. 612 10
Hivac Ltd. v. Park Royal Scientic Instruments Ltd. [1946] ch. 169 C.A. 189
Hoare & Co. Ltd. Re: [1904] 2 Ch. 208 C.A. 91
Hoare & Co. Ltd, Re: [1933] 150 LT.374 259
Hodgson v. N.A.L.G.O. [1972] 1 W.LR. 130 202
Hogg v. Cramphorn [1966] 3 All E.R. 420 167, 171, 174, 202, 205, 209
Holders Investments Ltd. Re: [1971] 2 All E.R.289 83, 84
Holdings (F.L.E.) Ltd. Re: [1967] 3 All E.R. 553 269
Homer Gold, Mines, Re: (1888) 39 Ch. D. 546 118
Holmes v. Keyes [1959] Ch. 199 41, 107, 250
Homes & Colonial Insurance Co. Ltd. Re: [1930] 1 Ch. 102 275

Home Remedies Ltd. Re: [1943] Ch. 1 266, 280
Hong Kong v. Glenn [1941] Ch. 527 66
Hooper v. Herts [1906] 1 Ch. 549 70
Hop & Mait Exchange & Ware House Co. Exp. Briggs (1866) L.R. 1 Eq. 483 79
Horsley & Weight, Re: [1982] Ch. 442 [1982] 3 All E.R. 1045 30, 32, 34
Houghton & Co. v. Horthard Lowe & Wills Ltd. [1928] A.C. 1 121, 127, 130, 131, 132
Houldsworth v. City of Glasgow Bank (1880) App. Cas. 60
House of Garments Ltd., Re: Companies Cause No. 2 of 1972 (Uganda) 262
Howard v. Patent Ivory Manufacturing Co. [1883] 38 Ch. D. 56 126
Howard Marine & Dredging Co. Ltd. v. Ogden & Sons Ltd. [1978] Q.B. 374 61
Howard Smith Ltd. v. Ampol Petroleum Ltd. [1974] A.C. 821 162, 170, 172-74, 192, 224
Hughes King (Nig.) Ltd. v. Harris (1972) U.I.L.R. 63 45
Hunter v. Revenue Authority (1938) E.A.C.A.65 55
Hutchful (George) v. Hamilton Kweku Biney [1971] All N.L.R. 268 111
Hutton v. Cork Railway (1883) 23 Ch. D. 654 34, 111, 159, 161-62, 202

**I**

Ibadan City Council v. Odukale (1972) 7 S.C.128 136
Icknield Re: [1973] 2 All E.R. 168 273
Illingworth v. Houldsworth [1904] A.C. 355 95
Imonioro v. Seemuth Electro Engineering (Nig.) Ltd. FRC/L/45/78 246
Imperial Chemical Industries Ltd. [1936] 2 All E.R. 463 76
Imperial Hydropathic Hotel Co. v. Hampson (1883) 23 Ch.D. 1 43, 199
Imperial Mercantile Credit Assoc. v. Coleman (18130 L.R. 6 H.L. 189 184, 185
Industrial Dev. Consultants v. Cooley [1972] 1. W.L.R. 443 178-82
Industrial & Commercial Bank, Re [1933] 10 N.L.R. 85 265, 268, 273
Industrial Growers (Ug.) v. Tamale C.S. No. 215 of 1963 118
International Construction Corp. Re: [1964} 1 All N.L. R. 131 28
International Paints (Q.A.F.) v. Akiwowo (1979) 1-3 CCHCJ 52 130
International Sales & Agencies Ltd. v. Marcus [1982] 3 All E.R. 551 133
Introductions, Re: [1969] 1 All E.R. 887 C.A. 30-32, 34, 38, 167, 273
I.R.C. v. Olive Mill Ltd., [1963] 1 All E.R. 130 275
Ireland v. Hart [1902] 1 Ch. 522 71
Iro v. Park (1972) 12 S.C. 93 8, 244
Irvine v. Union Bank of Australia (1877) 2 App. Cas. 266 P.C. 125
Irving Trust Co. v. Deutsch (1934) 73 F. 2d 121 178
Isle of Thanet Electric Co. Re: [1950] Ch. 161 81
Italcomm (W. Nig.) Ltd. Re; 1972 NCLR 293 226, 232, 262, 265

**J**

James Exp. (1803) 8 Ves. 337 43 Digest 779, 2193 175, 176
Jan Mohammed Kiisi Cinema Ltd. Re: [1971] E.A. 268 (Kenya) 277
Jarvis (Harrow) Ltd. v. Carrobot [1964] 3 all E.R. 89 38
Jermyn Street Turkish Baths Ltd., Re: [1970 1 W.L.R. 1194 225, 228-29
Jia Enterprises Ltd. v. B.I.C.I. [1962] 1 All NLR 363 95
Johnson v. Lyttle's Iron Agency (1877) 5 Ch. D. 687 202
Johnson (B) & Co. Ltd. Re: [1955] Ch. 634 C.A. 86, 102, 103, 237, 238
Johnston v. Greene 121A 2d 919 (S.D. Del) 180
Jon Beauforte, Re: [1953] 1 All E.R. 634 35, 36, 37, 92
Jones v. Lipman [1962] 1 W.LR. 832 10
Jubilee Cotton Mills v. Lewis [1924] A.C. 956 26

**K**

K.G. Meat Supplies (Guildford) Ltd. Re: [1966] 1 W.LR. 1112 233
Kampala Cotton co. Ltd. v. Madhvani (1954) 21 E.A.C.A. 129 6
Karameli & Barret Ltd. Re: [1917] 1 Ch. 203 229
Karsberg Ltd. Re: [1950] 1 W.LR. 57 C.A. 280
Kasikwu Farmers v. Male Construction Service Ltd., [1981] H.C.B. 26 100
Katate v. Nyakatura (1956) 7 U.L.R. 47 4, 14,
Kate Ent. Ltd. v. Daewoo Nig. Ltd. [1985] 5

Kasule Luyombo v. Ndikola Iga Ors [1977] H.C.B. 328 238, 239
Katherine et cie, Re: [1932] 1 Ch.70 271
Kaye v. Croydon Tramways Co. [1898] 1 Ch. 358 C.A. 207, 209, 247
Keech v. Sandford (1926) Sel. Cas. Ch. 61 175
Kehinde v. Registrar of Companies (1979) 3 L.R.N. 213 FRC 25-26, 27, 41, 111
Kelner v. Baxter (1866) LR. 2 C.P. 174 20-21, 22
Kent Outcrop Coal Co., Re: (1912) W.N. 26 243
Kerr v. Jon Mortram [1940] Ch. 657 45, 252
Kidner, Re: [1929] 2 Ch. 121 70
Kingston Cotton Mills Co. (No. 2) Re: [1896] 2 Ch. 278 C.A. 143-146, 148
Kinyaju v. Mkodo 1967 (1) A.L.R. Comm. 49 198
Kirkel v. Adam's (1934) 1 E.A.C.A. 26 237
Kitson & Co. Re: [1946] 1 All E.R. 435 236
Knigthsbridge Estates Trust Ltd. v. Byrne [1940] 2 All E.R. 401 93
Knowles v. Scott [1891] 1 Ch. 717 275
Kolchman v. Maurice [1903] K.B. 534 72
Kololo Curing Co. v. East Mengo Co-op. Union [1981] H.C.B. Co. 19
Kostoris (Gerald) Ltd. v. Ali Mansour & Sons Ltd. Lagos H.C./M/ 141/60 269
Kraus v. J.G. Lloyd Pty Ltd. (1965) V.R. 232 (Vict. S.C.) 205
Kreditbank Cassel G.M.B.H. v. Schenkers Ltd. [1927] 1 K.B. 826 127, 129-131, 133
Kushler, M. Re: [1943] Ch. 248 97, 270
Kwizu v. Iwuchukwu (Unreported) FCA/E/36/84 110
Kyaggwe Farmers Association Ltd. v. Kafero [1975] HCB 97 243, 246
Kylasant, Re: [1931] All E.R. Rep. 179 59

## L

Laceward Ltd. RE: [1981] 1 All E.R. 254 263
Lady Gwendolen, The [1965] p. 294 136
Lagos Chamber of Commerce v. Registrar of Companies 14 W.A.C.A.A. 197 28
Lalandia, The [1932] All E.R. Rep. 391 282
Lalji v. Ahmed [1933] 15 L.R.L. 16 254
Langley Construction (Brixham) Ltd. v. Wells [1969] 1 W.L.R. 503 267
Lapish v. Braithwaite [1926] A.C. 275 H.L. 185
Lasisi v. Registrar of Companies 1975 NCLR 483 24-25, 40
Latchford v. Beirne [1981] 3 All E.R. 705 103
Latchford Premier Cinema Ltd. v. Ennion [1931] 2 Ch. 409 109
Leadenhall General Hardware Stores Ltd., Re: [1971] 115 S.J. 202 233
Lee v. Lee's Air Farming Ltd. (1960) 3 All E.R. 420 5
Lee v. Neuchatel Asphalte Co. (1889) 41 Ch. D. 1 C.A. 90
Lee, Behrens & Co. Ltd. Re: [1932] 2 Ch. 46 34, 159-60
Lennard's Carrying Co. Ltd. v. Asiatic Petroleum [1915] A.C. 705 106, 136, 137
Leon v. York-O-Matic Ltd. [1966] 3 All E.R. 277 275
Leslie Engineers Co. Ltd. Re: [1976] 3 All E.R. 85 267
Lester v. Garland [1803-13) All E.R. Rep. 436 242
Levy v. Napeir 1962 S.C. 468 266
Lewis v. Haas (1970) S.L.T. (Notes) 67 235
Lewis Mertheyr Collieries Ltd. Re: [1929] 1 Ch. 498 C.A. 103
Licensed Victuallers Mutual Trading Assoc. Re: [1889] 42 Ch.D. 1 52
Ligett (B) Ltd. v. Barclays Bank Ltd. [1978] 1 K.B. 48 126
Lindgren v. L. & P. Estates Ltd. [1968] Ch. 572 150
Lindlar's Case [1910] Ch. 312 68
Littlewoods Stores v. I.R.C. [1969] 1 W.L.R. 1241 C.A. 10
Lloyd v. Grace, Smith & Co. [1912] A.C. 716 133
Lloyd Generale Italiano, Re: [1885] 29 Ch. D.219 282
Lloyds Bank Ltd. v. Bundy [1974] 3 All E.R. 757 155, 157
Loch v. Blackwood [1924] A. 783 226, 235-236, 265
Logan (Thomas) Ltd. v. David (1911) 104 L.T.914 114
London-Griffiths v. Smith [1951] 1 K.B. 295 252

London & Cheshire Insurance Co. v. Laplagrene Pty. Co. [1991] Ch. 499 98
London Founders Assoc. Ltd. v. Clarke [1888] 20 Q.B. 576 70
London & General Bank (No. 1) Re; [1895] 2 Ch. 166 C.A. 144, 148
London Greyhound Racecourses v. Wake [1931] A Ch. 496 133
London & Mashonaland Exploration Co. v. New Mashonaland and Exploration Co. [1891] W.N. 185 187
London Oil Storage Co. v. Scear Hasluck & Co. [1904] 31 The Accountant LR.1 145
London Overseas Trading Co. v. The Raleigh Cycle Co. Ltd. [1959] E.A. 1012 28
London & Paris Banking Co. [1875] L.R. 19 Eq. 444 263
London United Breweries Ltd. Re: [1907] 2 Ch.511 102
London Wharfing & Ware Housing Co. Ltd. Re: [1865] 35 Beav. 35 263
Longham Skating Rink Co. Re: (1877) 5 Ch. D. 669 236
Longham v. Bath Electric Tramways Ltd., [1905] 1 Ch. 646 70
Lornhro Export Ltd., v. Motorways (Nig.) Ltd. Suit No. FHC/L/M84/79 of 22/1/81 Unreported 262
Lubbock v. British Bank of South Africa [1892] 2 Ch. 198 91
Lubega (John) v. City Council of Kampala [1975] HCB 101 270
Lukerere Coffee Factory Ltd. c.c. No. 3 of 1991 (U) 277
Lucania Temperature Billiards Hall (London) Ltd. Re: [1966] Ch. 98 85
Lundie Brothers Ltd., Re: [1965] 1 W.L.R. 1050 226, 232-235
Lundy Granite Co. Ltd. Lewis' Case (1872) 26 L.J. 673 111
Lutaaya v. Gandesha & Anors [1986] HCB 46 56, 66
Lympne Investment Ltd. Re: [1972] 2 All E.R.385 123, 262
Lynde v. Anglo Italian Hemp Spinning Co. [1896] 1 Ch. 178 59
Lysons. v. Liquidator of Miraflores Gold Syndicate Ltd. [1895] 22 R. 605 273

## M

Macaura v. Northern Assurance Co. [1925] A.C. 619 H.L. 5-6
Maclonnel v. Prill (E) & Co. [1916] 2 Ch. 57 208, 247, 250
Macdougall v. Gardiner (1875) 1 Ch. D. 13 198, 201, 203-212
Mack Trucks (Britain) Ltd. Re: (1967) 1 W.LR. 780 102
Mackenzie, Re: [1916] 2 Ch. 450 83, 84
Mackereth v. Wigan Coal [1916] 2 Ch. 393 71
Mahony v. East Holyford Mining co. [1875] L.R. 7 H.L. 869 108, 125-26, 133
Maidstone Buildings Provisions Ltd. [1991] WLR 1085 122, 271
Mandilas v. Anglo Canadian Cement Co. 1967 (1) A.L.R. Comm.42 93, 95, 102
Mandilas & Kareberis Ltd. Commissioner of Policy (1958) W.N.L.R. 147 137
Mann v. Goldstein (1968) 1 W.L.R. 1091 263
Marina Nominee Ltd., v. F.B.I.R. [1986] 2 NWLR 48 4, 8, 9, 11
Marquis of Bute (The) Case [1892] 2 Ch. 100 192
Marshall's Valve Gear v. Manning, Wardle & Co. [1909] 1 Ch. 267 114-16, 200-201
Martins v. Ogunbadero 1967 NCLR 393 118-119, 248
Martin v. Ogunsanya 1962 (2) ALR Comm. 393 86
Mason v. Harris (1879) 11 Ch. D. 97 184, 202, 212
Matthews (F.P. & C.H.) Re: [1982] Ch. 257; [1982] 1 All E.R. 338 270
Matthew Ellis Ltd. Re: [1933] Ch. 458 C.A. 97
Mawogola Farmers & Growers Ltd. v. Kayanja [1971] E.A. 272 C.A. 55, 56, 66, 69, 76
Maxwell v. Dept. of Trade [1974] 2 All E.R. 122 239, 240
Mbene v. Ofili 1968 (1) A.L.R. Comm. 235 202, 203
McMahon v. North Kent co. [1891] 2 Ch. 148 101
McNeil v. Mcneil's Sheep Farming Co. Ltd. [1955] N.Z.I.R. 15 42
Measures v. Measures [1910] 2 Ch.248 267

Mechanisations Ltd. Re: [1966] Ch. 20 99
Medipharm Publications (Nig.) Ltd. Re: [1971] U.I.L.R. 421 236, 262
Menier v. Hooper's Telegraph Works (1874) L.R. 9 Ch. 350 194, 202, 206, 212
Mercantile Bank of India v. Chartered Bank of India [1937] 1 All E.R. 231 131
Metal Construction (W.A.) Ltd. v. Migliore [1977] 6-9 S.C. 1963 76
Metalimpex v. Levenits & Co. (Nig.) Ltd. 1974 NCLR 511 128-129
Metropolitan Railway Ware Housing co. Re: (1867) 36 L.J. Ch. 827 262
Meyer Douglas Pty Ltd. Re: [1965] V.R.638 225
Middlesbrough Assembly Rooms co. [1880] 14 Ch. D. 104 262
Midland Express Ltd. Re: [1947] 1 Ch. 41 94
Migliore v. Metal Construction Ltd. 121
Mills v. Mills [1938] 60 C.LR. 150 161-62, 168
Misango v. Musigire [1966] E.A. 390 198, 201, 202, 203, 207, 212, 246
Mitha v. Mitha [1967] E.A. 575 226, 228, 235
M'Leod (N) & Sons Ltd., Re: 1967 S.C. 16 245
Modern Retreading Co. Ltd. Re: 1966(1) ALR Comm. 494 30, 34, 35, 233, 236, 238, 271
Modikayo Oneka v. Wines & Spirits Ltd. [1974] HCB 263 89, 90, 111
Monolithic Building Co., Re: [1915] 1 Ch.643 100
Moore v. Bessler Ltd. [1944] 2 All E.R. 5151 137
Moore (Sir John) Gold Mining Co. Re: [1879] 12 Ch. D. 325 279
Moorgate Mercantile Holdings Ltd. Re: [1980] 1 All E.R. 40 249
Modern Retreading Co. Ltd., Re: [1966] (1) ALR Comm. 494 30, 34, 235
Morecambe Bowling Ltd. Re: [1969] 1 W.L.R. 133 238
Morgan v. Gray [1953] Ch. 83 65
Moriarty v. Regents Garage Co. Ltd. [1921] 1 K.B. 423 111
Morley (John) Building Co. v. Barass [1891] 2 Ch. 386 107, 199-200
Morris v. Kanssen [1946] A.C. 459 108, 126
Morrison, Jones & Taylor Ltd. Re: [1914] 1 Ch. 50 C.A. 96
Moseley v. Koffyfontein Mines Ltd. [1904] 2 Ch. 108 66, 94, 203, 214
Moss S.S. Co. v. Whinney [1912] A.C. 254 H.L. 101
Motabani v. Thobani [1945] 12 E.A. C.A.37 20, 22
Moukarim Metal Wood Factory v. Durojaiye 1976 NCLR 264 20, 21, 23
Moxham v. Grant [1900] 1 Q.B. 88 90
Mozeley v. Alson (1947) 1 Ph. 790 216
Musa v. Selemani 1968 (1) A.L.R. Comm. 392 198
Musselwhite v. Musselwhite & Sons [1963] 1 Ch. 964 209, 246
Mussini v. Balogun 1968 (2) A.L.R. Comm.197 99
Mutual Life & Citizens' Ass. Co. Ltd. v. Ebatt (1977) A.C. 793 60

## N

N.C.B. v. Gamble [1959] 1 Q.B. 11 138
Nakivubo Chemists (U) Ltd. [1977] HCB 312 226, 229-230
Nanji & Sons Ltd. Re: (1934) 25 KLR 124 262, 263
Nash v. Lynde [1929] A.C/ 158 53, 62
Nasr v. Berini Beirut Riyadh (Nig.) Bank Ltd. 1968 NCLR 370 118, 176, 184, 252
Natal Colonisation Co. Ltd. v. Pauline Colliery Dev. Syndicate Ltd. [1904] A.C. 120 P.C. 21
National Bank of Nigeria v. Are Brothers (Nig.) Ltd. 1977(1) A.L.R. Comm. 123 265
National Bank (Nig.) Ltd. v. Kuta Shipping Co. Ltd. [1978] 2 L.R.N 42 264
National Bank of Nig. Ltd. v. Sealion (Nig.) Ltd. 1976 NCLR 415 F.R.C. 264
National Bank of Nigeria Ltd. v. The Blue 5 Co. Ltd. FRC/L/M56/74 263
National Bank of Wales Re: [1899] 2 Ch. 269 C.A. 90
National Farmers' Union Dev. Trust Ltd. Re: [1972] 1 W.L.R. 1458 254
National & Grindlays Bank & Co. v. Kenfiles [1966] E.A. 17 136
National Provident Fund v. Midwest Cement Co. Ltd. 1971 (2) NCLR 337 102
National Savings Bank, Re: (1866) L.R. 1 Ch. App. 547 265
National Telephone Co. Re: [1891] 2 Ch. 317 80
Nelson v. James Nelson & Sons Ltd. [1914] 2 K.B. 770 46, 47

New Baliks Festeling Ltd. v. Randt Gold Mining Co. [1904] A.C. 165 86
New British Iron Co. Exp. Beckwith Re: [1898] Ch. 324 45, 111
New London & Brazilian Bank v. Brocklebank (1882) 21 Ch.D. 302 71
New Timbui Gold Mine Ltd. Re: (1974) 1 F.R.C.R. 125 277
New Zealand Netherlands Society, "Oranje" v. Kuys [1973] 2 N.Z.L.R. 163 157
Newborne v. Sensolid (G.B.) Ltd. [1953] 1 All E.R. 708 22-23
Newhart Developments v. Co-operatives & Comm. Bank 1978 (2) BCKR 337 102
Newman & Howard Ltd., Re: [1962] 1 Ch. 257 237, 265
Ngurli v. McCann (1953) 90 C.L.R. 425 168, 169, 170, 198
Nidditch v. Calico Printers Assoc. 1961 S.L.T. 282 259
Nigerian Commercial & Industrial Enterprises v. Hammond Project 1977 1 CCHCJ 31 267
Nigerian Commercial & Industrial Enterprises Ltd. v. Omagiafo 1976 NCLR 399 123, 262, 264
Nigerian Industrial Property Co. v. Bank of West Africa Ltd. [1962] 1 All NLR 556 F.S.C. 20, 22
N.I.P.C. v. Thompson Organisation Ltd. 1969 NCLR 110, [1960 1 Ail N.L.R. 138 (Supreme Court (Nigeria) 39-40, 101
Nigerian Ports Authority v. Construzioni Generali SPA 1972(2) ALR Comm. 199 130
Nigerian Stores Workers Union v. Uzor 1971 (2) NCLR 412 202-204
Njemanze v. Shell B.P. Port Harcourt [1966] All N.L.R. 8 SCN 6
Ngaremtoni Estate Ltd. v. C.I.I. 1966(1) ALR Comm. 186 21, 22
North (The) Molton Mining Co. Ltd. Re: (1886) 54 L.T. 602 273
Normandy v. Ind. Coope & Co. [1908] 1 Ch.84 208, 247
Nocton v. Lord Ashburton [1914] A.C. 932 H.L. 60, 148
Northern Nigerian Marketing Board, Re: 1964 N.N; L.R. 30 5
Northumberland Avenue Hotel Co. Re: (1886) 33 Ch. D. 16 21, 22
Northwest Transportation Co. v. Beatty (1887) 12 App. Cas. 589 161, 175, 184, 212
Norwest Holst v. Sec. of State for Trade [1978] 3 All E.R. 280 238, 239
Nyasaland Civil Servants Co-operative Soc., Re: (1923-60) A.L.R. Mal 278

## O

Oakes v. Turquand & Harding (1867) L.R. 2 H.L. 325 76
Obaseki v. African Continental Bank 1966 N.M.L.R. 35 125
Obasi v. Pureway Corporation (Nig.) Ltd. (1978) 4 F.R.C.R. 214 237, 265
Obikoya (A.O.) v. Ezenwa & Ors [1964] 2 All N.L.R. 133 43-44, 45, 47
Oceanic Steam Navigation Co. Ltd.. Re; [1939] Ch. 41 255
Oduduru v. National Union of Hotels & Personal Services FCA/L/226/83 Unreported 202, 203
Odumody v. Mohammed 1973 NCLR 52 7, 56, 64, 65
Official Receiver v. Sontag (1938) 5 EACA 95 270
Ogunade v. Mobile Films Ltd. 2 F.R.C.R. 101 226-29
Ogunyemi v. John Holt Ltd. 197(1) NCLR 115 72
Oilfield Supply Centre v. Johnson [1986] 2 N.W.L.R. 681 56
Okeowo v. Migliore (1979) 11 S.C. 138 115, 121, 242, 245
Olaolu Modern Bakery Ltd. v. Young & Ors (1977) F.R.C.R. 371 102, 199
Olathe Silver Mining Co. Re: (1884) 27 Ch.D.278 265
Oliver v. Dalgleish [1963] 1 W.L.R. 274 [1963] 3 All E.R. 330 209
Onuh v. United Nigeria Insurance Co. Ltd. 1975 NCLR 413 131-32
Onwuka v. Tayamani (1965) L.L.R.62 107, 130, 245, 246
Ooregum Gold Mining Co. of India v. Roper [1892] A.C. 125 52, 66
Oriental Inland Steam Co. Exp Scinde Rail Co. (1874) 9 Ch. App. 557 275
Ososanya v. Obadeji 1968 (2) A.L.R. Comm.431 246, 278, 280
Othery Construction Ltd. Re: [1966] 1 W.L.R. 514 232
Otongu v. Mogal (Nig.) Ltd. (1978) 4 F.R.C.R.88 9

Otuyemi v. Essol (W.A.) Ltd. (1961) W.N.L.R. 130 7
Oxford Benefit & Investment Society, Re: (1886) 35 Ch. 502 153
Re: Oxted Motor Co. Ltd. [1921] 3 K.B. 3 12
Oyekoya v. G.B. Ollivant (Nig.) Ltd. [1969] 1 All N.L.R. 80 243

**P**

Page v. International Agency & Industrial Trust Ltd. [1893] 62 L.J. Ch. 610 79
Pan African Pools (Nig.) Ltd. In the Matter of: M/110/66 of 11/4/69 Unrep. 268
Panorama Development (Guildford) Ltd. v. Fidelis Furnishing Fabrics [1971] 3 W.L.R. 440 122, 130, 132
Paper Conversion Co., Ltd., Re: 1972 NCLR 39 263, 267
Paraguassu Steam Tramrod Co. Black & Co.'s Case (1872) 8 Ch. App. 254 275
Paris Skating Rink, Re: (1877) 5 Ch. D. 959 265
Parke v. Daily News Ltd. [1962] Ch. 927 161-162, 165
Parker & Cooper Ltd. v. Reading [1926] Ch. 975 [1926] All E.R. 323 50, 246
Parker v. Mckenna [1874] 10 Ch. App..96 176
Parkes (Swadlincote) Ltd., Re: [1929] 1 Ch.139 99
Patrick & Lyon Ltd., Re: [1933] Ch.786 271
Paul (HR & Son) Ltd., Re: (1974) 118 S.J. 166 244
Pavlides v. Jensen [1956] Ch. 655 219
Peat v. Clayton [1906] 1 Ch. 659 71
Peat (W.H.) v. Gresham Trust Ltd. [1934] A.C.252 270
Pedley v. Inland Waterways Assocn. Ltd. [1977] 1 All E.R. 209 247
Peek v. Gurney (1873) L.R. 6 H.L. 377 58, 59
Peel v. L. & N.W. Rly Co. [1907] 1 Ch. 5 C.A. 251
Pender v. Lushington (1877) 6 Ch. D. 70 C.A. 64, 202-210
Pepper v. Litton 308 U.S. 295 (1939) 152
Percival v. Wright [1902] 2 Ch. 421 154-157
Pergamon Press Ltd. v. Maxwell [1970] 1 W.L.R. 1167 149, 239, 240
Peso Silver Mines Ltd. (N.P.L.) v. Cropper (1966) 58 D.L.R.1 (2d) 176-78, 180-82
Peter & Co. Ltd. Re: Companies Cause No. 18/1960 (Unreported) H.C. (U) 274, 275, 280
Peter's American Delicacy Co. Ltd. v. Health (1939) 61 C.L.R. 457 48-49
Peveril Gold Mines Ltd. Re: [1898] 1 Ch. 122 C.A. 265
Pharmaceutical Society v. Dickson [1968] 3 W.L.R. 286 169
Phillips v. Abou - Diwan (1976) 2 F.R.C.R. 24 F.H.C. 6
Phipps v. Boardman [1967] 2 A.C. 46 154, 182-184
Piercy v. Mills & Co. Ltd. [1920] 1 Ch. 277 56, 167, 170, 171, 202
Politis v. Okudzeto 1967 (3) A.L.R. Comm.178 225
Ponsford v. Financial Times [1900] 16 T.L.R. 248 252
Pool House Group (Nig.) Ltd. Re: Lagos H.Ct. M/190/70 of 25/1/71 236
Pool House (Nig.) Ltd. v. A.C.B. Ltd. 1969 NCLR 347 108, 130-31
Portman Building Society v. Galloway [1955] 1 W.L.R. 96 101
Portuguese Consolidated Copper Mines Ltd. Re: [1890] 45 Ch.D. 16 56
Powell v. Kempton Park Racecourse Ltd. [1899] A.C. 143 203
Press Caps. Ltd. Re: [1949] Ch. 434 C.A. 259
Price v. Kelsall [1957] E.A.. 752 21, 22
Prichlik v. Marsh & Ors (1961) 1 N.L.R. 59 108, 109, 118
President, Councillors & Rate Payers of Shire of Frankston & Hastings v. Cohen [1960] 102 C.L.R. 607 145
Produce Exchange Trust Co. v. Biebach 176 Mass 577 NE 162 (1900) 135
Prole v. Allen [1950] 1 All E.R. 476 15
Provident International Corpn Case [1969] 89 W.N. (Pt. 1) (N.S.W.) 370 169
Prudential Assurance v. Chatterley, Whitfied Collieries [1949] A.C. 512 81
Prudential Ass. Co. Ltd. v. Newman Industries Ltd. [1979] 3 All E.R. 507 199, 202
Prudential v. Newman Industries Ltd. (No. 2) [1980] 2 All E.R. 841 212-14
Pulbrook v. Richmond Consolidated Mining Co. (1878) 9 Ch. D. 610 118, 204

Pulsford v. Davenish [1903] 2 Ch. 625257, 275, 280
Punt v. Symons & Co. Ltd. [1903] 2. Ch. 506 47, 167, 170, 171, 202
Pyle Works, Re: (1890) 44 Ch.D. 534 79

**Q**

Queensland Mines Ltd. V. Hudson (1978) 52 A.L.J.R. 399 180-181
Quin & Axtens v. Salmon [1909] A.C. 442 45, 113, 203, 204-05, 210

**R**

Rev. Board of Trade [1965] 1 Q.B. 603 103
R.V. Camps [1962] E.A. 403 C.A. 107, 108
Rv. I.R.C. Haulage [1944] K.B. 551 137
Rv. McDonnell [1966] 1 Q.B. 233 138
Rv. Registrar of Companies Exp. Bowen [1914] 3 K.B. 1161 24
Rv. Registrar of Companies Exp. Moore [1931] 2 K.B. 197 26
Rv. Schacter [1960] 2 Q.B. 252 144
R. Various Accused Unreported (High Court, Tanzania) 136, 138
Rainford v. James Keith & Blackman [1905] 1 Ch. 296 72
Rama Corpn. Ltd. v. Proved Tin. General Investments [1952] 1 All E.R. 554 127
Ramsgate Victoria Co. Ltd. v. Montefiore (1866) L.R. Ex. 109 55
Rankin & Blackmore Ltd.; Petitioners 1950 S.C. 218 255
Rayfield v. Hands [1958] 2 All E.R. 194 45, 50
Read v. Astoria Garage (Streatham) Ltd. [1952] 1 All E.R. 922 46-47, 110
Realisations (R.R.) Ltd. Re: [1980] 1 All E.R. 1019 280
Regal (Hastings) Ltd. v. Gulliver [1967] 2 A.C.134 154, 174-78, 194-97, 219-20
Reid v. Explosives Co. (1887) 19 Q.B.D. 264 C.A. 102
Reigate v. Union Manufacturing Co. (Rambottom) Ltd. (1918) 1 K.B. 592 280
Reiss (Nig.) Ltd. v. F.B.I.R. (1979) 3 F.R.C.R.251 11
Rica Gold Washing Co. Ltd. Re: (1879) 11 Ch. D. 36 C.A. 232, 265
Richmond Gate Property Co. Ltd. Re: [1964] 3 All E.R. 939 111, 120, 205
Ridsel, Re: [1947] 2 All E.R. 312 145
Rights & Issue Investment Trust Ltd. v. Stylo Shoes [1964] 3 All E.R. 628 49-50
Robbie (N.W.) v. Whitney Warehouse Ltd. [1963] 3 All E.R. 613 C.A. 97
Roberta, The (1937) LI.L. Rep. 11
Roberts v. Hopwood [1925] 578 145
Roith (W & M), Re: [1967] 1 W.L.R. 432 162
Rolled Steel Products (Holdings) Ltd. v. B.S.C. [1982] 3 W.L.R. 715 32, 34, 50
Rosenblum v. Judson Engineering Corpn. (1954) 109 A (2d) 558 179
Rother Iron Works Ltd. v. Canterbury Precision Engineers [1974] Q.B.1 97
Roundwood Colliery Co., Re: [1897] 1 Ch. 373 C.A. 96
Rowell v. Rowell (J) & Sons Ltd. [1912] 2 Ch. 609 87
Royal British Bank v. Turquand [1956] 8E & B 327 124-33, 135
Ruben v. Great Fingall Consolidated [1906] A.C. 439 67, 132-33
Rudewa v. Commissioner of Stamp Duties [1966] E.A. 576 275, 280
Russel v. Wakefield Waterworks Co. [1875] 20 Eq. 474 153, 202

**S**

S.B.A. Properties Ltd., Re: [1967] 2 All E.R. 615 240
Saint Benoist Plantations Ltd. v. Felix [1959] 21 EACA 105 239
Salgitter (W.A.) Ltd. v. Registrar of Companies 1975 N.C.L.R. 149 249
Salmon v. Quin & Axtens [1909] 1 Ch. 311 C.A. 202
Salomon v. Salomon & Co. Ltd. [1897] A.C. 22 H.L. 4-5, 8, 10, 12, 60, 66
Saltdean Estate Co. Ltd. Re: [1968] 3 All E.R. 829 81, 85
Saltman Engineering Co. v. Campbell Engineering Co. [1948] R.P.C. 203 189
Sandwell Park Colliery Co. Re: [1914] 1 Ch. 589 258
Sarderet (Nig.) Ltd. v. Maiden Electronics Works Ltd. FRC/L/M119/78 263
Sarflax Ltd. Re: '1979] 1 All E.R. 529 271
Sartori [1961] All N.L.R. 534 20
Savoy Corpn. Ltd. v. Dev. Underwriting Co. Ltd. (1963) 80 W.N. (N.S.W.) 1021 170

Savoy Hotel Case (H.M.S.O. 1954) 161-162, 171
Savoy Hotel Ltd., Re: [1981] 3 All E.R. 646 254,255
Sentamu v. UCB [1983] H.C.B. 59 4, 6
Scholeý v. Central Rlwy Co. of Venezuela [1869] L.R. Eq. 266 59
Scott v. Frank Scott (London) Ltd. [1940] Ch. 394; [1940] All E.R. 508 50
Scott v. Scott [1943] J All E.R. 582 114-115
Scottish Cooperative Wholesale Sco. Ltd. v. Meyer [1959] A.C. 324 150, 187, 192, 227, 228, 230
Scottish Insurance Corpn. v. Wilson & Clyde Coal Co. [1949] AC. 462 80-81, 84-85
Scottish Petroleum Co. Re: [1883] 23 Ch. D. 413 59
Securities & Exchange Commission v. Texas Gulf Sulphur Co. 401F 2D 833 (1968) 157
Seddon v. North Eastern Salt Co. [1905] 1 Ch. 326 60
Sejpal Ltd., Re: [1957] E.A. 589 (Uganda) 265
Selangor United Rubber Estates Ltd. v. Craddorck (No. 3) [1968] 2 All E.R. 1073 88, 106, 186, 192
Shanley (M.J.) Contracting, Re: [1979] 124 S.J.239 246
Sharp v. Dawes [1976] 2 Q.B.D. 26 242, 248
Sharp v. Jackson [1899] A.C. 419 270
Sharpley v. Louth & East Coast Rlwy co. [1876] 2 Ch. D. 663 59
Shaw v. Shaw [1935] 2 K.B. 113 112, 199-200
Sheffied Corpn. v. Barclay [1905] A.C. 392 67, 72
Shepherd's Trustees v. Shepherd [1950] S.C. 60 69
Shindler v. Northern Raincoat Co. Ltd. [1960] 2 All E.R. 239 46, 110
Shonibare v. Mansour 1963 LHCR 1 22
Shonibare v. Probate Registrar 1966 (2) A.L.R. Comm. 389 6, 68
Shonibare v. Western Nigeria Finance Corpn. 1970 (1) A.LR. Comm.98 29, 35
Shonowo v. Adebayo 1969 NCLR 126 (Supreme Court of Nigeria) 105, 148, 191-193
Shuttleworth v. Cox Bros & Co. [1927] 2 K.B. 2 C.A. 48, 49, 223, 227
Sidebottom v. Kershaw, Leese & Co. Ltd. [1920] 1 Ch. 154 43, 48, 228
Siemens Bros & Co. v. Burns [1918] Ch. 324 72
Silber Light Co. v. Silber (1879) 12 Ch. D. 717 199
Simo Securities Trust Co. Re: [1971] 1 W.L.R. 1455 259
Simpson v. Molson Bank [1895] A.C. 270 76-77
Simpson v. Westminster Palace Hotel Co. [1860] 8 H.L. Cas. 712 203
Sinclair v. Brougham [1914] A.C. 398 35, 151
Smith & Fawcett, Re; [1942] Ch. 304 68, 159, 160, 161, 166-67, 172
Smith, Stone & Knight v. Birmingham Corpn. [1939] 4 All E.R. 116 9, 11-12
Smith (James) & Sons (Norwood) Ltd. v. Goodman [1936] Ch. 216 C.A. 274, 275
Smithfield Butchery Ltd. V.R. (1949) 23(2) KLR 81 137
Smyth v. Darley (1849) 2 H.L. Cas. 789 245
Societe Generale de Paris v. Tramways Union Co. (1884) 14 Q.B.D. 424 77
Sorbie v. Tea Corporation [1904] 1 Ch. 12 C.A. 258
South of England Natural Gas Co. Re: [1911] 1 Ch. 573 62
Southern Foundaries Ltd. v. Shirlaw [1940] 2 All E.R. 445 46, 110
Spargo's Case [1973] L.R. 8 Ch. App. 407 66
Sparks Electrics Ltd. v. Ponmile [1986] 2 N.W.L.R. 516 21, 56, 65, 66, 201, 202
Spencer v. Ashworth, Partington & Co. [1925] 1 K.B. 589 70
Spiraflite Ltd. Re: [1979] 2 All E.R. 1225 269
Spokes v. Grasvenor Hotels [1897] 2 Q.B. 124 C.A. 202, 212
Spottiswoods Dixon & Hunting Ltd. Re: [1912] 1 Ch. 410 276
Squire (Henry) Cash Chemist Ltd. v. Ball, Baker & Co [1911] 27 T.L.. 269 145
St. James' Court Estate Ltd. Re: [1944] Ch. 6 255
St. Thomas' Dock Co. Re: [1876] 2 Ch. D. 116 264

Standard Bank (Nig.) Ltd. v. B.G.C.Co. (Nig.) Ltd. Suit No. FRC/L/M89 262
Standard Bank (Nig.) Ltd. v. Balokor Enterprises Ltd. (1980) F.N.R. 114 124-26
Standard Bank of Nigeria Ltd. v. Communications Joint Services Ltd. 1975(2) ALR Comm. 264
Standard Bank v. Mehotor Farm Ltd. [1973] E.A. 78 88-89
Standard Chartered Bank v. Walhler [1982] 1 W.L.R.1410 102
Starcola (Nig.) Ltd. v. Taibatu Adeniji 1972 NMLR 69 56, 65, 66
Stephen v. Building Co. Ltd. 1 1968(2) ALR Comm. 242 21, 22, 66
Steele v. Gourley 1887 3 T.L.R. 772 15
Stephenson (H.A.) & Sons Ltd. v. Gillanders Arbuthnot & Co. [1931] 45 C.L.R. 33
Steen v. Law [1964] A.C. 287 P.C. 89
Steinberg v. Scola [1923] 2 Ch. 452 64
Stone Leigh Finance Ltd. v. Phillips [1965] 1 All E.R. 513 98
Stray v. Russel (1959) 1 E. & E 888, 890 70
Sutherland v. British Dominions Land Settlement Corpn [1926] Ch. 746 68
Swaledale Cleaners Ltd. [1968] 1 WLR 1710 69
Stevenson v. Wilson [1907] S. Aq. 445 70
Suerre Kang & Ors v. Buhemba Mines Ltd. [1935] 20 EACA 28 80, 28, 235
Survey v. Port Darwin Gold Mining Co. [1889] 1 Meg 385 C.A. 45-46
Sussex Brick, Re: [1961] Ch. 270 C.A. 76, 259
Standard Manufacturing Co. Re: [1891] 1 Ch.627 96
Strong v. Rapide 213 v. 419 (1909) 156, 157
Stevedoring (Nig.) Re: (1962) LLR 164 187, 236
Symington v. Symington's Quarries [1905) 8F 121 233
Steel Wing Co. Re: [1921] 1 Ch. 349 265
Stanley (G) & Co. Re: [1925] Ch. 148 270
Stead Hasel & Co. v. Cooper [1933] 1 K.B. 840 274
Swain (J.D.) Ltd. Re: [1965] 1 W.L.R. 909 C.A. 280

## T

Taff Vale Rlwy Co. v. Amalgamated Soc. of Servants [1901] A.C. 426 213
Taibatu Adeniji v. Starcola (Nig. Ltd. 1972 N.M.L.R. 69 19
Tamlin v. Hannaford [1950] 1 K.B. 18 C.A. 18
Tandy v. Harmony House Furniture Co. Ltd. [1964[ 1 All N.LR. 31 1, 263-264
Tanganyika Produce Agency Ltd. Re: [1957] E.A. 241 263
Tate v. Willaimson (1866) LR. 2 Ch. App. 55 157
Taupo Totara Timber Ltd. v. Rowe [1978] A.C. 537 112
Tavistock Iron Works Co. Re: (1871) 24 L.T. 605 273
Taylor v. Taylor 1977 N.C.L.R. 391 203
Teck Corporation Ltd. v. Millar [1972] 33 D.L.R. (3d) 288 B.C.S.C. 164-165, 171-73
Tejani v. Official Receiver [1960] E.A. 574 P.C. 269, 271
Tesco Supermarkets v. Natrass [1972] A.C. 153 H.L. 106, 137
Teso Cotton Co. Ltd. Re: Companies Cause No. 50 of 1960(U) 235
Texaco Africa Ltd. v. Nigerian Shipping Trading Co. [1962] L.L.R. 78 128
Thadani v. Thadani F.H.C. (unreported) F.H.C/L/M8/80 of 1.8.80 66
Thomas v. Corporation of Devonport [1900] 1 Q.B. 16 145
Thomas Garrard Ltd. [1967] All E.R. 525 146
Thomas Marshall v. Guinle [1979] 1 Ch. 227 187-190
Thomas Mortimer Ltd., Re: [1965] Ch. 186 97
Tiessen v. Henderson [1899] 1 Ch. 861 206, 207, 247
Tika-Tore Press v. Abina [1973] 1 All N.L.R. 244; 1973 NCLR 74 56, 65, 173
Tilt Cove Copper Co. Re: [1913] 2 Ch. 588 101
Tivoli Freeholds Ltd. Re: (1972) V.R. 445 31
Trade Links, Int. (Nig.) Ltd. v. Bank of America (1977) F.R.C.R. 285 113, 114, 125
Transatlantic Life Ass. Co. Ltd. Re: [1980] 1 W.LR. 79 76

Transbridge Co. Ltd. v. Survey Int. Ltd. [1986] 4 N.W.L.R. 576 21
Transplanters (Holding Co.) Ltd. Re: [1968] 2 Ch. 711 142
Transvaal Lands Co. v. New Belgium (Transvaal) Co. [1914] 2 Ch. 488 184, 185
Travel & Holiday Clubs Ltd. Re: [1967] 2 All E.R. 606 240
Trenco (Nig.) Ltd. v. African Real Estate [1978] 1 L.R.N. 146 126, 127, 128, 136
Trevor v. Whiteworth (1887) 12 App. Cas. 409 H.L. 65, 82, 84, 87, 152-53
Trinidad Oil Co. Ltd. Re: The Times April 13, 1957 259
Truculent (H.M.S.) [1952] p.1136
Tufton v. Sperni (1952) 2 T.L.R. 516 157
Tung v. Nig. Carton & Packaging Manufacturing Co. Ltd. FRC/L/M82/78 252
Tweeds Garages Ltd [1962] 1 Ch. 406 1, 263, 264
Twycross v. Grant (1877) 2 C.P.D. 469 19
Tymans Ltd. v. Graven [1952] 2 Q.B. 100 C.A.A. 277

U

Ukpilla Cement Co. Ltd. v. Igiekhume (1979) 1 F.C.A. 64 C.A.A. 106, 112, 115
Union Accident Insurance Co. Ltd. Re: [1972] 1 W.L.R. 503 267
Union National Bank v. Douglas 24 Fed Cas. 621 (1977) 152
Unit Construction Co. Ltd. v. Bullock [1960] A.C. 351 H.L. 13
United Bank for Africa Ltd. v. Registrar of Companies (1977) 3 F.R.C.R. 91 100
United Nig. Trading Co. Ltd. v. Registrar of Companies (1978) 4. F.R.C.R. 135 57
University of Nigeria v. E.W. Turner & Sons Ltd. 1968(1) A.L.R. Comm. 290 125
Urhobo v. Chief J.S. Tarka (1976) 11 CCHCJ 21
U.S. Brewing Co. v. Apthorpe (1898) 4 T.C. 17 11
United States v. Simon 425F (2d) 296 (2nd Circuit 1969) 147
Uxbridge Building Society v. Pickard [1939] 2 K.B. 248 133

V

Vanni v. Niger Park Ltd. (1979) 4-6 CCHCJ 148 124
Vatcher v. Paull [1915] A.C. 372 P.C. 168
Verner v. General & Commercial Investment Trust [1894] 2 Ch. 239 90
Victor Battery Co. Ltd. v. Curry's Ltd. [1946] 1 All E.R. 519 88, 186
Victoria Steamboats Co. Re: [1897] 1 Ch. 158 101, 103
Visinoni (B) Ltd. & Ors. v. National Bank of Nigeria 1975 NCLR 190 124
Vuma, Re: [1960] 1 W.L.R. 1233 266

W

W.A.A. (Nig.) Ltd. v. West African Pilot Ltd. 1968 (1) A.L.R. Comm. 65 130, 134
Wachukwu v. Cooperative Bank of Eastern Nigeria 1974 44, 45
Walji v. Shinyanga African Trading Co. Ltd. C.S. No. 18 of 1968 (Tanzania H.C.) 185
Walkden Sheet Metal Co. Ltd. [1960] Ch. 170 269
Walker v. Wimborne (1936) 50 A.L.J.R. 446 151-53, 162
Wall v. London & Northern Assets Corpn [1890] 2 Ch. 469 209
Wallersteiner v. Moir [1974] 1 W.L.R. 991 C.A. 11, 89, 214-217, 219-21, 222, 224
Wallis & Simmonds (Builders) Ltd., Re: [1974) 1 All E.R. 561 98
Wallworth v. Holt (1841) 2 My & Cr. 619 208
Wani v. Uganda Timbers & Joiners Ltd. H.C.C.C. 989 of 1972 5, 138
Warnford Investment Ltd. v. Duckworth [1978] 2 W.L.R. 741 271
Watson v. Duff Morgan & Vermont Ltd. [1974] 1 W.L.R. 450 100
Webb v. Alexandria Water Co. (1906) 21 T.L.R. 527 74
Wedgwood Coal & Iron Co. Re: (1877) Ch.D.75 41
Welsbach Incandescent Gas Light Co. Ltd. [1904] 1 Ch. 87 41, 42
Welton v. Saffery [1979] A.C. 299 45, 66
Wessex Dairies Ltd. v. Smith [1935] 2 K.B. 80 C.A. 189
West Canadian Collieries Ltd. Re: [1962] Ch.378 246

West End Hotel Syndicate v. Bayer [1912] 29 T.L.R. (Ch.) 199
Westbourne Galleries Ltd., Re: [1970] 1 W.L.R. 1378 229, 232-35
Westburn Sugar Refineries v. L.R.C. 1960 S.L.T. 297 91
Western Counties Steam Bakeries & Milling Co. Re: [1897] 1 Ch. 617 .. 144
Western Manufacturing (Reding) Ltd. Re: [1956] Ch. 436 259
Westminster C.C. v. Haste [1950] Ch. 442 103
Wheatley v. Silkstone Co. (1885) 29 Ch.D. 715 96
White v. Bristol Aeroplane Co. [1953] Ch. 65 83
White Church (George) Ltd. v. Cavanagh [1902] A.C. 117 121, 132
Whitfield v. Kern 192A 48 (1937) 152
Will v. Murray (1850) 4 Ex. Ch. 843 251
Will v. United Linkat Plantation Ltd. [1914] A.C. 11 80
William Jones & Sons Ltd. Re: [1969] 1 W.L.R.146 82, 85
William Mtcalfe & Sons, Re: [1933] Ch. 142 80
Wilson v. Bury (1880) 4 Q.B.D. 518 C.A. 150
Wilson v. Kelland [1910] 2 Ch. 306 96
Wilson v. L.M.S. Rlwy [1940] Ch. 169 185
Wilson v. Lovatt & Sons Ltd. (1977) 1 All E.R.274 276
Wincham Shipbuilding Boiler & Salt Co., Re: (1878) 1 Ch.d. 322 153
Windsor Steam Coal Co., Re: (1901) Ltd. [1921] 1 Ch. 151 275, 280
Winklaimer v. East African Plans Ltd. & Anors [1969] E.A. 415 207
Winthrop Investments Ltd. Winns Ltd. (1975) 2 N.S.W.L.R.66 207
Wise v. Perpetual Trustees Co. [1903] A.C. 139 15
Wiseman v. Borneman [1969] 3 All E.R. 275 239
Witu v. Peake (1913)/14) 5 E.A.L.R. 5 124
Wolverhampton Steel & Iron Co. Re: [1977] 1 W.L.R. 153 265
Wondoflex Textiles Pty Ltd. Re: 1951) V.L.R. 458 233, 237
Wood v. Odessa Waterworks Co. (1889) 42 Ch.D. 636 43, 50, 202
Wragg, Re: [1897] 1 Ch. 796 66
Wrexham Mold & Connah's Quay Rlwy Co. Re: [1899] 1 Ch. 440 35

## Y

Yagerphone Co. Ltd. Re: [1935] 1 Ch. 392 270
Yaskey v. Freetown City Council (1933) 1 W.A.C.A. 243
Yeovil Glove Co. Ltd. Re: [1965] 2 All E.R.849 96
Yenidje Tobacco Co. Ltd. [1916] 2 Ch. 426 C.A. 232, 233, 236
Yetton v. Eastwoods Froy [1967] 1 W.L.R. 104 120
York Tramways Co. Ltd. v. Willows (1882) 8 Q.B.D. 685 118
Yorkshire Mines Assoc. Howden [1905] A.C.256 202, 203
Yorkshire Woolcombers Assoc. Ltd. Re: [1903] 2 Ch. 284 95
Young v. Ladies Imperial Club [1920] 2 K.B.523 246

## Z

Zone Company Ltd. Re: (1962) L.L.R. 160 55, 76
Zwicker v. Stanbury (1954) 1. D.L.R. 257 182

# TABLE OF STATUTES


1571 Fraudulent Conveyances Act (UK) ........ 10
1845 Companies Clauses Act (8 & 9 Vict.c.16) S.71 ........ 247
1862 Companies Act (UK) ........ 125
1878 Dentists Act (UK) ........ 24
1881 Conveyancing Act, S.19 ........ 100
1883 Bankruptcy Act (UK) ........ 10
1890 Partnership Act (53 & 54 Vict.c.39)
S.32 ........ 233
S.33 ........ 233
S.34 ........ 233
S.35 ........ 233
Directors Liability Act ........ 60
1894 Merchant Shipping Act, 1894, S.502 ........ 136
1900 Companies Act (63 & 64 Vict. C. 48) ........ 145
1908 Companies (Consolidation) Act (8 Edw. 7 c.69) S.69 ........ 250
1934 Securities & Exchange Commission Act (US)
Rule 10b-5 ........ 159
1947 Companies Act 10 & 11 Geo. C.47)
S.9 ........ 224
1948 Companies Act (11 & 12 Geo. 6. C.38) ........ 2, 3
S.5 ........ 40
S.10 ........ 50
S.11 ........ 50
S.20 ........ 43-45
(1) ........ 205-206
S.54 ........ 88
S.74 ........ 75
S.132 ........ 266
S.165 ........
(b) (ii) ........ 239
S.184 ........ 234
S.191 ........ 193
S.199 ........ 184, 185
S.205 ........ 190
S.206 ........ 255
S.210 ........ 187, 224 - 30
S.222
(f) ........ 232 - 37
S.268 ........ 269
S.322 ........ 97
S.332 ........
(1) ........ 122
S.353 ........ 225
(6) ........ 225
S.448 ........ 193, 209
S.455 ........ 60
1958 Bills of Exchange Act (Cap.21 Laws of Nigeria) ........ 129
Companies Act (Cap.37 L/N) ........ 1, 69, 129
S.81 ........ 129
S.135 ........ 1
(e) ........ 1
S.137 ........ 1
S. 211 ........ 143
S.239 ........ 14
Criminal Code (Cap. 42 L/N) ........ 137
S.383 ........ 137
S.390 ........ 137
Sheriffs & Civil Processes Act (C.189 L/N) ........ 73
1959 Defamation Law (C.17 W.N.)
S.16 ........ 253
(I) ........ 253
(2) ........ 253
(3) ........ 253
(4) ........ 253
S.17 ........ 253
Sched. para. 11 ........ 253
Partnership Law (W.N.C. 86)
S.33 ........ 233
S.34 ........ 233
S.35 ........ 233
S.36 ........ 233
1960 British Columbia Companies Act (C.67) ........
S.185 ........ 244
Companies Act (N. Ireland) S.201
(6) ........ 224
South Carolina Code (S.12 - 22) S.15
(a) ........
(4) ........
(b) ........ 231
S.23 ........
(a) ........ 224
1961 Uniform Companies Act (Australia)
S.19 ........ 165
S.124 ........ 158, 159
(1) ........ 158
(2) ........ 158
(3) ........ 158
S.186 ........ 224
Companies Act (New South Wales)
S.367 B ........ 152
1963 Companies Code (Ghana) ........ 3, 183
S.202
(1) ........ 165
S.203

(3) .................................. 164
S.205
(a) .......................... 182 - 183
S.210 .......................................... 224
S.218 .................................. 224, 231
(1)
(a) ........................
(b) ........................ 231
(2) .................................. 232
1965 Companies Act (Malaysia) S.132
(2) .................................. 158
(4) .................................. 158
S.181 .......................................... 224
(1) ..................................
(b) ........................ 231
(2) .................................. 232
1966 French Loi Art 124 ...................... 134
(4) .............................................. 134
1967 Companies Act (Alberta)
S.82 ............................................ 158
S.83 ............................................ 158
S.84 ............................................ 158
S.85 ............................................ 158
S.87 ............................................ 158
S.88 ............................................ 158
Companies Act (Britain, C.81) ................ 148
S.14 ............................................
(3) ....................................
(a) ........................ 147
S.19 ............................................ 165
Companies Act (Singapore Am. 1971)
S.132 .................
(2) ................. 158
(4) ................. 158
S.132 A ...................................... 159
S.181 ........................................ 224
(1) ............................................
(b) .................................. 231
(2) ............................................ 232
Securities Act (British Columbia, Am: 1968 - 1976)
S.111 ........................................ 158
Part xi ........................................ 158
Exchange Control Act S.46 .................. 17, 68
1868 Companies Act (Nigeria)
............ 1, 14, 69, 262, 263, 281, 282
1964 Companies Act (Uganda) .............. 29
S.2 ............................ 1, 53, 92, 143
S.4 .............................................. 28
(1) .............................................. 23
(2)(a) .......................................... 23
(2)(b) ................................ 6, 23, 27
(2)(c) ........................................ 6, 23
S.5 .................................... 24, 27, 79
S.8 ........................................ 36, 39
(1) .................................... 40
(2) .................................... 40
(10) .................................. 40
(14) .................................. 40
S.9 .......................... 24, 42, 249, 256
S.10 ...................................... 24, 42
(1) ....................................
(2) .................................... 42
S.11 ...................................... 24, 42
S.12 .............................................. 43
S.13 .............................. 50, 113, 249
(1) .................................... 47
(2)....................................... 114
S.14 ...................................... 30, 42
S.15 .............................................. 24
(1) .................................... 24
S.16 ...................................... 5, 6, 7
(2) .................................... 24
S.17 .............................................. 26
(1) .................................... 24
(2) .................................... 24
S.20 ...................................... 28, 39
(1) ............................ 28, 249
(2) .................................... 28
S.21 ...................................... 28, 39
S.22 ...................................... 43 - 45
(1) ........................ 205 - 06
(2) ..............................
S.24 ...................................... 40, 47
S.25 .................................... 40, 249
S.26 .............................................. 42
S.27 .............................................. 84
S.28 .................................... 65, 225
S.29 ...................................... 65, 88
(2) .................................... 88
(3) .................................... 88
S.30 .................................. 7. 23, 68
S.32 ................................ 23, 54, 55
S.33 .................................. 8. 38, 39
S.35 .............................................. 129
S.38 .............................................. 123
S.39 .............................................. 8
S.40 ............. 8, 20, 51, 54, 55, 62, 79
(3) .................................... 62
(4)(a),(b) .......................... 62
(4) .................................... 62
S.41 .................................. 8. 54, 62
S.42 ........................................ 8, 61
(1) .................................... 54
(3) ....................................
S.43 ........................................ 8, 51
(1) .................................... 53
(2) ................................ 54, 62
(4) .................................... 63
S.44 .............................................. 8

S.45 .................... 8, 19, 58, 60, 61-62
(2) .................................... 61
(3) .................................... 61
S.46 ................................................ 8
(1) .................................... 63
S.47 ............................ 8, 51, 54, 55
(1) .................................... 53
S.48 ........................................ 8, 63
(a) .................................... 61
S.49 .................................. 8, 56, 57
(3) .............................. 56, 66
S.50 ........................ 8, 54, 55, 56, 57
S.51 ........................................ 8, 56
(2) .................................... 57
S.52 ............................ 8, 54, 55, 57
S.53 ........................................ 8, 57
(1) .................................... 57
(2) .................................... 57
(3) .................................... 57
(4) .................................... 57
S.54 .................................. 8, 57, 66
S.55 ........................................ 8, 52
(1) ....................................
S.56 .................................. 8, 88, 89
(1) .............................. 88, 89
S.57 ............................ 8, 53, 54, 55
(1) .................................... 53
S.58 ........................ 8, 66, 79, 82, 91
S.59 ........................................ 8, 66
S.60 ........................ 8, 39, 79, 82, 91
S.61 ....................................
(c) .................................... 64
S.62 .............................. 39, 79, 249
S.63 ............................................ 39
(c) .................................... 74
S.64 ............................................ 91
S.65 ............................................ 84
S.67 .................................... 88, 249
S.68 .............................. 84, 86, 249
S.69 ............................................ 85
(1) .................................... 85
S.70 ...................................... 39, 85
S.71 ............................................ 86
S.72 ............................................
(1) .................................... 86
(a) .................................... 86
(b) .................................... 86
S.74 ................................ 47, 82, 83
S.75 ........................................ 7, 64
S.76 ...................................... 74, 75
S.77 ................................ 69, 93, 94
S.78 ............................................ 65
S.80 .......................... 69, 70, 93, 94
S.81 ............................................
(2) .................................... 70
(3) .................................... 70
S.82 ................................ 67, 70, 93
S.83 ............................................ 67
S.84 ............................................ 65
S.85 ............................................ 74
S.91 ............................................ 93
S.92 ............................................ 93
S.94 ............................................ 94
S.95 .......................................... 103
S.96 .......................... 96, 98, 99, 100
S.97 ............................................ 99
S.98 ............................................ 99
S.99 ............................................ 99
S.100 ..........................................
(1) .................................... 99
(2) .................................... 99
S.101 ..........................................
(1) .................................... 10
S.102 .......................................... 100
S.103 ................................ 103, 104
S.104 .......................................... 98
S.105 .......................................... 97
S.107 ..........................................
(1) ....................................
(2) .................................... 28
S.109 ............................................ 9
S.111 .................................... 23, 92
S.112 .......................................... 75
(1) ....................................
(2) .................................... 73
(3) .................................... 75
S.113 .......................................... 75
S.114 .................................... 75, 89
S.115 .................................... 75, 89
S.117 .................................... 77, 89
S.118 ........................ 59, 69, 76, 275
S.119 ................ 71, 76, 77, 138, 139
S.120 .......................................... 77
S.125 .......................................... 77
S.126 .......................................... 77
S.127 .......................................... 77
S.130 .... ................................ 8, 23
(1) .................................. 242
(2) .................................. 242
(3) .................................. 242
(4) .................................. 243
(5) .................................. 243
(6) .................................. 243
(7) .................................. 243
(10) ................................ 261
S.131 .................................. 8, 243
(1) .................................. 243
(2) .......................... 243, 248

(3) .................................... 243
(4) ....................................
(5) .................................... 243
S.132 .............................................. 8
(1) .................................... 244
(2) .................................... 244
(5) .................................... 244
S.133 .............................................. 8
(1) .................................... 245
(3) .................................... 246
S.134 .......................... 8, 23, 248, 249
(d) .................................... 249
(e) .................................... 250
S.135 ...................... 8, 244 - 45, 248
S.136 ................................ 8, 23, 252
(1)(c) ........................ 250, 251
(2) ........................... 247, 251
(3) .................................... 251
(4) .................................... 251
S.137 .............................................. 8
(1) ....................................
(2) .................................... 251
S.138 ............................... 8, 250, 252
S.139 ...................................... 8, 252
S.140 ............................. 47, 247, 248
(1) .................................... 248
(2) .................................... 248
(4) .................................... 248
(a) ........................ 248
(5)(a) ................................ 248
S.141 .......................................... 113
(1) .................................... 246
(2) ........................... 246, 249
(3) .................................... 249
S.142 .................................. 110, 247
S.143 ...................................... 8, 249
S.144 .................................. 251, 252
S.145 .......................................... 118
(1) .................................... 252
(2) .................................... 252
(3) .................................... 252
S.146 .......................................... 252
S.147 .............................. 8, 138, 139
S.148 ...................................... 8, 139
S.149 ...................................... 8, 140
S.150 .......................................... 8, 9
(1) .................................... 140
(2) .................................... 140
S.151 ...................................... 8, 140
S.152 ...................................... 8, 140
(3) .................................... 141
S.153 .............................................. 8
S.154 ........................................ 8, 88
S.155 ...................................... 8, 139
S. 156 .............................. 8, 140, 247
S.157 ...................... 8, 138, 139, 140
(1) .................................... 141
(2) .................................... 141
S.158 .................................. 140, 247
S.159 .................................. 144, 243
(1) .................................... 141
(2) .................................... 141
(3) .................................... 142
(5) ....................................
(a) ........................ 141
(b) ........................ 141
(6) .................................... 142
S.160 .......................................... 247
(1) .................................... 141
S.161 ..........................................
(1) .................................... 142
(2) .................................... 142
(3) .................................... 142
S.162 ..........................................
(1) ........................... 144, 148
(2) .................................... 148
(3) ........................... 144, 145
S.163 ....................................
S.165 ........................... 238, 239, 266
(1) ..................
(a) ........................ 238
(b) ........................ 238
S.166 ........................... 239, 249, 266
(a) .................................... 238
(b) .................................... 238
S.167 .............................................. 9
S.168 .......................................... 144
(1) .................................... 239
(2) .................................... 239
(3) .................................... 239
S.169 .......................................... 240
(1) .................................... 240
(2) .................................... 240
S.170 .......................................... 266
(1) .................................... 240
(3) .................................... 240
S.171 .......................................... 241
S.172 .......................................... 240
S.173 .......................................... 241
S.174 .......................................... 241
S.175 .......................................... 241
S.176 .......................................... 240
(a) .................................... 240
(b) .................................... 240
S.A77 .................................... 8, 106
S.178 .............................. 8, 106, 120
S.179 .............................. 8, 120, 126
S.180 ...................................... 8, 120
S.181 .............................. 8, 108, 118

S.182 .......... 8
S.183 .......... 8, 74, 107
S.184 .......... 8, 107
S.185 .......... 8, 23, 110, 111, 120, 164, 234, 247
(2) .......... 110
S.186 .......... 8, 107, 109, 247
(5) .......... 109
(6) .......... 109
S.187 .......... 8, 107
S.188 .......... 8, 23, 107
S.189 .......... 8, 107
S.190 .......... 8, 186
(2) .......... 186
S.191 .......... 8, 186
(2) .......... 186
(3) .......... 186
S.192 .......... 8, 110, 111, 186, 193
S.193 .......... 8, 110, 111, 186
S.194 .......... 8, 111, 186
S.195 .......... 8, 109, 111
S.196 .......... 8, 109
(2) .......... 109
(5) .......... 109
S.195 .......... 8, 111, 140, 186
(3) .......... 186
(4) .......... 186
S.198 .......... 8, 122, 140, 186
S.199 .......... 8
S.200 .......... 5, 8, 184, 185, 190
(1) .......... 184
(2) .......... 184
(3) .......... 184
(4) .......... 184
(5) .......... 185
S.201 .......... 8, 105, 108, 109, 121
S.202 .......... 8, 109
S.203 .......... 8
S.204 .......... 8, 249
S.205 .......... 8, 249
S.206 .......... 122, 190, 191
S.207 .......... 39, 82, 245-256, 257
S.208 .......... 39, 254-56, 257
S.209 .......... 39, 254-56, 257
(1) ..........
(d) .......... 7
S.210 .......... 39, 258
(1) .......... 258, 259
(2) .......... 259
(3) .......... 259
(4) .......... 259
S.211 .......... 39, 47, 221, 224-30, 234, 235, 240
(2) .......... 225
S.212 .......... 261
(1) .......... 261
S.213 .......... 265, 272
S.214 .......... 265, 272
S.217 .......... 265
S.218 .......... 7, 266
S.222 .......... 249, 261, 265
(a) .......... 261, 264
(b) .......... 243
(f) .......... 232-37
S.223 ..........
(a) .......... 262
(b) .......... 262, 264
(c) .......... 262
S.224.......... 232, 261, 262, 265, 266, 281
S.225 .......... 7, 261, 266
S.226 .......... 263, 267, 280
S.227 .......... 103, 280, 282
S.228 .......... 267, 270, 282
S.229 .......... 267
(1) .......... 267, 281
(2) .......... 266
S.230 .......... 266
S.231 .......... 266, 267, 274
S.233 .......... 265
S.235 .......... 268
(1) .......... 268
S.236 .......... 268
S.237 .......... 274
S.238 .......... 267
S.239 .......... 268
S.240 .......... 268
S.241 .......... 268, 273
(1) ..........
(2) ..........
(4) .......... 268
S.242 .......... 266, 269, 274
S.243 .......... 269, 274
S.244 .......... 274, 275, 280
S.245 .......... 274, 276
S.247 .......... 274
S.248 .......... 274
S.250 .......... 274, 276
S.251 .......... 268
(1) .......... 268
(2) .......... 268
S.252 .......... 268
(1) .......... 268
(2) .......... 268
S.253 .......... 268
S.255 .......... 272, 274
S.256 .......... 269
S.257 .......... 272
S.258 .......... 274

S.261 .......... 267
S.263 .......... 274
S.267 .......... 269, 281
S.268 .......... 281
S.269 .......... 272
S.271 ..........
(a) .......... 274
S.272 .......... 276
S.276 .......... 249, 277
S.277 .......... 268
S.278 .......... 277
S.279 .......... 277, 280
S.280 .......... 280
S.281 .......... 278, 279
S.283 .......... 278, 280
S.284 .......... 278
S.285 .......... 39, 249, 254, 256-58
(1) .......... 257
(2) .......... 256
(3) .......... 256
S.286 .......... 278
S.287 .......... 278
S.288 .......... 278
S.289 .......... 279
S.291 .......... 279
S.292 .......... 279
S.293 .......... 279
S.294 .......... 279, 280
S.295 .......... 279
S.297 .......... 279
S.298 .......... 279, 280
(5) .......... 280
S.299 ..........
(4) .......... 280
S.300 .......... 280
S.301 .......... 249, 280
S.302 .......... 278, 279
S.303 .......... 278, 279
S.304 .......... 39, 249, 254
S.305 .......... 280, 282
S.306 .......... 280
S.307 .......... 281
S.308 .......... 281
S.309 .......... 282
S.310 .......... 282
S.311 .......... 282
(1) .......... 282
(2) .......... 282
(3) ..........
S.312 .......... 282
S.313 .......... 272
S.314 .......... 272
S.315 .......... 96, 103, 273, 280
S.316 .......... 97, 270
S.317 .......... 270
S.318 .......... 96, 97, 271
S.319 .......... 271
(1) ..........
S.320 .......... 269
S.321 ..........
(1) ..........
(2) .......... 269
(3) .......... 269
S.326 .......... 280
S.327 .......... 9, 107, 122, 138, 238, 271
S.328 .......... 102, 143, 237-238, 271, 275
S.329 ..........
(2) .......... 281
(3) .......... 281
S.330 .......... 273
S.331 .......... 101
S.333 .......... 367
S.336 .......... 249
S.337 ..........
(1) .......... 276
S.340 .......... 266
S.342 .......... 276
S.343 .......... 7, 225, 261, 276, 277
S.344 .......... 276
S.349 .......... 101
S.350 .......... 101
S.352 .......... 101, 102
S.353 .......... 102, 104
S.354 .......... 102
S.355 .......... 104
S.356 .......... 104
S.357 .......... 104
S.358 .......... 104
S.361 .......... 1
S.363 .......... 257
S.369 .......... 282
S.370 .......... 281, 282
S.377 (1) .......... 282
S.388 .......... 42
S.392 .......... 16
S.393 .......... 252
S.396 .......... 63
S.404 .......... 7
S.405 .......... 123, 193, 209
Shed. 1 ..........
Table A .......... 24, 42
Art. 2 .......... 79
Art. 4 .......... 83, 249, 252
Art. 5 .......... 83
Art. 6 .......... 52
Art. 7 .......... 71, 76
Art. 8 .......... 67
Art. 11 .......... 71
Art. 12 .......... 71
Art. 13 .......... 71

Art. 14 .......... 71
Art. 15 .......... 73
Art. 16 .......... 73
Art. 17 .......... 73
Art. 18 .......... 73, 74
Art. 19 .......... 73
Art. 20 .......... 73, 74
Art. 21 .......... 73, 74
Art. 22 .......... 68, 69
Art. 23 .......... 64, 68
Art. 24 .......... 68
Art. 25 .......... 68
Art. 26 .......... 68, 69
Art. 27 .......... 68
Art. 28 .......... 65
Art. 29 .......... 65
Art. 30 .......... 65, 69
Art. 31 .......... 65
Art. 32 .......... 65
Art. 33 .......... 86
Art. 34 .......... 86
Art. 35 .......... 86
Art. 36 .......... 86
Art. 37 .......... 86
Art 38 .......... 86
Art. 39 .......... 86
Art. 40 .......... 74, 83
Art. 44 .......... 83
Art. 45 .......... 83
Art. 46 .......... 83, 84
Art. 47 .......... 242, 243
Art. 48 .......... 242
Art. 49 .......... 242, 244
Art. 50 .......... 246
Art. 51 .......... 246
Art. 52 .......... 243
Art. 53 .......... 248, 251
Art. 54 .......... 248
Art. 55 .......... 248
Art. 56 .......... 248
Art. 57 .......... 250
Art. 58 .......... 250
Art. 59 .......... 250
Art. 60 .......... 249
Art. 61 .......... 250
Art. 62 .......... 250
Art. 67 .......... 250, 251
Art. 68 .......... 47, 251
Art. 69 .......... 251
Art. 70 .......... 251
Art. 71 .......... 251
Art. 72 .......... 251
Art. 73 .......... 251
Art. 74 .......... 252
Art. 75 .......... 106
Art. 76 .......... 111
Art. 77 .......... 107
Art. 78 .......... 190
Art. 79 .......... 92, 118
Art. 80 .......... 20, 112-118, 242
Art. 81 .......... 92, 118
Art. 84 .......... 5, 110, 184, 185, 190
Art. 88 .......... 109
Art. 89 .......... 107, 109
Art. 90 .......... 107, 109
Art. 91 .......... 107, 109
Art. 92 .......... 107, 109
Art. 93 .......... 107
Art. 94 .......... 107
Art. 95 .......... 107
Art. 96 .......... 107
Art. 97 .......... 107, 234
Art. 98 .......... 118
Art. 99 .......... 118
Art. 100 .......... 119
Art. 101 .......... 118
Art. 102 .......... 105
Art. 103 .......... 118
Art. 104 .......... 118
Art. 105 .......... 118, 126
Art. 106 .......... 118
Art. 107 .......... 46, 105, 110, 120
Art. 108 .......... 105, 120
Art. 109 .......... 105, 120
Art. 110 .......... 120
Art. 111 .......... 120
Art. 113 .......... 121
Art. 114 .......... 64, 89, 90
Art. 115 .......... 89, 90
Art. 116 .......... 89
Art. 117 .......... 16, 89
Art. 118 .......... 89, 90
Art. 119 .......... 89
Art. 120 .......... 89
Art. 121 .......... 89
Art. 122 .......... 89
Art. 128 .......... 16, 91
Art. 131 .......... 246
Art. 132 .......... 246
Art. 133 .......... 65, 246
Art. 134 .......... 246
Art. 135 .......... 144
Table A ..........
Part II ..........
Art. 3 .......... 68
Art. 4 .......... 248
Art. 5 .......... 246
Table B .......... 27, 30, 42
Table C .......... 27, 42
Table D .......... 27, 42

Table E ........................................... 27, 38, 42
Sched. 3, Part 1 .................. 20, 54-55, 62, 79
Sched. 4 ..................................................
Part 1 ........................................... 56
Sched. 5 .................................................. 77
Sched. 6 ....................................... 140 -141
Sched. 7 ....................................... 141, 144
Para (1) ....................................... 144
Para (2) ....................................... 144
Exchange Control Act. Cap. 158 ............... 17
S.8 ......................................... 17, 68
S.9 ............................................... 17
S.49 ............................................. 17
Accountants (Designations) Act ............... 142
Bills of Sales Act Cap. 77 ............................ 7
Partnership Act (Cap 86) ......................... 234
S.3 (1) ........................................ 234
S.34 ........................................... 186
Electricity Act (Cap.135) .......................... 17
(Cap. 136) ........................ 17
S.16 ............................................ 18
Land Transfer Act (Cap.202)...................... 92
Workmen's Compensation Act Cap. 197.... 273
Bankruptcy Act (Cap. 71) ....................... 272
S.34 ........................................... 272
1967 Judicature Act, S.3 (2)(b)(i), 5 ....... 29
1968 Trade Descriptions Act (UK)
C.29 ........................................... 137
1970 New York Corporations Act
S.202 ..........................................
(a) .................................. 165
Ontario Business Corporations Act (R.S.O)
S.16 ............................................ 37
S.99 ........................... 222, 223, 224
S.144 .......................................... 164
S.148 .......................................... 158
S.149 .......................................... 158
S.150 .......................................... 158
S.151 .......................................... 158
S.152 .......................................... 158
Securities Act (Alberta) .........................
S.108 .......................................... 158
S.109 .......................................... 158
S.110 .......................................... 158
S.111 .......................................... 158
S.112 .......................................... 158
S.113 .......................................... 158
S.114 .......................................... 158
S.115 .......................................... 158
1972 European Communities Act (UK C.68)
............................... 36, 133-134, 135
S.9 ..........................................
(1) ................................ 36 - 37
1973 British Columbia Companies Act (C.18)
........................................... 37
S.23 ............................................. 37
S.24 ............................................. 37
S.27 ............................................. 37
S.141 .......................................... 164
S.146 .......................................... 158
S.152 .......................................... 158
S.160 ..........................................
Companies Bill (UK) Clause 53 .............. 163
1974 Companies Bill (Bill 104), 1974
Clause 71 .................................. 230
1975 Canada Business Corporations Act
(Am 1976)
S.15(1) ........................................ 37
S.16 ..............................................
(2) ..................................... 37
(3) ..................................... 37
S.117 .......................................... 164
S.122 .......................................... 158
S.125 .......................................... 158
S.231 ................................... 37, 222
S.232 ................................... 37, 222
S.233 .......................................... 222
S.234 ..........................................
(2) .................................... 231
(3) .................................... 232
S.235 ................................. 222, 223
(1) .................................... 224
S.240 ............................................ 37
1976 Companies Act (Britain, C.69)
................................................ 2, 148
S.14 ............................................
(1) .................................... 147
(3) .....................................
1977 Nigerian Enterprises Promotion Act
(No. 3) ................................... 25, 26
S.5 ......................................... 25, 26
S.6 ......................................... 25, 26
1978 Companies Bill (UK) ........... 169, 184
Cl.44 ........................................... 170
(3) .................................... 182
(4) .................................... 182
Cl.45 ...........................................
(1) .................................... 193
Cl.46 .................................. 163 - 164
(1) .................................... 163
(2) .................................... 163
1979 British Columbia Companies Act
S.224 .......................................... 232
(1) ..................................

(a) ........................ 231
(b) ........................ 231
(2) .................................. 232
(6) ..................................
S.225 .......................................... 222
(7) .................... 222, 223, 224
1980 Companies Act (UK) ................ 2, 40, 87, 163
S.17 ............................................ 206
Ss. 48 - 66 .................................. 186
S.60 ............................................ 184
(1) .................................. 184
S.75 .................. 221, 223, 224, 230-32
Sched. 3 Para 4 ...................................... 140
1981 Companies Act (UK) .......... 2, 82, 148
1985 Companies Act (UK) ......................... 2
S.89 ........................................... 166
S.309 ............................................ 163
(1) ..................................... 163
(2) .................................. 163
S.459 ................ 165, 187, 221, 230-32
S.460 .................................. 221, 230
S.461 .................... 221, 222, 230, 232
S.462 .......................................... 230
S.659 ..........................................
(1) .................................. 165
(2) .................................. 165
1991 Co-operative Societies Act (Uganda) ...................................................... 16
Uganda Revenue Authority (Statute No. 6) .............................. 17
Exchange Control (Forex Bureau) Order ............................................... 3
1997 Income Tax Act No. 11 ..................... 9

# PREFACE

This book which has been in use in Uganda for about seven years requires no introduction. Its aim was to fill a gap then existing in Ugandan legal literature and to meet the needs of both law students offering the Law of Business Associations or Company Law courses at undergraduate and postgraduate levels as well as peripheral students of law pursuing courses in Commerce and Businees Administration in Ugandan universities. It is also beneficial to legal practioners mainly because of its analysis of the problems affecting Company Law, and possible areas of reform, as well as the inclusion of copious references to case.

The approach is basically functional. The introduction deals with general features affecting company law, namely, the law applicable, the relevance of company law to society, and aspects requiring reform. The nature and implications of incorporations as well as comparison of the registered corporations with other forms of associations are then considered before turning to the promotion and formation of a company. The most important documents required for incorporation, namely the memorandum and articles are examined before embarking on a consideration of corporate finance, the nature and implications of shareholding and the capital structure. In the context of corporate finance, the significance of allotment and the prospectus are appraised in much more detail then can be found elsewhere in literature on Company Law in Uganda. The treatment of corporate finance is extended to an analysis of debentures and borrowing by the company before examining the role of corporate directors and other officials and their individual capacity to saddle the company with liability. Official corporate responsibility is then considered in the context of the accounting, audit, duties of directors and their enforcement. The chapters on Directors' Duties and Enforcement of Cooperate Duties are concerned not only with the prevailing legal position, but also the probable course of development and reform in that area along trends in other common law jurisdictions in general and the commonwealth of nations in particular. This approach, which draws on my earlier research for my doctoral dissertation, is apposite given the common law and in particular English origin of Ugandan applicable principles of Company Law. The book winds up with a discussion of the meetings, proceedings, reconstruction and winding up of the registered company.

In addition to previsous acknowledgements recorded at the time the first impression of this text was produced, I wish to acknowledge Mr James Tumusime of Fountain Publishers for agreeing to publish this book with a view to giving it wider publicity, and Mr Alex Bangirana for speedy production of this impression.

***David J. Bakibinga***
Department of Commercial Law
Makerere University
December 2000

# 1
# INTRODUCTION

This text deals basically with companies as defined in the Companies Act, Cap 85, Laws of Uganda 1964 i.e. those companies formed and registered under that Act or incorporated under its predecessor Statute.[1] Some mention though is made of other types of business and other associations as well as public corporations, in chapter two, in the context of comparison of the registered company with those entities.

## Law applicable

Company Law in Uganda is an amalgam of the English Common Law, doctrines of equity and the Companies Act. The common law and doctrines of equity apply to Uganda by virtue of English Law reception Statute[2].

By virtue of the reception of the principles of English Common Law and the doctrines of equity reliance by Ugandan courts has continued to be made on English decisions, although this is done subject to local circumstances. Nevertheless, the courts are obliged to interpret and apply the Companies Act, as it stands without merely following English decisions on the relevant provision, although these may be relevant where the words being construed by the Uganda court are in *pari materia* with those of the English Statute considered earlier by an English Court. In this vein, in *Tandy V. Harmony House Furniture Co. Ltd*[3] Brett J.S.C. thus stated of an English decision[4] in interpreting a Nigerian Companies Statute:[5]

> This decision is, of course, not binding on any court in Nigeria but in the absence of Nigerian decisions on the relevant sections of the Nigerian companies Act, the reasoning of any decision on the equivalent provisions of the United Kingdom Act must command particular attention.[6]

The court then went on to follow the analysis of the Judge in the English decision. This explains the copious reference to English or other Commonwealth decisions in this text, in the absence of or supplement to Ugandan decisions.

## General features of company law

The purpose of Company Law is to regulate the formation, activity, officials and winding-up of an incorporated body created under the Companies Act. Specific attention is given to the basic documents required to be filed with the Companies Registry in Kampala upon incorporation. These are the Memorandum of Association, which defines generally the powers of the company and the Articles of Association which regulate the internal affairs of the company. The functions,

---

1. Companies Act, Cap 85, S.2; see also 361.
2. The reception date is 11 August, 1902
3. [1964] 1 All N.L.R.31 (Supreme Court of Nigeria)
4. *Re: Tweeds Garages Ltd. [1962] 1 Ch.406.*
5. Companies Act, (Cap.37 Law of Nigeria, 1958), Ss. 135(e),137. The quote is relevant to Uganda where Companies Law is substantially the same as that in Nigeria.
6. *Supra* n.4 at p.34

duties and liability of the company's officers, namely its directors, secretary as well as its promoters are appraised in addition to their capacity to bind the company by their acts.

The mechanisms by which the company, which is a distinct legal *persona* raises funds through the issue of shares to the public and borrowing by means of the issue of debentures are considered. The special position of shareholders as proportionate owners of the assets of the company together with their rights and duties such as entitlement to attend and vote at general meetings, entitlement to payment of dividends as well as surplus assets on winding-up of the company, is analysed.

As an addition to the principle of disclosure underlying company law, which manifests itself initially on the formation and raising of capital by means of the prospectus, the accounting, auditing and winding-up regulations of the company receive treatment. Finally the modes by which a company may be reorganised, reconstructed or amalgamated are also a subject for consideration.

## The company and society

From the foregoing exposition it is apparent that the company is essentially a creature of capital and, at that, private capital, It is an organisation by which capital is pooled together, invested and any resultant profits distributed among members by way of payment of dividend. In the exercise of their rights arising form their investment into the company as evidenced by shareholding, members are free to act solely in their interests to the exclusion of the company interest[7]. Nevertheless this feature, which smacks of *laissez fairism* is subject to the equitable principle that members must act *bona fide* in the interest of the company as a whole[8], a phrase whose exact connotation is a subject of controversy[9]. The rights of the members are moreover stringently regulated by the Act under the disclosure principles, essentially benefitting the public. Thus, while essentially a private organisation, the company apparently owes a statutory duty of disclosure of its activities to the society. The statutory intervention into the principle of *laissez faire* which logically underlies company philosophy appears to have arisen from the need for Government to have some control over these potentially powerful economic entities in the society and also in the context of the British origin of company law in Uganda to implement the principle of welfare statism by which the company is expected to make its contribution to the society.

The introduction of the registered company into Uganda was influenced partly by its being a colony of Britain where such an economic entity was widely recognised and accepted as a medium for conducting trade and manufacture and partly by the fact that with increased commercial activities in Uganda after the First World War, it became imperative to evolve and encourage credible commercial units. This explains the promulgation of the Companies Act. It is notable that the Ugandan Companies Act is largely a reenactment of the British Companies Act, 1948[10]. Consequently, although enacted by the Ugandan legislature, in strict historical jurisprudential terms, companies legislation has invariably been transplanted form Britain to the Ugandan soil and by that reasoning inefficacious owing to its alien origin. Nevertheless, this view is at best incomplete when compared with the much more compelling economic jurisprudential thesis that law is a superstructure over the socio-economic base. In this context, companies legislation must have some bearing on the socio-economic and political set-up of Uganda. This bearing stems

---

7 *North-West Transportation C. v. Beatty* (1887) 12 App. Cas.589

8 *Greenhalgh v. Ardene Cinemas Ltd.* /1951/ Ch.286 C.A.

9 See *infra* Chap.14

10 Now consolidated with the Companies Acts, 1967, 1976, 1980 and 1981 in the Companies Act, 1985.

from the fact that although nominally politically independent, the major economic activities and thereby control of the country lie with a powerful group of foreign multinational companies[11]. These Companies invariably control the manufacturing, banking and distributive sectors of the economy. The most recent manifestation of foreign influence on the economy was the decision to float the national currency, the shilling, in order to induce the re-scheduling of foreign debts owed by Uganda and also to enable the multinational companies to speedily repatriate their profits through purchase of foreign currency in the Forex Bureaux[12]. The relevance of companies legislation in the Uganda context as a means of regulating and taxing companies is thus obvious.

## The need for reform

It remains to add that the Companies legislation of Britain on which the Companies Act, is based has been overhauled several times over by amending and supplementing legislation in order to keep abreast of changes in that society. There has been no major attempt to reform company law in Uganda.

One fashionable suggestion is to codify both statutory and case law following the model of the Ghana Companies Code[13] Reform could also be effected through an overhaul of traditional company law in order to recognise the role and rights of labour or workers within the company by requirement that in exercising their duties, directors, should consider the interests of workers or that workers be represented on company boards and within the managerial stricture[14]. Given the importance of the company structure in the economic life of the country the suggestion for employee representation in the decision-making process of the company is a continuation of the process of democratization within the society.[15]

The other aspect requiring attention in the context of reform relates to the effectiveness of the general meeting and the board of directors in monitoring managerial performance. While in theory, the law provides for this, in practice owing to widely dispersed and insignificant shareholding as well as constraints of time, information and selection and tenure affecting the Board of Directors, the monitoring role of the general meeting and the board is illusory and perfunctory at best [16]. Consequently, it has been suggested that every publicly incorporated company should be required to have an audit committee consisting entirely of independent directors and empowered to (1) nominate and recommend the dismissal of the company's accountant on behalf of the main board and (2) direct the accountant's activities and determine the conditions of his employment[17]. That way, it is thought effective monitoring of management performance can be effected through the medium of the company's audit function.[18]

---

11 See *Budget Speech* 2nd July, 1991, Government Printer, Entebbe; *Background to the Budget*, Ministry of Planning and Economic Development, 1991.

12 See further The Exchange Control (Forex Bureau) Order, 1991.

13 Orojo, *Company Law and Practice in Nigeria* (2nd Ed.) p.11. The Code has influenced developments in other Commonwealth jurisdiction, principally Canada.

14 See further Bakibinga, *Analysis of Some Recent Trends Affecting the Legal Powers, Duties and Functions of Company Directors*, University of London Ph.d. Thesis (1981) Part four.

15 *ibid.*, p.5

16 *ibid.*,Chap.6

17 M.A. Eisenberg, "Legal Models of Management Structures in the Modern Corporation: Officers, Directors and Accountants" (1975) 63 *California Law Rev.* 375 pp.432-433.

18 For more detail on the history and role of the audit committee, see Bakibinga, *supra* chap.9

# 2

# NATURE AND CONSEQUENCES OF INCORPORATIONS

## Nature

A Company or Corporation is a legal entity separate and set apart from its members or shareholders. This legal personality is an artificial one which is distinguishable from natural personality. The possession of a legal personality implies that a company is capable of enjoying rights and being subject to duties, separately from its members. This principle was first distinctly articulated in the British House of Lords Judgment, *Salomon v. Salomon & Co. Ltd.*[1]

In that case, Salomon carried on business as a leather merchant, In 1892, he converted the business into a limited company by forming Salomon & Co. Ltd. The company consisted of Salomon, his wife and five children as members. Salomon was the Managing Director. The company then bought Salomon's business as a going concern for GBP39,000. The price was made up of (i) GBP 10,000 in debentures by which the company's assets were charged; (ii) GBP20,000 in fully paid GBP1 shares; (iii) the balance in cash. Seven shares were subscribed in cash by the members with the result that Salmon held 20,001 of the 20,007 issued shares. The remaining 6 shares were each held by a member of his family. Immediately after incorporation, the company experienced difficulties and a year later was wound up. It had sufficient assets to satisfy the debentures but nothing for the unsecured creditors.

As a result, following an action by the creditors, the court at first instance and the Court of Appeal held that the whole arrangement was contrary to the true intention of the Companies Act and that the company was a "mere sham" and an "alias", agent or trustee or nominee of Salomon, who remained the real proprietor of the business. Consequently, Salomon was liable to indemnify the company against its trading debts. However, on appeal to the House of Lords, this decision was reversed. The House of Lords held (i) that the company in question had been validly formed, since the Act merely required seven members holding at least one share each; (ii) the business belonged to the company and not to Salomon and Salomon was its agent and not it the agent of Salomon.

Lord Halsbury L.C. further stated:[2]

> Either the limited company was a legal entity or it was not. If it was, the business belonged to it and not to Mr. Salomon. If it was not, there was no person and nothing to be an agent at all; and it is impossible to say at the sametime that there is a company and there is not

In the words of Lord Macnaghten[3]

> The Company is at law a different person altogether form the subscribers.....; and though it may be that after incorporation the business is precisely the same as it was before, and the same persons are managers, and the same hands receive *the*

---

1 [1897] A.C. 22 H.L.; See too O.AKANKI, "Relevance of Corporate Personality Principle" (1977-80) 11 Nig. L.J.9, 14-16.

2 *ibid* at p.31; see also *Marina Nominees Ltd. v. F.B.* [1986] 2 N.W.L.R. 48, 55-56.

3 *ibid* at p.51 See also *Sentamu v. UCB [1983] HCB 59; Katate v. Nyakatura* (1956) 7 U.L.R.47

> profits, the company is not in law the agent of subscribers or trustees for them. Nor are the subscribers as members liable in any shape or form, except to the extent and in the manner provided by the Act.

This view has been re-echoed in *Dunlop Nigerian Industries Ltd. v. Forward Nigeria Enterprises Ltd. and Farore*[4] to the effect that a company has, in law, an identity distinct from that of its subscribers, irrespective of the number of shares held by any individual so that even if a member owns 90% of the shares and as Managing Director controls the company, he cannot usually be held jointly liable for its activities.

The principle of corporate personality has statutory backing[5] and also manifests itself in the following cases. In *Ebbw Vale U.D.C. v. South Wales Traffic Area Licensing Authority*[6] the issue arose as to whether a company which was a subsidiary of a corporation should be regarded as an agent of the corporation. It was held by Cohen L.J.[7] that the subsidiary company was not an agent of the parent company but a different entity. Consequently, its acts were not attributable to the parent company and the parent company was not responsible for its acts or omissions.

In *Lee v. Lee's Air Farming Ltd.*[8], the appellant's husband who founded Lee's Air Farming Ltd. was the controlling shareholder and governing director of the company. He was employed as its chief pilot. While piloting an aircraft of the company in the course of its business, he was killed. The issue arose in the course of litigation as to whether he was a worker for purposes of the Workmen's Compensation Act of New Zealand. The New Zealand Court of Appeal held that he was not. Upon appeal to the Privy Council it was held that he was a worker. Lord Morris thus stated:[9]

> ......... the active aerial operations were performed because the deceased was in some contractual relationship with the company. That relationship came about because the deceased as one legal person was willing to work for and to make a contract with the company which was another legal entity.

It is notable in this regard that a director of a company is not precluded form entering into a contract to serve the company, provided that such contract is disclosed to the company.[10]

Furthermore, in *Macaura v. Northern Assurance Co.*[11], it has been established that the property of a company belongs to it and not to its members. Consequently neither a shareholder nor a creditor of a company, unless secured has an insurable interest in the assets of the company. The facts were that Macaura, who was the owner of Killymoon estate in County Tyrore, sold the whole of the timber on the estate to a company, Irish Canadian Sawmills Ltd. in consideration for an allotment to him of 42,000 fully paid GBP1 shares. All the company's shares were held by Macaura and has nominees. He was also an unsecured creditor of the company for an amount of GBP19,000. Following the sale, Macaura effected policies in his own name with the respondent company and others covering the timber against fire. A claim brought by Macaura on the policies was disallowed on the ground that he had no insurable interest in the timber because if belonged to the Irish Canadian Saw Mills Ltd. In the words of Lord Sumner:[12]

---

4 1976 N.C.L.R. 243 (High Court of Lagos State: Ajoso-Adeogun, J.) pp. 248-249, 251-254 see also *Marina Nominees Ltd., supra n.2 Re: Northern Nigeria Marketing Board* 1964 NNLR 30.

5 Companies Act, S.16; See also *Kate Ent. Ltd. v. Daewoo Nig. Ltd.* (1985) 2 N.W.L.R.116

6 [1951] 2 K.B. 366 C.A.

7 ibid pp. 373-374

8 [1960] 3 All E.R 420; [1961] A.C. 12 P.C. See also *Wani v. Uganda Timbers & Joiners Ltd.* H.C.C.S.989 of 1972.

9 Sealy *Cases and Materials in Company Law* (2nd Ed., 1978), p.32

10 See S.200 Companies Act,Cap 85; Article 84 Table A, 1st Schedule to the Act.

11 [1925] A.C.619 H.L. see too *Gramophone & Typewriter Ltd. v. Stanley* (1908) 2 K.B.89

12 *ibid* [1925] A.C. at p.630

> Macaura stood in no 'legal or equitable relation' to the timber at all. He had no 'concern in' the subject insured. His relation was to the company, not to its goods...

## Consequences

The following consequences flow form the act of incorporation.

### Liability

The company being a distinct legal *persona* is liable for all its debts and obligations. The liability of the members or shareholders of the company is limited to the amount remaining unpaid on the shares. For instance where a shareholder has ben allotted 100 shares of shs1.00 each, and he pays shs50.00 to the company (i.e. 50cts on each share), at the time of winding up the company, if the shares remain not fully paid for, he will be required to pay shs.50.,00 (or 50ct on each share). It follows that the company's creditors can only sue the company and not the shareholders. In *Sentamu v. UCB* [12a], it was held that individual members of the Company are not liable for the Company's debts. Even a Managing Director of the company cannot be liable for its debts.

An exception exists in respect of an unlimited company. Members in such a company are liable for its obligations without any limitation on the amount payable.[13] With regard to a company limited by guarantee, each member is liable to contribute a specified amount of assets of the company in the event of its being wound up while he is a member or within one year after ceasing to be a member.[14]

### Property

An incorporated company is able to own property separately from its members[15]. The advantage of this is that members cannot directly interfere with the company's property. It is also settled that a company can occupy business premises as a tenant.[15a].

### Legal proceedings

As a legal person, a company can take action to enforce its legal rights or be sued for breach of its duties. However, the action for or against the company should be instituted in the company's registered name. Thus, in *Dennis Njemanze v. Shell B.P. Port Harcourt*[16], the plaintiff sued "Shell B.P. Port Harcourt". Counsel for the defendant objected that there was no company known as "Shell B.P. Port Harcourt". Counsel for the plaintiff asked for leave to amend the writ, but the court refused leave and struck out the claim. Upon appeal from the refusal, it was held[17] (dismissing the appeal) (i) that putting in an appearance did not prevent the company from objecting that the defendant sued was not a legal person; (ii) the plaintiff had a duty to show that there were reasonable grounds of excuse in naming the defendant wrongly and that the misnomer could not have given rise to any reasonable doubt as to which company was being sued, but he did not to so. Additionally, it is not enough to institute the action in the name of an officer of the company on behalf of the company[18], except where he has been expressly

---

[12a] *Supra* n.3

[13] Companies Act. S.4(2) (c)

[14] ibid S.4 (2) (b).

[15] ibid, S.16. See also *Phillips v. Abou-Diwan* (1976) 2FRCR 24 (F.H.C.); *Bozak v. Ziregbe* (1978) 4FRC.R.83; *Shonibare v. Probate Registrar* (1966) 2 A.L.R. Comm.389.

[15a] *Kampala Cotton Co. Ltd. v. Madhvani* (1954) 21 EACA 129; *Hindu Dispensary V. Patwa* [1958] E.A.74 C.A.

[16] [1966] All N.L.R.8 (S.C.N.)

[17] ibid pp.10 -11; See also *Govt. of Midwest State v. Midmotors (Nig.) Ltd. (1977)* 10 S.C.43.

[18] 012 Agbonmagbe Bank Ltd. v. General Manager, G.B. Ollivant *Ltd. & Anor* [1961] 1 All N.L.R. 166.

authorised so to defend.[19]. The only disadvantage about this consequence is that the limited company when suing may be required to give security for costs[20].

## Perpetual succession

A limited liability company is endowed with perpetual succession.[21] Consequently, changes in membership arising form the bankruptcy or death thereof do not affect the company's existence. The life of the company can only be ended either by winding up[22], striking off the register of Companies[23] or through amalgamation and reconstruction[24] as provided by the Companies Act.

## Transfer of shares

A share constitutes an item of property[25], which is freely transferable[26], except in the case of private companies. In private companies, the transfer of shares may be restricted to the existing members of the Company.[27]

## Borrowing[28]

A company can borrow money and provide security in the form of a floating charge. A floating charge is said to float like a cloud over the whole assets of the company at any given time.

However, the advantage of this to the company is that the charge does not prevent the company as mortgagor form disposing of the assets in the usual course of business. It is when something happens that the charge becomes crystallised or fixed over the existing assets of the company. The charge is also beneficial to the company especially when its business has no fixed assets such as land, which can be used in a normal mortgage, but has on the other hand, a large and valuable stock-in-trade. Since the stock-in-trade has to be turned over in the course of business, a fixed charge is inconvenient because the consent of the mortgagee would be needed every time anything was sold and a new charge would have to be entered into whenever anything was bought and added to the stock.

A floating charge takes care of these difficulties by (i) enabling the stock to be turned over but (ii) attaching to whatever it is converted into and to whatever stock is acquired. It is further notable that a floating charge is mostly restricted to companies and is not used by sole traders or partnerships because of the complicated procedure of registering mortgaged chattels under the Bills of Sale Act [29], which are inapplicable to charges by incorporated companies.

## Formalities, publicity and expenses

Apart form the advantages mentioned above, which accompany incorporation, certain disadvantages attend that exercise. These are (i) formalities have to be followed, (ii) there is publicity and therefore loss of privacy and (iii) the exercise is expensive.

In these respects a company differs from a partnership in the sense that no formalities are required for the formation of a partnership. A partnership can be formed orally, exist without publicity and be informally and cheaply dissolved.[30] However, with an incorporated company, promoters are required to file with the Registrar of Companies certain documents which include

---

19 *Otuyemi v. Essol (W.A.) Ltd.* (1961) W.N.L.R.130.
20 S.404 Companies Act, Cap 85
21 S.16 ibid
22 Ss. 218, 225 ibid
23 S.343 ibid
24 S.209 (1) (d)
25 *Odumody v. Mohammed* 1973 NCLR 52 (High Court of Lagos State).
26 S.75 Companies Act Cap. 85
27 S.30 ibid, Articles 23-25, Table A.
28 See further Gower, *Principles of Modern Company Law* (4th Ed. 1979) pp.107-108.
29 Cap 77 Laws of Uganda
30 See generally, Bakibinga, *Law of Partnership in Uganda* (1992) Chaps. 2,6.

the articles and memorandum of association and also to maintain registers at its registered office. All these documents are open to public inspection. Fees are paid for filing the documents. Additionally, meetings of the board of directors and the general meeting have to be held periodically and the minutes thereof kept.[31] Special and extra-ordinary resolutions must be filed at the Companies Registry.[32] Furthermore, all activities of the company must be conducted in the name of the company with the word *"limited"* at its end. "Limited" contrary to popular belief as to prestige in law acts as a warning to those dealing with the company as to the risk they run in transacting business with it.

A company is also required to keep accounts at its registered office.[33] Stringent provisions also govern the issue of shares[34] and the powers, rights and duties of directors.[35]

More information is required to be filed in respect of a public than a private company. For instance the former is required to publish and file a prospectus (i.e. an invitation to the public to purchase its shares). Furthermore, if a company makes a public issue of shares, these have to be listed on the stock exchange.

Finally, the company must be wound-up in the manner prescribed by the Companies Act.[36] The cost of winding up is normally more expensive than that in respect of formation. The policy behind these requirements of formality, and publicity is that incorporation should be accompanied by full disclosure.

# Lifting the veil of incorporation

A negative consequence of incorporation is that the legal personality of the company may be disregarded in certain circumstances by a device known as lifting the veil or mask of incorporation. In such a situation the law looks at the people behind the company rather than the cloak of incorporation. It has been observed in *Dunlop Nigerian Industries Ltd. v. Forward Nigerian Enterprises Ltd. & Farore*[37] that in particular circumstances e.g. where the device of incorporation is used for some illegal or improper purpose, the court may disregard the principle that a company is an independent legal entity and "lift the veil" of corporate identity so that if it is proved that a person used a company he controls as a "cloak" for an improper transaction he may be made personally liable to a third party. The Case of *Salomon*[38] and other cases supporting it *(supra)* may indeed be regarded as instances where the courts refused to lift the veil of incorporation. The legal technique of lifting the veil is recognised under two heads, (i) statute, (ii) case law.

## Statutory lifting of the Veil

### (a) Where the number of members is below legal minimum

Under S.33 of the Cap.85,if a company carries on business for more than 6 months after its membership has fallen below the statutory minimum (seven for public and two for private companies) every member during the time the business is carried on after the six months and

---

[31] Ss. 130-139 Companies Act Cap.85

[32] *ibid*,S.143

[33] Ss. 147-157 *ibid*

[34] Ss.39-60 *ibid*

[35] Ss. 177-205 *ibid*

[36] Reference hereinafter to this Act is Cap 85 unless otherwise indicated. See infra Chap.18

[37] Supra n.4 per Ajoso-Adeogun J. See also *Marina Nominees Ltd.V. F.B.I.R.* [1986] 2 NWLR 48, 56-58 (Supreme Court of Nigeria).

[38] Supra n.1. See also Gower, supra n.28, p.123

[38a] See also *Fadipe v. Manager, UBA* (1973), F.R.C.R..154, *Iro v. Park* (1972) 12 S.C. 93.

who knows that the company is carrying on business with less than the required minimum membership is severally liable for the company's debts incurred during that time.[38a]

**(b) Where the company is not mentioned in the Bill of Exchange**

By S.109 of Cap 85, an officer of the company is personally liable if he signs a bill of exchange cheque, etc. on behalf of company without mentioning the company's name on it in legible (clear) characters.

**(c) Holding and subsidiary companies**

According to S.150 of Cap 85, where Companies are in relationship of holding and subsidiary companies, group accounts should be presented before the holding company in general meeting. In this regard the holding and subsidiary companies are regarded as one for accounting purposes, and the separate nature of the subsidiary company is ignored.

**(d) Reckless or fraudulent trading**

It is provided under S.327 of Cap 85 that if during the winding up of a company it appears that any business of the company has been conducted recklessly or fraudulently, those responsible for such business may be held liable without limitation of liability for any of the company's debts or liabilities.[38b]

**(e) Investigation into related companies**

Where an inspector has been appointed by the Registrar to investigate the affairs of a company, he may if he thinks it fit also investigate into the affairs of any other related company and also report on the affairs of that other company so long as he feels that the results of his investigation of such related company are relevant to the main investigation. The related company may be a corporate body with a subsidiary or holding relationship to the company under primary investigation.[39]

**(f) Taxation**

Under the Income Tax Act, 1997 the veil of incorporation may be lifted to ascertain where the control and management of the company is exercised in order to determine whether it is a "Ugandan Company" for Income Tax Purposes.[40]

**Lifting the veil under case law**

**(a) Where the company acts as agent of the shareholders**

Where the shareholders of a company use the company as an agent, they will be liable for the debts of the company. Thus, in *Re: F. G. (Films) Ltd.*[41], an American company provided all the funds for producing a film, which it sought to register as a British film on the ground that the film was produced by arrangement with a British Company of which the American Company owned GBP90 of the GBP100 Capital. It was held - that the British Company was no more than a nominee or agent of the American Company which was the true maker of the film.

**(b) Company Deemed Trustee for Shareholders[42]**

Although uncommon, the courts are prepared in some cases to hold that the company holds property in trust from the shareholders. Thus in *The Abbey, Malvern Wells Ltd. V. Ministry*

---

38b See also *Abraham v. Tait (1935)* 2 EACA 51

39 S.167 Cap 85. See also *Otong V. Mogall* (Nig.) Ltd. (1978) 4 F.R.C.R.80

40 See, *Smith & Knight V. Birmingham Corporation* (1939) 161L.T. 371; *Marina Nominees Ltd. v. F.B.I.R.* (1986) NWLR 48 (Supreme Court of Nigeria). See also *Comm. I.T.v. Bjordal (1955) 22 EACA 156*

41 [1953] 1 W.L.R. 483 c.f. *Ebbw Vale U.D.C. v. South Wales Traffic Area Licensing Authority* (1951) 2K.B. 366 where the court refused to treat a subsidiary company as an agent of its holding company. See also Orojo *Nigerian Company Law & Practice* (1976) p.93. See further *Marina Nominees ltd. V.F.B.I.R.* 2 N.W.L.R.48, 63 per Nnamani J.S.C. (S.C.).

42 See further, Gower op.cit pp.125-126.

*of Local Government & Planning*[43], all the shares of the company were held on charitable trusts. The articles of association provided that the relevant trustees would be the governing body of the company. It was held that the company held all its property on charitable trusts. In *Littlewoods Stores v. IRC*[44] the court relied on trust doctrines as a means of ignoring the corporate personality principle in a tax case which concerned a holding and subsidiary company. Littlewoods, which was the holding company bought a capital asset and vested it in a property holding company, which was its wholly-owned subsidiary. It then tried to get a tax advantage by arguing that the subsidiary was a separate legal personality. It was held that the tax advantage could not be allowed and the veil of incorporation was lifted on the ground that the subsidiary held the property on trust for the holding company.

**(c) Where there has been fraud or improper conduct**

The veil of incorporation may also be lifted where the corporate personality is used as a mask for fraud or illegality. Thus in *Gilford Motor Co. v. Horne*[45] the defendant was the plaintiff's former employee. He agreed not to solicit its customers when he left the employment. He then formed a company which solicited the customers. Both the company and the defendant were held liable for breach of covenant not to solicit. The company the defendant formed was described as "a mere cloak or sham for the purpose of enabling him to commit a breach of the covenant!"[46] In *Jones v. Lipman*[47], the defendant, in order to avoid completion of a sale of his house to the plaintiff, formed a company and conveyed the house to it. The court ordered specific performance of the contract against both the defendant and the company. The company was described as "the creature of the first defendant, a device and a sham, a mask which he holds before his face in an attempt to avoid recognition by the eyes of equity".[48] In a *Bank of America National Trust & Savings Association v. Niger International Development Corporation Ltd.*[49], consequent upon the defendant company's failure to pay a judgment debt obtained against it by the plaintiff, its vehicle was attached pursuant to be plaintiff's writ. Another company, which had practically the same members as the defendant company and directors belonging to the same family inter pleaded and claimed to have bought the vehicle from the defendant, *bona fide* and without knowledge of any court action and for valuable consideration. The claimant argued that as the vehicle no longer belonged to the defendant it could not be attached. The plaintiff contended that (i) the transaction was intended to defeat it as a judgment creditor and (ii) as such it was ineffective against it.

Dosunmu J. held[50] that where an alienation with intent to defraud the grantor's creditors is made to company by an individual or another company and the grantor in either case is practically identical with the grantee company, the latter must be taken to have had full notice of the true nature of the transaction and cannot avail itself of the protection extended to a bona fide purchaser without notice, although the alienation is for valuable consideration. Accordingly, where two companies have practically the same members and their directors belong to the same family, such alienation between them may be impeached under the Fraudulent Conveyances Act, 1571 or Bankruptcy Act, 1883[51], amounting to lifting of the veil of incorporation. In *B.D. & Co. Ltd*

---

43 [1951] Ch.728 c.f. Butt V. Kelson (1952) Ch.197 C.A.

44 [1969] 1 W.L.R.1241 C.A. Refer too to *D.H.N. Ltd v. Tower Hamlets* (1976) 1 W.L.R. 852 C.A. discussed *infra.*

45 [1933] Ch.935

46 *ibid* at p.969

47 [1962] 1 W.L.R. 832

48 *ibid* p.836

49 1969 NCLR 268 (High Court of Lagos State)

50 *ibid* p.271

51 Relying on *Salomon v. Salomon* [1897] A/C/22. *In Re: Hirth* [1899] 1 Q.B.612; *Edmunds v. Edmunds* (1904) P.362. See also the Canadian case of *Einhorn v. West-Mount Investments Ltd.* (1969) 6 D.L.R.(3d) *371. c.f. Airlines Airspares Ltd. v. Handley Page Ltd. (1970) Ch.193 where there was no evidence of fraud or impropriety.*

*v. Commissioner, Income Tax* [51a] an arrangement for dividend stripping aimed at Tax avoidance and reduction was disallowed.

In *Wallersteiner v. Moir*[52], in a suit against Dr. Wallaersteiner, he filed a defence out of time to claims against him as director for misfeasance connected with contravening the Companies Act. It was held that the various companies through which Dr. Wallersteiner operated were his puppets. In the words of Lord Denning M.R. (as he then was):[53]

> The Companies were his agents to do as he commanded. He was the principal behind them. I am of the opinion that the court should pull aside the corporate veil and treat these concerns as being his creatures for whose doings he should be, and is, responsible

**(d) Cases of associated companies**

We have seen that there are situations where the courts are prepared to treat a subsidiary company as an agent of the holding company and as conducting the latter's business for it.[54] In other situations the veil is lifted in tax vases in the interest of revenue.[55] Others have nothing to do with revenue. Thus, in *Firestone Tyre & Rubber Co. v. Llewellin*[56], it was held that although the English subsidiary was a separate legal entity, which was selling its own goods, the sales were the means by which the American parent company carried on its European Business. In effect the parent company was trading in the United Kingdom through the agency of its subsidiary. In *The Roberta*[57] a parent company was held liable on a bill of lading signed on behalf of a wholly-owned subsidiary. Similarly, in *Smith, Stone and Knight v. Birmingham Corporation*[58], a parent company was held to be entitled to compensation on the compulsory acquisition of land owned by a wholly-owned subsidiary.

These approaches appear to derive justification from the words of Roskill C.J. in *The Albazero* where, while acknowledging he corporate entity principle, he thus stated:[59]

> Modern commerce is hampered and not helped by too rigid an adherence to the basic principle..... where the group is in truth the party interested and injured, the law should not be too astute not to recognise the realities of the position....

The problem, though, remains that it is difficult to predict the criteria by which the courts would lift the veil in respect of associated companies.[60] The cases considered are difficult to reconcile with the *Ebbw Vale Case*[61] where the court refused to lift the veil of incorporation because there was no express agency contract between the two affected companies. The issue then arises as to the criteria for lifting the veil in such cases. In the *Smith, Stone & Knight Case*[62], Atkinson J. attempted to lay down six principles which would guide the court as to whether or not to lift the veil of incorporation. These are (i) were the profits treated as those of the parent

---

51a (1959) Case No.66. See also *A.R. v. Commissioner, Income Tax, Case* No.44 (1956) 2 E.A.T.C.202

52 [1974] 1 W.L.R. 991 C.A.

53 *ibid* p.1013.

54 see op.cit. supra notes 41 and 44 and text thereof.

55 U.S.Brewing Co. v. Apthorpe (1898) 4T.C.17 *Apthorpe v. Peter Schoenfofen Brewing Co.* (1899) 4 T.C. 41 C.A.

56 [1957] 1 W.L.R.464 H.L.

57 [1937] Ll.L.Rep.

58 [1939] 4 All E.R.116

59 [1975] 3 W.L.R.491, 521, 534.

60 Gower, *op.cit* p. 129

61 Supra n.41

62 Supra n.58. See also Gower *op.cit.* p. 130; see too the Nigerian Case *Bank of America NAtional Trust Savings Association, supra n.50 and text thereof. Marina Nominees v. F.B.I.R. (1986) 2 N.W.L.R.*40; *Reiss (Nig.)Ltd. V.F.B.I.R.* (1979) 3 F.R. C.R.251,

company? (ii) were the persons conducting the business appointed by the parent company? (iii) was the parent company the head and brain of the trading venture? (iv) did the parent company govern the adventure and decide what should be done and what capital should be embarked upon it? (v) were the profits made by its skill and direction? (vi) was the parent company in effectual and constant control. It has been observed though that these guidelines are useful,but not decisive in determining whether or not to lift the veil.[63]

In *D.H.N. Food Distributors Ltd. v. Tower Hamlets London Borough Council*[64], the Court of Appeal was prepared to lift the veil of incorporation and instead to consider the economic entity of the whole group. In that case, DHN operated a wholesale cash and carry grocery business from premises owned by its wholly-owned subsidiary company ("Bronze"). Bronze had the same directors as DHN but did not itself carry on any business. Its only asset was the freehold properties which DHN occupied as licensee. Another wholly-owned subsidiary owned vehicles used by DHN in its business, but it too, carried on no operations of its own.

In 1970 the borough council, compulsorily acquired the premises. As a result, DHN had to close down its business. Compensation for disturbance was paid to the Bronze Subsidiary. DHN claimed the compensation. it was held by the Court of Appeal (reversing a ruling of the Lands Tribunal) that the group of companies should be treated as a single economic entity. As a result compensation for disturbance should be paid to DHN. The effect of the judgment was that DHN was treated as having owned the land itself, despite the fact that it was registered in the names of Bronze.

**(e) Ratifying Corporate Acts**

Normally, in law, a company is bound only by resolution of its organs such as the board of directors or a duly constituted general meeting, or duly authorised agents.[65] The issue therefore, arises as to whether a resolution which is passed by members without a properly convened meeting of the board or members binds the company. In *Re George Newman Ltd.*[66] Lindley L.J. indicated thus:

> Individual assents given separately may preclude those who have given them form complaining of what they have sanctioned, but for the purpose of binding a company in its corporate capacity, individual assents given separately are not equivalent to the assent of a meeting.[67]

However, in subsequent cases it appears to have been recognised that individual assents of all members given separately are equivalent to the assent of a general meeting, irrespective of a formally convened meeting.[68] Thus in essence the law looks at the collective actions of directors or members in order to determine the acts of the company. This approach is endorsed in the *Salomon* case itself, where Lord Davey indicated that "the company is bound in a matter *intra vires* by the unanimous agreement of its members"[69] In the words of Professor Gower though:[70]

> What now seems clear is that there does not have to be unanimous *agreement of all* members but merely agreement or tacit acquiescence of all members entitled to vote on the matter.

---

63 Gower, ibid

64 [1976] 5 All E.R. 462; 1 W.L.R.852 C.A. See also L. Sealy, *Cases and Materials in Company Law* (2nd Ed.1978) pp.54-55.

65 See infra, Chap.12

66 [1895] 1 Ch. 674 C.A.

67 ibid p.686

68 *Re: Oxted Motor Co. Ltd.* (1921) 3KB 32; *Re: Express Engineering Works Ltd.* (1920) 1 Ch.466 C.A. See also Article 5 Table A part II.

69 [1897] A.C. 22, 57.

70 Gower, op.cit supra n.28, p.134. His emphasis relying on *Re Duomatic Ltd.* (1969) 2 Ch.365 and *Re Bailey Hay and Co. Ltd.* [1971] 1 W.L.R.1357

**(f) Determination of residence**

The court may look behind the veil or facade of the company and its place of registration in order to determine its residence.[71] The test for determining residence is normally the place of its "central management and control". Usually this is the place where the board of directors operates. However, it might also be the place of business of the managing director where he holds a controlling interest, or that of the parent company. The problem is thus one of locating "control".

In *Unit Construction Co. Ltd. v. Bullock*[72], three wholly-owned subsidiaries of a company in the United Kingdom were registered in Kenya. The boards of the three subsidiaries were distinct from the board of the parent company. In addition, under the articles of association, directors' meetings could not be held in the United Kingdom. However, the management of the subsidiaries was in fact in the hands of the parent company in England. It was held by the House of Lords (reversing the Court of Appeal) (i) that for taxation purposes the three Kenyan Companies were resident in the United Kingdom; (ii) the issue was not, where according to the three constitutions of the three companies central management and control ought to have been, but where in fact they were; (iii) that for purposes of Kenyan Law, the companies might also be resident in Kenya, was irrelevant. In *De Beers Consolidated Mines v. Howe*[73], Lord Loreburn L.C. seemed to suggest that control of a company is determined by looking at its course of business or trading. He thus stated:[74]

> ...... in applying the conception of residence to a company, we ought, I think to proceed as nearly as we can upon the analogy of an individual. A company cannot eat or sleep, but it can keep house and do business. We ought therefore to see where it really keeps house and does business. An individual may be of foreign nationality and yet reside in the United Kingdom. So may a company. Otherwise, it might have its seat of management and its centre of trading in England under the protection of English Law and yet escape the appropriate taxation by the simple expedient of being registered abroad and distributing its dividends abroad..... A company resides for purposes of income tax where its real business is carried on. The real business is carried on where the central management and control actually abides.

The determination of residence is thus especially useful in relation to taxation. However, it may also govern enemy status or subjection of a company to the jurisdiction of Ugandan or foreign courts.

In *Daimler Co. Ltd v. Continental Tyre and Rubber Co.*[75], the plaintiff company (Continental Tyre) was incorporated in England for the purpose of selling in England tyres made in Germany by a German company which held majority shares in the English Company. The holders (except one) and all the directors were Germans resident in Germany. Following the outbreak of war between England and Germany in 1914, the plaintiff sued the defendant company (Daimler) for payment of a trade debt. The defendant company alleged that the plaintiff company was an alien enemy company and that payment of the debt would be trading with the enemy. In the course of delivering judgment, four law lords indicated that a company could have "an enemy character". In the words of Lord Parker:[76]

---

[71] Gower, *ibid* p. 135

[72] [1960] A.C. 351 H.L.

[73] [1906] A.C.455

[74] *ibid* p.458

[75] [916] 2 A.C. 307 H.L.

[76] *ibid*, p.345.

> .... for certain purposes a court must look behind the artificial persona - the corporation - and take account of and be guided by the personalities of the natural persons, the corporators.... such a company may, however, assume an enemy character. This will be so if its agents or persons in defacto control of its affairs, whether authorised or not are resident in an enemy country, or wherever resident are adhering to the enemy or taking instructions from or acting under the control of enemies. A person knowingly dealing with the company in such a case is trading with the enemy.

Furthermore, in *Gasque v. Commissioners of Inland Revenue*[77], Mrs Gasque transferred property to M.D. Company Ltd. which was incorporated in Guernsey but doing some business in England. She claimed that the company was domiciled in the United Kingdom and that the Finance Act, 1936 relating to her taxation did not apply. The Inland Revenue commissioners ruled that the company was domiciled in Guernsey and assessed her for tax in accordance with Section 18 of the Act. The ruling was upheld by the High Court, which indicated[78] that while a body corporate cannot have a domicile and residence in the same sense as an individual the attributes of residence, domicile and nationality can be given to it. However, in *Katete v. Nyakatura*[78a] it was held that a company being a distinct entity and abstract in nature was incapable of having racial attributes.

The available Nigerian cases on the issue of residence appear to emphasise the trading or carrying n business in Nigera as determinant of residence and therefore jurisdiction. Thus, in *Ezebube v. Aplin & Co. Ltd.*[79], the plaintiff sued the defendants in a Magistrates' court in Sapele, (Bendel State) for an amount owing to the plaintiff on his trading account with the defendant. The defendants had their head office at Onitsha outside the court's jurisdiction, but had an office in the court's jurisdiction which carried on occasional business with their trade customers. The defendant objected at the hearing in *limine* to the claim of the court to exercise jurisdiction where the cause of action arose outside the jurisdiction or alternatively to a cause which related to the defendant who was resident outside the jurisdiction. The objection was upheld by the Magistrate. Upon appeal to the High Court, the plaintiff contended that the court had jurisdiction over the matter in the circumstances. In upholding the appeal, Idigbe C.J. indicated[80] that a company, though domiciled outside the jurisdiction is deemed to be resident in the jurisdiction for the purpose of service of process, when it is conducting its business or a material part of it, at some fixed place in the country and this is more than mere casual dealing with customers remote from its headquarters. Similarly, in *Re: Gresham Life Assurance Society (Nig.) Ltd.*[81], the petitioner was incorporated as an insurance company outside Nigeria and registered in Nigeria Under S.239 of the then Companies Act (Cap. 37). The petitioner carried on business in Nigeria through the agency of another insurance company at a place of business which was occupied by the latter company. Following the coming into force of the Companies Act, 1968, the petitioner informed the Registrar of Companies that it did not intend to carry on business in Nigeria and instituted proceedings for winding up under the supervision of the Court. The petition was opposed on the ground that the petitioner had no established place of business in Nigeria. Accordingly, Section 369(3) of the Companies Act, 1968, did not apply and was discretionary. Consequently, that the order of winding up should be refused. The petition was dismissed on the ground that [82] a company incorporated outside Nigeria does not acquire an established place of business in

---

[77] [1940] 2K.B.80

[78] *ibid*, p.84

[78a] (1956) 7 U.L.R.47 Bennett, J.

[79] 1966 NCLR 39. (High Court of Midwestern State)

[80] *ibid*, p.42; see also *Dunlop Pneumatic Tyre Co. v. Motor Und A.G.* (1900-3) All E.R. Rep.197 per Collins M.R.

[81] 1970 NCLR 78 (High Court of Lagos State)

[82] See *ibid* pp.81-82,84.

Nigeria so as to make it a foreign company within the definition of S.368(a) of the Companies Act, 1968 by carrying on business in Nigeria through an agent at the agent's place of business. Furthermore, the Supreme Court of Nigeria has postulated in, *Aluminium Industries Aktein Gesselschaft v. Federal Board of Inland Revenue*[83], that[84] a foreign company does not become resident or carry on business in Nigeria merely by owning the share capital of a Nigerian Company. In that case the appellant company was a Swiss company which was non-resident in Nigeria. It was held that the fact of its being beneficial owner of share capital in Alumaco (the Nigerian company), did not make it carry on business here as Alumaco was a separate company form the appellant company.

# Incorporated company distinguished from other associations[85]

## Clubs and societies

These are unincorporated associations which are not subject to statutory regulation. Their constitution rests upon the ordinary law of contract between the members by which they agree either expressly or impliedly to be bound by the rules in force from time to time of the association.

In law a club has no legal existence separate from its members. However, there is a distinction between club property and property of the members. Club property is vested in trustees who are usually the club's governing committee. The property is held by the committee in accordance with club rules.

With respect to exercise of power, members normally delegate executive powers to certain officers and a committee. Consequently, the liability of the members for the acts of officers or committee depends on normal agency principles. These will determine (i) whether members are fully liable or only to the extent of club funds (ii) whether the officers and members of the committee are liable as such; (iii) if they are, whether they are entitled to be indemnified either by the members personally or out of club funds. Nevertheless, in normal circumstances, contracts made by officers in carrying on the club in the usual way will bind the committee personally, but not the members.[86] However, the committee will be entitled to be indemnified out of the club funds so far as they will go.[87] In other instances a third party may be taken to have agreed that the committee shall not be liable beyond the extent of club funds.[88]

Concerning the position of a club servant, he is not normally liable on club contracts but if he acts within the scope of his employment, he will bind his employers. Under normal contractual rules a club servant is treated as the servant of the club's committee[89], while in tort he is treated as a servant of the members as a whole and not of the committee.[90]

A member who is wrongfully expelled from the club can obtain redress by means of injunction or declaration and also recover damages from the committee and out of club funds. The action is usually framed in the form of representative action.[91]

The principles enumerated above in relation to clubs similarly apply to learned and similar societies. Most of such societies are normally recognised as charitable and therefore entitled to concessions of taxation and local rates. However, in many other respects their constitution is similar to that of clubs in the sense that they may be unincorporated or incorporated under the

83 1981(2) NCLR (Supreme Court of Nigeria)
84 *ibid* p.131 per Lewis J.S.C.
85 See further Gower op.cit. Chap 12; Orojo *op.cit* pp.13 to 16.
86 *Bradley Egg Farm v. Clifford* [1943] 2 All E.R. 378 C.A.
87 *Wise v. Perpetual Trustee Co.* [1903] A.C. 139 P.C.
88 *Steele v. Gourley* (1887) 3T.L.R.772,773, per Lindley L.J.
89 *Bradley Egg Farm* Case, supra n.86.
90 *Prole v. Allen* [1950] 1 All E.R. 476.
91 Gower, op.cit. p.261.

Companies Act and consequently legally indistinguishable from clubs. Finally, it may be noted that the legality of unincorporated clubs and societies may depend on their not carrying on business for their own gain or for that of their members. If this condition is unfulfilled they will be illegal if their membership exceeds 20 under section 392 of the Companies Act.[92]

## Partnerships[93]

A partnership is not a corporate body. Consequently, the partners, except in limited partnerships are personally liable for the debts of the partnership. Essentially this means that the partners have unlimited liability. With regard to legal proceedings, partners are sued jointly and severally for the liabilities of the business and this is possible even after they have retired or withdrawn from the partnership. In addition and in contrast to an incorporated company, a partnership has no perpetual succession. The death or bankruptcy of a partner, in the absence of a contrary agreement dissolves the partnership.

The property of the partnership is not vested in the partnership, not being a legal person. It is, instead vested in the partners as trustees. Furthermore, the borrowing powers of a partnership are limited in the sense that a partnership cannot issue debentures secured partly by charge on the floating assets of the firm.

## Co-operative societies

There exists legislation regulating the formation and operation of co-operative societies.[94] The criteria for registration of a co-operative society by the relevant Registrar is that the society must have as its object the promotion of the economic interests of it members in accordance with the object of facilitating the operations of such a society. Such a society may then be registered with or without limited liability.[95] Upon registration, the co-operative society then becomes a corporate body with perpetual succession and a common seal and power to hold property and enter into contracts. Co-operatives have been described as a bulwark against the capitalism which dominates the incorporated limited liability company in the sense that priority is placed on service to members rather than maximisation of profits.[96] Furthermore, [97] a co-operative is essentially a union of capital. The main purpose of an ordinary company is to realise a profit on investment, while that of a co-operative society is to provide a service to members on sound economic lines, avoiding loss. While the ownership of the number of shareholders is limited in a company, that is not generally the case with co-operatives whose membership is open. Again, while the control of a company is based on the number of shares held, with a co-operative, control is democratic, depending on the principle of one member, one vote. With respect to the interest or dividends on shares in a company, this is limited only by the company's profit earning! In contrast, in a co-operative, share capital is paid at a fixed and modest rate of dividend. With regard to surplus earnings, in the case of a company these belong to the corporation.[98] In the case of a co-operative these belong to the members or patrons. Although in a company, profits are divided in proportion to the shares held, surplus in respect of a co-operative is divided according to the number of its patrons. Lastly, while shares in a

---

92 See further Gower ibid, p.264

93 See further, Bakibinga, *Law of Partnership in Uganda* (1992)

94 Co-operative Societies Statute, 1991.

95 Orojo op.cit. p.15

96 D.G. Fauquet, *The Co-operative Sector* (Manchester Co-operative Union Ltd. 1951) pp.32-33.

97 See further "Differences between Co-operative Societies and other Forms of Business Organisations" (The Department for Co-operative Development, Kampala, 1966) in Katende, et al. *The Law of Business Organisations in East* and Central Africa. (Nairobi; East African Literature Bureau 1976) p.103. See also Bhalla and Bakibinga, "The Economics of Incorporation in Nigerian Law" (Paper presented at the 21st Annual Conference of the Nigerian Association of Law Teachers March, 1983.

98 Companies Act Table A Schedule 1 Articles 117 & 128.

company may be freely traded and fluctuate in value according to the profits made, shares in a cooperative are not traded for speculation and held in the name of members only.

## The unit trust

A unit trust is defined as [99]"any arrangement made for the purpose of having the effect of providing for persons having funds available for investment, facilities for the participation by them as beneficiaries under a trust in profits and income arising from the acquisition, holding, management or disposal of any property whatsoever".

Essentially then, the unit trust is an investment scheme by which persons pool their subscriptions under a trust deed.[100] The scheme involves a managing company and a trustee or trustees which is usually another company or bank. The practice is normally for the managing company to acquire securities such as shares or debentures which have been quoted on the stock exchange and to transfer them to trustees who become the sole custodians thereof. The securities are in turn divided into units and offered to the public for investment after quotation on the stock exchange. The investors then become beneficiaries under the trust deed and are entitled to the securities in proportion to their holdings. In addition, they are also entitled to dividends in proportion to their holdings. The unit trust may be fixed i.e. with the securities to be held strictly defined or it may be flexible or managed. In the latter case the managing company has wide powers and discretion to invest, subject to the provisions of the trust deed. The unit trust has the advantage of enabling people with small investments to spread the risk over a wide area. Sections 8 and 9 of the Exchange Control Act, 1964 impose restrictions on the creation or transfer of securities in favour of a or to a person resident outside Uganda. "Securities" are defined[101] to include units under a unit trust scheme.

## Public corporations

A public corporation has been defined[102] to mean a body set up to operate nationalised industries[103] or for the organisation of other public enterprises and services. Corporations are classified into commercial corporations i.e. those which are intended to operate an industry or public utility according to commercial principles, though subject to ministerial control.[104] An example is the Uganda Electricity Board.[105] Secondly are social service corporations i.e. those intended to carry out a particular social service on behalf of the government. An example is the Uganda Revenue Authority[106], a revenue collection agency.

Public corporations have emerged as a chosen legal instrument for the public control of basic industries in the economy.[107] In effect, though, public corporations are statutory companies created by individual statutes. They differ from the companies because the Companies Act does not apply to them.[108] It is suggested, however, that the ordinary common law of corporations applies to them except where expressly or by implication modified by the statute creating them. For instance, the *ultra vires* doctrine which restricts an incorporated company to the pursuit

---

99 Exchange Control Act, 1964,S.46.

100 See further Orojo, op.cit. pp. 15-16; Gower, op.cit. pp.266 to 272.

101 Exchange Control Act, 1964, S.46

102 Gower, op.cit. p.285

103 In the British Context though not necessarily in the Ugandan Context.

104 Gower, op cit. p. 286

105 Established Under Caps 135 and 136 Laws of Uganda, 1964.

106 Established under Statute No.6 of 1991.

107 W. Friedman, "The New Public Corporations and the Law" 10 M.L.R.p.233 (1946); A. Kiapi, "The Public Corporation as a Legal Instrument of Economic Policy in East Africa," Paper Presented at the East and Central African Conference on Law and Development, Kampala 1973, pp.1-2 in J.W.Katende, op.cit. Supra n.99, pp.105-106.

108 Gower, op.cit., p.287

only of its stated objects applies to public corporations[109] and they are required to keep trading accounts which should conform with the best commercial standards.[110]

The main difference between a public corporation and an ordinary registered company is that the former has neither shareholders nor share capital. In the words of Denning L.J. (as he then was) in *Tamlin v. Hannaford*, thus: [111]

> The significant difference is that there are no shareholders to subscribe the capital or to have any voice in its affairs. The money which the corporation needs is not raised by the issue of shares but by borrowing: and its borrowing is not secured by debentures but is guaranteed by the Treasury. If it cannot repay, the loss falls on the consolidated fund... i.e. on the tax-payer. There are no shareholders to elect the directors or to fix their remuneration. If it should make losses and be unable to pay its debts its property is liable to execution. but is not liable to be wound up at the suit of any creditors. The tax payer would. no doubt be expected to come to its rescue before the creditors stepped in.

[109] Katende. op.cit., p.1014.
[110] Electricity Act, Cap. 135, S.16; Gower, op.cit. pp.290-291.
[111] [1950] 1 K.B. 18, 23 C.A.

# 3
# PROMOTION AND FORMATION OF THE COMPANY

## Promotion

### Promoters defined

A "promoter" was defined in *Taibatu Adeniji and Others v. Starcola (Nig.) Ltd. & another* [1]as

> Any person who undertakes to take part in forming a company or who, with regard to a proposed newly formed company, undertakes a part in raising capital for it is, prima facie a promoter of the company, for he has taken part in setting going a company formed with reference to a given object. Thus a person may be a promoter though he has taken comparatively minor part in the promoting proceedings.

Consequently, a promoter may do anyone or more of the following activities, (i) arrange the preparation of the memorandum and articles of association; (ii) procure capital; (iii) prepare a prospectus; (iv) obtain directors for the company. However a person employed in a professional capacity (e.g. as a solicitor, valuer or accountant) is not a promoter.[2]

### Position of a promoter

A promoter stands in a fiduciary relationship to the company and consequently owes it certain fiduciary duties. It follows that a contract made between him and the company is voidable at the company's option unless he has disclosed all material facts relating to the contract to an independent board and the company has freely agreed to its terms. Thus in *Erlanger v. New Sombrero Phosphate Co.*[3]; a syndicate led by Erlanger, a Paris Banker, acquired for GBP55,000 the lease of an island in West Indies with the rights to work its phosphate deposits. The syndicate, acting through Erlanger then formed the respondent company and named its directors. Of these one, the Lord Mayor of London was independe nt of the syndicate, two were abroad and the remainder were mere puppets of Erlanger. The lease was then sold through a nominee to the company for GBP 110,000. The purchase was ratified without inquiry at the meeting of directors eight days after the incorporation of the company. Many members of the public subscribed for the shares, but the real circumstances of the sale and purchase were not disclosed until eight months later after the first phosphate shipments had proved a failure. The shareholders then removed the original directors and elected a new board. The board instituted this action to have the sale rescinded. It was held that the transaction should be rescinded because the promoter failed to remember their fiduciary position when they appointed directors who were in no way independent of themselves and who did not sustain the interests of the company with ordinary diligence and care.[4]

---

1 High Court of Lagos, 1972 NMLR 69-SCN, per Kazeem J. See also the definition by Cockburn, C.J. in Twycross v. Grant (1877) 2 CPD 469; *Kololo Curing Co. v. East Mengo Co-op. Union* [1981] 4 H.C.B 60.

2 Companies Act, S.45. See further Orojo, op.cit. pp.73-74; Gower *op.cit.* pp.324-326; Northey and Leigh's *Introduction to Company Law* (3rd Ed.1983) pp.30-31.

3 (1878) 3 App. Cas 1218 See also Sealy, Cases and Materials in Company Law (2nd Ed.1978) pp.13-15.

4 Per Lord O'Hagan at pp.1255-1256.

Furthermore, a promoter is not allowed to make a secret profit while acting as such. If he does so, the company may recover it form him. In *Gluckstein v. Barnes*[5], Gluckstein and three others bought the Olympia exhibition premises in liquidation proceedings for GBP 40,000. They then promoted a company, Olympia Ltd. to which they sold the property for GBP180,000. There were no independent directors. In a prospectus inviting applications for shares and debentures, the GBP40,000 profit was disclosed but not a further profit of some GBP20,000 which they had made by buying securities on the property at a discount and then enforcing them at their face value. The company was wound up within four years and the liquidator claimed in this action GBP 6,341 part of GBP20,000 received by Gluckstein. It was held that Gluckstein was accountable to the liquidator for the secret profit made.

It is evident from the above two cases that the remedies available to the company where a promoter is in breach of his fiduciary duties are (i) rescission of the contract if *restituo in integrum* in possible[6]; (ii) recovery of secret and undisclosed profit from the promoter and (iii) suit against the promoter for damages for breach of the fiduciary duty or for deceit.

## Remuneration of a promoter

Promoters do not possess an automatic right to remuneration from the company for their services since a company cannot enter into a contract before it comes into existence.[7] However, in practice, the company's articles allow directors' to pay preliminary expenses from the company's funds[8] Normally they exercise such power to pay promoters. Furthermore it is provided that payments to promoters must be disclosed in the company's prospectus[9] in the case of a public company.

## Pre-incorporation contracts

In promoting a company, promoters usually enter into contracts with third parties and when they do so they purport to do so on behalf of the unincorporated company. Such contracts are not binding on the company because it is not yet in existence and consequently has no capacity to contract. In addition, the company when it is incorporated cannot ratify contracts entered into by the promoter. Thus, in *Kelner v. Baxter*[10], A, B and C entered into a contract with the plaintiff to buy goods, "on behalf of the proposed Gravesend Royal Alexandra Hotel Co.". The goods were supplied and consumed in the business. Shortly after incorporation, the company collapsed and the plaintiff sued A,B, and C on the contract for the price of the goods. It was held that the defendants were personally liable on the contract.
Earle C.J. thus stated:[11]

> If Gravesend Royal Alexandra Hotel Company had been existing at the time of signing the agreement, the persons who signed the agreement would have signed as agents of the company. But as there was no company in existence at the time, the agreement was wholly inoperative unless it was held to be binding on the defendants.

---

5 (1900) A.C. 240 H.L.

6 *Re: Cape Breton Co.* (1885) 29 Ch.D,.798. The right to rescind a contract is governed by the general law of contract i.e. it may be lost if (i) the company has ratified the contract after full disclosure by the promoter and (ii) *if restituo in integrum* is impossible.

7 Kelner v.Baxter (1866) L.R.2 C.P.174; *Moukarim Metal Wood Factor Ltd. v. Durojaiye* 1976 NCLR 264 (High Court of Lagos State); *N.I.P.C. v. Bank of West Africa Ltd.* [1962] 1 All N.L.R.556 (Federal Supreme Court).

8 Article 80 Table A 1st Schedule to Companies Act 1968.

9 S.40, Companies Act, ibid; Schedule 3 part 1 para.13 Companies Act.

10 supra n.7 See also *Motabani v. Thobani* (1945) 12 E.A.C.A. 37

11 *ibid*, p. *Sartori & Co.* (1961) All N.L.R.534.

Willes, J. addressed himself to the issue of whether the company could have become liable by mere ratification of the defendants' acts and stated that it could not. He added:[12]

> Ratification can only be by a person ascertained at the time of the act done by a person in existence either actually or in contemplation of law...

Flowing from the above propositions of law is the idea that in order for a company to be bound by pre-incorporation contracts, fresh contracts in the same terms as the pre-incorporation contracts must be entered by it. In Natal & Colonisation Co. Ltd. v. Pauline Colliery & Development *Syndicate Ltd.*[13], the respondent company claimed specific performance of an agreement to lease certain coal mining rights initially made on 9 December 1897 by the appellant's agent, Rycroft with Mrs De Carey. Rycroft understood that Mrs de Carey was acting on behalf of a syndicate (then unincorporated) which was incorporated as the respondent company on 22nd January, 1898. On 31 January 1898, Rycroft's authorities to deal further with the land in dispute was stopped by a telegram from the appellant company's head office in London and he communicated this fact to the Syndicate's solicitors. In September 1898, the respondent company which had been prospecting the land in accordance with the terms of the agreement discovered coal and claimed its right to the lease. It was held by the Privy Council (reversing the lower court) that there was no contract to which the respondent company was a party. Consequently specific performance could not be decreed.

Similarly, in *Moukarim Metal Wood Factory Ltd. v. Durojaiye*[14], the defendant who traded in the name of Durmarking &Co., agreed to buy certain goods from the plaintiffs on behalf of "Durmarking & Co. ltd." The order was subsequently confirmed by a letter written on headed note paper purporting to come from the limited company. The plaintiffs delivered the goods and received part of the purchase price, the balance being covered by a post-dated cheque signed by the defendant in his personal capacity. The plaintiffs were unaware that at the date of the transaction Durmarking & Co. Ltd did not exist, although a company of that name was incorporated shortly afterwards with the defendant as Managing Director. Following the failure to honour the post-dated cheque, the plaintiffs brought the present proceedings against the defendant in his personal capacity contending that he should be made personally liable for the balance of the purchase prices since he had purported to act as agent for a non-existent principal in circumstances from which it might be inferred that he was himself the principal. Judgment was given for the plaintiffs on the ground that[15] a company is not bound by an agreement made before its incorporation; nor can it, after incorporation ratify or adopt such an agreement. In order that the company may be bound there must be a new contract to the same effect as the previous agreement, but the new contract may be inferred from the acts of the company when incorporated although not if such acts are done in the mistaken belief that the agreement is binding.

Furthermore, in the Uganda case of *Central Masaka Coffee Co. v. Masaka Farmers & Producers Ltd.*[16], it was held that the evidence showed that the company lacked the capacity to conclude an agreement for lease of a coffee processing factory made five days before its

---

[12] (1866) L.R.2C.P. 174, p.; See also *Caligari v. Giovanni, ibid, Urhobo v. Chief J.S. Tarka* (1976) IICCHCJ; *Sparks Electrics (Nig.) Ltd. v. S.B. Ponmile* [1986] 2 NWLR 516, 525 C.A. see also Osunbor, "A Critique of the Subtle Distinction in Pre-incorporation Contracts" (1985) *4 Journal of Private and Property Law pp.9-16.*

[13] [1904] A.C. 120 O,C,; *S.E. Ltd. v. Ponmile ibid.* See also *Price v. Kelsall* [1957] E.A.752; *Ngaremtoni Estate Ltd. v. C.I.I.* 1966(1) ALR Comm.186.

[14] 1976 NCLR 264 (High Court of Lagos State).

[15] ibid pp 268-271 per Ajose-Adeogun, J. following the Natal v. Pauline case supra n.13; Kelner v. Baxter supra n 10, In *Re Northumberland Avenue Hotel Co.* (1886) 33 Ch.D.16. See also *Stephen v. Build. Co. (Nig) Ltd* 1968(2) ALR. Comm 242 (Supreme Court of Nigeria). and *S.E.Ltd. v. Ponmile, supra* n.12, *Edopoulos v. Sem-Edo (1984) 7S.C. Trans Brige Co. Ltd v. Survey Int. ltd.* (1986) 4W.L.R. 1971 (1) NCLR 80 SCN.

[16] [1991] ULSLR 220

incorporation. Similarly in the Tanzania case. *Ngaremtoni Estate Ltd. v.Commissioner of Income Tax*[17],

Platt, J. (as he then was) held that a promoter had no right to indemnity from a company which he promoted in respect of an obligation undertaken on its behalf before its incorporation and he could not sue it upon a contract made by him with an agent or trustee on its behalf before its incorporation, even where the articles of association provide that the company shall defray the preliminary expenses. The court also reiterated the principles that a company cannot ratify an agreement purporting to have been made on its behalf before its incorporation, and that persons can only sue upon a new contract between the company and themselves.

In *Motani v. Theobani*[18], the appellant sought to enforce a claim against the second respondents to whom it was alleged the first respondent had sold his business in contravention of the Uganda Bulk Sales Ordinance. In actual fact, the first respondent had sold his business to one Narandas seven days before the second respondent company was incorporated. Narandas had bought the business with the object of transferring it to the company as soon as it was formed. However, there was no evidence of any agreement by the company after its formation to pay any debts due by the first respondent. It was held that the sale having been effected before the company was in existence was not a sale to the company and was incapable of ratification.

The principle that an incorporated company can only be bound by pre-incorporation contracts entered into afresh after its incorporation also applies to documents which may be registered in the company's name before its incorporation. Thus, in *N.I.P.C.Ltd & Anor v.Bank of West Africa Ltd.*[19], the plaintiffs (respondents) instituted an action in the High Court claiming *inter alia* a declaration that the NIPC Ltd. by registration in their name of a purported assignment to them of certain leaseholds by the second defendant (appellant), H. Mansour did not obtain any rights of priority against the plaintiffs as equitable mortgagees of the said leaseholds, on the ground that at the time of the assignment NIPC had not been incorporated. Judgment was given for the plaintiffs and upon appeal by the second defendant it was held by the Federal Supreme court[20] that registration of ownership of lands or leaseholds under the Registration of Titles Act, in the name of company which is not incorporated at the date of such registration is void and of no effect.

The issue of who is liable on a pre-incorporation contract purported to be entered into on behalf of an unformed company requires further examination. Although *Kelner v. Baxter*[21] in essence holds that the relevant promoters of the company are personally liable on such contracts that position appears to have been modified by the English Court of Appeal decision in *Newborne v. Sensolid (G.B.) Ltd.*[22] which seems to suggest that[23] in order to be liable under, or entitled to sue, on the purported contract of an unformed company, a person must have held himself out either as agent or as principal. In that case, the contract was for the sale to Sensolid of 200 cases of tinned ham. It was written on a printed form headed, "Leopold Newborne (London) Ltd." which ended with the words. "Yours faithfully Leopold Newborne (London) Ltd" and followed by the inscription "Leopold Newborne". The market fell and Sensolid refused to take delivery. When he was sued on the contract, he pleaded that on the date when the contract was made Leopold Newborne (London) Ltd. had not been incorporated and that neither the company nor Newborne personally could enforce it. The reason given was that Newborne did not purport to contract as agent or

---

17 1969(1) ARL Comm 186. *Platt J. See also Price v. Kelsall* [1957] E.A.752 C.A.

18 (1945) 12 EACA 37 applying *Re: Northumberland Avenue Hotel Co* (1886) 33 Ch.D.16; *Re: Express Engineering Co.(1880)* 16 Ch.D,125. See also *Stephen v. Build Co. (Nig.) Ltd.* 1968(2) ARL Comm.242

19 [1962] 1 All N.L.R.556 (Federal Supreme Court)

20 ibid, pp.559, 569

21 supra n.10

22 (1953) 1 All E.R. 708; (1954) 1Q.B. 45. See also *Shonibare v. Mansour* 1963 L.H.C R.1

23 See further Sealy, op.cit. p.8. The distinction between *Kelner* and *Newborne v. Sensolid* is criticised by Osunbor, *supra* n.12.

personally. He purported to sign for the company. Since the company was not in existence, when the contract was signed, there was then no contract.

In the Nigerian case of *Moukarim Metal Wood Factory Ltd. v. Durojaiye t/a Durmarking & co.*[24], *Newborne v. Sensolid* was distinguished on the ground that [25] "Lord Goddard had indicated that in that case the Court of Appeal could not find that the plaintiff purported to contract as agent or principal as in this case."

# Formation of a company

## Types of company

The Companies Act, makes provision for public and private companies on the one hand and limited and unlimited companies on the other.

A public company must have a minimum of seven members at its formation[26], but no maximum limit. A private company, on the other hand should have at least two members.[26] In addition, a private company should have provision in its articles of association for a restriction on the right of transfer of its shares and debentures to its existing members[27]. A private company may be converted into a public company by altering its articles to exclude the restrictive provisions on the transfer of shares.[28] While in the case of a public company minimum of two directors are required, only one is required in the case of a private company[29]. A private company can commence business immediately upon incorporation whereas a public company requires a trading certificate in order to do so[30]. Furthermore, it is not necessary for a private company to hold a statutory meeting and report thereon as is required of a public company[31]. In practice, though, Ss.111 and 130 of the Companies Act are avoided because public companies invariably incorporate as private companies and later convert to public ones. In addition the quorum at general meetings is two for a private company as contrasted to three for a public company[32]. With a private company a proxy can speak at the general meeting. This is not possible for a public company[33]. In further contrast with a public company, directors' appointment can be voted on together rather than individually[34]and there is no age limit on directors[35].

The company, whether public or private may be limited by shares, or by guarantee, or be an unlimited company. A company limited by shares is one where its memorandum of association limits the liability of its members to the amount, if any, unpaid on their shares.[36]A company limited by guarantee is one where the liability of members is limited to such amount as they may have undertaken to contribute to the assets of the company in the event of winding up[37]. An unlimited company is one in which there is no limit on the liability of members[38]. While a company limited by shares should have share capital, this is not required of a company limited by guarantee or an unlimited company.

---

24 supra n.14
25 *ibid* p.272.
26 Companies Act, S.4(1)
27 *ibid*, S.30
28 *ibid* S.32
29 *ibid*, S.188
30 *ibid*, S.111
31 *ibid*, S.130
32 *ibid* S.134.
33 *ibid*, S.136
34 *ibid* S.184
35 *ibid* S.4(2)(a)
36 *ibid* S.4(2)(a)
37 *ibid* S.4(2)(b)
38 *ibid*, S.4(2)(c)

## Mechanism of formation

A company is formed by registering it with the Registrar of Companies in Kampala and obtaining a certificate of Incorporation.[39]

In order to effect this the following documents must be submitted to the Registrar:

(a) Memorandum of Association;[40]

(b) Articles of Association;[41] (except where the company has adopted Table A).

(c) A statutory declaration by a legal practitioner engaged in the formation of the company or by a person named in the articles as director or secretary of compliance with the registration requirements of the Act.[42]

(d) A statement of nominal capital.

If the company is a public company the following additional documents are required to be registered:

(e) A statement with the names and particulars of directors and secretary and their undertakings by directors to take and pay for qualification shares, if any, unless they have signed the memorandum for at least that number of shares;[43]

(f) Prospectus or statement in lieu of prospectus.

## Effect of registration and the role of the Registrar

If the Registrar is satisfied that the documents are in order[44] and that stamp duties and fees have been paid, he enters the name of the company in the register of companies and issues a certificate of incorporation.[45] The issue of the certificate of incorporation is conclusive evidence that all registration requirements have been complied with and that the association is a company authorised to be registered and is duly registered under the Act.[46]

It is notable that the Registrar of Companies cannot refuse registration of a company whose objects are lawful and whose documents are in order. Thus in *R.v. Registrar of Companies Exparte Bowen*[47], an application was made to register a proposed company, named the United Dental Services Limited. The subscribers to the memorandum were seven unregistered dental practitioners. The registrar refused to register the company unless either the memorandum was altered so as to provide that the work of the company should be undertaken only by registered dentists, or the name of the company was amended so as not to include the word "dental" or "dentist". The applicants sought a writ of mandamus to compel the registrar to register the company. It was held that the Registrar's refusal was unjustified and the order of mandamus was granted on the grounds that (i) the use of the words "The United Dental Service" did not amount to an offence under the Dentists Act 1878 and (ii) such words did not imply a description of the acts to be performed and that the persons intended to perform them were persons specially qualified under the act of 1878. Similarly, in *Lasisi v. Registrar of Companies*[48], it has been indicated that a company which has among its objects the doing of something which cannot be lawfully be done without obtaining official permission may be formed without first obtaining the permission required for carrying out that particular object and the Registrar of Companies cannot refuse to register the company on the

---

39 *ibid,* S.16

40 *ibid* S.15 read together with S.5

41 *ibid,* S.15 read together with Ss.9,10 and 11.

42 *ibid* S.17(2)

43 *ibid,* S.182

44 i.e. that they comply with statutory requirements viz Ss.4(2),2,4,5,9,12 Companies Act.

45 *ibid.* S.15(1).

46 *ibid,* S.17(1) read together with S.16(2); See also Supra Cap.2

47 [1914] 3 K.B. 1161 K.B.

48 1975 NCLR 483 (Federal Revenue Court) at pp.485-486, 488.

ground that the permission has not been obtained and therefore the purpose of the company is unlawful. In the words of Belgore J.[49]:

> I cannot find any provision in the Companies Act which makes it incumbent on the applicant to obtain a permit as required by the Registrar before registration. What the provision of the Telegraphs Act says is that you cannot operate without permission and not that you cannot form a company to operate. Registration does not mean that the permit has been obtained, or that a further permit should not be obtained, where necessary....

In affirming the decision of the Federal Revenue Court (as it then was), the Supreme Court of Nigeria postulated that[50] the Registrar of Companies has a duty to register a company provided its objects are lawful and the promoters have complied with the requirements of the Companies Act, 1968. if the Registrar wrongfully refuses to register a company, the appellant having no other remedy to enforce his right is entitled to a writ of *mandamus* compelling the Registrar to register the Company and in these circumstances, the Court has no discretion to refuse the writ.

The issue of what constitutes lawful for purposes of registration came up again in *Kehinde v. Registrar of Companies*[51]. In that case, the applicants applied and obtained an order *nisi* for leave to apply for an order of mandamus directed at the Registrar of Companies to show cause why an order of mandamus should not issue commanding the respondent to register the memorandum and articles of association of Honda (Nig.) Ltd. submitted to him by the applicants for registration. The respondent objected to clauses 62 and 95 *inter alia* of the proposed company's articles of association which gave weighted voting rights to "B" shareholders as against "A" shareholders in proportion of 3 to 1 as infringing the Nigeria Enterprises Promotion Act, 1977. It was held that (i) since the memorandum is the fundamental document[52] required to be registered for purposes of registration and since it was in order the Registrar of Companies was under a duty to register it and consequently the company (ii) clauses 62, 94 and 95 of the articles of association, irrespective of their effect on the Nigeria Enterprises Promotion Act 1977[53], were inconsequential for purposes of registration not being in themselves illegal or unlawful. They may have offended government policy, but government policy is not the law.[54] In this vein while reiterating that by Sections 5 and 6 of the Nigeria Enterprises Promotion Act, 1977 foreign Companies seeking incorporation in Nigeria are required to have, on registration a 60% equity participation by Nigerian nationals, the court indicated in effect that the articles of such a company may validly give special voting rights to a class of non-Nigerian shareholders whereby those shareholders have control over the appointment and the determination of the conditions of service, the managing director and assistant managing director of the company. Although considering himself bound by the law in the decision he reached, Anyaegbunam P. nevertheless lamented this result as undermining the indiginesation policy of the Nigeria Enterprises Promotion Act, 1977.
In his words:[55]

> .... on reading clauses 4(1), (2) and (3) of the articles of association and Ss.5 and 6 of the Nigeria Enterprises Promotion Act, 1977, one may think that a great favour is being done to

---

49 *ibid*, p.488

50 *Lasisi v. Registrar of Companies* 1976 NCLR 7 (per Bell J.S.C.

51 [1979] 3 L.R.N. 213 (Federal Revenue Court). See also Goel, "Indigenisation: Corporate Control by Nigerians: a Plea for Company Law Reform" (1982) N.C.L. Review pp. 232-239; K.D. Barnes, "Incorporating Foreign Control Over Nigerian Companies: The Registrar's Refusal Considered" JPPL Vols. 1 & 2 (1984) pp.53-66.

52 Adopting the description by Orojo: op.cit.p64, ibid, pp.218, 224; See also *Guiness v. Land Corpn. of Ireland* (1882) 22 Ch.D.349, 381.

53 Ss.5 and 6

54 Following *Bushell v. Faith* (1970) A.C.1099 and *Lasisi (S.A.) v. Registrar of Companies* (1976) 7SC 73.

55 [1979] 3 L.R.N.213, pp.222-223. See also the *Lasisi* case *ibid.*

> Nigerians by giving them 70 percent equity participation instead of 60 per cent and 40 per cent as provided by Ss.5 and 6 of the (Act) respectively. it is only when one goes to clauses 94 and 95 that one discovers that it is all Greek gift. it is a ruse. I am of the view that Clauses 94 and 95 are calculated to cover up the effect of Ss.5 and 6. It may have been different if "A" and "B" shares were left to shareholders to make their choice. Unless clause 4(2) and (3) is altered, Nigerian Shareholders will be perpetually condemned to an inferior status and Japanese shareholder exalted to a superior overriding status when it comes to decisions as to who will be Managing Director of the Company and their conditions of service. The Managing Director will always be a Japanese and the Assistant Managing Director will always be a Nigerian. This is certainly contrary to the spirit of the Nigerian Enterprises Promotion Act, 1977..... Unless some amendment is made to these offensive clauses. the Federal Military Government's indigenisation programme will be wittingly or unwittingly frustrated..... it is unfortunate that compliance with the provisions of the Nigerian Enterprises Promotion Act, 1977 is not made a condition precedent to the registration of a new company.

However, the registrar may refuse to register a company whose objects are patently unlawful. Thus, in *R. v. Registrar of Companies Exparte More*[56], the Registrar refused to register a company formed to sell tickets in an Irish Lottery.

It was held that since the lottery was illegal in England, the refusal was right. Furthermore. registration does not establish conclusively that the objects of a company are lawful. However. after the issue of a certificate of incorporation the regularity of a corporation cannot be challenged on grounds of illegality except in proceedings specially brought in the name of the government to have registration cancelled.[57] In *Bowman v. Secular Society Ltd.*[58], the main object of the society, which was registered as a company limited by guarantee, was to "promote.... the principle that human conduct should be based upon natural knowledge and not upon supernatural belief and that human welfare in this world is the proper end of all thought and action...." It was alleged that this object which involves denial of Christianity was against public policy so that a bequest to the society was unlawful. It was held that the object in issue was lawful. In the course of delivering judgment, Lord Parker of Waddington considered the issue of conclusiveness of the certificate of incorporation under Section 17 of (Companies Act.) and said that[59] that section precludes the courts from going behind the certificate of incorporation or from alleging that the society is not a body corporate with the status and capacity conferred by the Act. On the danger of courts recognising the corporate existence of a company, all of whose objects in the Memorandum of Association are illegal, Lord Parker thus stated:[60]

> ... such a case is not likely to occur for the registrar fulfils a quasi-judi-cial function and his duty is to determine whether an association applying for registration is authorised to be registered under the acts. If such a case did occur it would be open to the court to stay its hand until an opportunity had been given for taking appropriate steps for the cancellation of the certificate of registration.... the Attorney General on behalf of the Government could institute proceedings by way of certiorari to cancel a registration which the registrar in affected discharge of his quasi-judicial duties had improperly or erroneously allowed....

---

56 [1931] 2 K.B. 197

57 See further, Sealy, op.cit. p.3

58 [1917] A.C. 406 H.L.

59 *ibid*, pp.438-439; see also *Jubilee Cotton Mills v. Lewis [1924] A.C. 958*

60 *ibid*. pp.439-440

# 4
# THE MEMORANDUM OF ASSOCIATION

## General

The Memorandum of Association of a Company, which is required to be registered for purposes of incorporation[1] is regarded as the company's most important document in the sense that it determines the powers of the company. Consequently, a company may only engage in activities and exercise powers which have been conferred upon it expressly by the memorandum or by implication therefrom i.e. the powers exercisable must be reasonably incidental to the fulfilment of the objects as contained in the memorandum[2]. All other activities would be regarded as *ultra vires,* void and therefore of no consequence. In the words of Bowen L.J. in *Guiness v. Land Corporation of Ireland*[3]

> ..... the Memorandum contains the fundamental conditions upon which alone the company is allowed to be incorporated. They are conditions introduced for the benefit of the creditors and the outside public as well as the shareholders....

This chapter will, therefore consider the contents of the memorandum and the scope of the *ultra vires rule.*

## Contents of the memorandum

The Memorandum of Association of a company limited by shares must state the following:[4]
(i) the name of the company with "limited' as the last word;
(ii) that the registered office of the company is situated in Uganda;
(iii) the objects of the company;
(iv) that the liability of the members is limited;
(v) the amount of share capital and division thereof into shares of a fixed amount.
If the company is limited by guarantee, the Memorandum should state that each member undertakes to contribute to the assets of the company in the event of its being wound up while he is a member or within one year after ceasing to be a member such amount as may be required not exceeding a specified amount.[5]

In addition, the Memorandum must state the names, addresses and descriptions of the subscribers thereof who must be at least two for a private company and seven for a public company. Furthermore, the Memorandum must bear stamp duty and must be signed by each subscriber in the presence of at least a witness who must attest to the signature[6]

---

1 See *supra* Chap.3
2 See Leigh *et al. Introduction to Company Law* (3rd Ed.1983), p.70
3 (1882) 22 Ch D 349 at p.381 C.A. See also *Kehinde v. Registrar of Companies* (1979) 5F.R.C.R.101, Co.6
4 Companies Act, S 5. The specimen form of the Memorandum appears in Table B, first schedule to the Act.
5 *ibid.* S.4(2)(b). The specimen form for the Memorandum of a Company limited by guarantee appears in Table C First schedule to the Act. The forms for a company limited by guarantee with share capital and that of an unlimited company with share capital appear in Tables D and E respectively of the first schedule.
6 *ibid.* S5.

## Name of the company

The promoters of the company may select the name of the company subject to the restrictions indicated in Section 20 of the Companies Act. It is indicated therein that a company will not be registered by a name which (i) is identical with that of an existing company or so nearly resemble it as to be calculated to deceive;[7] (ii) contains the words "Chamber of Commerce" unless it is to be registered under a licence granted under section 21 without the word limited.

Should a company by mistake be registered by name which is identical with that of an existing company, it may be required to change its name and if it defaults, it incurs a penalty[7a]. A company may change its name by special resolution and with the written approval of the Registrar[8].

The Minister for Trade may dispense with the use of the word "limited" if he is satisfied that the company's object is to promote commerce, art, science, religion, charity or any other useful object and intends to apply its profits, if any, or other income in promoting its objects and prohibits the payment of dividend to its members.[9]

In *London Overseas Trading Co. v. The Raleigh Cycle Co. Ltd*[9a], the appellant applied for registration of the word "Lale" in the register of Trade Marks. The respondents opposed the application on the ground that the word "Lale" was phonetically identical with the word Raleigh. The Registrar of Trade Marks upheld the objection. On appeal to the High Court, the appellant submitted that the Registrar was not entitled to take judicial notice that the type of bicycle manufactured by the respondent company was known in the trade and by the public in Uganda as "Raleigh" and that there was no evidence before him upon which he could base such a finding. It was held that it was open to the Registrar to find that the mark by being likely to deceive or cause confusion would be disentitled to protection by the court.

## Registered office of the company

As indicated above, the Memorandum must state that the registered office is situated in Uganda. However, the actual address must be communicated to the Registrar of Companies within fourteen days of the date of incorporation or from the day it commences business, whichever is the earlier[10].

## The objects clause

The Companies Act directs that the memorandum of every company shall state the objects of the company. The objects must be lawful and should include all the activities which the company is likely to pursue[11]. It has been said that the objects clause "must delimit and identify the objects in such plain and unambiguous manner as that the reader can identify the field of industry within which corporate activities are confined"[12]. The objects or powers of the company as laid down in the memorandum or implied therefrom determine what the company can do. Consequently "any activities not expressly or impliedly authorised by the memorandum are *ultra vires* the company[13]. The ultra vires doctrine restricts an incorporated company under

---

7 This requirement does not apply to a Company registered outside the country: *East African Electric Co. Ltd. v. Registrar of Companies* (1952) 25(1) KLR 2. (Supreme Court of Kenya). See also *Re: International Construction Corporation* (1964) 1 All N.L.R.131 (High Court of Lagos); *Lagos Chamber of Commerce v. Registrar of Companies* (1952) 14 WACA 197.

7a S.20(2)

8 S.20 (1)

9 *ibid*, S.21

9a [1959] EA 1012

10 *ibid*, S.107(2)

11 *ibid*, S. 4

12 *Cotman v. Broughman* [1918] A.C.514, 522 per Lord Wrenbury. See also Leigh, **op.cit.** p.75

13 Leigh, *ibid*, following *Ernest v. Nicholls* (1857) 6 H.L. Cas. 401.

the Companies Act[14] to the pursuit only of the objects outlined in its registered Memorandum of Association[15] and the exercise of powers expressly conferred upon it by the Memorandum or which are reasonably incidental to the achievement of its stated objects.[16] The doctrine which is basically a product of English Case Law applies to Uganda by virtue of the reception law which allow the common law, doctrines of equity and statutes of general application in force in England on 11th August 1902 to be applied in Uganda.[17] The issue arises as to whether this doctrine, which has wide acceptance both in England and Uganda shows any consistency in situations of its actual application and if not, whether it can be considered to be useful as a legal tool in company law, over one hundred and fifteen years after its first distinctive articulation by the English House of Lords in the case of *Ashbury Railway Carriage Co. Ltd. v. Riche.*

In this vein, an attempt is made to analyse the efforts at reforming or abolishing the doctrine with the aim of gauging their effect in making the rule viable or otherwise.

## The rule and its purpose

As we have already noted, the doctrine of *ultra vires* in Anglo-Ugandan Company Law was first laid down in so far as it applies to incorporated companies by the House of Lords in the *Ashbury Railway Carriage Case.*[18] In that case the company was incorporated under the then British Companies Act of 1862. Clause (3) of its Memorandum of Association provided that the objects for which the company was established was "to make and sell or lend on hire, railway carriages and waggons and all kinds of railway plant, fittings, machinery, and rolling stock; to carry on the business of mechanical engineers and general contractors; to purchase and sell as merchants, timber, coal, metals, or other materials, and to buy and sell any such materials on commission or as agents." Clause 4 of the Companies Articles of Association stated that "an extension of the Company's business beyond or for other than the objects or purposes expressed or implied in the Memorandum of Association shall take place on law in pursuance of a special resolution."

The company agreed to provide Riche with finance for the construction of a railway in Belgium. The company later repudiated the agreement. Riche sued the company for damages. The company pleaded that it was *ultra vires* for the company to enter into such a contract. The issue in the lower courts[19] was whether the contract though unauthorised had been approved or ratified by the shareholders under Article 4. It was emphatically held by the House of Lords that even if ratification had taken place, it would have been ineffective to cure an act which was clearly beyond the company's powers. Lotd Cairns L.C. indicated [20] that a company only comes into existence for the objects stated in the memorandum and this was the condition for its incorporation and existence. That form of existence has two aspects, the affirmative and the negative. It states affirmatively the ambit and extent of vitality and powers which by law are given to the corporation and negatively that nothing shall be done beyond that ambit, and that no attempt shall be made to use corporate life for any other purpose than that specified.

Lord Cairns also postulated [21] the dual purpose of the doctrine of *ultra vires,* namely the protection of investors in the company so that they know the objects for which their money is

---

14 Companies Act, Cap. 85. See also Bakibinga, Vol.1 *Ahmadu Bello University Law Journal* (1983) pp.110 - 121.

15 *Ashbury Railway Carriage Co. Ltd. v. Riche* (1875) L.R. 7H.L.653. See also *Shonibare V. Western Nigeria Finance Corporation* 1970 1A.L.R. Comm.98 in regard to a public corporation.

16 *A.G.v. Great Eastern Railway* (1880) App. Cas.473 H.L.

17 Judicature Act, 1967, S.3(2)(b)(i),(5)

18 See *Supra* note 15; for a brief history of the rule see Gower *etal. The Principles of Modern Company Law* (4th Ed., 1979), pp.162-165.

19 (1874) L.R. 9 Ex.224

20 (1875) L.R. 7H.L.653, 670.

21 *ibid at p.667*

used and secondly to protect creditors of the company so that the funds of the company are not used in authorised activities. Lord Parker of Waddington in a similar vein explained[22] that the purpose of a company's objects in the memorandum is firstly to give "protection to the subscribers who learn from it the purpose to which their money is applied" and secondly protects "persons who deal with the company and who can infer from it the extent of he company's powers". He added that the narrower the objects, the greater is the security of those who transact business with the company.

The rule as articulated in the *Ashbury Carriage Case* was extended in *Attorney General v. Great Eastern Railway*[23] to cover incidental powers necessary for executing the company's objects. Lord Selborne L.C. stated in this respect[24] that the doctrine of *ultra vires* as postulated in the *Ashbury Carriage Co. Case* ought to be reasonably understood "that whatever may fairly be regarded as incidental to or consequential upon those things which the legislature authorised ought not (unless expressly prohibited) to be held, by judicial construction to be *Ultra Vires...* ".

In *Re: Modern Retreading Co. Ltd.*[24a], it was held that it was *ultra vires* the company for directors to grant themselves bonus payments and rejected the attempt to prove these in the liquidation of the company. The identification of the nature and rationale of the doctrine now paves the way for an examination of its practical application.

## Application of the doctrine

As analysis of the practical application of the doctrine of *ultra vires* cannot escape the conclusion that the draftmen of Companies Memorandum of Association have invariably tried to circumvent the effect of the doctrine. The readiness with which the courts have accepted the schemes of evasion have, it is submitted, rendered the doctrine inconsistent and virtually useless.

The first method by which the doctrine has been by-passed is the modern practice of listing the objects of the company at great length so as to include every conceivable activity which the company may carry out. This practice appears to depart form the form of the Memorandum of Association envisaged by the Companies Act[25], in which the objects clause reads:[25a]

> The objects for which the Company is established are, "the conveyance of passengers and goods in ship or books between such place as the company may from time to time determine and the doing all such other things as are incidental or conductive to the attainment of the above object.

This clause may be contrasted with the multifarious modern objects clause which may run into several pages.[26]

The second method of evading the doctrine was to include in the objects clause, clauses whose aim was to ensure that none of the enumerated objects would be construed or interpreted restrictively by for example being read as ancillary to the other objects. A similarly worded clause in *Cotman v. Brougham*[27] was held effective for purposes of the *ultra vires* doctrine so

---

22 *Cotman v. Brougham* [1918] A.C. 514, 520, H.L.

23 See *supra* note 16.

24 ibid p.478.

24a 1966(1) ALR Comm.494

25 S.14 Companies Act. This section provides that the form of Memorandum of Association used in Table B, 1st Schedule to the Act should be used "as nearly as cirmustances admit".

25a Companies Act, Table B, Clause 3.

26 An example of the modern objects clause is given in L.S. Sealy *Cases & Materials in Company Law* (2nd Ed., Butterworths, 1978) pp.501-502. See also *Cotman v. Brougham (supra).*

27 See supra note 22. See also *Re: Introductions* infra n.29 and more recently *Re: Horsley & Weight* (30 July, 1980 unreported) Noted in (1981) 2 *Company Lawyer* 70.

as to render *intra vires* for Essequibo Rubber Company to underwrite shares in Anglo-Cuban Oil Bitumen Company in exercise of a general power given under the objects clause to underwrite.

The third way by which the doctrine has been rendered ineffective has been the practice of describing in the objects clause what essentially are powers as objects of the company. This practice has also received judicial blessing in *Cotman v. Brougham*[27]. Lord Parker stated in this respect.[28]

> ..... experience soon showed that persons who transact business which companies do not like having to depend on inference when the validity of a proposed transaction is in question. Even a power to borrow could not always be inferred, much less such a power as that of underwriting shares in another company. There thus arose the practice of specifying powers as objects, a practice rendered possible by the fact that there is statutory limit on the number of objects which may be specified.

An attempt was made to limit this practice in Re: *Introductions Ltd.*[29] In that case the company's objects clause empowered to company to borrow by means of issuing debentures and securing loans by means of charges. There was also a clause which stipulated that each sub-clause was to be construed independently of the other subclauses. The issue arose as to whether the company had an independent power to borrow money. The English Court of Appeal held that the company had no power to borrow except for the purposes of effecting or perpetuating its objects. Harman L.J. stated in this regard.[30]

> ......... a power or an object conferred on a company to borrow cannot mean something in the air: borrowing is not an end in itself and must be for some purpose of the company and since this borrowing was for an *ultra vires* purpose that is an end of the matter.

While this decision sought directly to limit the practice of specifying powers as objects it has been criticised in Australia as being "contrary to the actual decision and reasoning of the House of Lords in *Cotman v. Brougham*"[31] (supra), in so far as it is a Lower Court's decision in comparison to *Cotman v. Brougham,* it may be argued that the law on this point is still as laid down by the House of Lords. It follows that the practice of specifying powers as objects, drawing up a multifarious objects clause and insisting that each clause in the objects clause would be independently inter-preted are acceptable in law. The view in *Cotman v. Brougham* may, however, be doubted in view of the earlier decision in *Re David Payne & Co. Ltd.*[32] There, Buckley J. held that the lending company in this case was entitled to enforce the repayment of the loan even if the purpose was improper. In this case, the clause in the Company's Memorandum of Association gave it power to borrow and raise money for purposes of the company's business. The company borrowed money and used it to pay off certain debts. While the decision appears to support the view in *Cotman v. Brougham* that a power to borrow can exist on its own independently of the other objects of the company the remarks by Buckley J. appear to support the reasoning in *Re: Introductions*[33] Buckley J. was faced with the issue of whether it is a condition attached to the exercise of a power to borrow that the money should be used for the purposes of the company's business, or whether this was a question to be determined by the shareholders and directors.

---

28 *ibid* p. 520

29 [1969] 1 ALL E.R. 887 C.A.

30 *ibid* p. 889.

31 See Re *Tivoli Freeholds Ltd.* (1972) V.R. 445, 465.

32 (1904) 2Ch. 608 Ch.D. & C.A.

33 See *supra* note 29.

He remarked in this regard:[34]

> In my view, the introduction into any Memorandum of Association of a power to borrow is, generally speaking, unnecessary. Every trading company has power to borrow for the purpose of its business, and the introduction of this clause is only to express in words what would otherwise be the law. A limitation of the borrowing to borrowing for the purpose of the company's business is necessary, of course. A corporation cannot do anything except for the purposes of its business, borrowing or anything else; everything else is beyond it powers, and is *ultra vires.*

The decision in this case turned principally on Buckley, J.'s view that the power to borrow in this case was general. Consequently, the lender to the company was not required to investigate whether the money was borrowed for a property or improper purpose.

The attempt at limiting the practice of specifying powers as objects by clearly distinguishing what are powers and objects properly so called which is evident form the reasoning both in *Re: Introduction* and *Re: David Payne & Co. Ltd* (supra) appears to have been followed in the relatively more recent case of *Rolled Steel Products (Holdings) Ltd. v. British Steel Corporation*[35] where Vinelott J. thus stated.[36]

> Provisions though described as "objects" can be seen on construction of the Memorandum of Association as a whole and notwithstanding a "Separate objects clause" to be powers to be exercised in the furtherance of (the) purpose and add to, or may in some circumstances limit the powers that would otherwise be implied as reasonably incidental to them.

It is submitted that the treatment of a company's power as an object for purposes of the *ultra vires* doctrine in *Cotman v. Brougham, Re: Introductions* and *Re: David Payne & Co. Ltd.* (supra) clearly shows inconsistency at each level of the English Court's hierarchy.

The foremost attack on the effectiveness of the doctrine is the practice of inserting into the objects clause authority to the company itself or its directors to determine the limits to which the company's objects may from time to time be extended. What is regarded as "the high point in this development"[37] is to be found in *Bell Houses Ltd. v. City Wall Properties Ltd.*[38] In that case, both companies to the dispute carried on business as property developers. The plaintiff company agreed to introduce the defendants to a financier who could provide a bridging loan amounting to GBP 1 million in return for which the defendants promised to pay a fee of GBP20,000. When sued for the fee, the defendants pleaded that a mortgage broking transactions such as this was *ultra vires* the plaintiffs and that it was not expressly covered in the plaintiff Company's Memorandum of Association. The plaintiffs relied on sub-clause 3 (c) of their memorandum which stipulated:

---

34 [1904] 2 Ch.608, 612

35 An unreported decision of the British Companies Court given on 2nd December, 1981 and noted by J. Birds in (1982) 3 *Company Lawyer* 123-125.

36 Relying expressly on *Re Introductions* supra note 29 and *Re: Horsley and Weight* Supra note 27; Cited in *The Company Lawyer (ibid)* p.124.

37 Gower *supra* note 18, p.166

38 [1966] 2 All E.R. 674 C.A. See also Polack in (1966) *Camb. L.J.* 174; Wedderburn (1966) 29 *M.L.R.* 673 and Baker (1966) 82 *L.Q.R.* 463; The case has been followed in Canada in *H&A Logging Co. Ltd. v. Random Services Corpn Ltd.* (1967) 63 DLR (2d) 6.

> To carry on any other trade of business whatsoever which can, in the opinion of the Board of Directors, be advantageously carried on by the company in connection with or ancillary to....... the general business of the company.

Mocatta J. in the lower court [39] upheld the defendants' plea of *ultra vires,* but was reversed by the English Court of Appeal which held that clause 3(c) gave the company the necessary power. Salmon L.J. in a remark which virtually destroys the doctrine of *ultra vires* stated:[40]

> An object of the plaintiff company is to carry on any business which directors genuinely believe can be carried on advantageously in connection with or ancillary to the general business of the company. It may be that Directors take the wrong view and in fact the business in question cannot be carried on as directors believe. But it matters not how mistaken the directors may be providing they form their view honestly the business is within the company's objects and powers.

The effect of leaving to the directors the discretion to determine what may be regarded as within the company's objects is to enable companies to carry on any business which the directors choose. It should, however, be noted on this point that the law in England is different from that in Nigeria. The position in Nigeria is laid down in the Supreme Court case of *Continental Chemists v. Ifekandu*[41] In this case, the company's main business was that of chemists. The Memorandum of Association provided *inter alia.*

> (e) to enter into any business which the directors think will increase the profits of the company. The company can do all such business and things as maybe incidental and conducive to the attainment of the above objects and powers or any of them.

The main issue in the case was whether the company could validly carry on the business of running a hospital. The Supreme Court held[42] that the words "to enter into any business which the directors think will increase the profits of the company" are "indefinite and useless" and did not give power to the company to run a hospital. To this extent a clause like the one considered both in the *Bell Houses* case (supra) and the *Ifekandu Case* may be said to be ineffective in Nigeria for purposes of the doctrine of *ultra vires.*

The extreme diametrically opposed positions of both the *Bell Houses and Ifekandu* cases (supra) may be contrasted with the compromise position in the Australian case of *H.A. Stephenson & Sons Ltd. v. Gillanders Arbuthnot & Co.*[43] which, it is submitted, lies between the extreme positions adopted in the English and Nigerian cases respectively. In this case, the appellant company was established to carry on the trade of produce merchants in Western Australia. It entered into speculative contracts with the respondents in Calcutta for the purchase of Jute. The Memorandum of Association contained no express power to deal in Jute. However, Clause J, read:

> To carry on any other business whether manufacturing or otherwise as the company may deem expedient.

The main issue was whether the jute purchases were *intra vires* the company by virtue of this provision. The court held that they were. Dixon J. further observed on clause (J) that where you have a clause like this it has to be read in relation to the other objects specified in the Memorandum. This means that the business to be carried on should be connected with or arise

---

39 (1965) 3 All E.R. 427

40 [1966] 2 All E.R. 674, 687 C.A.

41 [1966] 1 All N.L.R.L. (Nig. S.C.).

42 Following *Re: Crown Bank* (1890) 44 Ch.D.634. This view is in line with those of Mocatta J. in *Bell Houses* [1965] 3 All E.R. 427. However, *Re: Crown Bank* was distinguished by the Court of Appeal in *Bell Houses* (*supra* note 38).

out of the business adopted by the company as stipulated in other objects. Thus rather than outrightly rejecting the clause as was the case in *Re: Crown Bank*[42] and the *Ifekandu* case [41] or, interpreting it to mean that anything determined by the company or its directors is *ultra vires* the company, the Australian case sought to connect such a clause to the other objects in the memorandum so as to arrive at a meaningful result. It should be noted that this approach is in line with that adopted in *Re: Introductions* which despite its being decided after *Bell Houses*[43] questions the approach in that case.[44] Harman L.J. stated in this respect:[45] "still you cannot have an object to do every mortal thing you want".

Again it is evident that the courts' approach to what is known as the subjective objects clause is not consistent.

## Extension of the rule?

Apart from the attempt to extend the *ultra vires doctrine* to enable a company to escape liability in tort or crime an attempt now regarded as a "heresy"[46], there is judicial opinion[47] to the effect that the doctrine extends to a position where, regardless of what the objects clause provides, an act of the company which is not *bona fide* aimed a benefitting the company is *ultra vires*[48]. This view has been rejected by Pennycuick J. in *Charterbridge Corporation Ltd. v. Lloyds Bank*[49] where he held that an act of the company which is within its expressed objects is *intra vires* the company whether or not it benefits the company. This approach has most recently been reinforced in *Re Horsley & Weight*[50] where Buckley L.J. indicatedthat a limitation on powers, expressly provided for in a company's objects, to the effect that they must benefit or promote the prosperity of the company was irrelevant. In this vein, while referring to Eve J.'s frequently cited and much relied on judgment in *Re Lee Behrens*[51] to the effect that both express and implied powers of the company must be exercised for the benefit of the company Buckley L.J. stated:[52]

> It is true that Mr. Justice Eve's observation expressly refers to both express and implied powers, but in relation to the former it was no more than *obiter dictum*

Further reinforcement of the rejection of attempts to extend the *ultra vires* doctrine[47] is evident from yet another decision, *Rolled Steel Products Holding) Ltd. v. British Steel Corporation*[53] where Vinelott J. stated:[54]

> ...... the answer to the question whether a disposition of the property of a company was made for the benefit and to promote the prosperity of the company, though directly relevant to the question whether that disposition if made by the directors without the sanction of the company in general meeting was either an excess or abuse of their powers, is not conclusive nor always even relevant to the question whether the disposition was *ultra vires* the company whether in the narrow or wider sense.

---

43 (1931) 45 C.L.R. 476 (High Court of Australia)
44 Supra n.29
45 [1970] Ch.199 at p.209 (C.A.)
46 Gower, *supra* note 18, pp.169-170.
47 *Hutton v. Cork Railway* (1883) 23 Ch.D.654 C.A.
48 See per Bowen LJ. (1881) 23 Ch.D. 673. See also *Re Modern Retreading Co. Ltd. 1966 (1) ALR Comm.494*
49 [1969] 2 All E.R. 1185.
50 *Supra* note 27.
51 [1932] 2 Ch.46 Ch.D.
52 Note M. Fitzgerald "Clarifying the tests laid down in *Re Lee Behrens*" (1981) 2 *Company Lawyer* 71.
53 See *supra* note 35.
54 *(1982) 3 The Company Lawyer 123 at p.125*

# Who may invoke the doctrine?

It has been observed from the decisions of *Ashbury Railway Carriage v. Riche and Cotman v. Brougham* (supra) that the ultra vires doctrine is aimed at protecting the company's investors and those dealing with it, principally the creditors. However, as has been more aptly put by Professor Gower, the doctrine is "designed to protect the company against itself (or rather against its organs) so as to safeguard its members and creditors"[55]. The issue then arises as to whether the doctrine should only be invoked by the company or whether a third party dealing with the company may also plead the doctrine. It has been held by Mocatta J. in *Bell Houses v. City Wall Properties*[56] that if a third party or the defendant in this case were to be sued by the company on a transaction, he is entitled to plead that the contract on which he is being sued is *ultra vires* the company. This view contrasts with the position in the Canadian Case of *Caledonia Community Credit Union Ltd. v. Halimand Feed Mill Ltd.*[57] Where it was held that a borrower cannot allege that a loan made by a company to him was *ultra vires* the lender. It was further suggested that a claim for repayment of the loan will lie on the ground of unjust enrichment. The converse view is evident from *Blackburn Building Society v. Cuncliffe Brooks and Co.*[58] which postulates that if a company has borrowed money *ultra vires* it, then the lender is entitled to have the loan treated as valid in that the money is applied to discharge the company's legal debts and obligations. This view is clearly reinforced in *Re: David Payne & Co. Ltd.*[59] though it may be doubted since *Re: Jon Beauforte (London) Ltd.*[59a] In that case a company's memorandum authorised it to carry on the business of costumers and gown-makers. It decided to undertake the business of veneered panel makers which admitedly was *ultra vires*. For this purpose it created a factory in Bristol. The issue *inter alia* arose as to the proof of a debt lodged in the liquidation of the company for the supply coke to the factory. Counsel for the supplier of the coke argued that the claimants were unaware of the purpose for which the coke would be used and that it was possible that the coke could be used for an *ultra vires* purpose. This plea failed because the coke had been ordered on note paper headed "Veneer Panel Manufacturers". The approach in this case finds support in *Re: Wrexham Mold & Connah's Quay Railway Co.*[60] where it has been said that a lender to a company on an ultra vires transaction it is not entitled to benefit form the securities or priorities which other creditors are entitled to upon the winding up of the company because the loan is invalid. In a similar vein, in *Sinclair v. Brougham*[61], the House of Lords said that a lender in an *ultra vires* transaction cannot bring an action in contract or quasi-contract for the repayment of the money lent. However, he may claim restitution of money which can be identified by a tracing order either at law or in equity. *Sinclair v. Brougham* thus appears to be a compromise between the positions taken by the courts in the *Blackburn Building Society case*[58] and *Re: Jon Beauforte Ltd.*[59a]. It is evident, though *on this point,* that again the courts are not consistent. The Nigerian Stand on this point is evident from *Afolabi v. Polymera Industries (Nig.)Ltd.*[62] which seems to suggest that if a person contracting with a company or its representatives makes a contract which to his knowledge,

---

55 Gower, supra note 18, p.171.

56 [1965] 3 All E.R. 427 Q.B.D. Note that the plea of *ultra vires* by a third party was raised without objection in the *Charterbridge Corporation* case *supra* note 4.

57 (1974) 4 D.L.R.(3d) 376, See also *Shonibare v. Western Nig. Finance Corp.* 1970 (1) A.L.R. Comm.98

58 (1882) 22 Ch. D.61 C.A.

59 Supra note 32

59a [1953] 1 ALL E.R. 634.

60 [1899] 1 Ch.440 C.A.

61 [1914] A.C. 398 H.L.

62 [1964] (2) A.L.R. Comm.205

actual or constructive is *ultra vires* the company, he cannot enforce it. This is an approach which is in line with the principle in *Re: Jon Beauforte Ltd.*[59a]

The inconsistency which is evident from the application, determination of scope and invocation of the *ultra vires* doctrine has in no small measure contributed to calls for its abolition[63]. The Cohen committee stated in this regard:

> ...... as now applied to companies, the *ultra vires* doctrine serves no positive purpose but is, on the other hand, a cause of unnecessary prolixity and vexation.

The Jenkins Committee, however, merely proposed a reform of the doctrine[64].

## Reform of the rule

In line with the recommendations of the Cohen Committee[65], section 5[66] of the British Companies Act, 1948 was enacted to enable companies to alter their objects in certain circumstances and provided certain conditions were fulfilled. To some extent this has mitigated the harshness of the rule. However, as has been noted by Professor Gower,[67] "(m) a king it easier to alter objects or other provisions in the memorandum does nothing to protect their parties or the company unless steps are taken before an otherwise *ultra vires* transaction is entered into".

It is further notable that the Cohen Committee's recommendation[65] that a company should have all the powers of a natural person was not implemented by the British 1948 Act which did not cater for the constructive notice rule i.e. that outsiders who deal with the company are deemed to have notice of its registered public documents, which include the Memorandum and Articles of Association. It follows then that although acts within the scope of the company's powers and objects would be valid they may be rendered invalid because they are beyond the company's officers' authority. To deal with this shortcoming, the Jenkins Committee[68] advocated the abolition of the constructive notice doctrine, and also suggested that actual knowledge of the contents of the memorandum and articles should not prevent a third part from enforcing the contract "if he honestly and reasonably failed to appreciate that they had the effect of precluding the company (or any director or other person on, its behalf, from entering into the contract in question".

Some attempt towards implementing this recommendation was made by S.9(1) of the European Communities Act, 1972 in Britain although in fact this provision was attempting to implement Article 9(1) of the E.E.C. First Council Directive on Companies[69] which stipulated:

> Acts done by the organs of the company shall be binding upon it even if those acts are not within the objects of the company unless such acts exceed the powers that the law confers or allow to be conferred on those organs.

Section 9(1) of the European Communities Act, 1972 stipulates:[70]

> In favour of a person dealing with a company in *good faith* any transaction *decided on by the directors* shall be deemed to be one which it is within the capacity of the company to enter into, and the power of the directors to bind the company shall be deemed to be free from any

63 *Report of the Cohen Committee on Company Law Reform* (Cmnd 6659) (1945) Para 12.
64 *Report of the Company Law Committee* (Cmnd 1749, 1962 Rep. (1973) para 41 to 42.
65 *Supra* n.63
66 S.8 Companies Act Cap. 85
67 Gower *etal supra* n.18 p.177
68 *Supra* n. 64, para 42.
69 No.68/151/EEC
70 Emphasis supplied

> limitation under the Memorandum or Article of Association; and a party to a transaction so decided on shall not be bound to enquire as to the capacity of the company to enter into it or as to any such limitation on the power of the directors and shall be presumed to have acted in good faith unless the contrary is proved.

This provision was so clumsily drafted that the *ultra vires* doctrine in fact still exists in Britain except in relation to outsiders who *in good faith* enter into transactions with a company and those transactions are *decided upon* by the directors[71] This tentative approach to the curtailment of the *ultra vires* doctrine may be contrasted with the far reaching measures in that respect, in Canada.[72] Section 15(1) of the Canada Business Corporations Act 1975 effectively abolished the *ultra vires* in so far as it applied to Canadian federally incorporated companies. The section provides that a corporation has the capacity, rights, powers and privileges of a natural person. Although subsection 16(2) of the same act provides for restrictions on powers in the corporation's article and stipulates that those restrictions shall not be contravened, subsection 16(3) undermines the effect of such contravention by providing:

> No act of a corporation...... is invalid by reason only that the act or transfer is contrary to its articles or this act.

However, the Canadian Act[73] contains remedial provisions for persons wishing to restrain or otherwise affect the corporation's behaviour with respect to express restriction in the article of a company. Those provisions allow a summary application to the court seeking compliance, restraint and any further order the court thinks fit. Section 232 defines complainant to include a registered or beneficial holder of the corporation's securities, directors and officer, former and present and "any other person who in the discretion of a court is a proper person to make an application."

However, it is clear that the effect of the Canadian Federal Act, though recognising the need to check corporate capacity is to abolish the *ultra vires* doctrine while maintaining a remedy for interested parties to enforce any existing articles or by-laws of the corporation. The grant to the corporation of natural capacity has the effect of eliminating the need for multifarious objects clauses. Section 16(2) allows for express restrictions on this capacity in the articles.[74]

## Conclusion

In view of the erosion of the doctrine of *ultra vires* by the practices of multifarious enumeration of the company's objects; providing that each sub-clause in the objects should be read independently of the other sub-clauses, specifying powers to be objects in the Memorandum of Association; leaving it to company or the directors to determine from time to time the scope of the rule it is questionable whether the rule any longer serves any useful purpose. Apart from these undermining practices to the rule, the inconsistent approach of the courts both in Nigeria and England, as well as other parts of the Commonwealth, to the application of the *ultra vires* doctrine and the ease with which they have accepted the schemes of evasion of the doctrine, leads to the conclusion that the rule is either a dead letter or one whose exact parameters cannot be easily determined and consequently varies according to given circumstances or the mood of the court in which the

---

71 For criticisms of the section. See (1973) 36 *Mod. L.R.* 270; (1973) *Camb. L.J.*: (1973) 89 *Law Q. Rev.* 518; (1973) *New L.J.* 312, 513.

72 See generally, F. Iacobucci *et. all. Canada Business Corporation: An Analysis of Recent Legislative* Developments (Law Book Co. Canada, 1977) pp.95-101.

73 Ss.231, 240

74 For provisions elsewhere in Canada to the same effect see Ss.23-24, 27 British Columbia Companies Act, 1973, C. 18S B.C. The updated Act is now known as the Company Act; 1979; See also S.16 Ontario Business Corporation Act, 1970, R.S.O.C. 89 which is not as far reaching as the Federal and the British Columbia Acts.

doctrine is sought to be invoked. In addition, the fact that there have been decisions like *Re Jon Beauforte Ltd.*[75] and *Re: Introduction Ltd.*[76] which clearly undermine the purpose of the *ultra vires* doctrine in protecting shareholders and creditors of the company as explained in the *Ashbury Railway Carriage case*[77] and *Cotman v. Brougham*[78] clearly puts the doctrine in the dock.

It is submitted that the way by which the doctrine has been dealt with in the Canadian Federal Business Corporations Act. i.e. by abolishing it, is the most realistic solution to the stigma and dilemma posed by its continued existence, albeit in an emasculated form in some jurisdictions. The result is that an incorporated company is endowed with the capacity, rights, powers and privileges of a natural person in contracting with third parties.

## The liability of members

The Memorandum of a company limited by shares or by guarantee should indicate that the liability of members is limited. With respect to a company limited by shares, the liability of a member is the amount, if any, unpaid on his shares. With regard to the liability of a member of a company limited by guarantee, this is limited to the amount he undertook to contribute to the assets of the company in the event of winding up. In the case of a company limited by guarantee having a share capital, the member thereof will also be liable to pay the amount, if any, unpaid on his shares.

A company may also be registered with unlimited liability. In such a situation the members thereof act as guarantors in respect of the company's obligations. While a creditor of such a company has no right of action against the member himself, his action being against the company, in turn looks to the members to discharge its debts by providing the necessary funds. The unlimited company may, however possess an advantage which for some family firms may be substantial, it can ensure privacy for its accounts.[79]

It is notable, though, that if a company carries on business for more than 6 months while the number of members is less than the minimum, then a member who is aware of this fact will be liable for all the debts contracted by the company following the lapse of the grace period of six months.[80]

In such a case the creditor can sue the members jointly and severally with the company.[81] It is further suggested[81] that while a "one man" company is legally possible, since the reduction in members below the required minimum does not of itself terminate the legal existence of the company[82] the effect of Section 33 would be to make such a company for practical purposes an unlimited company.

## Share Capital[83]

The memorandum requires that a company having a share capital must state the amount of share capital with which the company is to be registered and that such capital is divisible into shares of a fixed amount. The amount of capital with which a company is to be registered and

---

75 *Supra* note 59a.
76 *Supra* note 29.
77 *Supra* note 15
78 *Supra* note 22.
79 See First Schedule Table E
80 S.33 and *Supra* Chap.2 on lifting the veil
81 Leigh *op.cit.* p.95
82 *Jarvis (Harrow). Ltd. v Carrabott* [1964] 3 All \E.R. 89 *Re: Duomatic Ltd.* [1969] 2 Ch.365; [1969] 1 All E.R. 161

the amounts into which it is to be divided are matters to be decided upon by the promoters and will be determined by the needs of the company and finance available.[84]

## Alteration of the objects

Altering the objects of the company is an aspect of the alteration of the Memorandum of Association. Other aspects which include change of name;[85] alteration of capital;[86] creation of reserve capital [87] reduction of capital[88] making the directors' liability unlimited,[89] arrangements and reconstructions[90] as well as alteration pursuant to a court order aimed at stopping oppressive conduct[91] are considered elsewhere in this text. The treatment here restricts itself to alteration of objects.

A company may by special resolution alter the provisions in its memorandum with respect to the objects of the company to enable it[92]:

(a) to carry on its business more economically or more efficiently or
(b) to enlarge or change the local area of its operations or
(c) to attain any of its objects by new or improved means or
(d) to carry on some business which under existing circumstances may conveniently or advantageously be combined with the business of the company; or
(e) to restrict or abandon any of the objects specified in the memorandum; or
(f) to sell or dispose of the whole or any part of the undertaking of the company; or
(g) to amalgamate with any other company or body of persons.

A company cannot rely on ground(d) where the change is so fundamental that it amounts to changing the basic business of the company. Neither is alteration permissible where the company has completely given up the pursuit of its original objects.[93] The alteration should also not be incompatible with or opposed to the existing objects. Thus in *Re: Cyclist Touring Club,*[94] the Memorandum of the club indicated that its objects were to promote assist and protect the use of bicycle and other similar vehicles on public roads and to give legal assistance in the enforcement of members rights to use the roads. The club wanted to alter its memorandum in order to permit all tourists, including motorists, to join the club. The court declined to allow the alteration because (i) the change would have altered fundamentally the character of the club's activities, the new activities overwhelming the old and (ii) the protection of members against motorists was one of its original objects. In essence the new activity would have been inconsistent with the original purpose of the club.

Regarding ground (e) in *Re: Hampstead Garden Suburb Trust Ltd.*[95], the alteration of a provision of the objects clause which raised a secondary beneficiary to the position of a primary beneficiary on a winding up was held not to be an alteration enabling the company to restrict or abandon any of its objects. Consequently, the alteration was refused. In *N.I.P.C. Ltd. v. Thompson Organisation Limited, Amalgamated Press of Nigeria Ltd. & Ehren*[96], it was indicated that[97] the objects of a company stated in its Memorandum of Association are merely enabling provisions; if an activity of a company does not fall within any of its objects it is *ultra vires*, but an activity permitted by the objects clause is one which may, not must, be carried out.

---

83 See further *infra* Chap.9 for a discussion of share capital.
84 See also Leigh *op.cit.* p.95; Ayua *Nigerian Company Law (1984) pp.20-21*
85 Ss.20 and 21 Cap.85, considered *supra*
86 *ibid*, S.63 see *infra* Chap.9
87 *ibid* Ss. 60, 62. See *infra* Chap.9
88 *ibid*, S. 70. See *infra* Chap.9
89 S.33 Cap 85
90 Ss. 207-209, 210, 285, 304 *infra* Chap.9
91 S.211 *infra* Chap.15
92 See Section 8 of Cap. 85. Law of Uganda
93 *In Re Druges* (1942] 1 All E.R. 194
94 [1907] 1 Ch. 269

Accordingly, a resolution for ceasing to carry out an activity permitted by the objects is not an alteration of the objects. The alteration must be confirmed by the Court following an application by holders of not less than 15 percent in value of the shares or 15 per cent in value of the debentures or alternatively 15 percent of the members where the company is not limited by shares opposing the alteration[98]. However, such dissenting application cannot be made by any person who consented or voted in favour of the alteration.[99] The application should be made within twenty-eight days after the date on which the resolution altering the objects was passed. Following the expiration of the time limit the alteration cannot be challenged on the ground that it was not authorised by the section.[100]

Upon an application under the section the court may make an order confirming the alteration either wholly or in part and on such terms and conditions as it thinks fit. The court may adjourn the proceedings in order that an arrangement may be made to its satisfaction for the purchase of the interests of the dissentient members and also give such consequential orders as it may deem expedient for executing such arrangements. However, the company is forbidden from using its capital to buy dissentient members' shares[101].

The Jenkins Committee in its suggestions for reform of section 5 of Companies Act, 1948 of Britain, recommended[102] that there should be a general power to alter the objects and that an objection to an alteration should only require the support of 5 percent of the shareholders.There may arise a situation where an item in the objects clause is of such nature that it could have been included in the articles. Such an item may be altered by special resolution, subject to the right of 15 percent dissentients to apply to the court in the same manner as provided under section 8[103]. This does not, however, license the liability of a member to be increased without his consent.[104] In addition the section does not apply where the memorandum itself provides for or prohibits the alteration of any of its conditions.[105]

---

95 [1962] Ch.806; (1962) 2 All E.R. 879. See also Leigh *op.cit.* p.97

96 1969 NCLR 110; N.M.L.R. 99 (Supreme Court of Nigeria).

97 Per Lewis J.S.C. 1969 NCLR 117-118. See also *Edokpolo & co. Ltd. v. Sem Edo Wire Industries Ltd. (19840 7S.C.,119, Lasisi v. Registrar of Companies* (1974) 3 A.L.R. Comm.89

98 S.8(2)

99 S.8(2) Proviso

100 S.8(10)

101 S.8(14); the proscription of the Company from purchasing its members' shares has been removed in Britain by schedule 3 para. 4 Companies Act, 1980.

102 *Report of the Company Law Committee* 1749 (1962) para 48 See also B. Davis (1974) 90 *L.Q.R.*79.

103 Companies Act, S.25

104 The Section is subject to S.24

# 5
# ARTICLES OF ASSOCIATION

## Introduction

The Articles of Association contain regulations for managing the internal affairs of the company i.e the business of the company. They are applied and interpreted subject to the Memorandum of Association in that they cannot confer wider powers on the company than those stipulated in the memorandum. Thus, where there is a conflict or divergence between the Memorandum and Articles, the provisions of the memorandum must prevail. However, it has been suggested that where the memorandum is ambiguous or is silent on a particular issue it maybe permissable to resort to the articles in order to resolve the difficulty or supplement the memorandum[1]. This approach is supported by the statement of Jessel, M.R. in *Re: Wedgwood Coal and Iron Co.*[2] Thus[3]:

> Where there are two contemporaneous documents executed and assented to by the same persons at the sametime.... it appears to me that the ordinary rule applies according to which contemporaneous documents are read together, so that if there is an ambiguity in one it may be explained by the other.

However, if the difficulty arises from some matter which is by statute required to appear in the Memorandum, the Articles cannot be resorted to in order to modify the Memorandum.

In the words of Bowen L.J. in *Guinness v. Land Corporation of Ireland*:[4]

> The memorandum contains the fundamental conditions upon which alone the company is allowed to be incorporated. They are conditions introduced for the benefit of the creditors and the outside public, a well as the shareholders. The Articles of Association are the internal regulations of the company. How can it be said that in all cases the fundamental conditions of the charter of incorporation and the internal regulations are to be construed together?.... In any case it is, as it seems to me certain that for anything which the Act of Parliament says shall be in the memorandum you must look to the memorandum alone. If the legislature has said that one instrument is to be dominant, you cannot turn to another instrument and read it in order to modify the provisions of the dominant document......

Furthermore, since the Articles of Association are regarded as a business document, they should be interpreted where possible so as to give them reasonable business efficacy.[5]

---

1 Angostura Bitters, Ltd. V. Kerr (1933) A.C.550; *Re Duncan Gilmour & Co. Ltd* [1952]2. All E.R. 871; *Andrews v. Gas Meter Co.* [1897] 1 Ch.361; *Re: Welsbach Incandescent Gas Light Co. Ltd.* [1904] 1 Ch.87. See also Leigh, *op.cit.* P.99.

2 (1877) 7 Ch.D.75

3 Ibid.p.99

4 (1882) 22 Ch.D.349 at p.381; See also *Kehinde v. Registrar of Companies* (1979) 5 F.R.C.R.101, 1O6 per Anyaegbunam. C.J.

5 *Holmes v. Keyes* (1959) Ch.199, 215; (1958) 2 All E.R. 129

Copies of the Memorandum and Articles are required to be supplied to every member on request incorporating any changes.[6] Finally the Memorandum and Articles are open to inspection by the public.[7]

## Contents of the articles

It is provided that[8], except in the case of a company limited by shares, the Articles of Association shall follow the forms set out in the Tables in the first schedule or as near thereto as circumstances permit[9]. This implies that only slight divergences from those of the tables will be allowed. However, it has been suggested that "in practice the words of the section are not treated as imposing serious restraints on the draughtsmen."[10]

All companies, other than those limited by shares, must (the word "shall" is used) register Articles of Association together with the Memorandum of Association." The Articles should be signed by the subscribers to the Memorandum.[11] A company limited by shares "may" register articles. However, if it does not do so the provisions of Table A[12] apply as the company's regulations.[13] In practice, Table A is invariably modified with respect to quorums, rights attaching to different classes of shares, the number of Directors, and rotation thereof. Furthermore Table A is usually fully included for registration even if this involves duplication thereof because where Table A is allowed to apply it is the Table A that was in force at the time of the registration of the company that will govern the affairs of the company.

In the case of conflict or divergence between different provisions of the Articles of Association the courts should consider all of the articles in order to interpret a particular article and where possible reconcile it with the other provisions in the articles.[14].

The articles of an unlimited company must state the number of members with which it proposed to be registered and where it has a share capital, the amount of share capital with which it proposes be registered.[15]. With regard to a company limited by guarantee, the articles must state the number of members with which it proposes to be registered.[16]

Apart from the statutory prescriptions indicated the articles of a company may contain any rules decided upon by the members for regulating the business of the company, provided these are not illegal, contrary to the act or do not attempt to extend or modify the memorandum.[17] However, the rules may authorise something which is not expressly or impliedly forbidden by the memorandum. Thus, in *Andrews v. Gas Meter Co.*[18], the Memorandum and Articles were silent as regards the issue of preference shares. By special resolutions, the Articles were altered to authorize the issue of shares. Upon an increase of capital, preference shares were issued. The issue was upheld. The Court of Appeal indicated that in the absence of any provision to the contrary in the memorandum the rights of shareholders could be regulated by the articles. Consequently, the articles could be altered in order to provide for the issue of preference shares.

---

6 Companies Act, Ss.26, 27
7 *Ibid*, S.388
8 Companies Act. S.14
9 Tables B,C,D,E
10 Leigh, op.cit. P.100
11 C.A.S.9
12 First Schedule to the Act, ibid
13 *Ibid*, S.11
14 *McNeil v. McNeil's Sheep Farming Co. Ltd* (1955) N.Z.L.R.15 (Court of Appeal of New Zealand)
15 Companies Act, S.10(1)
16 *Ibid*, S.10 (2)
17 *Ashbury Railway Carriage and Iron Co. Ltd v. Riche*(1875) L.R.7 H.L.653, 671 per Lord Cairns L.C.
18 [1897] 1 Ch.361 C.A.; *Re Welsbach Gas Light Co. Ltd* [1920] 1 Ch. 154

The articles may also indicate conditions precedent for a person to continue to remain a member of the company. In this vein, a company may provide in its articles that any member who is engaged in competition with the company must transfer his shares, subject to payment therefor to a nominee of the directors. In addition, a company may alter its articles to include this power.[19]

The articles must be printed, divided into paragraphs numbered consecutively, be signed by each subscriber to the memorandum in the presence of at least one witness who must attest the signature.[20]

If the company intends to issue shares to the public for subscription, it should comply with the relevant provisions of the Stock Exchange.[21]

## The contractual effect of the memorandum and articles

Section 22(1) of the Companies Act provides that the Memorandum and Articles shall, when registered, "bind the company and the members therefore the same extent as if they respectively had been signed and sealed by each member and contained covenants on the part of each member to observe all the provisions of the Memorandum and of the Articles..."

While the effect of Section 22 cannot as yet be said to have been conclusively resolved by the courts[22], there have been serious attempts to fathorm its implications. Thus, in *Wood v. Odessa Waterworks Co.*[23], the article sand power to the directors to declare a dividend "to be paid" to the directors. The company passed an ordinary resolution proposing to pay no divided but instead to give shareholders debenture bonds redeemable at par by annual drawing, extending over thirty years. Wood, a shareholder, sought an injunction to restrain the company from acting on the resolution. It was held that the proposal was inconsistent with the articles. Consequently the injunction could be granted. Stirling J. Stated in this respect that.[24]

> The Articles of Association constitute a contract not merely between the shareholders and the company but between each individual shareholder and every other.......

Similarly, in *A.O. Obikoya v. Ezenwa & Ors*[25], the applicant and respondents were the permanent directors of a limited liability company, by virtue of Article 28 of the company's articles. Article 32 provided, that a permanent director shall not vote for the removal from office of another permanent director. In breach of both Articles 28 and 32, the respondents purported to alter article 28 by special resolution and inserted therefor Article 86 of Table A, at the same meeting which voted for the removal of the applicant form office as director of the company and thereafter prevented him from acting in that capacity. The applicant sued for damages against the respondents personally, for breach of the agreement contained in Article 32 and for an order of injunction to restrain the respondents from further preventing the applicant from acting as director of the company. It was held that when three members of the company who are also the three permanent

---

19 *Sidebottom v. Kershaw, Lees & Co. Ltd* [1920] 1 Ch.87

20 Companies Act, S.12

21 Stock Exchange Regulations Part A Schedule 6, Appendix II (Nigeria). Efforts are being mode to set up a Kampala Stock Exchange

22 See further Wedderburn, "Shareholders" Rights and the Rule in *Foss v. Harbottle"* (1957) *Camb. L.J.* 194; Goldberg. Enforcement of Outside Rights Under Section 20(1) of the Companies Act, 1948" (1972) 35 *Mod. Law. Rev.* 362-374 Baxter, "Irregular Company Meetings" (1976) *J. Bus Law;* Smith, "Minority Shareholders and Corporate Irregularities" (1978) 41 *M.L.R.*147 G. Practice, "The Enforcement of Outsiders' Rights" (1980) 1 *Co. Law* 179-185; Gower, *op.cit*,p.317.

23 (1889) 42 Ch.D. 636

24 *Ibid*, p.642

25 [1964] 2 All N.L.R.133. See also *Imperial Hydropathic Hotel Co. Blackpool v. Hampson* (1883) 23 Ch.D.1

directors agreed by virtue of article 32 not to vote for the removal of each other from office, they were agreeing between themselves as members, in which capacity they exercised their voting rights not so to vote. A contract did exist between them and that the applicant is within his right in making the application sought, because the action of the respondent in keeping the applicant away from his office as director was in breach of Articles 28 and 32.

Section 22 (or its equivalent) has also been construed to mean that the articles do not constitute a contract between a company and a non-member thereof. In *Eley v. Positive Government Life Assurance Co.*[26], the articles provided that Eley should be the company's solicitor for life, removable only for misconduct. Eley drafted the company's documents for registration and became a shareholder several months after incorporation. He sued the company for breach of contract in not employing him as a solicitor, pursuant to the articles. It was held that while the relevant article could be a stipulation which bound the members or a mandate to directors as to the appointment of a solicitor, it did not of itself constitute a contract between the plaintiff in his capacity as a solicitor and the company.

In a similar vein, it has been postulated that the contract in Section 22 which binds the company and the members only binds the latter in their capacity as member i.e. *qua members* and not in some other special capacity. *In Hickman v. Kent or Romney March Sheep Breeders Association*[27], the defendant association was incorporated as a non-profit making company. Article 49 of its articles provided that disputes between the association and any or its members should be referred to arbitration. Hickman, who was a member brought an action complaining about various irregularities in the affairs of the association including the refusal to register his sheep in its published flock book and a threat to expel him from membership. The defendant association successfully moved for a stay of the proceedings on the ground that the statutory provision corresponding to Section 22 of the Companies Act, made Article 49 an agreement to arbitrate enforceable as between the association and a member. In the course of his judgment, Astbury J. addressed himself to the issue as to whether the contract in the articles would bind the member in another capacity other than that of a member and concluded thus:[28]

> ...... first, that no article can constitute a contract between the company and a third person, secondly, that no right merely purporting to be given by an article to a person, whether a member or not, in a capacity other than that of a member, as, for instance as a solicitor, promoter or director can be enforced against the company and thirdly that the articles regulating the rights and obligations of the members generally as such do create rights and obligations between them and the company respectively.[29]

Furthermore, in *Beattie v. E. And F Beattie*[30], the plaintiff complained that certain sums had been improperly paid to Beattie, who was the Managing Director and Chairman of the Board of Directors. It was held[31] that since Beattie was being sued in his capacity as director and not that of member he could not invoke the equivalent of Section 22 to enforce an arbitration clause which was contained in the company's articles.

---

26 (1876) 1 Ex.D.83: See also *Wachukwu v. Co-operative Bank of Eastern Nigeria Ltd.* 1974 N.C.L.R.387, 398-399 per Balonwu C.J. (High Court of East Central State), though of doubtful authority.

27 [1915] 1 Ch. 881

28 *Ibid*, p.900

29 C.f *Wachukwu v. Co-operative Bank of Eastern Nig. Ltd* where it is indicated that a company and its employees are alike strangers to the Articles of Association of the Company, which are a contract only between the members *inter se* in respect of their rights as shareholders and not between the members and the company or the company and its employees *supra* n.26, pp.398-399.

30 [1938] Ch.708; [1938] 3 All E.R. 214 C.A

31 Following *Hickman v. Kent (supra n.28)*

From the foregoing, a conflict appears in the two propositions on Section 22. On the one hand, it is asserted that a member has a right to have provisions of the corporate constitution duly observed. On the other hand is the view that Section 22 cannot be relied upon to enforce the rights of a non-member or the "outsider" right of one who is a member which the articles purportedly confer on him in that capacity. This has been resolved by suggesting that a member has a right to enforce the observance of the articles even if that means indirectly the enforcement of "outsider" rights vested in himself or third parties so long as but only so long as he sues *qua* member and not *qua* outsider.[32]

A further issue, arising from Section 22, is whether the articles constitute a contract between the members *inter se*. In the words of Lord *Herschell in Welton v. Saffery*[33]

> ...... there is no contract in terms between the individual members of the company; but the articles do not any the less, in my opinion, regulate their rights *inter se*. Such rights can only be enforced by or against a member through the company, or through the liquidator representing the company; but I think that no member has as between himself and another member, any right beyond that which the contract with the company gives.

The implication is that although a member is "deemed to be in privity with the company, he is not deemed to be in privity with other individual members.[34] Such an approach, though, contradicts other case law authority[35], Thus, in *Rayfield v. Hands*[36]an article created pre-emptive rights in relation to the disposal of shares. Rayfield sought to compel the defendants who were the Directors of the company to buy his shares in accordance with the provision. It was held that the Directors were bound to buy the shares because the relationship was between the plaintiff as a member and the defendants not as directors but as members. The court also indicated that in the circumstances it was unnecessary to join the company as a party to the proceedings.

## Effects of articles incorporated into or underlying contracts

It is possible for a contract to be entered into between a company and person who is not a shareholder. The terms regulating such a contract can be based on the company's articles. The effect of this would be to incorporate the terms of the articles expressly or by implication into the contract. *In New British Iron Co. Exparte Beckwith*[37], the claimant had served the company as director without any express agreement for remuneration. However, paragraph 62 of the company's articles provided that the remuneration of the board should be an annual sum of GBP1,000. They claimed arrears of fees during the winding up of the company. It was held that they could succeed because the service contract incorporated paragraph 62 or part of its terms. However, where a contract has incorporated provisions of a company articles it must contemplate that the articles may be altered in the usual way provided such alteration is no retrospective. In *Survey v. Port Darwin Gold Mining Co.*[38], the company's articles provided that the directors were to be paid at the rate of GBP200 per annum. The company later passed a special resolution altering

---

[32] Wedderburn supra n.22, pp212-213 explaining *Quin & Axtens v. Salmon*(1909) A.C.442. See too Bakibinga, "Corporate Irregularities & Shareholders: Rights" in Bakibinga *Collected papers on company law and structures* (1984) p.57 (Mimeograph); see also *Gravitas Review of Business & Property Law* (Lagos) Vol.2 No.7 pp.15-21 (1989). See also *Obikoya v. Ezenwa, supra n.25*

[33] [1897] A.C. 299, p.315. See also *Wachukwu's case supra* n.26

[34] Leigh, *op cit* p.108

[35] *Eley's case, supra* n.26; *Borland Trustee v. Steel Bros & Co. Ltd.* [1901] 1 ch.279, 290; *Kerr v. John Mortram Ltd* [1940] Ch. 657, 660.

[36] [1958] 2 All E.R. 194. See also *Hughes King (Nig.) Ltd. V. Harris* (1972) U.I.L.R. 63 (Lagos High Court).

[37] [1898] 1 Ch. 324 Ch.D

[38] (1889) 1 Meg.385 C.A.

the articles so that directors were to receive GBP5 per month retrospectively from 31 December 1887. The plaintiff, who was a director thereupon resigned his office and claimed three months accrued fees at the old rate. It was held that his claim could succeed, since his contract for remuneration though based on the articles which were alterable, such alteration could only be effective with respect to the future. Similarly, in *Bailey v. British Equitable Assurance Co.*[39],the plaintiff, who was a non-member of the company took out a life policy with the company. The bye-laws of the company provided that profits form such policies should be distributed to policy holders without deduction. Later, it was proposed to register the company under the Companies Act with Articles of Association which altered the bye-laws so as to authorize the transfer of a percentage of such profits to a reserve fund. The plaintiff claimed a declaration that his policy was not affected by the altered articles. The court at first instance and the court of appeal granted the application on the ground that a company cannot by altering its articles justify a breach of contract. However, the House of Lords, in reversing the decision held that the alteration was valid because it was fair, honest and businesslike and was in the opinion of the directors, and shareholders of the company, beneficial to the policy holders. In addition, the alteration did not infringe the rights of policy holders. What appears to have been a retrospective alteration of the bye-laws was justified by the House of Lords on the basis of reasonableness.[40]

It is notable though, that a term cannot be incorporated into an express contract by implication from the articles if such terms conflict with an express provision of such contract. For example a contract appointing a Managing Director for a given period will prevail to revoke such an appointment. It follows, therefore, that if a person is removed from office, pursuant to such a power in the articles before his term has expired, the company will be in breach of the express contract.[41]

While a contract which incorporates or is based on the articles is subject to alteration in the usual way, such an alteration may amount to a breach of the contract. Thus, in *Southern Foundries Ltd. V. Shirlaw*[42], Shirlaw was, under a written agreement, appointed Managing Director of the appellant company for ten years, in 1933. In 1936, the appellant company was taken over by Federated Foundries Ltd. The appellant company then altered its articles in such away as to include a new paragraph 8. This paragraph gave Federated Foundries power by means of a written instrument to remove any director of the appellant company. In 1937 Federated Foundries exercised that power by removing Shirlaw form his directorship. He sued the appellant company for breach of contract and Federated Foundries for wrongfully procuring a breach of contract. It was held that he was entitled to damages for breach of contract because although Federated Foundries action was valid in so far as it was authorized by the articles of the appellant company, it amounted to a breach of contract with Shirlaw since it was contrary to a provision in the contract indicating that the employment was for ten years. However, where a service contract is based on the articles and the company exercises its powers under the articles to remove a director, there is no breach of contract. In *Read v. Astoria Garage (Streatham)* [43], Regulations included paragraph 68 which provided that the directors might appoint a Managing Director for such term and at such remuneration as they think fit, but his appointment shall be subject to determination *ipso facto* if he ceases from any cause to be a Director or if the company in general meeting resolve that his tenure of office of Managing Director be determined.[44]. Read was appointed Managing Director at a salary of GBP7 per week by a resolution of the Board of Directors.

---

39 [1904] 1 Ch.374 C.A. [1906] A.C.H.L.

40 See also Sealy, *op.cit* p.133

41 *Nelson v. James Nelson & Son Ltd.* [1914] 2 KB 770 C.A

42 [1940] 2 All E.R.445 H.L. See also *Shindler v. Northern Raincoat Co. Ltd* [1960] 2 All E.R. 239

43 [1952] Ch.637; [1952] 2 All E.R. 292 C.A. *Shindler v. Raincoat Co. Ibid*

44 This provision is equivalent to regulation 107 Table A first schedule to Companies Act, Cap.85

Seventeen years later, the board, acting with the approval of the company in general meeting terminated his appointment. It was held that the termination was valid and effective and did not amount to a wrongful dismissal. *Nelson v. James and Nelson & Sons Ltd.*[45] was distinguished on the ground that there was in that instance an express agreement with the plaintiff for a definite period whereas in this case there was no such contract. Consequently, the inference was that the contract was governed by Article 68.

## Alteration of the articles

It is provided that subject to the provisions of the Act and to the conditions contained in its Memorandum, a company may by special resolution alter or add to its articles. A special resolution is one which is passed by a majority of not less than three-fourths of such members as, being entitled to a vote in person, or where proxies are allowed, by proxy at a general meeting of which not less than twenty-one days notice specifying the intention to propose the resolution as a special one has been given.[46] An alteration so effected will be valid unless (I) it is illegal; (ii) it conflicts with provisions in the Companies Act, for instance by infringing conditions in the Memorandum of Association relating to entrenchment of certain provisions in the Articles. (iii) it extends or modified the memorandum[47]. (iv) it deprives members of rights conferred on them by the Act[48] which deal with class rights[49] or by the [50]court (v) requires a shareholder to take or subscribe, for more shares or increases his liability to contribute to the company[51] (vi) it amounts to a fraud on the minority. It is notable in this regard that conversely a company cannot contract itself out of the right to alter its articles[52].

The criteria for a valid alteration of the articles was first articulated in *Allen V. Gold Reefs of West Africa Ltd.*[53], where an alteration of the company's articles in order to give it a lien over fully-paid shares held by Zucani, the only such shareholder whose executors brought action to oppose the alteration, was upheld. In the course of delivering his judgement, Lord Lindley M.R. thus stated:[54]

> The power thus conferred on companies to alter the regulations contained in their articles is limited only by the provisions contained in the statute and the conditions in the company's Memorandum of Association.... It must, like all other powers, be exercised subject to those general principles of law and equity which are applicable to all powers conferred on majorities and enabling theM to bind manorities. It must be exercised not only in the manner required by law but also *bona fide* for the benefit of the company as a whole and it must not be exceeded. These conditions are always implied, and are seldom, if ever, expressed. But if they are complied with I can discover no ground for judicially putting any other restrictions on the power conferred by the section than those contained in it.

The case indicates that alterable articles may be altered even to the detriment of members' rights and retrospectively provided the alteration is not discriminatory and has been made *bona*

---

45 *Supra* n.41
46 Companies Act, s.13(1)
47 *Ibid* S.140
48 See discussion *supra*
49 Companies Act, S.74
50 *Ibid* S.211
51 *Ibid* S.24
52 *Punt v. Symons & Co. Ltd.* [1903] 2 Ch.506 per Byrne J.
53 [1900] 1 Ch.656 C.A. See also *Obikoya v. Ezenwa, supra* n.25
54 *Ibid*, pp.671-672

*fide* in the interests of the company. The issue arises as to what constitutes benefit to the company. In *Brown v. British Abrasive Steel Co.*[55], the court had to consider a proposed alteration of the articles which would have resulted into the expropriation of the shares of a minority. The alteration was disallowed since it could not be shown that it would benefit the company as a whole i.e the general body of shareholders taken as a whole. In contrast, *Dafen Tinplate Co. Ltd. v. Llanelly Steel Co. Ltd.*[56] appears to adopt an objective approach to what constitutes benefit to the company. In that instance, the defendant company altered its articles by introducing a power which allowed the majority of shareholders to require any member (excepting one) to transfer his shares at a fair value to an approved transferee. The plaintiff company which was a shareholder in the defendant company and which had stopped buying steel from the defendant company in favour of a rival company opposed the alteration. It was held that the objection was sustainable because in determining what constitutes "benefit of the company", it was necessary to show whether the alteration was genuinely for the benefit of the company. For this purpose, the power of the majority shareholders to expropriate any shareholder they think proper at their will and pleasure is not for the benefit of the company as a whole. Such an approach would be confusing the interests of majority shareholders with the benefit of the company as a whole. This objective approach was not followed in *Sidebottom v. Kershaw, Leese & Co. Ltd*[57]. In this case, the defendant company altered its articles by providing the directors with power to buy out at a fair price the shares of any member who competed with the company's business. The plaintiffs, who were minority shareholders and who carried on business in competition with that of the company, challenged the validity of the alteration on the ground that it did not benefit all the incorporators including himself. The action was dismissed and the alteration upheld because it was made *bona fide* for the benefit of the company with the aim of getting rid of members who would use their membership to compete with the company by obtaining crucial information. The approach in the *Dafen Tinplate Case*[58] was also disapproved in *Shuttleworth v. Cox Bros & Co.*[59],where the plaintiff was removed from his position of permanent director following the alteration of an article by which he had been appointed. The plaintiff challenged the dismissal on the ground that it was wrongful, although arising from discovery of irregularities in accounts between him and the company. The dismissal was upheld because since the relevant contract of employment was based on the articles, it was subject to alteration by special resolution changing the articles. Consequently, there was no breach of contract. Moreover, in considering the expression "bona fide for the benefit of the company", the court should be flexible, since the phrase is not a statutory provision. Consequently, if shareholders honestly altered the articles in the interest of the company, then the alteration must stand and the issue of benefit to the company is one of fact to be determined by the shareholders and not one of law.

The Australian case, *Peter's American Delicacy Co. Ltd. V Heath*[60], provides a synthesis and attempted resolution of the conflicting approaches in *Dafen Tinplate Case* and the subsequent cases mentioned above. While conceding (in line with *Dafen Tinplate*) that the power of alteration must be exercised *bona fide* with a view to the advancement of the interests of a majority of voters or of a section of the company only[61], and that the expression "bona fide for the benefit of the company as a whole" is meaningless and that "company as a whole" is a

55 [1919] 1. Ch.290
56 [1920] Ch.124
57 [1920] 1 Ch.154 C.A.
58 *Supra* n.56
59 [1927] 2 K.B.9 C.A.
60 (1939) 61. C.L.R.457 (High Court of Australia)
61 Per Rich J. Sealy, *Cases & Materials in Company Law* (2nd Ed.) p.153

corporate entity consisting of all shareholders[62] (in line with *Shuttleworth v. Cox Bros & Co.*), it was concluded[63] that in view of the conflicting interests inherent in the exercise of the property right attached to the share and the regulation of rights *inter se* the shareholders resulting from the alteration of the articles, it is left to those whose interests conflict to adjust them subject to an alteration by a three-fourth majority. Moreover, alteration here was upheld because it involved no oppression, no appropriation of an unjust or reprehensible nature and did not imply a purpose outside the scope of the power.[64] It would thus appear that the expression *"bona fide* in the interests or for the benefit of the company" means acting equitably in the interests of the shareholders without discrimination or oppression pursuant to the statutory power of alteration of the articles. This approach is evident in *Greenhalgh v. Ardene Cinemas Ltd.*[65] There the articles of the defendant, a private company stipulated that existing members should have pre-emptive rights if a member wished to sell his shares. The Managing Director of the company negotiated with a non-member of the company for the sale to that person of a controlling interest in the company at six shillings per share. To execute this agreement the Managing Director engineered the passing of a special resolution which destroyed the pre-emptive rights of the members.

One of the members, Greenhalgh, applied to the court for a declaration, the resolutions were invalid and were a fraud on the minority. It was held that the declaration could not be granted because the resolution was bona fide for the benefit of the company. Concerning the expression *"bona fide"* for the benefit of the company, Evershed M.R. thus stated.[66]

> ..... I think it is now plain that *bona fide* for the benefit of the company as a whole means not two things, but one thing. It means that the shareholder must proceed upon what, in his honest opinion, is for the benefit of the company as a whole. The second thing is that the phrase "company as a whole" does not (at any rate in such a case as the present) mean the company as a commercial entity, distinct form the corporators: it means the corporators as a general body. That is to say, the case may be taken of an individual hypothetical member and it may be asked whether what is proposed is, in the honest opinion of those who voted in its favour, for that person's benefit.

The court further indicated that in respect of a resolution altering articles, a member may vote in his interest and that when a person joins the company he should not assume that the articles will always remain in a particular form and that so long as the alteration does not unfairly discriminate, it is *bona fide.*

Similarly, in *Rights and Issue Investment Trust Ltd, v. Stylo Shoes*[67], the defendant company passed special resolutions by which the issued share capital was increased and the voting rights of the management shares were doubled. The aim was to preserve the voting strength of the management shares irrespective of the new issue. The resolutions were supported by a large majority of the general meeting and by a class meeting of the ordinary shareholders. However, the holders of management shares did not vote on each occasion. An ordinary shareholder applied for an injunction to stop the execution. The injunction was refused because the resolutions in issue were proper having been passed in good faith for the benefit of the company as a whole and without oppression of or discrimination against the ordinary shareholders. It was also notable that the majority of the members who voted in favour of the resolutions had themselves nothing to gain from the alteration. The court concluded that the alteration having complied with the Companies Act, the memorandum and the consent of the relevant shareholders, was

---

62 Per Dixon J. *Ibid* p.156

63 per Dixon, J.*ibid* p.156-157

64 See also the Allen case supra n.53, 54 and *Brown v. British Abrasive Co.* Supra n.55

65 [1950] 2 All E.R. 1120 C.A.

prompted by considerations of business policy, which the members were entitled to determine and in which case the court would not interfere.

Apart form alteration by resolution, the Articles of Association may be altered or overridden by unanimous agreement of the shareholders irrespective of non-compliance with Section 13 of the Companies Act. Thus, in *Cane v. Jones*[68], a company was incorporated by P. And H. Who were its only directors. Its articles provided, *inter alia,* that P. And H. Should be life directors. In addition, the directors were empowered to elect the chairman of the Board of Directors, who was to have a casting vote at board and general meetings. Later on, all of the ten shareholders entered into an agreement, which they did not meet or sign, providing *inter alia* that the chairman should not exercise a casting vote and where there was a tie in votes an independent chairman should be elected. Further on again, at a period when some of the shares had changed hands a dispute arose as to whether P was chairman, and, if so whether he had a casting vote. R, (who was a joint owner of some of the shares in the company) and P contended that the articles could only be altered by resolution under the Companies Act, 1948, Section 11[69] and that the agreement did not alter the articles. It was held (I) that P was not the chairman and (ii) the agreement in issue was effective to override the articles with respect to the chairman's casting vote. Consequently, any chairman of such a company would have no such vote. The court further indicated that [70] Section 10 ( Section 13 in the case of Uganda) only stipulated a procedure whereby some only of the shareholders can alter the articles since it is "a basic principle of company law that all of the corporators of a company acting together (whether they act simultaneously or at different times)[71] can do anything which is *intra vires* the company and Section 10 does not affect this principle[72]

Lastly, it remains to note that although the articles have been held to have a contractual affect[73] they cannot be rectified by the court on application of a member or other interested person. Thus, in *Scott v. Frank Scott (London)* Ltd[74], the defendants wished the Articles of Association to be rectified in order to reflect their intentions. It was held that rectification of both the Memorandum and Articles was not possible because the Act contains the powers of alteration and extension thereof. Such powers are purely statutory and there is no hint in the Act of any power to rectify. This may be regarded as the second major distinguishing feature of the contract in the Memorandum and Articles of Association from an ordinary contract. The first characteristic is that such a contract may be changed under section 13 of the Companies Act, without the consents of all parties thereto.

66 *Ibid* at p.1126

67 *[1964] 3 All E.R. 626 Ch.D.*

68 [1981] 1 All E.R. 535

69 In pari materia with S.13 Companies Act Cap 85

70 [1981] 1 All E.R. 535 at p.539

71 Relying on *Parker & Cooper Ltd. V. Reading* [1926] Ch.975 all E.R. Rep323, See also *Rolled Steel Products (Holdings) Ltd. V. British Steel Corporation* [1982] 3 W.L.R. 715

72 Leigh, op.cit. P. 116

73 *Wood v. Odessa Waterworks Co.* Supra n.23; *Rayfield v. Hands, supra,* n.36

74 [1940] Ch.794; [1940] 3 All E.R.508 C.A

# 6
# COMPANY FINANCE

The ways by which capital can be raised to run a company are considered in this chapter. It is notable at the outset that it is only public companies which can raise funds from the public through the sale of their shares. Invariably, the private company has limited sources of funding. These include banks, insurance companies and other financial institutions.

## Ways of raising capital

In view of the limited funds available to shareholders for purposes of running large companies with heavy capital involvement, it is normal to resort to the public, through invitation to subscribe for shares or debentures in the company, as a means of raising additional funds. There are three basic mechanisms by which this is effected:

(i) Direct offers to the public are usually done by means of a prospectus issued by the company. The offers could, however be made by an issuing house on behalf of the company.

In such cases the company bears the risk and may have to arrange ts own underwriting.1

(ii) Offers of sale. In such a situation the company sells the issue of shares or debentures to an issuing house, which then invites the public through a prospectus to buy the shares at a higher price. The issuing house bears the risk and is responsible for underwriting the issue[1]

(iii) Placing. This is done by the issuing house undertaking to place the securities with or without buying them itself. The issuing house will in effect try to persuade its clients (such as institutional investors) to buy the securities. Although no invitation is made to the public generally, the invitation is deemed to be a prospectus though not one issued by or on behalf of the company. Consequently, while not subject to Sections 40 and 43, it is subject to Section 47 of the Companies Act, which is applicable to an offer for sale.

In addition, funds may be raised by means of a rights issue. This is by way of inviting the company's existing shareholders to subscribe before additional shares in proportion to their original holding or the company issuing a provisional letter of allotment by which shareholders are allotted the number of shares which each is entitled to take up. The letter of allotment may be renounced by the shareholder signing the renunciation and handing the letter to a buyer, thereby selling his right to subscribe.[2]

A rights issue is distinguishable from a bonus or capitalisation issue. The latter "is not..... a method of raising new capital but merely increasing the nominal amount of the issued share capital by using undistributed profits to pay it up".[3]

## Underwriting

Upon the formation of a company, the promoter, where appropriate ensures that the shares offered to the public are underwritten. However, where an existing company is desirous of raising capital, it is the directors' duty to ensure that new shares are ůnderwritten. The aim of

---

1 See further S.47 *ibid* which is applicable.

2 See further Pennington, *The Investor and the Law* (1966)

3 Gower, *op cit, supra*, p.344

underwriting is to ensure that the issue of shares is successful. Underwriting is a form of insurance against possible poor reception of the issue by the public. In the words of Cotton L.J. in *Re: Licensed Victuallers' Mutual Trading Association.*[4]:

> an underwriting agreement means an agreement entered into before the shares are brought before the public, that in the event of the public, not taking the whole of them, or the number mentioned in the agreement, the underwriter will, for an agreed commission, take an allotment of such part of the shares as the public has not applied for.

In this context, underwriting commissions are different form brokerage "i.e. sums payable to a sharebroker who.agreed to *place* shares not to *take* shares[5]. It has been indicated that subject to the statutory minimum of 10 per cent[6], "the amount of commission payable to an underwriter will depend upon market conditions and the attractiveness of the investment to the public".

It is necessary for those involved in underwriting agreements to ensure that the underwriter has sufficient funds to meet the projected liability under the agreement. The relevant agreement may be a formal agreement signed by both parties or may be concluded by an exchange of letters.[7]

The underwriting commission is payable by a company to any person in respect of his subscription or agreement to subscribe for shares or procuring or agreeing to procure subscriptions for any shares in the company[8]. For such purpose, before such commission is paid the following conditions have to be satisfied:

(i) The payment of the commission must be authorised by the articles.[9]
(ii) The commission must not exceed 10 percent of the price at which the shares are issued or the amount or rate authorised by the articles, whichever is the less;
(iii) The amount paid or agreed to be paid must be:
- disclosed in the prospectus if the shares are offered to the public; or
- in other cases, disclosed in the prescribed form and delivered before payment of the commission to the Registrar and where a circular notice not being a prospectus is involved also disclosed in that circular or notice;

(iv) The number of shares which persons have agreed for a commission to subscribe for absolutely must be disclosed as in (iii)[10].

The section is inapplicable to the power of a company to pay brokerage charges which are fair and necessary. However, a commission which is unauthorised by the Act may not be paid in so far as this may amount to an unauthorised reduction of capital.[11]

## The principle of disclosure and the prospectus

Legal regulation of statements made for the purpose of advertising securities for purchase and sale is aimed at effecting full disclosure of the company's affairs to the investing public. In Nigeria, a company which is desirous of offering its securities to the public for subscription

4 (1889) 42 Ch.D.1,6
5 Leigh *etal op.cit.* p.43.
6 Companies Act, S.55
7 Leigh, *supra* n.6, p.43. See also *Re Consort Deep level Gold Mines Ltd.* [1897] 1 Ch.575: *Re Hannan's EmpressGold Mining and Development Company* [1896] 2 Ch.643
8 Companies Act, S.55
9 Table A, Art.6
10 Non-fulfilment of the conditions renders the contract to pay commission invalid: *Andrea v. Zinc Mines of Great Britain* [1918] 2 K.B.454
11 *Ooregum Gold Mining Co. of India v. Roper* [1892] A.C.125.

must fulfil either the prospectus provisions of the Companies Act, 1968 or the requirement of the Stock Exchange.

## The prospectus-nature

A prospectus is defined[12] as:

> any prospectus, notice, circular, advertisement or other invitation, offering to the public for subscription or purchase any shares or debentures of a company and includes any document which, save to the extent that it offers securities for consideration other than cash, is otherwise a prospectus.

The expressions *"invitation"* and *"offer"* in this context bear unique meanings in the sense that they "refer only to cases where application forms are sent out to be completed by potential subscribers for the acceptance or rejection of the company".[13] Consequently, when the form is sent out this in effect is an invitation to tender, while the completion and no despatch of he form constitutes the offer which has to be accepted by the company.

The expression "public" is restrictively defined to refer to any section of the public including persons already holding securities of the company of who are clients of the person issuing the prospectus.[14] It is understood, though that an offer of securities or an invitation to subscribe for securities which is addressed to existing holders of securities of a private company does not amount to a public issue[15]. In addition, a rights issue[16] may be convertible into a public issue where the rights are renounced in favour of a person other than the shareholder to whom the invitation (usually the provisional letter of allotment) is sent.[17]

Subscription or purchase under Section 2 means a subscription or purchase for cash. Consequently a proposal which offers shares in exchange for shares ( a common phenomenon in a situation or take-over) is not a prospectus[18] In *Nash v. Lynde*[19], it was indicated that an offer to the public is possible where the document is shown to a member of the public who is then invited to take shares upon the strength of it. Finally, it is provided[20]that where a company allots or agrees to allot any securities with a view to their offer to the public, any document by which the offer for sale to the public is made shall be deemed to be a prospectus issued by the company to which the statutory rules shall apply.

## Issue and contents of the prospectus

A prospectus issued by or an behalf of the company should be dated and such date, shall ,unless the contrary is shown, be taken to be the date of its publication[21]. In addition, a copy of every such prospectus, signed by every person named therein as a director should be delivered to the Registrar on or before the date of publication[22]. The prospectus should also state that a copy thereof has been delivered to and registered with the Registrar of Companies.[23] Furthermore,

---

12 Companies Act, S.2

13 *Orojo Nigerian Company Law & Practice* (1976) p.121

14 Companies Act, S.57(1)

15 *ibid*, s.57

16 See *supra* n.3 abd text thereof.

17 Leigh, *op. cit.* P.45

18 *Government Stock & other Securities Investment Co. Ltd. v. Christopher* [1956] 1 All E.R. 490; [1956] 1 W.L.R.237. The Jenkins Committee (Cmnd.1749 (1962) paras 236 and 237 recommend that such documents should be governed by the prospectus rules.

19 [1929] A.C. 158

20 Companies Act, s.47(1); Leigh *op. cit.* p.46.

21 Companies Act, *ibid* S.38

22 *ibid*, S.43(1)

the prospectus must disclose the information and set out the reports indicated in the Third Schedule to the Companies Act.[24]

The matters in part one of the Third Schedule which the prospectus should contain are as follows:

(a) the number of founders or management or deferred shares and the interest of the holders thereof in the company's property and profits;
(b) the share qualification of directors and provision in the articles as to their remuneration;
(c) names, descriptions and addresses of directors;
(d) if the shares are offered to the public for subscriptions, particulars as to:
(i) the minimum subscription i.e. minimum amount which in the opinion of directors must be raised by the issue of those shares to provide for:
- the purchase price of any property bought or to be bought and which is defrayed out of the proceeds of the issues;
- preliminary expenses payable by the company and any commission payable to any person who has subscribed or agreed to procure subscriptions for the company as shares;
- repayment of any money borrowed by the company for any of the foregoing matters;
- working capital
(ii) amount to be provided in respect of the above matters other than;
(e) Certain particulars of contracts relating to property acquired or to be acquired by the company and paid for wholly or partly out of the proceeds of the issue offered by the prospectus. This excludes (i) property, the contract for which acquisition was entered into in the ordinary course of the company's business; (ii) property the purchase money of which is not material. In respect of (i), the contract must not have been made in contemplation of the issue of shares nor the issue made in consequence of the contract.
(f) Any amount or benefit paid or given within two proceeding years or intended to be paid or given to any promoter and consideration for payment or benefit;
(g) The names and addresses of the auditors;
(h) If there are different classes of shares, the voting rights in respect of capital and dividend attached to various classes of shares.

The reports required to accompany the prospectus appear in part II of the Third Schedule to the Act. These are reports by the company's auditors showing (i) its assets and liabilities (ii) profits and losses of the company including its subsidiary, if any; (iii) dividends paid during each of the five financial years preceding the issue of the prospectus.

Schedule Three matters need not be contained in the prospectus where [25] (i) it is issued to existing members or debenture holders; (ii) it relates to securities which are uniform with those previously issued and for the time being dealt in or quoted on a recognised stock exchange (iii)[26] a certificate of exemption is granted by the stock exchange.

If the prospectus includes a statement purporting to be made by an expert[27], it should not be issued unless he consents and this fact must be stated in the prospectus and also that he has not withdrawn his consent[28]. The consent must be filed with the Registrar of Companies.[29]

The discussion above assumes a situation where the company's securities have in fact been issued to the public. This need not always be the case even for a public company. Even if an issue to the public is made it may not occur until sometime after the company's formation or its

23 *ibid* S.43(2)
24 *ibid*, S.40. See further Orojo, *op.cit.* pp. 123-127, Gower, *op.cit.*pp.354-359
25 S.40 *ibid.*
26 S.41 *ibid*
27 Defined to include "engineer, valuer, accountant, and any other person whose profession gives authority to a statement made by him; S.42(3) C.A. Under Schedule 3 a statement by an accountant is invariably required.
28 S.42(1) *ibid*
29 S.42(1) *ibid*

conversion from a private company to a public one. That notwithstanding, the Companies Act stipulates that a public company with share capital which does not issue a prospectus upon its incorporation or which issues a prospectus but does not allot its shares, must not proceed to allotment of it securities unless, at least three days before, it has filed with the Registrar of Companies a statement in lieu of prospectus containing particulars and reports in Schedule Four.[30] A similar requirement must be fulfilled when a private company converts into a public one and does not issue a prospectus within fourteen days.[31] It has been said that these provisions were made at a time when placing and offers of sale were not covered by the prospectus provisions and are now redundant in view of Section 47 and 57 of the Companies Act[32]. In Britain the Jenkins Committee recommended that they should be repealed.[33]

It is evident from the prospectus provisions that their purpose is to ensure that the company provides to the public, "the essential minimum information about its position when it is launched into the world, and that whenever it offers its securities to the public it fully and fairly discloses the relevant facts so that the risk of investment can be assessed".[34] In addition the provisions "prevent the company from getting underway until it has raised the capital needed to carry out the objects in which it has invited the public to participate."[35]

## Allotment

### Nature

An allotment of shares of a company may be made by the company upon application for them by a prospective subscriber. The application, in line with ordinary contractual principles is only an offer to the company, which may or may not be accepted by the company.[36a]

Where a prospectus has been used to invite subscription for shares by the public, the form of application issued by the company must be accompanied by the prospectus except where the statutory exemptions apply[36].

The normal contractual principle that an offer can be revoked any time before acceptance is communicated is modified by section 52 Companies Act, which says that the offer made pursuant to a prospectus cannot be revoked until after the third day following the opening of subscription lists. The object of this is[37] (i) "to give time for consideration, consultation and the study of press comments before submission of applications", (ii) to curtail the activities of "stags", "who apply hoping to sell for a quick profit if the securities rise, but who try to revoke their applications if a fall...... (is) likely." It is significant that an offer will normally lapse if it is not accepted within a reasonable time. Thus, in *Ramsgate Victoria Co. Ltd. v. Montefiore*[38] the period between June 8 and November 23 of the same year within which the company had to accept the applicant's offer was regarded by the court as too long. Consequently, the applicant was entitled to refuse to take the shares.

The application for shares is sometimes subject to a condition precedent. Consequently, if the condition is not fulfilled at the date of allotment, the allotment becomes void. This should

---

30 *ibid*, S.50

31 *ibid* S.32 and Fourth Schedule

32 Gower, *op cit.*, p.359

33 Cmnd. 1749 (1962) para 247, 248 and 252

34 Gower, op.cit. 38] EACA 65.

36 Companies Act, S.40. See *supra* notes 26 and 27 and text thereof.

37 Gower, op.cit. p. 357. See also *Re Zone Company Ltd.* (1962) L.L.R.160 *African Continental Seaways Ltd.* (1977) 3 F.R.C.R.363

38 (1866) L.R. 1Ex.109

be contrasted with a condition which is merely collateral to the contract of allotment. Such a condition will not invalidate the agreement if it is not fulfilled and an action under the separate collateral contract may instead be available. Thus in *Elkington's case*[39], an applicant applied for and was allotted shares upon signing the application form. He paid the stipulated sum and received a certificate of allotment. However, he refused to pay further calls on the shares on the ground that there was an understanding that he was not to pay any further calls until goods up to a certain amount had been taken and paid for by the company. It was held that he had become a member and such condition did not affect his membership. He was, therefore, liable for the call.

## Allotment by directors

The allotment of shares is normally made by directors at a meeting of the board thereof. Even if the allotment is irregular on the ground that the board is irregularly constituted or that it was made in bad faith, such irregularity can later be ratified by the company in general meeting.[40]

An allottee becomes a member of the company when his name is entered on the register of members[41]

## Restrictions on allotment

An allotment cannot be made of any share capital of a company offered to the public for subscription unless the amount stated on the share has been paid.[42] Such amount would normally be five per cent of the nominal amount of each share.[43] If the above condition is not complied with, within forty days after the first issue, all money must be repaid to the applicants without interest. If the money is not repaid within forty eight days of the issue of the prospectus the directors of the company shall be severally liable to repay it with interest of five percent per annum, unless they show that such failure was not due to any misconduct or negligence on their part.

A company with share capital which has not issued a prospectus on or with reference to its formation or which has issued the prospectus but has not issued any shares to the public for subscription must not allot any securities, unless three days before the first allotment of such securities, it delivers to the Registrar of Companies for registration, a statement in lieu of prospectus signed by every director or proposed director or by their authorised agents following the format in Part 1 of the Fourth Schedule to the Companies Act of [44].

## Consequences of improper allotment

An allotment which is made by a company contrary to Sections 49 and 50 of the Companies Act is voidable at the instance of the applicant, within one month after the holding of the statutory meeting of the company or where the company is not required to hold a statutory meeting, within one month of the date of allotment.[45] Furthermore, a director who knowingly contravenes

---

39 (1867) L.R. 2 Ch.511.

40 Re Portuguese Consolidated Copper Mines Ltd. (1890) 45 Ch.D.16; Tika Tore Press Ltd. v. Abina [1973] 4S.C.63; (1973) N.M.L.R. 220; 1973 NCLR 24, 35-38. *Abina v.Tika-Tore Press* 1968 NCLR 425, 429; *Bamford v. Bamford* [1969] 1 All E.R.420; *Piercy v. Mills & Co. Ltd.* [1920] 1 Ch.77. See further C.A. Olawoyin, "Directors Discretion to RefuSe Registration & Transfer of Shares" *Nig. Journal of Contemporary Law* (1972) 79-104.

41 *Odumody v. Mohammed & Ors* 1973 NCLR 452; *Sparks Electrics (Nig.) Ltd. & Anors V. S.B. Ponmile* [1986] 2 NWLR 516, 523 C.A.*Starcola (Nig.) Ltd. & Anor v. Taibatu Adeniji & Others* 1972 N.M.L.R. 69 (Supreme Court of Nigeria). See also *Oilfield Supply Centre v. Johnson (1986)* 2 N.W.L.R.681, 696, *Lutaaya v. Gandesha &Anors* [1986] HCB46 (Masika C.J.): This is, however, not conclusive evidence of membership: *Mawogola Farmers Ltd. v. Kayanja* [1971] E.A.272

42 Companies Act, S.49

43 *ibid* S.49 (3)

44 *ibid* S.50

'or permits or authorises the contravention of Sections 49 to 50 is liable to compensate the company and the allottee, respectively for any loss, damages or costs which the company or allottee has sustained. The recovery of such loss should be made within two years of the date of allotment.[46]

The allotment is required to be done after the third day (excluding Saturdays and Sundays) following that on which the prospectus was first issued[47]. Contravention of this requirement does not invalidate the allotment but is punishable by a fine of shs 1,000.00. In addition, the application in respect of the allotment cannot be revoked until after the third day following the opening of subscription lists.[48]

Where the prospectus offers to the public securities which have been quoted on the stock exchange, any application made in respect of such securities shall be void if permission to deal in such securities by the company has not been applied for before the third day after the issue of the prospectus or if permission is refused before the expiration of three weeks from the date of closure of the subscription lists.[49]If permission is not applied for, the company is required to repay, without interest, all money received from the applicant pursuant to the prospectus. If the money is not repaid within eight days after the company becomes liable to repay, the directors of the company shall be jointly and severally liable to repay the money with interest of five percent per annum from the eighth day unless failure to do so was not due to negligence or misconduct on the part of the relevant director(s)[50]. Money received pursuant to the prospectus should be kept in a separate bank account for so long as he company is liable to repay it. Failure to observe this requirement renders the company and every defaulting officer liable to a fine and any provision waiving compliance with Section 53 is void[51]

## Return of allotments

A company limited by shares, or by guarantee and having a share capital, must make a return of the allotment of shares to the Registrar of Companies within a one month of the allotment.[52] The return should give names, addresses and descriptions of the allottees, nominal amount of shares allotted and the amount paid or payable on each share. If the allotment is not made for cash, the contract and consideration in that respect must be stated. Failure to comply with the requirements attracts a fine of shs.100.00 for very day in default. The time for filing the information required may be extended.

---

45 *ibid* S.51

46 *ibid* S.51(2)

47 *ibid,* S.52

48 See *supra* under *Nature of Allotment* for policy reasons thereof.

49 Companies Act, S.53(1)

50 *ibid,* S.53(2)

51 *ibid* Ss.53(3),(4)

52 *ibid* S.54 See also *United Nig, Trading Co. Ltd. v. Registrar of Companies* (1978) 4 F.R.C.R.135

# 7
# LIABILITY IN RESPECT OF PROSPECTUS

The concern of this chapter is an analysis of the legal rights of subscribers and debentureholders and the liabilities of a company and its officers with respect to omissions or misstatements in a prospectus (as described in the foregoing chapter). Such rights and liabilities stem firstly from the general rules of common law and equity and secondly from statutory rules[1] forming a superstructure over case law. We shall firstly deal with civil liabilities created under the general rules of common law, equity and statute before considering criminal liabilities.

## Civil liabilities

### General remedies

Two main remedies are available under the common law and equity in respect of misstatement or omissions arising from a prospectus. These are an action for damages and rescission of the contract of allotment of shares. To these may be added an action for negligence a⁺ common law.

**(a) Damages for misrepresentation**

Where a statement in a prospectus, which induced a person to subscribe for shares on debentures contains a material misrepresentation resulting into loss or injury to the subscriber the company may be held liable following an action by the subscriber if any of its officers knew the statement to be false or had no reason to believe it to be true. This right is restricted to a direct allottee of the shares, who may sue the company or the relevant company officer for deceit. A person who has subsequently bought the shares on a market is not entitled to sue, the prospectus not having been addressed to him[2].

The shareholder will be unable to sue the company for damages, unless he rescinds the contract of allotment. In the absence of rescission, he can only sue the directors and other persons who were responsible for the issue of the prospectus.[3] Where the shareholder has rescinded but cannot recover his investment from an insolvent company, "an action against the directors and others for misrepresentation is a valuable additional remedy"[4]. To succeed in an action for deceit the plaintiff must show that a statement of fact was made, "to be acted upon by others which is false, and which is known to be false or is made by him recklessly or without care whether it be true or false"[5]. In *Derry v. Peek*[5], a director who honestly believed that the statement made in a prospectus was true, although he had no reasonable ground for such belief, was held not to be liable for fraud. The issue will always be whether the defendant" ... honestly believed the representation to be true in the sense in which he understood it albeit erroneously when it was made".[6]

Although only a direct allottee is entitled to sue for misrepresentation, following the principle in *Peek v. Gurney*[7], the case of *Andrews v. Mockford*[8], indicates that this does not apply where it

---

1 Principally deriving from the Companies Act
2 *Peek v. Gurney* (1873)L.R 6 H.L. 377
3 i.e in deceit or under Companies Act, S.45
4 Leigh, *et al op.cit.* pp.61-62
5 *Derry v. Peek* (1889) 14 App. Cas. 337 at p. 350 per Lord Dramwell. See also *Rolf De Mare and/or S V. Akerhielm* (1956) 23 EACA 214
6 *Akerhielm v. De Marc* [1959] A.C. 789 at p.805. See also *Friedman v. Njoro (1954) 21 EACA 172*
7 *Supra* n. 2.
8 [1896] 1 Q.B. 372 C.A.

is proved as a fact that the prospectus was intended to induce market dealings. Nonetheless, it is still maintained that the principle in *Peek v. Gurney* is still generally applicable.[9] Nevertheless, it is contended that this approach "fails to recognise the result of modern issuing techniques" in the sense that persons who issue the prospectus must be deemed to have contemplated the general public including subsequent buyers. Professor Gower adds in this vein:[10]

> Under modern conditions, those who advertise a prospectus know that it will be relied on indiscriminately by investors who apply on allotment and by those who buy on the market.

### (b) Rescission

In the event of a person subscribing for shares in or debenture of a company basing himself on a prospectus which contains an untrue or misleading but not necessarily fraudulent statement, such person may bring an action for rescission of the contract and the rectification of the register of members or debenture holders.[11] This is a general contractual remedy available to a person who has been induced by a misrepresentation to enter into a contract. As with damages, this remedy is not available to a person who has bought his shares on the market. It is only valuable to a direct allottee pursuant to the company's prospectus.[12] It is advisable for the relevant security holder to start his action against the company for rescission and rectification, as soon as he becomes aware of the misrepresentation. In the event of his success, he will be entitled to repayment of the money paid for the securities to the company. To be able to succeed the security holder must prove

(i) that the prospectus contained an untrue or misleading statement or misrepresentation;[13]
(ii) that the untrue or misleading statement or misrepresentation was in respect of a material matter and was one of the inducements to apply for shares or debentures;[14]
(iii) that the company is liable for the statement or misrepresentation.[15]

A company will be liable for misrepresentations or statements made by its directors and servants within their authority and for contents of a prospectus issued before its incorporation where the shares or debentures were subscribed for or allotted on the basis of such a prospectus. Finally, the security holder must show that he has acted promptly to rescind the contract.[16] For this purpose he does not need to act on rumour. He can wait until he has sufficient knowledge. He is not deemed to know the falsity of a prospectus simply "because the prospectus refers to sources from which its accuracy could be verified."[17]

Should a security holder, after becoming aware of the misstatement or misrepresentation do any act which is inconsistent with his right to rescind, he loses the right to rescind. Instances of such acts include the attendance of meetings, the paying calls or accepting dividends[18] or attempting to sell shares.[19] However, if a shareholder who possesses separate grounds for rescission has lost his right to rescind on one ground, he is not prevented from rescinding on another ground.[20] A security holder who has rescinded the contract should also apply to have the register of members

---

9 Gower, *op. cit.* p.374

10 *ibid*, p.375

11 See Companies Act, S. 118 for rectification procedure which is without prejudice to the court's general jurisdiction over the matter. See further Leigh, *op.cit.* pp. 57-61; Gower *op.cit.* pp. 376-382.

12 *Peek v. Gurney* (1873) L.R. 6 H.L. 377. For the controversy over this rule see previous section on damages.

13 See *Greenwood v. Leather Shod Wheel Co.* [1900] 1 Ch. 421.

14 See *Re: Kylsant* [1931] All E.R. Rep. 179

15 *Lynde v. Anglo - Italian Hemp Spinning Co.* [1896] 1 Ch. 178

16 In *Re: Scottish Petroleum Co.* (1883) 23 Ch. D. 413; *Sharpley v. Louth and East Cost Rly Co.* (1876) 2 Ch. D. 663, 785

17 Leigh, op. cit. p. 551 see also *Central Rly Co. of Venezuela v. Kisch* (1867) L.R. 2 H.L. 99.

18 *Scholey v. Central Rly Co. of Venezuela*(1869) L.R. 9 Eq. 266

19 *Re: Hop & Malt Exchange & Warehouse Co. Exparte Briggs* (1866) L.R. 1 Eq. 483

20 *Elder's Trustee & Executor Co. Ltd. v. Commonwealth Homes and investment Co. Ltd.* (1941) 65 C.L.R. 603

security holder who has rescinded the contract should also apply to have the register of members rectified. Furthermore, the right to rescind must be taken before winding-up of the company has started[21].

The right to rescind a contract of allotment is also subject to general contractual principles affecting rescission. Thus the contract cannot be rescinded once it has been executed.[22]

Furthermore, delay in bringing an action for rescission is sufficient, on ground of lapse ot time, to deny a security holder the remedy. The presence of shareholder's name on the register of members by which persons may be induced to advance credit to the company may also be a ground for refusing rescission especially where steps have not been taken by the shareholder to have his name removed from the register.[23] Where a shareholder has lost his right to rescind as a result of delay or otherwise he cannot obtain damages for misrepresentation from the company.[24] The rationale for this is that since a shareholder is part and parcel of the company, he may not recover damages from himself and his fellow shareholders.[25] However, such a shareholder can, without rescinding the contract, sue the directors or other persons with responsibility for issuing the prospectus.[26]

**(c) Actions for negligence at Common Law**

Prior to 1890 the common law did not recognise an action for damages in respect of loss or damage arising from negligent misstatement.[27] This was remedied by the Directors Liability Act 1890 which is in *pari materia* with Section 45 of the Companies Act. Section 45, however, only creates a remedy in respect of prospectus inviting the public to subscribe for shares and debentures of the company. It has no application to documents which, "because they offer shares for purchase or sale, or because they offer shares for other than cash consideration are not prospectuses within the meaning of the Companies Acts".[28] In addition, before 1964, it was thought on the authority of *Derry v. Peek* that no duty of care could arise unless there was a pre-existing contractual or fiduciary relationship.[29] However, in *Hedley Byrne & Co. Ltd. v. Heller & Partners Ltd.*[30], the House of Lords established that liability exists at common law for negligent misstatements provided that a duty of care is owed by the maker thereof to the recipient of the statement. In that case the plaintiffs sought advice from professional men. It was held that the law implies a duty of care "when the party seeking information from a person possessed of special skill trusts him to exercise due care and that person knew or ought to have known that reliance was being placed on his skill and judgment".[31] It would presumably follow from this that a duty of care will not arise unless advice or information is sought. Consequently, it would be rare to establish a duty of care with regards to prospectuses not usually solicited by the recipients. This is, however, regarded as a restrictive interpretation of *Hedley Byrne & Co. case*[32] and though supported by authority[33] would still appear to cover those who publish a prospectus. This is much more evident with

21 *Cakes v. Turquand & Harding* (1867) L.R. 2 H.L. 325

22 *Seddon v. North Eastern Salt Co.* [1905] Ch. 326. This principle has been altered in Britain by Misrepresentation Act, 1967, S.1 to the effect that the fact that the misrepresentation has become a term of the contract, does not preclude rescission. See further Gower, *op.cit.* pp. 378, 380

23 See *Aaron's Reefs Ltd. v. Twiss* [1896] A.C. 273, 294 per Lord Davey; *Re: Scottish Petroleum Co.* (1883) 23 Ch. D. 413, 439 per Fry L.J.

24 *Houldsworth v. City of Glasgow Bank (1880) 5 App. Cas. 317. The rule does not apply to debenture holders.*

25 The principle may need recasting in the light of the subsequent principle of separate company personality established in *Solomon v. Solomon* (1897) A.C. 22

26 *Arnison v. Smith* (1889) 41 Ch D. 348

27 *Derry v. Peek (supra); Candler v. Crane & Christmas Co. [1961] 2 KB 164*

28 Leigh, *op. cit* p. 64 referring to Companies Acts, S. 455 (Britain), S.2 (Uganda)

29 Gower, op. cit. p. 371. See also *Nocton v. Lord Ashburton* [1914] A.C.A.C. 932 H.L.

30 [1964] A.C. 465; [1963] 2 All E.R 575

31 Gower *op.cit.*, p.371, following Lord Morris, *ibid* [1964] A.C. 465 at p.503

32 Gower, *ibid*

33 *Mutual Life and Citizen's Assurance Co. Ltd. v. Evatt* [1971] A.C. 793 P.C. Per Lord Diplock at P. 805

respect to a prospectus which is published in the form of a stock exchange advertisement. The rubric which the Stock Exchange insist shall be placed at the head of the advertisement essentially invites the public to rely on it and indicates that the directors accept responsibility. Furthermore an expert such as a surveyor, accountant or engineer who agrees to his report appearing in the prospectus, essentially invites the public to rely on his expert opinion[34].

In a subsequent case, *Howard Marine and Dredging Co. Ltd. v. Ogden & Sons (Excavations) Ltd.*[35], Lord Denning indicated that duty of care arises where the representation concerns a business or professional transaction whose nature makes clear the gravity of the inequity and the importance attached to the answer. Such obligation goes beyond an obligation to the initial inquirer and extends to those to whom it is reasonably foreseeable it will be furnished by whom it will be acted upon.

## Statutory remedies

### (a) Compensation under Section 45 Companies Act

Section 45 indicates that compensation is available to persons who suffer loss or damage arising from an untrue statement in a prospectus inviting persons to subscribe for shares or debentures of a company. The claim for compensation may be made against any director, person named as director in the prospectus, promoter of the company or any other person authorizing the issue of a prospectus. However, an expert whose consent to be named in a prospectus had been obtained under Section 42 will be liable only in respect of an untrue statement purporting to be made by him as an expert. It is thus clear that this remedy is only available against the company's officers in the circumstances indicated and not against the company itself. A "promoter" in this context includes a person who was party to the preparation of the prospectus.[36]

Any of the persons potentially liable under the section other than an expert can escape liability by proving either that he publicly dissociated himself from the prospectus or that he believed on reasonable grounds that the statement made therein was true.[37] An expert will be exonerated from liability if he can prove that he withdrew his consent in writing either (i) before registration of the prospectus, or (ii) upon registration but before allotment, provided that in the latter case he gave reasonable public notice of his withdrawal and reasons thereof[38]. The expert will also not be liable if he can prove his competence to make the statement and that up to the time of allotment he reasonably believed it. In effect, the expert must actually be both competent and careful before he can escape liability under the section. It is suggested that the section provides a subscriber with a better remedy than an attempt to establish a duty of care under *Hedley Byrne & Co. Ltd. v. Heller & Partners Ltd.*[39]

Even where the untrue statement is that of an expert, the other parties to the prospectus have to show that it "fairly represents what the expert said, and that they believed on reasonable grounds that the expert was competent and had consented to its publication."[40] In effect, they are obliged to be both honest and diligent and have to prove discharge of that duty.

A statement included in the prospectus is deemed to be untrue for the purposes of section 45, if it is misleading in form and context in which it is included.[41]

---

34 Gower, *op.cit.* p. 371

35 [1978] Q.B. 374; [1978] 2 All E.R. 1134. See also the New Zealand case *Diamond Manufacturing Co., Ltd. v. Hamilton* (1969) N.Z.L.R. 609, where it was held that buyers of a company's shares could maintain an action against the company's auditors where the auditor handed a copy of the audited balance sheet to the buyer's agent for use in negotiations. This amounted to an implied representation as to the correctness of the balance sheet to purchasers, who, it could be foreseen would act on it.

36 S. 45, Companies Act

37 *ibid*; S. 45 (2)

38 *ibid*, S. 45 (3)

39 [1964] A.C. 365 H.L. considered *supra* above.

40 Gower, *op. cit.* p. 386

41 Companies Act, Section 48 (a)

Section 45 also indicates that directors are liable to indemnify anyone who is held liable because he is wrongly described as a director in the prospectus or because his expert report has, been published following his withdrawal of his consent.

**(b) Non compliance with Section 40 of The Companies Act**

Section 40 requires that the information set out in schedule 3 to the Act must be disclosed in the prospectus, failure of which attracts criminal sanction.[42] However, it is provided further that where there is contravention or non-compliance with the section, "a director or other person responsible for the prospectus shall not incur any liability" if he brings himself under certain defences. This implies that if he cannot avail himself at least of one of the defences he will be civilly liable.[43] This approach is open to doubt[44] and it has been suggested that when it was indicated that the section might confer a right of action, "non-compliance with its provisions was deemed by statute to be fraud."[45] This apparently is not the case, the obligation being simply a statutory duty of disclosure.[46]

A director or other person responsible under the section can be exonerated from liability by proving[47] (i) that he was not aware of any matter omitted or (ii) that the non-compliance or contravention of the section stemmed from an honest mistake. Where the omission is of the director's interest in the promotion, the plaintiff is obliged to prove that the defendant had knowledge.[48] A potentially liable person under the section can also avoid liability if in the opinion of the court, the error was immaterial or ought in the circumstances to be reasonably excused.[49]

**(c) Liabilities under sections of the Companies Act**

Other civil liabilities which are provided for by the Companies Act have been dealt with earlier.[50]

# Criminal liabilities

## Non compliance with The Companies Act

It is an offence for a person to issue a form of application for a company's shares or debentures without a prospectus and without having been so exempted under section 41. Such person is liable on conviction to a fine not exceeding shs. 10,000/-.[51] However, a director or other person responsible for a prospectus will not be liable for the failure to issue a prospectus pursuant to Schedule Three if (i) he proves that with respect to any matter not disclosed, he was unaware of it or that the failure to comply arose from an honest mistake of fact on his part or (ii) the court is satisfied that the matters involved are not material and are excusable in the circumstances.[52]

It is also an offence attracting a fine of up to Shs. 10,000/- to issue a prospectus containing the statement of an expert without his consent.[53] Where a prospectus is issued without complying with registration provisions, i.e. delivering a copy to the Registrar, and without making the necessary endorsements and attachments, the company and every person who is knowingly a party to the

---

42 *ibid* S. 40 (3)
43 *Re South of England Natural Gas Co.* [1911] 1 Ch.573
44 *Nash v. Lynde* (1929) A.C. 158 H.L.
45 Leigh, op. cit. p. 64
46 *ibid*
47 S.40 (4) (a), (b)
48 S.40 (4) Proviso
49 S. 40(4) (c) *c.f.* S.405
50 See Chapter 6 under heading *"Consequences of Improper Allotment"*
51 Companies Act, S.40 (3)
52 ibid, S. 40(4)
53 ibid, S 43 (2)

issue is liable to a fine not exceeding one hundred shillings for every day from the date of issue until a copy is so delivered with the required endorsements or attachments.[54]

## Liability for misstatements

Any person who authorises the issue of a prospectus containing any untrue statement is liable on conviction in the High Court to a fine of shs. 10,000/- or two years imprisonment or both or on summary conviction to imprisonment for three months unless he proves either that the statement was immaterial or that he had reasonable ground to believe and did up to the time of issue of the prospectus, believe the statement was true.[55] A statement shall be deemed to be untrue if it is misleading in the form and context in which it is included and shall be deemed to be contained in a prospectus if it is in any report or memorandum therein incorporated by reference or issued therewith.[56]

It is also an offence for a promoter, director, officer or auditor of the company to circulate a written statement of account which he knows to be false in material particular with intent to defraud a member or induce any person to advance or entrust property to the company. [57] Criminal liability is also created in respect of false statements in matters and reports which are required to be set out in the prospectus.[58]

---

54 *ibid*, S. 43(4)

55 *ibid* S.46(1)

56 *ibid* S.48, adopting *Rv. Kylsant* [1932] 1 KB 442

57 Penal Code

58 Companies Act, S.396

# 8
# SHARES

It is proposed here to examine the nature of shares, the mode of their issue [1], the mechanism of becoming a shareholder and other legal problems and rules which affect shares generally.

## Nature of shares

The idea that a shareholder is a proportionate owner of the company stems from the view that a share is a personal estate of a member, and not real estate, which is transferrable in accordance with the articles.[1] It is also provided that money paid in respect of shares under the memorandum and articles of association constitutes a debt due from the shareholder to the company and is in the nature of a specialty debt.[2] A share has also been defined in *Borland's Trustee v. Steel Bros. & Co. Ltd.*[3] as:

> ... the interest of a shareholder in the company measured by a sum of money for the purpose of liability in the first place and of interest in the second, but also consisting of a series of mutual covenants entered into by all the shareholders interest...

The holding of a share therefore carries with it certain property rights and liabilities in the company. These include the right to proportionate share in the profits of the company commensurate with the shareholding;[4] the right to vote at the company's general meeting.[5]

## The mode of issue of shares and becoming a shareholder

### Issue of shares

Shares are invariably issued by directors at a duly convened meeting of the board, in the manner described in chapter 6 herein.[6]

### Becoming a shareholder

#### (a) Who can be a shareholder?

**Infants**

A minor can be a member of the company, except where the articles of association prevent this. If he is a member, he is subject to the general contractual rights and liabilities of a minor. This means that if he has bought shares, he can repudiate the contract at any time before he reaches twenty-one years of age or within a reasonable time thereafter. However, if he repudiates, he cannot recover money paid, unless there has been total failure of consideration.[7]

---

1 Companies Act, S. 75 and Table A, Art. 23

2 *ibid.*, S. 22 (2)

3 [1901] 1 Ch. 279, 288 per Farwell J. See also *Odumody v. Mohamed & Ors.* (1973) NCLR 452, 460 (High Court of Lagos State).

4 Companies Act, S. 61(c), Table A, Art. 114

5 *Pender v. Lushington* (1877) 6 Ch. D. 70 C.A.; *Odumody v. Mohamed supra* n.4;

6 See section on allotment.

7 *Steinberg v. Scala* [1923] 2 Ch. 452

**Personal representatives**

A personal representative of a deceased shareholder can be registered as a member. This is subject though to the directors' right to refuse registration.[8] Furthermore, a personal representative, can transfer shares of a deceased member without himself being registered.[9] The estate of the deceased shareholder is liable on calls while the personal representative will be personally liable where he has become a member. In this regard, directors may require the personal representative to choose between being personally liable and making the estate liable.[10] The production by a personal representative of the probate of the will or letters of administration of the deceased is sufficient evidence to the company of the grant thereof.[11] Subsequently the personal representative is entitled to receive dividends and benefits accruing from the shares.

Although not having a right to vote at meetings, the personal representative is nonetheless entitled to notice of such meetings.[12] Thus, in *Tika Tore Press Ltd. v. Abina*[13], the plaintiffs were executors of the deceased shareholder. They applied to be registered as shareholders in the place of the deceased. However, before registration could be effected, they attended and voted at a meeting of the company contrary to Article 23 of the then Companies Act of Nigeria[14]. It was held that the executors had no right to attend or vote at the meeting which was to that extent, in any case, irregular.

**Trustee in bankruptcy**

A bankrupt shareholder remains a member. However, he votes as directed by his trustee in bankruptcy.[15] Generally the position of a trustee is similar to that of a personal representative (above). For instance, the trustee may opt to be registered himself and the directors have discretion to refuse registration., etc.

**Another company**

Another company can become a member of a company be appointing a representative thereon[16] However, a company cannot be a member of itself i.e. it cannot buy its own shares, as this is likely to lead to reduction in its registered capital.[17] Furthermore, section 29 of the Companies Act, restricts the ability of a subsidiary company to become a member of its holding company. This is subject to the exceptions that (i) it can hold its holding company's shares as trustee or personal representative provided that the holding company is not beneficially interested in the trust and (ii) the subsidiary was at the commencement of the Act a member of the holding company, in which case, though, it will have no voting rights.

## The process of becoming a member

A person may become a member[18] of the company by subscribing to the memorandum of association. Under section 28 of the Companies Act, upon registration of the company the

---

8 Table A, Arts 29-30

9 Companies Act, S. 78

10 *ibid.*, Table A, Art. 31

11 *ibid*, S. 84

12 *ibid*, Table A., Art. 32

13 (1973) II 1All N.L.R. 244; (1973) 1 N.M.L.R. 220; 1973 NCLR 24 (Supreme Court of Nigeria). See also *supra n.4 Dipcharima v. Borno Holding Co. Ltd.* (1969) (3) ALR Comm 112.

14 Cap. 37 which is equivalent to Table A, Art. 31 Companies Act

15 Table A, Arts. 30-32, 133; *Morgan v. Gray* [1953] Ch. 83

16 *Hillman v. Crystal Bowl* [1973] 1 All E.R. 379

17 *Trevor v. Whitworth* (1887) 12 App. Cas. 409 H.L. per Lord Watson

18 Becoming a member may not necessarily mean becoming a shareholder as some companies have no share capital. See also *Odumody v. Mohammed* (1973) NCLR 452, 460-461, c.f. *Sparks Electrics (Nig.) Ltd. v. S.B. Ponmile* (1986) 2 NWLR 516, 522 C.A. See also *Starcola (Nig.) Ltd v. Taibatu Adeneji* 1972 NMLR 69

subscribers to the memorandum become members. Alternatively, membership is achieved through agreement to be a member.[19] This includes (i) those who apply for allotment of shares,[20] (ii) those to whom shares are transferred or transmitted and (iii) directors who have signed and delivered to the Registrar of Companies an undertaking to take and pay for their qualification shares.[21] In *Lutaya v. Gandesha*[22a], it was held that holding of a share certificate and appearance of one's name on the company's annual return may be evidence of membership.

**(c) Payment for shares**

Normally shares are paid for in cash. However, they may also be paid for in kind. In *Spargo's case*[22], X sold a lease to a Company which was formed for the purpose of adopting the lease. The company then credited the purchase price of the lease against X's liability on the shares for which he had subscribed. It was held that this amounted to payment in cash for the shares.

It is further notable that an allottee must pay five per cent of the nominal value as minimum subscription.[23] In payments made otherwise than in cash, registration thereof at the company registry is required[24] and the court will not inquire into the adequacy of the consideration given, unless it is obvious that the consideration is inadequate or is illusory or fraudulent.[25] For this purpose past consideration is not regarded as consideration.[26] Where shares are allotted after incorporation and the agreement between the allottee and the company is silent as to time of payment, payment must be made within a reasonable time.[27]

**(d) Issue of shares at a discount**

The law does not allow the issue of shares at a discount. The full nominal value of the shares must be paid because otherwise the capital yardstick of the company would be misleading. In *Ooregum Gold Mining Co. of India Ltd. v. Roper*[28], a company which was in need of money and whose original shares stood at a discount issued preference shares of £ 1.00 each with Shs. 15/- credited as paid, leaving a liability of shs. 5/- per share. It was held that the issue was beyond the powers of the company. The position with regard to shares may be contrasted with that in respect of debentures which may be issued at a discount provided that they are not rapidly converted into shares.[29] However, shares may be issued at a discount provided the conditions stipulated under section 59 of the Companies Act are fulfilled.

**(e) Issue of shares at a premium**

The issue of shares above their nominal value is permissible.[30] However, the amount of the premium thereby realised, whether in cash or otherwise must be transferred to a share premium account in the company's balance sheet.[31] Such account can only be used for the following purposes,[32] (i) to pay off bonus shares which are issued to members of the company as fully

---

19 See too *Stephen v. Build Co.* (Nig.) Ltd. (1968) NCLR 249, 251-253; *Mawogola Farmers & Growers Ltd. v. Kayanja* [1971] EA 272

20 See chapter 6 for procedure.

21 Companies Act, S. 182 *S.E. Ltd. v. Ponmile* (1986) 2 NWLR 516, 523 C.A. *Thadani v. Thadani* suit No. FHC/L/M/8/80 of 1/8/80 unreported; *Haslir v. Zard & Co. Ltd* (1978-74) *1F* R.C.R 235 F.H.C. See also *Starcola (Nig.) Ltd. v. Adeniji supra* n. 17

22a [1986] HCB 46

22 (1873) L.R. 8 Ch. App. 407

23 Companies Act, S. 49(3)

24 *ibid*, S. 54

25 *Salomon v. Salomon* [1897] A.C. 22; *Re: Wragg Ltd.* [1897] 1 Ch. 796; *Hong Kong v. Glen* [1941] Ch. 527

26 Re: *Eddystone Marine [1893] 3 Ch 9*

27 *Stephen v. Build Co. (Nig.) Ltd.* 1968 NCLR 249, 251-253, (Supreme Court of Nigeria)

28 [1892] A.C. 125 H.L. See also *Welton v. Saffery* [1897] A.C. 299

29 *Moseley v. Koffyfontein Mines Ltd.* [1904] 2 Ch. 108

30 Companies Act, s. 58

31 *ibid.* See too *Head v. Ropner Holdings Ltd.* (1951) 2 All E.R. 994

32 *ibid* S. 58

paid up; (ii) to write off preliminary expenses of the company and expenses of any commission paid on discount allowed on any issue of shares of debentures of the company; (iii) to provide for the premium payable on redemption of redeemable preference shares or of debentures of the company.

**(f) Share certificate and Estoppel**

Within two months of allotment or transfer of shares, a company is required to issue a share certificate in respect thereof.[33] The certificate constitutes a statement by the company that the holder owns shares which are described in the certificate and is also *prima facie* evidence of the title of that person to the shares.[34]

The certificate operates as an estoppel against the company in two instances viz. (i) that the person to whom it is granted is a registered shareholder who is entitled to the shares mentioned in the certificate and (ii) that the amount certified to be paid has been paid.[35] In respect of the first, a person deceived on the basis of the certificate can recover damages from the company. With regard to the second, it provides a defence to a claim for calls made by the company. However, the estoppel will not operate where the transferee of the shares has submitted a forged transfer, even if in good faith. In such a case, he is required to indemnify the company for any liability it incurs as a result of registering the transfer.[36] Exceptionally, though, a company may be estopped from denying the accuracy of a share certificate against a person to whom it is issued. This will be so where that person on the faith of the certificate issued to him enters into a contract to sell the shares or fails to pursue his remedies against the person who has arranged the transfer to him. In such a case he may be entitled to damages or indemnity from the company. Thus, in *Balkis Consolidated Co. v. Tomkinson*[37], X the original proprietor of the shares transferred them to Y, who was thereby registered. X, then fraudulently, transferred to Z, who took the shares in good faith. The company issued Z with a certificate but did not place his name on the register of members. Z then entered into a contract to sell the shares to A, but was unable to perform the contract without buying other shares. It was held that he was entitled to recover from the company the price paid for these other shares. Furthermore, in *Dixon v. Kennaway* & Co.,[38] a broker who was also employed by the company got money from a client for the purchase of the shares and arranged the issue of a certificate indicating that the client was the owner of shares which were actually owned by another member. Later, the fraud was discovered and by that time the broker had gone bankrupt. It was held that the company was liable in damages, the client having relied on the certificate to such an extent that it became too late to recover from the fraudulent broker. The court indicated that the reliance and detriment had to be proved by the plaintiff and that even so she would have failed if the company had proved that the action against the broker would have been fruitless were she to pursue it at once. It is notable that in both cases "the original recipient of the certificate had in fact changed his position in reliance on the certificate and neither had he put forward a forged transfer."[39] Consequently, where the certificate itself is forged, no estoppel against the company can arise.[40] However, it is maintained that "if the genuineness of the certificate has been expressly or impliedly warranted by an official acting within the actual or apparent scope of his authority, this warranty will bind the company even though that official has committed forgery.[41]

---

33 ibid., S.82; Table A. Art. 8.

34 ibid., S. 83

35 *Re: Bahia & San Francisco Rly Co.* (1868) L.R. 30.8.584, *Bloomenthal v. Ford* [1897] A.C.156

36 *Sheffield Corporation v. Barclay* [1905] A.C. 392

37 [1893] A.C. 396 H.L.

38 [1900] 1 Ch. 833. See also Gower, *op.cit.* p. 438

39 Gower, *ibid*

40 *Ruben v, Great Fingall Consolidated* [1906] A.C. 439

41 Gower, *op. cit.* p. 440

# Transfer of shares

## Restrictions on transfer

It has been noted[42] that shares are in the nature of a personal estate or chose in action and are transferable in the mode prescribed by the articles.[43] Practically, companies which are listed on the stock exchange should have no restrictions on transfer. However, public unlisted companies may have restrictions to transfer in their articles. Private companies are by definition[44] entities which place restrictions on the transfer of their shares and invariably provide for rights of pre-emption i.e. that the shares should be offered to existing members of the company for sale. In such a case it is normal to make provision for determining what is a fair value to be attached to the shares in the event of a dispute. In *Shonibare v. Probate Registrar*[45], the appellants who were executors of an estate sued the Probate Registrar disputing his valuation of some shares forming part of the assets of the company. It was held[46] that in the valuation of shares in a private company for estate duty purposes the executors must prove any circumstances which would justify valuing the shares at a less than par. Furthermore,[47] that the net value of the assets of the company at a given point in time is one of the matters to be considered in estimating the market value of the shares. It is notable that the par or face value of a share is distinguishable from its market value.[48]

There is also other statutory restriction on the transfer of shares to the effect that the transfer of any security or creation of or transfer of any interest in a security to or in favour of a person resident outside Uganda is invalid except where it has been sanctioned by the Minister of Finance.[49] In *Bread Ltd. v. Uganda Co. Ltd.*[50], it was held that the complete transfer of shares and the subsequent acquisition of the first defendant's assets and property amounted to a complete takeover of the company.

## The role of directors

Directors are invariably given absolute discretion to refuse registration of any transfer of shares without giving reasons.[51] In *Ferris George & Sons. V. Khoury*[52], a similar article to Article 3 of Part II, Table A was interpreted to give directors an absolute power to refuse registration of shares limited only by the requirement of *bona fides*.

Where in exercise of the discretion to allow registration of transfer of shares, directors give reasons for refusal and these are adjudged to be in bad faith, the court may interfere.[53] However, if the articles give the directors power to decline registration of transfers on certain grounds,[54] but without giving reasons, they may subject to provision in the article be questioned as to the ground for refusal but not as to the reasons.[55] As a corollary, where the articles provide that

---

42 *supra* n. 2 and text thereof;

43 Table A. Arts 22-27. See also *Lindlars case* [1910] Ch. 312, 316 per Buckley L.J.

44 Companies Act. S. 30

45 1966 (2) A.L.R. Comm 389; 1966 NCLR 389, Supreme Court of Nigeria,

46 *ibid* 1966 NCLR. p. 393 per Brett J.S.C.

47 *ibid.*, p. 397

48 *Eguekweh v. Barclays Bank of Nigeria Ltd.* (1973) NCLR 432

49 Exchange Control Act, S.8

50 [1975] HCB 218

51 See e.g. Table A, Part II Art. 3. See also G.A.. Olawoyin, "Directors Discretion to Refuse Registration and Transfer and Transmission of Shares" *Nigerian Journal of Contemporary Law* (1972) pp. 79-104. Table A Art. 24

52 [1965] 1 All NLR, See also *Coker v. Iro & Ors* (1976) 2 F.R.C.R. 136

53 *Re: Bell Bros.* (1891) 65 L.T. 245; *Re: Smith & Fawcett* [1942] Ch. 304, 306

54 e.g. that it is not in the interest of the company to register the proposed transferee.

55 *Sutherland v. British Dominions Land Settlement Corporation* [1926] Ch. 746; *Re: Bede Steam Shipping Co.* [1917] 1 Ch. 123 C.A.

directors "shall not be bound to specify the grounds" on which they have decided to refuse a transfer, they cannot be forced by interrogatories to disclose the grounds.[56]

The right to refuse registration must be formally and positively exercised before registration is confirmed to have been refused. Thus, in *Abina and Others v. Tika-Tore Press*[57], the applicants were administrators of the estate of a deceased person who held shares in the respondent company during his lifetime. Article 22 of Table A First Schedule to the Companies Act[58] was part of the Respondent's articles of association. It gave anyone becoming entitled to a share by reasons of death of shareholder a right to be registered as a member in respect of the share, but it reserved to the directors the same right to decline registration as they would have had in the case of a transfer of the shares by the deceased before his death. Article 2 of the respondent's articles gave directors an absolute discretion as to the acceptance or rejection of any transfer of shares *inter vivos*. The applicants asked the respondents to register their names as successors to the deceased's shares. The respondent acknowledged this request and stated that further communications would be addressed to them but took no further action in the matter and its directors took no decision as to the registration of the applicant's names or exercise of their right not to do so. The applicants thereafter applied to court to rectify the register by entering their names thereon.[59] In holding that the applicants were entitled to registration, Kazeem, J. indicated[60] that where directors have a right to decline registration of a holder of shares by transmission on death, there must be, to authorise a refusal to register, a formal active exercise of the right by means of a vote of the board; mere failure to pass a resolution being insufficient. Furthermore, if the directors have had sufficient time to make a decision, the absence of any formal exercise of the right to decline entitles the shareholder to be registered.

In the event of registration being refused by the directors, notice of refusal thereof should given to the transferee within two months of lodgment of the transfer[61]. Where there is a division of the board of directors as to whether or not to refuse registration, the decision is not positive. Consequently, the transfer must be registered.[62] In addition, the refusal to register the transfer must occur within a reasonable time; otherwise it will be regarded as void. In *Re: Swaledale Cleaners Ltd.*[63], it was held that a delay of four months was unreasonable.

Where the company has unreasonably failed to register a transfer of shares, the transferee has a right to apply to court for rectification of the register of members so as to substitute his name for that of the transferor.[64]

## Form of transfer

A proper instrument of transfer is required to be used in effecting the transfer of shares.[65] A proper instrument is one which is executed by or on behalf of the transferor and transferee respectively[66]. In *Re: Greene*[67], it was held that a provision in the articles which provides for automatic transfer to a designated party upon the shareholder's death is not a proper instrument of transfer.

---

56 *Berry & Stewart v. Tottenham Hotspur & Athletic Co. Ltd.* [1935] 1 Ch. 318 193; *Re: Bede Steam Shipping Co., ibid*

57 1968 NCLR 475 (High Court of Lagos State) See also *Chief Toye Coker v. Paul Iro, Tarstone & Co. Ltd (Ors* (1976) 2 F.R.C.R. 136

58 Cap. 37. Laws of Nigeria. See Table A Art. 30, Companies Act, Cap 85

59 A remedy now available under Companies Act, S.118; *Mawogola Farmers & Growers Ltd. v. Kayanja [1971]* EA 272

60 1968 NCLR 475 at pp. 480-481

61 Companies Act, S. 80

62 *Shepherds Trustees v. Shepherd* (1950) S.C. 60; *Re: Hackney Pavillion Ltd.* [1924] 1 Ch. 276

63 [1968] 1 WLR 1710. See also Table A, Art. 26; Companies Act, 1968, S. 80

64 See *supra* notes 54 to 56 and text thereof; Companies Act, *ibid*, S. 118

65 Companies Act, *ibid.*, S. 77

## Procedure for transfer

### (a) Sale of all shares on a share certificate

If the transfer involves the sale of all the shares which are mentioned in a share certificate, the seller is required to hand to the buyer the instrument of transfer as well as the share certificate. The buyer then sends there documents to the company with the requisite fee. The company will in turn send to the buyer a new certificate[68] or notify him of the decision to refuse registration within two months of request therefor.[69]

### (b) Sale of only part of shares on a certificate

If the seller is only selling some of his shares which are mentioned in a single certificate, the procedure of certification must be complied with. Essentially, the seller executes the instrument of transfer and sends it together with the share certificate to the company. The company will then endorse on the transfer instrument, "certificate lodged" and return it to the seller.[70] The seller then hands the instrument to the buyer who pays him and then forwards the instrument tot he company for registration. The company will in turn send a new certificate to the buyer[71] or notify him of the refusal to register.[72]

The certification of the transfer instrument amounts to a representation by the company to any person acting on it that documents showing a *prima facie* title to the shares in the transferor have been produced to the company. It is not a representation that the seller has title to the shares.[73] Nevertheless, if the company fraudulently or negligently makes a false certification, anyone who acts on it can sue it.[74] However, if the company negligently returns the original certificate to the seller of shares, who then fraudulently sells the same shares, the company is not liable. An action will instead lie against the seller for fraud.[75]

### (c) The duties of seller and buyer

Under the contract of sale of shares, the seller must hand over to the buyer a valid instrument of transfer and relevant share certificate. In return the buyer must pay the price for the shares.[76] There is an implied undertaking on the part of the seller that the certificate carries the rights and interests which it purports to convert.[77] The seller should do nothing to prevent the buyer from having the transfer registered or to delay its registration.[78] However, if the directors refuse to register the transfer, the buyer has no remedy against the seller unless the seller had guaranteed registration.[79]

Following the conclusion of the contract of sale but before registration, the buyer holds the equitable title to the shares. The seller holds the legal title to them but as trustee for the buyer.[80] Where directors have declined registration of the transfer the seller will hold the shares on trust for the buyer. This means that the buyer is entitled to dividend as from the date of sale.[81] He will also be liable to indemnify the seller on calls, unless there is a contrary agreement.[82] Finally, at meetings the seller is entitled to vote in accordance with the buyer's instructions.

---

66 *ibid*, S. 77; Table A, Art. 22
67 [1949] Ch. 333
68 Companies Act, S. 82
69 *ibid*, S.80
70 *ibid*, S. 81(3)
71 *supra* n. 64
72 *supra* n.65
73 Companies Act, S.82
74 *ibid* S. 81 (2)
75 *Longman v. Bath Electric Tramways Ltd.* [1905] 1 Ch. 646
76 *Stray v. Russel* (1859) 1 E&E 888, 890
77 *ibid*
78 *Hooper v. Herts* [1906] 1 Ch. 54g
79 *London Founders Association Ltd. & Palmer v. Clarke* (1888) 20 QBD 576
80 *Stevenson v. Wilson* (1907) S.G. 445

### (d) Priorities

There may be competing claims to the shares. If one of the claimants is on the register, he will have priority over the shares unless he had notice of the prior equitable claim. Thus in *Ireland v. Hart*,[83] the equitable interest prevailed over the legal mortgagee as notice thereof had already been given to him. However, where none of the claimants is on the register, the one whose title was first in time has priority. Thus, in *Peat v. Clayton*,[84] X, the registered owner, executed a transfer in favour of Y, but did not hand over the certificates, saying that they were abroad. Y gave notice to the company but did not attempt to secure registration,[85] X then transferred the same shares to Z and handed the certificates to him. Z's transfer was lodged with the company and registered. At this stage, it would be assumed that Z had an unimpeachable title because of the registration. However, the company then remembered Y's notice and took Z's name off the register and refused to give her a certificate. Z then applied to her brokers for restitution and they bought other shares in the company for her. The brokers then claimed a lien on the original shares to reimburse them for their expenditure. It was held that although Z might have had legal title which would prevail over Y, the brokers had at most only an equitable lien and as this had arisen after Y's equity, it did not prevail against Y.

It is also established[86] that a transfer of shares, though improper under the articles (providing for pre-emption) has the effect of transferring an equitable interest which prevails over another equitable right arising at a later date *e.g.* a charging order of an execution creditor or of the seller.

In practical terms it is desirable for a transferee or buyer of shares to ensure quick registration of himself by the company. Otherwise, he risks losing his priority to a subsequent transferee of the shares who obtains registration before him or where some earlier equity had been detected. The practice though is for directors to withhold registration where they have become aware of an adverse equitable claim.[87]

### (e) The company's lien

This is usually regulated by the company's articles,[88] which give the company a lien on the shares of a member who has not fully. paid for them. The lien covers the amount unpaid on the shares. A lien is regarded as an equitable charge. It is enforceable by the sale of the shares following nomination by the company of someone (usually a director) to execute the transfer. However, before the sale is effected notice should be given to the shareholder. Following the sale, any money left after satisfaction of the lien is paid to the shareholder.[89]

Where a shareholder has borrowed money using his shares as security, the lender will have priority over the company's lien irrespective of what the articles say. This will be so if the lender has given notice of his security before the company's lien arose.[90] The same principle is applicable where a shareholder is a trustee of the shares and notice of the lender's interest has been given to the company.[91] Where, however, notice of the lender's interest has not been given, the company's lien will prevail.[92]

---

81 *Black v. Homersham* (1878) EX.D.24; *Re Kidner* [1929] 2 Ch. 121

82 *Spencer v. Ashworth, Partington & Co.* [1925] 1 K.B. 589 C.A.

83 [1902] 1 Ch. 522

84 [1906] 1 Ch. 659

85 Admittedly such a notice was of no legal effect.

86 *Hawks v. McArthur* [1951] All ER 22

87 Orojo, *op.cit.* p. 218.

88 See e.g. Companies Act, Table A, Arts 11-14

89 *ibid*, Arts 12 and 13

90 *Bradford Banking Co. v. Briggs* (1886) 12 App. Cas. 29; H.L. overriding Companies Act, S. 119 and Table A, Art. 7.

91 *Mackereth v. Wigan Coal* [1916] 2 Ch. 393

92 *New London & Brazilian Bank v. Brocklebank* (1882) 21 Ch. D. 302

### (f) Forged transfers

These are null and void in that they do not affect the real owner. Consequently, a person who lodges a transfer for registration, impliedly warrants that it is genuine. If it is not, he is liable to indemnify the company from liability.[93]

### (g) Mortgage of shares

There are two types of mortgages - legal and equitable.

A legal mortgage is one where upon borrowing money, a borrower executes a transfer of his shares, by way of mortgage, to the lender. The transfer is registered with the registrar of companies and the company. The instrument of transfer indicates the terms of the mortgage and also provides for re-transfer when the loan has been repaid. The lender is entitled to payment of dividends on the shares and to vote at the company's general meetings. However, if the transfer restricts these rights, then he is not entitled to enjoy them.[94] Should the mortgagor default in repaying the loan, the mortgagee may sell the shares without recourse to the court, since he is legal owner thereof.

Legal mortgages of shares are rare and consequently use is made of equitable mortgages.[95] Normally the borrower deposits his share certificates with the lender as a security. If the borrower defaults, the lender can apply to the court for the sale of shares. The usual practice is for the borrower to deposit the relevant share certificate plus a blank transfer signed by him, with the lender. If the borrower defaults, the lender has an implied power to sell the shares. Thus, in *Ogunyemi v. John Holt Ltd*[96], A deposited a stock certificate accompanied by a blank transfer with the first defendant as security for payment in respect of a trading venture. Upon A's default in payment, the first defendant completed the blank transfer in favour of the second defendant. It was held that the first defendant (who was the mortgagee) had an implied power to fill in the blank transfer, thereby transferring the legal interest in the shares, the articles not having provided for a formal deed.

The equitable mortgage is, however, a tenuous security. Thus, in *Rainford v. James Keith & Blackman*,[97] the borrower was able to get a buyer of shares registered without producing a share-certificate, which had been deposited with the lender. As a result, the lender lost his rights because the buyer was a *bona fide* purchase for value without notice of the lender's rights. In such a situation, it is advisable for an equitable mortgagee of shares to serve a stop notice both at the registry of the companies and the company's registered office.[98]

Finally, a judgment creditor may obtain a charging order[99] on the debtor's shares by way of equitable execution. This has the effect of vesting in the creditor such title as the debtor had at the date of the order.[100] However, the court may, upon independent application[101] order a sale of the shares.[102] In *Bank of West Africa Ltd. & Ors v. Louis Fadoul*[103], an application was made for (i) an order against one of the respondends who held 30,500 GBP1 ordinary shares in Ferris George & Sons Ltd..., to hand over the share certificates he held in the company to the court's sheriff so that the shares could be sold in execution of the judgment obtained by the applicants; (ii) an order that the directors of Ferris George & Sons Ltd. accept the transfer of the shares to a purchaser and register them in the books of the company irrespective of regulation 6 of the

---

93 *Sheffield Corporation v. Barclay* [1905] A.C. 392

94 *Siemens Brothers & Co. Ltd. v. Burns* [1918] Ch. 324.

95 Gower, *op.cit.* p. 464

96 1971 (1) NCLR 115 (High Court of Lagos State)

97 [1905] 1 Ch. 296

98 See English Supreme Court Practice, Order 50, rr. 11-15 and Orojo, *op.cit* p.221

99 Under Rules of the English Supreme Court Order 50, r.2.

100 *Hawks v. McArthur* [1951] 1 All E.R. 22

101 *Kolchman v. Maurice* [1903] 1 KB 534 C.A.

102 It cannot though order foreclosure: *Daponte v. Schuber* [1939] Ch.958

103 1960 NRNLR 15

company's articles which gave other directors an absolute discretion as to the acceptance or rejection of any transfer. It was held that (i) physical possession of share certificates by the court sheriff is not necessary though desirable for purposes of execution; (ii) a private company may be regarded as public for purposes of the Judgments (Enforcement) Rules[104] which allow sale in execution of shares to any person and (iii) where the purchase of shares sold under execution has a remedy against the holder (as provided by the Judgments'(Enforcement Rules), the court will not grant any remedy (such as an order to directors to register shares) unless and until the purchaser had pursued the remedy open to him. The third holding was prompted by the court's realisation that under the rules,[105] the court had power, upon application of the buyer (and where the property in execution consisted of shares) to issue an order prohibiting the person in whose name the shares stood from transferring the shares to any person except the purchaser or receiving any dividend thereon and the manager, secretary or other company officer from permitting any such transfer or making any such payment to any person except the purchaser. The effect of this, in the court's estimation was to give the purchaser of shares sold in execution a remedy in the form of a court order and to make the shares valueless to the holder unless and until he accepts the purchase price and transfers the shares to the purchaser.

**(h) Transmission of shares**

This is a form of transfer of shares by operation of law arising either from the death or bankruptcy of the shareholder. Its implications have been considered earlier in this chapter.[106]

## Calls on shares

It is common for the articles to give the directors power to make calls on members regarding sums of money which remain unpaid on their shares.[107] Where the shares are issued on the understanding that 30 per cent of their value shall be paid upon application, 20 per cent on allotment and a further 20 per cent within a given period following allotment, a call will be made only in respect of the remaining 30 per cent of the sum unpaid on the shares. However, the articles may provide that sums payable on allotment or within a fixed period thereafter shall be deemed to be calls.[108] The debt due on calls is regarded as a specialty debt.[109]

The call must be made in accordance with the articles, otherwise it will be regarded as null and void. Although mere irregularities affecting the issue of the call will not nullify it[110], it is necessary for a resolution making the call to be passed[111], which must specify the amount of the call, to whom payable and the time and place of payment.[112] Similar to other situations, where they are exercising their powers, the directors must make the calls *bona fide* in the interest and for the benefit of the company as a whole. Thus, in *Alexander v. Automatic Telephone Co.*[113], a resolution was passed by the company's directors allotting shares to some of themselves on which nothing was to be paid on application and allotment. However, the other members were required to pay 3 shillings on each share upon application and allotment. It was held that the allotment to the directors was improper and an abuse of the directors' power. In this vein, Lindley M.R. stated that:[114]

---

[104] Under Order 50 rr. 2-10 British Rules of the Supreme Court, the distinction between public and private companies for purposes of charging shares is now irrelevant. See further Orojo, op. cit. pp. 221-222.

[105] Order 5 rule 1, made under Sherrifs & Civil Processes Act, Cap. 189 Laws of Nigeria, 1958

[106] See discussion under Titles, *Personal Representatives and Trustee In Bankruptcy*, supra notes 9 to 16 and text thereof.

[107] See e.g. Companies Act, Table A, Arts 15-21

[108] ibid, Table A, Art. 19.

[109] ibid S. 22(2)

[110] *Dawson v. African Consolidated Land and Trading Co.* (1898) 1 Ch. 6

[111] Table A, Art. 16

[112] *Re: Cawley & Co.* (1889) 42 Ch.D. 209 (C.A.) See too *Palmer's Company Law* (22nd Ed. 1976) pp. 369-374.

[113] [1900] 2 Ch. 56 C.A.

[114] *ibid*, pp. 66-67

> The court ... has always exacted from directors the observance of good faith towards their shareholders and towards those who take shares from the company and become co-adventurers with themselves and others who may join them. The maxim *Caveat emptor* has no application to such cases, and directors who so use their powers as to obtain benefits for themselves at the expense of the shareholders, without informing them of the fact, cannot retain those benefits and must account for them to the company, so that all the shareholders may participate in them.

The articles may also provide that interest be paid on calls which have not been paid.[115] Calls are required to be paid in cash. The directors may be empowered by the articles to accept calls in advance or to make calls so that there is a difference between the holders in the amount of calls to be paid or in times of payment.[116] A shareholder who is sued in respect of calls on shares and whose defence is based on mispresentation has to prove not only his prompt repudiation of the shares but also that he has taken steps to get his name removed from the register.[117]

## Share warrants

A company which is limited by shares may, if empowered by its articles issue share warrants respecting fully paid-up shares.[118] Share warrants are regarded as negotiable instruments.[119] Essentially the shareholder is handed, in the place of a share certificate, a document indicating that the bearer is entitled to the shares ordered in the warrant. Such bearer is entitled to all the rights of a shareholder, except where there is contrary provision in the articles. His name, will not, however, appear on the register of members. Instead an entry will be made on the register indicating the details relating to the issue of the warrant.[120] Dividends will normally be paid in the form of coupons or otherwise to the holder of the warrant. Shares which are included in a share-warrant are not regarded as qualification for a director in case of articles requiring the holding of qualification shares.[121]

## Conversion of shares into stock

Fully paid shares or any class of them may be converted into stock by the company if there is authority for doing so in its articles of association.[122] Conversion into stock has the effect of merging "into one fund of a nominal value equivalent to that of the total of the shares"[123] with the member instead of holding particular identified shares (e.g. 100 shares of shs 1/= each numbered 1 to 100) holding shs 100/= stock.

The theoretical advantage of this arrangement from a member's perspective is that the stock is easily divisible into fractions of any amount. However, in practice the articles invariably provide that the stock cannot be transferred in units which are less than a prescribed amount. This is to avoid inevitable administrative difficulties.[124]

From the company's point of view the existence of stock simplifies the duty of maintaining the register and issuing certificates. If the capital is divided into shares, the register would have to keep surveillance over each share identifiable by a separate number,[125] this leading to

---

115 e.g. Table A, Art. 18

116 *ibid*, Arts 20 and 21

117 *First National Re-Insurance Co. v. Greenfield* [1921] 2 KB 260

118 Companies Act, S.85

119 *Bechuanaland Exploration Co. v. London Trading Bank Ltd.* [1898] 2 QB 658; *Webb, Hale & Co. v. Alexandria Water Co.* (1905) 21 T.L.R. 572

120 Companies Act, S. 114

121 *ibid*, S. 183(2)

122 *ibid* S 63(c) Table A, Art 40

123 Gower, *op. cit.* p. 433

124 *ibid*

125 Companies Act, S. 76

considerable untidiness. On the other hand, upon conversion into stock the difficulty is removed in that the register merely shows the amount of stock which is held by each member. Nevertheless, in view of provision in the Companies Act[126] that if all the issued shares of a class are fully paid, none of those shares need have a distinguishing number so long as it remains fully paid and ranks *paripassu* for all purposes with all the shares of that class, it becomes difficult to fathom the practical advantage achieved by conversion into stock.[127] Consequently, the Jenkins Committee suggested an amendment to the equivalent section under the British Companies Act[128] to forestall the problem which could arise if a new issue of shares is not to rank for the next dividend but is in every other way *pari passu* with the existing unnumbered shares.[129] Given that section 76 of the Companies Act is in *pari materia* with section 74 of the British Act, this is a recommendation worth considering in the Ugandan context for purposes of reform of the existing law.

The purported advantage of converting shares into stock is also questionable on the basis that it does not change the relationship between the holder thereof and the company in that he remains a member and the nature of his interest in the company is unaltered since under the Companies Act "share" includes "stock".[130] As a result the Jenkins Committee in appreciating that the whole distinction between shares and stock has become confusing recommended that the term stock should be abolished.[131]

## The register of members

Every company is under a duty to maintain a register of members[132]in which is entered their names, addresses and descriptions. The register has to be kept at the registered office of the company. However, if the maintenance of the register is done at another office of the company (other than the registered office), or is done on behalf of the company by some other person, it may be kept where the work is done[133], provided that this not outside Uganda. In addition, a company should give to the Registrar of Companies notice of where the register is kept except where this is done at its registered office.[134]

Companies with share capital are also required to show in the register the number of shares held by each member and the amounts paid or agreed to be treated as paid on those shares. The date at which each member was entered in the register and the date he ceased to be a member must also be included. In the event of shares having been converted into stock, the register should indicate the amount of stock held by each member. Where the number of members is more than fifty and the register is not arranged alphabetically, the company must keep an index.[135] The register, index and any unregistered transfers must be made available for inspection by any person including non-members.[136]

Upon the issue of share warrants, the company is required to strike out the name of the member to whom the warrant is issued and enter details of the warrant in the register.[137] The

---

126 *ibid* S. 76 *proviso*

127 Gower, *op. cit.* pp. 433-43

128 Companies Act,1948 S.74

129 *Report of the Company Law Committee Cmnd* 1749 para 473 (1962)

130 S.2

131 supra n. 129, para 472

132 Companies Act, S. 112; see also Leigh, *op.cit.* pp. 301-3

133 *ibid*, S. 112 (2)

134 *ibid.*, S. 112 (3). See further Orojo, *op. cit.* p.177

135 Companies Act, S. 113

136 *ibid.*, S. 115

137 *ibid.*, S. 114

bearer of a share warrant may, subject to provision in the articles, be entered on the register upon surrendering the warrant for cancellation. The holder of a share warrant is entitled, subject to the Act and the articles, to the ordinary rights and privileges of membership.[138]

The court has power under the Companies Act,[139] to rectify the register of members, upon application by an aggrieved person or any member of the company if:

(i) the name of any person is, without sufficient cause, entered in or omitted from the register; or

(ii) default is made or unnecessary delay takes place in entering on the register the fact that a person has ceased to be a member.

The above grounds are not conclusive and the court has power to order rectification in other circumstances.[140] The court may intervene in all cases where a name is on the register "without sufficient cause".[141] Thus, in *Re: Imperial Chemical Industries Ltd.*[142], the registered holder of shares executed a transfer in favour of another person who was duly registered. The transferor then applied to court for the transferee to be struck off and the register rectified on the ground that the transfer was obtained by deception. It was held that rectification was proper in the circumstances. The court may also refuse rectification or order rectification together with the payment of damages to the injured party. Additionally, the court can determine issues relating to the title to shares and other matters which are incidental to rectification. Rectification is possible with regard to some part of a member's shareholding. In a case where shares have not been validly issued, rectification does not necessarily involve a reduction of capital.[143] In *Re Zone Company Ltd.*[144], an applicant asked for his name to be removed from the register of members of Zone Company Ltd. on the ground that his application for shares in the company was not accepted before he withdrew it. It was held that consequent upon the withdrawal of the application before its acceptance, there was no contract for the allotment of shares and the resulting allotment of shares to him was null and void. In the result, no shares were allotted to the applicant and his name should be removed from the register.

In *Busoga Millers & Industries Ltd. v. Patel*[145], it was held that a court cannot order the name of a *bonafide* purchaser of shares to be removed from the company's register without its being made party to the proceedings. On the facts no ground for rectification was disclosed and the lower court should not have ordered rectification.

If an allottee has been induced to take shares through fraudulent statements or misrepresentations contained in a prospectus, he should rescind the contract before commencement of the company's winding-up. Otherwise, he loses his right to rectification. Rescission must be accompanied by rectification of the register.[146]

It is also provided that[147] no notice of any trust, expressed, implied or constructive, shall be entered on the register or be receivable by the registrar of companies. Consequently, a company is not liable if it sells shares in breach of a trust of which it has notice, unless a stop notice had previously been filed with it. Thus, in *Simpson v. Molson's Bank*[148], the bank registered a

---

[138] Leigh. *op. cit.* p. 301

[139] S. 118 See also *Metal Construction (W.A.) Ltd. V.D.A. Migliore* (1977) 6-9 S.C. 163; *Mawogola Farmers & Growers Ltd. v. Kayanja* [1971] EA 272

[140] *Burns v. Siemen Bros. Dynamo Works* [1919] 1 Ch 225

[141] Leigh, *op. cit.* p. 302

[142] [1936] 2 All E.R. 463

[143] In *Re: Transatlantic Life Assurance Co. Ltd.* [1980] 1 WLR 79

[144] (1962) L.L.R. 160. See also Ayua, *Nigerian Company Law* (1984) p. 104

[145] (1955) 22 EACA 348

[146] *Oakes v. Turquand and Harding* (1867) L.R. 2H. L. 325 c.f. *Re: Sussex Brick. [1904] 1 Ch. 598 where rectification for delay was permitted even thought the company was being wound up.*

[147] Companies Act, S 119 Table A, Art. 7.

[148] [1895] A.C. 270 P.C. See also Leigh, *op.cit.* p. 303

transfer of its shares, executed by trustees and executors to one of the residuary legatees, in breach of the provisions of the will. The bank possessed a copy of the will and its president was an executor under the will. The legatee, thereafter disposed of the shares to a third party. The issues arose as to whether the bank had notice of the trust and if so whether it should have declined to register the transfer. The statute setting up the bank had a provision in it similar to section 119 of the Companies Act. It was held that although the bank had notice of the trust, it was not bound by it. The transfer was, therefore, valid.

To deal with that result, there has been suggestion that directors who permit a shareholder to transfer shares in breach of trust of which they have actual notice are personally liable to the beneficiary.[149] However, this has been criticised on the ground that it detracts from the principle of finality which attaches to the register.[150] Furthermore, such liability cannot be imposed except where the directors are fraudulent in relation to the trust.[151]

It is evident that the aim of section 119 is to ensure smooth transfers since the company and the transferee are not obliged to inquire whether the transfer is in breach of trust. Nevertheless, to be able to affect the register with a non-registrable equitable interest, the claimant may file and serve on the company a document known as a stop notice.[152] Such a notice will prevent the company from allowing the shares to be transferred by the registered holder without first giving notice to the claimant.[153]

Finally, the register is regarded as *prima facie* evidence of the matters registered thereon.[154] Consequently, this does not prevent the production of evidence to disprove the statements contained therein.[155] Additionally, the company has power to close the register for a period not exceeding 30 days in a year, provided that due notice is given of the fact to the public (usually through newspaper and media advertisements).[156]

## Annual return

Every company must deliver an annual return to the registrar of companies within 42 days after the holding of an annual general meeting. Where the company has a share capital, the return should contain matters which are specified in schedule 5 to the Companies Act and should also comply with the form indicated in part II of that schedule. However, if the company is without share capital, the return must be in the form indicated in section 126 to the Act.[157] Essentially, details relating to members and their shareholding must be supplied.[158]

---

149 *Societe Generale de Paris v. Tramways Union* Co. (1884), 14 Q.B.D. 424 C.A. per Cotton, L.J.
150 Leigh, *op.cit.* p. 303
151 *supra* n. 149, pp. 453-454 per Lindley L.J.
152 Under Rules of Supreme Court 1965 0.50 rr. 11-14 (Britain).
153 *Societe Generale de Paris v. Tramways Union Co. supra* n. 149
154 Companies Act, S. 120
155 *Re British Medical and General Life Association* (1888) 39Ch.D.61
156 Companies Act, S. 117
157 *ibid.* Ss. 126, 127
158 *ibid* Ss. 125-126

# 9
# CAPITAL

The use of the term capital varies in its legal, economic and accounting contexts.[1] However, expressed simply, it refers to property which has been invested into a business. The property may be tangible (patents, copyrights, trade secrets or the goodwill and business connections of the existing going concern.) Monetary value is normally place on such property in order to facilitate the preparation of accounts and to allow the proprietor to be able to estimate what return he is getting out of his investment. In the normal business sense, "capital" refers to the networth of the business viz. "the amount by which the value of the assets exceeds the liabilities."[2] This conception is especially relevant for sole and partnership business undertakings.

With a limited liability company, the "usual" conception of "capital" is inappropriate. Consequently, the law has formulated principles relating to the raising and maintenance of a limited liability company's capital.[3] In the words of Professor Gower:[4]

> In effect, capital has ceased to be a name given to the fluctuating net worth of the business and has become a rigid yardstick fixing the minimum value of the net assets which must be raised initially and then, so far as possible, retained in the business.

The requirement of minimum capital and retention thereof by the company is aimed at protecting its creditors and shareholders. In this regard the concept of maintenance of a company's capital is comparable to the doctrine of *ultra vires*.

## Types of share capital

### Nominal capital

This is the amount with which a limited liability company is registered. At registration a company limited by shares or guarantee and with a share capital is required to state the nominal capital, which is divisible into shares of a fixed amount in the memorandum of association.[5] The amount remains constant until it is increased or reduced pursuant to the Companies Act[6]

### Issued capital

This is a portion of the nominal capital, which has been issued out to the shareholders. It may be the whole nominal capital. However, usually only a part is issued, leaving the company to issue further shares normally at a premium.

### Paid up capital

This is the amount which has been issued by the company and actually paid for by the shareholders. For instance if the issued capital is worth shs. 10,000.00 and shs. 50/= has been paid up capital will be shs. 5,000.00, leaving uncalled capital of shs. 5,000.00. The company

---

1 Gower, *op.cit.* p. 214
2 *ibid*.p. 215
3 These have no application to an unlimited company. They only apply to companies limited by *shares:* Gower, *ibid.*, p. 216
4 *ibid*
5 Companies Act, S.5
6 See *infra*.

may later resolve to make a call of shs.50/= on each share. Uncalled capital will not be regarded as an asset of the company until the company has actually made a call,[7] although apparently the company may mortgage it.[8]

### Reserve capital

A company may, by special resolution decide that any part of its share capital which has not been called up shall not be called up except in the event of its winding up.[9] Such capital is known as reserve capital and as such it cannot be mortgaged. It is distinguishable from (i) capital reserve which constitutes the share premium account[10] and the capital redemption reserve fund.[11]

## Classes of share capital

Shares may be issued with special rights relating to payment of dividend, voting, return of capital or otherwise as the company may by ordinary resolution decide.[12] Provision in relation thereto is usually made in the terms of issue of the shares, the articles or memorandum of association.[13] However, it is normal to divide shares into three main classes viz; ordinary, founders (deferred) and preference shares.

### Ordinary shares

Ordinary shares comprise the residuary class of shares "in which is vested everything after the special rights of other classes, if any, have been satisfied."[14] They do not have special rights or restrictions attaching to them. Consequently, they bear the main financial risk of the business in the event of the company failing, and the greatest reward, if it is successful. Furthermore, upon the company's winding up, after paying all the liabilities of the company and returning the capital of other classes, ordinary shares are entitled to all the surplus assets save where preference shares have the right to participate in the distribution of such assets.[15]

### Founder's or deferred shares

These shares are entitled to a fixed dividend relative to the profits available to the company following the declaration of dividends on the preference and ordinary shares. Provision is usually made in the articles to the effect that profits which remain un-distributed after the preferential and ordinary shares have received dividends at fixed rates shall be divided among the ordinary and deferred shareholders.

These shares are normally held by the promoters and directors of the company or vendors who have sold their business to the company. Consequently, such people have a direct interest in the success of the company. It follows that the greater the profits the company makes the higher their entitlement to dividends will be. In addition, since special rights are given to these shares, their particulars are required to be stated in the prospectus.[16]

---

7 *Page v. International Agency and Industrial Trust Ltd.* (1893) 62 L.J. Ch. 610
8 *Re Pyle Works* (1890), 44 Ch. D. 534
9 Companies Act, S. 62
10 See Companies ACt, S.58 Table A, Art 117
11 *ibid.*, S. 60
12 See e.g Table A, 1st Schedule to Companies Act, Art 2; *Andrews v. Gas Meter Co. [1897]* 1 Ch.36 C.A.
13 See also *Campbell v. Rofe* [1933] A.C. 91, 98 P.C.
14 Gower, *op. cit.* p. 423
15 Orojo, *op.cit.* p. 185
16 Companies Act, Schedule 3 para 1 and S. 40

## Preference shares

Although lacking precise legal meaning the expression "preference share" refers to the rights of preference shareholders as determined by the memorandum and articles of association as well as the terms of the issue. Additionally though varying in character the main identifying features of preference shares are that they confer on the holders some preference over other classes in respect either of dividend or of repayment of capital or both.[17] This characteristic places them in a similar class with debentures in the capacity of "prior charges" in respect of the company's assets. It is possible, though for preference shares to participate together with the other shares following satisfaction of their preferential rights. There may, for instance, be provision that preference shares confer the right to preferential dividend of 6 per cent and the right to participate with other shareholders in any dividends after the latter have in turn received 6 per cent. Alternatively or additionally, it may be provided that the capital paid up on the shares shall be repaid in preference to others and that they shall also participate in the surplus assets after the others have received back their paid-up capital. In such a case the shares are described as participating preference (or preferred ordinary) shares possessing all the advantages of usual prior charges and some or all of the advantages of equities.

With regard to preferential rights as to dividend, preference shares rank in priority over ordinary shares in payment of dividend. This will, however, only be possible if (i) there is profit which can be distributed and (ii) there is declaration of dividend by the directors in accordance with the articles.

Preference shares may also be entitled to cumulative dividend i.e. if no dividend has been declared in one year, such shares will be entitled to arrears the following year and will, in that respect have priority over ordinary shares. However, if it is provided that shares are non-cumulative, then if no dividend is declared in one year, it cannot be carried over to the following year. A cumulative preferential dividend may also be paid upon the company's winding up as an arrear especially where it has not been declared and therefore carried over.[18] The arrears are invariably paid out of the company's assets after payment of all the company's liabilities.

The issue may arise as to whether preferential shareholders are entitled to share in the distribution of surplus assets after all the debts have been paid and all capital has been returned to shareholders.[19] This will depend on the interpretation of the termsof issue. In *Birch v. Cropper*[20], it was established[21] that where the terms of issue make no express distinction between the rights of different categories of shareholders in respect of (i) dividend, (ii) the return of capital (and participation in "surplus assets," in a winding-up, or (iii) yoting, the rule of construction in each case is that *prima facie*, all shareholders rank equally. The mere fact that a preference in respect of any one of these matters is conferred does not imply any right to preference in some other respect and the presumption of equality remains undisturbed. However, if the terms of issue actually make express provision as to the rights of a class of shareholders in respect of (i) dividend, (ii) the return of capital (and participation in "surplus assets") or (iii) voting, then that provision is exhaustive of the rights of the class in that particular respect.[22] This approach was dissented from in *Re: William Metcalf & Sons Ltd.*[23] which held that the principle of construction in *Will's* case[22] did not apply to capital rights. *Re: William Metcalfe Ltd*[23] was overruled by *Scottish Insurance Corporation v. Wilsons & Clyde Coal Co.*[24] which maintained that no such distinction existed.

---

17 Gower, *op.cit* p. 412; *Suerre Hang v. Buhemba Mines Ltd* (1935) 20 EACA 28

18 For a useful discussion of difficulties attendant to this procedure see Gower, *ibid.*, pp. 419-421. See also Leigh, *op.cit.*, pp. 286-288

19 Leigh, *ibid.*, p. 289

20 (1889) 14 App Cas 525 H.L.

21 See also L. Sealy, *Cases and Materials in Company Law* (2nd Ed. 1978) p. 273

22 *Will v. United Linkat Plantations Ltd.* [1914] A.C. 11 H.L.; *Re National Telephone Co.* [1914] 1 Ch. 755 Ch. D.

23 [1933] Ch. 142

24 [1949] A.C. 462; [1949] 1 All E.R. 1068 H.L.

The existing position can be gathered from the statement by Wynn-Parry J. in *Re Isle Thanet Electric Co.*,[25] thus:

> First, that, in construing an article which deals with rights to share in profits, that is dividend rights, and rights to share in the company's property in a liquidation, the same principle is applicable and second, that the principle is that where the article sets out the rights attached to a class of shares to participate in profits while the company is a going concern or to share in the property of the company in a liquidation, prima facie, the rights so set out are in each case exhaustive.

This formula does not though cater for all situations which may arise. Thus, in *ReBridgewater Navigation Co*[26], the surplus assets upon winding up represented ploughed back profits of previous years which could have been distributed by way of dividend to the ordinary shareholders but which instead were placed on reserve. The issue arose as to whether these were to be regarded as belonging to the ordinary shareholders and therefore belonging to them alone. The Court of Appeal answered the issue in the affirmative. However, that case was distinguished in *Dimbula Valley (Ceylon) Tea Co. Ltd v. Laurie*[27] on the ground that while there provision was made for the undistributed profits to "belong" to the ordinary shareholders, in this case provision was simply made for such profits to be "divisible" among such shareholders. Essentially, the *Dimbula Valley Tea* case indicates that where the articles of a company clearly create a right for preference shareholders to share rateably in the surplus assets with ordinary shares after prior repayment of capital and dividend, preference shareholders are entitled to share in the surplus.[28] Nevertheless, should the articles give preference shareholders the right to prior repayment of capital and accumulated dividends, then the preference shareholders are not entitled to an additional right to participate in the surplus assets.[29]

The effect of decisions, like *Scottish Insurance Corporation and Prudential Assurance*[30], have been to render preference shares a "less secure form of investment" [31] than had hitherto been thought. In the words of Professor Leigh, Joffe and Goldberg:[32]

> The effect of these decisions is to place the holders of preference shares, and especially redeemable preference shares, in very much the same position as debentureholders. If a preference shareholder has no voting rights in general meetings and is entitled under the terms of issue only to a fixed cumulative dividend and to repayment of capital in a winding-up, he is to all intents and purposes a debentureholder. An important difference, and that to the disadvantage of the preference shareholder is that, having loaned monies to the company, debentureholders are paid off before any shareholder receives any payment, whether in respect of arrears of dividend or of capital.

Ever since those decisions, the practice has grown up in Britain of expressly stipulating in the terms of new preference issues by companies whose shares are quoted on the stock exchange that in the event of a return of capital the amount to be repaid should be geared to the market

---

25 [1950] Ch. 161, p.171 C.A. applying the *Scottish Insurance Corporation* case, *ibid.* See also *Prudential Assurance v. Chatterley - Whitfield Collieries* [1949] A.C. 512 H.L.

26 [1891] 2 Ch. 317 C.A.

27 (1961) Ch. 353. See also Rice (1961) 24 *Mod. L.R.* 525

28 See also Leigh, *op. cit.* pp. 290-291

29 Re *Saltdean Estate Co. Ltd.* [1968] 3 All E.R. 829

30 See *supra* n. 25

31 Sealy, *op. cit.*, p. 380

32 Leigh, *op. cit.*, p. 291; See also Gower, *op.cit.* pp. 417-419 and further M.A. Pickering, "The Problem of the Preference Share" (1963) 26 *Mod. L.R.* 499

quotation at the time.[33] This assumes though that shareholders are not prejudiced if they receive payment for their shares, which is equivalent to the open market rate then prevailing. In *Re: William Jones & Sons Ltd.*[34], the court allowed repayment of capital on preference shares, which were entitled to participate on winding-up to a stipulated amount, on the ground that they were not less than par. By being repaid at par the preference shareholders got more than they would have obtained on a sale at that time. In the absence, moreover of any objection the court decided that the reduction was fair in the circumstances. The case thus undermines the assumption which may also be mis-conceived when in practice the preference shareholders may be un-willing to sell their shares at the prevailing market rate.

### Redeemable preference shares[35]

These are preference shares which may be bought out by the company in exception to the general rule relating to the maintenance of a company's capital that a company must not buy its own shares.[36] However, there are certain conditions attached to a company's redemption of its shares viz.[37] (i) the shares must be fully paid up; (ii) the redemption must be out of the company's profits or fresh issue of shares done for purposes of redemption; (iii) if a premium is payable on the shares, it should, before redemption be provided for out of the profits of the company or the company's share premium account[38]; (iv) where redemption is made out of profits, a sum equal to the nominal amount of shares redeemed, must be transferred out of the profits which would otherwise be available for dividend to a fund known as the capital redemption reserve fund.

In *Suerre Kang & Others v. Buhemba Mines Ltd.*[39], it was held that the power to issue preference shares in place of redeemed preference shares as though the latter "had never been issued" is expressly conferred by the Companies Law so long as the terms on which they are issued are justified by the company's articles.

## Variation of class rights

It has already been indicated that shares may be issued with certain rights.[40] The issues to be considered here are the circumstances and mode by which such rights may be altered.

Where the class rights are defined in the company's memorandum of association, they can only be varied if the memorandum provides a method of alteration. Alternatively, provision for variation may be made in the articles provided such articles are mentioned.

Where a variation procedure is stipulated in the memorandum or articles, it requires the consent of a specified proportion of the class or the consent of a class meeting. Then where the rights are varied in line with that procedure, the holders of not less than 15 per cent of the shares of that class, who did not support the resolution for variation, may apply to the court within thirty days of the consent or sanction for the variation to be cancelled. Where such application has been lodged, the variation will be ineffective unless and until it is confirmed by the court.[41] Variation is also possible under a scheme of arrangement or reconstruction.[42]

---

33 Gower, *ibid.*, Sealy, *supra* n. 31
34 (1969) 1 W.L.R. 146
35 The position in Britain is considerably modified by the Companies Act, 1981. See Leigh, *op. cit.* pp. 291-295
36 *Trevor v. Whitworth* (1887) 12 App. Cas. 409 H.L
37 Companies Act, S.60
38 *ibid.*, S. 58. See also *supra* chap. 8 under *Issue of Shares at a Premium*
39 (1935) 20 EACA 28
40 *supra* n. 12 and text thereof
41 Companies Act, S. 74
42 *ibid.*, S. 207

The normal practice though, is for class rights to be set out in the articles of association. Nevertheless, the authority to modify such rights may be either in the memorandum or the articles. The model articles allow for variation of class rights to be effected with 75 per cent written consent of the class members or by extra-ordinary resolution at a meeting of the class.[43] The consent of the relevant class of shareholders must be *bona fide* and should not be motivated by any influence or other interests. Thus, in *Re: Holders Investment Trust Ltd.*[44], the company petitioned for confirmation of a reduction of capital, under which it was proposed to cancel its redeemable preference shares and to allot to the holders an equivalent amount of unsecured stock. The reduction was sanctioned by a special resolution of the company and an extra-ordinary resolution of a separate class meeting of the preference shareholders. At the latter meeting, 90 per cent of the votes cast were held by certain trustees who also held 52 per cent of the ordinary stock and shares, and in that respect stood to gain substantially from the reduction. It was held by the court that the vote at the class meeting was ineffectual since the majority preference shareholders had considered their own interests, without regard to what was best for the preference share-holders as a class.

Where the variation of rights is impeachable on grounds of *bona fide*, section 74 of the Companies Act is still applicable in allowing the stipulated percentage of shareholders of that class to petition the court for cancellation of the variation.

A further question relates to what constitutes "variation". Judicial opinion appears to have taken a very technical view of what "variation" or "effected" connotes in the context of alteration of class rights. It has, for instance ,been suggested that variation of enjoyment or rights is not synonymous with "variation". Thus, in *White v. Bristol Aeroplane Co.*[45], new preference shares were issued to ordinary shareholders. This resulted into loss of voting control for the preference shareholders. It was held that the proposal was permissible since the rights attaching to the shares themselves (as distinguished from the enjoyment or the effectiveness of those rights) were not "affected" by the proposal.

The model articles also indicate[46] that the creation or issue of additional shares of equal rank with the existing ones is not variation of class rights. Finally, in *Re: Mackenzie*[47], it was postulated that a reduction of capital or dividend was only a variation of enjoyment and not variation of class rights.

## Alteration of share capital

Authority for the alteration of a company's capital other than reduction is governed by section 63 of the Companies Act,[48] as follows by: (i) increasing its share capital by new shares of such amount as it thinks expedient; (ii) consolidating and dividing all of or any of its share capital into shares of larger amount than its existing shares; (iii) converting all or any of its paid-up shares into stock and reconverting that stock into paid-up share of any denomination (iv) subdividing its shares, or any of them, into shares of smaller amount than is fixed by the memorandum; (v) cancelling the shares which, at the date of passing the resolution, have not been taken or agreed to be taken by any person, and diminish the amount of its share capital by the

---

43 Table A, Art. 4

44 [1971] 1 W.L.R. 583 [1971] 2 All E.R. 289. See also Sealy, *op.cit.* p. 338. See too *Re: Hellenic and General Trust* [1975] 2 All E.R. 382; *British America Nickel Corporation Ltd. v. O'Brien* [1927] A.C. 269 P.C.; *Carruth v. Imperial Chemical Industries Ltd.* [1937] 2 All E.R. 422 H.L

45 [1953] Ch. 65 [1953] 1 All E.R. 40 C.A.

46 Table A, Art 5. See also *Greenhalgh v. Ardene Cinemas* [1946] 1 All E.R. 512

47 [1916] 2 Ch. 450

48 See also Table A, Arts. 40, 44-46

amount of the shares so cancelled. Such cancellation is not deemed to be a reduction of share capital within the meaning of the Act.

The powers can only be exercised by the company in general meeting by means of an ordinary resolution except where the articles indicate a special or an extraordinary resolution. Every copy of the memorandum which is issued after the date of the resolution must include it.[49]

Where the articles do not provide for the power of alteration, they should first be altered by special resolution in order to provide for that power. This can be done at the same meeting as one where the resolution for the alteration is to be made.[50]

After the passing of the resolution for alteration, the company should, within fifteen days thereof, give notice to the Registrar of Companies of the alteration,[51] and a copy of the resolution authorising the increase.[52]

## Reduction of capital

By Section 68 of the Companies Act, the procedure for reduction of a company's capital is enumerated. It is notable that a company has no power to reduce its capital except in accordance with the Act.[53]This is necessary in order to ensure that creditors have reliable fund for satisfying their claims by preventing undue depletion thereof by the company. Furthermore, there is need to guarantee justice and fair play between the various classes of shareholders.[54]

Under Section 68, the reduction of capital must be authorised by the company's articles.[55] If there is no such authority, the company must then pass a resolution authorising reduction. The company is then required to petition the court for confirmation of the reduction. Although the section creates a general power of reduction, it mentions three specific instances of reduction namely: (i) extinction or reduction of liability on any of its shares in respect of share capital which is not yet paid up; (ii) with or without extinguishing or reducing liability on any of is shares, cancelling any paid-up share capital which is lost or is unrepresented by available assets; (iii) with or without extinguishing liability on any of its shares, paying off any paid-up share capital which is in excess of the needs of the company.

The court will sanction the reduction, unless it considers the proposed reduction to be unfair in the interests of creditors, shareholders and the public. In that regard, the court considers the investing public and the fairness of the reduction as between different classes of shareholders. Concerning the latter aspect, the court would estimate what would happen to the capital in the event of the company being wound-up, that is who would bear the loss and who is bearing the loss under the proposed reduction.[56]

Those who oppose the reduction must show that it is unfair in relation to the modification of their rights[57]. Additionally, the reduction should conform with modification of rights clauses in the articles. Where there is any surplus capital it should be returned to those who are entitled to priority in a winding up. In *Scottish Insurance Corporation Ltd. v. Wilsons & Clyde Coal Co. Ltd.*[58], the company's business was nationalised with the result that it could no longer earn profits.

---

49 Companies Act, S. 27

50 *Campbell's case* (1873) L.R. 9 Ch. App. 1

51 Companies Act, S. 65

52 See further Orojo, *op. cit.*, pp. 194-197 for a more detailed practical exposition

53 Companies Act, S.68

54 *Trevor v. Whitworth* (1887) 12App. Cas. 409. p.423 per Lord Watson

55 See e.g. Table A, Art. 46

56 See e.g. *Re: Mackenzie, supra* n.45 and text thereof.

57 *Re: Holders Investment Trusts Ltd., supra* n.44 and text thereof; *Carruth v. I.C.I.* [1937] A.C. 707, [1937] 2 All E.R. 422

58 [1949] A.C. 462 H.L. (S), Sealy, *op.cit.*, p.330

It proposed to pay off the preference capital in anticipation of liquidation. This was opposed in part because it was believed that this would deprive preference shareholders of a right to participate in "surplus assets" in a liquidation. It was held that[59] the proposal for reduction was fair and it was unnecessary for the court to intervene. Furthermore, that the preference shareholders had in any case no right to participate in "surplus assets" in a liquidation. In *Re: Chatterley - Whitfield Collieries Ltd.*,[60] Lord Greene M.R. thus stated:[61]

> It is a clearly recognised principle that the court, in confirming a reduction by the payment off of capital surplus to a company's needs, will allow, or rather require, that the reduction shall be effected in the first instance by payment off of capital which is entitled to priority in a winding-up. Apart from special cases where by agreement between classes the incidence of reduction is arranged in a different manner, this is and has for years been the normal and recognised practice of the courts, accepted by the courts and by businessmen as the fair and equitable method of carrying out a reduction by payment off of surplus capital. I know of no case where this method has, apart from agreement, been departed from ...

Furthermore, in *Re: Saltdean Estate Co. Ltd.*[62] the company's preferred shareholders were entitled to participate in the "balance of profits" in each year after a 10 per cent preferred dividend and an equivalent sum in dividends on the ordinary shares had been paid; but in a winding-up they had no right to participate in surplus capital. The ordinary shareholders possessed voting control. The court was petitioned to confirm a reduction of capital which was to be effected by paying off the preferred shares at 15s per 10s. share. The reduction was approved by the court which indicated that there was no "variation" of the preferred shareholders' rights which required approval by a separate class meeting. Buckley J. further added:[63]

> The fact is that every holder of preferred shares of the company has always been at risk that his hope of participating in undrawn or future profits of the company might be frustrated at any time by a liquidation of the company or a reduction of its capital properly resolved upon by sufficient majority of his fellow members. This vulnerability is, and always has been, a characteristic of the preferred shares. Now that the event has occurred, none of the preferred shareholders can in my judgment, assert that the resulting state of affairs is unfair to him.

## Creditors objection to reduction

The company's creditors may object to the reduction if it involves (i) diminution of liability in respect of unpaid share capital; (ii) payment to any shareholder of any unpaid up capital and (iii) any other case as may be directed by the court.[64]

With respect to the procedure for objection, the court will upon lodgement of objection settle a list of creditors and ascertain their names and the nature and amount of the claims.[65]

The court may, however, dispense with the list in certain special circumstances such as where the company is in a very strong financial position and no creditor who is entitled to object is prejudiced[66] or where the company intends to write off capital not lost or unrepresented by

59 Lord President Cooper (dissenting) in the Court Session (Scotland)
60 [1948] 2 All E.R. 593 C.A. affirmed [1949] 1 All E.R. 1094 H.L.;
61 *ibid* p. Sealy, *op. cit.* p. 335
62 [1968] 3 All E.R. (Ch.D.) Sealy, *ibid.*, p. 336
63 *ibid.*, p. ; Sealy *op.cit.*, p. 337. See also *Re: William Jones & Sons Ltd.* [1969] 1 All E.R. 913
64 Companies Act, S. 69
65 *ibid.*, S. 69 (1)
66 *Re: Lucania Temperature Billiards Hall (London) Ltd* [1966] Ch. 98
67 Companies Act, S. 70

available assets. The court may confirm the reduction after being satisfied that the creditors have consented or adequate provision has been made to discharge or secure their debts or claims.[67] The order of reduction must be filed with the registrar of companies showing the particulars of capital alteration. The registrar then registers them and issues a certificate of registration of the particulars substituting the relevant part of the memorandum of association.[68]

It is notable that when the court is considering whether or not to sanction a reduction, it is not concerned with broad questions of whether the reduction is in the public interest. Thus in *Re: Westburn Sugar Refineries, Ltd.*[69], the purpose of reduction was to place some of the company's assets outside the reach of nationalisation and to avoid profits tax. It was held that provided that the reduction was not objectionable as being prejudicial to creditors or shareholders, it would not refuse to confirm it in the light of wider considerations of public policy.

Following the reduction of capital, the liability of members in respect of reduced shares is limited to the difference, if any, between the amount of the share as fixed by the minute and the amount paid, or the reduced amount deemed to have been paid on the share.[70] If, however, the company cannot pay the claim of any creditor who is entitled to object but who has not done so out of ignorance of the proceedings for reduction or of their nature and effect and who was not entered on the list of creditors, every member at the date of registration of the order for reduction will remain liable to contribute to the assets of the company as though the company had been wound up on the day before the date of registration of the court order[71].

## Forfeiture and surrender of shares[72]

Forfeiture and surrender of shares are effectually reductions of capital without the court's consent although the shares can be reissued.

The directors have power to forfeit the shares of members if so authorised by the articles.[73] The power is only exercisable in respect of non-payment of a call or an instalment. In any other event the forfeiture will be a reduction of capital contrary to the Companies Act[73a].

Upon the forfeiture of shares, they may be sold or otherwise disposed of in a manner decided upon by the directors. Before such disposition, though, the forfeiture may be cancelled[74] with the consent of the holder thereof.[75] The power of forfeiture is fiduciary and should, therefore, be exercised in the interest of the company.[76]

Forfeiture effectively vests the ownership of the shares into the company which may sell or reissue them.[77] The buyer thereof, if any, becomes liable for future calls[78], while the forfeiting shareholder ceases to be a member in respect of the forfeited shares. However, he remains liable in respect of liabilities on such shares which were incurred before the date of forfeiture[79].

Essentially, forfeiture is in nature a penalty. Consequently, the provisions in the articles relating to it must be strictly observed. If not, the purported forfeiture will be void.[80]

---

[68] *ibid;* S. 71

[69] [1951] A.C. 625; [1951] 1 All E.R. 881; Gower [1951] 14 M.L.R. 330

[70] Companies Act, S. 72(1)

[71] S. 72(1)(a)(b)

[72] See generall Act, 1980. See Leigh, *op.cit.*, pp. 330-331.

[73] E.g. Table A Arts 33-39.

[73a] S.68; See also also *Martin v. Ogunsanya* 1962(2) A.L.R.Comm.393

[74] Table A Art. 36

[75] Larkworth's Case [1903] 1 Ch. 711

[76] *Re: Esparto's Trading Co.* (1879) 12 Ch. D. 191

[77] Table A Art. 36

[78] *New Baliks Festeling Ltd. v. Randt Gold Mining Co.* [1904] A.C. 165

[79] Table A. Art. 37

[80] *Johnson v. Lythleson Iron Agency* (1877) 5 Ch. D. 687; *Garden Gully Mining Co. V. Melister* (1875) 1 App. Cas.39

With regard to the surrender of shares, the company's articles may empower directors to accept a surrender of shares in situations where a forfeiture is proper. A surrender is permissible if its aim is to avoid forfeiture procedure,[81] or where the surrender of fully paid shares is being accepted in return for new shares of the same nominal value[82] Partly paid shares which are not liable to forfeiture cannot be surrendered as this has the effect of exonerating the shareholder from further liability on the shares and also amount to the purchase by the company of its own shares thereby resulting into a reduction of capital without the court's confirmation[83]. Surrendered shares may be reissued if the articles so allow.

# Maintenance of capital

Companies legislation and case law try to ensure that the company's capital is maintained. Such attempts are considered under four heads namely the rules that (i) a company cannot return its capital to its members by buying its own shares; (ii) a subsidiary company is forbidden from being a member of its holding company; (iii) a company is forbidden from providing financial assistance to purchase its shares; and (iv) dividends can only be paid out of the profits of the company.

## Acquisition by a company of its own shares

A company is precluded from becoming a member of itself by buying its shares. Thus in *Trevor v. Whitworth*[84] a company went into liquidation. A former shareholder then claimed from the company the balance of the price of his shares which he had sold before the liquidation and which had not been wholly paid for. The claim was disallowed. Lord Watson indicated[85]that the intention of the legislature in restricting the power of limited companies to reduce the amount of their capital as stated in the memorandum is to protect the interests of creditors. Additionally, that the effect of the restriction is to prevent transactions between the company and shareholder by which money already paid to the company in respect of the shares is returned to him, save where the court has sanctioned this. Allowing the company to buy its own shares amounts to a return of capital to the shareholder and is misleading as far as the capital holding of the company is concerned.

However, there are exceptions to the rule in *Trevor v. Whitworth*. First, under the alternative remedy to the rule in *Foss v. Harbottle*[86] in Section 211 of the Companies Act,[87] the court may order the company to buy shares from an aggrieved oppressed shareholder. Second, the company is permitted to buy its redeemable preference shares.[88] Third, a company may transfer its shares to a trustee for it provided they are fully paid up[89]. Finally, the principle in *Trevor v. Whitworth* is not contravened when the shares in the company are held on trust for the company itself as a result of a gift or bequest. In such a situation legal title to the shares is held by the trustees.[90]

---

81 *Trevor v. Whitworth* (1887) 12 App. Cas. 409, p. 429

82 *Rowell v. John Rowell & Sons Ltd.* [1912] 2 Ch. 609

83 *Bellerby v. Rowland and Marword's Steamship Co. Ltd.* [1902] 2 Ch. 14 C.A.

84 (1887) 12 App Cas 409 H.L.. The principle in this case has been placed on statutory footing in Britain. See Companies Act, 1980 and Leigh, *op. cit.*, pp. 329-330

85 *ibid.*, 12 App. Cas. 409 at pp. 423-424

86 (1843) 2 Hare 461 V.C.

87 See *infra* Ch. 15

88 Companies Act, S. 60, See supra for discussion thereof; notes 34a to 37 and text thereof.

89 *Kirby v. Wilkins* [1929] Ch. 444

90 *Re: Castiglione's Will Trusts, Hunter v. Mackenzie* [1958] Ch. 549; [1958] 1 All E.R. 480

## Subsidiary company cannot be member of holding company

A subsidiary[91] is precluded from being a member of its holding company. However, exceptionally a subsidiary can hold its holding company's shares as trustee or personal representative provided that the holding company is not beneficially interested in the trust.[92] Additionally, a subsidiary can be a member of its parent where at the commencement of the Act[93] it was a member thereof. However, in such a case it is deprived of its voting rights.[94]

## Financial assistance by a company to acquire its shares

In order to prevent a breach of Section 29 of the Companies Act, Section 56(1) provides that it is unlawful for a company to give any financial assistance by way of loan guarantee or the provision of security to any person for subscription or purchase of its own shares or those of its holding company, if any. Breach of Section 56 renders the company and every officer in default liable to a fine. Any security given by a company in breach of Section 56 is invalid. Thus, in *Selangor United Rubber Estates Ltd. v. Cradock* (No.3)[95], the plaintiff company sold its rubber estates and was, therefore, without business. However, between 1957 and 1958 it had liquid assets worth GBP235,800. Acting through a banking firm, Contanglo Banking and Trading Company Limited, Cradock made an offer for the shares in the plaintiff company. The offer was accepted by 79 percent of the shareholders. The plaintiff company provided the funds for the purchase of its shares by Cradock by lending GBP232,500 to a Mr Woodstock. Mr Woodstock in turn lent the money to Cradock on the latter's instructions. In 1961, the plaintiff company went into liquidation. The Board of Trade acting with the liquidator's permission instituted an action against Barlow-Lawson and Jacob, two directors of the plaintiff company who as Cradock's puppets had effected the transfer of the company's funds. It was held that the two directors were liable for the misapplication of the company's funds. Similarly, in *Heald v. O'Connor*[96], it was held that a debenture which was given by a company as security for moneys lent to enable a person to buy shares in a company contrary to Section 54, of the British Companies Act, 1948[97] was illegal and, therefore, void. For purposes of Section 54, it was indicated[98] that a company is deemed to give financial assistance to the purchaser of shares whether the security is valid or not. All that is required to make the financial assistance effective is that the lender should believe the security to be valid and on the strength of it make a loan.

In the Kenyan case of *Standard Bank Ltd. v. Mehotor Farm Ltd.*[99], a private company owed Sh. 203,309.95 by way of overdraft to the bank. The debt was secured by equitable mortgages over the company's land which had been duly stamped for Sh. 320,000/-. The shareholders of the company agreed to sell all the shares to Mr & Mrs Kamau for sh. 456,690.05 i.e. Shs. 660,000/- less the Shs. 203, 309.95 owing on the overdraft. The bank advanced this sum to the company to be used as finance for Mr & Mrs Kamau on the purchase. The vendors of the shares were released from their existing guarantees of the company's debt to the bank. The equitable mortgage were "unstamped" to the extent of Shs 660,000/- with Mr & Mrs Kamau executing guarantees of the company's debt to the bank to that extent. Subsequently, the bank sued the company for the amount outstanding on the overdraft, which had risen to shs 841,051.85 and also sued Mr & Mrs Kamau for Sh. 660,000/- due under the guarantees. The three defendants invoked S.56 of the Companies Act. The High Court held that this section provided a complete defence to all the

91 defined in Companies Act, S. 154
92 *ibid.*, S. 29(2)
93 January 1, 1961
94 Companies Act., S. 29(3)
95 [1968] 2 All E.R. 1073
96 [1971] 1 W.L.R. 497; [1971] 2 ALL E.R. 1105
97 *in pari materia* with Companies Act, S. 56 (Uganda)
98 per Fisher, J. distinguishing and disapproving *Victor Battery Co. Ltd. v. Curry's Ltd.* [1946] 1 ALL E.R. 519
99 [1973] E.A. 78 C.A.

bank's claims. The bank appealed. It was held (per Spry V-P) that Section 56 is a provision which was introduced as a matter of public policy to prevent fraud and accordingly was drafted in very wide terms. It renders offending companies liable to penalties which, in relation to the present value of money are hardly more than nominal, but by making transactions illegal, it may make very large sums of money irrecoverable. In some circumstances, such as the present, it may operate most harshly, heavily penalising persons who have acted in all innocence and giving undeserved windfalls to the persons whose debts are irrecoverable. For this reason, Section 56 ought to be interpreted very strictly and should not be extended to apply to any transaction which is not expressly covered by it.

The appeal against the company was allowed but disallowed against Mr & Mrs Kamau. Furthermore, in *Wallersteiner v. Moir*[100], in March 1962 Hartley Bird Ltd. was a public company. Ten million of its shares worth GBP 500,000 were held by Camp Bird Ltd. Camp Bird had charged them to Pearl Assurance Company Ltd. to secure a loan of GBP 125,000. It would have cost an honest buyer GBP625,000 to get them for his own benefit free of charge. By September, 1972, Dr Wallersteiner (in the name of his creature Rothschild Trust) had acquired all those shares for his own benefit and free of any charge. But he did not pay any penny for them. He achieved this in two ways: (i) by loans which Hartley Bird made to him (in the name of his company IFT) of Nassau); (ii) by Commissions which he said he earned in the name Liechtenstein Co. The loans to IFT were for £ 284,981 11s. 4d. and £ 50,000. They were repayable by IFT by instalments over the succeeding years. One or two instalments were paid, but none thereafter. IFT had assets left, so the sums were lost to Hartley Bird. The loans by Hartley Bird to IFT greatly assisted the acquisition of shares by Rothschild Trust and Dr Wallersteiner was the moving spirit behind it. It was held that Dr. Wallersteiner was guilty of misfeasance and breach of Section 54 of the British Companies Act 1948[101]

Apart from the statutory fine of Shs. 2,000/-, it has been suggested[102] that every director who is guilty of Section 56 is guilty of misfeasance and breach of trust and is liable to recoup to the company any loss occasioned to it by the default.

However, Section 56 is inapplicable in three instances: (i) where the company lends money as part of its ordinary course of business;[103] (ii) where the money is provided by the company following a scheme for the purchase or subscription by trustees of fully paid shares in the company or its holding company and is to be held by or for the benefit of employees of the company including a salaried director.[104] (iii) where the company makes loans to employees other than directors to enable them to buy shares in the company.[105]

## Dividends payable out of profits

A dividend is essentially a share of the company's declared profits relative to a member's shareholding. The payment of dividends is usually regulated by the company's articles of association.[106]

The basic rule is that dividends should not be paid out of capital. In *Re: Exchange Banking Co. Flitcroft's Case,*[107] the directors had for several years made it appear that the company had

---

100 [1974] 3 ALL E.R. 217 C.A. For discussion thereof see J.H. Farrar and N.V. Lowe (1975) 38 *Mod. L.R. 455.* The facts are culled from the judgment of Lord Denning M.R. (as he then was).

101 See supra n. 97

102 per Lord Denning, supra n. 100. See also Sealy, *op. cit.*, p. 322 and *Report of the Company Law Committee* (Jenkins Committee) 1962 Cmnd 1749, paras 170-187. *Steen v. Law* [1964] A.C. 287 P.C.

103 S. 56 (1) proviso (a); *Steen v. Law ibid*

104 Ss. 56 (1) proviso (b)

105 *ibid.*, proviso (c)

106 See e.g. Table A, Arts 114-122

107 (1882) 21 Ch. D. 519 C.A. Table A. Art. 116, Companies Act, S.67. See also *Modikayo Oneka v. Wines & Spirits (U) Ltd* (1974) HCB 263

made profits, when in fact it had not, by laying before the shareholder's reports and balance sheets in which debts known to be bad were entered as assets. Acting on the faith of these reports, the shareholders passed resolutions declaring dividends, which the directors then paid. Upon the winding-up of the company, the liquidator successfully applied to have the directors who had been responsible on each occasion to be made accountable to the company for the sums which were wrongly paid.

While that is the basic proposition, exceptionally, the directors in such circumstances may claim an indemnity from shareholders who are aware of the breach.[108]

Dividends are normally declared at the company's general meeting. However, they should not be higher than those recommended by the directors.[109] Interim dividends may be paid to the members provided the articles so permit.[110] Even where the company has made profits, a dividend may not be declared. Instead the profits may be transferred to a reserve account and applied for the company's proper purposes.[111] Additionally, the payment of dividends may be based on the amount paid up on the shares[112], although the usual practice is to base the calculation on the nominal value of the shares.

The legal rules relating to the payment of dividends may be summarised as follows:

(a) Dividends should not be paid if this would lead to the company being unable to pay its debts as they fall due.

(b) It is permissible to pay dividends out of the profits without making up for losses on fixed capital.[113] Thus, in *Lee v. Neuchatel Asphalt Co.*[114], a wasting asset resulted into loss of capital. It was held that this could not prevent the payment of dividend. This means that it is unnecessary to provide for depreciation of capital before paying dividends although the normal commercial practice is to provide for depreciation. In *Verner v. General & Commercial Investment Trust*[115], the defendant, an investment company sustained losses in the value of its investments as a result of fall in the market. However, the annual income received from its investments considerably exceeded the expenses for the year. It was held that in the circumstances, it was proper to pay dividends. The dividends could be paid from current trading profits without having to make good the losses in fixed capital. Lindley L.J. stated in this regard:[116]

> ...fixed capital may be sums and lost, and yet that the excess of current receipts over current payments may be dividend, but that floating or circulating capital must be kept up, as otherwise it will enter into and form part of such excess, in which case to divide such excess without deducting the capital which forms part of it will be contrary to law ...

(c) Dividends should only be paid after making good the loss of circulating capital[117] during the year.

(d) Losses of previous years, however great need not be made good before payment of dividend. It is sufficient that a particular year produces a profit.[118]

---

108 *Moxham v. Grant* [1900] 1 Q.B. 88 C.A

109 Table A., Art. 114

110 *ibid*, Art. 115

111 *ibid*, Art. 117

112 Companies Act, S. 61 (c). Table A. Art. 118

113 Viz. permanent asset of the company which are used to produce income e.g. plant, machinery and premises: *Ammonia Soda Co. v. Chamberlain* [1918] 1 Ch. 266, 286.

114 [1889] 41 Ch. D. C.A.

115 [1894] 2 Ch. 239 C.A.

116 *ibid.* p. 266 See also *Modikayo case supra* n. 107

117 This is capital which is intended to be turned over i.e. for Sale e.g. stock in hand, raw materials. See *Ammonia Soda Co. Case supra* n. 11. p. 286

118 *Ammonia Soda Co. Case ibid; Re: National Bank of Wales* [1899] 2 Ch. 629 C.A.

(e) Profits of previous years may be distributed by way of dividend from a reserve fund. They continue to be regarded as the company's profits until capitalised.[119]

(f) A profit which has been made on the sale of the company's fixed assets can be distributed to members by way of dividend.[120]. In so doing, though, all the capital items must be considered and not just one.[121]

(g) A company is permitted to distribute a surplus on its capital account which results from a revaluation of the company's assets made in good faith by competent valuers. This means that a profit on the capital account can be distributed by way of dividend.[122] The Jenkins Committee in Britain recommended that this should not be the case.[123]

## Capitalisation of profits

It is permissible to capitalise profits as contained in the company's reserve or profit and loss accounts by (i) fully paying up shares or (ii) distributing fully paid unissued shares[124]. This may be done instead of paying dividends. The distribution is made relative to existing shareholdings. It is notable in this regard that the share premium account and capital redemption reserve fund may only be used to pay up unissued shares or bonus shares.[125]

---

119 *Re: Hoare & Co. Ltd.* [1904] 2 Ch. 208 C.A

120 *Lubbock v. British Bank of South Africa* [1892] 2 Ch. 108

121 *Foster v. New Trinidad Lake Asphalt Co. Ltd* [1901] 1 Ch. 208, 212 per Bymer, J.

122 *Dimbula Valley (Ceylon) Tea Co. Ltd. v, Laurie* [1961] 1 All E.R. 769

123 *Supra* n. 99, para 350 (b). See also the Scottish Case, *Westburn Sugar Refineries v. I.R.C.* 1960 S.C.T. 297; (1960) T.R. 105. The position in Britain is modified by Companies Act, 1980.

124 Table A. Art. 128 *Dimbula Valley* (Ceylon) *Tea Co. Case, supra* n. 20

125 Companies Act, Ss. 58, 60; Table A, Art. 128; *Dimbula Case ibid*

# 10

# DEBENTURES AND BORROWING

## Authority to borrow

Generally, a company's powers are laid down in the statute under which it is incorporated, its memorandum and to some extent its articles. Trading companies have an implied power to borrow and charge their property as security.[1] Other companies require authorisation by their memorandum. Restrictions may be imposed by the memorandum on the power to borrow money. In practice the power to borrow money is inserted in provisions of the articles with an indication that the directors may borrow money up to a certain limit. The excess over that limit requires the sanction of the general meeting.[2] Once it is established that the company has power to borrow money, then there is an implied power to charge its property for purposes of securing the repayment of the money borrowed.[3] However, this power is subject to express restrictions contained in the memorandum and articles of association or statute. With regard to statutory restrictions on charges, provision may be made to the effect that where the property mortgaged or charged includes land and the chargee or mortgagee is an alien, the approval of the relevant Minister is necessary.[4] The company's borrowing powers can only be exercised after it has become entitled to commence business.[5]

Where the company borrows in excess of the powers given to it by its memorandum, the borrowing is regarded as *ultra vires*. In such a case the lender will be unable to sue the company on the contract to recover the sums advanced.[6]

## Debentures

### Definition

Debentures are defined in Section 2 of the Companies Act, including "debenture stock bonds, and any other securities of a company whether constituting a charge on the assets of the company or not." This definition is not helpful. A debenture may be more usefully defined as a document acknowledging the indebtedness of the company, "which is normally, but not necessarily secured by a charge over property".[7] Where the debenture is not secured the document will be referred to as a naked debenture or unsecured loan stock.

The document will also contain a promise to repay the principal sum borrowed on a given date with interest at specified intervals. In *British India Steam Navigation Co. v. I.R.C.*[8], Lindley J., while conceding that the expression "debenture" had no precise meaning, indicated thus:[9]

---

1 See e.g Table A, Art. 79 which gives directors such power. *General Auction Estate & Monetary Co. v. Smith* [1891] 3 Ch. 432

2 *ibid.*, Art. 79 Provisio

3 *Australian Auxiliary Steam Clipper Co. v. Mounsey* (1858) 4 K & J. 733

4 Land Transfer Act, Cap 202

5 Companies Act, S. 111

6 *Re: Jon Beauorte (London) Ltd.* [1953]Ch. 131. See generally Chap. 4 on *Ultra vires*

7 Gower *op. cit.* p. 401

8 (1881) 7 Q.B.D. 165 Q.B.D.

9 *ibid.*, at pp. 172-173

> ... We know that there are various kinds of instruments commonly called debentures. You may have mortgage debentures, which are charges of some kind on property. You may have debentures which are bonds;... You may have debenture which is nothing more than an acknowledgment of indebtedness. And you may have a thing like this, which is something more; it is a statement by two directors that the company will pay a certain sum of money on a given day, and will also pay interest half-yearly at certain times and at a certain place, upon production of certain coupons by the holder of the instrument. I think any of these things which I have referred to may be debentures within the Act.

The Act defines debenture to include "debenture stock bonds." The company may "instead of issuing individual debentures, evidencing separate and distinct debts, create one loan fund known as 'debenture stock' divisible among a class of lenders each of whom is given a debenture stock certificate, evidencing the *aliquot* parts of the loan to which he is entitled.[10] The debenture stock becomes the indebtedness itself, with the certificates evidencing the stockholder's interests in it. A point of distinction arises between a debenture and debenture stock. While a debenture is a single item which can be legally transferred as an entity, debenture stock can be subdivided and transferred in fractions as the holder deems fit.[11] The normal practice is for the company to issue debenture stock backed up by a trust deed giving trustees a charge on the company's property.

## The trust deed

The trust deed contains the company's covenant to repay with interest the money borrowed. It will specifically charge the company's property and indicate when the charge becomes enforceable. This is usually done where the company defaults in the payment of interest. The deed also provides powers to deal with the charged property and to appoint a receiver to enforce the security.

The advantages of a trust deed are that because of the large sums involved, a legal fixed charge is possible. In addition, competent trustees can deal professionally with relevant matters when the charge is enforced. Furthermore, a company can usually deal with property while it is still charged and the insurance covenants of the company are enforceable by the trustees.

## Issue and transfer of debentures

The procedures of transfer, certification of transfers and the issue of certificates which were considered in relation to shares[12] equally apply to debentures.[13].

Irredeemable debentures may be issued irrespective of this being contrary to the equity of redemption[14]. The company has power to reissue redeemed debentures.[15]

With regard to the essential nature of debentures, some contrast with shares[16], may be useful. In contrast to shareholders, debenture holders are not members of the company. Their interest can be paid out of the company's capital in contrast dividends on shares which can only be paid out of profits.[17] Again in contradistinction with shares[18], debentures can be issued at a discount since they are not part of the company's capital. In the same way, a company can buy its own debentures, whereas it cannot buy its own shares[19].

---

10 Gower, *op.cit.* p.401

11 *ibid.*, p. 402

12 See *supra* chap. 8.

13 Companies Act, Ss. 77, 80 and 82; *Mandilas & Karaberis v. Anglo Canadian Cement Co.* 1967(1) A.L.R. Comm. 42; 1967 NCLR 42.

14 *ibid.*, S. 91; *Knightsbridge Estates Trust Ltd. v. Byrne* [1940] 2 ALL E.R. 401 H.L.

15 *ibid.*, S. 92

16 See *supra* Chap. 8.

17 See *supra* chap. 9.

18 Chap. 8

A contract to take up shares is enforceable by an order of specific performance[20]. Finally, debentures are convertible into shares.[21]

### Priority

Debentures may be issued with each ranking *pari passu* with others in the series. In such a case, if there are insufficient assets to pay all the debentureholders in full, the available amount would be distributed in proportion to the amounts owing to each of them. The arrears of interest which are payable on some of the debentures may be withheld so as to make equal interest payments.[22] However, if a series of debentures are issued without indicating that they rank *pari passu*, they will be repaid according to the date of issue. Where they are all issued on the same date, they are repayable according to the number given to each of them. Where the holder of a debenture in a series ranking *pari passu* enforces the security, he is under an obligation to do so on behalf of all the shareholders of debentures in that series.[23]

### Classes of debentures

Debentures may be classified relative to the person who is entitled to them.

#### (a) Registered Debentures

These are debentures which are payable to the registered holder. They indicate that the money secured and interest thereof are payable to the person named therein or the registered holder for the time being. They may be transferred in the manner prescribed in the debenture. However, registration must be accompanied by a proper instrument of transfer.[24] Refusal of transfer by the company must be notified to the transferee within two months thereof.[25] A transferee will take the debenture subject to equities which may be enforced against the transferor. However, the company may decline to enforce the equities.[26]

#### (b) Bearer debentures

These are payable to the bearer thereof or to the holder for the time being. Interest thereon is normally payable on production of coupons which are attached to the debentures. This type of debenture is essentially a negotiable instrument.[27] Consequently, it is transferable by mere delivery and a transferee in due course obtains title free from the defects in title of the transferor.

Debentures may also be classified according to the nature of the security underlying them whether as specific property or a floating charge.

## Charges

### Fixed charge

This is a mortgage of defined property and the company cannot deal with it without the mortgagee's consent. Examples of the specific property charged are the company's factory, land or interests therein, ship and similar property. In the words of Lord Macnaghten, in *Illingworth v. Houldsworth*:[28]

---

19 *Supra* chap. 9
20 Companies Act, S. 94
21 *Moseley v. Koffyfontein Mines Ltd.* [1904] 2 Ch. 108
22 *Re: Midland Express Ltd* [1914] 1 Ch. 41
23 Leigh, *op.cit.*, p. 358
24 Companies Act, S. 77
25 *ibid.*, S. 80
26 *Re: Goy & Co.; Ltd.*, [1900] 2 Ch. 149
27 *Bechuanaland Exploration Co. v. London Trading Bank Ltd.* [1898] 2 Q.B. 658
28 [1904] A.C. 355, at p. 358 H.L.

> A specific charge ... is one that without more fastens on ascertained and definite property or property capable of being ascertained and defined.

On the winding up of the company, the debenture holder whose debenture is secured by a fixed charge will rank as a secured creditor.

## Floating charge

### (a) Nature and advantages

The floating charge affects the company's property which is constantly changing, such as its stock in trade. The company is free to deal with the property until the charge crystallises. In *Governments Stock and other Securities Investment Co. v. Manila Railway Co.*[29], Lord Macnaghten described the floating charge as follows:[30]

> A floating security is an equitable charge on the assets for the time being of a going concern. It attaches to the subject charged in the varying condition in which it happens to be from time to time. It is of the essence of such a charge that it remains dormant until the undertaking charged ceases to be a going concern, or until the person in whose favour the charge is created intervenes...

In *Illingworth v. Houldsworth*[31], Lord Macnaghten indicated that:[32]

> ... a floating charge, ... is ambulatory and shifting in its nature, hovering over and so to speak floating with the property which it is intended to affect until some event occurs or some act is done which causes it to settle and fasten on the subject of the charge within its reach and grasp ...

In Re: *Yorkshire Woolcombers' Association Ltd.*[33], Romer L. J. indicated[34] that a floating charge has the following three characteristics: (i) it is a charge on a class of assets of a company present and future; (ii) the class of assets is one which in the ordinary course of the company's business would be changing from time to time; (iii) where, it is contemplated by the company that until its holders take steps to enforce it the company may carry on its business in the ordinary way regarding the particular class of assets charged.

The floating charge in effect covers all the property of the company even if it is acquired after the charge was created. However, on certain events occurring the charge is said to crystallize and will henceforth take effect as a fixed charge.[35] The generally recognised events which would result into crystallisation are (i) cessation of the company's business; (ii) commencement of winding up or reconstruction of the company; (iii) default in the payment of interest or principal sum and steps are taken to enforce the security.

The principal advantage for a company of a floating charge is that it can charge assets which could not be easily made the subject of a fixed charge, such as stock-in-trade. In addition it can deal with its assets and even sell its business without the chargee's consent, if so authorised by its memorandum of association.[36] The company may also create legal mortgages and equitable charges in priority to the floating charge.[37]

---

29 [1897] A.C. 81 H.L.
30 *ibid*, p. 86. See also R. Pennington, *"The Genesis of the Floating Charge"* (1960) 23 *M.L.R.* 630
31 [1904] A.C. 355 H.L.
32 *ibid.*, p. 358; See too *Jia Enterprises Ltd. v. B.I.C.I.* [1962] 1 All N.L.R. 363
33 [1903] 2 Ch. 284
34 *ibid.*, p. 295
35 *Mandilas & Karaberis v. Anglo-Canadian Co. Ltd.* [1967] (1) A.L.R 42
36 *Re: Boraxco.* [1901] 1 Ch. 326
37 *Wheatley v. Siltstone Co.* (1885) 29 Ch. D 715

However, there are certain disadvantages from the perspective of the floating chargee. The floating charge may be avoided or invalidated under the circumstances stipulated by Section 318.[38] Additionally, it can very easily lose priority to other charges or creditors.[39]

**(b) Priority**

As between floating charges, a later one can only have priority or rank *pari passu* if the earlier charge expressly provides for this.[40] However, a later fixed charge will have priority over an earlier floating charge unless the latter has a provision preventing this of which the later chargee has notice.[41]

The floating chargee will also lose priority to:

(i) an execution creditor where the goods of the company are sold by a court sheriff[42] or the company pays out the sheriff in order to avoid the sale[43] or the creditor obtains a garnishee order absolute before crystallisation[44].

(ii) a landlord's distress for rent levied before crystallization[45]

(iii) the vendor of goods under a hire-purchase agreement;[46]

(iv) preferential creditors during a winding up, such as the Internal Revenue Office, local authority, employee's wages[47];

(v) a vendor who reserves his title in the goods sold until payment[48]; In such case the goods are not available to the company's chargees.

**(c) Avoidance of the floating charge**

Where a company is being wound up a floating charge created within three months of the commencement of the winding up is unless the company was solvent immediately after the charge was created, invalid except to the amount of any cash paid to the company at or after the time the charge was created and in consideration of the charge.[49] The aim of the section is to prevent one or more creditors, particularly directors from obtaining priority over general creditors, all with past debts.

Where cash is paid to the company before the creation of the charge, then, provided that the lender has not procured or acquiesced in the delay of the creation of the charge this will still be valid as paid at the date of creation. *In Re: F & E. Stanton*[50], advances of cash which were made fifty-four and five days respectively before the charge was created were not enough to avoid the charge because the payments were made in consideration of the security. In *Re: Yeovil Glove Co. Ltd.*[51], the company went into liquidation after having unsecured debts amounting to GBP 94,000 and an overdraft with the National Provincial Bank totalling GBP 67,000. The overdraft was secured by a floating charge which was given less than twelve months before. During the subsistence of the charge, the bank met cheques drawn by the company, totalling GBP 110,000

---

38 Companies Act; See *infra* note 50 and text thereof.

39 See e.g. *Re: Castell & Brown Ltd.* [1898] 1 Ch. 315

40 *Re: Automatic Bottle Makers* [1926] Ch. 412 C.A.

41 *Supra* n. 40; Registration of the charge under S. 96 Companies Act, does not of itself constitute such notice: *Wilson v. Kelland* [1910] 2 Ch. 306. See also *English & Scottish Mercantile Co. v. Brunton* [1898] 1 Ch. 315 Ch. D

42 *Re: Standard Manufacturing Co.* [1891] 1 Ch. 627

43 *Heaton and Duggard Ltd. v. Cutting Bros.* [1925] 1 K.B. 655

44 *Evans v. Rival Granite Quarries ltd.* [1910] 2 K.B. 979 C.A.

45 *Re: Roundwood Colliery Co.* [1897] 1 Ch. 373 C.A.

46 *Re: Morrison, Jones and Taylor Ltd.* [1941] 1 Ch. 50 C.A.

47 Companies Act, S. 315

48 *Aluminium Industry v. Romalpa* [1976] 2 All E.R. 553

49 Companies Act, S. 318

50 [1929] 1 Ch. 180

51 [1965] Ch.148; [1964] 2 All E.R.849 C.A.; Sealy, *op.cit* pp 362-3

and received GBP 111,000 for payment into the company's account. The unsecured creditors objected to the security under the British equivalent of Section 318 Companies Act,[52], alleging that no cash had been paid to the company by the bank within the meaning of the section. However, the bank treated the bank's acts in meeting the company's cheques as equivalent. It then followed that by virtue of the rule in *Clayton's case*[53] that the bank could claim that the whole of the £ 67,000 was cash advanced subsequently to the creation of the charge, so that the security was valid for this sum.[54]

It is further significant that a floating or fixed charge which is made within six months before the winding up commences is void if it is a fraudulent preference of a creditor.[55] In this instance the charge or conveyance must have been made voluntarily i.e. without threat of legal action and at a time when the company is unable to pay its debts as they fall due and with intent to prefer a particular creditor.[56] With regard to the effect of crystallisation of the floating charge and the issue of set-off, it appears that each debt which accrues to the company after a floating charge which affects its future property had crystallised becomes immediately fixed with an equity in favour of the debenture holders. It follows that no debt which becomes due after crystallisation by a company may be set off by a creditor so as to give him priority over the debenture holders.[57] Thus, in *N.W. Robbie & Co. Ltd. v. Whitney Warehouse Co. Ltd.*[58], the plaintiff company gave out a debenture, secured by a floating charge to the Bank of Ireland. The bank appointed a receiver who allowed the company to continue trading. The company sold goods to the defendants worth GBP 1,346. In the instant suit the receiver asked for payment of the price. In the meantime, the defendants had taken an assignment of a debt of GBP 852 due by the plaintiffs to English Spinners Ltd., and claimed to be entitled to set off this sum against the GBP 1,346 sued for. It was held that the set-off failed because the debentureholder's equity had priority. This case may be contrasted with the later case of *Rother Iron Works Ltd. v. Canterbury Precision Engineers Ltd.*[59] In this instance, the plaintiff company agreed to sell goods to the defendant company for GBP 159 at a time when it already owed the defendant GBP 124 under a previous contract. A receiver was appointed by the plaintiff's bank some two weeks later, under a power contained in a floating charge; and the goods were delivered to the defendant after a further two weeks. It was held that the defendant had a right to set off the earlier debt. The decision turned on the fact that the debt sought to be set off was incurred before the crystallisation of the floating charge.

## Registration of charges

A company is required to register all charges created by it on its property, in its own register and with the registrar of companies.

### (a) Registration in the company's register

Every company is required to keep at its registered office a register of charges for purposes of entering all charges which affect its property and all floating charges affecting its undertaking or property. The register should indicate[60] (i) a short description of the property charged, (ii)

---

52 Companies Act 1948 (UK) S. 322

53 (1816) 1 Mer 572

54 See also *Re: Thomas Mortimer Ltd.* [1965] Ch. 186; see further *Re: Destone Fabrics ltd.* [1941] Ch. 319 C.A. *Re: Matthew Ellis Ltd.* [1933] Ch. 458 C.A.

55 Companies Act, S. 316

56 *Re: F.L.E Holdings* [1967] 1 W.L.R. 1409; *Re: Eric Holmes* [1965] Ch. 1052 Re: *M. Kushler* [1943] Ch. 248

57 Sealy, *op.cit.*, p. 357

58 [1963] 1 W.L.R. 1324; [1963] 3 ALL E.R. 613 C.A.

59 [1974] Q.B. 1, [1973] 1 ALL E.R. 394 C.A. See also *Geo Barker v. Eynon* [1974] 1 ALL E.R. 900; *Business Computers Ltd. v. Anglo African* [1977] 2 ALL E.R. 741

60 Companies Act, S. 105

the name of the chargee and (iii) the amount charged. Failure to observe this attracts a default fine, although the charge is not thereby invalidated. In addition, the company is required to keep a copy of every instrument creating the charge.[61]

**(b) Registration with the Registrar**

A copy of all the charges created by a company and falling under Section 96 of the Companies Act must be registered with the Registrar. The copy has to be accompanied by a statutory declaration relating to the execution of the charge and verifying it as a true copy. A copy of the following charges is required to be registered:

(i) a charge securing any issue of debentures;

(ii) a charge on uncalled share capital;

(iii) a charge created or evidenced by an instrument which, if executed by an individual, would require registration as a bill of sale.[62]

(iv) a charge on land, wherever situate, or any interest therein, but not including a charge for any rent or other periodical sum issuing out of land;

(v) a charge on the book debts of the company;

(vi) a floating charge on the undertaking or property of the company;

(vii) a charge on calls made but not paid;

(viii) a charge on a ship or any share in a ship;

(ix) a charge on goodwill, on a patent or a licence under a patent, on a trade mark or a copyright or licence under a copyright.

Particulars relating to the charge and the instrument creating it must be delivered to the registrar for registration within forty-two days after their creation.

If a series of debentures ranking *pari passu* has been issued the Act is deemed to have been complied with if they are registered with the following particulars:[63]

(i) the total amount secured by the series;

(ii) the dates of the resolutions authorising the issue of the series and the date of the covering deed, by which the security is created or defined;

(iii) a general description of the property charged;

(iv) the names of the trustees, if any, for the debenture holders; together with a copy of the deed containing the charge, or if there is no such deed, copy of one of the debentures of the series accompanied by a statutory declaration as to the execution and verification as a true copy.

Where there is more than one issue of debentures in the series, particulars of the date and amount of each issue must be sent to the registrar. However, omission to do so will not invalidate the debentures so issued. If any commission, allowance, or discount has been paid by the company in consideration of a person subscribing or agreeing to subscribe for debentures, the particulars as to the amount or rate of percentage of the commission, discount or allowance so made must be supplied to the Registrar.

It is notable that it is only a charge *created* by a company which requires registration. In *London and Cheshire Insurance Co. v. Laplagrene Property Co. Ltd.*[64], the unpaid vendor's lien which arose by operation of law was held not to be registrable. However, in *Re: Wallis and Simmonds (Builders) Ltd.*[65], the deposit of title deeds was held to create an equitable charge which arose by presumption and not by operation of law. Consequently it was registrable.

---

61 *ibid.*, S. 104

62 Under Bills of Sales Act, Cap 77 Laws of Uganda. See also *Stoneleigh Finance, Ltd. v. Phillips* [1965] 1 ALL E.R. 513

63 Companies Act, S. 96(7)

64 [1971] Ch. 499; [1971] 1 All E.R.

65 [1974] 1 W.L.R. 391; [1974] 1 All E.R. 561

Where a registrable charge is created but is not registered, the lender will not avoid the consequences of section 96 by claiming to be subrogated to the unpaid vendor's lien on the ground that the money advanced was used by the company to pay the vendor of the land.[66]

With regard to other charges other than those indicated above, particulars relating to the date of creation, the amount secured, the property charged and chargees must be given to the registrar.[67]

If the company defaults in effecting registration of the charges a person who is interested therein can carry out the registration and recover the necessary fees from the company.[68]Where a company acquires any property which is already subject to a charge and which, if created by the company would have required registration, the company must register the particulars and copy of the charge within forty-two days of acquisition.[69] Failure to do so attracts a default fine but does not affect the validity of the charge.

If the charge comprises property situated in Uganda but is required to be registered elsewhere in Uganda other than the Companies Registry[70], it is permissible if instead of the original instrument a true copy of the instrument creating the charge duly certified by the secretary of the company is delivered to or received by the Registrar of Companies for registration. The registrar has discretion to inspect the original instrument.[71]

Where the charge is in respect of property situated outside Uganda and is created outside Uganda, Section 96 will be duly complied with if a duly verified copy of the instrument is delivered to the registrar within forty-two days from the time when the instrument if despatched by post would ordinarily have reached the registrar.[72]

### (c) Effect of registration

Upon the registration of a charge, the registrar issues a certificate of registration which is conclusive evidence that the requirements of the Act regarding registration have been complied with[73], this will be so even if the particulars delivered by the company are incorrect. However, the inaccuracy in the registered particulars and in the registrar's certificate does not affect the validity of the charge to which they relate. The terms of the charge are to be found in the instrument itself alone.[74] Although this approach leaves room for fraudulent submission of particulars, it has been indicated[75] that Section 99 would not operate against third parties.

Furthermore the certificate of registration must be endorsed on every debenture by the company. Default thereof attracts a fine.[76]

### (d) Effect of non-registration

Where a copy of the charge is not registered as required by Section 96, it is void as against any liquidator and any creditor of the company. However, this does not affect the obligation to repay. The consequence is that the chargee becomes an unsecured creditor and the contract to repay becomes immediately enforceable.[77] It is further notable that a registered charge has priority over an earlier unregistered charge, even when the holder of the later charge has notice of the

[66] *Burston Finance Ltd v. Speirway Ltd.* [1974] 1 W.L.R. 1648; [1974] 3 All E.R 1358
[67] Companies Act, S. 99
[68] *ibid.*, S. 97
[69] *ibid.* S. 98
[70] e.g. registration of mortgage of land in a District Land Registry.
[71] Companies Act, S. 96
[72] *ibid.*, S. 98 Proviso
[73] Companies Act, S. 99
[74] *Re: Eric Holmes Ltd.* [1965] Ch. 1052; [1965] 2 ALL E.R. 333; *Re: Mechnisations Ltd.* [1966] Ch. 20 Ch. D. *Mussini v. Balogun* (1968) (2) A.L.R. Comm. 197; *Re: C.L. Nye Ltd.* [1970] 3 ALL E.R 1061
[75] *Re: C.L. Nye Ltd.*, ibid
[76] Companies Act, S. 100 (1) (2)
[77] *Re: Parkes (Swadlincote) Ltd.* [1929] 1 Ch. 139; *Capital Finance Co. Ltd. v. Stokes* [1968] 3 ALL E.R. 625

unregistered security.[78] This approach was distinguished in *Watson v. Duff Morgan & Vermont Ltd.*[79], where it was held that if two mortgages were created consecutively on the same day, the second being registered within twenty-one days and the first sometime later under an order containing the usual provision, the priority which the second obtained when the first became void for non-registration was not protected. While acknowledging that on the particular facts the decision was fair, Professor Gower nevertheless adds this rider:[80]

> It surely cannot be right that a second mortgage created 22 days after the first (unregistered) mortgage is protected whereas one created within 21 days is not.

In *Kasozi Ddambi v. Male Construction Service Co.*[81], it was held that the debenture, by failure to be registered within the prescribed period under section 96(1) of the Companies Act, was void as against the liquidator and any creditors of the company and could not be enforced against the judgment creditors.

**(e) Late registration**

If the charge is not registered as required, the court[82] has power to extend time for its registration or rectify the register on the application of the company or any other interested person. However, for this purpose the omission must have been accidental or due to inadvertence or some other sufficient cause or not of a nature to prejudice creditors or shareholders or on other grounds where it is just and equitable to grant the relief[83]. The relief would also only be granted if it does not prejudice the rights of any party which were acquired prior to the time when the charge was actually registered.[84] However, this will not affect rights acquired when the first debenture became void.[85]

# Remedies of debenture holders

## Mode of Enforcement

The mode of enforcement of a debenture is dependent upon the type of security underlying it. Whatever the case, the normal procedure is for the debenture holders or their trustees to arrange the appointment of a receiver. Alternatively if the financial position is such that the receiver's remuneration cannot be met, it may be preferable for the trustees to take possession of the security. Where the "debenture" is in effect an ordinary mortgage of a specified piece of property the debenture holder may exercise his power of sale[86] without necessarily having to appoint a receiver.

In *Multiholdings Ltd. v. UCB*[87], it was held that the acceptance of promissory notes by a bank, which had given out a loan on security of debentures, did not suspend the right to demand repayment. The demand was valid and the appointment of receivers and managers was proper.

The appointment of a receiver may be effected by the debentureholder himself pursuant to express or implied powers in the debenture, or by the court. However, even when there is no

---

78 *Re: Monolithic Building Co.* [1915] 1 Ch. 643 C.A.

79 [1974] 1 W.L.R. 450

80 Gower, *op. cit.*, p. 484

81 [1981] HCB 26, Kantinti J.

82 High Court

83 Companies Act, S. 102; See also *UBA Ltd. v. Registrar of Companies* 1977 3 FRCR 91, *Bank of the North Ltd. v. Registrar of Companies (1973-74) 1 FRCR 56*

84 *Re: Monolithic supra* n. 80. See further *Development Finance Co. Ltd. v. Registrar of Companies* 1973 NCLR 497; Orojo *op. cit.* (2nd Ed 1984), p. 370

85 *Watson v. Duff Morgan supra* n. 79

86 Pursuant to a term in the debenture or trust deed or the implied power of sale by a mortgagee: Conveyancing Act, 1881., S. 19;

occurrence which would make the security enforceable, but the debentureholder's position is in jeopardy, an application may be made to court, which has a discretionary power to appoint a receiver in such a situation, although usually it has no such power except where the debentures are secured by a charge.[88] The procedure is then for a debenture holder on behalf of himself and the other holders to start a debentureholders' action. The action is normally for the enforcement of the charge and the appointment of a receiver and or manager and an order for sale or foreclosure. "Jeopardy" in this instance is established where for instance execution is about to be levied against the company[89], or when it intends to distribute to its members its only remaining asset.[90]

The appointment of a receiver out of court is advantageous from the perspective of the debentureholders as a body. This is so because "the procedure in a debentureholders' action is lamentably expensive and dilatory, since the receiver, as an officer of the court will have to work under its closest supervision and constant applications will have to be made in chambers throughout the duration of the receivership, which may last years if a complicated realisation is involved"[91]. Consequently, in view of provision for an out-of-court appointed receiver to seek the court's directions[92] an application to court for appointment of a receiver may be unnecessary and unduly expensive.

A receiver's function is to take possession of the assets charged, collect rents and profits, exercise the debentureholders' powers of realisation and pay the net proceeds to the holders in reduction of their charge. He has no authority to carry on the business of the company. Consequently, where the charge involved is a floating one and carrying on the company's business is thereby necessary for its realisation, the receiver's position will be precarious. To resolve the difficulty, the receiver needs, in addition, to be appointed a manager. Express power for such appointment is usually to be found in the terms of the debenture. The appointment may also be made by the court, exercising its inherent powers.

Neither a body corporate[93] or an undischarged bankrupt[94] may be appointed receiver or manager. Attempted appointment of such persons is null and void.[95] However, if the company is already in liquidation, it is permissible to appoint the official receiver for such purpose.[96]

## Status and position of receiver or manager

A receiver is distinguishable from the company's liquidator on winding up. It is not necessary to wind up the company before appointing a debentureholders' receiver. Where, however, a receiver and a manager is appointed in respect of the whole of the company's undertaking, the board of directors will effectively cease to function just as on winding up.[97]

A receiver who is appointed by the court is not anybody's agent, but is simply an independent officer of the court. However, a receiver who is appointed out of court may be an agent of the appointor, i.e. the debentureholder or trustee. This will be so where no express or implied term to the contrary, (to be found in the terms of the debenture or circumstances), applies.[98] In

---

87 1971 ULR 241 Russel Ag. J.

88 *Harris v. Beauchamp Bros.* [1894] 1 Q.B. 801 C.A.

89 *McMahon v. North Kent Co.* [1891] 2 Ch. 143; *Edwards v. Standard Rolling Stock* [1893] 1 Ch. 574; *Re Victoria Steamboats Co.* [1897] 1 Ch. 158; Gower, *op. cit.* p. 487: *NIPC v. Thompson Organisation 2 Ors* (1969) 1All N.L.R. 138 (S.C.)

90 *Re: Tilt Cove Copper Co.* [1913] 2 Ch. 588; Gower, *ibid; Dipcharima v. Bornu Holding Co. Ltd* (1965) (3) A.L.R. Comm 112

91 Gower, *ibid*; See also *Akinbobola v. Fisko (Nig) Ltd.* (1986) 4 NWLR

92 Companies Act, S. 352

93 *ibid.*, S. 349

94 *ibid.*, S. 350

95 *Portman Building Society v. Gallwey* [1955] 1 W.L.R. 96 (Company)

96 Companies Act, S. 331. The official receiver's functions are discussed *infra* chap. 18

97 *Moss S.S. Co. v. Whinney* [1912] A.C. 254 H.L

98 *Gosling v. Gaskell* [1897] A.C. 575 H.L.

practice, there is usually provision in the debenture expressly or impliedly that the receiver is deemed to be the agent of the company. The issue as to whether the receiver is an agent of the appointor or the company is now insignificant in view of Section 352[99] in the sense that for most purposes the position of the two is identical. The only significant difference is that a court-appointed receiver is obliged to act under the court's supervision whereas the one appointed out of court is not, although he can obtain the court's directions if he so wishes.[100] The other minor difference is that interference with a receiver appointed by the court, will amount to contempt of court although with leave of the court he may be sued by the debenture holder at whose behest he was appointed.[101] Invariably, though, the primary duties of an out-of court appointed receiver are owed to the debentureholders and not to the company. The company, may, for instance be unable to complain that upon the realisation of the assets, the receiver has not sought the best possible price.[102] He is also free from summary misfeasance proceedings[103] being taken against him as an officer of the company.[104]

With respect to liability, a receiver is not bound by contracts entered into by the company even where he oversees their performance.[105] However, if he enters into new contracts pursuant to the receivership, he, together with the company would be personally liable on them except where the contract otherwise provides, though he retains a right of indemnity out of the assets.[106] The effect of this is that whereas existing unsecured creditors will be unable to recover subsequent to the appointment of the receiver, they will be able to recover if they enter into new contracts with him since, "they will have the personal liability of a responsible professional man and, by a process of subrogation, can take advantage of his right of indemnity as a first claim on the assets".[107]

The effect of appointing a receiver is firstly that any floating charges crystallise and become fixed charges with the result that the company cannot deal with the relevant assets without the consent of the receiver.[108] Secondly, the directors' powers of control over the security cease.[109] Thirdly the employees of the company are automatically dismissed,[110] although the receiver may re-employ them. However, there is authority to the effect that mere appointment of a receiver does not automatically terminate contracts of employment with the company[111]e, although a sale by him of the company's business does.[112] Upon re-employment, the employees continue to be regarded as engaged by the company, whose agent the receiver is.[113] Fourthly, all business letters, invoices, or orders for goods must indicate the fact of appointment of the receiver or manager.[114]

An out-of court appointed receiver or manage is liable as a trespasser if there is any defect in his appointment. It is, therefore, necessary for him to ensure that the necessary formalities are

---

99 Companies Act; See also *National Provident Fund v. MidWest Cement Co. Ltd.* 1971(2) NCLR 337

100 *ibid., S. 352.* His remuneration may also be fixed by the court upon application of the liquidator: S. 354

101 *Arthur (Insurance) Ltd. v. Sisson* [1966] 1 W.L.R. 1384

102 *Re: B. Johnson & Co. Ltd* (1955) Ch. 354 c.f. *Cuckmere Brick Co. Ltd. v. Mutual Finance Ltd.* [1971] Ch. 949 C.A.

103 Pursuant to S. 328 Cap 85

104 See *Re: B. Johnson & Co. Ltd. supra* n. 102.

105 Gower, *op. cit.*, p. 489; *Airlines Airspares v. Handley Page* [1970] 1 ALL E.R. 29. See also *National Provident Fund v. Midwest Cement Co. Ltd. supra* n. 98

106 Companies Act, S. 352

107 Gower, *op.cit.*, p. 490; See also *Re: London United Breweries Ltd.* [1907] 2 Ch. 511.

108 *Mandilas & Karaberis Ltd. v. Anglo-Canadian Cement Co. Ltd.* (1967) (1) A.L.R. Comm. 42

109 See further *Newhart Developments v. Cooperative Commercial Bank* 1978 2 NCLR 337; *Olaolu Modern Bakery Ltd. v. Young, & Ors* (1977) FRCR 371

110 *Reid v. Explosives Co.* (1887) 19 Q.B.D. 264 C.A.

111 *Re: Mack Trucks (Britain) Ltd.* [1967] 1 W.L.R. 780 *Griffiths v. Social Services Secretary [1974] Q.B. 468*

112 *Re: Foster Clark's Indenture* [1966] 1 WLR 125

113 *Re: Mack Trucks (Britain) Ltd. supra* n. 10

114 Companies Act, S. 353

observed and the power of appointment has become exercisable. It has been suggested[115] that the court should be authorised in such circumstances to relieve the receiver of liability and to impose it on his appointor.

Although the receiver's principal function is the collection and distribution of assets which are subject to the debenture, the court may authorize him to borrow money for purposes of running the business. However, this is conditional on the court being satisfied that such expenditure is necessary.[116] Where the borrowing has been authorised, the lenders in such instances will have priority over the claims of other creditors, including the debentureholders. The receiver cannot dispose of the company's property after the commencement of winding-up without the court's sanction.[117] However, where the disposition has been made in good faith and effectively improves (or does not worsen) the company's position, it may be validated by the court.[118]

## Application of assets on realisation

A receiver, who is appointed on behalf of debentureholders who are entitled to a floating charge[119] must pay the creditors entitled to a preferential claim upon winding-up before paying out the debentureholders' claim for principal or interest.[120] Failure to do so renders the receiver to be personally liable[121]. However, fixed charges are not subject to preferential debts.[122]

In other respects, the assets realised by the receiver or manager must be applied in the following order:

(i) the cost of realisation;
(ii) the costs, including remuneration, of the receiver;
(iii) the costs, charges and expenses of the debenture trust deed, including the trustee's remuneration;
(iv) the plaintiff's costs;
(v) the preferential creditors;[123]
(vi) the debenture holders;[124]with the surplus being paid to the company for the unsecured creditor.

In the performance of his duties, a receiver is regarded as standing in a fiduciary position to the debentureholders who have appointed him under the debenture.[125] He also owes to the debenture holders a duty of care[126], which extends to the company over whose assets he superintends.[127] In addition, he owes a duty to the general creditors of the company i.e. creditors other than those who appoint him or preferential creditors to obtain the best price possible for the assets.[128]

## Publicity of receivership

Upon appointment of a receiver, notice thereof must be given to the Registrar of Companies.[129] Similarly, when the receiver vacates the appointment, notice must be given to the Registrar[130].

115 *Report of the Company Law Committee (*Cmnd 1749 Britain 1962) para. 299
116 *Greenwood v. Algeciras (Gibraltar) Rail Co.,* [1894] 2 Ch. 205 (effecting repairs).
117 Companies Act Cap 85 S.227
118 *Re: Clifton Place Garage Ltd.,.* [1970] Ch. 477; (1970) 1 ALL E.R. 353; See also Leigh, *op.cit;* p. 366
119 *See Re Victoria Steamboats Co., Ltd.,* [1897] 1 Ch. 158
120 Companies Act S. 95
121 *Westminster C.C. v. Haste* (1950) Ch. 442
122 *Re: Lewis Merthyr Collieries Ltd. [1929] 1 Ch.498 C.A.*
123 Companies Act Ss. 95, 315
124 *Re: Glyncorrwg Co., Ltd.,* [1926] Ch. 951
125 *Re: B. Johnson & Co. (Builders), Ltd* [1955] Ch. 634; [1955] 2 ALL E.R. 776
126 *R. v. Board of Trade, exparte St. Martin's Preserving Co. Ltd.* [1965] 1 Q.B. 603; [1964] 2 ALL E.R. 561
127 *Expo International Property Ltd. v. Chant.* [1979] 4 ACLR 679
128 *Standard Chartered Bank v. Walker* [1982] 1 WLR 1410; c.f. *Latchford v. Beirne* [1981] 3 ALL E.R. 705
129 Companies Act S. 103 (1)
130 *ibid,* S. 103 (2)

As already noted[131], all the company's business documents, bearing its name should indicate the fact of the receiver's appointment.[132] Since in respect of a floating charge over the undertaking of the company, the receiver is practically the liquidator[133], accounts and statements similar to those required on liquidation must be supplied.[134] However, in other respects, the duties of disclosure are less strict[135], although the receiver is obliged to file at the companies registry bi annual abstracts of his receipts and payments.[136]

These requirements do not apply where the debenture holder himself enters into possession instead of appointing a receiver.[137] This state of circumstances is unsatisfactory in that although mortgagees usually avoid taking possession, there have been situations where trustees have been compelled to do so in the absence of a willing receiver. Consequently, it is suggested that the publicity requirements should equally apply to a debenture holder who has taken possession.[138]

131 Above under *Status and Position of Receiver*
132 Companies Act, S. 353
133 c.f. *Cohen Report* Cmd 6659 (1945) para 66
134 Companies Act, Ss. 355 - 356. 358
135 Gower, *op. cit.* p. 491
136 Companies Act Ss. 357-358, Gower, *op.cit.* p. 491
36a Gower, *op.cit.* p.491
137 Gower, *ibid.* p, 486 note 54
138 Gower, *ibid.*, p. 491; The Jenkins Report in Britain (Cmnd, 1749), para 306K recommends that the equivalent of the Ugandan Companies Act, S. 103 should be extended to such a case.

# 11

# DIRECTORS AND OFFICERS OF THE COMPANY

## Introduction: Position of directors

The control of the modern registered company is normally distributed among its principal organs, viz. the general meeting, the managing director (where he exists) and the board of directors. Contrary to the legal prescription that the board of directors manages the affairs of the company[1], empirical studies indicates that the board of directors largely exercises only general policy control and invariably leaves the detailed management and policy implementation to the managing director or chief executive of the company and his managerial staff[1]. This is made possible by the ability of the board of directors to delegate its functions to a single managing director,[2] or a director.[3]

The expression "director" is defined[4] to include "any person occupying the position of a director by whatever name called." For certain purposes, "director" is also defined to include "any person in accordance with whose directions or instructions the directors of the company are accustomed to act".[5] These definitions are clearly vague and inadequate. The true nature of who a "director" is, may, therefore, have to be sought elsewhere other than the Companies Act. Directors have invariably been described either as agents[6] of the company or as trustees[7] or as both agents and trustees.[8] Modern writers either dissent from or qualify such classifications.

Professor Gower has stated thus:[9]

> ... the directors have ceased to be mere agents of company. Both they and the members in general meeting are primary organs of the company between whom the company's powers are divided.

Later on he adds, when refuting the notion that directors are trustees:[10]

> to describe directors as trustees seems today to be neither strictly correct nor invariably helpful .... In truth directors are agents of the company rather than

---

1 See D.J. Bakibinga, *"An Analysis of Some Recent Trends Affecting The Legal Powers, Duties and Functions of Company Directors"*, University of London Ph.D. Thesis (1981), Chapter 6 "The Reality of Corporate Power."

2 Table A. Art. 107-109

3 *ibid.*, Art. 102

4 Companies Act, S. 2

5 *ibid.*, s. 125. See also S. 201(9) (a)

6 *Ferguson v. Wilson* (1866) L.R. 2 Ch. 77, at p. 89 per Cairns L.J.; *Higgs v. West African Airways Corp. (Nig.) Ltd.* 1969 NCLR 304, 311 per Taylor C.J. (High Court of Lagos State).

7 *Charitable Corporation v. Sutton* (1742) 2 Atk 400

8 *G.E. Ry v. Turner* (1872) L.R. 8 Ch. 149, at p. 152 per Lord Selborne

9 Gower, *Principles of Company Law* (3rd Ed., 1969), p. 136; (4th Ed, 1979), p. 152. See also Wurdinger, *German Company Law* (Oyez 1975). p. 47 See also *Ukpilla Cement Co. Ltd. v. Igiekhume* (1979) 1FCA 64

10 *ibid* (3rd Ed.) pp. 515-516; (4th Ed.) pp. 571-572 relying on Romer J. in *Re: City Equitable Fire Insurance Co.* [1925] Ch. 407 at p. 426. He acknowledges, though that they would be treated as trustees of the company's property if they misapply it. See further *Shonowo v. Adebayo* 1969 NCLR 126, pp. 137-139 (Supreme Court of Nigeria). See also *Atewologun v. Metro Motors Ltd.* (1978) 2 LRN 46, FRC

> trustees of it or its property. But as agents they stand ....... in a fiduciary relationship to their principal, the company.

Gower's views are concurred in by Professor E.E. Palmer[11] and Professor K.E. Lindgren who observes:[12]

> But analysis of the theoretical status of directors demonstrates that they are not properly classified either as agents or trustees, but are suis generis ... like the shareholders in general meeting, it (the board of directors) is a 'constitutional organ' of the body corporate.

The above observations serve to highlight the difficulty of conclusively classifying directors. It is quite clear that since they act for a body, they must necessarily be agents of that body. However, because of the artificial nature of their principal, it is difficult to discern the normal agency-principal relationship. Between directors and a company, the directors control the company.[13] Even assuming that shareholders are the principals, the control aspect is difficult to discern, since directors are not necessarily subject to the wishes of the majority of shareholders.[14] Neither can one comfortably regard them as trustees since the ordinary rules applicable to trustees do not affect them.[15] The directors are only deemed trustees if they misapply the company's property.[16] The most apt description of company directors would appear to be that they are a *Suis generis* entity on equal footing with shareholders in general meeting in the corporate structure, possessing powers and duties whose exercise may procedurally render them agents or trustees of the company. Herein lies their fiduciary characteristic. This description may derive some support from the requirement that directors act collectively as a board.[17]

## Appointment

Every public company registered under the Companies Act must have at least two directors, while other Companies must have at least one director.[18] However, a sole director cannot be secretary at the same time.[19]

The appointment of directors is regulated by the company's articles of association. The first directors may be named in the articles.[20] This means that they are usually appointed by the

---

11 J.C. Ziegel (Ed.), *Studies in Canadian Company Law* Vol. 1. 1967 (Toronto) at pp. 367-368.

12 K.E. Lindgren, "The Fiduciary Nature of a Company Board's Power to Issue Shares" (1971-1972) 10 *West. Aust. L. Rev.* 364 at p. 366

13 See E.E. Palmer, *supra* n. 12, at p. 367. See also per Lord Reid in *Tesco Supermarkets Ltd. v. Natrass* [1972] A.C. 153 (H.L.) and Viscount Haldane in *Leonard's Carrying Co. Ltd. v. Asiatic Petroleum* [1915] A.C. 705.

14 *Automatic Self-Cleansing Filter Syndicate Co. Ltd. v. Cunninghame* [1906] 2 Ch. 34, per Cozen-Hardy L.J. at p. 44: "... I cannot see anything in principle to justify the contention that the directors are bound to comply with the votes of resolutions of a simple majority of an ordinary meeting of shareholders. It is not true to say that directors are mere agents. Directors are managing partners ..."

15 C.M. Schmitthoff (Ed.) *Palmer's Company Law* (22nd Ed, 1976) p. 628. Professor Palmer in Ziegel, *supra* n. 12 at p. 367 thus states:"the basic technical argument rests on the fact that a trustee is the legal owner of the trust *res*, while title to corporate property is not vested in the directors but in the corporate entity". See also *Selangor United Rubber Estates v. Cradock* (No. 3) [1968] 1 WLR. 1555, per Ungoed - Thomas, J.

16 *Palmer's Company Law ibid*, p. 629. See also *supra* n. 11

17 Gower, *supra* n. 10, pp. 138, 517 (3rd Ed); pp. 52, 572-573 (4th Ed); Pennington, *Company Law* (3rd Ed, 1973) p. 502; Wurdinger *supra* n. 10, p. 44; *c.f.* position in the French private company; J. Legall, *French Company Law* (Oyez 1974), p. 197. See also Sealy "The Director as Trustee" (1967) *Camb. L.J.* 83-103.

18 Companies Act, S. 177

19 *ibid*, S. 178(1)

20 *ibid.*, Table A, Art. 75

subscribers to the memorandum of association. The proper procedure is for the subscribers to meet and for a majority of them to sign a document at the meeting indicating the number of directors and the names of the first directors.[21]

However, in the absence of a meeting all the subscribers should sign the appointment except where there is contrary provision in the articles.[22] It is suggested that any appointment of the first directors by the articles is void, unless the persons named in the articles are also those named in the statement.[23]

Subsequent directors may be appointed in accordance with the articles which normally regulate the mode of increase, reduction, casual vacancies and retirements.[24] Such directors should be appointed at a general meeting and should be voted for individually unless a unanimous resolution to the contrary has been passed.[25]

The company is required to notify the Registrar of Companies of any change among its directors or secretary and the notification must contain a consent signed by the new director or secretary, to act in that capacity.[26]

Unless there is contrary provision in the articles, an ordinary resolution (i.e. support by a majority of shareholding) offices to elect a director or all of the directors.

As regards qualifications for appointment, a person of over seventy years of age cannot be appointed a director unless (i) the company is a private one; (ii) the company is not a subsidiary of a public company; (iii) the articles otherwise provide or (iv) the appointment has been made or approved by a resolution with special notice stating his age having been given.[27]

An undischarged bankrupt is also precluded from acting as director without the leave of the court.[28] Additionally, a person who is convicted of the following offences cannot be a director.[29] (i) an offence connected with the promotion, formation and management of a company; (ii) if during winding up a person has been guilty of an offence for which he is liable under Section 327, i.e. where the business of the company has been carried on with intent to defraud creditors of the company or creditors of any person or for fraudulent purposes; (iii) if the person has otherwise been guilty while an officer of the company of any fraud in relation to the company or of any breach of his duty to the company. The court would normally indicate the period of disqualification.

Where a share qualification is required for appointment[30], the shares should be taken up within two months of assumption of office or such shorter period as may be prescribed by the articles.[31] Failure to do so leads to vacation of the office.

A director need not be a natural person; a corporation may be so appointed[32], this being found useful to enable a holding company to maintain complete control of a subsidiary.[33]

The articles may also authorise a director to appoint an alternate director to act for him at any board meeting where he is absent. The scope of the alternative director's powers and whether he is entitled to remuneration will depend on the terms of the relevant article.[34] There is also the

---

21 *Onwuka v. Tayamani* (1965) L.L.R. 62, 66

22 *John Morley Building Co. v. Barras* [1891] 2 Ch. 386

23 Leigh, *op.cit.*, p. 120

24 Table A, Arts 89-97

25 Companies Act, S. 184

26 *ibid*, S. 201

27 *ibid*, Ss. 186, 187

28 *ibid*, S. 188

29 *ibid*, S. 189

30 Table A, Art. 77

31 Companies Act, S. 183; See also *Holmes v. Keyes* [1959] Ch. 199; [1958] 2 ALL E.R. 129; *Rv Camps* [1962] EA 403 (CA) Sinclair J.A

32 *ibid*. S. 186

33 Gower, *op. cit.* (4th Ed.) p. 143

34 *ibid.*

practice of giving employees status without responsibility by designating them "special" or "executive" or "associate" directors. While the powers of such employee directors may be so limited as to exclude them from the definition of "director" under the Companies Act,[35] it has been suggested that alternate directors properly fall within such definition.[36]

It is also provided[37] that the acts of a director are valid notwithstanding any defect that may afterwards be discovered in his appointment or qualification. This provision does not apply where there has been no appointment at all[38] In *Dawson v. African Consolidated Land and Trading* Co.[39], it was held that an equivalent Section validated the actions of a duly appointed director who at the time of the relevant transaction had ceased to hold qualification shares but had later reacquired them. Any person, be it a member or an outsider can rely on the provision to validate a transaction or proceeding if he was unaware of the irregularity or was not put on inquiry.[40] In *Pool House Group (Nig). Ltd. v. ACB Ltd,* it was indicated[41] that an equivalent provision to Section 181 applies not only where there has been non-compliance with the articles of association which the company could put right, but where the director's disqualification is statutory. Actual appointment or attempt at appointment is crucial to the operation of Section 181. Thus it will not apply where there is mere holding out of the "director". In *Joseph Asabaro Ltd. v. Western Finance Corporation*[42], proceedings in the name of the company were instituted against the defendant corporation after the plaintiff company's first directors had died. The proceedings were not authorised by the members of the company in general meeting. The defendant objected that the plaintiff had no directors who could sue. The two witnesses who claimed to be directors of the plaintiff company were not supported by any minutes of their appointment or minutes of any directors' resolution authorising the institution of proceedings. The action was accordingly dismissed as there was no evidence of appointment of directors and consequently the action in the company's name was instituted without authority. There was thus no plaintiff before the court. The court further observed that[43] a person cannot become a director of a company, so as to authorise the bringing of an action in the name of the company by holding himself out as a director or calling himself a director; he must be appointed a director in accordance with the procedure laid down by the articles of association of the company; and where the burden of proving the appointment lies on the company, it cannot be discharged by oral evidence, but by producing the record of appointment.

## Publicity requirements of directors and secretaries

A register of directors and secretaries must be kept at the registered office of the company.[44] It should contain the present names, former names, residential address, nationality, business occupation and particulars of any other directorships held by each director. Where Section 186 applies to the company (i.e. a public company), the date of birth of the director should also be indicated.[45] Where a corporation is a director, its corporate name and registered or principal

35 S. 2

36 Orojo, op. cit. p. 262

37 Companies Act, S. 181; Rv. Camps [1962] E.A. 403 C.A

38 Morris v. Kanssen [1946] A.C. 459; [1946] 1 ALL ER 586; *Dipcharima v. Ali (1914) 1 ALL NLR, Bozak (Nig) Ltd. v. Ziregbe* (1978) 4 FRCR 84

39 [1898] 1 Ch. 6. C.A. See also Leigh, *op.cit.*p. 127

40 *Mahony v. East Holyford Mining Co.* (1875), L.R. 7 H.L. 869; *Pool House Group (Nig) Ltd. v. A.C.B. Ltd. 1969 NCLR* 347. See also *Prichlik v. Marsh & Ors* [1961] 1N. L.R. 59

41 *ibid,* 354-355

42 1974 NCLR 266 (High Court of Western Nigeria)

43 *ibid*; pp. 274-276

44 Companies Act, S. 201

45 *ibid* S. 201 (2) (a)

office must be supplied.[46] Similar particulars should be registered in respect of a secretary to the company.[47] the above details should be sent by way of return to the Registrar of Companies within 14 days of appointment of directors or secretaries or change thereof.[48]

The company is also required to maintain a register which shows for each director the number, description and amount of shares or debentures of the company or its subsidiary or holding company or a subsidiary of the company's holding company, which are held by or in trust for him or which he has a right to become the holder.[49] Particulars of the date of, and consideration for, any dealings with the director's holding after the commencement of the Act should also be entered into the register.[50]

The register, which is kept at the company's registered office is open to inspection by members and debenture holders for a period commencing 14 days before and ending three days after the annual general meeting.[51]

The director's name, former name, and nationality should also be stated in all trade catalogues, circulars, showcards and business letters of the company.[52]

# Termination of directorship

## Resignation

A director may resign his office at any time. The company's articles usually make provision for resignation. Article 88 (e)[53] indicates that the office of a director shall be vacated if the director resigns his office by notice in writing to the company. Where such notice of resignation has been given, it cannot be withdrawn without the approval of the remaining directors.[54] Even where the articles require the resignation to be in writing, the company can validly accept a verbal resignation tendered before it in general meeting.[55]

## Retirement

There is usually provision in the articles for the retirement of directors by rotation.[56] For instance, Article 89 of Table A stipulates that one-third of the directors shall retire by rotation in each year. Such retiring directors are eligible for re-election. Where Table A is followed, it is indicated that a retiring director who offers himself for re-election will be deemed to be re-elected unless at such meeting it is expressly resolved not to fill the vacated office, or a resolution for the re-election of such director has been put to the vote at the meeting and lost.[57]

Under Section 186, a director of the company which is subject to the section (viz a public company) must vacate his office at the conclusion of the general meeting commencing next after he attains the age of 70 years. This provision may be waived by a resolution, of which special notice has been give to the general meeting.[58]

---

46 *ibid*, S. 201 (2) (b)

47 *ibid*, S. 201 (3)

48 *ibid* .s 201 (4), (5)

49 *ibid*., S. 195 (1)

50 *ibid*., S. 196 (2)

51 *ibid*., S. 196 (5)

52 *ibid*. S. 202

53 Table A.

54 *Glossop v. Glossop* [1907] 2 Ch. 370 *Prichlik v. Marsh* (1961) WNLR 59

55 *Latchford Premier Cinema Ltd v. Ennion* [1931] 2 Ch. 409

56 Table A. Arts 89-92

57 *ibid*. Art. 92. See also *Grundt v. Great Boulder Pty Gold Mines Ltd*. [1948] Ch. 145; [1948] 1 ALL ER 21.

58 Companies Act, S. 186 (5)

## Removal

The shareholders have authority to remove a director by ordinary resolution at a general meeting.[59] This power supersedes anything contained in the articles or in any agreement between the company and the director although it does not affect a director in a private company holding office for life on 1st January, 1961. Special notice has to be given of any such resolution and the affected director must be availed a copy of such notice and entitled to a hearing at the meeting.[60] The affected director is also entitled to circulation of his representations regarding the resolution.[61] The dismissal of the director is without prejudice to any claim he may have for compensation or damages arising from the termination of his services.[62] This may prove onerous to the company if it is appreciated that the contract of service between the company and the director is in practice effected by the directors on behalf of the company. Consequently, there is a possibility of the directors entrenching their positions.[63] This disadvantage may be partly offset by provision that the board of directors refer to the general meeting the amount of compensation to be paid to a dismissed director.[64] The affected director can only legally claim compensation if he has a binding contract entitling him either to hold his position for a fixed term or to be dismissed only after a prescribed notice.[65] If such a contract exists then the company cannot evade it by altering its articles of association and if an alteration is carried out giving the company power to dismiss contrary to the terms of the service agreement, this will amount to a breach of contract.[66]

In a situation, though, where a managing director has an informal service agreement or one of an unspecified duration, it is apparent that the agreement is deemed to be on the terms of the articles with only such security and tenure as there provided.[67] The implication is that "many informal service agreements can be ended by either party at a moment's notice without giving rise to any claim for damages."[68] This is exemplified by Article 107 of Table A, which stipulates that the appointment of a managing director "shall automatically determine if he ceases from any cause to be a director." There is an apparent contrast to a situation where a director is appointed to another office of profit (e.g. secretary consultant etc.) under Article 84 (3). As is put by Gower:

> If his express contract provides that he shall be entitled to remain a director so long as he retains the other office, he will, apparently be entitled to damages under Section [185(6)] if the company removes him from the directorship.[69]

---

59 *ibid.*, S. 185; See also *Eronini v. Harbor.* (1952) 2 FSC 43: *Kwizu v. Iwuchukwu* (Unreported) FCA/E/36/84; *Ali El-Khadra v. International Metal Industries Ltd.* (1973) 2FRCR 84; *Assoc. Reg. Eng. Contractors Ltd. v. Amaye*, (1986) 3 NWLR

60 S. 185 (2) read together with S. 142 of Cap 85. See also B.J. Cartoon, *The Removal of Company Directors Journal of Business Law* pp. 17-23; *Awoyemi v. Salomon* (1976) 2 FRCR 165 FHC

61 *ibid.* S. 185

62 *ibid.* S. 185 (6)

63 Gower, *op. cit*, (3rd Ed.), p. 134; (4th Ed), p. 150

64 Companies Act, Ss. 192 and 193

65 *Supra* n. 64

66 *Southern Foundries v. Shirlaw* [1940] A.C. 701 H.L.; It was held that there is an implied undertaking in the contract of service of a managing director for a given period that the company will not during that period revoke his appointment as director and will not resolve that his tenure of office be determined. See also *Shindler v. Northern Raincoat Co. Ltd.* [1960] 1 WLR 1038

67 *Read Astoria Garage (Streatham) Ltd.* [1952] 1 ALL ER 922. See also *supra* chap. 5 on the effect of alteration of articles.

68 Gower, *supra* n. 64, p. 135

69 *ibid.*, p. 136; (4th Ed.) pp. 151-152

The object of Section 185 can be frustrated by providing in the articles for weighted votes in respect of a director's shares on a resolution to remove him,[70] with the result that the director is enabled to survive a resolution intended to remove him.

Where the articles indicate the mode of removal, they must be strictly implied with in order to achieve a valid removal. Thus, in *George Hutchful v. Hamilton Kweku Biney, W. Biney & Co.*[71], the plaintiff applied for a declaration that his purported removal by the first defendant as and general manager of the second defendant company was *ultra vires* the first defendant.

It was held that irrespective of article 12(a) of the company's articles, which authorised the governing director, "to remove any director however appointed, and at any time," since the first defendant purported to act as general manager, he was confined to the powers of that office, which powers did not embrace the right to remove a director. Consequently, the purported removal of the plaintiff as director was *ultra vires* and illegal.

## Remuneration of directors

Directors are in principle not regarded as servants of the company. Rather they are its controllers.[72] Consequently, they are not entitled to remuneration except where there is provision to that effect in its articles of association.[73] Articles[74] usually indicate that directors shall be entitled to such remuneration as shall be determined by the company in general meeting by resolution. A director is entitled to sue for the remuneration which the company has agreed to pay him and may prove it in a winding-up.[75] The articles may provide for directors to be paid a fixed sum per annum. However, the directors will not be able to sue for such remuneration unless they can prove existence of a contract with the company. For that purpose provision in the articles is not sufficient[76], although an implied contract might be inferred on the basis of such articles, where the director has accepted office on the basis thereof.[77] Where the remuneration is thus provided for, it constitutes a debt due from the company to the directors for which they may sue. However, in the absence of a valid agreement, a director who, in addition, holds a service position such as that of managing director may recover payment for his services on *quantum meruit,* based on an implied undertaking to pay for services rendered on behalf of and accepted by the company.[78]

Director's remuneration must be stated in the prospectus, if any[79] and disclosed in accounts laid before the company in general meeting.[80] Compensation for loss of office must also be disclosed to members and approved by them in general meeting.[81] However, this only applies to payments which have not been agreed upon. Consequently, if the director's service contract

---

70 *Bushell v. Faith* [1970] A.C. 1099 H.L. See also *Kehinde v. Registrar of Companies* (1979) 3 LRN 213 where a similar approach had the effect of frustrating the *Nigeria Enterprises promotion Act,* 1977, with respect to indigenous control of the company See too the criticisms by Prentice, (1969) 32 MLR 693

71 [1971] ALL NLR 268 (Supreme Court of Nigeria).

72 See supra n. 13 to 18 and text thereof.

73 *Hutton v. West Cork Rail Co.* (1883) 23 Ch. D 654; *Moriarty v. Regent's Garage Co. Ltd.* [1921] 1 K.B. 423, p. 446, per McCardie J.; *Re: George Newman & Co.* [1895] 1 Ch. 674 at p. 686, per Lindley LJ. See also *Modikayo Oneka v. Wines & Spirits (U) Ltd.* [1974] HCB 263

74 e.g. Table A., Art. 76

75 c.f. *Re: Richmond Gate Property Co. Ltd.*, [1964] 3 ALL ER 939 discussed *infra*

76 *Re: Lundy Granite Co., Ltd., Lewis Case* (1872) 26 L.J. 673

77 *Re: New British Iron Co.* [1898] 1 Ch. 324, p. 326 per Wright J. See further *Re: T.N. Farrer, Ltd.* [1937] Ch. 352; [1937] 2 ALL ER 505

78 *Craven-Ellis v. Canons Ltd.* [1936] 2 KB 103; [1936] 2 ALL ER 1066

79 Schedule 3 Para 2. Companies Act,

80 *ibid.*, S. 197

81 *ibid.*, S. 192-195

provides for compensation upon termination of his office, no general meeting approval is necessary for the payment.[82]

# Powers of directors

The powers of directors usually stem from provision in the principal statute and the articles. It is common for the relevant Section or article to grant to the directors all powers of the company which are not reserved by the Act or regulations to the shareholders in general meeting.

For instance Article 80 of Table A stipulates:

> The business of the company shall be managed by the directors who ... may exercise all such powers of the company as are not, by the Act or by these regulations, required to be exercised by the company in general meeting, subject, nevertheless, to any of these regulations, to the provisions of the Act and to such regulations, being not inconsistent with the aforesaid regulations or provisions, as may be prescribed by the company in general meeting; but no regulation made by the company in general meeting shall invalidate any prior act of the directors which would have been valid if that regulation had not been made.

**Is the board subordinate to the general meeting under Article 80?**

Sullivan has argued[83] that although Table A grants to the directors some specific powers in relation to liens, calls, share transfers, borrowing and dividends, the rest of their powers have to be deduced from Article 80.

He adds:[84]

> Thus it is not a residual regulation supplementing a range of powers specifically conferred but the prime source of directors' authority within the company.

Hence in examining the scope of the directors' powers in relation to Article 80, the crucial issue is "whether in the sphere of management, directors are autonomous representatives or more in the nature of delegates"[85]

A number of decisions highlight the controversy inherent in tackling the above issue. In *Automatic Self-Cleansing Filter Syndicate Co. v. Cunninghame*[85], Cozen-Hardy LJ rejected the notion that a similarly worded article to Article 80 had the effect of making directors agents of the general meeting, susceptible to control and direction by that body.[86] This approach was supported shortly afterwards by the Court of Appeal in *Gramophone and Typewriter Ltd. v. Stanley*[87], where Buckley L.J. stated[88]

> The directors are not servants to obey directions given by the shareholders as individuals; they are not agents appointed by and bound to serve their shareholders as their principals. They are persons who may by the regulations be entrusted with the control of the business,

---

82 *Taupo Totara Timber Co., Ltd. v. Rowe* [1978] A.C. 537; [1977] 3 ALL ER 123

83 "The Relationship Between The Board of Directors and General Meeting In Limited Companies" (1977) 93 *LQR* 569. See also Bakibinga, *Punjab Univ. Law J.* Volume 44, pp.61-70 (1987); *Review of Business & Property Law* (Lagos) March 1989, pp.13-17.

84 *ibid.* p . 571

85 [1906] 2 Ch. 34, hereinafter *Automatic.*

86 *ibid* p. 44

87 [1908] 2 KB 89 See also *Ukpilla Cement Co. Ltd. v. Igiekhume, supra* n. 10

88 *ibid.* pp. 105-106. Buckley L.J. here departed from his earlier view that the general meeting had power to control the board of director: *Companies Act* (6th Ed. 1891) p. 492; (7th Ed. 1897) p. 530. See also *Shaw v. Shaw* [1935] 2 K.B. 113, 134 per Green L.J.

> and if so entrusted they can be dispossessed from that control only by the statutory authority which can alter the articles. Directors are not I think bound to comply with the directions even of all corporators acting as individuals.

The views expressed in those cases and others which will be considered form the majority approach to Article 80.[89] Sullivan's objection to the *Automatic* decision is twofold. In the first place, of the two relevant articles considered by the court, Article 97 empowered the directors to "sell any property", but unlike Article 80 it was not "hedged around" with "subject to" qualifications. Secondly that Article 96 was identical in effect to Article 80 but the power to manage was "subject to such resolutions as may be made by extra-ordinary resolution." In addition, Collins M.R. found that this clause entitled the shareholders to intervene in management (though not with the exclusive power to sell property) provided that the constitutional requirements were observed. As regards the *Gramophone Typewriter* case, Sullivan notes that Buckley L.J.'s "assertion" was not only *obiter*, but was based on the decision in *Automatic* rather than an express interpretation of Article 80,.

It is respectfully submitted that Sullivan's attempt to distinguish the *Automatic* decision from the purport of Article 80 on the ground that the provision in issue there talked of "resolutions... made extraordinary resolution" is not significant. If it is accepted, as we contend here, that in order to change the directors powers in Article 80 the company in general meeting has to pass a special resolution (pursuant to Section 13 of the Companies Act), which requires at least a three-fourths majority of shareholders, the same majority as for an extra-ordinary resolution (S. 141, Companies Act), then the case for distinguishing the reasoning in the *Automatic* decision from Article 80 appears inconsequential. It would also follow that the criticism of Buckley LJ's observations in the *Gramophone Typewriter* case which were based on the *Automatic* case, also lacks force.

The third case tending towards the "majority" view of Article 80 is *Quin and Axtens v. Salmon*[90], which laid down that the effect of Article 80 is to render the general meeting incapable of interfering with a decision of the directors unless they are acting contrary to the provision of the act or the Articles. Professor Gower notes[91] that the effect of the decision was to deprive the last words of Article 80 (referring to prescription by the general meeting) of any meaning. Sullivan[92] regards the case as significant for Lord Loreburn's equation of the word "regulations" in phrase "subject nevertheless... to such regulations" in Article 80 with "articles"[93]. He objects to such an interpretation on the ground that "the articles are clearly referred to in the preceding 'these regulations'."

He adds:

> ... if the dictum is correct the seemingly vital words of limitation are but pointless repetition.

Mr Sullivan further points out that Lord Loreburn's interpretation was *obiter* in "the strictest sense", his judgment resting on the reason that the right of veto of the managing director was in absolute terms and therefore independent from shareholder regulation.

While conceding the nature of Lord Loreburn's interpretation in relation to Article 80, Sullivan's objection to it, is with respect inconsequential. Regardless of whether the interpretation was *obiter*, it is clear that his understanding of the word, "regulations" in the expression "subject

89 Sullivan, *op. cit.* pp. 573-577. See also *Atewologun v. Metro Motors Ltd.* (1978) 2 LRN 46, *Trade Links Int. (Nig) Ltd. v. Bank of America (Nig) Ltd.* 3 FRCR 79

90 [1909] 1 Ch. 311 C.A. [1909] A.C. 442 H.L.

91 *The Principles of Modern Company Law* (3rd Ed. 1969), p. 131.

92 *op. cit. supra* pp. 575-576

93 [1909] A.C. at pp. 444

nevertheless ... to such regulations or provision as may be prescribed by the company in general meeting" is consistent with a correct analysis of Article 80. The correct analysis is that since the powers given to the directors are contained in an article, a variation of, or interference with, those powers must of necessity involve an alteration of that article.[94] Such an alteration, (which under Section 13 of the Companies Act must be made by special resolution) would essentially amount to a substitution or replacement of the article with regulations constituting a new article. This is borne out by the wording of Section 13(2):

> Any alteration or addition so made in the articles shall, subject to the provisions of this Act, be as valid as if originally contained therein, and be subject in like manner to alteration by special resolution.

Thus, while from a narrow draughtsman's point of view, the phrase "regulations" appears to carry a different import from that of "articles", an examination of the legal effect of interfering with the directors' powers in Article 80 leads to a result which makes "regulations" synonymous with "articles"[95]

In *Scott v. Scott*[96], the majority shareholders passed ordinary resolutions purporting to declare interim dividends and to cause the financial affairs of the company to be investigated by outside auditors. In either case, the powers had been conferred by Table A upon the directors. Lord Clauson held that such resolutions were void and refused to be persuaded that the limiting words, "subject nevertheless" etc, in Article 80 had anything to do with the directors' duty to manage the company and in effect appraised the contradiction inherent in that regulation. To the extent that this case conclusively[97] supports the view that the power of directors to manage the business of the company is inviolable and not susceptible to control by the general meeting. it may be said to be contrasting to the leading judicial authority supporting the "minority view" of Article 80, viz. *Marshall's Valve Gear v. Manning, Wardle and Co.*[98]
In that case, Neville J. thus stated:[99]

> Under (Article 80) the majority of the shareholders within the company at a general meeting have a right to control the actions of the directors *so long as they do not affect the control in a direction contrary to any of the provisions of the articles which bind the company.*

Although its not *prima facie* clear what type of majority Neville J. had in mind, if that "majority of shareholders" is interpreted in the light of the subsequent phrase that they have to affect the control of the directors pursuant to "the articles which bind the company", then it is obvious that a special majority of three "fourths of the shareholders was envisaged.[100] If this interpretation is accepted, it would then follow that Neville J.'s statement is nothing more than a paraphrase of Article 80 and consequently gives us little assistance in understanding that article. In this context, Sullivan's reliance on the *Marshall's Valve* case as giving a straightforward meaning to Article 80 in comparison with the *Scott* case[101] may be doubted. Furthermore, the learned writer's view that "whatever practical difficulties a division of power between directors and

---

94 See also K.A. Aickin, "Division of Power Between Directors and General Meeting As a Matter of Law, and as a Matter of Fact & Policy" (1967) 5 *Melbourne University L. Rev. 448, 458*

95 For a contrary view, see Goldberg, "Article 80 Table A Companies Act 1948" (1970) 33 *M.L.R* 177, 172-8

96 [1943] 1 ALL ER 582; hereinafter *Scott*

97 Although described as not "very strong": Mackenzie (1983) 4 *Co. Law*, 99.

98 [1909] 1 Ch. 267. See also Sullivan, *op. cit.* pp. 572-573; 577-8

99 *ibid* at p. 267. EMPHASIS SUPPLIED. See also *Logan (Thomas) Ltd. v. Davis* (1911) 104 L.T. 914 and *Dowse v. Marks* (1913) S.R. (N.S.W.) 332; *Trade Links* case, supra n. 89

100 especially where the control affects powers given to directors by the Articles of Association. See discussion *supra*.

101 *op. cit.* p. 578

shareholders may give rise to, it seems clear that Article 80 was not intended to give the directors a free hand in management" is, with respect, too sweeping and neither supported by the *Marshall's Valve* case nor the phraseology of Article 80 itself. To read into Article 80 a lack of "free hand in management" for the directors is to ignore the fact that the phrase, "subject, nevertheless, to ... such regulations ... as may be prescribed by the company in general meeting", is only a limiting provision and does not divest the directors of their discretion in management.

**Article 80 and the residual powers of the general meeting**

It has been suggested[102] that "Article 80 is a compromise between securing some degree of directoral autonomy and preserving the residual authority of the general meeting as the supreme organ of the company."

It is submitted that, where a company has adopted Article 80, the issue of residual authority of the general meeting does not arise as all powers not required to be exercised by shareholders in general meeting are given to the board of directors. In this context, the attempt once again to invoke[103] the *Marshall's Valve* case as indicating that the residual powers of the general meeting are relevant in relation to article 80 is unconvincing. In that case, Neville J. thus stated:[104]

> I take it that prior to the decision in the case of *Automatic self-Cleansing Filter Syndicate Co. v. Cunninghame* [1906] 2 Ch. 34, the law was established to the effect that the majority of shareholders, *in the absence of a contract to the contrary*, had the ultimate control of the affairs of the company and could assert their rights in general meeting.

While the learned judge's interpretation of the equivalent of Article 80, as to the distribution of power between the general meeting and the board of directors, may be questioned,[105] it would appear that he is correct when he says that *"in the absence of any contract to the contrary* the majority of the shareholders in a company have the ultimate control of the affairs, and are entitled to decide whether or not an action in the name of the company shall proceed..."[106] Consequently, where there is a contrary provision in the articles of association the question of residual authority of the general meeting will not arise, especially where the company has adopted Article 80.

Admittedly, there are situations where the residual authority of the general meeting becomes operative. These include instances where directors act contrary to their duties or exceed their authority[107]; where there is a dispute as to the use of the company's name in litigation.[108] Professor Wedderburn maintains that on the issue of initiation of proceedings on behalf of the company both the directors and the shareholders in general meeting retain parallel authority notwithstanding the form of the articles.[109] The residual authority of the general meeting will also arise where the directors are unable to act or are non-existent, in which case their powers will revert to the general meeting.[110] The situations in which the residual authority of the general meeting would be exercised have strictly speaking nothing to do with Article 80, except possibly where there is a dispute between the board of directors and the general meeting as to the

---

102 Sullivan, *op. cit.* p. 577

103 Mackenzie, *op. cit.* pp. 99-100

104 [1909] 1 Ch. 267 at p. 272; emphasis supplied

105 See *supra,* notes 98 to 99 and text thereof

106 [1909] 1 Ch. 267, 272; emphasis supplied

107 *Bamford v. Bamford* [1970] Ch. 212

108 *Danish Mercantile Co. Ltd. v. Beaumont* [1951] Ch. 680

109 (1957) *Camb. L.J.* 194, 200-203; (1976) 39 *MLR* 327, 28, Gower 4th Ed, p. 147

110 *Alexander Ward & Co. Ltd v. Samyang Navigation Ltd.* [1975] 1 WLR 673 H.L. See also Lord Wedderburn, (1976) 39 *M.L.R.* 327,328; *Okeowo v. Migliore* [1979]11 S.C. 138; per Idigbe, J.S.C.; *Ukpilla Cement Co. v. Igiekhume, supra n.10.*

commencement of proceedings in the name of the company. This is resolved by admitting that since both bodies have parallel authority in the matter, Article 80 is inapplicable. Strictly speaking though, where Article 80 has been adopted and there is no other authority in the articles empowering the general meeting to initiate litigation in the company's name, then such a power, being managerial, lies with the board of directors[111], except in situations of impropriety on the part of the board.

**Company control and managerial control**

Sullivan has suggested the direction in which he sees the resolution of the two competing views of Article 80. He thus stated:[112]

> ... when an appellate court does resolve this issue it will find that under Article 80 shareholders in general meeting by passing ordinary resolutions can give controlling directions to the board in matters of management. Such intervention will be subject to the proviso that the management function must reside in the directors.

This prescription is unsatisfactory in the least and at worst contradictory. It is difficult to appreciate how a management function can reside in directors who are nevertheless subject to control by the general meeting giving controlling directions to the board on management matters appears to suggest that the board is an agent of the general meeting, a notion which is inconsistent with case law authority.[113] It would be feasible to talk of the general meeting controlling the company's affairs for tax purposes but such "control" is interpreted to mean "ultimate control of the composition of directors" rather than control over the manner in which the directors manage the company's business.[114]

**A liberal interpretation of Article 80**

It has, however, been suggested that rather than emphasizing a rigid interpretation of Article 80, it should be recognised that there are instances (e.g regarding the institution of suit by the shareholders in general meeting) where justice and equity requires a more flexible appreciation of the division of powers between the board of directors and shareholders in general meeting.[115] This approach is based on Lord Wilberforce's observation in *Ebrahimi v. Westbourne Galleries thus:*[116]

> There is room in company law that behind it or amongst it there are individuals with rights, expectations and obligations *inter se* which are not necessarily submerged in the company structure ... (the just and equitable principle) enables the court to subject the exercise of legal rights to equitable considerations, that is of a personal character arising between one individual and another which may make it unjust or inequitable to insist on legal rights or to exercise them in a particular way.

It is respectfully submitted, though, that this dictum is much more relevant in the context of the just and equitable winding up remedy under Section 222 (f) of the Companies Act, than one of the relationship between the board of directors and the general meeting.

---

111 *c.f. Bamford v. Bamford* [1969] 1 ALL ER 969 at p. 976

112 *op. cit.* pp. 579-580

113 *Automatic* decision, *supra* note 86 *Gramophone Typewriter* case, *supra* note 88

114 Aickin, *op. cit. supra* note 95 pp. 461-462; See also *British American Tobacco Co. v. IRC* [1942] AC 335, 340

115 B.I. Mordsley and R.A. Weidberg, "Shareholders' Right or Directors' Might - Who Rules Within A Company" (1977) *City of London Law Review*, 45, 57

116 [1973] A.C. 360, 379 (H.L)

**The continental position**

It may be interesting to consider the significance of the two conflicting views of the relationship between directors and shareholders in general meeting in two other distinctive company law systems.

With regard to the *Societe Anonyme* public company in France, its board of directors is given wide powers to act on behalf of the company.

However, these must be exercised within the limits of the objects and subject to powers which are expressly reserved by law to the general meeting. The inference here is that the directors' powers are exclusive to themselves but they must not in exercising them encroach on those of the general meeting. There is no suggestion that the directors are subject to control in their exercise of powers. A similar position is discernible with respect to managers of SARLS or private companies.[117]

In Germany[118], the board of directors in a public company is empowered with managing the business of the company or managing the company. In so doing, Professor Wurdinger notes[119] that it "is sovereign in making decisions ... and since it acts on its own responsibility, it is subject to the directions of neither the supervisory board as a supervisory organ is inherently incapable of giving directions to the board. It can only supervise, but not direct, and the statutes can do nothing to change this..."

It is further notable that the board's management freedom of action only exists within the scope of management activities and ancillary to the business of the company. It is evident that the directors' powers of management are not subject to interior control by the general meeting.

Concerning the private company (GmBHG), the managers' powers to manage may be subjected to the directions of the supervisory board or the shareholders.[120] This approach is consonant with the "minority view" of Article 80, and would presumably take care of the "hard case" posited by Ms Mackenzie with respect to the dilemma of a major shareholder who is not a board member in a small private company.[121] Overall though, it is clear that the exclusive managerial powers of the board of directors in French companies and German public companies conform with the majority view of the Article 80

While conceding that there may be some merit in the minority view of Article 80, a closer analysis of that view reveals shortcomings relating largely to, the analysis of the relevant cases; the confusion of the residual powers of the general meeting with the import of Article 80; and the failure to appreciate the distinction between company and managerial control. It is submitted that while ultimate control of the company lies with the general meeting through its power to remove directors (s. 185 of the Companies Act) and alter the articles of association (s. 13 of the 1968 Act), where the company has adopted Article 80, managerial control rests with the board of directors.

Ultimately, the minority view of Article 80 rests on the policy that an investor in a company should have some control over the way in which his investment is used.[122] This policy, which should be distinguished from the legal effect of Article 80, is achieved by empowering the general meeting to appoint and dismiss directors. In addition, the shareholders have the option not to adopt Article 80 where it is found inconvenient for their purposes.

The directors may, if permitted by the articles, delegate some of their powers[123] or appoint a managing director to whom they may entrust any of their powers.[124] They may also appoint

117 See generally, J. Legall, *French Company Law* (London: Oyez, 1974) pp. 133-136; 196-197

118 See generally, H. Wurdinger, *German Company Law* (London Oyez, 1975) pp. 44-47; 198-199

119 *ibid* p. 45

120 *ibid* p. 199

121 Mackenzie, *op. cit.* p. 101

122 *ibid*, p. 102

123 Table A. Art. 102

124 See *infra*

attorneys[125] and exercise all the borrowing powers of the company, subject to restrictions as to the amount which may be imposed by the company.[126]

Directors' powers end when upon winding up of the company, a liquidator is appointed.[127]

# Proceedings of the directors

The directors normally act as a board, unless the articles otherwise provide, at a meeting.[30a] They decide issues arising by a majority of votes cast. Any director can call a meeting.[128] Every director is entitled to reasonable notice of the directors' meeting. Otherwise, proceedings at the meeting will be void.[129] Nevertheless, in *Bentley Stevens v. Jones*[130], a director was removed in the course of irregular proceedings, this being so because no valid notice was served on him. It was held that an injunction could not be granted to restrain the removal since the irregularity could be cured by going through the proper processes and serving a valid notice. The result would, in any case, be the same.

The quorum at a board meeting is normally fixed by the articles. Thus, it may be provided that such quorum shall be fixed by the directors, and if not so fixed, shall be two,[131] who must remain throughout the meeting. A decision of the board may be invalidated if it is voted on by directors who are disqualified from voting.[132] The directors may also elect a chairman of the meeting, among themselves, who may have a casting vote.[133] In addition, they may delegate their powers to committees,[134] whose activities may be regulated by the articles.[135] Nevertheless, where the directors of a company delegate their powers to a committee and there is no provision for a quorum, the whole committee must meet and then act by a majority. They have no power to add to their number or supply a vacancy.[38a]

The board may dispense with an actual meeting by getting a resolution signed by all the directors. Such resolution will be valid and effectual as if it had been passed at a board meeting, duly convened and held.[136] The articles may also validate acts of directors, even if it is afterwards discovered that there was some defect in the appointment of them or that any of them was disqualified as a director.[137]

The minutes of the board's meetings must be kept and should be signed by the chairman.[138]

It is also established that a director may bring a personal action against his fellow directors to restrain them from wrongfully excluding him from the board.[139] In *Martins v. Ogungbadero & Ors*[140], following deterioration of the relationship between the plaintiff and the other directors

---

[125] e.g Table A. Art. 81

[126] *ibid.* Art. 79. See also *supra* chap. 10

[127] See *infra* Chap 18

[30a] *Carib Construction Co. Ltd. v. Lynch* CCHCJ/12/73/29, 32 Per Savage, J.

[128] See e.g. Table A. Art. 98

[129] *Re: Homer Gold Mines* (1888) 39 Ch. D. 546; See also *Haslir v. Zard & Co. Ltd.* 1976 2 FRCR 235; 1976 NCLR 149; *Industrial Growers (Ug) v. Tamale* Cs. No. 215 of 1963 (Unreported) (High Court of Uganda)

[130] [1914] 1 WLR 638; See also *Ellis v. Bailey & Co. (EA) Ltd.* [1962] EA 626

[131] Table A. Art. 99

[132] *Re: Greymouth Point Elizabeth Railway & Coal Co., Ltd.* [1904] 1 Ch. 32; See also Companies Act, S. 183

[133] Table A. Art. 98 and 101 read together.

[134] *ibid.* Art. 102

[135] *ibid*, Arts 103-105; See also *Higgs v. W.A.A.C (Nig) Ltd.* 1969 NCLR 394

[38a] *Higgs v. WAAC ibid*, pp. 312-313 See too 6 *Halsbury's Laws of England* 3rd Ed. p. 296 para 600.

[136] *ibid.* Art. 106 See also *Re: Bonnelli's Telegraph Co.* (1871) L.R. 12 Eq. 246, *Okeowo v. Migliore* (1979) 1 S.C. 138

[137] Table A, Art 105. See also S. 181 of the Companies Act.

[138] *ibid* S. 145 *Nasr v. Berini Beirut-Riyadi (Nig) Bank Ltd.* 1968 NCLR 370

[139] *Pulbrook v. Richmond Consolidated Mining Co.* (1878) 9 Ch.D. 610

[140] 1967 NCLR 393 (High Court of Lagos State). See also *York Tramways Co. Ltd. v. Willows* (1882) 8 Q.B.D. 685 and *Pricklik v. Marsh* (1961) WNLR 59

when he attempted to divert money to his use. The company held a meeting to consider the plaintiff's conduct and possible disciplinary action against him. Notice of the meeting was given to him, but the plaintiff did not attend. The other directors decided to deprive him of his directorship and informed him of such by letter. The plaintiff sued the defendants for, *inter alia,* a declaration of his status as a director and an injunction restraining the defendants from excluding him from the exercise of his rights and duties as a director. It was held, *inter alia,* that the plaintiff was validly dismissed as a director of the company in line with the relevant company's article which provided that two members in person could form a quorum and transact the company's business. Consequently, the claim for injunction failed.[141]

Where the number of directors is reduced to below the minimum required for a quorum the director or directors will be precluded from acting except where the articles otherwise provide.[142] In *Martins v. Ogungbadero*[143], at a meeting at which the first defendant, the deceased and another were present, it was decided that shareholders should pay for their shares. The plaintiff was informed of the decision by letter, but declined to pay up. Following the death of the deceased, the first defendant and the plaintiff were the remaining shareholders. The first defendant, acting alone and in breach of the company's articles, gave the plaintiff notice of forfeiture of shares and confirmed this by letter. The plaintiff instituted an action for a declaration, *inter alia,* that he was still a shareholder of the company. It was held that[144] as there was no provision in the articles and memorandum of association of the company for a sole surviving director to act otherwise than in conformity with the relevant article, providing for a quorum of two members to transact the company's business, the call on the plaintiff shareholder was invalid and consequently the decision forfeiting his shares was wholly void. It followed that the plaintiff was entitled to the declaration sought.

## The managing director

While the law gives most of the company's powers to the general meeting and the board of directors, in practice, the detailed and regular decisions affecting the company's business are taken by persons to whom the board of directors delegates its powers of management. The person to whom such powers are delegated is normally the managing director. It has in this regard been observed:

> In large companies the day to day management decisions are left to one or more managing directors...[145]

In a similar vein, Iacono commented:

> It is also common knowledge (at least in business circles) that directors rarely do in fact manage the company, except perhaps in closely held corporations... and that this task is generally entrusted to the management, and more specifically to the President and other executive officers.[146]

Furthermore, Goel noted that in large companies:

---

141 *ibid,* at p. 396. See also *Ellis v. Bailey & Co, (EA) Ltd.* [1962] EA 626

142 Under Table A. Art. 100 the continuing directors are authorised to act only for the purpose of increasing the number of directors to the number required for a quorum or summoning a general meeting of the company.

143 *Supra* n. 140

144 *ibid* p. 397. See also *Inre: Alma Spinning Co. Bottomley Case* (1880) 16 Ch. D. 681

145 *Palmer's Company Law (22nd Ed., 1976)* p. 665, para 60-07; See also Gower, *op cit.* (4th Ed.) p. 154

146 Iacono, The Strict Ethic of the Equitable Principle: Comments on *Canadian Aero Services v. O'Malley* (1975) 2 *McGill L.J.* 445.

> It is neither customary nor feasible for the directors to manage the corporate business in the sense that they themselves conduct its day-to-day operations.[147]

Management is thus a reality and significant factor within the corporate power structure. It is notable though that "a Managing Director as such has no specific powers or duties recognised by the law. What powers and duties he is to have must be derived from the company itself."[148] The powers entrusted to a managing director derive from provisions in the articles of association which empower the directors to appoint from among themselves a managing director.[149] Subject to these articles, the other powers and rights of the managing director may be stipulated in an agreement between him and the company, but he remains subject to the company's power to terminate his appointment under Section 185 of the Companies Act.[150]In addition, the managing director's power and duties may be limited in that the board of directors reserves to itself the power to curtail his functions. This was the case in *Harold Holdsworth & Co. (Wakefield) Ltd. v. Caddies.*[151] Caddies' contract of employment with the company provided that he should perform the duties and exercise the powers in relation to the business of the company and the businesses of its existing subsidiaries "which may from time to time be assigned to or vested in him by the board of directors of the company." It was held by the House of Lords that it was permissible for the board of directors to instruct Caddies to manage a subsidiary company instead of the principal holding company, which he had then been managing. It is significant though that under "the more usual terms of employment"[152], such an interference by the board would amount to a breach of contract on its part.[153]

The remuneration of the managing director is determined by the board of directors.[154] It has been decided that Article 108 is independent of Article 107 and applies whether the managing director is appointed by the articles or the board under Article 107.[155] However, if the contract appointing him is invalid, a claim on *quantum meruit* is permissible.[156]

## The secretary

The other significant officer of the company who may be said to form part of the management of the company is the secretary.

It is mandatory on the company to have a secretary who at the same time must not be its sole director.[157] Anything required to be executed by a director and the secretary cannot be done by the same person acting in both capacities.[158]

The secretary, as Gower notes[159], "can be appointed with less formality than a director." Thus, he will be appointed by the board of directors rather than the general meeting and any officer of the company may be empowered by the board to act in the absence of the secretary.[160] In order to

---

147 Goel, "Delegation of Directors" Powers and Duties - A Comparative Analysis (1969) 18 *ICLQ* 152

148 *Palmer's Company Law supra* n. 145

149 e.g. Articles 107 to 109 Table A,

150 See *supra*, Under removal of directors.

151 [1955] 1 WLR 352 (H.L.). See also *Ellis v. Bailey & Co (EA) Ltd* [1962] EA 626

152 *Gore Browne on Companies* (43 Ed. 1977) para. 26-8

153 *Yetton v. Eastwoods Froy* [1967] 1 WLR 104. A managing director was dismissed and then offered the position of assistant managing director at the same salary. It was held that he was entitled to refuse the offer because of the loss of status involved.

154 Article 108 Table A

155 *Re: Richmond Gate Property Co. Ltd.* [1965] 1 WLR 335

156 *Craven-Ellis v. Canons Ltd.* [1936] 2 KB 403

157 Ss. 178 (1), 179, Companies Act, Table A. Art. 111

158 S. 180 ibid

159 LCB Gower, *Principles of Modern Company Law* (4th Ed. 1979) p. 158

160 S. 178 Table A. Art. 110. See also *Adebesin v. May & Baker (Nig) Ltd.* (1978) 4 FRCR 232

publicise the secretary, it is stipulated that the statement of the first directors (which must be delivered to the Companies Registry at the time of registration), must also give the name of the first secretary (or joint secretaries). The statement should bear the signatures of persons named as a director and secretary consenting to act in those capacities.[161]

The Secretary is entrusted with ensuring that the documentation of the company is accurate and orderly and that the necessary requisite returns are made to the Companies' Registry and that the Company's registers are in proper form.[162] In addition, he carries out the orders of the directors and the company's clerical work such as issuing notices of meetings, sending circulars, writing letters, preparing the agenda for directors' meetings and general meetings of the company and writing up the minutes of these meetings.[163] Furthermore, the Secretary is under a duty to certify share transfers,[164] and the articles of association may provide that the Secretary countersign deeds of the company.[165]

The functions of the Secretary raise the issue as to his status and position within the company. While he is an officer of the company within Section 2 of the Companies Act, his exact position has been of some controversy.

Thus, in the nineteenth century, the secretary was regarded to be no more than a servant or "office boy"[166] of the company. In this regard, Lord Egher M.R. in *Barnet Hoares & Co. v. South London Tramways Co.*[167] stated[168] that the secretary of a company:

> is a mere servant; his position is that he is to do what he is told, and no person can assume that he has any authority to represent anything at all; nor can anyone assume that statements made by him are necessarily to be accepted as trustworthy without further inquiry, any more than in the case of a merchant it can be assumed that one who is only a clerk has authority to make representations to induce persons to enter into contracts.

At the turn of the century and in a similar vein, Lord Macnaghten said in *George Whitechurch Ltd. v. Cavanagh*:[169]

> Now, the duties of a company's secretary are well understood. They are of a limited and of a somewhat humble character.

Such views have been described as "both unrealistic and out of harmony with the legislative trends.[170] However, as early as 1916, Lord Parker had described the secretary as one of the company's organs.[171] This was followed by Lord Parker CJ in *John Henshall (Quarries) Ltd. v. Harvey*[172] where he stated thus:

> There is no doubt that there are many cases where the knowledge of somebody in the position of the brain, may be the directors, the managing director, the secretary, the responsible officers of the company, has been held to be the knowledge of the company.

---

[161] Companies Act, S.201

[162] Gower, *supra* n. 159, p. 157; Gore-Browne, *supra*, n. 152, para. 26-9 See also *Okeowo v. Migliore* (1975) 11 S.C 138

[163] Gore-Browne, *ibid; Okeowo v. Migliore, ibid*

[164] Gore-Browne, *ibid*, para. 16-17 to 16-18. *Okeowo v. Migliore, ibid; Migliore v. Metal Construction (West Africa) Ltd.*

[165] Article 113 Table A

[166] Note (1971) 87 *LQR* 457

[167] (1887) 18 QBD 815

[168] at p. 817

[169] [1902] AC 117 at p. 124; see also *J.C. Houghton & Co. v. Northard, Lowe and Wills Ltd.* [1928] AC1 *Re Cleadon Trust Ltd.* [1939] Ch. 286

[170] Gower, *supra*, n. 62 p. 158; see also *Buckley on the Companies Acts* (13th Ed., 1957) p. 373

[171] *Daimler Company Ltd. v. Continental Tyre & Rubber Company* [1916] 2 AC 307 HL at p. 340

[172] [1965] 2 QB 233 at p. 241

The much more recent decision of the British Court of Appeal, in *Panorama Development (Guildford) Ltd. v. Fidelis Furnishing Fabrics Ltd.*[173], has reinforced that approach to the status of the secretary. In that case, the secretary of the defendant company hired cars from the plaintiff company, using hiring agreements which he signed and stamped ostensibly for the defendant company's business, although in reality for his own purposes. The plaintiffs sued for the outstanding charges and the defendant company denied liability contending that the secretary was acting for himself and was not in a position to bind the company at all. The defendants expressly relied on the *Barnett case.*[174] The defendants were held liable for the hiring charges.

Lord Denning, M.R. observed in relation to the position of the company secretary:

> Times have changed. A company secretary is a much more important person nowadays than he was in 1887 ... He is an officer of the company with extensive duties and responsibilities... He is certainly entitled to sign contracts connected with the administrative side of a company's affairs, such as employing staff, and ordering cars and so forth. All such matters now come within the ostensible authority of a company's secretary.[175]

*Salmon, L.J.* concurred referring to the secretary as "the chief administrative officer of the company." He, however, expressly reserved for future consideration "whether the secretary would have any authority to sign a contract relating to the commercial management of the company for example a contract for the sale and purchase of goods in which the company deals.[176]

This reservation has prompted the view that "it would be going too far to assume that a company secretary must be regarded as charged with the general management of the company."[177] This may help to explain the decision of Pennycuick V.C., in *Re: Maidstone Buildings Provisions Ltd.*[178], at first instance. In that case, it was held that a chartered accountant who acted as secretary and financial adviser to a company, was not a person who was knowingly a party to the carrying on of the business of the company with intent to defraud creditors. contrary to the Companies Act, 1948, S. 332(1)[81a] He could only be said to have failed to take steps to prevent the company trading fraudulently, when he was aware of its relevant condition. Hence "mere inertia on the part of a secretary does not, however, make him party to the carrying on of the company's business."[179] The usual functions of a secretary, though, are communication with the shareholders; keeping the books of the company and sending all necessary returns to the registrar of companies.[82a]

Since the secretary is an officer of the company[180], particulars of any loans made to him by the company must be shown in the company's accounts which are laid before the general meeting.[181] Furthermore, any attempt by the company's articles to exempt an officer of the company from or indemnifying him against any liability which would attach to him in respect of any negligence, default, breach of trust in relation to the company is void.[182] He may, as an officer of the company

---

173 [1971] 3 WLR 440

174 (1887) 18 QBD 815

175 [1971] 3 WLR 440 at p. 443

176 *ibid* at p. 444. See also *Adebesin v. May & Baker (Nig) Ltd supra* n. 63

177 Note (1971) 87 *LQR* 457-458; see also J.G. Collier, "Authority of a Company's Secretary to Enter Into Contracts On its behalf" (1972 A) 30 *C.L.J.* 44-47

178 [1971] 1 WLR 1085; in the light of the *Panorama case* it is doubtful whether this decision is still good law: J.H. Farrar, (1976) *J.B.L.* 214 at p. 226

81a Companies Act, S. 327

179 *supra* n. 177, p. 458

82a See further Orojo op. cit. pp. 285-287

180 Companies Act, S. 2

181 *ibid.* S. 198

182 *ibid.*, S. 206

be relieved from liability in respect of negligence; default, breach of duty or trust, where he has acted honestly or reasonably in relation to the liability arising.[183]

It is also established that appearance in court by a company should be done by its secretary.[184] In addition demand, where the company is unable to pay its debts, must where the creditor is also a company be authenticated under Section 38 of the Companies Act, by being signed by a director, secretary or other officer of the creditor company.[185]

## The auditors

The other significant official within the company whose functions impinge on management is the auditor. His legal role is discussed in detail elsewhere.[186]

---

183 *ibid.*, S. 405

184 *Ayodeji v. Lagos City Council* 1974 NCLR 299 (High court of Lagos State)

185 *Nigerian Commercial & Industrial Enterprises Ltd. v. Omagiafo Builders Ltd. & Anor* 1976 NCLR 399 (Federal Revenue Court) at pp. 402-403 per Belgore, J. See also *In Re Lympne Investments Ltd.* [1972] 1 WLR 523; [1972] 2 ALL ER 385.

186 See *infra* Chap. 13

# 12

# AUTHORITY OF CORPORATE INDIVIDUAL DIRECTORS AND OFFICERS*

## Introduction

It is clear that as a primary organ of the company, the directors' collective exercise of power as a board binds the company, which in relation to that exercise may be regarded as the principal. Similarly, a managing director, to whom the board has delegated its functions can bind the company.[1] The difficulty affecting the capacity to bind the company is most pronounced with regard to the actions of an individual director or official of the company. In the words of D.G. Rice:[2]

> Little difficulty attends the actions of the directors when they are acting jointly ... as a board. For in this capacity they clearly constitute one of the primary organs of the company whose powers are expressly defined for all to see in the company's constitution i.e., in its memorandum and articles of association. But as soon as an individual director purports to enter into a transaction on behalf of the company, considerable doubts are liable to arise as to the degree of authority.

## The indoor management rule

Nevertheless, an individual director may be able to bind the company in transactions with outsiders on the basis of the application of the constructive notice doctrine as modified by the indoor management rule or the rule in *Royal British Bank v. Turquand*[3]. In that case, the constitution of the company stipulated that the directors could borrow on bond such sums as should, from time to time by a general resolution of the company, be authorised to be borrowed. Without such resolutions, two bonds for £ 2,000 were issued to the bank under the common seal of the company and were signed by two directors. In liquidation proceedings, the bank sued Turquand, the liquidator on the security bonds. The defendant pleaded that since the borrowing had not been authorised by the requisite resolutions, the bonds were not binding on the company. It was held that the bonds were binding on the company. It was indicated[4] that, while persons dealing with a company are fixed with notice of its public documents, in this case the deed and statute of settlement, they are not bound to do more. In this respect all that the bank was required to do was to read the settlement. In so doing, it found that there was permission to borrow by the company on certain conditions, that is by resolution of the company. The bank then had a right to infer that a resolution authorising the borrowing had been passed. The essence of the rule then is that persons who are dealing with the company are assumed to know the contents of its

---

* See also Bakibinga, Volume 13, No.3 *Commonwealth Law Bulletin* (1987) pp.1062-1075

1 *B. Visinoni Ltd. & Ors V. National Bank of Nigeria* 1975 NCLR 198 (High Court of North Central State of Nigeria)

2 D.G. Rice, "Power of a Director to Bind The Company" (1959) *Journal of Bus. Law, 332*

3 (1856) 6E & 8 327. See also *Standard Bank Nig. Ltd. v. Bolokor Enterprises ltd.* (1980) FNR 114, 123-124 (High Court of Bendal State (Warri)

4 *African Development Corporation Ltd. v. Lagos Executive Dev. Board* 1966 NCLR; *Vanni v. Niger Pak Ltd.* (1979) 4-6 CCHCJ 148; See also *Witu v. Peake* 1913/1914 5 E.A.L.R 17

public documents, and that therefore any transaction they enter into with the company is authorised by those documents. However, they are not bound to do any more i.e. they need not inquire into the regularity of internal proceedings and may assume internal regularity.

The relevant documents, for purposes of the constructive notice doctrine, include the memorandum and articles of association and special and extraordinary resolutions of the company. Registration of such documents constitutes notice to the world.[5]

The indoor management rule has been considerably qualified in view of subsequent case law formulation and the application of agency principles.

# The application of agency principles[5a]

## Rule 1

Although an outsider who is dealing with a company is deemed to know the contents of its public documents, where the act proposed to be done is explicitly contrary to the documents, it cannot bind the company unless it has been ratified. Thus, in *Irvine V. Union Bank of Australia*[6] the articles of a company authorised the directors to borrow any sums up to one half of its paid-up capital. The articles could be altered by a simple majority. However, under the operative Companies Act,[7] such alteration had to be registered.

The directors borrowed money from the bank in excess of the authorised limit and handed to the bank certain property deeds as security. The articles were not altered and the shareholders did not ratify the directors' actions. The bank sought to enforce the security given to it by way of sale of the relevant property in order to satisfy the full value of the loan. It was held that, as there was no ratification, the bank could claim only up to the limit of the borrowing authorised by the articles. This was so because it was evident to the bank from the articles that the directors' borrowing powers were limited. Furthermore, an extension of such powers by resolution was required to be registered. Consequently, the transaction could not be protected by the indoor management rule.

Similarly, in *Obaseki v. African Continental Bank*[8], Obaseki purchased a piece of land, at an auction sale from the defendant company. The sale was authorised by a branch manager of the bank. However, under the articles of association, it was the board of directors which was authorised to approve the sale and execute the conveyance. Upon discovery of the irregularity in the procedure of sale, the board declined to give its approval. The plaintiff applied for specific performance of the contract and damages for refusal to execute. It was held that an act done in excess of actual authority by an agent is not binding especially where he is dealing with persons who are aware of the excess of authority.

## Rule 2

A second modification of the indoor management rule is to the effect that it is inapplicable where the relevant third party has knowledge that the internal procedures required have not been complied with or they are șuspicious circumstances putting him on inquiry in that regard. Thus, in *Mahony v. East Holyford* Mining Co.[9], a bank paid a cheque pursuant to a resolution sent to it by a company purporting to authorise the payment of cheques, if signed by two or three

---

5 *Ernest v. Nicholls* (1857) 6 HLC 401; *University of Nigeria v. E.W. Turner & Son Ltd.* (1968) (1) ALR Comm 290; See also *Tradelinks International (Nig) Ltd v. Bank of America (Nig) Ltd* (1977) 3 FRCR 285; Director's particulars

5a See generally, Gower, *Principles of Modern Company Law (4th Ed. 1979)* chap. 9 and *Orojo, Nigerian Company Law and Practice* (1976) pp. 112-117

6 (1877) 2App Cas. 266 P.C. See also *Standard Bank (Nig.) case supra n. 3*

7 Companies Act, 1862, S. 53

8 1966 NMLR 35 (Supreme Court of Nigeria)

9 (1875) LR 7 HL 869

named directors and secretary. In actual fact no directors or secretary had ever been appointed and no meetings had been held. In liquidation proceedings, the liquidator sought to recover the money paid from the bank. It was held that he could not succeed because it appeared to the bank that the resolution authorising the payment was regular and the bank was not put on inquiry nor suspicious as to the regularity of the resolution. In contrast, in *B. Liggett Ltd. v. Barclays Bank Ltd.*[10], the original directors of the plaintiff company were Liggett and Melia. The articles authorised the directors at any time to appoint an additional director. The bank was instructed to honour cheques signed by the two directors. However, Liggett was in the habit of issuing cheques signed only by himself which Melia would subsequently countersign at the bank, sometimes after they had been paid. In July, 1925 Melia instructed the bank that cheques were not to be paid without his signature. However, the former practice was still followed at times. In September 1925, Liggett as chairman of the board, wrote informing the bank that his wife had been appointed an additional director. Melia was unaware of this letter and of the alleged "appointment" of Mrs Liggett. The bank thereafter honoured cheques signed by Mr and Mrs Liggett. The company sued the bank for paying cheques without authority. It was held that the bank was liable since it had been put on inquiry about lack of compliance with internal procedures.

In *Afolabi v. Polymera Industries (Nig) Ltd.*[11], the plaintiff received from the defendants a letter, which he accepted as an agreement for remuneration between himself and the company. The company applied for the cancellation of the letter on the ground that it was only the managing director who could authorise such a letter.

It was held that the letter could not be repudiated since the plaintiff had no knowledge of the company's or its agent's lack of authority.

A director of the company may be regarded as an outsider and therefore benefit from the indoor management rule, provided that at the relevant time he is not acting as a director.[12] However, the general rule is that insiders, that is persons who by virtue of their position in the company are in a position to know whether or not the internal regulations of the company have been observed, cannot benefit from the indoor management rule. They are deemed to know the internal set up and procedures of the company.[13]

## Rule 3

A third limitation on the rule in *Turquand* is that an officer of the company who is held out by it is having authority to represent it will bind the company irrespective of defective appointment[14] or excess of authority, except (i) where the outsider knows that the officer has been irregularly appointed or is exceeding his authority; (ii) Circumstances are such as to put him on inquiry; (iii) It is clear from the public documents that the officer has no actual authority. Thus, in *Freeman & Lockyer v. Buckhurst Park Properties (Mangal) Ltd.*[15], the plaintiff company was set up for the purpose of buying and reselling a large estate by Kapoor, a property developer and Hoon who contributed one-half of capital but did not play an active part in the company's business. Kapoor, Hoon and a nominee of each of them were appointed the four directors of the company. Under the articles, all the four were required to form a quorum of the board. Hoon was most of the time abroad, and left all the day-to-day management of the company' affairs in Kapoor's hands. The initial plan to immediately resell the land did not materialize. Consequently, Kapoor decided to develop the estate and engage the plaintiffs, a firm of architects and surveyors to apply for planning permission. Later on, the company refused to pay the plaintiff's fees on the ground that

---

10 (1928) 1K.B. 48 KBD

11 1964 (2) ALR Comm 205; See also *Trenco (Nig) Ltd v. African Real Estate* (1978) 1 LRN 146

12 *Hely - Hutchninson v. Brayhead [1968] 1 QB 549*

13 Howard v. Patent Ivory Manufacturing Co. (1883) 38 Ch D 56 *Morris v. Kanssen* [1946] 1 ALL ER 586

14 See also. Companies Act, S. 179 Table A. Art. 105

15 [1964] 2 QB 480; [1964] 1 All ER 630 C.A. See also *Standard bank (Nig) Ltd. case, supra n. 3*

Kapoor had no authority to engage them. It was held that the company was bound on the ground that Kapoor had apparent authority to bind the company by his acts. In the course of judgment, Diplock L.J. formulated four criteria by which a company would be bound by the act of its agent. It must be shown that:[16]

(i) a representation that the agent had authority to enter on behalf of the company into a contract sought to be enforced was made to the contractor;

(ii) such representation was made by a person or persons who had "actual" authority to manage the business of the company either generally or in respect of those matters to which the contract relates;

(iii) the third party was induced by the representation to enter into the contract, that is that he in fact relied upon it;

(iv) under its memorandum or articles of association the company was not deprived of the capacity either to enter into a contract of the kind sought to be enforced or to delegate authority to enter into a contract of that kind to the agent.

Kapoor's actions fell within the articulated criteria. Diplock L.J. also explained away four hitherto irreconcilable cases in the light of these principles.[17] In the *Houghton* case,[17] the directors had under the articles power to "delegate to any managing director, local board, head manager, manager, attorney or agent, any of the powers .. .. for the time being vested in the directors." In addition, there was another article which authorised the board to delegate any of its powers to committees consisting of a member or members. The issue arose as to whether the plaintiff could rely upon the articles of which they had no knowledge, to bind the company through its director. It was held that they could not, because the transaction in question was of such unusual character that it was necessary for them to ensure that the power to enter into such a contract had actually been conferred upon the purported agent. This approach was also evident in the *Kreditbank Cassel Case*[17], where it was held that the drawing of bills of exchange by a branch manager upon his company is an unusual transaction sufficient to put a third party on inquiry with regard to his authority to do so. Consequently, even though there is a power of delegation contained in the articles which a person dealing with the company is deemed to know, he cannot rely on that presumption, unless it is proved that he had knowledge of the existence of the powers. A similar trend also manifested itself in the *Rama Corporation case*[17]. In all the three cases criteria (i) and (iii)[18] as formulated by Diplock L.J. were not satisfied viz. there was no representation to the third party as to the company's authority for its agent to act on its behalf and the third party was not induced by such representation to act. As a result the outsiders in those cases could not succeed against the respective companies.

In contrast, in the *British Thomson - Houston case*[19], the directors of the defendant company had powers under the articles to delegate to one or more of their own body certain powers. Additionally, they were empowered to determine who should be entitled to sign contracts and documents on the company's behalf.

The chairman of the defendant's board variously described himself to the plaintiff by signing - "for and on behalf of the company, N.P. chairman." A document purporting to be a guarantee executed by the defendant company was given to the plaintiff and signed thus: "The FEB Ltd

---

16 *ibid* [1964] 2 QB at p. 506 See also *Ekweozor v. Building & Civil Construction Co. of Nig. Ltd.* (1980) 7-9 CCHCJ 301 (High Court of Lagos)

17 *Houghton & Co. v. Northard Lowe & Wills Ltd.* [1927] 1 KB 246; *Kreditbank Cassel GMBH v. Schenkers Ltd.* (1927) 1 KB 826 *British Thomson - Houston Co. Ltd. v. Federated European Bank Ltd.* [1932] 2 KB 176; *Rama Corporation Ltd. v. Proved Tin Gen. Investments Ltd.* [1952] 1 All ER 554. See also S.R. Brown, *Company Directors (Australia, 2nd, Ed, 1965) pp. 108-109*

18 *Supra* n. 16

19 *Supra* n. 17 See also *Trenco (Nig) Ltd. v. African Real Estate* (1978) 1 LRN 146 where a company chairman bound the company by his letter, irrespective of the absence of a formal contract.

(signed) N.P." The plaintiff brought an action on the guarantee. The defendant company denied executing any guarantee, which it alleged had to be signed by two directors.

It was held that the plaintiffs were dealing with the defendant's chairman in a matter which normally a director would have power to act and the plaintiffs were entitled to presume that the defendant's directors had authorised him to sign on behalf of the company and the company was therefore liable on the guarantee. This approach is also evident in a later English Court of Appeal case, *Hely-Hutchinson v. Brayhead Ltd.*[20] In this case, the plaintiff obtained a controlling interest in Perdio Electronics Ltd. (Perdio) and became chairman and managing director. He subsequently met Richards the second defendant who acquired control of and became chairman of the first defendant company. Later Perdio started experiencing difficulties and obtained overdraft facilities of £ 50,000.00 from Guiness Mahon and Co. Ltd. The plaintiff gave his personal guarantee in respect of the overdraft, but as the sum was insufficient for Perdio's needs he arranged with Richards to have the first defendant company acquire shares in Perdio. Persistent difficulties for Perdio's led it to acquire more money from the first defendant company and Kleinwort & Benson Limited. Additionally, the plaintiff agreed with Richards to advance his own money to Perdio if the defendant company would guarantee such loans and gave him an indemnity in respect of his personal guarantee to Guiness Mahon.

The defendant company's directors approved the purchase of shares in Perdio, but no disclosure was made of the other transactions. Shortly afterwards, two documents on the company's headed notepaper and signed by Richards as chairman, materialised. One gave an indemnity in respect of the Guiness Mahon guarantee and the other guaranteed the plaintiff's loans to Perdio. There was no evidence that the existence of these documents was ever disclosed to the Brayhead board of directors. The plaintiff having advanced £45,000.00 of his own money to Perdio and paid £ 510,000.00 to Guiness Mahon brought an action against both Brayhead and Richards relying on the documents. The principal issue in regard to the defendant company was whether the actions of Richards who purported to act as managing director but had never been formally appointed, and although the articles of association contained power to make such an appointment, bound the company. It is notable that on many occasions he had acted with the subsequent approval and acquiescence of the other directors. It was held that upon the facts Richards had actual implied authority which bound the company. It was indicated[21] that authority is implied from the circumstances of the case and from the conduct of the parties such as when a board of directors appoint one of their members to be a managing director, they thereby authorise him to do all such things as fall within the usual scope of that office.

The Nigerian cases are conflicting with regard to the application of the criteria formulated in the *Freeman and Lockyer case.*[22] Thus, in *Metalimpex v. A.G. Leventis & Co. (Nig) Ltd*[23], an indorsement over the defendant company's rubber stamp on a bill of exchange was made by a director who signed the undertaking to the debtor that the defendants would pay the relevant instalments to the plaintiff. The articles of association of the defendant company conferred power and imposed duties on the "directors" in plural without exception, and there was no provision for the exercise by a single director of the defendant's powers of dealing with a bill of exchange. It was also not shown that the director who indorsed the bill had been authorised to do so or to guarantee payment of the debt, in the name or on behalf of the defendant. In action by the plaintiff against the defendant on the bill, it was held that a single director had no

---

20 [1968] 1 QB 549; [1967] 3 All E.R. 98. See also R.S. Nock, "When is a Director Not A Director" (1967) 30 *Mod. Law. Rev.* 705, 706, 707. See also the *Trenco Case ibid.*

21 [1967] 3 All E.R at p. 102 per Lord Denning M.R. See also *Texaco Africa Ltd. v. Nigerian Trading Co. Ltd.* [1962] LLR 78

22 *Supra* n. 16

23 1974 NCLR 511 (High Court of Lagos State)

authority to endorse the company's bills of exchange. Dosunmu. J. reasoned that[24] authority for a single director to accept bills of exchange cannot be implied in the articles of association of a company, empowered to deal in bills of exchange, which confer powers and impose duties only on "the directors" in plural. This approach is sensible and is in fact supported by the reasoning in the *Kreditbank Cassel Case*[25] on the basis that the acceptance by a single director of a bill of exchange is an unusual transaction sufficient to place an outsider dealing with the company on inquiry as to his authority to do so. However, on appeal, Dosunmu J. was reversed by the Supreme Court of Nigeria.[26] It was contended by the appellant plaintiff that if the articles did in fact authorise dealings with bills of exchange by single directors then the respondent would be liable on the bill in question whether or not the director who signed the bill was actually authorised or not. In effect, it was being suggested that this situation fell within the rule in *Royal British Bank v. Turquand*[27] and not outside it by the application of agency principles under *Freeman & Lockyer*[28] and other cases.[29] It was held that the appellant's contention was the legal position and the respondents were liable on the bill. It was indicated[30] that a bill of exchange is deemed to have been signed on behalf of a company if it is signed by a person acting on its authority, and if a director without authority accepts bills on behalf of a company whose articles of association give power to delegate the duty of accepting bills to one director, the company is liable to the holder in due course even though the delegation has not in fact taken place. This approach may be compared with the one in *Daarnhouwer & Co. Ltd. v. J. Christian & Co. Ltd. & Anor*[31]. In this case, the first defendant company asked for a loan from the plaintiff company and the second defendant company agreed to guarantee the loan. The instrument of guarantee was signed by a director of the second defendant without any form of words after the signature. The letter renewing it was merely signed by the director's personal assistant. The plaintiff drew six bills of exchange on the first defendant. Each bill was accepted and signed by one of the first defendant's employees but the first defendant's name only appeared. The plaintiff sued the defendants to recover the principal sum advanced together with interest and damages arising from the first defendant's breach of contract. The issue arose, *inter alia,* as to whether the bills of exchange signed by a director were effective to bind the first defendant company. It was held that they were not. Kazeem Ag. J. indicated[32] that where a director of a company signs a bill of exchange without adding words to indicate that he is signing for and on behalf of the company, that is not sufficient acceptance to bind the company under section 81 Companies Act[33] and section 26(1) of the Bills of Exchange Act.[34] The director is personally liable even if the company's seal is fixed to the bill.[35] This result may be said to be in consonance with the original decision of Dosunmu J. in *Metalimpex*[36] and the *Kreditbank Cassel case*[37], but at variance with the supreme court decision in *Metalimpex*[38]

---

24 *ibid.* at pp. 520 - 521

25 *Supra* n. 17

26 See 1976 NCLR 20

27 *Supra* n. 3 See also ibid pp. 32-33 where the court restated the rule.

28 *Supra* n. 16

29 *Supra* n. 17

30 *supra* n. 26, at pp. 34-36. See also 7 *Halsbury's Laws of England* 4th Ed. para 743 p. 444

31 1967 NCLR 434 (High Court of Lagos: Kazeem Ag. J.)

32 *ibid.* pp. 442-444. See also *Dutton v. Marsh* L.R. 6 QB 364 24 L.T. 472

33 Cap 37 Laws of Federation 1958, See Companies Act S. 35 and Table A., Art 105

34 Cap 21 Laws of Federation of Nigeria, 1958

35 The use of the company's seal is usually regulated by the articles. See e.g. Table A, Art. 113 which requires authority by the board or committee of directors and signature by a director and secretary. See also *Containers (Ng) Ltd. v. Niglasco Ltd.* (1979) 4-6/CCHCJ 290, 316 (High Court of Lagos State)

36 See *supra* n. 28

37 *Supra* n. 17

38 *Supra* n. 26

The other curious case is *W.A.A. (Nig) Ltd. v. West African Pilot Ltd.*[39] Upon the application of the defendant's general manager, the plaintiff advanced to the defendant credit facilities for the transportation of the defendant's newspapers. As a result the defendant was indebted to the plaintiff, who sued to recover the debt. The defendant argued that the general manager had no authority to procure the contract. The plaintiff countered that the power exercised by the general manager was one which a general manager would usually have. Furthermore that the plaintiff was unaware that the general manager had no authority and that it had no reason to suspect that he had none. This submission was accepted by the court which held the defendants liable. This decision may be said to be curious in the light of the *Houghton* and *Kreditbank Cassel* cases.[40]In *Houghton,* a director and a secretary were held not to have authority to make the representations in issue in a transaction of an unusual character likely to put the outsiders on inquiry. In *Kreditbank Cassel*, a branch manager was adjudged incapable of drawing bills of exchange so as to bind the company, the whole practice being unusual as to put an outsider on inquiry as to his actual authority to do so. Given the results, it is doubtful whether a general manager in a company can enter into a contract on its behalf without the outsider being put on inquiry as to his actual authority. Even if there is such authority, it would appear on the authority of *Houghton* and *Kreditbank Cassel* that the outsider must be aware of such authority or its express representation which he must have relied upon in order to render the defendant company liable.[40a]

There is also Nigerian authority to the effect that defective appointment does not affect the power of a director or officer who is held out by the company as having usual authority, to bind it. In *Pool House Group (Nig) Ltd. v. ACB Ltd.*[41], the plaintiff company's memorandum of association gave it power to carry on the business of Pool agents, and in order to do this, to borrow money on security. Its articles indicated that its first directors should hold office for life and that the seal of the company when affixed to an instrument by the authority of a resolution of the company in the presence of one of its directors and the secretary, who should sign the instrument should bind the company. The articles were dated before the coming into force of the Immigration Act, 1963. One of its first directors, a Lebanese, was given written permission by the Chief Immigration Officer to continue in office. He was, however, not reappointed as a director. The plaintiffs were customers of the defendant bank and the Lebanese director was one of the persons whom they had authorised to sign their cheques. In order to cover a proposed overdraft, a deed of mortgage in favour of the defendants, comprising certain leasehold land was sealed with the plaintiff's seal and signed by the Lebanese director, another director and the company's secretary.

The plaintiffs alleged that the deed was ineffectual in so far as it purported to confer a leasehold title on the defendants because the Lebanese director, being an alien and not having the permission of the Minister was prohibited by law from acting as or performing the functions of a director of the plaintiff. The issues arose as to whether (i) the holding out by the plaintiff company of the Lebanese as a director made him a *defacto* director regardless of statutory contravention and (ii) even if the Lebanese was a *defacto* director, his act (of signing the mortgage deed) amounted to an act done in the ordinary course of the plaintiff's business. Both issues were answered in the affirmative. In his rationalisation, Adeferasin J. indicated that[42], if persons are held out and act as directors of a company and the shareholders do not prevent this from happening,

---

39 1968 (1) A.L.R. Comm. 65. See also *International Paints (W.A.F) Ltd. v. Akiwowo & Anors* (1979) 1-3 CCHCJ 52, 54 (High Court of Lagos State); office manager; *Nigerian Ports Authority v. Construction Generali S.P.A. & McEwan* 1922 (2) ALR Comm 199

40 *supra* n. 17

40a The rationalisation of this decision is still possible along the lines of *Panorama Developments v. Fidelis Furnishing Fabrics* [1971] 2QB 711 See also *Ajayi v. Lagos City Council* 1967(3) ALR Comm 213

41 1969 NCLR 347 (High Court of Lagos State. See also Companies Act, S. 181; Table A. Art. 105. See also *Onwukwa v. Taymani* (1965) LLR 62

42 *ibid* at pp. 355-356

a third party dealing *bona fide* with them is entitled to assume that they are directors and as between the company and the third party the acts of such directors *defacto* in the ordinary course of the company's business will bind the company. Giving its bankers security for an over-draft is an act in the ordinary course of the business of a company empowered to raise money in order to carry out its objects.

## Rule 4

A fourth qualification of the indoor management rule is that where an officer purports to exercise authority which he does not usually have, an outsider is not protected, if the officer exceeds his authority unless the company has held him out as having authority to act in the matter and the outsider has relied on the representation in which case the company is estopped. However, a provision in the memorandum or articles or other public document cannot create the estoppel except where the outsider actually knows and relies on it. Consequently, mere registration at the company's registry does not for this purpose constitute notice.

The difference between this rule and the preceding rule 3 is that under the preceding rule "the officer is held out as having power to enter into the transaction in issue because he has been allowed to occupy a position in which it would be usual to have that power; while under the present rule he is held out as having authority to enter into the transaction although an agent in his position would not usually have authority to do so."[43] Furthermore, the main importance of the distinction is that it provides an answer "to the vexed question of how far it matters whether or not the other party has read the company's articles."[44] When rule 3 applies, the issue is irrelevant since if the officer is doing what that sort of officer would usually be authorised to do, the company is bound unless the third party knows or ought to know that the officer is exceeding his authority. Additionally, where the articles or other public documents clearly indicate that the officer is exceeding his authority, the company is not liable whether or not the other party has read the articles. Consequently, reliance on rule 3 does not depend on having read the articles.[45] Where, however, rule 4 applies, a third party cannot rely on a provision in the articles to establish that the officer has been held out as having authority unless he has in fact read and relied on that provision.[46]

As a result of this approach by rule 4 it has been difficult for outsiders to succeed under it. However, in *Mercantile Bank of India v. Chartered Bank of India*[47] a company which was authorised by its memorandum and articles of association to borrow and appoint agents, appointed agents by powers of attorney and empowered them to borrow and charge the company' property. The directors placed a limit on the amounts which the agents could borrow, although this did not appear in the powers of attorney. It was held that a charge which was granted to secure a borrowing in excess of the limit bound the company because the powers of attorney, in the absence of any prohibition in the articles, estopped the company. This result may be compared with the one reached in *Onuh v. United Nigeria Insurance Co. Ltd.*[48] In this case, the plaintiff applied for and obtained the defendant's consent to the removal of goods consequent upon which they were lost. A letter under the defendant's letter-heading stated over the bare signature of an employee of the defendant company that the policy covered the new store to which the

---

43 Gower, *op.cit.* (4th Ed.) p. 197

44 Gower, *ibid.* See further the treatment in the *Houghton, Kreditbank Cassel, British Thomson - Houston and Rama Corporation Cases* cited *supra* n. 17. See also the *Freeman & Lockyer* case, *supra* n. 15 and Montrose (1934), 50 *ICLQ* 224; Thompson (1956), 11U. *Toronto L.J.* 248; Campbell, (1959) 75 *ICLQ* 469; (1960) 76 *ICLQ* 115; Nock, (1966) 30 *Conv. (N.S.)* 123; Barak (1969) 18 *ICLQ* 152

45 *Freeman & Lockyer* case, *ibid*

46 Gower, *Supra* n. 44, p. 198. See further *Houghton's case* and *Kreditbank Cassel* case *supra* n. 17

47 [1937] 1 All ER 231

48 1975 NCLR 413 (High Court of East Central State of Nigeria)

goods were being conveyed. Evidence adduced indicated that the employee in question was a clerk and was not authorised to waive any alteration in the terms of the policy. The plaintiff instituted the action to recover the sum insured for the goods under a policy of insurance issued to him by the defendant. The issue arose as to whether the employee of the company was authorised to alter the terms of the policy so as to bind the company. It was held that he was not and the company was not bound by the alteration. Phil Ebosie J. indicated that[49]an insurance company is liable for the acts of its agents or servants if they have the actual or ostensible authority to do the act, notwithstanding any internal arrangements; but for a claimant to succeed, he must show that the company's agent or servant had the actual or apparent authority and that he relied on that authority. It is not enough to assume that the servant or agent has the authority even if he says so.

It may be said that although the courts were initially reluctant to recognise the ability of the company secretary to bind the company[50], since the case of *Panorama Developments (Guildford) v. Fidelis Furnishing Fabrics Ltd.*[51], it may be assumed confidently that a company secretary possesses ostensible authority to enter into contracts relating to the administrative aspects of the company's affairs such as the hiring of cars for the use of the company's staff and customers.[52] The position with regard to his capacity to make commercial contracts on the company's behalf is still unclear.[53]

## Rule 5

The last qualification of the *Turquand* rule in the Ugandan context is that if a document purporting to be sealed or signed on the company's behalf turns out to be a forgery it does not bind the company. Nevertheless, the company may be estopped from disclaiming the document as a forgery if it has been put forward as genuine by an officer acting within his actual, usual or apparent authority. Furthermore, if the transaction is binding under the preceding rules, considered, the company is liable irrespective of the officer having acted fraudulently or committed the forgery.[54]

The view has been maintained that the *Turquand* rule is inapplicable where there is a forgery affecting a transaction. Thus, in *Ruben v. Great Fingall Consolidated*[55], a company secretary issued a share certificate to which he had affixed the company's seal and forged the signatures of the directors in whose presence it purported to be fixed.[56] It was held that the document was a forgery and therefore could not bind the company unless some officer acting within his authority had warranted that it was genuine. Even though the secretary could be presumed to have by implication warranted this, he had no authority to do so and the company was not bound. The case, therefore appears simply to decide that the secretary's acts fell outside the scope of his authority.[57] However, Lord Loreburn stated, *Obiter*[58], that the *Turquand* rule does not apply to a forgery. This proposition appears to be based on the idea that an act could not be within the ambit of authority of an agent or servant if it has been done fraudulently and for his own benefit rather

---

49 *ibid.* pp. 421-422, applying the *Turquand case, Supra* n. 3 and *MacGillivray Insurance Law* 5th Ed. para. 595 pp. 291 (1961)

50 *Barnet Hoares & Co. v. South London Tramways Co. [1887]* 18 QBD 815; *George Whitechurch Ltd. v. Cavanagh* (1902) A.C. 117 H.L. *Houghton case, supra* n. 17; *Re: Cleadon Trust Ltd.* [1939] Ch. 286.

51 [1971] 2 QB 711

52 Gower, *Supra* n. 46, p. 196

53 [1971] 2 QB at 718 per Salmon L.J. See also *Houghton case Supra* n. 17

54 See also Campbell, (1960) 76, *Law Q. Rev.* pp. 130-136; Lindgren (1973-1974) 9 *Melbourne U.L. Rev.* 192; *Ekweazor v. Building & Civil Construction Co. of Nig. Ltd. (1980) 7-9 CCHCJ 301*

55 [1906] AC 439 HL See also Gower *op.cit.* pp. 203-204

56 Note the procedure for using the company's seal: Table A. Art. 113

57 Gower, *Supra* n. 55

58 [1906] AC at p. 443

than that of his principal or master.[59] This approach, has, however been rejected in *Uxbridge Building Society v. Pickard*[60] In this case a solicitor was held liable for the frauds of his managing clerk irrespective of their having involved forgery. Lord Greene M.R. distinguished the company cases on the ground that the *Turquand* rule does not depend on agency principles.[61] Professor Gower disagrees on the ground that[62] the *Turquand* rule has always been expressed as an agency principle.

Furthermore, that to contend that it does not apply to fraud is incorrect since the case of *Mahony v. East Holyford Mining Co.*[63], on which Lord Green M.R. relied, was a case of fraud. Professor Gower concludes:[64]

> The truth seems to be that there are no reasons why the fact that there is a forgery should exclude the Turquand rule. All the decisions can be explained on the ground either that the forged document was not put forward as genuine by an officer acting within his actual or apparent authority, or that the outsider was put on inquiry.

## Some aspects of reform and trends in other jurisdictions

In Britain, the Jenkins Committee[65] advocated the abolition of the constructive notice doctrine and also suggested that actual knowledge of the contents of the memorandum and articles should not prevent a third party from enforcing the contract, "if he honestly and reasonably failed to appreciate that they had the effect of precluding the company (or any director or other person on its behalf) from entering into the contract in question." In Britain, some attempt towards implementing this recommendation was made by section 9 (1) of the European Communities Act, 1972, which provides thus:[66]

> In favour of a person dealing with a company in *good faith* any transaction *decided on by the directors* shall be deemed to be one which it is within the capacity of the company to enter into, and the power of the directors to bind the company shall be deemed to be free from any limitation under the memorandum or articles of association; and a party to a transaction so decided on shall not be bound to enquire as to the capacity of the company to enter into it or as to any such limitation on the power of the directors and shall be presumed to have acted in good faith unless the contrary is proved.

As regards the capacity of a single director to bind the company, it has been suggested that, in so far as the section relates to transactions "*decided on by the directors*", it has no effect on the position of a single director in this respect. Consequently, the common law will continue to

---

59 See also *Kreditbank Cassel v. Schenkers* [1927] 1 KB 826 CA. *S. London Greyhound Racecourses v. Wake* [1931] 1 Ch. 496 *c.f. Lloyd v. Grace, Smith & Co.* [1912] A.C. 716 HL.

60 [1939] 2 KB 248 CA. See also *Ekweazor case supra* n. 54

61 *ibid.* p. 257

62 Gower, *op. cit.* p. 204

63 (1875) LR 7 HL 869, see also *supra* n. 9 and text thereof.

64 Gower, *op. cit.* p. 205. See also *Uxbridge Building Society v. Pickard* [1939] 2 KB at p. 249 per Mackinnon L.J. *Ekweazor v. Building & Civil Construction Co. of Nigeria Ltd.* (1980) 7-8 CCHCJ 301 (High Court of Lagos)

65 Report of the Company Law Committee (Cmnd 1749, 1962, Rep. 1973), para 42. See also D.J. Bakibinga Vol. 1 *Ahmadu Bello University Law Journal*, pp. 119-120 (1983) and Anifalaje, "The Lacunae In The Nigerian Companies Amendment Bill, 1981" (1982) *Nig. CL. Rev. 287-301*

66 Emphasis supplied. See further *International Sales and Agencies Ltd. v. Marcus* [1982] 2 All E.R. 551 which interpreted the provision in the light of EEC Directive 68/151

apply;[67] *viz.* if a director acts consistently with the usual authority of a single director, the company would be bound but, if he acts outside thereof, it would not. It is further argued[68] that the device employed by the modern cases, i.e to contend that a single director is either impliedly or ostensibly given greater powers than those of an ordinary director, though not actually appointed to that position, may be used. With respect to the effect of section 9 (1) on the tests formulated in the *Freeman and Lockyer case*[69], Thompson thus observed:[70]

> In the light of section 9 (1) it appears that test (iv) need no longer be satisfied so that the company may still be held bound even if by its articles it has no power to appoint a managing director. On the other hand, if there is no 'holding out' and no implication of authority arising from the circumstances, it would appear that the present rule will continue to apply and the company will be able to avoid liability.

It is thus apparent that the effect of Section 9(1) on the common law position affecting the capacity of a single director to bind the company, is limited.

In France,[71] the law indicates that any restrictions placed on the powers of the board of directors of a public company by the company's statutes may not be invoked against a person who deals with the board whether he is cognisant of them or not. However, if the authority conferred, upon the president of *Societe Anonyme* to give guarantees on behalf of the company, or to create mortgages or charges over its assets up to a given limit is exceeded, the company can repudiate the transaction involved without incurring liability to a third party even if he was unaware of the prescribed limit. Otherwise, the restrictions placed upon the president's powers are only effective as between him and the company and cannot be enforced against third-parties. This rationale appears to apply to the general manager or *directeur general* as well, a position which is consistent with the result in *WAA v. West African Pilot Ltd.*[72] Even within the two-tier structure of management introduced by the Law of 1966, limitations upon the powers of the executive board or sole managers cannot be invoked against third parties.[73] Furthermore, similar to the president in the traditional *Societe Anonyme*, limitations upon the powers of the chairman of the executive board, while effective within the company, cannot be enforced against third parties.

In Germany the director's power of representation is illimitable. Professor Wurdinger has pointed out that[74] this is aimed at protecting contracting parties. It, therefore, follows that the company is bound by contracts entered into by the board, "outside the scope of the company's business as specified in the statutes, including contracts to which the consent of the supervisory board was required but was not obtained."

The United States' approach is that in most cases the directors have wide discretionary powers whose exercise is free from shareholder control and would bind the company if exercised by an unauthorised person, are acquiesced in by the board of directors.[75] However, there may be instances in which, as is put by Professor Cary:[75]

---

67 Thompson, "Directors' Powers Under the European Communities Act" (1973) 123 *New Law Journal* 593. For other comments on S.9. (1) European Communities Act, 1972 see (1973) 36 *Mod. Law Rev.* 270; (1973) *(1973) New Law J. 312, 513; Wedderburn, (1983) 46 Mod L.R.* 204, at pp. 211-212

68 Thompson, *ibid.* p. 594 referring to *Freeman & Lockyer (Supra* n. 15)

69 *Supra n. 16*

70 *Supra* n. 68. See also Gower, *op cit.* (4th Ed.) pp 184-191

71 See generally J. Le Gall, *French Company Law* (Oyez, London, 1974) pp. 134-135; 139-140; 142-143.

72 *supra* n. 39

73 Art. 124 (4) of 1966 Loi

74 H. Wurdinger, *German Company Law* (Oyez, London 1975) p. 47

75 *W.L. Cary, Cases and Materials on Corporations (U.S.A)* 4th Ed.-(1969), pp. 189-190. This is consistent with the *Hely-Hutchinson v. Brayhead decision, supra* n. 20

> ... the applicable statute requires that the act have the consent of the shareholders, under some statutes their consent given at a meeting, under other statutes their written consent. Such consent is usually required for sale or lease of all or substantially all the corporate property ... certain kinds of guarantees, .... corporate mortgages .., where such statutes exist, questions ... arise as to the validity of action taken by directors without obtaining the consent of shareholders. Most cases relate to corporate mortgages. ... It has frequently been held that only the shareholders can take advantage of a failure to obtain shareholders' consent to a corporate mortgage ...

Similar to the British position, in the United States, where a power is one which would otherwise be exercisable by a person to whom directors have delegated powers, any by-law restricting his authority is not effective against an outsider who has no actual notice of it.[76] There is a contrary view to the effect that the existence of a restrictive by-law would be binding on an outsider who would be fixed with notice of the restriction upon the officer's powers.[77]

# Conclusion

Ugandan law in this area continues to follow the position in Britain with the exception of the effect of the European Communities Act, 1972, which is a post-1900 British statute. The result is that the capacity of a director, other company officer or directors' delegates to bind the company is still regulated by the *Turquand* doctrine, as modified by the *Freeman and Lockyer* decision[78] and analogous Nigerian cases.[79] It is significant that some Nigerian cases[80] have not strictly adhered to the British position. The positions in France and Germany are radically different and very favourable to the third party affected by directors' exercise of powers whether authorised or not. The tendency in the United States is inconsistent and may be said to vacillate between the Anglo-Ugandan and Continental European approaches. It is further complicated by the existence of management contracts with people from outside the corporate structure.[81]

Ugandan law may be considerably simplified by explicitly abolishing the constructive notice doctrine and adopting approaches similar to those in France and Western Germany. The position as it is presently is still rather complicated and uncertain as the cases discussed under rules 3 and 4 show. The simplification would accord with the social-economic realities of Uganda where face-to-face transactions are the norm rather than documentary reliance.

# Liability under the organic theory

While the liability of the company may be established through the normal application of agency principles[82] especially with respect to contractual transactions, given that the company is an artificial entity which acts through human agents and servants, difficulty may arise in establishing its liability where this is predicated upon personal fault as is the case with criminal responsibility. To overcome situations where the company would escape liability on ground of lack of personal fault or intention the courts have created a device whereby "the acts and thoughts of certain

76 *Produce Exchange Trust Co, v. Biebach*, 176 Mass. 577, 58 n.E. 162 (1900). See also Cary, *ibid* p. 191

77 *Bloomingdale v. Cushman* 134 Minn. 455, 159 N.W. 1076 (1916). See also Cary, *ibid.*

78 *supra* notes 15 and 16

79 See generally notes 22 to 48 and text thereof.

80 See *supra* notes 23 and 26; 39-40a and text thereof.

81 See Cary, *Supra* n. 75

82 See *supra* section C.

agencies of a company may be regarded as those of the company itself"[83] Those agencies are then regarded as the organic parts of the company.

## The organic theory

Ordinarily the general meeting, the board of directors and sometimes the managing director are regarded as the organs of the company.[84] However, there is a line of judicial development which runs counter to that tendency. Thus, in *Lennard's Carrying Co. v. Asiatic Petroleum Co. Ltd.*;[85] The company which was the owner of a ship sought to take advantage of the limitation of liability under the Merchant Shipping Act, 1894.[86] The limitation can only be used where the injury is caused without the owner's "actual fault or privity". The relevant loss actually arose from default of Lennard, the company's managing director. Nevertheless, the company was held liable.

In his rationalisation, of the decision Viscount Haldane LC. thus stated:[87]

> My lords, a corporation is an abstraction. It has no mind of its own any more than it has a body of its own; its active and directing will must consequently be sought in the person of somebody *who for some purposes may be called an agent, but who is really the directing mind and will of the corporation, the very ego and centre of the personality of the corporation*......... If Mr. Lennard was the directing mind of the company, then his action must unless a corporation is not to be liable at all, have been an action which *was the action of the company itself* within the meaning of section 502 ..... It must be upon the true construction of that section in such a case as the present one that the fault or privity of somebody *who is not merely a servant or agent for whom the company is liable upon the footing respondeat superior, but somebody for whom the company* is liable because his action is the very action of the company itself.

Similarly, in *HMS Truculent*[88], a Third Sea Lord was adjudged the "directing mind" of the British Admiralty for purposes of establishing liability for a collision between S.S. Divine and HMS Truculent, which resulted into the death of over sixty persons. In *The Lady Gwendolen*[89], it was indicated that the person whose fault is attributable to the corporation need not be a director. In this particular case, the assistant managing director of a shipping company was held to be an *alter ego* of the company. Following this trend, Professor Olawoyin has thus concluded:[90]

> Accordingly a company could be held liable for the actions of any of its officers who need not be directors, but with formally delegated authority over some aspect of the company's business, on the basis that such actions are those of the company itself, provided the delegation is in fact of a primary character.

This trend has in fact been used to extend the liability of the company beyond that arising from normal agency principles.[91]

---

83 Gower, *supra* n. 70, p. 205. See too Olawoyin, Status and Duties of Company Directors (1977) pp. 22-28

84 See *supra* chap. 11

85 [1915] A.C. 705 HL. See also *Bath v. Standard Land Co.* [1910] 2 Ch. 408, 416 per Neville J.

86 S. 502

87 [1915] AC at pp. 713-714. Emphasis supplied. See also *Trenco (Nig) Ltd. v. African Real Estate* [1978] 1 LRN 146, p. 153 (Supreme Court of Nigeria) and *Bolton Engineering) Co. Ltd. v. Graham & Sons* [1957] 1 QB 159 pp. 172-173 per Denning LJ. See also *Rv. Various Accused Unreported HC Tanzania; National & Grindlays Bank & Co. v. Kenfiles [1966] EA 17*

88 [1952] p. 1

89 [1965] p. 294. See also Leigh (1965) 28 *Mod. LR* 584

90 *Supra* n. 83, p. 25. See also *Ibadan City council v. Odukale* (1972) 7 S.C. 128, pp. 146-147 per Udo Udoma JSC

91 Gower, *supra* n. 83, p. 206

## Criminal responsibility

The principle in *Lennard's* case[92] has been especially employed with respect to the criminal liability of companies. Prior to 1944 it was thought that the concept of vicarious liability did not apply to criminal law since *mens rea* on the part of the accused person was essential to establish responsibility. However, in 1944 a general principle emerged to the effect that a company could be liable personally for the acts of its officers and not merely on the basis of *respondeat superior*. Thus, in *Director of Public Prosecutions v. Kent & Sussex Contractors Ltd.*[93], a company was charged under the Defence Regulations for using a document with intent to deceive and for making a statement known to it to be false, in order to obtain petrol coupons. The presiding justice dismissed the information on the ground that the company could not be guilty of the offences charged since *mens rea* was required and the *mens rea* or a servant could not be attributed to a corporate body as master. However, this decision was reversed by the Divisional Court which reasoned thus:[94]

> It is true that a corporation can only have knowledge and form an intention through its human agents, but circumstances may be such that the knowledge and intention of the agent must be imputed to the body corporate... If the responsible agent of a company acting within the scope of his authority, puts forward on its behalf a document which he knows to be false and by which he intends to deceive, I apprehend that ... his knowledge and intention must be imputed to the company.

This approach was approved by the Court of Criminal Appeal in *Rv. IRC Haulage*[95]. In this case, the company was indicted for a common law conspiracy to defraud. It was held that it could be convicted irrespective of *mens rea* being an essential element of the offence. The acts of the managing director were adjudged to be those of the company while his fraud was imputed to the company. Similarly, in *Moore v. Bessler Ltd.*[96], a company was held liable for the acts of its secretary and branch manager which amounted to using a document with intent to deceive. Furthermore, in *Mandilas & Karaberis Ltd. v. Commissioner of Police*[97], a company was convicted of stealing by fraudulent conversion contrary to sections 390 and 383 of the criminal code. This was so despite the fact that the relevant action was that of a branch manager of the company.[98] The Nigerian approach in this respect appears to depart from the English trend where "a limitation has been put on the ambit of the [organic theory] by making it clear that it is not the act or knowledge of every agent or servant of the company which will be attributed to the company,[99] but only of those whom the company has made its 'responsible officers' for the action in question."[100] This is buttressed by the House of Lords decision in *Tesco Supermarkets v. Nattrass*[101], where an attempt was made to make the company liable under the Trade Descriptions Act, 1968, for the failure of one of its shop managers to ensure that goods advertised for sale at a specified price were actually being sold at that price. The justices found that the company had exercised all due diligence in devising a proper system for the operation of the store.

---

92 *Supra* n. 87
93 [1944] KB 146
94 *ibid* p. 156 per Macnaghten J. See also *Smithfield Butchery Ltd. v. R* (1949) 23 (2) KLR 81 which applied this case
95 [1944] KB 551 CCA. See also *Smithfield Butchery Ltd. v. R* (1949) 23 (2) KLR 81
96 [1944] 2 All ER 515
97 [1958] WNLR 147
98 c.f. *Hanshall (Quarries) Ltd v. Harvey* [1965] QB 233, where the Divisional Court refused to impute the knowledge of weighbridge man to his company on the ground that he was not a responsible officer of the company whose mind could be regarded as the mind of the company itself.
99 As suggested in *Moore v. Bessler Ltd.*, *supra* n. 96
100 Gower, *op. cit.* (4th Ed.) pp. 208-209
101 [1972] AC 153 HL

On appeal, the House of Lords finally held that the shop manager, one of several hundred, could not be identified with the company. Consequently, the offence was due to the oral default of another person. It is apparent from this decision that where necessary, the court will carry out a factual inquiry into the workings of the company's management in order to ascertain who the "responsible officers" are.[102] For this purpose, the question to be asked by the tribunal is whether the function in question "is a primary managerial one, and whether the person to whom it is entrusted enjoys primary control."[103]

The organic theory may be said to have reached its logical conclusion in *R. V. McDonnell,*[104]where it was held that a company was not guilty of conspiring with the sole officer responsible for its acts and intentions. The theory could also work in reverse *viz.* the acts of the company may be treated as those of its directors.[105] The theory is also relevant to the determination of the company's residence[106] in that those who control the management of the company are deemed to be the company's "brains" and wherever they operate is the residence of the company.

However, the trend in East Africa is that a limited liability company cannot be imprisoned[107] or arrested[108]because of its artificial nature.

---

102 As was the case in *NCB v. Gamble* [1959] 1 QB 11.

103 See further Gower, *op. cit.* p. 209

104 [1966] 1 QB 233; Gower *op. cit.* p. 208

105 *Biba Ltd. v. Stratford Investments, Ltd.* [1973] Ch. 281. See also Companies Act, Ss. 327 (1), 119 (2), 147 (4), 157 (3)

106 See *supra* n. Chap. 2 under *Lifting the Veil of Incorporation.*

107 *R.V. Various Accused* Unreported, 1965 (High Court of Tanzania)

108 *Wani v. Uganda Timbers & Joiners Ltd* CS No. 989 of 1972 (High Court of Uganda)

# 13

# ACCOUNTS AND AUDIT OF THE COMPANY

## Introduction

A company with share capital is required, at least once in each year to make a return to the registrar of companies. The return should include details of its registered office, register of members, debenture holders, indebtedness, members and directors.[1] Failure to make the return attracts a fine against the company and any officer who is responsible in that regard.[1] Every company is also required to maintain two types of accounts viz: (i) the accounting records of its day to day transactions which should reflect the continuous history of the company's dealings; (ii) regular annual accounts, comprising the profit and loss account and the balance sheet, both of which should give an overall view of its financial performance. The responsibility for the preparation and maintenance of the accounts lies with the directors.[2]

This chapter will examine the accounting requirements under the Companies Act, as well as the related aspect of auditing which includes the mode of auditing as well as duties, powers and rights of auditors.

## Accounts

Every company must keep proper books of account relating to: (i) all moneys received and expended by it in respect of which the receipt and expenditure takes place; (ii) all sales and purchases of goods; (iii) its assets and liabilities.[3] For this purpose, the books kept must give a true and fair view of the state of the company's affairs and explain its transactions.[4] The books must be kept at the company's registered office or such place in Uganda as the directors may decide, and should at all times be open to inspection by the directors.[5] In addition, notice of the place where the books are kept should be given by the company to the Registrar. Should the directors fail to secure compliance with the above requirements, they are criminally liable.[6]

### Directors duties in relation to the accounts

The company's directors should within eighteen months after incorporation and, subsequently, once at least in every year lay before the company in general meeting a profit and loss account or income and expenditure account in case of a company not trading for profit. The first account must date from the company's incorporation and subsequent accounts must be made up from the preceding account to date not earlier than nine months before the meeting or twelve months if the company has interests abroad.[7] The directors should also lay, before the general meeting in every year, a balance sheet made up to date of the profit and loss account or income expenditure account as the case may be.[8]

---

1 *ibid*, S. 119 (2)
2 *ibid*, Ss. 148, 155, 157
3 *ibid*. S. 147 (1)
4 *ibid*. S. 147 (2)
5 *ibid*. S. 147 (3). See also *Conway v. Petronius Clothing Co. Ltd.* [1978] 1 ALL ER 185
6 *ibid*. S. 147 (4)
7 *ibid* S. 148 (1)
8 *ibid* S. 148 (2)

## The balance sheet

The balance sheet should give a true and fair view of the company's state of affairs as at the end of its financial year.[9] The balance sheet must be signed on behalf of the board by at least two directors or if there is one director by that director.[10]

Every balance sheet must comply with the requirements of Schedule 6 of the companies Act except where the Registrar approves a modification.[11] Schedule 6 contains a list of matters to be included in the balance sheet. These are designed to give a true and fair view of the company's financial position. The documents to be attached to the balance sheet are the profit and loss account, any group accounts, the auditors' report and the directors' report.[12] A copy of every balance sheet and documents attached thereto to be laid before the general meeting must, not less than twenty one days before such meeting, be sent to every member, debentureholder or other persons entitled to receive notices of the general meeting.[13]

## Profit and loss account

The profit and loss account must give a true and fair view of the profit or loss of the company for the financial year[14] and should comply with the requirements of Schedule 6 of the Companies Act.[15] The information required to be shown in the profit and loss account by Schedule 6 includes amounts: (i) charges to revenue by way of provision for depreciation: (ii) of interest on debentures and other fixed loans: (iii) of the charge for Ugandan income tax and taxation on profits: (iv) of income from investments, distinguishing between trade investments and other investments.[16]

In addition, the accounts of the company laid before the general meeting must show the amount of emoluments and pensions of directors and the amount of compensation to the directors for loss of office[17]. The accounts should also indicate the amount of any loans made during the company's financial year to any officer of the company.[18]

## Group accounts

Where companies are in the relationship of holding and subsidiary companies,[19] when the holding company lays its own balance sheet and profit and loss account before the general meeting, it must, in addition, lay before it group accounts, dealing with the state of affairs, and profit and loss of itself and its subsidiaries.[20] The group accounts shall not be required where the company is at the end of its financial year the wholly owned subsidiary of another body incorporated in Uganda.[21]

The group accounts shall be in the form of consolidated balance sheets and profit and loss accounts of both the holding company and its subsidiaries.[22] The accounts, should also give a true and fair view of the state of affairs and profit and loss of the company and its subsidiaries.[23] However, where the accounts are consolidated they should comply with the requirements of

---

9 *ibid* S. 149 (1)
10 *ibid*, S. 149 (1) and Schedule 6
11 *ibid*, S. 149 (2) (4)
12 *ibid*, Ss. 156, 157
13 *ibid*, S. 158
14 *ibid*, S. 149 (1)
15 *ibid*. S. 149 (2)
16 for other requirements see Schedule 6
17 *ibid*, S.197
18 *ibid* S. 198
19 See definition thereof in S. 154 *ibid*. See also *Supra* chap. 2 under *"Lifting the Veil."*
20 *ibid*, S. 150 (1)
21 - *ibid*, S. 150 (2) and other exceptions thereunder.
22 *ibid*, S. 151
23 *ibid*, S. 152 (1)

Schedule 6 to the Companies Act, and if not so prepared should give the same equivalent information.[24]

## Directors' report

The directors' report should be attached to the balance sheet, circulated to members and publicised by way of return to the Registrar of Companies and maintenance at the company's registered office.

The report is required to show the state of affairs of the company; the amount, if any, which they recommend as dividend: and the amount, if any, which they propose to carry to reserves as defined in Schedule 6 to the Companies Act[25]. The report should also, so far as is material for the appreciation of the company's state of affairs by its members, and provided this is not harmful to the company's business or that of its subsidiaries, deal with any charge during the financial year in the nature of the company;s business in which the company has an interest.[26] Default by any director in ensuring compliance with the requirements in respect of the directors' report attracts criminal liability.[27]

## Auditors' report

The auditors are required to make a report to the members on the accounts examined by them, and on every balance sheet, profit and loss account and all group accounts laid before the company in general meeting during their tenure of office. The report, which should be read before the general meeting and is open to inspection by any member, must contain the matters indicated in Schedule 7 to the Companies Act.[28]

## Auditors

### Appointment

The first auditors of the company are appointed by the directors at any time before the first annual general meeting and hold office until the end of that meeting. However, if they have not been appointed before the meeting, the general meeting may appoint them.[29] The general meeting may also remove any auditor appointed by the directors and replace him with another nominated and chosen at the general meeting.[30]

Subsequently, every company is required at each annual general meeting to appoint an auditor or auditors who hold office until the end of the next general meeting.[31] A retiring auditor may be re-appointed at any annual general meeting without the passing of a resolution unless he is not qualified for reappointment; a resolution has been passed at that meeting appointing some other person in his place or indicating expressly that he shall not be reappointed; he has given the company written notice of his unwillingness to be reappointed.[32] Special notice of a resolution intended to appoint a new auditor should be given to all members.[33]

24 *ibid.* S. 152 (3)
25 *ibid.* S. 157 (1)
26 *ibid,* S. 157 (2)
27 *ibid.* S. 157
28 *ibid.* S. 162 (1), (2)
29 *ibid* S. 159 (5) (b)
30 *ibid.* S. 159 (5) (a)
31 *ibid* S. 159 (1)
32 *ibid.* S. 159 (2)
33 *ibid.* S. 160 (1)

Where no auditor has been appointed at an annual general meeting or reappointed, as the case may be, the Registrar of Companies may appoint a person to fill the vacancy.[34] The directors are empowered to fill a casual vacancy of an auditor, but while such vacancy continues, the surviving or continuing auditors may act.[35]

## Qualification

An auditor must be a member of the professional bodies specified in the Accountants (Designations) Act.[36] The following persons are disqualified from acting as auditor:[37]

(i) an officer or servant of the company;
(ii) a person who is a partner of or in the employment of an officer or servant of the company;
(iii) a body corporate;
(iv) a person who by reason of being an officer or servant of the company or a partner or servant of an officer or servant of the company cannot be appointed auditor of the company's holding company or its subsidiary or another subsidiary of its holding company.

The aim of the legislation is to ensure the auditor's independence in carrying out his check. In the words of Profession Baxt:[38a]

> This implies that there is some concern that the auditor should be independent. An audit is an independent check of information which is contained in a company's annual accounts and the company's records which are used in the preparation of these accounts. The auditor provides some assurance that the disclosure made by the company to its shareholders, pursuant to its obligations is reliable and in the auditor's opinion represents a 'true and fair view' of the company's financial state of affairs. Thus apart from specific requirements in statutes it is clear that a company auditor is not permitted merely to rely on the work carried out by the company accountant in the preparation of annual accounts.

This latter view appears to be supported by a New South Wales case, *Dominion Freeholders Ltd. v. Spargo Aird* (Third Party)[38] where the Court of Appeal rejected an argument by a company auditor that his statutory obligation was fulfilled by a mere sole reliance on the work which had been done by the company accountant in the preparation of annual accounts.

In *Re: Transplanters (Holding Co ) Ltd.*[39] Wynn-Parry J. distinguished the auditors from the accountant of the company. The latter was in every respect an agent of the company; the auditor, however, was not to be regarded for all purposes as an agent. It had also been observed that 'once a man takes upon himself a position of auditor ... he must stand aloof and divorced from the aims, objects and activities of the company."[40]

In reality, however, the auditor may be inhibited towards his prescribed independent role of objectively assessing a company's accounting records. This may stem from the fact that he's also a consultant to the company and therefore in a way financially dependent upon it. Thus although as Baxt has noted[41] the auditor should not be concerned with this aspect of the company's activities, "but the lucrative contract which usually accompanies the appointment as managerial consultants may be too much an inducement to allow for a completely unbiased approach to the

---

34 *ibid.* S. 159(3)
35 *ibid* .S. 159 (6)
36 See S. 161(1)
37 *ibid.* S. 161(2),(3)
38a R. Baxt, "The Modern Company Auditor - A Nineteenth Century Watchdog" (1970) 33 *MLR* 413 at p. 415. See also Bakibinga "The Audit Function" *Review of Business & Property Law* (Lagos) Vol.2 No.6.pp.18-23 (1989).
38 (1966) 2 NSWR 293
39 [1968] 2 Ch. 711
40 Arnold, "The Neutrality of an Auditor" (1959) 26 *The Solicitor* pp. 37-38

audit, especially where the issue of a qualified report may lead to the directors refusing to review the appointment as managerial consultants and influencing, as they can so easily do in most cases the appointment of another firm of consultants." Baxt concludes that while the notion of independence is desirable, it is at the same time "an unobtainable one, as it involves not just the absence of any direct relationship between the auditor to the company but requires the auditor to act with a state of mind that his work as an auditor will not affect his future situation as auditor of the company, or his other work for the company. There is no specific provision in the Act or in the case law which demands that an auditor be independent' in this abstract sense."

It is, nonetheless, respectfully submitted that an auditor should not be a management consultant and should be independent. The practice of having auditors qualify accounts and then not resign is bad. Nigel Savage[42] has noted that in the United States the view that the auditor must be independent of all parties in the corporate structure, has gained currency consistent with trends towards monitoring corporate social responsibility. While discussing the same subject, Dr Savage criticises the United Kingdom accountancy bodies' guidelines as to auditing not only for lacking enforceability but also for being "vague aspirations resting on the auditor using his own judgement in particular situations." In this vein, Dr Savage reacts to the suggestion that, "Independence is purely a state of mind and cannot be defined beyond vague guidelines and in terms of situations where the auditor prejudices his independence." He states:[42]

> ... it might be argued that independence in this context has two elements, the substantive and the appearance. In the first instance it relates to the objectivity of the individual auditor in terms of his state of mind. This is developed and guaranteed by personal qualities such as strength of character and professional integrity and may not be necessarily achieved by legislation or rules. The appearance of independence is, however of equal importance in terms of preserving and improving the credibility of the auditor's function in the eyes of the public. Independence in this respect is rather like justice, it must not only be accomplished but it must be seen to be accomplished.

Dr Savage concludes that given public suspicion as to the performance of auditors[43]consideration must be given to strengthening the legislative provisions designed to safeguard the independence and integrity of accounts.

Thus a measure of independence and competence (evidenced by the requirement that an auditor belong to one of the established professional bodies of accountants)[44] are required of an auditor.

## Position of the auditor

A company's auditor is not an officer of the company within the meaning of Section 2 of the Companies Act, nor for purposes of Section 161 (1). However, he is an officer for purposes of the misfeasance proceedings regulated by Section 328 of the Act.[45] In *Shonowo v. Adebayo*[46], it was held that in respect of misfeasance proceedings under the operative Companies Act[47], an auditor who is not the company's regular auditor, but was engaged to conduct an *adhoc* inquiry

---

41 Baxt, *supra*, n. 38, p. 416; See too Nigel Savage, "New Teeth for The Watchdog" (1980) *JBL* 393, 399-400

42 *ibid* at, p. 339

43 *ibid* at p. 400 and p. 393-394, citing the Department of Trade Inspectors' Reports on *Roadship Ltd.* (HMSO, 1976) p. 256; Lonrho Ltd. (HMSO 1976) p. *London* and *Counties Securities Ltd.* (HMSO 1976) p. 229 and *London and Capital Group* (HMSO, 1977) p. 368

44 See *supra* n. 37 and text thereof.

45 *Re: Kingston Cotton Mill Co. (No. 2)* [1896] 2 Ch. 279

46 1969 NCLR 126; 1969 (2) ALR Comm. 419; 1969 1 NMLR 82 (Supreme Court of Nigeria).

47 Cap. 37 Laws of the Federation, 1958, S. 211

into the company's affairs is not an officer of the company and an order cannot be made against him under the relevant section.[48]

Furthermore, a company is precluded through provision in its articles or any contract from relieving auditors of liability for negligence, breach of duty or breach of trust but they can be indemnified against liability incurred by them in defending proceedings brought against the company.[49] Additionally, the court may grant auditors relief, if they have acted honestly and reasonably or ought to be fairly excused.[50]

However, where inspectors have been appointed to investigate the affairs of the company under Section 168 of the Companies Act, they are regarded as agents of the company for purposes of compliance with provisions of that section.[51]

## Duties of the auditor

The primary duty of an auditor is to audit the accounts of the company including its annual balance sheet and profit and loss statement and to prepare a report which states *inter alia* whether the accounts have been properly prepared and whether they give a true and fair view of the state of affairs and profit and loss aspects of the company.[52] To achieve this, the auditor must carry out investigations which will assist him to determine whether proper accounting records have been kept and whether they comply with the entries.[53] For this purpose, the auditor has right of access to all relevant documents to enable him to do his duty.[54] The duty to investigate, gives rise on the part of the auditor to exercise care in carrying out that function. R. Baxt suggests that this standard of care has two aspects. The first stems from the legal requirement that the auditors are appointed by[54] and report to[55] the shareholders in general meeting. The object of this arrangement is to ensure that shareholders received "independent and reliable information respecting the true financial position of the company at the time of the audit."[56] The second aspect, which stems from the first, relates to the manner of carrying out this duty. The fist guidance on this point was put forward by Lindley L.J. when he stated:

> Such I take to be the duty of the auditor: he must be honest - i.e. he must not certify what he does not believe to be true, and he must take reasonable care and skill before he believes what he certifies to, is true. What is reasonable care in any particular case must depend upon the circumstances of that case. Where there is nothing to excite suspicion very little inquiry will be reasonably sufficient, and in practice I believe business men select a few cases at haphazard, see that they are right, and assume that others like them are correct also. Where suspicion is aroused more care is obviously necessary; but the auditor is not bound to exercise more than reasonable care and skill, even in a case of suspicion, and he is perfectly justified in acting on the opinion of an expert where special knowledge is required.[57]

This theme was expanded upon by Lopes L.J. in *Re: Kingston Cotton Mill Co. (No. 2).*,[58] when he made his famous watchdog formulation. He stated:

---

48 1969 NCLR, at pp. 143-144. See also *In Re: Western Counties Steam Bakeries & Milling Co.* [1897] 1 Ch. 617, 627 per Lindley L.J.; *R v. Shacter* [1960] 2 QB 252

49 Companies Act, S. 206; Table A. Art. 135

50 *ibid.* S. 405

51 *ibid* S. 168

52 *ibid.* S. 162 (1); Schedule 7

53 *ibid* S. 162 (3), Schedule 7 Paras 1, 2.

54 Companies Act, S. 159

55 Companies Act, S. 162(1)

56 per Lindley L.J. in *Re: London & General Bank (No. 2)* [1895] 2 Ch. 673 at p. 682

57 *ibid*, at p. 683

58 [1896] 2 Ch. 278

> .... It is the duty of an auditor to bring to bear on the work he has to perform that skill, care, and caution which a reasonably competent, careful and cautious auditor would use. What is reasonable skill, care and caution must depend on the particular circumstances of each case. An auditor is not bound to be a detective, or, as was said, to approach his work with suspicion or with a foregone conclusion that there is something wrong. He is a watchdog, but not a bloodhound. He is justified in believing tried servants of the company in whom confidence is placed by the company. He is entitled to assume that they are honest, and to rely upon their representations, provided he takes reasonable care. If there is anything calculated to excite suspicion he should probe it to the bottom: but in the absence of anything of that kind he is only bound to be reasonably cautious and careful.[59]

Although reliance on theses cases has been consistent ever since they were decided as indicating the auditor's duty of care and its implications, it is notable that at the time they were decided there was no statutory requirement on the part of a trading company (other than certain banking companies) to file annual accounts at the companies registry,[60] although the articles may have required the company to supply annual accounts to shareholders. In addition, there was no legal obligation on the part of the company to appoint an auditor until 1900.[61]

Baxt further notes[62] that the introduction of legislation requiring accounts to be prepared, filed, distributed, together with the requirement that these be audited, (and the very substantial development of statutory law in relation to the information that companies supply to the company registry and to their own shareholders) is one of the landmarks in the developments of company law. Accordingly, Professor Baxt is of the view that with this background in mind "it is nether real nor acceptable to view the common law principles of 1896 as exactly applicable today.[63] The views of Lord Lindley and Lopes L.J. must, therefore, be subjected to the statutory provisions and the understanding which required that accurate and meaningful information be supplied.[64] Indeed, Lopes L.J.'s watchdog theme has through the years been doubted[65] in the light of the evolving formal status of the auditor.[66]The problem of determining the scope of the auditor's duty of care has been compounded by the lack of clarity among the professional accounting bodies of the standards of auditing. In fact, some of the guidelines do not reflect what would be acceptable as accounting standards.[67]

What would be regarded as the most radical departure from Lopes L.J.'s watchdog formula in case law is to be found in *dicta* by Lord Denning in *Fomento (Sterling Area) Ltd. v. Selsdon Foundation Pen Co. Ltd.*,[68] where in analysing the obligations of the auditor, he remarked:

---

59 *ibid* at pp. 288-289

60 Edey & Panitpakdi, *British Company Accounting And the Law* (1844-1900 (p. 357) in Littleton and Yamey, *Studies in the History of Accounting* (1956); see also Baxt, *supra*, n. 38a p. 418

61 63 & 64 Vict. C. 48

62 *supra* n. 38a, pp. 418-9, following Gower, *Principles of Modern Company Law* (2nd Ed. 1954), p. 54

63 *ibid*, p. 419

64 Companies Act, S. 162(3)

65 *London Oil Storage Co. v. Seear Hasluck & Co.* (1904) 31. *The Accountant L.R.I., in Dicksee's Auditing* (17th Ed.) at p. 634 per Lord Alverstone; *Henry Squire (Cash Chemist) Ltd. v. Ball, Baker & Co.* (1911) 27 L.R. 269, 271

66 Baxt, *supra* n. 38a, p. 420. In *Re: City Equitable Fire Insurance Co; Ltd.* [1925] 1 Ch. 407, Romer J. observed (at pp. 497-498) "that it is the duty of a company's auditor in general to satisfy himself that the securities of a company in fact exist and are in safe custody, cannot, I think be gain said." See also *Thomas v. Corporation of Devonport* [1900] 1 QB 16, 21 per Lord Russel of Killowen C.J. *Re: Ridsel, Ridsel v. Rawlingson* [1947] 2 ALL ER 312 per *Jenkins J.; Roberts v. Hopwood* [1925] 578, 605 per Lord Sumner; see also the Australian case, *President, Councillors and Rate Payers of the Shire of Frankston & Hastings v. Cohen* (1960) 102 CLR 607 per Fullager J. at pp. 619-20

67 See e.g. *Recommendations of Accounting Principles* issued by the Institute of Chartered Accountants in England & Wales; see also Baxt, *ibid*, p. 22; Chambers, Financial Information and Securities Market" *Abacus* Vol. 1 No. 1. p: 3

> What is the proper function of an auditor? It is said that he is bound only to verify the sum, the arithmetical conclusion, by reference to the books, and all necessary vouching material and oral explanations; and that it is no part of his function to inquire whether an article is covered by patents or not. I think this too narrow a view. An auditor is not to be confined to the mechanics of checking vouchers and making arithmetical computations. He is not to be written off as a professional 'adder-upper and substractor.' His vital task is to take care to see that errors are not made, be they errors of computation or errors of omission or commission or down-right untruths. To perform this task properly, he must come to it with an inquiring mind, not suspicious of dishonesty, I agree but suspecting that someone may have made a mistake somewhere and that a check must be made to ensure that there has been none.[69]

Lord Denning further suggests that if in the course of his inquiries the auditor requires expert knowledge, like legal advice on patents, he may obtain it and rely on it.[70] Lord Denning's approach thus has strong ingredients of conceiving the auditor as a "bloodhound" rather than mere watchdog, and it is submitted that this would appear to accord with his current statutory obligation to investigate.[70]

The relatively more recent case of *Re: Thomas Garrard Ltd.*[71]appears to accept the watchdog theme in principle although its holding, based on the peculiar facts of the case and modern conception of the role of the auditor, departs from the "watchdog" notion. The decision is criticised for by passing "an opportunity to up-date the law" and for failing to positively analyse the position of auditors and thus denying guidance to the accounting profession and those connected with it.[72]

Thus, the trend in the development of the role of an auditor underlies his importance within the corporate structure as an investigator, detective and ultimately as an assessor. This is all the more significant when the concept of auditing is understood.

## The essence of auditing

Essentially, auditing involves forms of measurement of given indexes in order to determine the performance of the audited subject. Professor Eisenberg has thus observed in relation to monitoring corporate management:[73]

> To the extent that the autonomy of corporate management ultimately rests on notions of efficiency and to the extent that the board's major role is to monitor management, the institutions by which managerial efficiency is measured - whether by the Board or by others must be a central concern of the corporate system.

It is further recognised that the techniques currently used to measure managerial efficiency centre on indexes involving corporate profits which are essentially numerical. In addition the methods employed to determine such profits cannot be objective or comparable unless they are part of a choice or accounting principles which are used to prepare financial statements.[74] While in theory this objectivity and comparability is achievable through independent accountants or auditors, the practice has belied this assumption. The major cause of this is that the task of determining accounting principles has been left with management rather than accountants. In turn,

---

68 [1958] 1 ALL ER 11

69 *ibid*, at p. 23, Viscount Simonds expressed a slightly different view following *Re Kingston Cotton Mill* (No. 2), *supra*, n. 59

70 *supra*, notes 53 to 54 and text thereof.

71 [1967] ALL ER 525

72 R. *Baxt, supra* n. 38a, p. 429. For a more detailed discussion see Baxt, pp. 425-429

73 *Eisenberg* (1975) *California Law Review*. 375

74 *ibid*, pp. 417-424 especially true of the United States position

management has been given a wide discretion of principles to choose from by major accounting bodies.[74] The third shortcoming is that management selects, determines the tenure of and dismisses the accountants and auditors of the company.[75] The inevitable result is that the process of auditing management performance is neither objective or comparative principally because the body to be audited decides the criterion and mode by which it is to be judged and in practice demands acquiescent reports from the auditors.[76]

Such structural shortcomings within the corporation have to be remedied before the function of monitoring management is made viable through the framework of accountants and auditors.

The first remedy suggested is to leave to the accountants the task of determining objective accounting principles[77], since they alone are qualified to do this. Furthermore, this removes from management the power to determine how it is to be assessed, thus ensuring a measure of objectivity.

Secondly, the criterion of auditing i.e the accounting principles themselves must be standardised in one major respect which is to ensure that the accounting and auditing function reflects the true picture of what is being assessed as a whole.

Professor Eisenberg's summary of two important United States civil cases in this regard is pertinent:

> ... just as Barchris[78] held in effect that an accountant cannot rely on general acceptance to support his certification of a principle that does not fairly account for the transaction being described, Simon[79] held that an accountant cannot rely on the general acceptance of each principle employed in the preparation of a financial statement to support his certification of a statement that is not fair as a whole.[80]

Thus the view is held that in order to comply with those decisions accountants have to significantly increase their control over the financial statement they certify. This position appears to have been reached in the United Kingdom.[81]

The last remedy would be to remove the power of selecting and dismissing the accountants and auditors from management and transferring it to another body. This would further increase the independence of the auditors and also ensure more objective assessment of management. One suggestion is that this power should lie with the shareholders in general meeting[82] as is the case in Uganda and Britain.[83] Objection is expressed to this idea in that in practice the shareholders would depend on the board of directors for guidance on selection and dismissal, and would be unable to determine the scope of the audit, nor the compensation of the accountant, and could not give the accountant periodic direction and support.

Another suggestion is that every publicly incorporated company should be required to have an audit committee consisting entirely of independent directors, empowered to (1) nominate and recommend the dismissal of the company's accountant on behalf of the main board and (2), to direct the accountant's activities and determine the conditions of his employment.[84]

---

75 *ibid*,. p. 424-426

76 *ibid*, p. 427; see also Report by P. Legatt and D.C. Hobson, on London and County Securities Ltd. (*HMSO* 1976) caps. 7 & 13

77 *ibid*, pp. 427-432

78 *Escott v. Barchris Construction Corporation, 283F Supp* 643 (SDNY 1968)

79 *United States v. Simon* 425F. 2d 796 (2nd Circuit 1969) certificate denied 397 US 1006 (1970)

80 Eisenberg, *op.cit., supra* n. 78, p. 432

81 S. 14(3) (a) Companies Act, 1967; see also Keith J. Louden, *The Effective Director in Action* New York (1975) pp. 24-28.

82 D. Hawes, "Stockholder Appointment of Independent Auditors" (1974) 74 *Columbia L. Rev*. 39

83 See S. 14(1) Companies Act, 1976; S. 159 Companies Act, Cap. 85

84 Eisenberg, *op. cit.* n. 74, pp. 432-433

The audit function has to be appreciated within the framework of the role, rights and powers of the auditor, and subsequently, his impact on management, through his scrutiny of the company's financial information.

The Companies Act, gives the auditor wide powers of investigation, a role which though somewhat restricted by case law standards of care, is nonetheless considerable, and much more so as the courts are beginning to appreciate that he is more than a "watchdog", and perhaps approaching the role of "bloodhound". Concomitant to these powers is the detailed protection of the auditor from arbitrary dismissal and interference with his work. All this is aimed at ensuring objectivity, an aspect which is enhanced (at least in theory) by the fact that he is appointed by the general meeting of shareholders rather than management.

The practice, particularly that in the United States, still allows considerable interference by management in the audit function through appointing, or at least influencing the appointment of auditors, determining the accounting principles to be used and, consequently casting doubt on the objectivity of financial auditing and as a corollary, management audit.

The solutions suggested accord in large measure with the statutory provisions in the United Kingdom Companies Acts.[85] These are, however, inadequate in that the shareholders, to whom the task of choosing auditors is given, are invariably passive and subject to manipulation, in that task by management. Hence the suggestion of an audit committee consisting predominantly of independent directors, and having the power to appoint, supervise and dismiss the auditor. This has the additional advantage that company financial affairs are reviewed on a regular basis rather than carrying out postmortems after irregularities have arisen.

Finally, may be asked to whom does an auditor essentially owe the duty of care? The primary duty of an auditor is to the company with whom he is in contractual relationship.[86] Consequently, auditors have been held liable in actions instituted by the company usually through its liquidator.[87] Nevertheless, it is notable that the auditor's report has to be made to the members in general meeting, each of whom is entitled to inspection thereof.[88] As a result, it has been suggested that a duty of care is owed to each individual member[89], who could sue irrespective of the rule in *Foss v. Harbottle*[90]. It follows then that an auditor stands in a fiduciary relationship to both the company and its members.[91] Furthermore, given that the accounts are prepared and published for the benefit, not only of members and creditors but also for the public generally who rely on them, an audit thereof should give wider liability for the auditor. Indeed, it appears that the auditor owes a duty to a non-member of the company or outsider, if he knows that his audited accounts are likely to be relied on by a potential investor,[92] except where there is express disclaimer of responsibility. It is also evident that he owes a duty of care where he is required to value shares for purposes of their acquisition under pre-emptive rights under the company's articles.[93]

---

85 See Companies Acts 1967, 1976, 1981, Consolidating Act, 1985

86 See generally Gower, *op.cit.* (4th Ed), p. 523-524; Leigh, *op. cit.* pp. 185-186

87 *Re London & General Bank* (No.1) [1895] 2 Ch. 166 C.A., *Re Kingston Cotton Mills Co.* (No. 1) [1896] 1 Ch. 6. C.A. *Shonowo v. Adebayo, supra* n. 47

88 Companies Act, S. 162 (1) (2).

89 Gower, *op. cit* p. 523

90 See *infra* chap. 15

91 *Nocton v. Ashburton* [1914] A.C. 932, 971, in contrast to the position of directors. See *infra* chap. 14

92 *Hedley Byrne & Co. Ltd. v. Heller & Partners Ltd.* [1964] A.C. 465 H.L. *J.E.B Fasteners v. Marks, Bloom & Co. [1981] 3 ALL ER 289*

93 *Arenson v. Arenson* [1977] A.C. 405 H.L.

# 14*

# DIRECTOR'S DUTIES

The present discussion restricts itself to a consideration of issues affecting the scope and extent of directors' duties.

It appears to be settled that a director's fiduciary duties are owed only to the company.[1] However, recent developments affecting disclosure of information to shareholders and the general area of insider dealing in corporate securities have tended to question, if not undermine this legal concept, which is, basically a product of case law. We shall examine some significant cases which tend to support the concept and afterwards go on to analyse in what respects, if any, the principles enunciated in those cases have been questioned or undermined.

## Duty to a holding company or subsidiary

In *Bell v. Lever Bros. Ltd*[2] a holding company (L) held more than 99 per cent of the share capital of its subsidiary (N). Two directors of N, who had service agreements with L, engaged in secret speculations in cocoa, a commodity in which N company dealt. This was conduct which would have justified their dismissal as directors by N company and termination of their service agreements with L. With regard to the issue as to whether they were in breach of duty to the holding company, it was held by the House of Lords that they were not. Lord Atkin stated in this respect;[3]

> It will be noticed that Bell was not a director of Levers, and with respect, I cannot accept the view of Greer L.J. that if he was in a similar fiduciary relationship to the Niger Company he was in a similar fiduciary relationship to the shareholders or the particular shareholder (Levers) who held 99 per cent of the shares.

In essence, Lord Atkin's statement rejects the notion that a director of a subsidiary company owes duties either to its shareholders or its holding company. The inference is that the director's duties are owed only to the company of which he is director. This position was also reached by Pennycuick. J. sitting at first instance in *Pergamon Press Ltd. v. Maxwell.*[4] This was a case where the plaintiff holding company held 70% of the shares of a subsidiary in New York of which the defendant director was president. To the suggestion that the court should interfere with the discretionary powers of the defendant to vote in a manner adverse to the plaintiff company, Pennycuick J. replied:[5]

> the court would not at the instance of some only of the members of an incorporated company make a mandatory order upon the defendant directing him to exercise his discretion in a certain manner.

* Partly based on the Author's Ph.D. Thesis submitted to the University of London 1981, Chap. 4

1 *Gore Browne on companies* 43rd Ed. 1977) para 27-8 L.C.B. Gower, *Principles of Modern Company Law* (4th Ed 1979) p. 573

2 [1932] A.C. 161 H.L.

3 *ibid* at p. 228 following Avory J. in *Healey v. Societe Anonyme Francaise Rubastic* [1917] 1KB 946

4 [1970] 1 WLR 1167

5 *ibid* at p. 1172

Likewise, it seems to be the law that a director of a holding company owes no duty to any of its subsidiaries. Harman L.J., in the Court of Appeal judgment, in *Lindgren v. L. & P. Estates Ltd.*[6], thus observed:[7]

> ... but Lindgren was a director not of the defendant company but of CCP. He may have been in breach of his duty to that company, but he owed no duty to the defendant company although it was about to become a subsidiary of CCP. To Hold that Lindgren, a director of CCP, was bound to protect the interests of one of its subsidiaries which had an independent board is to stretch the principle altogether beyond reason.

This view, is however, qualified in the House of Lord's decision, *Scottish Cooperative Wholesale Society Ltd. v. Meyer*[8] where Viscount Simmonds indicated[9] that when a subsidiary company is formed with an independent minority of shareholders, the parent company is under an obligation so to conduct its own affairs as to deal fairly with its subsidiary. In essence, the directors of the parent company in exercising their duties must have regard to the interests of such a subsidiary.

## Duty to a person or body in a fiduciary position to the company

The other controversial proposition of law is that a director does not owe duties to a person to whom the company stands is a fiduciary relationship. This was the majority view of the Court of Appeal in *Wilson v. Bury.*[10] In that case, a company was formed for the purpose of receiving money from depositors and investing it upon security. The defendants were directors of the company. The plaintiff deposited £ 1,000 with the company upon certain terms. The company went into liquidation and the plaintiff sued the defendants to recover the £ 1,000 upon the ground that this sum was lost to him as a result of the negligence of the defendants. The Court of Appeal held that the defendants were not liable to the plaintiff. Thus in this vein Bramley L.J. stated:[11]

> for assuming that there is a trust and a breach of it, I can see no reason on which the directors can be held personally responsible for it to the plaintiff.

Brett L.J. found[12] that a contract existed between the plaintiff and the company, but the defendants could not be held liable as constructive trustees for aiding and abetting in the breach of a trust. In so doing, the learned Lord Justice relied on a statement in *Archer v. Lavender*[13] thus:[14]

> The general rule of the court is, that an agent employed by a trustee is answerable only to the trustee who employed him and that he cannot be considered a constructive trustee and be held liable as such merely because he knew of the trusts. Such an agent is not bound to see to the application of the trust fund received by him and paid over to the trustee at least unless he is aware that the trustee is about to misapply the same fraudulently.

---

6 [1968] Ch. 572
7 *ibid* at p. 595
8 [1959] A.C. 324
9 *ibid* at p. 343. For a more detailed treatment of this case see *infra* chap. 15
10 (1880) 5 QBD 518 (C.A.)
11 *ibid* at p. 537
12 *ibid* at p. 530
13 Ir Rep I Eq. 220
14 *ibid* at p. 225

To these forceful expositions of the law may be compared an equally forceful dissent by Baggallay L.J. who was of the view that on the facts of this case the relation of trustee and *Cestui que trust* existed between the company and plaintiff and that a breach of trust had been committed by the company and the defendants were parties to the breach of trust. He added:[15]

> I fully recognise as a general rule that an agent employed by a trustee is accountable to his principal only, and cannot be made responsible as a constructive trustee to the *Cestui que trust, but I think that a distinction may and ought to be drawn between the case of a company necessarily acting by its directors and an individual trustee, acting through an agent over whose actions he can exercise control.*

Baggallay L.J.'s view, with which the present writer is most sympathetic was shared about a generation later by Fletcher-Moulton L.J. in his dissenting judgment in the Court of Appeal decision, *Bath v. Standard Land Company Ltd.*[16] The learned Lord Justice stated:[17]

> The simple question is whether, where a limited company undertakes the administration of a trust, the directors as individuals may come under a duty to the *Cestui que trust*, and if so under what circumstances and to what extent? In the first place, I am of opinion that although the *directors of a company are properly described as its agents and act as such, there is a broad distinction of degree between them and ordinary agents which is of importance in deciding such a question as this. It is that so far as knowledge are concerned, the company is an abstraction. Where directors actually perform their part in the management of the company they are both the brains and hands of the company and they cannot shelter themselves under the plea that the knowledge of the trustee is not their knowledge, or that the nature and intention of the acts of the trustee were unknown* to them. Contrast their position with that of an agent for sale such as a broker employed by a company or a person to affect a sale of trust property. He can know nothing more than he is told, and the courts have rightly held that it would be intolerable if he were bound to refuse to act in the ordinary course of his profession or business by reason of mere suspicions as to the intentions of the persons employing him.

He concluded that:[18]

> directors are liable for matters of personal conduct inconsistent with their full knowledge of the fiduciary character of the duties which, in the name of the company, they have to carry out.

If the views of Baggallay L.J. and Fletcher-Moulton L.J. *(supra)* are to be accepted there is the implication that directors may owe duties to the creditors of the company they manage. Indeed, there is judicial opinion which would seem to suggest that directors owe a fiduciary duty to creditors in respect of an *ultra vires* loan.[19] A much more recent judicial development in this direction is to be found in *Walker v. Wimborne*,[20] a decision of the High Court of Australia. This was an appeal by a liquidator against the dismissal of a misfeasance summons brought against the

---

[15] (1880) 6 QBD 518 at p. 535 *Emphasis supplied*

[16] [1911] 1 Ch. 618

[17] *ibid* at p. 636 *Emphasis supplied.*

[18] *ibid* at p. 637

[19] *Sinclair v. Brougham* [1914] A.C. 398 at pp. 443-44; per Lord Parker of Waddington. It is notable though that this case related to an incorporated building society governed by statute (see p. 439).

[20] (1976) 50 A.L.J.R. 446

former directors of Asiatic Electric Co. Pty Ltd. ("Asiatica") under the equivalent of section 328 of the Companies Act [21] The respondents were directors and controllers of other companies which included Australian Sound & Communications Pty. Ltd. (Sound) and Estoril Pty. Ltd. (Estoril). There were two transactions. In one, the respondents caused "Asiatic" to pay $ 10,000 to Sound without security and without any express undertaking by "Sound" to repay. Asiatic did not benefit from this transaction, as in the words of Mason J. the transaction "offered the probable prospect of loss", since Sound was then insolvent. In the second transaction, Asiatic received $ 10,000 from Estoril and granted an equitable charge securing repayment thus putting Estoril on a more favourable footing than Asiatic's other creditors. However, Asiatic was at all relevant times insolvent as its ability to pay its debts punctually depended on receipt of an amount owing by a fourth company (controlled by the respondents) which could not pay.

The Australian High Court held by a majority that the directors of Asiatic were guilty of misfeasance. Thus, Mason J. stated:[22]

> The transaction offered no prospect of advantage to Asiatic, it exposed Asiatic to the probable prospect of substantial loss and thereby seriously prejudiced the unsecured creditors of Asiatic. It was more than an improvident transaction reflecting an error of judgement; it was undertaken in accordance with a policy adopted by the creditors in total disregard of the interests of the company and its creditors.

The learned Justice then postulated the principle which effectually recognises the relevance of creditor's interests of the discharge of directors' fiduciary duties to the company. He stated:[23]

> ... the directors of a company in discharging their duty to the company *must take account of the interest of its shareholders and its creditors.* Any failure by the directors to take into account the interests of creditors will have adverse consequence for the company as well as for them. the creditor of a company must look to that company for payment. His interest may be prejudiced by the movement of funds between companies *in the event that the companies* become insolvent.

Ultimately, Mason J's approach sees the consideration of creditor interests as beneficial in the first instance to the company and secondly to the creditors. Thus while his judgment *appears* to create a duty by directors towards company's creditors, this is regarded as perpetuating the recognised duty they owe the company generally.[24]

Furthermore, Mason J.'s postulation suggests that creditor interests may be considered even before the company has gone into liquidation. It is enough that there exists the mere possibility of insolvency. This view contrasts with that in the United States, where directors are deemed **quasi** trustees for creditors in situations of insolvency.[25] However, this concept is largely justified by reference to rules as to the maintenance of the capital of the corporation.[26] To that extent there is similarity with the English approach. Thus, *Trevor v. Whitworth*[27] postulates that

---

21 S. 367B (1) Companies Act 1961 (New South Wales)

22 *supra* n. 20 at p. 449

23 *ibid* Emphasis supplied

24 See also Note R. Barret, "Directors' Duties to Creditors" (1977) 40 *M.L.R* 226 at pp. 228-229

25 The general rule in the U.S is that "upon insolvency of the ordinary private corporation a quasi trust relationship arises between its director and creditors *(Whitfield v. Kern* 192 A 48-1937). See also 19 *Corpus Juris Secundum, Corporations,* para 837 and *Pepper v. Litton* 308 U.S. (1939)

26 *Brooks v. Buys,* 186 N.W. 472 (1921). In *Eastern National Bank v. American Brick & Tile Co.* C.A. 917 (1906) Pitney J. indicated that the statutory scheme (relating to maintenance of capital) "required stock subscriptions to be made good for the benefit of creditors of insolvent companies". In *Union National Bank v. Douglas* 24 Fed. Cas. 621 1977 Love D.J. was of the view that "the capital stock property and assets of a corporation are to be deemed a trust fund secretly pledged for the payment of the debts of the corporation."

27 (1887) 12 App. Cas. 409

creditors may rely on the capital remaining undiminished by and expenditure outside the limits of the authorised objects or by the return of any part of it to shareholders. The English position as compared with the United States' one has thus been aptly summarised by R. Barrett:[28]

> English courts have developed their own version of the American 'Trust Fund' doctrine, but without any clear identification of creditors as the beneficiaries of the trust. The notion of *quasi* trustees is recognised in a number of cases, but it is the company itself that is the beneficiary.[29] Reference to the interests of creditors have done no more than reflect their standing under earlier versions of section 328 to institute proceedings based on wrongs done to the company by misapplication of moneys or breach of trust. There has been no clear indication that directors are obliged to have regard to the interests of creditors in all circumstances. What is recognised, however, is that the rules as to the maintenance of capital exist for the benefit of creditors and that after liquidation has commenced creditors have a statutory right to seek the assistance of the court in compelling directors to make good to the company such loss as it has sustained through breach of their duties.

In summary, the *Walker v. Wimborne*[20] decision is capable of three interpretations. The first is that in insisting on the relevance of creditors' interests in the discharge of directors' fiduciary duties, the decision merely confirms the statutory requirements as to maintenance of capital which recognise creditors' rights. The second interpretation is that creditors' interests may only be recognised in situations of insolvency.[30] However, and this third interpretation may be the most accurate, if the Australian High Court merely indicates the theoretical possibility of insolvency[31] as one ground for requiring directors' regard for creditors' interests then the court is not merely confirming statutory schemes as to creditor protection but laying down a distinct duty owed to creditors. However, an analysis of Mason J.'s statement[31] shows that although the learned judge indicates that directors should take into account the interests of both the shareholders and creditors, such an account is necessary to prevent "adverse consequences" for the company. Furthermore, it is indicated that a creditor should look for payment to the company. It is, therefore, submitted that the duty of directors to the company is paramount and the *Walker v. Wimborne*[20] decision only provides for the interests of creditors to the extent that these relate to the directors' fiduciary duties to the company. Such an approach would appear to be in line with English authority[32], and would appear to avoid the problems of reconciling the conflicting interests of shareholders and creditors, the two groups whose interests Mason J. suggests should be considered.[33] As a result, the rule that a director owes no duties to his company's fiduciary remains intact.

---

28 *supra*, n. 24 at pp. 229-30

29 Following *Russel v. Wakefield Waterworks Co.* (1875) 20 Eq. 474 per Jessel M.R: "In this court the money of the company is a trust fund because it is applicable only to the special purpose of the company in the hands of the agents of the company and it is in that sense a trust fund applicable by them to those special purposes" and *Re: Oxford Benefit and Investment Society* (1886) 35 Ch. 502 per Kay J.: "directors are quasi trustees of the capital of the company." However, Jessel. M.R. in the *Wakefield Case* (ibid) insists that only the company can sue in respect of such trust fund.

30 Following Gower, *Principles of Modern Company Law* (3rd Ed. 1969) p.523 and Ford, *Principles of Company Law* (1974) p.340

31 See *supra* n. 23 and accompanying text.

32 See cases at n. 29 *supra*. See also per Jessel M.R. in *Re: Wincham Ship building Boiler and Salt Co.* (1878) 1 Ch. D 322 where he says that "directors are trustees for the shareholders that is for the company... but directors are not trustees for the creditor of the company."

33 See also Barrett, *supra* n. 24 at p. 231

## Duty to shareholders[33a]

A much more pertinent legal concept is that a director does not owe duties to individual shareholders. This is largely a consequence of the decision at first instance ow Swinfen-Eady J. in *Percival v. Wright.*[34] In that case, a director was approached by shareholders to purchase their shares at a quoted price. The director was aware of an impending take-over bid which envisaged a much higher price being offered by the prospective purchaser of the company. The director did not disclose to the shareholders his inside information about the impending take-over and he accepted the shareholders' offer. Swinfen-Eady J. held that since a director owed no fiduciary duty to shareholders he was not liable for the non-disclosure. The *Percival v. Wright* decision has been the subject of much criticism.[35] The chief objection to the decision is that it is in conflict with commercial morality and inconsistent by analogy with the fiduciary duty of directors not to use the property or confidential information of the company for personal profit.[36] Indeed both the Cohen and Jenkins committees[35] recommended *Percival's* abrogation by the enactment of new legislation.

Upon closer analysis of *Percival v. Wright* the decision is possibly not as monstrous as some criticisms have made it look. Thus, it is notable that the judgment of Swinfen Eady J. emphasizes that there was no "unfair dealing" by the directors and appears to suggest that it was significant that the initial approach in the matter was made by the shareholders.[37] The most forthright confrontation of *Percival v. Wright* is to be found in the New Zealand case, *Coleman v. Myers.*[38] It is in this decision that the above "mitigating" view of the *Percival* decision is adverted to. Thus Mahon J. comments of it:[39]

> ... the undisclosed facts in *Percival v. Wright* involved a possible sale which in the end proved abortive so that the defendants appeared to derive no profit from the transaction and the learned judge specifically acquitted the defendants of any suggestion of "unfair" dealing, a conclusion which, for my own part, I think might have been stated in the judgment as mitigating what may have appeared to be the palpable injustice of the principle applied in the ultimate decision.

However, in his approach to the peculiar facts of *Coleman v. Myers* he did not think that the fact that the initial approach, with regard to the purchase of shares, in *Percival* was made by the shareholders was significant enough to distinguish it from the case before him where a take-over offer was made by the defendant director.[40]
Thus he stated:[39]

> ... I find myself unable, in the last resort, to find that the present case is distinguishable from *Percival v. Wright*. In each case there were negotiations between directors and shareholders for the purchase of shares in their own company. It seems immaterial to me that the party

[33a] See also Bakibinga, *GRBPL* (Lagos) Vol. 2. No. 12 pp 22-26 (1989)

[34] [1902] 2 Ch. 421

[35] See *Report of the Company Law committee* (Cohen Committee) Cmnd 6659 (1945) paras. 86 and 87; *Report of the Company Law Committee* (Jenkins Committee) Cmnd 749 (1962) paras. 89 and 99(b). P.R. Adams *Company Directors in Australia* (2nd Ed) pp. 146-147; Loss, "The Fiduciary concept as Applied to Trading by corporate 'Insiders' in the United States" (1970) 33 *M.L.R* 34, 40-41

[36] *Coleman v. Myers* [1977] 1 NZLR 225 at pp. 268-9 following *Regal (Hastings) Ltd.v. Gulliver* [1967] 2 AC 134 (HL) and *Phipps v. Boardman [1967] 2 AC 46*

[37] [1902] 2 Ch. 421, 426-7; *Gore Browne on Companies* (43rd Ed.- 1977) para. 27-8

[38] [1977] 2 NZLR 225; see also notes by BAK Rider, *Percival v. Wright* - per incuriam" [1977] 40 *MLR* 471-6; "A special Relationship on special facts" (1978) 41 *MLR* 585 BAK Rider "Partnership Law and its impact on Domestic Companies" [1979] *CLJ* 148 at pp. 166-8

[39] [1977] 2 NZLR 225 at p. 274

> making the initial approach was a director in one case and shareholders in the other, and that in the one case the proposal was for sale of one parcel of shares while in other there was an unconditional bid for the purchase of the entire shareholding for in the latter case the bidder is making a separate offer to each shareholder. The key fact is that in both cases there was a contemplated and later executed transaction for the purchase of shares by a director and I can find no ground for holding that the cases are, in principle distinguishable.

Having thus held *Percival v. Wright (supra)* and *Coleman v. Myers (supra)* to be indistinguishable in principle, Mahon J. went on to observe that the former decision was incorrectly decided. In the *Percival* case the plaintiffs had contended that although no fiduciary situation exists in dealings between a director and a shareholder before the take-over situation arises, as soon as that possibility arose, a fiduciary situation is created. To this proposition, Swinfen-Eady J. retorted that a shareholder is fixed with the knowledge of all the powers of directors and should have no more reason to assume that they were not negotiating a sale of the undertaking than to assume that they were not exercising any other powers. Further that the contrary views would place directors in a most invidious position as they could not buy or sell shares without disclosing negotiations of which a premature disclosure might well be against the best interests of the company.

To these conflicting propositions, Mahon J. thus observed:[41]

> ... but in my opinion, it was not necessary for the plaintiffs to assert that the fiduciary position brought into operation by the negotiations for purchase of the shareholders' shares was in any specific category. The judge seems to me to have not considered the further question whether this approach by the plaintiff shareholders to sell their shares to the directors did not create a fiduciary position of a more general kind in that the shareholders were not dealing with potential purchasers who alone had access to the knowledge of a material fact which unknown to the shareholders controlled the value of the shares which they desired to sell.

Thus the basis for a "breach of fiduciary duty is the improper advantage taken by the defendant of a confidence reposed in him either by or for the benefit of, the plaintiff."[42] Applying this test to the relationship between a shareholder and a director, Mahon J. thus observed:[42]

---

[40] Briefly the facts in *Coleman v. Myers (ibid)* were that the plaintiff, who were minority shareholders in a small private company, reluctantly sold out their shares to A.D. Myers who was the company's managing director. This was in line with a take-over offer by Myers for the entire equity capital. After he became close shareholder, Myers sold the company's surplus assets and declared a dividend to himself thus reimbursing himself the acquisition expenses. The plaintiffs submitted that their shares and those of others had been sold at a gross undervaluation through a scheme and strategy by which the value of the company's assets had been concealed. The plaintiffs *(inter alia)* asked that the contract of sale be set aside and damages awarded on the basis of actionable non-disclosure (i.e. that the defendants should have disclosed "all relevant information in their possession bearing on the fair price of shares").

[41] *ibid* at p. 275, this approach, in Mahon J.'s view is justified by the practice of the Courts of Equity where "the original concept of fiduciary obligation ... rested upon the court's jurisdiction ... to intervene in any case where there had been an abuse by one party of trust or confidence reposed in him by another (*ibid* p. 275). See also L.S. Sealy "Fiduciary Relationships" (1962) *C.L.J.* 69. Mahon J. particularly relied upon *Erlanger v. New Sombrero Phosphate Company* (1878) 3 App. Cas. 1218 (H.L) where promoters were held liable for non-disclosure of material facts in relation to the original purchase price of a property which they sold to the company. This was not because they were trustees for the company but because they stood in a fiduciary position to the company. Mahon J.'s reliance on this case is criticised on the ground that the relationship between a promoter and controller of a company is different from that between a director and a shareholder (see Rider *supra* n. 38 (1977) 40 *MLR* 474).

[42] [1977 2 NZLR p. 277. In so doing Mahon J. rejected the notion advanced by Lord Denning M.R. in *Lloyds Bank Ltd v. Bundy* [1974] 3 All ER 757 that a fiduciary obligation could arise in a situation of unequal bargaining power.

> When one considers the legal relationship between the shareholder in a limited liability company and the directors entrusted with the management of that company, it appears to me that in any transaction involving the sale of shares between director and shareholder, the director is the repository of confidence and trust necessarily vested in him by the shareholder, or by his legal status in relation to the existence of information affecting the true value of those shares. I say this because a shareholder who is not a director has not in the absence of any special provision in the articles any right to intervene in the management of the company.

Mahon J. restricted his conception of the fiduciary duty between a director and shareholder "to private companies and to such transactions in public company shares, listed or otherwise, where the identity of the shareholder is known to the director at the time of sale."[43] He thereby excluded stock exchange transactions which should be regulated by statute. The learned judge further draws a distinction between the "special facts" doctrine as applied in the United States[44] and his postulation. He says that while in the former situation directorial liability is established by the existence of special facts, his *"opinion is founded upon the legal status and powers of a director as being the originating cause of liability."*[43]

The New Zealand Court of Appeal took a different approach on the outstanding points raised in Mahon J.'s decision.

In the first place, the Court of Appeal expressed the view that the *Percival v. Wright* decision was correct on its facts. Woodhouse J. said of it:[45]

> ... the very limited point put to the court was simply that fortuitous negotiations for the sale of the undertaking altered the whole position. That, in my view, could not possibly be the test and, with respect, the decision of the judge in that particular case, restricted as I think it was to that one point, was inevitable.

Cooke J. observed that "the actual outcome of the decision does not shock the conscience",[46] while Casey J. indicated thus with regard to Mahon J.'s finding that Percival was wrongly decided:[47]

> In so far as it may suggest that a director can never be in a fiduciary relationship with a shareholder, I concur. But in view of its own facts and of the concessions made the case may have been correctly decided on the basis that the relation of director/shareholder does not by itself give rise to a fiduciary duty and that Swinfen-Eady J. did not consider the circumstances warranted such a finding.

Secondly, the Court of Appeal thought that *Percival v. Wright* had little if any relevance to the instant case.[48] Thirdly, with regard to Mahon J.'s test that the basis of the fiduciary duty is the confidence reposed in the director by the shareholders to disclose information affecting a transaction which the director acquires by virtue of his status and powers as director. The Court of Appeal regarded such a formula as too wide. It thought that such a duty "depends upon all the surrounding circumstances and the nature of the responsibility which in a real and practical sense

[43] *ibid* p. 278 Emphasis supplied

[44] See *Strong v. Rapide* 213 V5 419 (1909) where the U.S. Supreme Court, though cognisant that the ordinary relationship between directors and shareholders does not impose any fiduciary obligations on directors, nonetheless held that where special circumstances exist as in that case, a duty of disclosure upon the directors to the shareholders would be recognised.

[45] [1977] 2 NZLR p. 324

[46] *ibid* at p. 329

[47] *ibid* at p. 370

[48] per Cooke J. (at p. 330 *ibid)* and Casey J. (ibid p. 371)

the director has assumed towards the shareholder.[49] These circumstances would vary and while the court could not lay down a general test as to when the duty would arise and how it would be discharged, certain factors could be considered in this respect. These include:

> ... dependence upon information and advice, the existence of a relationship of confidence, the significance of some particular transaction for the parties, and ... the extent of any positive action taken by or on behalf of the director or directors to promote it.[49]

Cooke J.[50] thought that in the present case a fiduciary duty arose by virtue of the family character of the company, the positions of father and son in the company and the family; their high degree of inside knowledge and the way in which they went about the take-over and the persuasion of shareholders. In this vein, Cooke J. ventured that this case fell within "the broad class of fiduciary relationships arising from special facts."[51]

In essence, the Court of Appeal, in *Coleman v. Myers,* acknowledges that the *Percival v. Wright* decision was correct. However, the court declined to accept that the *Percival* decision is authority for the proposition that a director can never be in a fiduciary relationship with a shareholder.[52] The test as to the existence of a fiduciary obligation between a director and a shareholder does not depend on the status of the director within the company *viz-a-viz* the shareholder. To that extent, the test is similar to the "special facts" doctrine applied in the United States by virtue of the *Strong v. Rapide*[44] decision of the Supreme Court and consistent with common law authorities establishing fiduciary obligations on the basis of special facts. To the extent that the duty of disclosure by directors is to be gathered from all surrounding circumstances one detects a similarity with the "materiality" test established by case law under Rule 10b-5 which operates by virtue of Section 10 of the United States Securities Exchange Act of 1934. Rule 10b-5 states:

> It shall be unlawful for any person directly or indirectly, by the use of any means or instrumentality of interstate commerce, or of the mails, or of any facility of any national securities exchange:

(1) to employ any device, scheme or artifice to defraud,
(2) to make any untrue statement of a material fact or to omit to state a material fact necessary in order to make the statements made, in the light of the circumstances under which they were made, not misleading, or
(3) to engage in any act, practice, or course of business which operates or would operate as a fraud or deceit upon any person, in connection with the purchase or sale of any security."

Thus, in the United States decision on this rule, *Securities and Exchange Commission v. Texas Gulf Sulphur Co.*[53] it was held that the test of materiality of disclosure is objective in that the relevant question always is whether there has been non-disclosure of any fact which in reasonable and objective contemplation might affect the value of a security. The case essentially recognises a private right of action under Rule 10b-5. To that extent a duty of disclosure of

---

49 per Woodhouse J. at *ibid* pp. 324-325.

50 *ibid* at p. 330; See also Casey J. *ibid* at p. 371

51 *ibid* pp. 331-332 following *Tate v. Williamson* (1866) L.R. 2 Ch. App. 55, *Tufton v. Sperni* 1952 2 TLR 516; *Lloyds Bank v. Bundy* [1975] QB 326; *New Zealand Netherlands Society "Oranje" Inc. v. Kuys* [1973] 2 NZLR 163; Note by D. Sugarman, "Seeing Through The Double Dutch of Corporate Opportunity?" (1974) 52 *Can. Bar. Rev.* 280-291.

52 *ibid* per Woodhouse J. at p. 324. Reference was in this respect made to the Privy Council decision in the Canadian case, *Allen v. Hyatt* [1914] 30 TLR 444 (P.C.) where it was held that where directors, by their conduct place themselves in the position of agents for individual shareholders then a fiduciary duty on the part of the directors towards the shareholders arises. See also *Briess v. Wooley* [1954] A.C. 333 (H.L) and *Glaisden v. Bennetto* [1913] 9 DLR 719.

53 401F 2D 833 (1968) at pp. 848-9

material infirmation may be established on the part of a director towards shareholders in his company.

The attempts at creating a fiduciary duty owed to shareholders by a director and other officers of a company receive further expression in Canadian legislation dealing with insider trading. This legislation stems largely from the *Report of the Attorney General's Committee on Securities Legislation in Ontario (1965) (Kimber Report)*. The legislation has a two-pronged approach. In the first place, it requires an insider to report his beneficial holdings in the corporation and any changes in those holdings to the relevant securities commission, failure of which would result into criminal liability.[54] Secondly, the legislation stipulates that every insider of a corporation and every associate or affiliate of an insider who, in connection with a transaction relating to the capital securities of the corporation, makes use of any specific confidential information for his own benefit or advantage that, if generally known, might reasonably be expected to affect materially the value of such securities:

(a) is liable to compensate any person or company for any direct loss suffered by such person or company as a result of such transaction unless such information was known or ought reasonably to have been known to such person or company at the time of such transaction and

(b) is also accountable to the corporation for any direct benefit and/or advantage received or receivable by such insider, associate or affiliate as a result of such transaction.[55]

To the extent that directors fall within the meaning of insiders for purposes of Canadian insider dealing legislation, they have duties of disclosure of material information, not only to shareholders, but also to other people with whom they are likely to deal in securities. Such duties are enforceable either by those people or the companies with which the directors are connected, by civil action. The legislation would also appear to create duties of disclosure on the part of directors in regard to securities transaction towards their holding or subsidiary companies as the case may be, or to persons standing in a fiduciary relationship to the company of which they are directors.

In Australia, the insider dealing provision which was enacted in 1971 following recommendations of the Eggleston Committee stipulates:[56]

> 124A(1) An officer of a corporation who in or in relation to a dealing in securities of the corporation by himself or another person makes use to gain directly or indirectly an advantage for himself or another person of specific confidential information acquired by virtue of his position as such officer, which if generally known, might reasonably be expected to affect materially the value of the subject matter of the dealing is liable to a person for loss suffered by that person by reason of the payment by him of a consideration in respect of the securities greater than the consideration that would have been reasonable if the information had been generally known at the time of the dealing.

---

[54] Alberta *Companies Act* 1967 Ss. 82 to 84, 87 to 88 and generally Alberta *Securities Act* Ss. 108 to 115; British Columbia *Securities Act*, Part XI. Ontario *Business Corporation Act*, Ss. 148 to 152; *Canada Business' Corporations Act* 1974-1976 S. 122

[55] S. 85 of Alberta *Companies Act* 1967: British Columbia *Companies Act* S. 152; British Columbia *Securities Act* S. 111; Ontario *Business Corporations Act* 1970 Ss. 150-151; *Canada Business Corporations Act* S. 125; see generally F. Iacobucci, *et al Canadian Business Corporations; An analysis of Recent Legislative Developments* (Canada Law Book Ltd. 1977) Cap. 8. In Australia, the duty not to use any information by a director for his benefit or to the Company's detriment is still owed to the Company: S. 124(2) (3) *Uniform Companies Act, 1961*. In Singapore this duty may be owed to *any person*: S. 132 (2), (4) *Companies Act* 1967 presumably including shareholders. See also S. 132 (2), (4) Malaysian *Companies* Act, 1965

[56] S. 124(A) (1) *Uniform Companies Act* 1961

Apart from this provision being broadly similar to the North American legislation affecting insider dealing, it creates a right on the part of a third party, dealing with a corporate officer, in respect of any loss suffered as a result of the officer using material information, unknown to the third party (who may be a shareholder) to gain from such a transaction. The Singaporean provision is identical to this Australian section.[57]

Essentially the common law position that a director's fiduciary duties are owed to the company only is undermined in regard to insider dealing. It may, however, be contended that the findings of the Court of Appeal in *Coleman v. Myers (supra)* as to the circumstances which would give rise to a fiduciary obligation between a director and shareholders are consistent with the requirements of both Rule 10b-5 of the United States Securities Exchange Commission Act 1934 and Canadian insider trading legislation. It is notable, though, that the latter legislation has much wider impact, especially in its effect on publicly incorporated companies. *Coleman v. Myers* appears to be limited to closely held or private companies.

It is now pertinent to consider the controversial criterion for the exercise of directors' duties whether owed to the company or other interests, as the case may be.

## The duty to act bona fide in the interest of the company[57a]

In 1942 Lord Greene M.R. postulated in Re: *Smith & Fawcett Ltd.*[58] that directors have to act "*bona fide* in what they consider - not what a court may consider - is in the interests of the company and not for any collateral purpose." This statement clearly gives directors the power and discretion to determine what is in the interests of the company and thereby respects their business and commercial judgment.

With regard to the phrase *bona fide* in the postulated test, Bowen L.J. observed as early as 1883 that,[59] "*bona fides* cannot be the sole test, otherwise you might have a lunatic conducting the affairs of the company and paying away its money with both hands in a manner perfectly *bona fide* yet perfectly irrational. The test must be what is reasonably incidental to, and within the reasonable scope of carrying on, the business of the company."

Thus, the director's duty to act honestly and in good faith is pegged to the execution of functions in pursuance of the business of the company. In this vein, Bowen L.J. repeated:[60]

> ... The test ... is not whether it is *bona fide*, but whether as well as being *bona fide* it is done within the ordinary scope of the company's business and whether it is reasonably incidental to the carrying on of the company's business for the company's benefit.

A similar test was advances some fifty years later by Eve J. in *Re: Lee, Behrens and Co. Ltd.*[61]in regard to the expenditure of a company's money for the benefit of employees, former employees and the widows and other dependants of such persons. He stated in this respect:[62]

> But whether they be made under an express or implied power all such grants involve an expenditure of the company's money and that money can only be spent forpurposes reasonably incidental to thecarrying on of the company's business,

57 S. 132A *Singaporean Companies Act* 1967-1971

57a See also Bakibinga (1990) 39 *ICLQ* pp. 451-460

58 [1942] Ch. 304 at p. 306 CA

59 *Hutton v. West Cork Ry. Co. (1883) 23 Ch.D 654 at p. 671 (C.A.)*

60 *ibid* at p. 672

61 [1932] 2 Ch. 46

62 *ibid* at pp. 51 following *Hampson v. Price's Patent Candle* 45 LJ (ch) 437; *Hutton v. West Cork Ry. Co. (supra* n. 66); *Henderson v. Bank of Australasia* (1890) 45 Ch. D. 330

and the validity of such grants is to be tested, as is shown in all the authorities, by the answers to three pertinent questions:

(i) Is the transaction reasonably incidental to the carrying on of the company's business?
(ii) Is it a *bona fide* transaction? and
(iii) Is it done for the benefit and to promote the prosperity of the company?

Pennycuik J. in his judgment at first instance in *Charterbridge Corporation v. Lloyds Bank Ltd.*[63] sought to limit the application of that test to situations where a company's powers could only be implied. In this case, Castleford Ltd., was one of a large group of companies headed by Pomeroy Ltd., and was empowered by the objects to trade in land and "to secure or guarantee by mortgages, charges, or otherwise the performance and discharge of any contract, obligations or liability of Castleford Ltd., or any other person - or corporation with whom or with which Castleford Ltd., has dealings or having a business undertaking in which Castleford Ltd., is concerned or interested whether directly or indirectly." Castleford Ltd., entered into guarantee and mortgage arrangements with Lloyds bank to secure the indebtedness of Pomeroy Ltd. The plaintiff challenged the *Vires* of these arrangements and also asserted that they were not beneficial to Castleford Ltd. (following *Re: Lee Behrens Ltd.)*

Having satisfied himself that this was a situation where express power had been conferred by the memorandum of association, Pennycuik J. went on to deal with Eve J.'s test in these terms:[64]

> It seems to me on the best consideration I can give to this passage, that the judge must have been directing his mind to both the issues raised by the liquidator without differentiating them. In truth, the first of the three pertinent questions which he raises is probably appropriate in part, and perhaps principally, to the duty of directors. Question (iii) is, I think, quite inappropriate to the scope of express powers and notwithstanding the words whether they be made under an express or implied power at the beginning of the paragraph, I doubt very much whether the judge really intended to apply this last question to express powers.

In the Court of Appeal decision, *Bell Houses Ltd. v. City Wall Properties Ltd.*,[65] the objects of the plaintiff company were *inter alia:*

(c) to carry on any other trade or business whatsoever which can, in the opinion of the board of directors, be advantageously carried on by the company in connection with or ancillary to any of the above businesses or the general business of the company.

It may be contended that "the opinion" of the directors in this clause must be formed subject to the equitable doctrine formulated by Lord Greene M.R. in *Re: Fawcett & Smith (supra)* i.e it must be honest and in good faith in the interests of the company. However, the Court of Appeal in Bell Houses seems to lay emphasis on "the opinion" of the directors as the sole test of validity rather than any connection of that exercise of discretion to the interest or benefit of the company. In essence where a company has in its constitution a subjective object clause like (c) above, the test of the validity of any transaction effected by a director is his subjective opinion irrespective of the relevance of the transaction to the interests or benefit of the company. This appears to be the gist of Salmon L.J.'s construction of the above object. Thus, he observed:[66]

> As a matter of pure construction, the meaning of these words seems to me to be obvious. An object of the plaintiff company is to carry on any business which the directors genuinely

---

63 [1970] 1 Ch. 62
64 *ibid* at pp. 70-71
65 [1966] 2 QB 656 C.A.
66 *ibid* at p. 690; and per Danckwerts L.J. at p. 650. See also L.S. Sealy, "The Director as Trustee" [1967] *C.L.J.* 83 at p. 92

> believe can be carried on advantageously in connection with or as ancillary to the general business of the company. It may be that the directors take the wrong view and in fact the business in question cannot be carried on as the directors believe. But it matters not how mistaken the directors may be. Providing they form their view honestly the business is within the plaintiff company's power and objects.

This is precisely the situation which Bowen L.J.[59] wished to avoid when he said *bona fides* alone cannot be the sole test since it would be possible for a lunatic to act *bona fide* and be irrational at the same time. Thus his insistence that there must be a connection between the *bona fides* of a director and the benefit and or interests of the company. It is submitted that Salmon L.J.'s approach in *Bell Houses*[65] has the effect of validating a transaction provided it satisfied a director's *bona fides* rather than because it affects the interests of the company. Admittedly, the *Hutton* case and the *Bell Houses* case had different factual contexts, the former being concerned with corporate gifts, while the latter was an *ultra vires* case. Our interest, however, lies in the way the *bona fides* of the directors were considered, in relation to their exercise of power and duty.

In summary, the cases show a consistent recognition of and adherence to the thesis by Bowen L.J. in *Hutton's* case[59] which received firm expression by Lord Greene M.R. in *Re: Smith & Fawcett (supra)*. The issue now arises as to what constitute the interests or benefits of the company.

The question has thus been succinctly put by Gower:[67]

> But what exactly is meant by saying that they must act in the interest of the *company?* Despite the separate personality of the company it is clear that directors are not expected to act on the basis of what is for the economic advantage of the corporate entity disregarding the interests of the members.

In the *Savoy Hotel Case*[68], the inspector indicated that the term "company" did not mean "the sectional interest of some (it may be the majority) of the present members or even ... of all the members but of present and future members of the company ... on the footing that it would be continued as a doing concern, balancing a long term view against the short term interests of the present members."

This approach is accepted by *Gower*[69] and *Gore-Browne*[70] in each case with supporting references to *Hutton v. West Cork Railway Co.*[71] and *Parke v. Daily News Ltd.*[72] Indeed, *Gower*[69] goes further to contend that directors who are shareholders have a right to consider their own interests in the exercise of their duties. Such a view is the judicial consequence of the Australian High Court Case, *Mills v. Mills*[73] where Latham C.J. stated:[74]

> A director who holds one or both classes of shares is not in my opinion required by the court to live in an unreal region of detached altruism and to act in a vague mood of ideal abstraction from obvious facts which must be present to the mind of any honest and intelligent man when he exercises his powers as a director.

---

67 Gower. *supra* n. 1, p. 577. His emphasis on the term "Company".

68 *The Savoy Hotel Limited and the Berkeley Hotel Company Limited: Investigation under S. 165 (6) of the Companies Act 1948.* Report of Mr. E. Milner Holland, QC (HMSO 1954) at p. 16

69 Gower *supra* n. 1 p. 578

70 Gore-Browne, . 927

73 (1938) 60 CLR 150. See also *N.W. Transportation Co. v. Beatty* (1887) 12 App. Cap. 586

74 *ibid* at p; 164

That may well be. However, objection is expressed to the equation of "company" with present and future members of the company. It is contended in this respect that neither *Parke v. Daily News Ltd. (supra) nor Hutton v. West Cork Railway Co. (supra)* support this definition of "company".[75]. It is true that Plowman J. in the *Parke Case (supra)* indicated that Lord Evershed's comment to the effect that "benefit of the company as a hole" means the corporators as a general body[76] applied to the case before him.[77] However, this construction has been criticised as "an aberration which cannot be supported".[75] Indeed such a restricted interpretation in relation to Directors' duties and discretion has been disapproved by Lord Wilberforce in *Howard Smith Ltd. v. Ampol Ltd.*[78] When he indicated that directors' discretion is not limited by employing a phrase such as "bona fide in the interests of the company as a whole" or "for some corporate purpose." He added:

> Such phrases if they do anything more than restate the general principle applicable to fiduciary powers, at best serve negatively to exclude from the area of validity cases where the directors are acting sectionally, or partially, i.e. improperly favouring one section of shareholders against another.

Indirectly, Lord Wilberforce is rejecting the idea of directors acting for themselves in their capacity as shareholders or for any class of shareholders[79] as indicative of the fact that "company" is synonymous with shareholders. However, by implication his statement appears to support the notion that "company" means all the shareholders. This is so because if the expression "bona fide in the interests of the company as a whole" has the effect of invalidating directorial actions favouring only a section of the shareholders, then it follows that the expression is equating "company" with all the shareholders.

If this interpretation is correct, then it is consistent with the definition of "company as a whole" given by Lord Evershed[76] and accepted by Plowman J. in *Parke v. Daily News.*[77] To the extent that the *Parke Case (supra)* followed *Hutton v. West Cork Railway Co.*[71] it is submitted that both *Gower*[69] and *Gore-Browne*[70] are correct in supporting the definition of "company" in the *Savoy Hotel Case*[68] with reference to those judicial decisions. It is respectfully, submitted[80] that merely because Plowman J. refused to equate the benefit of employees with that of the company,[81] does not mean that the expression "company as a whole" cannot be equated with all the shareholders of the company.

Ever since the Australian High Court decision, *Walker v. Wimborne,*[82] it would appear that in exercising their duties directors should take into account the interests of creditors, as well as those of shareholders. Closer examination of that case, however, shows that such interests will only be relevant in the context of the wider interests of the company.

Up to now in Uganda and Britain, the law does not recognise the interests of employees as forming part of the interests of the company. The interests of employees would only be considered if they are reasonably incidental to the carrying on of the business of the company.[83]

---

75 Ralph Instone, "The Duty of Directors" [1979] *JBL* 221, 227; see also H. Mason; (1979) 53 *Aust. LJ.* at pp. 30-33; For an incisive critique of Instone's arguments see Bird, *infra* n. 84, pp. 69-72.

76 Greenhalgh v. Ardene Cinemas Ltd. *[1951] Ch. 286, 291.*

77 *Supra* n. 72 at p. 963

78 [1974] AC 821, 835 PC. Emphasis supplied

79 See *supra* notes 69 and 74 and accompanying text.

80 Contrary to R. Instone. *supra* n. 75

81 *supra* n. 77. The learned judge said "... the directors of the defendant company are proposing that a very large part of its funds should be given to its former employees in order to benefit those employees *rather than the company*, and that is an application of the company's funds which the law as I understand it will not allow (emphasis added).

82 (1976) 50 AJLR 446 (Aust. HC) see discussion thereof at *supra* notes 20 to 33 and accompanying text.

83 *Hampson v. Price's Patent Candle Company* (1876) 45 LJ Ch. 437 *Hutton v. West Cork Railway Co.* (*supra* n. 59 at pp. 672-673). See also *Re: W. & M. Roith* (1967) 1 WLR 432

However, the British Companies Act, 1985[84] attempts to create a duty upon directors to consider the interests of both the employees and shareholders. Section 309 of the Act stipulates:

(1) The matters to which the directors of a company are to have regard in the performance of their functions shall include the interests of the company's employees in general as well as the interests of its members.

(2) Accordingly, the duty imposed by subsection (1) above on the directors of a company is owed by them to the company (and the company alone) and is enforceable in the same way as any other fiduciary owed to a company by its directors.

While the provision does not clearly create a duty owed by directors to shareholders and employees, it at least recognises the interests of both these two groups as relevant to the exercise of duties owed by the directors to the company. It is submitted that merely requiring directors to have regard to the interests of employees and shareholders does not mean they owe a duty to those interest groups. Subsection 309(2) emphasises the fact that the matters to be considered in subsection 309(1) are in execution or perpetuation of the directors' duty to the company. Furthermore, it is only the company which can enforce such a duty. It follows that the interests of employees and members are subordinate to the primary duty the directors owe to the company. To this extent section 309 hardly changes the common law position. In commenting on a similar provision in the *Companies Bill 1973*[85] Ralph Instone thus observed:[86]

> This formulation evokes three comments. First, it would have added nothing to long established case law, e.g. *Hampson v. Price's Patent Candle Co.*[83] Secondly, it neither states nor implies anything about the duties of directors or to whom these duties are owed. Thirdly, it erroneously pre-supposes that in all companies the members have relevant interests...

Instone's first and third objections appear to be still valid in regard to section 309 of the 1985 Companies Act. However, sub-section 309(2) meets his second criticism. To that extent, subsection 309(2) is an improvement on the 1973 Bill as well as the innocuous clause 46(2) on clause 46 of the Companies Bill 1978 which provided as follows:[87]

> Where in any proceedings it falls to a Court to determine whether a director of a company is in breach of his duty to have regard, in the performance of his functions, to the interests of the company's members the court shall take into account the fact that the director is also required to comply with the duty imposed by this section.

The problem with this provision is that although it interprets sub-clause 46(1) as creating a duty by directors towards the employees and shareholders, apparently that "duty" is subordinate to the directors' duty in regard to the interests of the company. However, it is also possible to contend that if that is the case, then this clause was enlarging the scope of the "interests of the company" to include those of the employees and shareholders. Gower has thus commented on clause 46 of the Companies bill, 1978 as follows:[88]

> A provision on these lines as well as being desirable in any event, will obviously be essential if we introduce employee representations on boards of directors.[89] If that occurs, however,

[84] Companies Act, 1985; see also J. Bird, "Making Directors Do Their Duties" (1980) 1 *The Company Lawyer, 67, 72-73.*

[85] Clause 53 provided that "the matters to which the directors of a company are *entitled* to have regard in exercising their powers shall include the interests of the company's employees generally as well as the interests of its members". Emphasis added.

[86] *supra* n. 75 at p. 229; Bird, *supra* n. 84, at p. 72

[87] Cl. 46(1) is identical to S. 46(1) of the 1980 Act (*supra* n. 84).

[88] supra n. 1 pp. 577-8

> it will add a further class to that of shareholders or debenture holders. Clearly, the intention is that such a director shall act primarily in what he conceives to be the interests of the security holders who appointed him, and if he does not he is likely to lose his office.

It is also notable that the affected director could lose his office by virtue of an ordinary resolution passed in general meeting.[90] Gower regards his "legal position as an invidious one." It is presumably in reaction to these difficulties that Professor Gower formulated Section 203(3) of the Ghana Companies Code 1963[91] which stipulates:

> In considering whether a particular transaction or course of action is in the best interests of the company as a whole, a director when appointed by or as a representative of a special class of members, employees or creditors may give special, but not exclusive, consideration to the interests of that class.

The nearest English law has come to this position is through an observation by Lord Denning M.R. in *Boulting v. ACTAT*[92] Although acknowledging that mandating a director to act in any way is illegal,[93] the Master of Rolls conceded that a nominee director of a large shareholder could solely act in that person's interest and adds:[94]

> There is nothing wrong in it. It is done everyday. Nothing wrong that is so long as the director is left free to exercise his judgement in the interests of the company which her serves. But if he is put upon terms that he is bound to act in the affairs of the company in accordance with the directions of his patron, it is beyond doubt unlawful.

Canadian legislation merely restates the common law position that directors should act *bona fide* in the interests of the company, without clarifying what those interest are.[95] The British Columbia Supreme Court in the *Teck Corporation Ltd. v. Millar*[96] however, appears to expand the scope of the interests of the company. F. Iacobucci had thus commented on that decision:[97]

> Berger J. in a very courageous way rejected the classical view of directors looking only to the shareholders and said modern circumstances have changed the traditional approach. In his view, if directors consider the interests of employees or of the community on a particular question so long as such consideration is not exclusive or in disregard of shareholders the directors could be said to be acting *bona fide* with the interests of shareholders.

Such an approach obviously overlooks the problems (supra) inherent in equating the term "Company" in the expression "interests of the company" with shareholders. That equation, as we have seen, is by no means a settled principle of law either in the United Kingdom or Canada.[98]

---

89 Following recommendations of the *Report of the Committee of Inquiry on Industrial Democracy* (Bullock Report) Cmnd 6706 (1977) cap. 8, para 38

90 Companies Act S. 185

91 Act 179

92 [1963] 2QB 606

93 A view also held by the Bullock Committee, supra n. 89, cap.8, para 40, and the last Labour Government, White Paper *Industrial Democracy*, Cmnd 7231 para 25 (1978)

94 [1963] 2QB 606 at p. 626

95 See British Columbia *Companies Act*, 1973 S.141; Ontario *Business Corporation Act*, 1970 S. 144; Canada *Business Corporations Act*, 1974-1976 S. 117

96 [1972] 33 D.L.R (3d) 288 (BCSC)

97 F. Iacobucci, "The Exercise of Director' Powers: the Battle of Afton Mines" *Osgoode Hall L.J.* (1973) 353 at p. 369; see also J.C. Ziegel, "Directors' Powers and Proper Purposes" [1947] *J.B.L.* 85

98 See F. Iacobucci, *et al supra* n. 55 at p. 295

The true position remains that the interest of employees may only be considered if they are reasonably incidental to the carrying on of the business of the company.[99]

In Britain, this position has been altered in regard to the interests of employees where the business of the company is about to cease or be transferred and with respect to the interests of members where the directors' conduct of their duties is prejudicial to the members' interests. Thus Section 659 of the British Companies Act 1985 states:

> (1) The powers of a company shall, if they would not otherwise do so, be deemed to include power to make the following provision for the benefit of persons employed or formerly employed by the company or any of its subsidiaries, that is to say, provision in connection with the cessation or the transfer to any person of the whole or part of the undertaking of that company or subsidiary.
>
> (2) The power conferred by subsection (1) above to make any such provision may be exercised notwithstanding that its exercise is not in the best interests of the company.

Such a provision is obviously a reversal of Plowman J.'s contention, in *Parke v. Daily News*[100], that an application of the company's fund for the benefit of former employees rather than the company was inconsistent with the law even if sanctioned by the shareholders in general meeting. Furthermore, apart from recognising that in given circumstances (e.g. when the business of the company is about to cease or be transferred) company funds may be used to benefit employees of the company thus derogating from the strict common law principle that only the company's interests are relevant to the exercise of directorial powers and duties, it is clear that subsection 659(1) may be invoked to the exclusion of the interests of the company.[101] It is notable though, that this is an enabling power vested in the company in general meeting rather than the directors.

With regard to shareholders, Section 459 of the British Act, 1985 stipulates:

> (1) Any member of a company may apply to the court by petition for an order under this section on the found that the affairs of the company are *being conducted* in a manner which is unfairly prejudicial to the interests of some part of the members (including at least himself) or that any actual or proposed act or omission of the company (including an act or omission on its behalf) is or would be so prejudicial (emphasis added).

This provision appears to recognise the separate interests of shareholders apart from those of the company as relevant to the directors exercise of their duties. Thus if such exercise or conduct is prejudicial to the interests of any section of the shareholders, then any member has a right to petition the court for relief. In essence, the provision creates a duty on the part of those people entrusted with the conduct of the company's affairs (invariably directors) to consider the interests of shareholders in such conduct. They are also under an obligation not to do or omit to do an act which would be prejudicial to the interests of some of the members. It remains to be seen how the courts will interpret conduct which is regarded as "prejudicial" to the interests of shareholders. Professor Boyle has observed that Section 459 appears "to open the way to a petition for a breach of duty by directors or others which, though not of a continuing nature, does sufficient harm to the company to affect the value of the complainant's shareholding..."[102]

---

[99] See *supra* n. 83 and accompanying text. For trends elsewhere which indicate that a company may give chargeable gifts irrespective of benefit to the company see S. 19 Companies Act, 1967 (UK) S. 19 Companies Act (Australia); S. 202(a) *New York Corporations Act,* S. 202(1) Ghana Companies Act, 179

[100] *Supra* n. 81; see also H. Mason, 53 *Aust. L.J.* pp. 32-33

[101] Subsection 659(2). This section again raises the issue as to what constitute a company's interests. Can it be said that in this context the interests of the company are separate from those of its employees?

[102] A.J. Boyle, "Power of Court to Grant Relief on a Petition Alleging Unfair Practice" (1980) 1 *Co. Lawyer* 280, *281*.

Another aspect of legal reform which appears to enhance the interests of shareholders is provided by Section 89 of the British Companies Act[103] with regard to pre-emption rights.

Thus it is provided:

> Subject to the following provisions of this section and sections 90 and 91 below, a company proposing to allot any equity securities -
> (a) shall not allot any of these securities on any terms to any person unless it has made an offer to each person who holds relevant shares or relevant employee shares to allow him on the same or more favourable terms a proportion of those securities which is as nearly as practicable equal to the proportion in nominal value held by him of the aggregate of relevant shares and relevant employee shares...

The provision essentially creates a duty upon the company and through it its officers (who include directors) to consider first the interests of shareholders before allotting any equity securities. To that extent the provision derogates from the general equitable principle formulated by Lord Greene M.R.[104] that directors must act bona fide in what they consider to be the interests of the company. Section 89 (1) of the British 1985 Act clearly requires the company's instrumentalities (invariably directors) as a matter of compulsion (the term "shall" is used) to offer equity securities first to shareholders before allotting them. This would presumably be in disregard of the directors' *bona fides* and the interests of the company respecting the allotment. Contravention of Subsection 89 (1) is enforceable by civil action.[105] It is notable that if the allotments are by a private company, Subsection 89(1) may be excluded by a provision contained in "the memorandum or articles of that company.[106]

## Duty to exercise powers for a proper purpose[8a]

Lord Green M.R., in his formulation of the test for exercising directors' powers to transfer shares, indicated that in addition to exercising their discretion in the interests of the company, they may not so act "for any collateral purpose."[107] The implication is that directors' powers must be exercised for a given purpose, which judged relative to that prescription must be proper.

It has been argued that *Re: Smith & Fawcett*[9] has nothing to do with the proper purpose duty, K.C.K. Chow adds in this respect regarding the phrase in Lord Green's dictum, "and not for a collateral purpose" as being the basis for the proper purpose duty:

> But, 'collateral purpose' by definition means that there must be at least two purposes, one of which is 'collateral' to the other. Hence if the directors issue shares in order to ward off a take-over bid solely because they think that it is in the interests of the company, it is difficult to see how there can be any 'collateral purpose.' It may be termed as an 'improper purpose', but it certainly is not 'collateral'"[108]

103 *Supra* n. 84

104 See *supra* n. 58 and text thereof

105 Subsection 89(9)

106 Subsection 89(8) N.B. S 89 is subject generally to section 95 which provides: (1) where the directors of a company are generally authorised for the purposes of section 80 above they may be given power by the articles or by a special resolution of the company to allot equity securities pursuant to that authority as if -
(a) section 89 (1) above did not apply to the allotment; or
(b) that subsection applied to the allotment with such modifications as the directors may determine and where the directors make an allotment under this subsection the said section 89 shall have effect accordingly.

8a See also *Bakibinga, Gravitas Review of Business & Property Law* (Lagos) Vol 2 No. 10 pp. 16-22 (1989)

107 See note 58 (*supra*)

108 KCK Chow "Proper Purpose Doctrine and the Companies Bill I" (1979) 129 *NLJ* 123 at p. 124

Chow concludes that *Re: Smith & Fawcett* was only concerned with the *bona fides* of directors. He notes in this regard that the proper purpose duty "was an additional duty which was superimposed by later decisions like *Hogg v. Cramphorn*"[109] and this may be the reason why *Re: Smith & Fawcett* never considered "the classic proper purpose doctrine cases" like *Piercy v. S. Mills*[110] and *Punt v. Symons*[111] Conversely that the "leading proper purpose cases" like *Hogg v. Cramphorn* and *Bamford v. Bamford*[112] did not refer to *Re: Smith & Fawcett* and this was because the latter "held that the directors' good faith should be decided by a subjective test, whereas as an additional duty to the duty of bona fide, the proper purpose doctrine essentially administers an objective test. This means that had the judges in those proper purpose cases chosen to follow *Re: Smith & Fawcett*, they would have to administer the subjective test which could run contrary to the very basis of the proper purpose doctrine itself."[113]

Before examining what constitutes the exercise of power for a proper purpose, it is pertinent to consider briefly the nature of directors' powers and whether their delineation within the framework of proper purpose is justified.

The treatise *Farwell on Powers* defines power as "an authority reserved by, or limited to, a person to dispose ... of real or personal property, either for his own benefit or that of others".[114] It is notable that this definition refers to a power of appointment. It is possible to distinguish such powers from powers given to a person for the purpose of general management of a going concern J.H. Farrar notes in this respect:

> ... these may not be to use Farwell's Australian language, 'powers properly so called.' Without ... following that language down the path of essentialism... there are significant differences between powers 'properly so called' and directors' powers. The latter are part and parcel of an established fiduciary relationship which is of a continuing nature. Shareholders can change the purpose of the power and objects from time to time by special resolution. Apart from the question of corporate personality the director-shareholder relationship is a bilateral one, whereas a power situation is a triangular one where the settler/donor is different from the donee. Hence the notion of purpose is more relevant to the latter.

The learned writer adds that the notion of purpose if it has any use at all has to be more sophisticated and read in the light of the objects of the company as a whole.[115]

If this postulation is valid, it follows that the purpose behind the directors' exercise of power must have a connection with the objects of the company. This presupposes that powers are delegated by the company to directors to perpetuate or effectuate the objects of the company. It is in this regard that Lord Greene's test gains relevance. It has indeed, received additional articulation and support from a line of judicial authorities. Thus, commenting on the exercise of directors' powers, Isaacs J., in *Australian Metropolitan Life Assurance Company Ltd. v. Ure,* stated:

109 [1967] ch. 277

110 [1920] 1 Ch. 277

111 [1903] 2 Ch. 506

112 [1970] Ch. 212 (C.A.)

113 Chow, *supra*, n. 108 pp. 124-125; these views contrast with those of Gower who interprets *Re: Smith & Fawcett* as holding "that the appropriate article was expressed sufficiently widely to enable the directors to exercise the power to refuse transfers for *any purpose* which they bona fide believed to be in the interests of the company", *supra*, n.1 (3rd Ed.) p. 524; see also Prentice, (1970) 33 *MLR* 700; Slutsky, (1974) 37 *MLR* 460 and Birds, (1976) 39 *MLR* 400

114 (3rd ed) at p.1

115 J.H. Farrar, Note: Abuse of Power By Directors (1974) *CLJ* 221 at pp. 222-3. For a similar judicial view, see *Introductions v. National Provincial Bank Ltd.* [1968] 2 All ER. 1221 where Buckley J. says that a power to borrow must be used to effect the objects of the company.

> ..it must be exercised as all such powers must be, bona fide, that is, *for the purpose for which it was conferred*, not arbitrarily or at the absolute will of the directors, *but honestly* in the interests of the shareholders as a whole.[116]

In a similar vein, in *Mills v. Mills,* Rich J. observed:

> The validity of the directors' resolution, therefore, must depend on the question whether they exercised the power in good faith for the purpose for which the power was given.[117]

The High Court of Australia in *Ngurli Ltd. v. McCann* commented thus:

> The power must be used *bona fide* for the purpose for which it was conferred...[118]

A notable feature of the above *dicta* as Professor Lindgren has noted[119] is "the linking of propriety of purpose with the notion of subjective good faith." He argues that this is understandable because in many cases the particular improper purpose in question is that the directors are seeking to benefit themselves at the expense of the company, i.e. "on the facts of the particular cases, impropriety of purpose was co-extensive with a kind of directorial culpability, if not amounting to fraud at common law."

Three other factors explain the connection between improper purpose and lack of good faith. The first is the categoris,ation of directors' powers into two: an ostensible and legitimate purpose on the one hand, and a "real" and illegitimate purpose on the other. This is shown by the statement of the Australian High Court in *Ngurli v. McCann* thus:

> (The power to issue shares) must not be used under the cloak of (raising sufficient capital for the benefit of the company as a whole) for the real purpose of benefitting some shareholders or their friends at the expense of other shareholders[120]

The second factor is the tendency to describe directors' use of power for unwarranted purpose in "morally charged terms like "improper", "cloaks" and "ulterior" purposes. This is despite the observation, in *Vatcher v. Paull,* by Lord Parker that:[121]

> The term 'fraud' in connection with fraud on a power does not necessarily denote any conduct on the part of the appointor amounting to fraud in the common law meaning of the term or any conduct which could properly be termed dishonest or immoral. It merely means that the power has been exercised for a purpose, or with an intention, beyond the scope of or not justified by the instrument creating the power.

The third element is the moral colour given to actions by legal sanctions attaching to them where there has been an impropriety of purpose.[122]

Professor Lindgren argues that the effect of the above three factors has been to raise propriety of purpose from its position as a demonstration of subjective good faith into an independent and objective test of validity. This may pose the difficulty that "proper purpose" "suspiciously" resembles the objective notion "for the benefit of the company" which the courts had rejected.

---

116 (1923) 33 *CLR* 199 at p. 217, emphasis supplied

117 (1938) 60 CLR 150, 169

118 (1953) 90 CLR 425, 439-440; See also Afterman & Baxt, *Cases and Materials on Corporations* (Australia, 1972) pp. 432-433

119 Lindgren, The Fiduciary Nature of a Company Board's Power to Issue Shares (1971-72) 10 *West Aust. L. Rev.* 364 at p. 371

120 (1953) 90 CLR 425 at p. 440 and Afterman & Baxt, *op. cit., supra,* note 118 at p. 433

121 [1915] AC 372 at p. 378 (PC)

122 The three factors are formulated by KE Lindgren, *op. cit., supra,* note 119 at pp. 371-372

He suggests that a solution may lie in appreciating that there was always an objective element in "bona fide for the benefit of the company as a whole", to wit that the directors must have "truly and *reasonably* believed at the time that what they did was for the benefit of the company".[123] Consequently, the directors cannot claim that they reasonably believed that it was *bona fide* for the benefit of the company for them to exercise a power for an improper purpose. This approach appears to be supported by Helsham J. when he said:[124]

> ... it is my opinion that the requirement of *bona fides* of a director must be considered in relation to the power and exercise of it, not his belief or state of mind.

Professor Lindgren further contends that his suggested solution "enables the requirements that directors act honestly and that they exercise their powers for a proper purpose to be viewed as sub classes of the general formula that they act '*bona fide* for the benefit of the company as a whole.' The alternative is to treat the latter formula as synonymous with the requirement that directors act honestly, so that there are but two independent rules: honesty and propriety of purposes.

It is clear in this text that we are following the alternative formula. What essentially then is the "proper purpose" test?

Directors will be regarded as liable for exercising their powers for purposes other than those for which they are conferred. In this respect, Gower submits that it would clarify matters if a distinction is made between an act *ultra vires* the directors because they have usurped a power which they never had, and an act which *prima facie* is within the powers delegated to them but which they have abused by exercising it for an improper purpose.[125] Sometimes their purpose may be improper because it is illegal or contrary to public policy.[126] However, very often the impropriety will derive from the purpose not being contemplated by the article or regulation conferring it. How then is the directors' exercise of powers to be judged relative to the purpose so conferred? Gower says that "... it is for the Court to decide on a true interpretation of the articles what the purpose was for which the power was conferred.[27] Afterman postulates in this regard:[127]

> There appears to be a subjective and an objective aspect to the 'improper purpose' rule. The Court will interpret for itself what is the purpose of the power delegated to the director in the articles of memorandum. Once this is determined, the Court will find as a question of *fact* the purpose behind the director's actions. In order to sustain the director's position, both purposes must coincide. The question of honesty is collateral.

This approach appears to make the proper purpose test a 'mere rule of interpretation of the articles'[128] although it is argued with some force that the proper purpose duty is a fiduciary duty superimposed by the Court and therefore capable of independent existence of the articles.[129] However, the fact that it was omitted from the *British Companies Bill 1978* as a director's duty would appear to lend weight to the analyses of the majority of scholars that the test only exists in relation to the articles.[130] Thus, in the same vein, Farrar conceptualizes:[131]

---

[123] Per Earl of Selborne in *Hirsche v. Sims* [1894] AC 654 at 661, emphasis supplied.

[124] *Provident International Corporation case* (1969) 89 WN (Pt. 1) (NSW) 370, 377, following *Ngurli Ltd. v. McCann* and *Vatcher v. Paull (supra).*

[125] *op. cit. supra*, note 15 at p. 524

[126] *Pharmaceutical Society v. Dickson* [1968] 3 WLR 286

[127] Afterman, *Company Directors & Controllers* (Australia), at p. 64; see also Afterman & Baxt, *op cit., supra* note 118 at p. 430; see also Prentice (1970) 33 *MLR* 703; Slutsky (1974) 37 *MLR* 457 at 460; Birds (1974) 37 *MLR* p. 580, n. 2; *Gore-Browne on Companies* (43rd 1977) para 27.10

[128] Chow, *supra*, n. 108 p. 123

[129] Chow, *ibid*, pp. 123-4

> In practical terms the Court should first consider the nature of the power and prescribe 'in the light of modern conditions' the limits within which it must be exercised. Then it must examine the 'substantial purpose' for which it is in fact exercised and reach a conclusion whether that was proper or not. This then remains a question of law. In reaching such a conclusion it will necessarily give credit to the *bona fide* opinion of the directors and respect their judgment in matters of management.

The above formula for determining the propriety of purpose in directors' exercise of their powers has received varied judicial application especially in situations dealing with their power to issue shares or authorise their transfer.

In the Australian High Court case, *Australian Metropolitan Life Assurance Co. Ltd. v. Ure,*[132] the directors refused to register a transfer of shares which would have resulted in the board losing control of the company. Following a stipulation in the articles, they refused to give their reasons. They then proposed to issue shares with the aim of preventing the challenging group from gaining control of the company. It was held that the directors were entitled to remain silent as no improper inference could be drawn from their silence and that being so the plaintiffs failed to discharge their burden of proving 'improper purpose' or *mala fides.*

In another Australian case, *Anselt v. Butler Air Transport Ltd. (No. 1)*[133], the defendant directors issued shares to employees of the corporation with the aim of preventing Anselt from gaining control as a majority shareholder. No question arose as to raising capital by allotment. It was found that the purpose of this sale was to put shares in the hands of people, loyal to the directors of Butler Air Transport. Butler's directors honestly believed that a take-over by Anselt would be calamitous to the interest of the company. Their action was nevertheless invalidated by the Court which concluded that the power to issue shares was not given to the directors for the purpose of ensuring the continuance of their policies or depriving the majority of their right to control. Here the board's purpose was totally improper in that there was no consideration for the capital to be raised by the issue. This case may be contrasted with *Savoy Corporation Ltd. v. Development Underwriting Ltd.*[134] A call was made by directors on partly paid shares while a merger of the company appeared imminent. The call contributed to a defeat of the plaintiff's take-over bid. The plaintiff submitted that the directors' actions were designed to facilitate the merger, and, in so doing, to protect their positions as directors. It was held that the call was for the legitimate purpose of raising capital. It was, however, indicated that if the call had been for the sole or primary purpose of effectuating the merger, the directors would have violated their duty.

In this regard controversy centres around how to judge the "sole" or "primary" purpose or the "moving cause" of a director's exercise of power for instance to issue shares. The view is held that an exercise of the director's powers to issue shares must be aimed at raising capital.[135]

---

[130] See clause 44 and Chow, *supra,* (1979) 129 *NLJ.,* pp. 136-137

[131] (1974) *Camb LJ* at p. 223 following *Howard Smith Ltd. v. Ampol Petroleum Ltd. and Others* (PC) [1974] 2 *W.L.R* 689 at p. 697f.

[132] 33 CLR 199 (1923)

[133] (1958) 75 WN (NSW) 299. A similar fact situation is to be found in *Bamford v. Bamford* [1968] 2 All ER 655, which is noted in [1968] 31 *M.L.R* 688 by KW Wedderburn.

[134] (1963) 80 WN (NSW) 1021

[135] See per Williams J. in *Grant v. John Grant & Sons Pty. Ltd.* (1950) 82 CLR 1 where following *Piercy v. S. Mills & Co. Ltd.* [1920] 1 Ch. 77 said,
"When a company is not in need of further capital, directors are not entitled to use this power for the purpose of maintaining their control or the control of themselves and friends."
In *Ngurli Ltd. v. McCann* it was observed that "the power must be used *bona fide* for the purpose for which it was conferred, i.e. to raise sufficient capital for the benefit of the company as whole."

This view is contradicted in another Australian case, *Harlowe's Nominees Property Ltd. v. Woodside (Lake Entrance) Oil Co.*[136] where the High court upheld an issue of shares to a large oil company which was found to have been made to secure the financial stability of the issuing company. This was so in spite of the fact that this had the effect of defeating the attempt of the plaintiff to secure control. It was indicated that although as a proposition of fact, it may be true that an exercise of directors' power to issue shares is not maintainable unless the company has at the time of such exercise, immediate need of capital, it is not conclusive as a general proposition of law.

This judicial authority appears to contrast with the leading English decision, *Hogg v. Cramphorn Ltd.*[137] where directors issued shares in order to set up a trust scheme which would discourage a take-over bid and also ensure their continued control of the company. Buckley J. held following *Punt v.*

*Symons and Co.' Ltd.*[138] and *Piercy v. S. Mills and Co. Ltd.*[139] that:

> directors are not entitled to use their powers in issuing shares merely for the purpose of maintaining their control or the control of themselves and their friends over the affairs of the company, or merely for the purpose of defeating the wishes of the existing majority of shareholders.

Professor Wedderburn notes that this "clearly reinforced the broad rule that directors must not make use of their powers for a "collateral purpose."[140] It is notable that the directors' good faith was regarded in this case as irrelevant to the determination of propriety of purpose. The *Hogg* decision stands in contra distinction to the Canadian case, *Teck Corporation Ltd. v. Miller*[141] where Berger J. in the Supreme Court of British Columbia upheld the validity of an exploitation agreement made by the directors of Afton Mines ltd., which *inter alia* provided for the issue to Canex of a large block of shares. This was in spite of the fact that the issue of shares had the effect of displacing the majority held by Teck Corporation, which was planning to remove the board and exploit Afton's mineral rights. The learned judge held that the directors' object was to obtain the best agreement they could while still in control. Furthermore, that they acted in what they honestly and in good faith believed to be in the company's best interest and were not bound to defer to Teck's wishes as a majority, or prospective shareholder. This was a rejection of the *Hogg v. Cramphorn ratio* that directors are not entitled to exercise their share issuing powers to frustrate a take-over bid even though they believe themselves to be acting in the ompany's best interests. Thus, he stated:[142]

> directors are entitled to consider the reputation, experience and policies of anyone seeking to take the company. If they decide on reasonable grounds, a take-over will cause substantial damage to the company's interests, they are entitled to use their powers to protect the company.

Specifically on the "propriety of purpose" ratio, Berger J. thought that the basis of the Court's intervention was not the type of impact the directors' decision had on shareholders' rights but

136 (1968) 121 CLR 483

137 [1966] 3 All ER 420, noted by K.W. Wedderburn in (1967) 30 *MLR* 77. The findings there are consistent with the opinion of the Inspector in the *Savoy Hotel* case, *supra* note 68 where he indicated that the disposal of an asset by the directors was improper as the object was to deprive the shareholders of such control, as under the regulations of the company they may have over the company's assets.

138 [1903] 2 Ch. 506

139 [1920] 1 Ch. 277. See also *Abina v. Tika Press Ltd.* 1968 NCLR 425, 429.

140 Note: "Shareholders' control of Directors' Powers: A judicial Innovation?" (1967) 30 *MLR* 77 at p. 79

141 [1973] 33 DLR (3d) 288; noted in (1974) 37 *MLR* 457, 580 at 583. Discussed by Farrar in (1974) *CLJ* 221 at p; 224; JC Ziegel, (1974) *JBL* 85; and F. Iacobucci in (1973) 11 *Osgoode Hall Law Journal* 354; Bennum in (1975) 24 *ICLQ* 359; S. Ahmed in (1974) 124 *NLJ* 1111.

142 (1973) 33 DLR (3d) 288 at 317

the impropriety of the directors' purpose. "Impropriety" in his view is, dependent "upon proof that the directors were actuated by a collateral purpose", it does not depend upon the nature of any shareholders' rights that may be affected by the directors' powers".[143]

Professor J. Ziegel objects to Berger J.'s approach as being too favourable to management and says:[144]

> The recognition that a company has responsibilities and loyalties to a wider constituency is commendable, but it should be possible to accommodate this range of interests without giving management a virtual veto power over control changes.

The other objection to the *Teck Corporation case* is that it relied on the subjective test in *Re: Smith & Fawcett* viz. "(Directors) must exercise their discretion *bona fide* in what they consider - not what a Court may consider - is in the interests of the company and not for any collateral purpose." Thus K. Chow has stated in this respect:[145]

> To rely, as the Canadian *Teck Corporation case* did, on the relevance of *Re: Smith & Fawcett* to the proper purpose doctrine would necessarily involve the Court in denying the essential independent existence to the very doctrine of which the Court was trying to uphold.

The above discussion shows that being fiduciaries, company directors have to exercise their powers, subject to fiduciary obligations i.e. in the interests of the company. Secondly, their powers are sometimes regarded as being subject to equitable rules relating to powers in the technical sense, although this appears not to be the true position. Thirdly some writers view the consequent duty to exercise their powers for a proper purpose as an aspect of their obligations which is independent from the requirement of *bona fides.* These points were considered by the Judicial Committee of the Privy Council in *Howard Smith Ltd. v. Ampol Petroleum Ltd. and Others*,[146] an appeal from New South Wales. The case arose out of the death of the patriarch of RW Miller (Holdings) Ltd (Millers) and the sale of his large block of shares in Millers to Ampol. Following the sale, Ampol indicated its intention to bid for the remainder of the shares. Millers' directors rejected Ampol's offer as too low. Howard Smith Ltd., then announced a rival bid at higher price which the majority of the directors were in favour. This led to Ampol combining with another substantial shareholder and indicated an intention to reject the Howard Smith offer. In the meantime, Millers needed capital which it was in the process of raising by means of *loan* capital. The directors of Millers after taking legal advice resolved to issue shares to Howard Smith at a premium, which would have the effect of diluting the holdings of Ampol and its associate. Street C.J. found that the directors' *primary* purpose was to dilute Ampol's holding and to facilitate Howard Smith's bid, and held the issue invalid. His decision was upheld by the Privy Council.

The case is especially significant for its treatment of the possibility of directorial share issuing powers being used for a mixture of purposes. Lord Wilberforce's opinion rejects two opposing arguments *viz.* on the one hand that if directors are not found to have acted from self-interest, the matter would be determined in their favour and the Court will not inquire into the validity of their reasons for making the issue and on the other that the purpose for which the power to issue shares is given is in order to raise capital, and an issue is invalid if is found that it is not make for that purpose. Their lordships postulated that self-interest was one of the instances of improper

143 *ibid* at p. 312

144 J.C. Ziegel, "Directors Powers & Proper Purpose" [1974] *JBL* 85 at pp. 88-89

145 *supra* n. 10 at p. 125

146 [1974] 2 WLR 689; [1974] 1 All ER 1126; note by J.H. Farrar in (1974) CLJ 221; discussed by JR Birds in (1974) 37 *MLR* 583; ME Bennum in (1975) 24 *ICLQ* 359; S. Ahmed, "Fiduciary Powers of Directors" (1974) 124 *NLJ* 1111. Consult also Harper & Browne, "The Duties & Liabilities of a Director in 1973" (1973) 47 *ALJ* 447

motive, though no doubt the commonest, but on the other hand, they were not prepared to say that shares could only be issued in order to raise capital and held that the law should impose no such limitation on the directors' powers. Then they went on to postulate a formula for determining directors' exercise of power for a proper purpose.[147]

With regard to directors' possibility of acting for a multiplicity of purposes Lord Wilberforce said that in order to ascertain the "substantial or primary" one "... the Court ... is entitled to look at the situation objectively in order to estimate how critical or pressing or substantial, or *per contra,* insubstantial an alleged requirement, may have been. If it finds that a particular requirement, though real, was not urgent or critical, at the relevant time, it may have reason to doubt or discount, the assertion of individuals that they acted solely in order to deal with it, particularly when the action they took was unusual or even extreme."[148]

This statement has not gone uncriticised. J.H. Farrar comments of it:[149]

> Substantial purpose' is of course a crypt value judgment of the kind which the Courts find useful but which the Courts find useful but which produces flexibility at the price of certainty.

The learned writer favours the phrase "moving cause."

In a similar tone, Bennum observes that to require the Court to look "objectively" at for instance the liquidity of a company in order to assess how substantial its requirements may be appears to envisage its waking the value judgment castigated by Lord Eldon in *Carlen v. Drury.*[150]

In addition, the case is significant for its distinguishing of the controversial cases *Harlowe's Nominees Pty. Ltd. (supra) and Teck Corporation v, Millar (supra)* on the ground that in the present case the purpose was "simply and solely to dilute" Ampol and its associate holdings, a practice condemned by the authorities and which amounted to an interference with an element of the constitution "set from and separate against their powers." Together with the immediate purpose was the ulterior purpose to let Howard Smith's bid proceed when it could have been blocked by Ampol, which amounted to an interference with the shareholder's individual right to dispose of his shares at a given price. Directors can advise shareholders" in a take-over bid but must not use their powers solely to shift shareholder power. Such actions are not only improper but also outside their powers as directors altogether.

*Howard Smith v. Ampol* may be regarded as a judicial synthesis of the law and controversy surrounding the criterion for the exercise of directors' powers. It reinforces but modifies (in the light of possible directorial multiplicity of purpose exercise of power) the view common in the United States, United Kingdom, Australia and Canada that directorial exercise of power to issue shares for control purposes is assailable.[151] This may suggest that the "bona fide" and "proper purpose" tests of directors' exercise of power, taken singly or together have a considerable influence in this area of law. However, professor Slutsky advocates their substitution by "the

---

[147] See *supra,* note 131 and text thereof

[148] [1974] 1 All ER at 1131-1132. See also *Tika-Tore Press v. Abina* 1973 NCLR 24 pp. 35-38 (Supreme Court of Nigeria)

[149] *op.cit. supra,* note 146 at pp. 223-224. The expression "moving cause" is also used by Latham J. in *Mills v. Mills* (1938) 60 CLR 150, following Lord Shaw in *Hindle v. John Cotton Ltd.* [1919] 56 Sc. LR 625. In *Mills v. Mills* the court appears to lay down the proposition that if a legitimate purpose is primary the directors' actions would not be invalidated because of a subsidiary improper motive. It was stated that if a "substantial object" of the directors was to increase their control their resolution might be invalid. It was found that their action was *bona fide* designed to capitalise earnings.

[150] (1812) IV & B., 154

[151] See F. Iacobucci, *op.cit., supra,* note 141 at p. 364-367: *The Exercise of Directors' Powers - The Battle of Afton Mines;* see also on this point Afterman, *op cit., supra* note 127 at p. 65, footnote 60: "American law has tended to deal with types of cases covered by the general 'bona fide in the interest of the company' standard in more specific terms. For example there is a large body of law concerned with the propriety of share issue designed to maintain the control of directors. The results however have been consistent with those reached under Anglo-Australian law". Consult in this regard *Cummings v. United Artists Theatre Circuit inc.* (1964) 204A (2d) 795

conflict of interest and duty" principle. The result of its application is that a court is concerned only with the *effect* of a board's decision, which is better than the subjective "improper purpose" doctrine "which required judicial penetration of a director's mental processes in order to determine his actuating motive." It is also better than the "bona fide" factor considering that the Court will not be asked to exercise a business judgment function. The learned author concludes:

> A combination of the equitable principles requiring directors to act *bona fide* in the interests of the company and to avoid conflicts of interest and duty would appear to be more than adequate to enable the courts to deal satisfactorily with those situations in respect of which they now rely upon the 'improper purposes' rule, and at the same time would give the directors a sufficient degree of freedom of action.[152]

This view is theoretically tenable although lacking judicial authoritative backing. It is further notable that there is a distinction between situations where directors obtain secret profits or indulge in self-dealing amounting to a conflict of their duty to the company and their interests and situations where they exercise their powers improperly.

## The requirement upon a director to avoid conflict of duty to the company and his interests[152a]

There are three aspects to this fiduciary principle. The first involves use by a director of a company's property, information or opportunity. The second affects contracts made between a director and his company, while the third impinges on situations where a director competes with the company which employs him. We shall examine the first aspect in some detail, considering its controversial nature and as shown by the case law generated in that area over the past generation as well as attempts at codification. Treatment of the second aspect will hinge mainly on attempts at codification of principles relating to a director's contracts with his company. Some attention will also be given to the third aspect of the fiduciary principle to avoid a conflict of duty and interest situation on the part of a director, especially in the light of case law developments.

### The use of a company's property, information or opportunity

A director of a company is precluded from benefitting from the company's property, information or opportunity in circumstances in which his duty to the company and his interests conflict. If he does so he is liable to account for any such benefit to the company.[153] This principle was thus put by Lord Buckmaster in the Privy Council:[154]

> But ... men who assume the complete control of a company's business must remember that they are not at liberty to sacrifice the interests which they are bound to protect, and, while ostensibly acting for the company divert in their (own) favour business which should properly belong to the company they represent.

In that case, three directors of a company carrying on the business of a railway construction contractor obtained a contract in their own names to the exclusion of the company. The contract was obtained under circumstances which amounted to a breach of trust by the directors and

---

152 Note, Canadian Rejection of the *Hogg v. Cramphorn* "Improper Purposes" Principle - A Step Forward? (1974) 37 *MLR* 457 at p. 462

152a See also Bakibinga, *Review of Business & Property Law* (Lagos) Vol 3 No. 14 pp 63-71 (1990)

153 *Cook v. Deeks* [1916] AC 554 (PC) *Regal Hastings v. Gulliver* [1942] 1 All ER 378 (HL)

154 *Cook v. Deeks ibid* at p. 563

constituted them trustees to its benefits on behalf of the company. By their votes as holders of three-fourths of the issued shares, they subsequently passed a resolution at a general meeting declaring that the company had no interest in the contract. The Privy Council held[155] that the benefit of the contract belonged in equity to the company and directors could not validly use their voting power to vest it in themselves. Lord Buckmaster added in this respect:

> ... the defendants ... were guilty of a distinct breach of duty in the course they took to secure the contract and that they cannot retain the benefit of such contract for themselves, but must be regarded as holding it on behalf of the company.[156]
>
> If ... the contract in question was entered into under such circumstances that the directors could not retain the benefit of it themselves, then it belonged in equity to the company and ought to have been dealt with as an asset of the company.[157]

Similar reasoning appears from the leading English decision, *Regal (Hastings) v. Gulliver*[158] apart from views on ratification of directors' acts by the general meeting, to which we shall advert later.[159] In this case, the company owned a cinema and the director decided to acquire two others with a view to the sale of the undertaking of the company as a going concern. For that purpose they formed a subsidiary company (A) with a capital of £5,000 in £ 1 shares. The owner of the two cinemas offered them a lease but insisted on a personal guarantee of the rent by the directors unless the paid up capital of the company was £ 5,000. The directors were unwilling to give the guarantee, so the company subscribed for 2,000 shares in the subsidiary at par and the remaining 3,000 shares were taken up by the directors and their friends, the company being unable to subscribe for more than 2,000 shares. Later all the three cinemas were sold by way of sale of all the shares in the company and its subsidiary. The shares in A were sold at a profit of £ 2.16s.1d. per share. The new owners of the company successfully sued the defendant directors for the profit realized.

In reversing the lower courts which had dismissed the action, the House of Lords held that the directors were in breach of their fiduciary duty to the company. The law Lords indicated[160] that directors in a fiduciary position to the company are bound to account for any secret profits they make to the company in the course of their duties, and in ascertaining their liability to account, questions as to their *bona fides* or *mala fides* are irrelevant. Lord Russel of Killowen added in this vein:[161]

> The rule of equity, which insists on those who by use of a fiduciary position make a profit, being liable to account for that profit in no way depends on fraud, or absence of *bona fides,* or upon such questions or considerations as whether the profiteer was under a duty to obtain the source of the profit for the plaintiff, or whether he took a risk or acted as he did for the benefit of the plaintiff or whether the plaintiff has in fact been damaged or benefitted by his action. *The liability arises from the mere fact of a profit having in the stated circumstances, been made.*

---

155 Distinguishing *N.W. Transportation Co. v. Beatty* (1887) 12 App. Cas. 589 and *Burland v. Earle [1902]* AC 83; see also H. Mason "Misappropriation of a Company's Property and Gifts by a Company; An Anglo-Australian comparison" (1979) 53 *Aust. LJ* 27, pp. 28-29; NA Bastin, "Honest Director and Secret Profits" (1978) 128 *NLJ* 527-9

156 *supra* n. 154 pp. 563

157 *ibid* p. 564

158 [1942] 1 All ER (HL) and Bastin, *supra* n. 155

159 See *infra*

160 ibid per Lord Russel p. 389 and per Lords MacMillan (pp. 391-2) Porter (p. 394)

161 *supra* n. 158 at p. 386 following *Keech v. Sandford* (1726) Sel. Cas. Ch. 61; 43 Digest 633, 720 and *Ex. P. James* (1803) 8 Vas. 337 43 Digest 779, 2193 Emphasis supplied; see also per Lord Wright at p. 392; Prentice, *infra* n. 170 at p. 631

> The profiteer, however honest and well intentioned cannot escape the risk of being called upon to account.

The above principle would apparently apply whether a director is regarded as a trustee or agent of the company.[162] The core of the principle applied in this case to render the directors liable was aptly summarised by Lord MacMillan thus:[163]

> The sole ground on which it was sought to render them accountable was *that, being directors of the plaintiff company and therefore in a fiduciary relation to it they entered in the course of their management into a transaction in which they utilised the position and knowledge possessed by them in virtue of their office as directors and that the transaction resulted in a profit to themselves.* (Emphasis added)

This formula is regarded by Gower[164] as "carrying equitable principles to an inequitable conclusion" and was not followed in the Canadian Supreme Court Case, *Peso Silver Mines Ltd. (NPL) v. Cropper.*[165] In this case, the company dealt in silver mining claims. Next to its claims its consulting geologist (A) discovered other claims and approached both the defendant managing director and the *Peso* board of directors to acquire the claims. The board decided that the company, because of its financial position, could not acquire the claims. Later the defendant and the consultant geologist purchased the claims at the price at which they had been offered to the plaintiff company and formed a new company, Cross Bow Mines Ltd., to take them over. Later new directors of *Peso* sued the defendant to account to the company for the shares held by him in Cross Bow Mines Ltd. The action was dismissed by all the courts. In affirming the decisions of the lower courts Cartwright J. stated:[166]

> When Dickson at A's suggestion, offered his claims to the appellant it was the duty of the respondent as director to take part in the decision of the board as to whether that offer should be accepted or rejected. At that point he stood in a fiduciary relationship to the appellant. *There are affirmative findings of fact that he and his co-directors acted in good faith, solely in the interests of the appellant and with sound business reasons in rejecting the offer.* There is no suggestion in the evidence that the offer to the appellant was accompanied by any confidential information unavailable to any prospective purchaser or that the respondent as director had access to any such information by reason of his office. When later A approached the appellant it was not in his capacity as a director of the appellant, but as an individual member of the public whom, A was seeking to interest as a co-adventurer.

It is easy to see why this reasoning is unsatisfactory.[167] The *Regal* (supra) case and the authorities it follows make it clear that the duty to account in respect of a profit made is independent of the

---

[162] *ibid* n. 158 per Lord Russell (pp. 386-389) Lord Wright (p. 392), following *Parker v. McKenna* (1874) 10 Ch. App. 96 per Lord Cairns LC (at p. 118) and James LJ (at pp. 124-5)

[163] *ibid* n.158 at p. 391. See also per Lord porter (at p. 395): "... Directors, no doubt, are not trustees but they occupy a fiduciary position towards the company, whose board they form. Their liability in this respect, does not, depend upon breach of duty but upon the proposition that a director must not make profit out of the property acquired by reason of his relationship to the company of which he is a director It matters not that he could not have acquired the property for the company itself - the profit which he makes is the company's even though the property by means of which he made it was not and could not be acquired on its behalf" (following Lord Eldon in *Ex P. James supra* n. 63). See also *Nasr v. Berini Beirut Riyadh (Nig.) Bank Ltd.* 1968 NCLR 370 (Supreme - Court of Nigeria)

[164] *supra* n. 1. p. 594

[165] [1966] 58 DLR 1 (2d) (SCC); although the Court purported to follow to the letter the *Regal* principles.

[166] *ibid* at p. 8 *Emphasis added*

[167] Gower, *supra* n. 1 p. 595 n. 65; Prentice, *infra* n. 170 at pp. 623 631-2

question of *bona fides* of the director in a fiduciary position of the company. It is enough that a director uses his fiduciary position to use knowledge acquired in the course of his duties to benefit himself. The *Regal* case makes it clear that it is immaterial that the benefit acquired was incapable of acquisition by the company. The distinction made in the *Peso* case between a director acting in his individual capacity as opposed to his capacity as a director is dubious.

In commenting upon Bull J.A.'s judgment in the Court of Appeal (which judgment is in contradistinction to that of Norris J.A. and whose criticism is also relevant to Cartwright J.'s judgment in the Supreme Court of Canada), Professor Beck thus observed:[168] (at p. 101)

> There was ample evidence that *Peso* was in exactly the same position as the *Regal* company - it wanted the property but could not finance its purchase. The company President testified to that effect when asked the question by the trial judge... Professor Beck adds (at p. 102):[70]
> In purchasing the claims so short a time after rejection by the company when the company was interested but financially unable to purchase, Cropper put himself in a position in which his interest and duty were in conflict and he ought to have been required to account. Once a conflict of interest is found, a finding of prior *bona fide* rejection of the property becomes irrelevant, and Equity's rigid rule should have been applied.

Professor Beck further criticised[70] (p. 111-112) the reference by Cartwright J. to the idea of confidential information being relevant in this context. He said:[70]

> It is not clear what relevance the question of confidentiality has. If the information relates, or may possibly relate to the affairs of the company and the director acquired it while in the course of acting for the company, he is bound to give the opportunity of making use of it to the company. If he makes use of it personally he will have made a profit out of his office and must account. If the information was given to him confidentially on behalf of the company the position is exactly the same... It is the use that is made of the information that comes to a director in his capacity as such that matters, whether it is confidential or not.

Indeed, Norris J.A., in his dissenting judgment in the British Columbia Court of Appeal thus observed:[70]

> It is clear from... the evidence that at the time of the acquisition of the claims the respondent (and his fellow director) in substance acknowledged and were aware that:
>
> (1) the information as to the claims came to them in the course of and in the execution of their duties as director;
> (2) in that sense the information was "confidential";
> (3) they owed a duty to the shareholders to 'protect' their interests in respect of the potential value of the claims;
> (4) whatever action was taken with regard to the claims must be taken on behalf of the Peso shareholders;
> (5) they were consequently trustees for the shareholders;
> (6) they had a duty to account to the shareholders in respect of the claims.
>
> ... It is not necessary that there be proof of an actual conflict in interest. It is sufficient that the interests 'possibly may conflict' as Lord Cranworth said in

---

168 [1966] 56 DLR (2d) 117 (BCCA); see also S.M. Beck "The Saga of Peso Silver Mines", (1971) 49 *Can. B. Rev.* 80; 100-2 D.D. Prentice (1967) *MLR* 450; HR Hahlo (1968) 85 *SALJ* 71

> *Aberdeen Ry Co. v. Blaike Brothers* (1854) 1 Macq 461 ... That case shows that it is not of importance that the company could not avail itself of the opportunity to take claims.

Norris J.A. was essentially insisting that the strict equitable principle enunciated in the *Regal* case *(supra)* should be adhered to. Such an approach is evident in another English decision, *Industrial Development Consultants Ltd. v. Cooley.*[169] In that case, the defendant was a managing director of the plaintiff company. In the course of his duties for the plaintiffs, the defendant sought to obtain supervision contracts for the company from the Eastern Gas Board. The board were disinclined to do business with the company, but indicated that they could engage the defendant personally. The defendant resigned his post with the plaintiffs on pretext of ill-health and accepted work from the Gas Board. The court held him liable to account to the plaintiff company for all benefits accruing under the contract with the Easter Gas Board.

A similar argument to the one in the *Peso* case (*supra*) was advanced for the defendant to the effect that the information communicated to the defendant was received by him privately and not in his capacity as the defendant company's managing director. To that proposition, Roskill J. answered thus:[170]

> The defendant had one capacity and one capacity only in which he was carrying on business at that time. That capacity was as managing director of the plaintiffs. Information which came to him while he was a managing director and which was of concern to the plaintiffs and was relevant for the plaintiffs to know was information which it was his duty to pass on to the plaintiffs because between himself and the plaintiffs a fiduciary relationship existed.

The learned Judge went on to observe that by holding onto the information he gained for his own personal purposes and profit he put himself into the position when his duty and his interests conflicted. Then he posed the dilemma implicit in applying the strict equitable doctrine:[171]

> The remarkable position then arises that if one applies the equitable doctrine on which the plaintiffs rely to oblige the defendant to account, they will receive a benefit which ... it is unlikely they would have got for themselves had the defendant complied with his duty to them. On the other hand, if the defendant is not required to account he will have made a large profit as a result of having deliberately put himself into a position in which his duty to the plaintiff who were employing him and his personal interests conflicted.

Roskill J. went on to affirm the principle in the cases "that the question whether or not the benefit would have been obtained but for the breach of trust has always been treated as irrelevant."[73]

This approach is justified by the policy considerations that any other approach would tempt the directors "to refrain from exerting their strongest efforts on behalf of the corporation" by affording them an "opportunity to profit"[172] at the company's expense. In this vein, Roskill J. indicated that it would have been the defendant's duty to have tried to persuade Eastern Gas Board "to change their mind" about dealing with the plaintiffs and that it would have been a "curious position" if "he whose duty it would have been to seek them to change their mind should now say that the plaintiffs suffered no loss because he would never have succeeded in

---

[169] [1972] 1 WLR 443

[170] *ibid* at p. 451; see also D.D. Prentice (1972) 50 *Can. B Rev.* 623; A. Rajak 91972) 35 *MLR* 655 J.G. Collier [1972] 30 *CLJ* 222; A. Yoran (1973) 89 *LQR* 187

[171] *ibid* p. 453; see also *Furs Ltd. v. Tomkies* (1936) 154 *CLR* 583 at p. 592

[172] *Irving Trust Co. v. Deutsch* (1934) 73F 2d 121, at p. 124; see also Prentice *supra* n. 170 at p. 630

persuading them to change their mind."[173] Dr Prentice[174] argues that similar reasoning would require the rejection of other possible available defences to the defendant such as commercial liability on the part of the company to exploit the opportunity[175] or the fact that the opportunity was *ultra vires* the company.[176]

The effect of the *Cooley (supra)* decision was to bring English law on corporate opportunity closer to the American position.[177] The doctrine in Dr Prentice's words appears to be that:[178]

> ... where there is presented to a corporate officer a business opportunity which the corporation is financially able to undertake, and which, by its nature, falls into the line of the corporation's business and is of practical advantage to it, or is an opportunity in which the corporation had an actual or expectant interest the office is prohibited from permitting his self-interest to be brought into conflict with the corporation's interest and may not take the opportunity for himself.

Before the *Cooley* case *(supra)*, English and American law on corporate opportunity had developed differently. As Yoran put it,[179] English law, "emphasised that the fiduciary duty is based upon the information having had its source with the company while American law emphasised the property rights of the company to opportunity as being property belonging to the company, to which it had expectancies or which were essential to the maintenance of its business." The American approach was criticised by Ballantine as being too narrow to sustain the fiduciary duty. He stated:[180]

> the true basis of the doctrine should not be found in any expectancy or property interest concept, but in the unfairness on the particular facts of a fiduciary taking advantage of an opportunity when the interests of the corporation justly call for protection. This calls for the application of ethical standards of what is fair and equitable to particular sets of facts.

Ballantine's approach has since received some judicial affirmation in the United States[181] and is very similar to the one adopted by Roskill J. in the *Cooley* case *(supra)* to the extent that he postulated that the basis of Cooley's accountability and liability was that "a man must not be allowed to put himself in a position in which his fiduciary duty and his interests conflict."[182]

Such an approach may explain the difference between the *Cooley* case and the *Peso* case *(supra)* the latter of which seems to have followed the old American concept as to corporate

---

173 *supra* n. 169 at p. 451

174 *supra* n. 170 at p. 630

175 Following the *Regal* case *supra* n. 158

176 Following *Fine Industrial Commodities v. Powling* (1954) 71 RPC 153

177 *Equity Corp. v. Milton* (1966) 221 A. 2d 494 at P. 497; *Greene v. Dunhill International Inc.* (1968) 249A 2d 427, Beck, *supra* n. 168 at pp. 92-93; The test should be whether the opportunity was so closely associated with the existing and prospective activities of the corporation that the director should have fairly acquired it for, or made it available to the corporation.

178 *Supra* n. 170 at pp. 629-30; see also *Yoran, supra* n. 170 pp. 189-192

179 *ibid* at p. 191

180 Ballantine, Corporations (1946) p. 204

181 *Durfee v. Durfee and Canning Inc.* 80 N.E 2d 522 (Mass 1948) see also *Equity Corporation v. Milton* (1966) 221 A 2D 494 (SC Del) where it was stated that "whether or not the director has appropriated something for himself that, in all fairness, should belong to his corporation. The determination of this question is always one of fact to be determined from the objective facts and surrounding circumstances." In *Rosenblum v. Judson Engineering Corporation* (1954) 109A. 2d 558 (S.C.N.H.) the court observed (at p. 563) That "the fact that a business opportunity is itself of such a nature that under the particular circumstances of the case it should fairly belong to the corporation is sufficient to establish a duty ... to acquire it for the corporation."

182 *supra* n. 169 at p. 453

opportunities, as advanced by cases like *Johnston v. Green.*[183] In this case a businessman, who was director of numerous companies was offered personally shares in a certain company and patents connected with the business of the company. The businessman revealed the information as to the acquisition of the shares to one of the companies on whose board he served but appropriated the business of his friends, associates and himself. A derivative action filed by a shareholder of the company to whom the director disclosed the information concerning the acquisition of shares, claiming the profits from the sale of the patent was dismissed by the Delaware Supreme Court.

Following the old American conception, the court laid weight upon the fact that the opportunity in this case, was presented to the director in this private capacity. In addition, the court thought that there was not a close connection between the business of the company, in whose name the action was filed and business of the company to which the patents were related. Furthermore, the company filing the action had no interest nor real expectancy to receive the opportunity and it was not essential for its existence. While conceding that the company attempted to obtain investment opportunities through the defendant director, the court did not think that this was indicative that the company had "a specific interest attaching in equity to any and every business opportunity that may come to any of its directors in his individual capacity."[184]

Thus, in this vein, the supreme court of Canada in *Peso* found Cropper and his friends not liable to account to the plaintiff company because he did not make use of confidential information and the contract he acquired was made after the rejection of the offer by the company's board and was made to directors in their private capacities and not in their capacities as directors of the company. The contrast between the *Johnston v. Greene and Peso* cases (supra) with the *Cooley* case has aptly been summaried by Yoran thus:[185]

> In the Cooley case, the opportunity was one which the company greatly desired, and made considerable efforts to acquire. It even employed Cooley with the specific intention that he help in acquiring opportunities of that type. Putting it in the terms used in the American cases, although the company did not have an expectancy of receiving the opportunity as the result of any acquired right, to a great extent the opportunity was essential for the existence of the company in the market it was attempting to enter. Emphasis must also be given to Cooley's lack of good faith, which was manifested in the way in which he obtained his release from the position of General Manager of the plaintiff company.

It is thus clear that while the *Cooley* case follows the approach advocated by Professor Ballantine[186] (*viz.* taking into account "the unfairness on the particular facts of a fiduciary taking advantage of an opportunity" contrary to the company's interest) the *Peso and Johnston v. Green* cases base themselves on the expectancy and property interest concepts previously applied in the United States. The Australian case, *Queensland Mines Ltd. v. Hudson*[187] also appears to follow the *Peso* and *Johnston v. Greene* cases line of reasoning. In that case, *Queensland Mines Ltd.* brought an action against its former managing director, Mr Hudson. The company alleged that Hudson had abused his position as managing director to make a profit for himself. It was claimed that Hudson had obtained the benefit of certain exploration licences which he had acquired in his own name

---

183 121A 2d 919 (Supreme Court of Delaware); see also *Guth v. Loft* (1939), 5A 2d 503 (SC Del) where it was postulated that if an opportunity comes to a director in his individual capacity and is one, (at p. 511) "... which by its nature falls into the line of the corporation's business and is of practical advantage to it, or is an opportunity in which the corporation has an actual or expectant interest, the officer is prohibited from permitting self interest to be brought into conflict with the corporation's interest and may not take the opportunity for himself."

184 *ibid* at p. 924

185 *supra* n. 170 at p. 190

186 *supra* n. 180 and accompanying text.

187 (1978) 52 ALJR 399 noted in 52 ALJ 574; see also (1979) 8 *Sydney L. Rev.* 668-77; (1977-1978) 3 ACLR 176-184.

rather than on behalf of the plaintiff company. In the supreme court of New South Wales, Wooten J. held that there had been a breach of fiduciary duty by Hudson, but that the company's claim was barred by lapse of time. Upon appeal by the company to the Privy Council the appeal was dismissed on the ground that the company had been fully informed of all relevant facts but had renounced all interest in the development of the licences and had in effect assented to Hudson "going it alone."

The Canadian Supreme Court case, *Canadian Aero Service Ltd. v. O'Malley*[188] which considered both the *Cooley* case (*supra*) and the *Peso* case (*supra*), while applying the strict equitable principle on the particular facts there, appears to concede that there may be instances depending on given circumstances when that principle may be relaxed. In this case, the two defendants were directors of the plaintiff company and were engaged in carrying out preparatory work for the plaintiff in connection with a project in Guyana. The Canadian government invited the plaintiff company and others to submit tenders for this project. At about this time, the defendants resigned their offices with the plaintiff company, formed their surveying company, which was later awarded the contract. Since the plaintiff company was a subsidiary of a United States company, the chances of its getting the contract (in line with Canadian government policy) were minimal. The Canadian Supreme Court, nonetheless, held the defendants liable for the loss of the contract. Having satisfied himself that the defendants held analogous positions to those of directors in the company and thereby stood in a fiduciary relationship to it, Laskin J. (as he was then) thus observed of the application of the strict equitable principle:[189]

> An examination of the case law ... shows the pervasiveness of a strict ethic in this area of the law. In my opinion this ethic disqualifies a director or a senior officer from usurping for himself or diverting to another person or company with whom or with which it is associated a maturing business opportunity which his company is actively pursuing; he is also precluded from so acting even after his resignation where the resignation may fairly be said to have been prompted or influenced by a wish to acquire for himself the opportunity sought by the company, or where it was his position with the company rather than a fresh initiative that led him to the opportunity which he later acquired.

Thus, while acknowledging that the general equitable principle applied to the case before him, Laskin J. did not think that it applied in all situations. Thus, he stated:[190]

> In this, as in other branches of the law, new fact situations may require a reformulation of existing principle to maintain the vigour in the new setting.

In this vein he added:[191]

> In holding that on the facts found by the trial judge, there was a breach of fiduciary duty by O'Malley and Zarsyck which survived their resignations, I am not to be taken as laying down any rule of liability to be read as if it were a statute. The general standards of loyalty, good faith and avoidance of a conflict of duty and self-interest to which the conduct of a director or senior officer must conform, must be tested in each case by many factors which it would be reckless to attempt to enumerate exhaustively. Among them are the factor of position or office held, the nature of the corporate opportunity, its ripeness, its specificness and the director's or managerial officer's relation to it, the amount of knowledge possessed, the circumstances in which it was obtained and whether it was special or indeed even

---

188 [1974] 40 DLR (3d) 371; see also Prentice (1974) 37 *MLR* 464; - SM Beck (1975) 53 *Can. Bar. Review* 771 and *Canada Safeway Ltd. v. Thompson* (1951) 3 DLR 295; (1976) 54 *Can. Bar. Rev.* 224-228; Darla Hunter, (1976-1977) 41 *Sask-Law Rev.* 159-167.

189 [1974] 40 DLR (3D) 371, At P. 382

190 *ibid* at p. 383

191 *ibid* at p. 391

> private, the factor of time in the continuation of fiduciary duty where the alleged breach occurs after termination of the relationship with the company, and the relationship under which the relationship was terminated, that is whether by retirement or resignation or discharge...

This approach appears to be in line with the reasoning in the *Cooley* case (*supra*) and consistent with the formula advocated by Professor Ballantine.[88] It had indeed been followed in the Alberta supreme court decision *Abbey Glen Property Corp. v. Stamborg*[192] where it was emphasised that the duty of directors to account to their company for profits arising out of the performance of their office with the company (e.g. the personal exploitation of information acquired in the course of their duties with the company) exists irrespective of the company's ability to exploit the opportunity. Professor Hahlo has thus concluded of the *Cooley, O'Malley and Abbey Glen Property Corp.* cases *(supra)*:[193]

> These three decisions now appear to make clear that a company's right to an accounting from its directors for so-called "secret" profits does not depend on an "expectancy" or property interest of the company in the opportunity or any direct conflict of interest between the company and its directors but on broad ethical standards of what is fair and equitable.

In the United Kingdom, the Jenkins Committee recommended that future companies legislation should provide that:[194]

> a director should not make use of any money or other property of the company or any information acquired by virtue of his position as a director or officer of the company to gain directly or indirectly an improper advantage for himself at the expense of the company.

This recommendation has not yet been enacted although the lapsed 1978 British Companies Bill attempted to formulate the fiduciary equitable principle in much more width.[195] The formulation attempted to synthesise the principles on corporate opportunity, information and property which are derived from commonwealth decisions, which have applied the *Regal* case *(supra)*[196] and appears to be consistent with Professor Ballantine's formula[197].

Other legislative attempts on the corporate opportunity doctrine appear in the British Columbia Act[198] which stipulates that when a director or officer who holds any office or possesses any property which might give rise, directly or indirectly to conflicts with his duties to the corporation, he must disclose the fact and the nature character and extent of such conflict. It is notable that this provision does not actually prohibit such conflicts. It merely requires disclosure of their existence.

Section 205(a) of the *Ghanaian Companies Code*[199] has some similarity with Clause 44 (3) of the United Kingdom 1978 Companies Bill. It provides that a director shall not:

---

192 [1976] 2 WWR 1; (1978) 85 DLR (3d) Alb. Sup. Ct. App Div); see also Prentice; Note (1978) 42 *MLR* 215-219

193 H.R.Hahlo and M.J. Trebilcock, *Hahlo's Casebook On Company Law* (2nd Ed. 1977) p. 483

194 *supra* n. 35 para 99(a) (ii)

195 Clause 44 (3), (4)

196 e.g. *Zwicker v. Stanbury* (1954) 1 DLR 257; *Canada Safeway Ltd. v. Thompson*, *supra* n. 188 *Fine Industrial Commodities v. Powling supra* n. 176; the *Peso* case, supra n. 165 *Phipps v. Boardman* [1967] 2 AC 46 HL; The *Cooley* case *supra* n. 169. The *Canadian Aero Service Case supra* n. 189 and the *Abbey Glen Corporation Case supra* n. 192

197 *supra* n. 180 and accompanying text.

198 British Columbia Companies Act, Ss 146, 160

199 Act. 179

(a) use for his own advantage any money or property of the company or any confidential information or special knowledge obtained by him in his capacity of director.

It is significant that both the United Kingdom Companies Bill 1978 and the Ghana Companies Code lay weight on prohibiting use of information obtained by a director in such a capacity. The use by the Ghana Code of "confidential information" is subject to Professor Beck's criticism[200] to the effect that the addition of "confidential" is superfluous and that what matters is the use to which a director obtaining such information in his capacity as a director puts it.

The British Bill 1978 was an improvement on the Ghana Code to the extent that it did not allude to "confidential" information but referred to "relevant" information as defined. Furthermore both the Ghana Code and the British Bill draw a distinction in the former case between information and the company's assets and in the latter between information or opportunity and the assets of the company. To that extent they avoid the confusing equation between information and property which was advanced both in the English Court of Appeal and House of Lords in *Phipps v. Boardman.*[201] In this context, while agreeing that information could be property, Lord Upjohn, in his dissenting judgment, sought to limit the instances in which such an equation can be made. He stated:[202]

> In general information is not property at all. It is normally open to all who have eyes and ears to hear. The true test is to determine in what circumstances the information has been acquired... The real rule, is in my view, that knowledge learnt by a trustee in the course of his duties as such is not the least property of the trust and in general may be used by him for his own benefit or for the benefit of other trusts unless it is confidential information which is given to him (1) in circumstances which, regardless of his position as a trustee, would make it a breach of confidence for him to communicate to anyone for it has been given to him expressly or impliedly as confidential, or (2) in fiduciary capacity and its use would place him in a position where his duty and his interest might possibly conflict.

This formulation, which has close similarity to clause 44(3) and (4) of the British Bill, 1978 in so far as it relates to information was further qualified by Lord Upjohn in regard to the second rule. He stated in this respect;[203]

> ... you have to look and see whether the knowledge acquired was capable of being used for his own benefit ot *injure* the trust.

The attempt by the Master of Rolls and the majority of the law Lords in *Phipps* to draw a connection between information and property in the context of situations of conflicts of duty and interest by persons in fiduciary positions has thus been criticised by Professor Beck:[204]

---

200 *Supra* n. 168

201 [1965] Ch. 992 (C.A. per Lord Denning (at pp 1018-1019): "Likewise with *Information or Knowledge which he has* been employed by his principal to collect or discover, or which *he has otherwise acquired*, for the use of his principal, then again if he turns it for himself, he is accountable ... for such information or knowledge is the property of his principal just as much as an intention is (his emphasis). In the House of Lords [1967] AC 46, Viscount Dilhorne (at pp. 89-90) Lord Hudson (at. p. 107) and Lord Guest (at p. 115) agreed that knowledge acquired while acting for the principal could be regarded as the principal's property. See also per Lord Cohen (pp. 102-103). In the trial Court, Wilberforce J. (as he then was) observed of the information gathered by Phipps and Boardman [1964] 2 All ER. 187 at p. 204: "This knowledge was (so far as the expression can be used) essentially the property of the trust."

202 [1967] AC 46 at pp. 127-129

203 *ibid* at p. 129 His emphasis. This qualification is difficult to justify in so far as it introduces subjective elements in determining the conflict of duty and interest rule. The *Regal* case *(supra)* and the cases that buttress it make it clear that injury or profit to the principal in a conflict situation are irrelevant. see *supra* n. 63 and accompanying text.

204 *supra* n. 168 at p. 110

> It is unfortunate that the idea of information as property was introduced in *Phipps* to further tangle the problem of fiduciary obligations. It is unfortunate because it was unnecessary. The question is not whether the information acquired by the agent is the property of the trust, but is whether the agent used his position to make a profit without the informed consent of his principal.

The British Companies Bill 1978 formulation thus meets this criticism by clearly drawing a distinction between relevant information and property of the company and instances in which that information may not be used i.e. situations where use of such information would place a director in a conflict of duty and interest situation and which information would be expected to be disclosed to the company. The formulation has further similarities with Lord Upjohn's postulation,[205] save for the law Lord's allusion to "confidential" information.

## Contracts with the company

The issue as to the effect of contracts made by a director with a company of which he is a director is contentious. The position at common law is that unless the company's articles permit, a director cannot validly enter into a contract with his company except where, following full disclosure, the general meeting has approved or ratified the contract.[206] In this regard, a director is free to use his voting power to effect the approval or ratification by the company,[207] unless the effect thereof is fraudulent or oppressive to the other members.[208] Should the articles require that before contracting with the company a director should declare his interests therein, the nature of the interest rather than mere declaration that the director is interested is required.[209]

However, with time the necessity for full disclosure to be made to a general meeting was thought by directors to be excessively rigorous. Consequently, exception clauses were inserted into the articles which invariably required disclosure to be made to a meeting of the directors. The relevant aspects are now governed by section 200 of the Ugandan Companies Act, and Article 84 of Table A.

A director who is directly or indirectly interested in a contract or proposed contract with the company is under a duty to declare the nature of his interest at a meeting of the directors.[210] In the case of a proposed contract, the declaration should be made at the meeting of the directors at which the issue of entering into the contract is first taken into consideration or where the director was not so interested then at the meeting after he becomes interested.[211] For this purpose, it is sufficient for the director to give general notice to the directors of the company that he is a member of a specified company or firm and is to be regarded as interested in any contract which may subsequently be made with that company or firm provided the notice is given at a meeting of the directors or that reasonably necessary steps are taken to ensure that it is brought and read at the next meeting of the directors after it is given.[212] A defaulting director is liable to a fine of two thousand shillings.[213] This is clearly inadequate deterrent, given the possible windfall benefits derived by a director from the contract in issue.

---

205 *Supra* n. 202

206 *Transvaal Lands Co. v. New Belgium (Transvaal) Land and Development* Co., [1914] 2 Ch. 488; *Nasr v. Berini-Beirut - Riyadh (Nig.) Bank* 1969 (2) ALR Comm 78; 1968 NCLR 370 (Supreme Court of Nigeria).

207 *North-West Transportation Co., Ltd. v. Beatty* (1887), 12 App Cas. 589

208 *Mason v. Harris* (1879), 11 Ch. D. 97

209 *Imperial Mercantile Credit Association v. Coleman* (1873), L.R. 6 HL 189

210 Companies Act, Cap 85 S. 200 (1). In Britain the equivalent provision (C.A. 1948 S. 199 (1) has been extended to cover transactions or arrangements in which directors are interested: Companies Act, 1980, S. 60 (1).

211 *ibid* S. 200 (2)

212 *ibid* S. 200 (3)

213 *ibid* S. 200(4)

In *Walji v. Shinyanga African Trading Co. Ltd*[16a], it was held that as the managing director was fully authorised to conduct the day-to-day business of the company, he had a duty to ensure adequate supplies of beer for the company to enable it to carry on business. He was not, in fact, making a secret profit since the directors knew fully well and approved of the purchases of beer by the managing director.

Where the company has adopted the articles in the form of Table A, a director will be allowed to contract with the company provided that he makes disclosure in line with section 200. However, subject to given exceptions affecting contracts indemnifying a director against loss in connection with obligations accepted by him for the benefit of the company or to underwrite securities of the company, a director is precluded from voting in respect of any contract in which he is interested, neither can he be counted towards a quorum at the directors' meeting at which such contract is considered.[214]

A contract entered into by the company and with regard to which a director's interest has not been disclosed is not ineffective. It is merely voidable at the option of the company.[215] Disclosure which validates the contract is more than that of the director's interest. The nature of the relevant interest should be indicated and this depends on relevant circumstances,[216] although generally understood to refer to the exact extent of the profit which the director will realise as a result of the contract.[217] It is also significant that it is only the nature of the interest and not all material facts which has to be disclosed.[218]

The issue may arise as to what constitutes "interested" for purposes of Section 200. An interest as trustee is enough to bring the basic equitable principle (to avoid a conflict of interest and duty) into operation.[219] However, there is a holding to the effect that a director of another company who is paid only by salary is not deemed to be "interested" in a contract with that other company for purposes of a provision stipulating that an interested director should vacate office.[220] If this approach is applied to Section 200 the term "interested" would exclude anyone (e.g. a trustee or salaried director other than a shareholder) who has no *pecuniary* interest.[221] This interpretation appears not to have been the intention of the draftsman in so far as section 200 (1) refers to any director "who is in any way whether directly or indirectly, interested in a contract or proposed contract." This view also receives support from Table A, Article 84(2) (d) which authorises voting by a director in connection with any contract with another company "in which he is interested only as an officer" or shareholder. The implication is that holding an office is a sufficient interest for general purposes and in particular for purposes of disclosure under Section 200 and Article 84(1) of Table A.[222]

It may also be noted that Section 200 by itself does not validate the contract in issue, even if fully complied with. Its effect is negative, thereby limiting the scope of any exclusion clause in the articles by expressly indicating that[223]"nothing in this section shall be taken to prejudice the operation of any rule of law restricting directors of a company from having any interest in contracts with the company." Consequently, such contracts can only be valid if ratified by the general meeting following full disclosure or as a result of exclusion of the general rule under provision in the articles.[25]

16a Civil Case No.18 of 1968 Unreported (High Court of Tanzania)

214 Table A, Art. 84

215 *Hely-Hutchinson v. Brayhead, Ltd.* [1968] 1 QB 549; [1968] 3 All ER 98

216 *Gray v. New Angurita Porcupine Mines, Ltd.*, [1952] 3 DLR 1 PC

217 *Imperial Mercantile Credit Association v. Coleman, supra* n. 12

218 Gower, *op.cit.* (4th Ed.) p. 587

219 *Transvaal Lands Co. v. New Belgium (T.) Land Co., supra* n. 206

220 *Wilson v. LMS Ry* [1940] Ch. 169; *Lapish v. Braithwaite* [1926] AC 275 HL

221 Gower,*op.cit.* p. 588. his emphasis. referring to S. 199 of the British Companies Act, 1948, which is in *Pari materia* with S. 200 (Uganda)

222 Gower *ibid.* referring to British Companies Act, 1948, S. 199 and Article 84 of Table A to that Act.

223 S. 200 (5)

## Other statutory complements to the general equitable principle

A number of sections in the Companies Act Cap 85 provide for additional restraints on certain types of contracts or arrangements between a company and its directors. Under Section 190 a company is forbidden from paying a director remuneration (whether as director or otherwise) free from income tax[224] Any agreement to that effect will be read as if it allowed for payment subject to the relevant tax of the sums involved.[225] In addition, Section 197 of the Companies Act requires disclosure to the members, through annual accounts presented to them, of the aggregate amounts of the directors' emoluments,[226] pensions,[227] and payments by way of compensation for loss of office.[228] Under Section 198, similar particulars must be given of the amount of any loans made by the company or its subsidiary to any officer.

As regards the issue by the company of loans to its directors, this is regulated by Section 191 of the Companies Act. By virtue thereof, a company is precluded from making a loan to a director of the company or a director of its holding company or to enter into any guarantee or provide any security in connection with a loan to such a person by any other person. However such prohibitions are inapplicable to (i) anything done by a subsidiary where the director is its holding company; (ii) anything done to provide any such person with funds to meet expenses incurred by him on behalf of the company or in the performance of his duties provided that the company at a general meeting had approved the expenditure or where such approval is not given before or at the next annual general meeting, the loan is repaid or the obligation discharged within six months after the meeting;[229] (iii) anything done in the course of the company's ordinary business by a company whose ordinary business includes money lending and guaranteeing of loans. Where the relevant approval by the general meeting is not given, the directors who authorise the issue of the loan, entry into guarantee or provision for security shall be jointly and severally liable to indemnify the company against any loss arising therefrom.[230] It is further notable that a loan made in contravention of Section 191 renders the transaction illegal so that neither the borrower nor the company can sue on it. However, this may not always be the case.[231]

Finally, under Section 192, payment to a director by way of compensation for loss of office must be disclosed to the general meeting and ratified. Otherwise, it is illegal. Furthermore, under Section 193, if the payment to a director for loss of office is connected with the transfer of the whole or any part of the under-taking or property of the company, where the payment is subsequently declared to be illegal, on account of non disclosure to and ratification by the general meeting, the amount received by the relevant director is deemed to have been received by him in trust for the company.[232]

## Competing with the company

Although in general a fiduciary without the consent of his beneficiaries is forbidden to compete with them,[233] it is not certain that the same rule applies to company directors. Indeed, there is

---

224 *ibid* s. 190
225 *ibid* S. 190 (2)
226 See definition in S. 197
227 *ibid* s. 197 (3)
228 *ibid* S. 197 (4)
229 *ibid.* S. 191 (2). The position in Britain is considerably changed by Companies Act, 1980 Ss. 48-66
230 *ibid* s. 191 (3)
231 See *Victor Battery Co. Ltd. v. Curry's Ltd.* [1946] 1 Ch 242 at p. 248; *Selangor United Rubber Estate Ltd. v. Cradock* (No. 3) [1968] 1 WLR 1555 at pp. 1654-1659
232 S. 194 regulates disclosure of payment for loss of office connected with the transfer of shares.
233 See e.g. Partnership Act Cap.86. S.34

authority for the proposition that a director cannot be prevented from acting for a rival company.[234] Such an approach appears to be inconsistent with the equitable requirement upon a director not to place himself in a situation giving rise to a conflict between his private interests and his duties. This appears to be the effect of *Industrial Development Consultants Ltd. v. Cooley*[235] and *Canadian Aero Services Ltd. v. O'Malley*[236] In both cases, a director who engaged in a competitive business with his company was subjected to the equitable doctrine to account for profits derived from his position as a director. As Dr Prentice has put it:[237]

> A director in such a situation will, by definition divert to himself economic opportunities which would have been exploited by his company and therefore will fall within the prescription of [the *Cooley* Case]

Dr Prentice adds that even if the director discloses the fact of his association with a rival company or business, he would still be in breach of duty to his company following the *Cooley* case:[238]

It is submitted that the same result is achieved by applying the *O'Malley* case. This reasoning receives justification from the strict application of the duty and interest conflict doctrine. In the words of Dr Prentice:[41]

> The application of the fiduciary principles to this situation underscores the positive obligations of directors to actively pursue the interests of their companies, the dilution of this duty has very little to recommend it.

However, presumably the holding by a director of multiple directorships will continue to be permissible and not lead to a breach of duty, provided the company consents to such conduct.[239] Furthermore, unless otherwise agreed or expressly provided, the duty not to compete would exist only during the continuation of the fiduciary relationship and not after its end.[240] The most recent decision in this area appears to show that in the absence of any provision to the contrary in a service agreement between a director and his company, a director is free to use knowledge and information acquired in his capacity as an employee of that company, to compete with it. Thus, in *Thomas Marshall v. Guinle,*[43] under an agreement between the defendant managing director and the plaintiff company, the defendant was not to engage in any other business without the company's consent, while employed as a managing director. Additionally, he was not "to disclose" confidential information in relation to the affairs, customers or trade secrets of the company and its group; and that after ceasing to be managing director he was neither "to use or disclose" confidential information about the suppliers and customers of the group nor for a period of five years to employ any person who had worked for the company during the last two years of his employment. Without the company's knowledge, the defendant traded on his own account and on behalf of his two companies in competition with the company and, in so doing, he bought form the company's suppliers and sold to the company's customers. It also appeared that some of the company's former employees were associated with the defendant or his companies. The

234 *London and Mashonaland Exploration Co. v. New Mashonaland Exploration Co.* [1891] WN 185, followed and approved by Lord Blanesburgh, in *Bell v. Rever Bros.* [1932] AC 161, 195 HL. This could, however, lead to an action under the then S. 210 of 1948 Act (now S. 459 1985 Act): per Lord Denning in Scottish Cooperative Society v. Meyer [1959] AC 324 (S. 211 Uganda Act, Cap.85)

235 [1972] 1 WLR 443; See also *Re: Stevedoring (Nig)* (1962) LLR 164

236 [1973] 40 DLR (3d) 371

237 DD Prentice, Note (1972) 50 *Can. Bar Rev.* 623, 632-633

238 *ibid*

239 Gower, *Principles of Modern Company Law* (4th Ed. 1979), p. 600; Prentice, *ibid* at pp. 633, 635

240 *Canadian Aero Service v. O'Malley (supra). Thomas Marshall (Exporters) Ltd. v. Guinle* [1979] 1 Ch. 227. See too Afterman & Baxt, *Cases & Materials on Corporations & Associations* (Butterworths, Australia, 1980) p. 578; *Re Stevedoring (Nig) Ltd. supra* n. 235

defendant purported to resign when his contract had another 4 years to run. The company applied for an injunction to restrain the defendant from soliciting orders from or otherwise dealing with any customer of the company for goods of the nature sold by the company and from soliciting orders for the supply of goods of such nature or otherwise dealing with any supplier of such goods to the company and secondly from disclosing or using any confidential information or trade secret of the company during or after his employment as managing director.

Megarry VC granted the first arm of the application. With regard to the effect of the defendant's unilateral repudiation of the contract with the company, on his obligations thereunder, Mr Hutchinson for the defendant thus contended:[241]

> ... the general rule was that a contract was not determined merely by the wrongful repudiation of it by one party, and that it was for the innocent party to decide whether to treat the contract as having determined or as continuing in existence. That rule, however, did not apply to contracts of employment, for they were subject to a special exception. Under the exception, any contract of employment could at any time be brought to an end by either party repudiating it. This exception however, was itself subject to an exception and that was where despite the repudiation the mutual confidence between the parties remained unimpaired. In that exceptional case the normal rule for contracts still applied, and the contract remained in being unless the innocent party elected to treat the repudiation as terminating it.

This contention was rejected by Megarry VC after an involved, albeit dutiful, discussion of the authorities.[242] The Vice Chancellor thus held:[243]

> .... in my judgment the service agreement between the parties has not been determined but remains still in force. Second, the defendant is subject to all the obligations that flow from his being bound by the service agreement. Third, as the service agreement is still in force, clause J.2 which provides for the defendant to be free from restrictions when he ceases to be a managing director, has not come into operation and that is so whether or not the two provisos are satisfied. Fourth, there is ample jurisdiction in the court to grant an injunction to restrain the defendant from doing acts contrary to his obligations under the service agreement, subject always to the exercise of the Court's discretion whether to grant an injunction at all, and, if so, in what width.

On the question of restraining the defendant from disclosing or using information or secrets of the company, acquired in his capacity as managing director, Megarry VC held that while under the agreement between the defendant and the company, the defendant could be restrained from disclosing confidential information and trade secrets of the company, he would not be prevented from using that information as such a restriction would lead to "remarkable" and "odd" results.[244] In this regard, the learned Vice Chancellor astutely observed:[245]

> ... I think 'disclose' means what it says, and does not extend to 'use'. Of course, I can conceive of methods of use which would amount to making a disclosure. If an employee were to use his secret knowledge in such a way as to make it plain to others what the secret process or information was, that might well amount to disclosure. The mode and

241 [1978] 1 Ch. 227, 236-237

242 *ibid*, pp. 237-243

243 *ibid*, at p. 243

244 *ibid*, pp. 245 to 247

245 *ibid*, p.247

> circumstances of use may be so ostentatious that they plainly constitute a disclosure. But apart from such cases I do not think that a prohibition on disclosure prevents use. It therefore seems to me that [there is] no basis for granting an injunction to restrain the defendant from using confidential information or trade secrets, as distinct from disclosing them.

Additionally, Megarry VC advanced four guidelines "in principle" which would guide the Court in identifying confidential information on trade secrets, which the court would protect.[246] First, the owner must believe that the release of the information would be injurious to him or of advantage to his rivals. Second, the owner must believe that the information is confidential or secret. Third, the owner's belief under the previous two heads must be reasonable. Fourthly, the information must be judged in the light of the usage and practices of the particular industry or trade concerned. These guidelines were apart from those provided by the authorities,[247] which the Vice Chancellor did not find particularly helpful in the context of the matters before him.

Lastly, Counsel for the plaintiff company had contended that the defendant was in breach of (i) his fiduciary duty as a director of the plaintiff company, to apply the company's property for the benefit of the company and not himself and (ii) the servant's implied duty of fidelity and good faith to his master.[248] While expressing his reluctance to base his holding on *Cook v. Deeks*[51], Megarry VC, nonetheless held that plaintiff's counsel's submissions in this regard were valid. He added:[249]

> It is impossible to deny that the defendant has been guilty of gross and repeated breaches of his implied obligation to be faithful to the company. While still in office as managing director of the company he travelled abroad, ostensibly on the company's business, and without the company's knowledge placed orders for the benefit of himself and his companies with the company's suppliers. He also, while still managing director and without the company's knowledge, sold goods for the benefit of himself and his companies to customers of the company. In the *Boston* case, the receipt by the managing director of what may have been a single secret commission was said ... to be dishonest and a fraud. I can apply no milder description to the defendant's prolonged duplicity.

On the question of fiduciary duty to the company, the Vice Chancellor concluded:[250]

> Applying the *Cynamid* principles ... I think the balance of convenience, and not least the *status quo* existing before the defendant began the conduct of which the company complained so promptly on discovering it, point to granting a suitable injunction to enforce this duty.

It is thus clear that the *Thomas Marshall v. Guinle* case does not create a general duty on a director not to compete with their companies. Apart from its being an inte-locutory judgment,

---

246 *ibid*, p. 248

247 See e.g *Saltman Engineering Co. Ltd. v. Campbell Engineering Co. Ltd* (1948) 65 RPC 203, 215 per Lord Greene MR; "Something which is public property and public knowledge" is not confidential *Coco v. AN Clark (Engineers) Ltd* [1969] RPC 41, 47; "something that has been constituted solely from materials in the public domain may possess the necessary quality of confidentiality for something new and confidential may have been brought into being by the application of the skill and ingenuity of the human brain. Novelty depends on the thing itself and not upon the quality of the constituent parts." In *Herbert Morris Ltd. v. Saxelby* [1916] 1 AC 688, 705, it was suggested that costs and prices which are not generally known may constitute trade secrets or confidential information.

248 [1979] 1 Ch. 227, 244-245, relying on *Wessex Diaries Ltd. v. Smith [1935] 2 KB 80 (CA) Hivac Ltd v. Park Royal Scientific Instruments Ltd.* [1946] Ch. 169 (CA) *Cook v. Deeks [1916] 1 AC 554 PC*

249 [1979] 1 Ch. p. 244, following *Boston Deep Sea Fishing Advice Co. v. Ansell* (1888) 39 Ch. D. 339 CA

250 [1979] 1 Ch. pp. 236, 245, following *American Cynamid Co. v. Ethicon Ltd.* [1975] A.C. 396 HL (E)

that case is closely circumscribed especially in its reliance upon the terms of the contract of employment between the plaintiff company and the defendant managing director. The implication is that the duty not to use or disclose confidential information, acquired by a director in his course of employment of the company, will only exist if so provided in his service agreement with the company and only for so long as that agreement subsists. In determining whether for purposes of any remedy sought to enforce that duty, the agreement is still in force, the Court will have regard not only to the arbitrary and unilateral conduct of the offending party but also to the general rules regulating the repudiation of contracts of employment. Megarry VC's reluctance to base his decision on *Cook v. Deeks*[51] with respect to the defendant's breach of fiduciary duty to act *bona fide* in the interests of the company, is understandable considering that *Cook v. Deeks* was a general breach of duty (amounting to a breach of trust) case whereas in *Guinle* that duty was somewhat circumscribed by provisions in the defendant's service agreement with the plaintiff company. Furthermore, while *Cook v. Deeks* involved appropriation by directors of contracts which would otherwise have gone to the company, *Guinle's* behaviour was more limited to the use of confidential information and secrets which he had obtained in the course of his employment as managing director for the company. A blanket application of *Cook v. Deeks* to the Guinle case would, therefore, it is submitted, have been inappropriate.

## Exempting directors from liability

Possible breach of a director's fiduciary duties may be avoided through the company consenting to the relevant act or omission amounting to the breach of duty. Such consent may be manifested through relevant authority given in the articles for the act or omission in question.[251] Before the promulgation of the equivalent of Section 206 of the Companies Act[252], it was accepted that articles "could effectively exempt from liability except for breaches which were 'fraudulent'"[253] However, Section 206 provides thus:

> Subject as hereinafter provided, any provision, whether contained in the articles of a company or in any contract with a company or otherwise, for exempting any officer of the company ... from or indemnifying him against any liability which by virtue of any rule of law would otherwise attach to him in respect of any negligence, default, breach of duty or breach of trust of which he may be guilty in relation to the company shall be void.

The issue has arisen[254] as to how to reconcile this provision and other statutory provision and other statutory provisions[255] relating to the directors' duty of disclosure of their interests in contracts, with articles which invariably limit or attempt to abrogate that duty.[256] With regard to the relationship between the statutory provisions and waiver clauses inserted in the articles[59], Professor Gower has thus observed of the latter:[257]

> they must be regarded as permissible and, at any rate to some extent, as effective. Presumably that is so because, if the articles permit a director to place himself in certain situations and to retain the benefits he derives thereby, it can no longer be said that the situations are ones

[251] Birds, "The Permissible Scope of Articles Excluding The Duties of Company Directors" (1976) 39 *MLR* 394. Baker, "Disclosure of Directors' Interests in Contracts" [1975] *JBL* 181; Birds "Making Directors Do Their Duties" (1980) 1 *Co. Lawyer* 67.

[252] Companies Act, 1948, S. 205 (United Kingdom).

[253] Gower, *op. cit.* (4th Ed.) p. 601; *Re City Equitable Fire insurance* Co. [1925] Ch. 407

[254] See *supra* n. 251

[255] e.g. Companies Act, S. 200

[256] *ibid.* Table A, Arts 78 84(3)

[257] *supra* n. 253, pp. 601-602. See also Birds *supra* n. 251, (1976) 39 *MLR* at p. 401 and Baker, *supra* n. 251, *at p. 194*

> in which there could be a conflict with his duty in the light of that permission. If, however, blanket waiver clauses of this sort are effective, it enables a considerable hole to be driven in the equitable principle... while articles clearly cannot relieve directors of the duty to display subjective good faith, they could if worded sufficiently widely relieve them of any obligation not to place themselves in a position whereby their personal interests could conflict with their duty. That, however, is tantamount to saying that section [206] has achieved nothing in relation to fiduciary duties and merely prevents exclusion of liability for breach of the minimal duty of care and skill.

Apart from consent to a breach of duty arising from the articles, it could also be achieved through the company in general meeting authorising or ratifying a particular act or omission, amounting to a breach of duty.[258] It is argued that this form of consent is not a "provision " within the meaning of section 206 and is therefore permissible to exclude liability arising from a director's breach of duty.[259]

## The duties of care and skill

In contrast to the director's fiduciary duties which are stringently enforced, laxity attends the prescription of a director's duty of care and skill. As a result of this, with regard to the duty of care and skill, "the trustee analogy breaks down for the type of skill required of a cautious trustee is quite different from that which an enterprising director needs to display"[260] In other words the recognised director's duty of care and skill is at variance with his descriptions as a trustee in his relationship to the company. However, a director may be regarded as agent for purposes of this duty.[261] With respect to agency, it is usual to distinguish between agents who exercise a particular trade or profession and who must show a degree of skill and diligence consistent with that of reasonably competent and conscientious members of that trade or profession as is the case with auditors,[262] and other agents who are simply required to exhibit such skill as they possess and such diligence as would be displayed by a reasonable man in the circumstances.[64] The issue which logically arises is whether a directorship is a profession within this distinction. The answer would be affirmative in the sense that a directorship is an office of profit. However, the courts have been realistic in recognising that both historically and traditionally "the possession of a title was often regarded as a greater qualification for office than any amount of business acumen and drive, and that the ordinary part time director was only expected to display such skill (if any) as he happened to possess, and such attention to duty as he thought fit to offer." [64]

This approach is different with respect to holders of other offices in the company. Thus full-time employees are expected to devote their whole time and attention during the usual working hours to the business of the company. Similarly the company's solicitors, accountants and secretaries are expected to exhibit the normal skill of members of their professions. Managing directors are also required to show analogous diligence, although the standard of skill required of them has not been determined. In *Shonowo v. Adebayo*[263], it was indicated[264] that the chairman of the board of directors and managing director occupied special positions within the company. Consequently, they were expected to be better informed with regard to the detailed machinery of control than other directors.

---

258 See *infra* on ratification

259 Gower, *op. cit.* p. 602

260 *ibid* See also *Shonowo v. Adebayo* 1969 NCLR 126

261 *ibid* p. 603

262 See *supra* chap. 13

263 1969 NCLR 126 (Supreme Court of Nigeria)

264 *ibid.* p. 144

Apart from those contributory factors to a lax standard of directors' duties of care and skill, the attitude of the courts is another notable cause. In the words of Professor Gower:[265]

> Whereas their[266] training and experience make them well equipped to adjudicate on questions of loyalty and good faith, they move with less assurance among complicated problems of economics and business administration. Hence, they display an understandable reluctance to interfere with the directors' business judgment - a reluctance of which many examples will be found throughout the whole area of Company Law.

In this vein, the Privy Council in *Howard Smith Ltd. v. Ampol Ltd.*[267] thus stated:

> There is no appeal on merits from management decisions to courts of law; nor will courts of law assume to act as a kind of supervisory board over decisions within the powers of management honestly arrived at.

The common law duties of care expected of a director towards his company were first distinctly stated by Romer J. in *Re: City Equitable Fire Insurance Co.*[268] In this case a company lost a lot of money as a result of the fraud of its managing director. The action attempted to make the other directors of the company liable in negligence for leaving the managing director without any control. In the course of judgment, Romer J. distilled from the law three propositions respecting a director's duties of care and skill thus:

(i) A director need not exhibit in the performance of his duties a greater degree of skill than may reasonably be expected from a person of his knowledge and experience.

(ii) A director is not bound to give continuous attention to the affairs of his company. His duties are of an intermittent nature to be performed at periodical board meetings and at meetings of any committee of the board upon which he happens to be placed. He is not, however, bound to attend all such meetings, though he ought to attend whenever in the circumstances he is reasonably able to do so.

(iii) In respect of all duties that, having regard to the exigencies of business and the articles of association, may properly be left to some other official, a director is, in the absence of grounds for suspicion, justified in trusting that official to perform such duties honestly.

With regard to the first proposition a standard of skill to be shown by a director in actions undertaken by him is postulated. The test indicated, is partly objective (the standard of the reasonable man) and partly subjective (the reasonable man is taken to have the knowledge and experience of the particular individual).

With respect to the second proposition; it does not apply to a managing director, who is expected to be better informed with regard to the detailed machinery of control than the other directors.[269] However, with the case of an ordinary director, although liable for a negligent decision to which he was a party he will not be liable in respect of a decision taken at a meeting at which he was not present.[270] Thus, in *Marquis of Bute's Case*[73], Stirling J. stated:[271]

> Neglect or omission to attend meetings is not, in my opinion, the same thing as neglect or omission of a duty which ought to be performed at those meetings.

There may be doubt as to the extent of the second proposition. It is presumably applicable "in cases where the director had knowledge or notice that a duty which ought to have been performed

---

[265] Gower, *op.cit.* (4th Ed.) pp. 603-604

[266] referring to court judges.

[267] [1974] AC 821 at p. 832. See also *Scottish Insurance Corporation v. Wilsons & Clyde Coal Co.* 1948 SC 360 at p. 375 per Lord Cooper affirmed [1949] AC 462 HL

[268] [1925] Ch. 407. These are restated by the Supreme Court of Nigeria in *Shonowo v. Adebayo supra* n. 263

[269] *Shonowo v. Adebayo supra* n. 263

[270] *The Marquis of Bute's Case* [1892] 2 ch. 100. See also *Re Denham* & Co. (1883) 25 Ch. D. 752

[271] *ibid.* p. 109. See further *Selangor United Rubber Estates Ltd. v. Cradock* (No.3) [1968] 1 WLR 1555 at p. *1614*.

at the meeting was not being performed".[272] The attempt at statutory codification of the duties of care and skill in Britain prescribed a duty to exercise such care and diligence as could reasonably be expected of a reasonably prudent person.[273] This is an objective standard, which improves upon the common law position. In addition the Bill recognised that the degree of care and diligence which a director or official ought to have varies with circumstances relative to his position as either an executive or non-executive director and the nature of the duties the company requires him to perform. In similar vein, the Supreme Court of Nigeria, in *Shonowo v. Adebayo*[274] indicated that directors' responsibilities vary with the nature of the company and provisions of the articles of association.

Concerning the third proposition. The permission for directors to rely on expert officials is predicated upon the first proposition that directors are not required to show any particular skill yet the running of a business entails a certain measure of skill. Such officials are in law agents and servants of the company rather than the directors. Consequently, the directors are not vicariously responsible for their errors or misjudgment. The directors would only be rendered liable on the basis of personal negligence. Nevertheless, the particular circumstances are a relevant consideration. Directors should not delegate their duties to "an obviously unqualified official; the handling of the investments of a finance company must not be left to an office boy".[275] It is significant that one of the bases for holding the directors liable for breach of duty in the *Re: City Equitable Case*[276] was that they permitted the managing director to assume functions which were not delegated to him and allowed the company's stockbrokers to keep a large amount of money without requisite security in a way common to bankers than brokers. Thus, though failing even to observe the low standard of care and skill at common law, the directors were exonerated from liability as a result of a clause exempting them from wilful default, in the articles.

In *Shonowo v. Adebayo*, the Nigerian Supreme Court indicated[277] that a company director may rely on the competence and judgment of responsible and qualified staff and may escape liability for losses which have accumulated without coming to his knowledge. However, inaction amounting to gross negligence after he has become aware of the position will render him liable for supervening losses which businesslike management could have avoided. In *Re: Duomatic, Ltd.*[278], the director paid a former director compensation for loss of office without notifying the shareholders as required by section 191 of the Companies Act 1948[279] and without considering whether the director's conduct qualified him for the payment and if so what amount. The directors did not take legal advice on the point. It was held that they had acted unreasonably by failure to take advice. Consequently, they were liable to repay the relevant amount of money to the company. Their unreasonable behaviour also precluded them from indemnification under Companies Act 1948, Section 448.[280]

---

272 Leigh, *op cit* p. 188
273 Companies Bill, 1978, Clause 45(1)
274 *supra* n. 263
275 Gower, *op.cit.* p. 606
276 *supra* n. 268
277 *supra* n. 66 at pp. 137, 148-150
278 [1969] 2 Ch. 365
279 identical to Companies Act, S. 192
280 in *pari materia* to Companies Act, S. 405

# Ratification: Reconciling Cook v. Deeks and Regal (Hastings) Ltd. v. Gulliver[281]

Professor Gower's insistence[282] that on the issue of ratification by the general meeting of directors improprieties, there is a distinction between *Cook v. Deeks*[283] and *Regal (Hastings) v. Gulliver*[284] against some formidable opposition, was vindicated in the carefully reasoned judgment of Templeman J. (as he then was) in *Daniels v. Daniels*.[285]

**Cook and Regal**

It will be recalled that in *Cook v. Deeks* the directors obtained for themselves the benefit of a contract which might otherwise have gone to the company. They effected this through a resolution at a general meeting supported by their votes as holders of three-fourths of the issued shares. The resolution had the effect of depriving the company of any interest in the contract. Although fraud on the part of the directors was not proved, the Judicial Committee of the Privy Council nonetheless held them trustees for the company of the benefits of the contract. In essence, the conduct of the directors, though lacking fraud, amounted to a breach of trust towards the company and was incapable of ratification by themselves in their capacity as shareholders in general meeting. In *Regal (Hastings) v. Gulliver*, on the other hand, the company owned a cinema and the directors decided to acquired two others with a view to the sale of the undertaking of the company as a going concern. For that purpose, they formed a subsidiary company (A) with a capital of £ 5,000 in £ 1 shares. The owner of the two cinemas offered them a lease, but insisted on a personal guarantee of the rent by the directors, unless the paid-up capital of the company was £5,000. The directors were unwilling to give the guarantee, so the company subscribed for 2,000 shares in the subsidiary at par and the remaining 3,000 shares were taken up by the directors and their friends, the company being unable to subscribe for more than 2,000 shares. Later all the three cinemas were sold by way of sale of all the shares in the company and its subsidiary. The shares in (A) were sold at a profit. The new owners of the company successfully sued the defendant directors for the profit realised. The House of Lords held that the directors were in breach of their duty to the company and were accountable for the profits obtained to the company. A notable feature of this decision is Lord Russel's *dictum* that the directors "could, had they wished, have protected themselves by a resolution (either antecedent or subsequent) of the *Regal* shareholders in general meeting. In default of such approval, the liability to account must remain."[286]

**Academic controversy**

What has troubled some legal writers[287] is that if the directors' conduct in *Regal* is ratifiable, how does one reconcile that case with *Cook v. Deeks* and cases like *Menier v. Hooper's Telegraph Works*[288] which effectually proscribe majority shareholder ratification of directors' expropriation of corporate assets? Professor Gower's solution is that the problem could be better

---

281 Reproduced from Bakibinga *Nigerian Law Journal* Vol.13 pp. 121-127. (1986)

282 LCB Gower, *Principles of Modern Company Law* (3rd Ed. 1969). p.. 565-566; (4th Ed. 1979) pp. 617-619.

283 [1916] AC 554 PC

284 [1942] 1 All ER 378 HL

285 [1978] Ch.406

286 (1942) 1 All ER 378 at p. 389. See also *Furs Ltd. v. Tomkins* (1936) 54 CLR 583 p. 599

287 K.W. Wedderburn, "Shareholders' Rights and the Rule in *Foss v. Harbottle*" (1957) CLJ 194; (1958) CLJ 93, 103-105; SM Beck, "The Saga of Peso Silver Mines" (1971) 49 *Can. Bar Rev.* 80, 116-117; R. Baxt, "Judges in their own cause: The Ratification of Director' Breaches of Duty", (1978) *Monash U. Law Rev.* 16, 45-48; Afterman, *Company Directors and Controllers* (Law Book Co. Australia, 1970) pp. 149ff; Beck in J. Ziegel (Ed.) *Studies in Canadian Company Law* (Butterworths, Toronto, 1973), Vol. II, pp. 232-238; Sealy [1967] *CLJ* 83, 102-103

288 (1874) LR 9 Ch. 350

appreciated if a distinction is drawn between "(i) misappropriating the company's property and (ii) merely making an incidental profit for which directors are liable to account." In this vein, it is contended that *Cook v. Deeks* (and presumably analogous cases) fell within (i) in that it was the duty of directors to acquire the contracts on behalf of the company. In such a situation ratification by the general meeting would be to allow the company to give away part of its assets. On the other hand, Gower contends that in *Regal* "the directors can be said not to have misappropriated any property of the company" and therefore ratification was possible. This approach is criticised by Professor Beck in these terms:[289]

> With great respect, it is difficult to accept this distinction between *Cook* and *Regal*. In *Cook* the company was in the construction business and would clearly have been interested in the new contract which the two directors entered into with its primary client. In *Regal* the company owned theatres and the directors took up shares in the subsidiary which was used to acquire the lease in a new theatre. In both cases, the directors in the course of acting as such took for themselves opportunities with respect to which they had a duty to use their best efforts to acquire for the company.

Furthermore, Professor Beck adds that accepting that information may be property *(Phipps v. Boardman)*[290] and therefore belonging in equity to the company (*Cook v. Deeks*), the shareholders in *Regal* could not ratify its use by the directors as this would amount to giving away corporate assets.

It is respectfully submitted that while there is some merit in seeing both the *Regal* and *Cook v. Deeks* fact situations in terms of directors' breaches of duty resulting into benefits to the directors, it is also necessary to gauge how far such breaches affect the company for purposes of ratification. In essence a distinction has to be drawn between a breach of duty *per se* and a breach of duty resulting into harm to the company - in effect a breach of trust. KW Wedderburn (as he then was) first stumbled on a similar solution when attempting to explain the impact of *Cook v. Deeks* on *Alexander v. Automatic Telephone Co.*[291] Thus, he observed:[292]

> ... it might be thought that cases like *Alexander's* case could be explained by the formula *(Cook v. Deeks)* as being cases where the company had an equitable "property" in the benefits obtained by the directors and therefore minority action was possible. But it is this ... point which exposed the difficulty at the root of the formula. Is it a distinction between the *Cook* case and the *Regal* case that in the first the property belonged *abinitio* in equity to the company? Was that not so in *Regal* as well?

**Daniels v. Daniels - a solution?**

It is this writer's view that Wedderburn's query has been answered, though, belatedly by Templeman J. in *Daniels v. Daniels*.[293] In this case, it will be recalled that the company sold land to the second defendant (who, together with the first defendant were majority shareholders and directors of the company) for £4,250 on the instructions of the first and second defendant as directors. Later the land was sold by the second defendant for £120,000. The plaintiffs, who were minority shareholders brought an action against the defendants alleging that the land was sold to the defendant at an under value. The defendants applied to strike out the action as not disclosing a reasonable cause of action. Templeman J. (as he then was) held that a minority

289 (1972) 49 *Can. Bar Rev.* 116-117
290 [1967] 2 AC 46 HL
291 [1900] 2 Ch. 56
292 *op cit supra*, [1958] CLJ 93, 103
293 [1978] Ch. 406

shareholder's action was maintainable, as in this case, where "directors use their powers intentionally or unintentionally, fraudulently or negligently *in a manner which benefits them at the expense of the company*"[294] (Emphasis added). In reaching this decision, Templeman J. was clearly influenced by *Alexander v. Automatic Telephone Co.* case and *Cook v. Deeks*. Indeed *Daniels v. Daniels* is a synthesis of the ratios in those two cases. It will be recalled that in the *Alexander* case, the directors issued shares and requested some people who took up the shares to make payments in respect of those shares, but the directors did not themselves make payments on the shares which they had taken up. A minority shareholder's action was allowed and, although fraud was discounted, the basis of the action was said to be "breach of duty". Lindley M.R. observed, in this regard, that "the charge is that the directors were guilty of a breach of duty in procuring contracts and in taking advantage of them so as to benefit themselves at the expense of the shareholders.[295] He added that "the directors who so use their powers to obtain benefits to themselves at the expense of the shareholders without informing them of the fact, cannot retain those benefits and must account for them to the company so that all shareholders may participate in them.[296] This latter proposition amounts to an exception to the rule in *Foss v. Harbottle* allowing an individual shareholder to enforce his personal rights in that capacity. However, Lindley M.R. thought that the breach of duty here also involved a wrong to the company which was derivatively actionable. He stated:[297]

> *The breach of duty to the company consists in depriving it of the use of the money which the directors ought to have paid up sooner than they did.* I cannot regard the case as one of internal management, which, according to *Foss v. Harbottle* and numerous other cases, the court leaves the shareholders to settle among themselves. It was ascertained and admitted at the trial that when this action was commenced, the defendants held such a preponderance of shares that they could not be controlled by the other shareholders. Under these circumstances an action by some shareholders on behalf of themselves and the others against the defendants is in accordance with the authorities and unobjectionable in form. (Emphasis added)

It would thus appear that while Wedderburn tried to explain the *Alexander* case in terms of *Cook v. Deeks,* the most apt explanation is that of *Cook* in terms of *Alexander*. The result is that the *Alexander ratio* to the effect that the directors' breach of duty which results into harm to the company is not ratifiable and therefore individually and derivatively actionable, covers the *Cook* fact situation, which was essentially a breach of trust. The synthesis of the two cases produced the result in *Daniels v. Daniels*. It is submitted that *Daniels v. Daniels* reinforces Professor Gower's distinction between *Cook v. Deeks* as a case where the company's property was misappropriated and therefore incapable of ratification by the company in general meeting and the *Regal* case where the directors' conduct, though resulting into secret profits to themselves, it was not certain that this harmed the company. In essence, *Cook v. Deeks* is a case where the directors, by their conduct were in breach of trust to the company, whereas those in *Regal* were not. It was, therefore, possible to ratify their breach of duty in the latter case.

---

294 (1978) Ch. 406, 414

295 [1900] 2 Ch. 56, 64

296 *ibid,* pp. 66-67

297 *ibid,* p. 69; In the Australian case, *Ngurli Ltd. v. McCann* (1953) 90 CLR. 425, the *High* Court observed (at p. 477) that:
"... even in general meeting a majority of shareholders cannot exercise their votes for the purpose of appropriating to themselves property or advantages which belong to the company for that would be for the majority ,to oppress the minority. The right to issue new capital is an advantage which belongs to the company."

This approach is at variance with Dr Prentice's explanation of *Daniels v. Daniels* in relation to the *Regal* case. In the first place, he is of the view that "the net result of *Daniels v. Daniels* is that the rule in *Foss v. Harbottle* is confined to a very narrow compass to situations where a director's breach of duty does not result in personal fain."[298] It follows from this that "breaches of duty by directors constituting self-serving negligence are not ratifiable" and consequently, a minority shareholder can sue in respect of such breaches. Dr Prentice then attempts to illustrate this point by reference to the *Regal* case and Lord Russel's dictum that the general meeting could have ratified the directors' act in that case. He concludes that Lord Russel's dictum was "unfortunate" and a minority action would have been possible since the breach of duty in *Regal* was self-serving and therefore not ratifiable.

The first objection to Dr Prentice's thesis is that in *Daniels v. Daniel*, Templeman J. explicitly rejected the plaintiff's counsel's submission that a minority shareholder had a right to sue for any and every breach of director's fiduciary duty to the company.[299] To the extent that the directors' acts in the *Regal* case only amounted to a breach of their duty to the company, *Daniels v. Daniels* has no application to that case. Secondly, Templeman J. in *Daniels v. Daniels* appears to think that there is a distinction between the position of a director who is merely negligent or foolish that he makes a profit and that of one whose negligence or foolishness results into his making a profit at the expense of the company. Thus, he said that "to put up with foolish directors is one thing; to put up with directors who are so foolish that they make a profit of £115,000 odd at the expense of the company is something different."[300] If that distinction is accepted, then it clearly distinguishes the fact situation in *Daniels v. Daniels* from that in the *Regal* case. It was not alleged nor was it proved that the directors' conduct in *Regal* harmed the company as was the case in *Daniels*. It follows that while the directors' conduct in *Regal* was in Lord Russel's view ratifiable, the same could not be said of the directors' alleged conduct in *Daniels v. Daniels*. It is notable in this regard that Templeman J. clearly had in mind the issue of ratification in *Daniels*. This is borne out by his citation of a passage by Lord Davey in *Burland v. Earle*[301] which touches upon the possibility of ratification by the general meeting of directorial conduct.

In conclusion, it is submitted that Professor Gower's distinction between *Cook v. Deeks* and *Regal (Hastings) v. Gulliver* on a ratifiablitiy basis has at last received judicial recognition by the Chancery Court in *Daniels v. Daniels*. The *Cook* case is explained in terms of directorial breach of duty amounting to a breach of trust which is incapable of ratification, while the *Regal* case amounts to a breach of duty resulting into the realisation of secret profits to the directors, but not in any way harming the company, conduct which does not amount to a breach of trust to the company and which in view of *Daniels v. Daniels* is ratifiable to the extent of precluding a minority shareholder action.

---

298 D.D Prentice, "Self-serving Negligence and the Rule in *Foss v. Harbottle* (1979) 43 *Conveyancer* (NS) 47, 51

299 [1978] Ch. 409-414

300 *ibid*, p. 414

301 [1902] AC 83, 93

# 15
# ENFORCEMENT OF CORPORATE DUTIES*

It is intended to consider how corporate duties either on the part of shareholders or its officials are enforced. Although the effect of incorporation has been to overcome several procedural problems[1], it has not totally eliminated those which manifest themselves when there is a dispute within the corporate power structure. In contrast to a breach of duty within the partnership structure which entails an action by the wronged partner for an account;[2] where the breach of duty is on the part of company directors or controllers, the other shareholders have no *locus standi.* This is because corporate duties are owed not to them but to the company itself. Consequently, it is only the Company which is capable of suing in respect of breach thereof. However, a difficulty arises when those to be sued are the proper authority for instituting the proceedings in the company's name. Exceptions to the general rule inevitably arise to accommodate certain circumstances in which a corporate organ cannot proceed, by virtue or equitable and legislative intervention.

Treatment here is not restricted to litigation but extends to statutory inspection and investigation of companies, which is an administrative remedy sufficient in its own right or as a preparation for legal action. The alternative remedy to winding up and Section 211 of the Companies Act as well as winding up on the just and equitable ground under Section 222(f) are also considered.

## Litigation by the company

It has for a long time been the law that where it is legally necessary to enforce a duty owing to the company, the only plaintiff is the company itself. This notion stems from the Rule in *Foss v. Harbottle.*[3]. However, since the company is in reality a fiction the power to litigate on its behalf must be vested in some person or group. It has, in this respect, been suggested that the Rule in *Foss v. Harbottle* "rests on the basic premise of majority rule, and control by the majority in general meeting of the use of the corporate name in litigation"[4]. This approach appears to have been reinforced initially in *McDougall v. Gardiner*[5] and subsequently in *Edwards v. Halliwell*[6] where Jenkins L.J. stated:[7]

---

* Partly based on the author's Ph.D. Thesis submitted to the University of London February, 1981, Chapters 1 and 2.

1 See *supra* Chap.2

2 See Bakibinga, *Partnership Law in Uganda*(1992) Chap.5 and *Kinyaju v. Mkodo* 1967 (1) A.L.R. Comm. 49; *Mussa v. Selemani* 1968(1) ALR Comm.392, 394 (High Court of Tanzania).

3 (1843 2 Hare 461, 67 E.R. 189 (Ch.). See also *Edwards v. Halliwell* [1950] 2 All E.R. 1064, pp.1066-1067 per Jenkins L.J.; *Tika-Tore Press v. Abina* 1973 NCLR 24: (S.C.N.); *Kalo Dipcharima v. Bornu Holding Co. Ltd and Anors.* 1969 NCLR 322; *Eternal Sacred Order of Cherubim & Seraphim v. Adewunmi* 1969 NCLR 73 (Supreme Court of Nigeria); *Misango v. Musigire* [1966] E.A.390 (High Court of Uganda)

4 Beck, "Analysis of Foss v. Harbottle", *Studies in Canadian Company Law,* (Ed. J.Ziegel, 1967) 545 at p.548 Wedderburn, "Shareholders" Rights and the Rule in *Foss v. Harbottle*", (1957) C.L.J. at p.198 thinks that the Rule's limits "lie along the boundaries of majority rule".

5 (1875) 1 Ch.D.13 (C.A.)

6 [1950] 2 All E.R. 1064

7 *ibid,* p.1066

> In my judgment, it is implicit in the rule that the matter relied on as constituting the cause of action should be a cause of action belonging to the general body of corporators or members of the company or association as opposed to a cause of action which some individual member can assert in his own right.

The trend in the latter part of the nineteenth century and the early years of this century had indeed been, (when objection was raised as to the use of the company's name as a plaintiff in an action), for the court to act on the majority's views regarding the litigation if they were ascertainable[8] or to postpone a decision on the objection until a general meeting was called to ascertain the majority's wishes.[9] Such a practice has been endorsed in relatively recent cases. *Pavlides v. Jensen*[10] indicates that the majority of shareholders have the right to decide on litigation, while in *Danish Merchantile Co. Ltd. v. Beaumont*[11] Jenkins L.J., alluded to the court's "well-settled practice" of adjourning "any motion brought to strike out the company's name with a view to a meeting being called to see whether the company desires the action to be brought or not". Much more recently, one member of the English Court of Appeal in *Bamford v. Bamford*[12] reaffirmed the right of the majority shareholders to bring an action in the company's name. Russel L.J. indicated that it is "for the company by ordinary resolution" to decide whether or not to sue in respect of a wrong done to the company:[13]

> to litigate or not to litigate, apart from very special circumstances is for decision by such a resolution.

The concept of majority shareholder control over company litigation, however, stands in contradistinction to the view, stemming largely from interpretation of Article 80 of Table A to the Companies Act,[14] to the effect that the board of directors has power over litigation.

It may be contended in this respect that since Article 80 vests in the board of directors *all* the company's powers which are not required to be exercised by the shareholders in general meeting, it follows that in the absence of authorisation to the contrary in the principal act or articles, the power over litigation vests in the board of directors. *Dicta* to this effects are evident in *John Morley Building Co. v. Barras*[15] and *Shaw & Sons (Salford) Ltd v. Shaw*,[16] where an identical article to article 80 was interpreted to give power to the board of directors to bring a suit. Greer L.J. stated in this respect[17]

> when the permanent directors decided to instruct the company's solicitors to bring these actions on behalf of the company, they had power under the articles.

---

8 *Silber Light Co. v. Silber* (1879) 12 Ch.D.7171; *East Pant Du United Lead Mining Co. Ltd. v. Merryweather* (1864) 2 H & M 254, 71 E.R. (thought a minority action was possible): *Atwool v. Merryweather* (1867) L.R.5 Eq. 464; *West End Hotel Syndicate Ltd. v. Bayer* [1912] 29 T.L.R.(Ch.)

9 *Exeter & Crediton Railway v. Butler* (1847) 16 L.J. Ch.449; *Pender v. Lushington* (1877) 6 Ch.D.70; *Duckett v. Gover* (1877) 6 Ch.D.82; *Imperial Hydropathic Hotel v. Hampson* (1882) 23 Ch.D. 14 (C.A.); See also Wedderburn, *supra*, n.4 (1957) *C.L.J.*, p.201.

10 [1956] Ch.565, pp.576-7

11 [1951] 1 Ch.680, pp.686-87. See also, *Olaolu Modern Bakery Ltd. v. Arthur Young, Osindero & Co.* (1977) 3 F.R.C.R.37

12 [1969] 1 All E.R. 969 (C.A.)

13 *ibid* at p.976

14 See *supra* Chap. 11 under "*Powers of Directors*"

15 [1891] 2 Ch.386

16 [1935] 2 K.B. 113 for a critique of this case see cap.11, *supra*; For a recent allusion to this view see *Prudential v. Newman Industries* [1980] 2 All E.R.841, 875; However, it has been held by Brightman J. in *Re: Emmadart* [1979] 1 All E.R.599 that a receiver invested with the board of directors' managerial powers under Articles 80 (1st Schedule Table A, Companies Act 1948) has no power to present a petition for winding up the company without the approval of the company in general meeting.

17 *ibid* p.133

Slesser L.J., relying on *John Morley Building Co. v. Barass*[15] said:[18]

> I read the judgment of Stirling, J., to indicate that the directors as such are the proper persons to authorise proceedings in the name of the company.

The issue arises as to whether this power over litigation is exclusive to the Board of Directors, an aspect raised by the *Automatic Self-cleansing*[19] line of cases which tend to establish that when a particular power is vested in the board of directors either by a specific article or under the general delegation clause, the directors' right to exercise that power is exclusive and not susceptible to interference by the shareholders' in general meeting.[20] The implication is that once a clause like article 80 appears in the company's regulations the members in general meeting are precluded from initiating litigation.

There thus appears to be a conflict between the *Automatic Self-Cleansing*[21] line of decisions which establish the board's exclusive right to institute legal proceedings in the name of the company on the one hand, and on the other, those decisions which buttress the Rule in *Foss v. Harbottle*[22] which indicate that the general meeting can authorise litigation. It has been observed of the two trends of case law evolution:[23]

> as is not uncommon in the development of English Law, the two lines of authority have substantially developed independently and with little cross reference.

Professor Slutsky adds in this vein[24]:

> The fact that the two lines evolved quite separately is not really surprising. Whereas in *Foss v. Harbottle* cases, the conflict was generally between the *majority and the minority*, in the *Automatic Self-cleansing* decisions the dispute was invariably between the *majority and the board*. (emphasis his)

While this rationalisation is valid an additional explanation would appear to be that in most of the *Foss v. Harbottle*[22] line of decision, the issue concerning the effect of Articles of Association and particularly an article like Article 80 did not arise and indeed first arose with the *Automatic Self-cleansing*[19] decision. This was recognised by Neville J. in *Marshall's Valve Gear Co. Ltd. v. Manning Wardle & Co. Ltd.*[25] where the observed:[26]

> I take it that prior to the decision in the case of *Automatic Self-cleansing Filter Syndicate Co. v. Cunninghame* [1906] 2 Ch.34, the law was established to the effect that the majority of shareholders, in the absence of a contract to the contrary, had the ultimate control of the affairs of the company and could assert their rights in general meeting.

While Neville J.'s interpretation of the equivalent of Article 80 Table A (1st Schedule to the Companies Act), as to the distribution of power between the general meeting and the board of

---

18 *ibid* p.143; see also Gower, *supra,* (3rd Ed.) p.583, Pennington *Company Law* (1973), p.482; *Palmer's Company Law* 21st Ed. (1968) pp.529-30.

19 [1906] 2 Ch.34

20 See Cap.11 (*supra*) Greer L.J. thus stated in *Shaw v. Shaw* (*supra* n.16) at p.134: "If powers of management are vested in the directors, they and they *alone* can exercise those powers".

21 *supra,* n.20

22 *supra* n.3

23 Aickin, "Division of Power Between Directors and General Meeting as a Matter of law, and as a matter of fact and policy (1967) 5 *Melbourne University Law Review,* 448 at p.462.

24 Slutsky, *The Duties and Powers of Management in the Company Law of Canada and England,* University of London Ph.D. Thesis (1971) p.19

25 [1909] 1 Ch.267

26 *ibid* p.272

directors, may be questioned,[27] it would appear that he is correct when he says that "in the absence of any contract to the contrary the majority of the shareholders in a company have the ultimate control of the affairs, and are entitled to decide whether or not an action in the name of the company shall proceed...."[28]. This position is consistent with Professor Lord Wedderburn's view that both the directors and the shareholders in general meeting retain parallel authority to initiate proceedings on behalf of the company, notwithstanding the form of the articles.[29] Such an approach has also been endorsed (albeit indirectly) in the case of *Alexander Ward & Co. v. Samyang Navigation Co.*[30] where a liquidator was held to be entitled to commence or authorise proceedings in the name of the company where the board of directors is unable to do so.

It may be concluded that while the *Foss v. Harbottle* line of cases establish the right of the general meeting to authorise litigation, the importance of the contractual effect of the Articles of Association which give wide powers to the board or directors has tended to undermine that assumption. Consequently the *Automatic Self-cleansing* line of cases would appear to suggest that the power over litigation where a company has an article like Article 80 in Table A, lies with the board of directors. On a strict construction of that article this view is valid, but conflicts with those of some leading scholars to the effect that both the general meeting and the board of directors have parallel authority over litigation.

Regardless of the proper view as to which of the company's primary organs has power over litigation, it is quite clear that the company is the property plaintiff in respect of an action brought to enforce a duty owed to it. Nevertheless, the requirement that an action be instituted by the company itself has been rationalised on two major premises. First, that it prevents a multiplicity of suits in the sense that if each shareholder was permitted to sue, the company would be harassed by numerous actions commenced and discontinued by several plaintiffs.[31] Second, if the irregularity complained of is one which can be effectively ratified by the general meeting it is useless to have litigation about it except with the consent of the general meeting.[32]

## Litigation by a member

It has been said that "the rule in *Foss v. Harbottle* greatly strengthens the position of the majority, indeed if there were no exceptions to it the minority would be completely in their hands."[33] Consequently, certain exceptions are recognised under which an individual shareholder may sue in place of the company. These are:[34]

---

27 See *supra* Cap.3

28 [1909] 1 Ch.267, 272

29 Note, "Control of corporate litigation (1976) 39 M.L.R.327, 328; Wedderburn *supra* n.4 pp.200-203; see too Gower, supra (3rd Ed.) pp.137-128 (4th Ed.1979), p.147 and Pennington, *supra* n.18, pp.501,561.

30 [1975] 1 W.L.R.673 [H.L.Sc.]. See also *Joseph Asaboro Ltd. v. Western Nigeria Finance Corporation* 1976 NCLR 266 (High Court of Western Nigeria) where it is indicated that a corporate action may be instituted by either the general meeting or board of directors. See further *Economic Exports Ltd. v. Kasumu* 1966 NCLR 104.

31 *Gray v. Lewis* (1873) L.R. 8 Ch.App. 1035. See also *Misango v. Musigire, supra.* n.3

32 *Macdougall v. Gardiner* (1875) 1 Ch. D.13 C.A. See criticism thereof *infra* under "Corporate Irregularities and Personal Shareholders". See also *Sparks Electric (Nig.) Ltd. v. Ponmile* [1986] 2 NWLR 516, 526 C.A.; *Cole v. R.C. Irving & Co. Ltd.* 1970 NCLR 472, 482-483 (High Court of Lagos State); Tika Tore Press Ltd. v. Abina (1973) 4 S.C.63

33 Gower, *op.cit.* (4th Ed.) p.644

34 See *Edwards v. Halliwell, supra* n.3. See also *Daniels v. Daniels* [1978] Ch.406; [1978] 2 All E.R. 89 considered *supra* Chap.14; *Edokpolor v. Edo S.C.* 89/1983 unreported.

(i) When it is complained that the company is acting or proposing to act *ultra vires,* since the matter is one which the members cannot ratify;[35]
(ii) Where the act complained of, though not *ultra vires* the company, could be effective only if resolved upon by a special majority vote, usually where a special or extra-ordinary resolution is required and it is alleged that it has not been validly passed;[36]
(iii) Where it is alleged that the personal rights of the plaintiff shareholder have been infringed or are about to be infringed in such a way that the wrong to the plaintiff cannot be ratified by an ordinary resolution of the company;[37]
(iv) Where those who control the company are perpetrating a fraud on the minority;[38]
(v) (Arguably) any other case where the interests of justice require that the general rule prescribing suit by the company should be disregarded.[39]

With the exception of the fifth "exception", which is not so well established, all the others could be summarised by saying that "an individual shareholder can always sue, notwithstanding the rule in *Foss v. Harbottle,* when what he complains of could not be validly effected or ratified by an ordinary resolution."[40]

The difficulty, however, arises in applying this principle by preventing a member's action simply because the company could have rectified, the wrong complained of, when in fact it has not had an opportunity to decide whether or not to do so. This has been resolved by the court staying the relevant action until the general meeting has been given the opportunity to decide on the matter complained of. Thus, in *Hogg v. Cramphorn Ltd.*[41],it was held that an individual shareholder could sue on the ground that directors, in issuing additional shares had exercised their powers improperly. However, the court also held that their action could be confirmed by the general meeting and gave the company the opportunity to do so provided that the directors undertook not to exercise their votes on the new shares. This would suggest that simply because an action could be ratified by the general meeting will not necessarily preclude a minority shareholder's action either in a personal capacity or on behalf of the company from being commenced. However, it would be stayed, if it is subsequently ratified.

Little difficulty attends the operation in practice of the first and second exceptions that is those based on *ultra vires* and special majority. An *ultra vires* act cannot be ratified by the company[42]. Additionally, each member has a right to ensure that the funds of the company are

---

35 *Russel v. Wakefield Water-works Co.* (1875) L.R.20 Eq.474; *Hutton v. W.Cork Ry* (1883) 23 Ch.D. 654; *Yorkshire Miners Association v. Howden* [1905] A.C.256; *Nigerian Stores Workers Union v. Uzor* 1971(2) NCLR 412, 426,430 (High Court of Lagos State) *Mbene v. Ofili* 1968(1) ALR Comm.235; *Oduduru Anor. v. National Union of Hotels & Personal Services Workers & Or.* FCA/L/226/83. Unreported; *Misango v. Musigire, supra* n.3

36 *Baillie v. Oriental Telephone Co.* [1915] Ch.503 C.A.; *Cotter v. National Union of Seamen* [1929] 2 Ch.58, 69-70. *Edwards v. Halliwell, supra* n.34; *Nigerian Stores Workers Union* case *ibid. Mbene v. Ofili, ibid.*

37 *Johnson v. Lyttle's Iron Agency* (1877) 5 Ch.D.687 C.A. *Pender v. Lushington* (1877) 6 Ch.D.70; *Wood v. Odessa Waterworks Co.* (1889) 42 Ch.D. 636; *Salmon v. Quin & Axtens* [1909] 1 Ch.311 C.A. [1909] A.C. 442 H.L.; *British America Nickel Corporation v. O'Brien* [1927] A.C. 369, P.C. *Edwards v. Halliwell ibid.*

38 *Atwool v. Merryweather* (1967) L.R.5 Eq. 464n., *Menier v. Hooper's Telegraph Works* (1874) 9 Ch. App.350; *Mason v. Harris* (1879) 11 Ch.D. 97 C.A. *Spokes v. Grosvenor Hotel* [1897] 2 Q.B. 124 C.A.; *Burland v. Earle* [1902] A.C.83 P.C. *Cook v. Deeks* [1916] A.C.554 P.C. *Daniels v. Daniels supra* n.34; *Sparks Electric (Nig.) Ltd. & Anor v. S.B. Ponmile* [1986] 2 N.W.L.R.516, 526-527, C.A.; *Misango v. Musigire supra* n.3

39 *Heyting v. Dupont* [1964] 1 W.L.R.843; [1964] 2 All E.R.273 *Prudential Assurance Co. Ltd v. Newman Industries Ltd. & Ors.* [1979] 3 All E.R.507; (No.2) [1980] 2 All E.R. 841; *Eastmanco (Kilner House Ltd)* v. *G.L.C.* [1982] 1 All E.R. 437; *Edokpolo & Co. Ltd. v. Sem - Edo Industries Ltd.* (1984) 7 S.C.119

40 Gower, *supra* n.33 at p.645.

41 [1967] Ch.254. See also *Punt v. Symons & Co.* [1903] 2 Ch.506; *Galloway v. Halle Concerts Society* [1915] 2 Ch.233; *Piercy v. Mills* [1920] 1 Ch.77; *Bamford v. Bamford* [1970] Ch.212 C.A.; *Hodgson v. NALGO* [1972] 1 W.L.R. 130; *Tika-Tore Press Ltd. v. Abina* (1973) 4 S.C.63

42 *Ashbury Carriage Co. v. Riche* (1875) L.R.H.L. 653. See *supra* Chap.4; *Cole v. R.C. Irving &Co. Ltd., supra* n.32; *Nigerian Stores Workers Union Case supra,* n.35; *Mbene v. Ofili supra* n.35. *Oduduru case supra* n.35

used for its proper objects.[43] In this respect, the court is only concerned with whether the activity is *ultra vires* and not as to its character in terms of merit or otherwise.[44] Relative to this right is that a member can institute a personal action where the act complained of is illegal.[45] The capacity on the part of a member to restrain an *ultra vires* or illegal act exists even when a member has in the past been privy to the act complained of.[46]

With regard to the special majority exception, the best illustration is provided by *Edwards v. Halliwell*[47]. In that case, the constitution of a trade union indicated that contributions by members were not to be altered until a ballot vote of the members had been taken and two-thirds majority secured. A delegate meeting of the union, without taking any ballot, passed a resolution increasing the contributions of members. The plaintiffs, who were members of the union, instituted this action against two executive committee members of the union and the union itself for a declaration that the resolution was null and void. It was held that the resolution was invalid. Jenkins L.J. indicated that if the company alone were allowed to sue in cases of this nature, a company which had broken its own rules by doing something without a special resolution which could only be done validly by a special resolution, would effectually be allowed to do by ordinary resolution that which, according to its own regulations, could only be done by special resolution. The court also concluded that the matter complained of amounted to an invasion of the personal rights of members.

The most controversial exceptions are those relating to the invasion of personal rights of the shareholders and fraud on the minority entailing a derivative action. To these we now turn.

## Corporate irregularities and personal shareholders' rights[47a]

The basic difficulty here stems from the need to reconcile case law which seems to limit corporate litigation as a right predominantly belonging to the majority of shareholders in general meeting,[48] with the personal shareholder's right to enforce the Articles of Association, as a basic contractual obligation.[49] The majority shareholder rule essentially prescribes an individual shareholder's action where the matter complained of can be put right by the shareholders in general meeting. The issue, however, arises as to which matters can be rectified by the majority in general meeting, and which cannot.

### (a) The MacDougall and Pender Dilemma

In *McDougall v. Gardiner*[48] the Court of Appeal held that a member had no *locus standi* to complain about the breach of an article entitling him to demand a poll in general meeting. James L.J. stated thus:[50]

> I cannot conceive that there is any equity on the part of the shareholder, on behalf of himself and the minority, to say....... we have a right..... and every

[43] *Simpson v. Westminster Palace Hotel Co.* (1860) 8 H.L.Cas.712

[44] *Yorkshire Miners Association v. Howden* [1905] A.C.256

[45] *Powel v. Kempton Park Racecourse, Ltd.* [1899] A.C.143

[46] *Moseley v. Koffyfontein Mines Ltd.* [1911] 1 Ch.73 C.A. Affd. [1911] A.C.409 H.L. *Oduduru v. National Union of Hotels & Personal Services Workers, & Ors Supra n.35*

[47] *Supra* n.3. See also *Nigerian Stores Workers Union v. Uzor* 1971 (2) NCLR 412, 426-427 (High Court of Lagos State); *Taylor v. Taylor* (1977) NCAR 391,394-395 (Federal Court of Appeal, Enugu); *Mbene v. Ofili* 1968(1) ALR Comm.235 (High Court of Lagos State).

[48] [47a]See also Bakibinga, *Gravitas Review of Business & Property Law* (Lagos), Vol.2, No.7 pp.15-21 (1989)

*Foss v. Harbottle* (1843) Hare 461; *MacDougall v. Gardiner* (1875) 1 Ch.D.13; *Mozley v. Alston* (1847) 1 Ph.790; *Cotter v. National Union of Seamen* [1929] 2 Ch.58; See also *Burland v. Earle* [1902] A.C. 83 and the Ugandan Case, *Misango v. Musigire* [1966] E.A. 390, 396-397; *Eternal Sacred Order of the Cherubim & Seraphim* 1969 NCLR 73, 87, 89-90 (S.C.N.)

[49] S.20(1) Companies Act 1948 (United Kingdom) S.22 Ugandan Companies Act. *Quin and Axtens Ltd. v. Salmon* (1909) A.C. 442; *Nigerian Stores Workers v. Uzor* 1971(2) NCLR 412, 427-8

[50] *Supra*, n.48 at p.23. See also *Cole v. R.C. Irving & Co. Ltd.* 1970 NCLR 472. 482-483 (High Court of Lagos State).

> individual has a right to have a meeting held in strict form in accordance with the articles,

Essentially, the Court of Appeal was saying that where you have irregularities relating to the internal management of the company (in this instance its conduct of a general meeting) these are capable of being corrected by the majority of members and should not be subject of litigation by an individual member, even if they are at the same time breaches of the articles of association. Apart from the ratifiability aspect of the irregularity in question in this case, certain *dicta* appear to suggest that the irregularity may have been seen as a wrong to the company only rather than something affecting an individual shareholder's right. Thus, James L.J. stated:[51]

> Everything in this bill, so far I can see, if it is a wrong it is a wrong to the company, because every meeting that is called must be for some purpose or other.

This view is reiterated by Jessel M.R. when he said:[52]

> The plaintiff in that case *(MacDougall v. Gardiner)* did not complain that his own vote was excluded; he was suing, on behalf of the company. Here the plaintiff sues in his own name.

R.J. Smith has observed[53] that the above two *dicta* could lead to two conflicting conclusions as regards *McDougall v. Gardiner.* One is that it can be distinguished out of existence as not being relevant to a personal action. Or secondly, that it is an example of the limitation of the personal action. The former view appears to underlie the leading authority standing in contra-distinction to *Macdougall v. Gardiner,* namely, *Pender v. Lushington.* We shall advert to the second view later on.

**Is Foss v. Harbottle irrelevant to the personal action?**

In *Pender v. Lushington*[54], the right of a shareholder to vote according to the Company's Articles of Association was upheld by the English Court of Appeal. Jessel M.R. stated in this vein:

> ...... whether he votes with the majority or the minority, he is entitled to have his vote recorded - an individual right in respect of which he has a right to sue.

It is implicit in this reasoning that a shareholder's individual right to enforce his rights which derive from the Articles of Association is independent of any limitation implicit in the rule in *Foss v. Harbottle*[48] *Mozley v. Alston*[48] and *MacDougall v. Gardiner.* This approach was more recently evident in *Edwards v. Halliwell,*[55] where an alteration in the regulations of a Union, which had the effect of increasing a member's subscription, irregularly, was restrained by the Court at the suit of a member. Earlier this century the Court of Appeal had explicitly held that a member of a company can enforce a right conferred upon him *qua* Managing Director by the Articles of Association.[56] In the words of Professor Wedderburn, *Quin & Axtens Ltd. v. Salmon* is authority for the proposition "that a member can compel the company not to depart from the contract with him under the articles even if that means indirectly the enforcement of "outsider" rights vested either in third parties or

---

51 *ibid* at p.22

52 *Pulbrook v. Richmond Consolidated Mining Co.* (1878) 48 L.J. Ch.65 C.A. In this case the plaintiff was personally affected by the irregularity.

53 R.J. Smith, "Minority Shareholders and Corporate Irregularities" (1978) 41 *M.L.R.147*; See also S.M Beck, "The Shareholder Derivative Action" (1974) *Can. Bar. Rev.* 159, 187-95.

54 (1877) 6 Ch.d 70 C.A., especially at 81; See also K.W. Wedderburn, "Shareholders' Right and the rule in *Foss v. Harbottle*" (1957) *C.L.J.* 194, pp.214-215; C.R. Baxter "Irregular Company Meetings" (1976) *J.B.L.* Smith, *ibid.* pp.147-159 *Nigerian Stores Workers Union v. Uzor supra* n.49, pp.427-428.

55 [1950] 2 All E.R. 1664 C.A.

56 *Quin & Axtens Ltd. v. Salmon, supra* n.49

himself, so long as, but only so long as he sues *qua* member and not *qua*"outsider"[57]. Dr Goldberg's alternative interpretation of S.20(1) is formulated thus:[58]

> "A member of a company has under section 20(1) of the Act a contractual right to have any of the affairs conducted by the particular organ of the company specified in the Act or the company's Memorandum or Articles, even though the enforcement of that right (and the correlative obligation) may incidentally enforce also a right or power bestowed by the Memorandum or Articles on a person in a capacity otherwise than as a member of the company, be that person in fact be a member or not; but a member has no right under the sub-section to have enforced a right or power bestowed by the Memorandum or Articles on a person otherwise than in his capacity as a member, of the company, whether or not that person is in fact a member, unless the enforcement of the latter right or power is incidental to the enforcement of the member's contractual right under the said subsection to have any of the company's affairs conducted by the particular organ of the company specified in the Act or in the Memorandum or Articles.

This was an attempt at narrowing down Professor Wedderburn's formulation which was regarded as too wide and amplifying Professor Gower's which was said to be too narrow. Professor Gower's view is that "it is settled, as an overriding principle that [section 22] gives the Memorandum and Articles contractual effect only in so far as they confer rights or obligations on the member in his capacity as member.[59]

While acknowledging the force of Dr Goldberg's approach, Gower nevertheless favours the Wedderburn approach as being consistent with principles formulated by Judicial decisions and producing a result which "(can) be arrived at by any accepted Canons of Statutory Interpretation".[60] Prentice thinks[61] that Lord Wedderburn's formulation is correct "provided (it is) not understood to refer to every term of the articles, but only to those terms which form part of the [S.22(1)] contract as being definitive of the power of the company to function". He concludes with an attempt at reconciling Professor Gower, Lord Wedderburn and Dr Goldberg thus:[62] "outsider" rights are capable of enforcement, but only if the member sues *qua* member as Lord Wedderburn suggests in respect of a term of the [s.22(1)] contract, as Professor Gower would have, and the enforcement of the 'outsider' right is incidental to the compliance by the company on some limitation of the power of the company to function under the terms of the constitution". This writer is of the view that both Dr Goldberg and Graham Prentice's variations of Lord Wedderburn's approach are inconsequential as it is difficult to distinguish between instances in which the non-observance of the company's memorandum and articles in [S.22(1)] which are contractually binding between the company and its members) would or would not affect a member in any capacity.

However, apart form the *Pender v. Lushington, Edwards v. Halliwell* and the *Salmon* cases', illustrations of instances where a personal action has been upheld irrespective of the rule in

---

[57] Wedderburn, *supra* n.54, pp.212-213. For contrary views see G.D. Goldberg "*The Enforcement of Outside Rights Under Section 20(1) of the Companies Act, 1948* (1972) 35 *Mod. Law Rev.* 362-374.

[58] Goldberg, *ibid* p.363. S.22 of the Ugandan Act is identical to S.20

[59] Gower, *Principles of Modern Company Law* (4th Ed. 1979) at p.317

[60] Gower, *ibid*, pp.319-329. For other cases supporting Lord Wedderburn's construction see *Re H.R.Harmer* [1959] 1 W.L.R. 62 (C.A.) at pp.858-89; *Re Richmond Gate Property Co. Ltd.* [1965] 1W.L.R. 355 (the Company relied on an article in defending a claim by a director, who was also a member). For notes thereon see (1965) 28 *M.L.R.* 34) and (1966) 29 *M.L.R.* 608, 612; *Kraus v. J.G. Lloyd Pty. Ltd.* [1965] V.R. 232, 235-237 (Vict. S.C.); *Hogg v. Cramphorn* [1967] Ch. 254 and *Bamford v. Bamford* [1975] Ch.212 C.A. For a much more recent attempt at grappling wih this interpretive problem see Graham Prentice, *"The Enforcement of Outsiders' Rights"* (1980) 1 *Co. Law 179-185.*

*Foss v. Harbottle*. Professor Wedderburn argues with force that other cases go much further than this. In his words.[63]

> ...... they have recognised not merely the member's contractual rights in general terms under the articles and the right to enforce his rights as a member, but in particular, personal rights obtained from the articles to transfer shares and to vote; to protect preferential rights and class interests such as the right to have shares offered to him to be registered and to enforce delivery of a share certificate in accordance with the articles, to enforce a declared dividend as a legal debt, and if none is declared, at least to prevent dividends from being distributed otherwise than in accordance with the articles; to prevent an irregular forfeiture to prevent directors holding office in breach of the articles and other "procedural" irregularities. Similarly, a member has a *personal* right to prevent alterations in the articles which would constitute a fraud on the minority; and probably has a similar right to enforce proper notice of meetings and business to be conducted at them.

While little difficulty attends actions brought by individual shareholders to enforce what from Professor Wedderburn's list are mainly substantive shareholder rights, controversy surrounds their position where the so called *"procedural"* irregularities mainly affecting the convening and conduct of meetings by the company's organs are concerned. This latter situation is the classic point of difference between *Pender v. Lushington* and *MacDougall v. Gardiner (supra).* It is notable though, that even in this area, the cases supporting *Pender v. Lushington* and by implication the thesis that where a personal right deriving from the articles is infringed, a member has a right to bring an action, irrespective of *Foss v. Harbottle,* are legion.[64] Indeed there is a contention that the *Foss v. Harbottle* rule relating to majority control is premised upon procedural requirements governing company meetings being observed. In this vein Kekewich J. Observed:[65]

> The application of the doctrine of *Foss v. Harbottle* to joint stock Companies involves as a necessary corollary the proposition that the vote of the majority at a general meeting, as it binds both dissentient and absent shareholders, must be a vote given with the utmost fairness - that not only must the matter be fairly put before the meeting, but the meeting itself must be conducted in the fairest possible manner.

We now examine those cases which support the *Pender v. Lushington* line of reasoning in relation to a member's right to protest procedural irregularities.

In *Alexander v. Simpson*[66], the Articles of Association of a company stipulated that "Seven days notice in writing specifying the place, day and hour of meeting and in case of special business the general nature of such business, shall be given to the members before every general meeting." A notice was given to the effect that an extra-ordinary general meeting would be

61 Prentice, *ibid* p.184

62 *ibid* p.185

63 *ibid* pp.210-211 and cases there cited. His emphasis. In regard to pre-emption rights see now ss.17-19 *Companies Act*, 1980 (U.K.)

64 Admittedly, these cases may be explicable on their facts either as being situations where a special majority vote or sanction for an act was required, or as an illustration of the requirement that a majority may convene a meeting openly and without deception.

65 *Tiessen v. Henderson* [1899] 1 Ch.862 at p. 866, following *Menier v. Hooper's Telegraph Works* (1874) L.R.9 Ch.350. *In Bretts & Co. v. Macnaghten* [1910] 1 Ch.430. Eve J. said (at p.435) that the Court is entitled to look at the notice convening the meeting as part of *res gestae,* to see if the proceedings are regular.

66 (1890) 43 Ch.D.139 C.A.

held on 12 July at the hour and place therein mentioned for the purpose of considering, and if deemed advisable of passing the resolution set forth in the notice and it concluded: "Should such resolutions be duly passed the same will be submitted for confirmation as special resolutions to a subsequent extra-ordinary general meeting which will be held on 29 July at the sametime and place."

It was held by the Court of Appeal (affirming Chitty J. at first instance) that the said meeting was invalid. Further, that though it was possible to put on the notice the construction that a meeting would be held on 29 July, whether the resolutions were passed on the 12th or not, the construction which an ordinary businessman would put upon the notice would be that the meeting would be held only if the resolution was passed at the first meeting. Consequently, the notice of the second meeting was conditional, and being bad, when sent, could not be made good by shareholders acquiring information *aliunde* that the resolutions had been passed at the first meeting.

It is notable, however, in relation to this case that Chitty J. had indicated that the defect could be rectified by the majority, thus allowing for the injunction, which had been granted, to be stayed.[67]

The *Tiessen v. Henderson* case, [68]while distinguishing *Alexander v. Simpson*[66] as to the conditional notice, nevertheless postulated that the notice of an extra-ordinary general meeting must disclose all facts necessary to enable the shareholder receiving it to determine in his own interest whether or not he ought to attend the meetings and that the preliminary interest of a director in the matter of a special resolution to be proposed at the meeting is a material fact for this purpose. On this latter point Kekewich J. was following *Kaye v. Croydon Tramways Co.*[69]

In this case, a provisional agreement was made between two companies for the sale of an undertaking of the one to the other. The purchasing company agreed to pay in addition to the sum payable to the selling company, a substantial sum to the directors of the selling company as compensation for loss of office and the agreement was made conditional upon its adoption by the shareholders of the selling company. The notice convening the meeting of shareholders to consider the agreement described it simply as an agreement for the sale of the undertaking. It did not mention the directors' remuneration. The selling company was governed by the Companies Clauses Act 1845. It was held[70] by the Court of Appeal (reversing Kekewich J.) that while the provision in favour of the directors did not render the agreement *ultra vires,* the notice by reason of its omission to refer to this provision did not fairly disclose the purpose for which the meeting was convened, and did not comply with Section 71 of the Companies Clauses Act, 1845.

Similar reasoning is evident from another powerful Court of Appeal decision, *Baillie v. Oriental Telephone & Electric Co. Ltd.*[71] In this case, special resolutions were passed altering the Articles of Association in order to sanction the retention by directors of payments previously received in breach of trust. The notice convening the meeting at which the resolutions were passed did not give particulars of the amount of remuneration received by the director. The plaintiff shareholder brought an action on behalf of himself and all other shareholders of the defendant company for a declaration that the resolutions were not binding on the ground of insufficient notice of the

---

67 *ibid*, pp.144-145

68 [1899] 1 Ch.861

69 [1898] 1. Ch.358 C.A. See also the Ugandan case, *Winklamier v. East Africa Plans Ltd. & anors.* [1969] E.A.415. The *Kaye v. Croydon Trmways Co.* Case was more recently applied by Samuels J.A. in the Australian case, *Winthrop Investments Ltd. v. Winns Ltd.*(1975) 2 N.S.W.L.R.66 (noted D. prentice (1977) 40 *M.L.R.*557 in his dissenting judgment.

70 See especially Lindley M.R. at p.370 *(ibid)* and Rigby L.J. at p.373 *ibid.*

71 (1915) 1 Ch.503 C.A. See also the Ugandan case, *Misango v. Musigire* [1966] E.A.390

meeting at which they were passed and for an injunction to restrain the company and the directors from acting upon them.

Astbury J., following *Normandy v. Ind. Coope & Co.*[72], dismissed the action on the ground that the company had not been joined as plaintiffs. The implication was that the wrong complained of was a wrong to that company. The Court of Appeal reversed Astbury J. and held[73] that the plaintiff's action was well conceived. The Court further agreed that the notice complained of did not give a sufficiently full and frank disclosure to the shareholders of the facts upon which they were asked to vote and the resolutions were not therefore binding. Swinfen-Eady L.J. thought[74] that the plaintiff could maintain the action because his private rights as a shareholder had been infringed and justice required that he be entitled to bring the action. In this respect, he relied upon the statement by Wigram V.C. in *Foss v. Harbottle* thus:[75]

> If a case should arise of injury to a corporation by some of its members, for which no adequate remedy remained except that of a suit by individual corporators in their private character, and asking in such character the protection of those rights to which in their corporate character they are entitled, I cannot but think that the principle so forcibly laid down by Lord Cottenham in *Wallworth v. Holt*[76] and other cases would apply and the claims of justice would be found superior to any difficulties arising out of the technical rules respecting the mode in which corporations are required to sue.

The essence of Swinfen-Eady L.J.'s reliance upon this statement would appear to be that where a corporate irregularity affecting the convening and conduct of a company's meeting is committed, an individual shareholder has a personal right to bring an action to challenge that irregularity. The basis of the action is not only the corporate right deriving from the member's contract with the company, but also the interests of justice. The right to bring the action is independent of the shackles imposed by the rule in *Foss v. Harbottle,* as Wigram V.C. himself recognised.

In *McConnel v. Prill (E) & Co.*[77], it was alleged that the notice convening the meeting did not firstly, specify the resolution and secondly, the intention to pass the resolution as an extra-ordinary resolution within Section 69 of the Companies Act, 1908. Sargant J. upheld both objections and observed:[78]

> As regards the first objection, it is obvious that the notice signifies merely an intention to propose some increase or other in the capital of the company and not an intention to make the specific increase embodied in the resolution that was actually passed. It seems to me of great importance that shareholders should be protected in matters of this kind by specific notice of what is intended to be done.

The cases hitherto considered relate largely to notices of corporate meetings. Similar results to those in those cases are evident from situations where the irreguralities complained of took place during the actual conduct of a meeting.

---

72 [1908] 1 Ch.84

73 *Supra* n.71. See per Cozens - Hardy M.R. at pp.514-5

74 *ibid* at p.518

75 (1843) 2 Hare 461, 492

76 (1841) 4 My & Cr. 619,635

77 (1916) 2 Ch.57

78 *ibid* p.61; contrast with *Bretts & Co. Ltd. v. Macnaghten* [1910] 1 Ch.430, where it was held that having regard to the terms of the Articles of Association, the meeting transacted at the meeting was within the scope of special business as indicated in the notice and the notice was therefore sufficient. The Articles of Association of the company *inter alia* provided (54) that the notice of an ordinary general meeting at which special business was to be transacted should specify generally the nature of such special transactions.

Thus in the Court of Appeal decision, *Henderson v. Bank of Australasia,*[79] the plaintiff was prevented by the chairman at a meeting, from moving an amendment to a resolution by which the article of the company were altered. The Court of Appeal held that the plaintiff was entitled to have the resolution set aside as the chairman's refusal to accept the amendment had the effect of withdrawing a material and relevant question from the consideration of the meeting. In *Oliver v. Dalgleish,*[80] a member successfully challenged the exclusion of certain proxy votes, which had resulted into resolutions replacing directors being defeated instead of carried. In *Musselwhite & Anors. v. Musselwhite & Sons,*[81] the omission to give notice of a meeting to the plaintiffs was held to invalidate the proceedings at the meeting.

An interesting feature of all the above cases is their lack of, or scanty mention of *Foss v. Harbottle*. The justification may lie in the realization that that rule was in those instances irrelevant.[82] Thus while referring to *Kaye v. Croydon Tramways*[83] where the rule had not been adverted to, Cozens-Hardy M.R. in *Baillie v. Oriental Telephone* said[84]that no-one would suggest that the very learned Counsel who argued the case there had never heard of the doctrine. In *Henderson v. Bank of Australasia*[85], the only person to mention the rule was the plaintiff, appearing in person.

In the *Baillie* case[84] itself, the *Foss v. Harbottle* decision was referred to only in justifying the plaintiff's personal right to bring the action. The inescapable conclusion is that the *Foss v. Harbottle* doctrine is irrelevant where a member seeks to challenge an irregularity, however technical, arising from a breach of the company's Articles of Association. This approach appears to be supported by Lord Wedderburn in his seminal article when he states thus:[86]

> .... the mere fact that a breach of the articles can be expressed to be an "internal irregularity" is not reason, without more, for saying that the wrong had been "done to the corporation" alone and for denying an individual member a personal right of action in respect of the wrong.

Bowen L.J., in *Alexander v. Simpson,* seemed to be of the same view regarding the need for a proper notice to be given of a meeting to shareholders. He observed thus:[87]

> I regret very much that our decision will cause a great deal of inconvenience and trouble in the affairs of this company, but it is not a mere technical matter. The difficulty cannot be described as a technical one. The construction of a notice convening an extra-ordinary general meeting of a company is not a technical point....

---

79 (1890) 45 Ch.D.330 C.A.

80 [1963] 1 W.L.R.274; [1963] 3 All E.R. 330

81 [1962] 1 Ch. 964

82 Baxter, *supra* n.54 p.325

83 *supra* note 69

84 [1915] 1 Ch. 503 at p.515

85 *Supra* note 79

86 *Supra* p.54 at p.215. It is tempting to draw a distinction between improprieties which would justify a personal action and irregularities which would not. However, when does an irregularity which amounts to a departure from a company's Articles of Association lead to a personal action and when does it not? The positon would be clarified if it is accepted that any departure form the articles, however "technical" or "irregular" is actionable by a shareholder or member by virtue of the contractual effect of the articles. However, it would then be up to the Court to exercise its discretion as to what relief to grant. In so doing it may entertain policy considerations, including an adoption of the majority shareholder view on the dispute in question. The court clearly has such jurisdiction (S.448, 1948 Act (U.K.), S. 365 Uniform Companies Act (Australia) S. 405 Ugandan Act. An analogous position was reached in *Hogg v. Cramphorn Ltd.* [1967] Ch.254 which established that a matter which is ratifiable can still lead to litigation. To paraphrase Professor Weaderburn (1967) 30 M.L.R.77, 82) the minority may sue yet the majority ratify; see also *Grant v. John Grant & Sons Pty. Ltd. infra* n.96 and text thereof; Gower, *supra note 59, p.646.*

In referring to most of the cases in the *Pender v. Lushington* mould, which we have considered, R.Smith concluded:[88]

> The important point is that they do not involve irregularities which are sufficiently personal in their effect as to survive any of the ratifiability analyses. They support, therefore, the argument that ratifiability is not relevant to the personal action.

Notwithstanding these powerful views, the idea persists that there must be a way of reconciling *MacDougall v. Gardiner* and, through it, *Foss v. Harbottle with Pender v. Lushington* and similar cases.

**(c) Is MacDougall v. Gardiner a limitation on the personal action?**

In *Boschoek Proprietary Ltd. v. Fuke*[89], Swinfen-Eady J. tried to tackle the problem by saying that the majority can ratify a breach of an article where the article in question amounts only to "a limitation of the authority of the directors... and not a limitation of the general powers of the company". Other attempts at dealing with the problem indicate that a majority cannot ratify what in substance is an alteration of the articles or what is a breach amounting to a "complete transformation of the company - a fundamental alteration of policy."[90] Such suggestions, however, still leave the issue as to which breaches are ratifiable and which are not, largely unresolved. Nigel Bastin[91] attempted to put forward a solution. In his words:[92]

> The rule *(Foss v. Harbottle)* will only apply where the alleged irregularity is capable of being cured by ordinary resolution of the company in general meeting. In situations like *Wood v. Odessa Waterworks Co.* and *Quin & Axtens v. Salmon* the general meeting could not pass the resolution in dispute because of the provision in the articles. The power of the general meeting was expressly limited. The majority, therefore, could not bind the minority. The rule in *Foss v. harbottle* was inapplicable, and thus as individual member was entitled to bring an action to restrain the company from acting on the resolution. On the other hand, the irregularities in *Mozley v. Alston* and *MacDougall v. Gardiner* did not involve articles which limited the power of the general meeting. They were concerned with matters of form and procedure, the breach of which could be corrected by an ordinary resolution of the company at a subsequent general meeting. Thus a shareholder could not sue. Therefore the solution to the problem is to be found in ascertaining whether the matter is one which may be determined by the majority going through the proper process. If it is, the rule in *Foss v. Harbottle* will apply - if it is not, then the member has a right to sue and thus compel the company to act in accordance with the provisions of its Articles of Association.

To this proposition R. Smith has pointed out that "most irregularities constitute once and for all contraventions of articles and do not purport to change them.[93] Furthermore, even if Bastin's distinction between articles which limit the powers of the general meeting and those which regulate form and procedure[94] is tenable, how does it explain the different results in *MacDougall v. Gardiner* on the one hand and *Pender v. Lushington*, on the other?

---

87 (1890) 43 Ch.D.139 at p.149; see also *Wall v. London & Northern Assets Corporation* [1890] 2 Ch.469

88 *supra* n.53 at p.159

89 [1906] 1 Ch.148, 163

90 Wedderburn, *supra* n.54 at p.214. See cases there cited.

91 N.A.Bastin, "The Enforcement of a Member's Rights" (1977) *J.B.L.*17

92 *ibid* pp.23-24

93 Smith *supra* n.53 p.152

94 A distinction which is strikingly similar to the one attempted some seventy years earlier by Swinfen-Eady J. See *supra* n.89 and text thereof.

The other consideration in this context is that a breach of an article is a wrong to and by the company.[95] Hence, while the company can ratify a wrong done to it, it is doubtful whether it can ratify a wrong done to an individual member. This then means that however technical the breach, an individual member can challenge it through court litigation. This reasoning appear to be supported by a statement in the Australian case, *Grant v. John Grant & Sons Pty. Ltd.* where Fullager J. suggested that:[96]

> (where).... there have been breaches of the provisions of the Articles of Association and.... any member of the company who has not assented to such breaches is *prima facie* entitled to enlist the aid of the courts for the purpose of undoing the effect of such breaches.... a general meeting has no power to override Articles of Association. A departure from the articles is *prime facie* challengeable, unless all the members of the company have agreed to the departure and the transaction in not otherwise objectionable.

The effect of such reasoning may lead to the paralysis of corporate activity and indeed calls to mind Lawrence L.J.'s objections in *Cotter v. National Union of Seamen*[97] thus:[98]

> I think it would be lamentable if a technical breach of the rules were held to entitle a dissentient member or minority to obtain an injunction to restrain the carrying out of a resolution.

A solution to such a possibility is reached by arguing that invariably courts would not grant relief to a member where this does not lead to any concrete results.[99] This appears to be the reasoning in cases like *Bentley-Stevens v. Jones*[100] and *Browne v. Le Trinidad*[101]. In *Bentley-Stevens*, the plaintiff moved the court for an injunction to restrain the defendants from acting on a resolution because of its underlying irregularities. It was held by Plowman J. dismissing the motion, that even if the plaintiff's complaint of irregularities was correct, the irregularities could be cured by going through the proper processes and the ultimate result would be the same. Consequently, the court would not interfere. In *Browne v. La Trinidad,* Lindley L.J. thus observed:[102]

> I think it is most important that the court should hold fast to the rule upon which it has always acted, not to interfere for the purpose of forcing companies to conduct their business according to the strictest rules where the irregularity complained of can be set right at any moment.

Apart from these predominantly policy considerations which may be said to be a reaction to Lord Wedderburn's rhetorical question; "Was this an irregularity such that we will allow an ordinary majority to put it right?"[103], the persistent view is that where corporate irregularities deriving from the non-observance of articles are committed, *Foss v. Harbottle* is inapplicable as the shareholder has a personal right to ensure that the Articles of Association of the company are observed.[104] Admittedly, it may be said that the considerations which led to the results in the

---

95 *Pender v. Lushington* (1877) Ch.D.70; Smith, *supra* n.53, pp.155-6; Weddebrun, *supra* n.54, pp.215. Baxter, *supra* n.54, p.329.

96 (1951) 82 C.L.R.1,48

97 *supra* n.48

98 [1929] 2 Ch. 58, 107

99 Baxter, *supra* n.54, at p.332; Smith, *supra* n.53 p.156

100 [1974] 1 W.L.R. 638

101 (1887) 37 Ch.D.1

102 *ibid* at p.17

103 Wedderburn, *supra* n.54. (1957) C.L.J. 194, 215

104 Smith, *ibid* pp.159-160; Beck, *supra* n.53, p.195

*Bentley Stevens*[105] and *La Trinidad*[106] cases explain the result in MacDougall v. Gardiner. To that extent, the latter case is a limitation on the personal action.

## The derivative action and the rule in Foss v. Harbottle

The prerequisites for a derivative action in company law have been amply canvassed, by Professor Gower[107]. In essence they are six. First, the wrong complained of must involve a fraud on the minority resulting into the expropriation of the property of the company or the minority shareholders, a breach of the directors' duties of subjective good faith or conduct which leads to the passing of resolutions which are not *bonafide* in the interests of the company as a whole.[108] Secondly, the plaintiff in a derivative action must show that the alleged wrong-doers control the company.[109] The decision by Vinelott J., in *Prudential Assurance Co. Ltd. v. Newman Industries*[110], attempted to modify this requirement. The Chancery Court postulated that an exception to the rule in *Foss v. Harbottle* which allows a minority shareholder action is not limited to situations where the alleged wrongdoer has voting control of the company, but applies wherever the wrongdoer, though not holding the majority of the shares in the company, was shown to be able by manipulating his position in the company to ensure that the majority would not allow a claim to be brought for the alleged wrong. This exception was said to found in the court's general jurisdiction to allow a minority shareholder's claim where it was in the interests of justice[11a]. Furthermore, the principle underlying the exception was that in ascertaining the view of the majority in regard to bringing the claim, the court would disregard votes cast or capable of being cast by a shareholder whose interests directly conflicted with those of the company,[11b] and would have regard to circumstances which showed that the majority would not be relied upon to determine in a disinterested way whether it was in the company's interests to bring the claim. Vinelott J.'s approach would clearly cover a situation where domineering directors or a Managing Director used their positions to manipulate the proxy votes of shareholders in order to obtain their way. Third, the company must be joined to the action as a defendant.[111] Fourth, the plaintiff shareholder should sue in a representative capacity on behalf of himself and the other members.[112]

A further procedural development in this direction has been provided by the decisions of Vinelott J. in *Prudential v. Newman Industries.*[113] In the first case[114], the first defendant company (Newman) proposed to acquire assets of the fourth defendant company. *Newman* issued a circular to the shareholders, signed by the chairman (Bartlett, the second defendant) explaining the proposed transaction, and at a general meeting of *Newman* a majority of shareholders passed a resolution approving the transaction. The plaintiff company which was a

[105] *supra* n.100

[106] *supra* n.101

[107] L.C.B. Gower & others, *"The Principles of Modern Company Law"* (4th Ed., 1979) pp.647-653. See also *Gore Browne on Companies* (43rd Ed., 1977) paras.28-4, 28-8.

[108] *ibid* pp.616-630; 648-649

[109] *Atwool v. Merryweather* (1867) L.R. 5 Eq. 464 n; *Menier v. Hooper's telegraph Works* (1874) L.R. 9 Ch. App.350; Mason v. Harris (1879) 11 Ch.D.97 and others; *Wallersteiner v. Moir* (No.2) [1975] 1 All E.R. 849 C.A. *Daniels v. Daniels* [1978] Ch.406, 408; *Misango v. Musigire* [1966] E.A. 390.

[110] [1980] 2 All E.R. 841, 872, 874-6. This approach, though commendable was rejected in the Court of Appeal. See [1982] 2 W.L.R.31. See also Gregory, Note (1982) 45 *M.L.R.*584-588; Boyle "The Prudential, the Court of Appeal and *Foss v. Harbottle*" (1981) 2 *Company Lawyer* 264-266.

[11a]This was rejected by the Court of Appeal as impractical [1982] 2 W.L.R. at p.47

[11b]*c.f. N.W. Transportation v. Beatty* (1887) 12 App Cas.589

[111] *Spokes v. Grosvenor Hotel Co.* [1897] 26 D.124, 128-129 C.A.; *Misango v Musigire* [1966] E.A. 390, 400 (Uganda)

[112] *Mozley v. Alston* (1847) 1 Ph.790. *Burland v. Earle* [1902] A.C. 83, 93 P.C.

[113] [1979] 3 All E.R. 507 [1980] 2 All E.R. 841 858-860; See also A.J. Boyle, *Representative* and *Derivative Actions are Combined in Prudential Case* (1980) 1 *Co. Lawyer*, 97-99.

minority shareholder in *Newman* voted against the resolution. It then brought an action claiming, *inter alia,* damages for conspiracy against the defendants, the chairman and vice chairman, in respect of the transaction, alleging that the circular was tricky, misleading and contained statements which the defendants could not honestly have believed and further alleging misconduct on the part of the defendants as directors of *Newman*. The action was originally framed as a derivative action by the plaintiff minority shareholder claiming damages on behalf of Newman. It was also framed to enable the plaintiff to bring a personal claim for damages against the defendants. The plaintiff proposed an amendment to the writ and a statement of claim to enable it to bring a representative action on behalf of the shareholders of Newman at the date the resolution was passed, seeking (i) on behalf of such shareholders who had suffered damage as a result of the passing of the resolution, a declaration that they were entitled to damages for conspiracy from the defendants and (ii) damages on their own behalf.

The defendants averred that the court had no jurisdiction to entertain a representative action, where the cause of action of each member of the class purported to be represented, was a separate cause founded, in tort in respect of which proof of damage was a necessary ingredient, or alternatively, if there was jurisdiction to order a representative action, the court in its discretion ought not to accede to the plaintiff's application to amend.

Vinelott J. held that the court had jurisdiction to entertain a representative action by a plaintiff suing on behalf of a class where the cause of action of the plaintiff and each member of the class was alleged to be a separate cause of action in tort. Three conditions had, however, to be satisfied.[115] The first was that an order for a representative action would not have the effect either of conferring on any member of the class a right he could not have claimed in a separate action. Consequently a plaintiff in his representative capacity would normally only be able to obtain a declaratory relief. Second, there had to be an interest shared by all the members of the class viz. a common ingredient in the cause of action of each member as was evident in the instant case. Third, the court had to be satisfied that it is for the benefit of the class that the plaintiff be permitted to sue in a representative capacity. Consequently, the court had to be satisfied that the issues common to every member of the class would be decided after full discovery and in the light of all evidence capable of being adduced in favour of the claim.

As to the objection to the court to use its discretion to allow the plaintiff's amendment, Vinelott J. held[116] that the court would allow the amendments in principle because to allow the plaintiff to sue in a representative capacity would not enlarge the limitation period available to members of the class represented for they would still have to bring their own actions to establish damage within six years from the date when the cause of action accrued, and the only effect of an order in favour of the plaintiff in its representative capacity would be that the issues covered by that order would be *res judicata* between members of the class and the defendants. Furthermore, since the allegations of misconduct and conspiracy on the part of the defendants had been made in the statement of claim as originally framed, the amendment would not add to the action "numberless claims in fraud" but would merely allow a common element in the causes of action of all members of the class to be established in a representative action.

Additionally, to the contention that if the claim had been originally formulated as a representative claim the defendants might have wished to adduce evidence that no member of

---

[114] [1979] 3 All E.R.507; See also the Canadian Case, *Goldex Mines Ltd. v. Revill* [1974] 54 D.L.R. (3d) 672 (Ont. Court of Appeal), where it was established that "misleading information" circulated by management can lead to a breach of both personal and corporate rights thereby resulting into a continued personal and derivative action. For comments thereon see B.V. Slutsky, "Shareholders Personal Actions - New Horizons" (1976) 39 *M.L.R.331*; D.D.Prentice Note, "*Goldex Mines v Revill:* Some Reflections on the Statutory Derivative Action" (1976) 15 *Univ. of West Ont.* 225-237; M. Mason, "Ratification of the Directors' Acts: An Anglo-Australian Comparison (1978) *41 M.L.R.*161, 171-172.

[115] *ibid* pp.519-520; following *Taff Vale Railway Co. V. Amalgamated Society of Railway Servants* [1901] A.C. 426.

[116] [1979] 3 All E.R. 507, 520-521

the class has suffered damage, Vinelott J. was of the view that this objection was misconceived. He added:

> The court cannot in a representative action make an order for damages, though, of course, the plaintiff in its own non-representative capacity will be entitled to pursue its claim for damages. It would be as wrong to permit the defendants to adduce evidence that other members of the class represented, who are not actually parties, have not suffered damage, as it would be to allow a representative action to proceed as a claim for damages on behalf of all members of the class.

Finally, to the objection that the plaintiff could not be allowed to pursue two representative claims, one on behalf of the present shareholders and one on behalf of the shareholders at the date of the resolution, Vinelott J. thus answered:[117].

> That objection is, in my judgment, founded on the form and not the substantial effect of the amendment. The derivative claim is framed in the conventional way as a claim on behalf of all the shareholders in the defendant company except the second and third defendants. But the claim is in effect a claim for recovery of damages or equitable compensation by Newman, the first defendant. If it succeeds, the plaintiff may not wish to pursue its claim for damages for conspiracy. But I can see no reason why that claim, whether alternative or cumulative should not be pursued in the representative capacity, at least to the extent of the issues that would be raised in an action for damages for conspiracy by any member of the class represented.

Fifthly, the plaintiff must come to court with clean hands and should not be implicated in the wrong of which he complains.[118] Lastly, the plaintiff shareholder is always at liberty to discontinue the proceedings, but presumably only for good reason.[119]

The derivative action is a procedure allowed to a shareholder in exception to the majority shareholder rule in *Foss v. Harbottle*[120]. Its essence was summarised by Lord Denning M.R. in *Wallersteiner v. Moir* (No.2) where he stated:[121]

> It is a fundamental principle of law that a company is a legal person with its own corporate identity, separate and distinct from the Directors or shareholders and with its own property rights and interests to which alone it is entitled. If it is defrauded by a wrong-doer, the company itself is the one person to sue for the damage. Such is the rule in *Foss v. Harbottle*.

---

117 *ibid* at p.521. This view was re-echoed by Vinelott J. in *Prudential v. Newman Industries Ltd.* (No.2) [1980] 2 All E.R. 841, 860: "It is true that a derivative action is,in form, an action brought on behalf of the members of the defendant company except the person against whom relief is sought and it may seem odd at first sight that a plaintiff should seek to represent two sets of shareholders, those as at 29 July, 1975 and those at the date of the action, which may not coincide. (Shares may have changed hands between 29 July, 1975 and the issue of the second writ). *But, although a derivative action is in form a representative action, it differs from other representative actions in that if the action succeeds property or damages are recovered not by the plaintiff or the class whom he represents, but by the company and only indirectly by the shareholders through the accretion of the company's assets* (following per Lord Denning M.R. in *Wallersteiner v. Moir* (No.2) [1975] 1 All E.R. 849, 858). In substance there is only one truly representative action, the direct action, which is joined with a derivative action brought on behalf of the company..."

118 *Moseley v. Koffyfontein Mines* [1911] 1 Ch.73, C.A. affirmed [1911] A.C. 409 H.L.

119 Gower, *supra* n.107 at p.453

120 (1843) 2 Hare 461

121 [1975] 1 All E.R. 849, at p.857, following *East Pant Du Lead Mining Co. v. Merryweather* (1864) 2H 8 M. 254 and *Atwool v. Merryweather, supra* n.10 and *Foss v. Harbottle* (1843) 2 Hare 461 per Wigram V.C. (p.492). See also *Bornu Holding Co. Ltd. v. Dipharima* (1976) 1.S.C.63 (Supreme Court of *Nigeria) See also* Bakibinga, "The Derivative Action in Nigeria Law" *The Company Lawyer,* Vol.10 No.5, pp.121-122 (1989)

> The rule is easy enough to apply when the company is defrauded by outsiders. The company itself is the only person who can sue. Likewise, when it is defrauded by insiders of a minor kind, once again the company is the only person who can sue. But suppose it is defrauded by insiders who control its affairs - by directors who hold a majority of shares - who can sue for damages? Those Directors are themselves the wrongdoers. If a board meeting is held they will not authorise proceedings to be taken by the company against themselves. If a general meeting is called, they will vote down any suggestion that the company should sue themselves. Yet the company is the one person who is damnified. It is the one person who should sue. In one way or another some means must be found for the company, to sue. Otherwise the law would fail in its purpose. Injustice would be done without redress.

Hence, the derivative action - an action brought by an individual shareholder on behalf of himself and other members except the wrongdoers to remedy a wrong done to the company and which cannot otherwise be corrected because of the reluctance or refusal of the majority wrong-doers to rectify the wrong.

**(a) Wallersteiner v. Moir - a sixth exception to Foss v. Harbottle**

Apart from explicitly, recognising the derivative action in English Company Law, the *Wallersteiner v. Moir*[22] decision has been interpreted, as it were, introducing a sixth exception to the rule in *Foss v. Harbottle*, to wit that an individual shareholder can bring a derivative action to remedy a wrong done to the company arising from any breach of duty irrespective of whether the wrongdoers are in control. Thus Mr. David Sugarman stated:[122]

> Here then is a new exception to the rule in Foss v. Harbottle. Although it embraces "fraud on a minority" it is not so limited... in this sense, it comes close to giving effect to what has been called a *Justice* exception. This, however, is to express the ambit of the decision in traditional terms which minimise its innovative nature. The judgments are not defined by reference to the perimeter of directors' fiduciary duties nor to the "exceptions" to the rule in *Foss v. Harbottle*. In substance, a general right to litigate for corporate wrongs on behalf of the company is recognised. This cuts across both the scope of Directors' duties and the 'exceptions'. All 'exceptions' are subsumed into this more pontent derivative action.

Earlier on, he had stated "... in effect, therefore the breach by directors of their fiduciary duties has been elevated to one of the exceptions to the rule in *Foss v. Harbottle*"[123]. Professor Lord Wedderburn objected to this analysis in these terms:[124]

> But the earlier authorities establish that a derivative action can be brought only where the 'fraud' involved acts by directors or other controllers which either are *mala fide* or evince an expropriation of property, money or advantages belonging to the company. Mere breach of directors' fiduciary duty may not involve either of these.

This is obviously a very orthodox approach to Sugarman's contention and is an attempt to explain the derivative action in terms of well established criteria for its invocation and totally though, authoritatively, ignores Sugarman's appeal that *Wallersteiner v. Moir* (No.2) be seen not in a "traditional" perspective, but in an "innovative" light.

---

122 Note, (1975) 91 *L.Q.R.* 482, pp.484-485

123 *ibid* p.483

124 Wedderburn, Note: "Control of Corporate Litigation" (1976) 39 *M.L.R.*327, p.330, following *Burland v. Earle* [1902] A.C. 83,93 per Lord Davey.

Another attempt at seeing *Wallersteiner v. Moir* (No.2) in an innovative light as far as *Foss v. Harbottle* is concerned, is provided by Dr Daniel Prentice. While admitting that the Court of Appeal decision could be interpreted to have only dealt with the issue of costs and not one of standing, nevertheless he concludes that its effect was to introduce a new criterion (exception?) for determining standing irrespective of *Foss v. Harbottle*. Thus he states:[125]

> Although the judgment of the Court of Appeal in *Wallersteiner v. Moir* (No.2) has the hallmark of one that was carefully crafted, on one critical point it is far from clear. It could plausibly he argued that the court only dealt with the issue of costs and its decision has no bearing on the problem of the standing of a minority shareholder to commence an action, a point that went by default in *Wallersteiner v. Moir* (No.2) where no objection was raised to the standing of Mr. Moir to maintain the counterclaim. This reservation about the reach of the decision is strengthened by the fact that the breach of duty by Dr. Wallersteiner clearly fell within the fraud on the company exception to the rule in *Foss v. Harbottle*. In other words, would the indemnity procedure apply if the alleged wrong was manifestly ratifiable?

Having thus posed the question, Dr Prentice adds that[26] the language of the judgments in *Wallersteiner v. Moir* (No.2) "is capable of extension to cover both the issues of costs and that of standing and it is hard to imagine that the court did not have the latter issue squarely in mind in the light of the fact that *Foss v. Harbottle* and its progeny were cited to it". He concludes:[126]

> *if* this broader interpretation is given to the case, then the question of a shareholder's standing will not be dependent on the ratifiability of the wrong in question. *The question to be asked on any application is whether or not it is reasonable for the shareholder to commence the action.*

If that is the test to be gleaned from *Wallersteiner v. Moir* (No.2). Dr Prentice further contends[127] that test would *probably* be satisfied in all cases of directors' breach of duty except where the breach was trivial or *perhaps* where an independent board had decided not to take any action, or a meeting of independent shareholders had ratified the wrong. He concludes that "the result of this is that we now have a procedural mechanism for circumventing the rule in *Foss v. Harbottle* which enable a shareholder.... to bring a derivative action without first having to fit himself within the exceptions to the rule in *Foss v. Harbottle*".

That bold interpretation of *Wallersteiner v. Noir* has not gone uncriticised. Dr Rider[128] regards Dr Prentice's approach as merely an emphasis on the procedure suggested by the Court of Appeal as to how to assess the merits of a prospective shareholder action for purposes of indemnity. Accordingly, the

*Wallersteiner v. Moir* decision does not substantively alter the rule in *Foss v. Harbottle*. He concluded:[129]

> The Court of Appeal's observations on the law were thus concerned solely with the question of costs and not the standing of minority shareholders to assert derivative actions for wrongs committed against the company - therefore a minority shareholder to succeed in this

---

[125] D.D. Prentice, "*Wallersteiner v. Moir*: The Demise of the Rule in *Foss v. Harbotte*" (1976) 40 Conv. (N.S.) 51 at p.61.

[126] *ibid. Emphasis supplied*, presumably following Buckley L.J. [1975] 2 W.L.R. pp.407-408 when he said that the question is whether the action is one "which it would have been *reasonable* for an *independent* Board of Directors to bring in the Company's name" *(Emphasis supplied).*

[127] *ibid* p.63 *(Emphasis supplied).*

[128] B.A.K. Rider, "Amiable lunatics and the rule in" *Foss v. Harbottle*" [1987] 37 *C.L.J.*270, pp.280-281.

[129] *ibid* p.280

> action would still have to bring himself within one of the "exceptions" to the rule in *Foss v. Harbottle*.

Dr Rider's approach has a lot to commend it. Apart from its being possible to reconcile it with Dr. Prentice's views, which are qualified by some doubts,[130] it is quite clear that the major concern of *Wallerstainer v. Moir* No.2) was the question of indemnifying a shareholder who has brought a derivative action in respect of his costs. This view is held by Professor Boyle.[131] The Professor's major objection to the "innovatory" interpretations of *Wallersteiner v. Moir* by both Mr Sugarman and Dr Prentice is that "there is no discussion in any of the judgments in *Wallersteiner* (No.2) of the precise issue of *locus standi* whether in terms of established categories (i.e. the "exceptions", including the invocation of the 'justice' principle) or in terms of an alleged 'new principle'.[132] In this vein, the reference by Sugarman and Prentice to Lord Denning's discussion of the derivative action as supporting their thesis is also criticised in that to that extent that the discussion emphasised that a derivative action stems from a corporate cause of action, it was a necessary justification if not prelude for "the innovatory 'translation' to a company law context of a right of indemnity long known in the law of trusts (and also of agency). It is the familiar type of analogical reasoning which often produces important legal developments. The references to good faith (or honesty) and to the minority shareholder having reasonable ground to commence suit are obviously consequences of relying upon that analogy".[133]

Professor Boyle's second objection to Sugarman and Prentice is that "there is no evidence that it was the Court of Appeal's intention to engage upon a fundamental restatement of the *Foss v. Harbottle* rule as it impinges upon the breach of directors' duties.... The Court of Appeal, it might be surmised, may have thought that it had sufficient novel issues to settle in respect of the costs in derivative litigation without taking up the question of *locus standi,* when that was not an issue between the parties or necessary for the court's decision.".[134]

The views of Professor Boyle and Dr Rider, with which the present writer is in agreement, clearly show that where a wrong is done to the company in circumstances which would give rise to the right to institute a derivative action,[135] it is by no means easy to by-pass *Foss v. Harbottle.* In order to do so, one has to place himself within the four established "exceptions" to the majority shareholder rule in that case. Such a thesis is vindicated by the approach of the Chancery Division of the English High Court to the issue of *locus standi* in a derivative action; in *Daniels v. Daniels.*[136]

**(b) Daniels v. Daniels - an exception for negligence/breach of duty?**

In *Daniels v. Daniels,* the company sold land to the second defendant (who with the first defendant were majority shareholders and directors of the company) for GBP4,250 on the instructions of the first and second defendants as directors. Later the land was sold by the second defendant for GBP 120,000. The plaintiffs, who were minority shareholders brought an action against the defendants alleging that the land was sold to the second defendant at an undervalue. The defendants applied to strike out the action as not disclosing a reasonable cause of action as it did not allege fraud or any other cause justifying a minority shareholder action. Templeman J. (as he then was) held that the minority shareholder action was maintainable where "directors use

---

[130] *supra* notes 125-127 and accompanying text.

[131] A.J. Boyle, "Indemnifying the Minority Shareholder" [1967] *J.B.L.* 18, p.19, A.J. Boyle, "Minority Shareholders" suits for Breach of Directors' Duties" (1980) 1 *The Company Lawyer,* 3 pp.4-5.

[132] (1980) 1 p.4

[133] *ibid* p.5, following *Re Beddoe* [1893] 1 Ch.547,567 C.A.

[134] *ibid* p.5

[135] As unquestionably was the case in *Wallersteiner v. Moir* (No.1) [1974] 1 W.L.R. 991

[136] [1978] Ch.406

their powers intentionally or unintentionally, fraudulently or negligently in a *manner which benefits them at the expense of the company.* "[137]

This is the principle which Templeman J. "gleaned" from a careful analysis of earlier and pertinent cases. Two of those cases stand out as having clearly influenced the learned Judge. In *Alexander v. Automatic Telephone Co.*[138], the directors issued shares and required some people who took up the shares to make payments in respect of those shares, but the directors did not themselves make payments on the shares which they had taken up. A minority shareholders action was allowed and although fraud was discounted, the basis of the action was said to be "breach of duty". Lindley M.R. observed in this regard that "the charge is that the directors were guilty of a breach of duty in procuring those contracts and in taking advantage of them so as to benefit themselves at the expense of the shareholders."[139] He added that "directors who so use their powers as to obtain benefits to themselves at the expense of the shareholders, without informing them of the fact, cannot retain those benefits and must account for them to the company, so that all shareholders may participate in them".[140] This latter proposition is an exception to the *Foss v. Harbottle* rule allowing an individual shareholder to enforce his personal rights as shareholder. However, Lindley M.R. though that the breach of duty here also involved a wrong to the company which was derivatively actionable. He stated: [141]

> The breach of duty to the company consists in depriving it of the use of the money which the directors ought to have paid up sooner than they did. I cannot regard the case as one of mere internal management, which, according to *Foss v. Harbottle* and numerous other cases, the court leaves the shareholders to settle amongst themselves. It was ascertained and admitted at the trial that, when this action was commenced, the defendants held such a preponderance of shares that they could not be controlled by the other shareholders. Under these circumstances an action by some shareholders on behalf of themselves and the others against the defendants is in accordance with the authorities and is unobjectionable in form.

Professor Lord Wedderburn regards the *Alexander v. Automatic Telephone Co.* case [39] as providing the only real exception to *Foss v. Harbottle.* Thus he observed of it:[142]

> .....*Alexander's* case suggested that some breaches open to sanction by disclosure (and, therefore, one would have thought to ratification), allow for a minority action in spite of the Rule in *Foss v. Harbottle.* It is (this) proposition which is critical because, if it is correct, it is the only *real exception* to the Rule in *Foss v. Harbottle* which we have discovered; a case where the majority might ratify, yet the minority can sue."

The other outstanding case, upon which Templeman J. relied was *Cook v. Deeks*,[143] where the directors obtained for themselves a contract which should have gone to the company. Minority shareholders were allowed to sue, although fraud was not proved. In this regard, Lord Buckmaster L.C. thus postulated:[144]

---

137 *ibid*, p.414. *Emphasis supplied.*

138 [1900] 2Ch.56.

139 *ibid*, p.64.

140 *ibid*, pp.66-67.

141 *ibid*, p.69.

142 K.W. Wedderburn "Shareholders" and the Rule in *Foss v. Harbottle" Rights* [1958] *C.L.J.*93, 105-106. *his emphasis.*

143 [1916] A.C. 554 P.C.

144 *ibid*, p.563.

> ..... men who assume the complete control of a company's business must remember that they are not at liberty to sacrifice the interests which they are bound to protect, and, while ostensibly acting for the company, divert in their own favour business which should properly belong to the company they represent.

Consequently, it would appear that far from introducing a new exception of negligence or breach of duty by directors as entitling a minority shareholder action, notwithstanding *Foss v. Harbottle*, *Daniels v. Daniels* is carefully moulded into the "fraud on the minority" exception to *Foss v. Harbottle* as established by earlier cases. Professor, Lord Wedderburn subscribes to this view in yet another orthodox stance by saying that although the directors in *Daniels v. Daniels* were not alleged to be guilty of 'simple fraud' they were, on the facts alleged guilty of 'fraud' in the extended sense that allows for a minority shareholders' derivative action".[145] While reaching a similar conclusion, Professor Boyle, similar to his handling of *Wallersteiner v. Moir* (No.2) *(supra)* examines the Chancery Court's handling of the facts before it in the light of decided cases and concludes:[146]

> Templeman J.'s decision is valuable in clarifying the meaning of 'fraud in a minority' and restricting the scope of *Pavlides v. Jensen.*[147] The citation and handling of earlier cases is entirely orthodox...... The court's reasoning was clearly intended to be within the principles laid down by those courts, while taking advantage of the leeway they might allow in the way of further clarification. The facts alleged in the pleadings could well have led to the conclusion at a full hearing that the defendants had either misappropriated property belonging in equity to the company *(Cook v. Deeks)* or had acted in bad faith in exercising their power to sell the company's property *(Alexander v. Automatic Telephone Company)*.

The views of Professors Boyle and Wedderburn, which, it is submitted, correctly explain *Daniels v. Daniels* appear to be at variance with Dr Prentice's understanding of that case. Thus he says of it:[148]

> The net result of *Daniels v. Daniels* is that the rule in *Foss v. Harbottle* is confined to a very narrow compass to situations where a director's breach of duty does not result in any personal gain.

In essence, Dr Prentice thinks that "breaches of duty by directors constituting self-serving negligence are not ratifiable" and consequently a minority shareholder can sue in respect of such breaches. Dr Prentice tries to illustrate his point by reference to *Regal (Hastings) Ltd. v. Gulliver*[149] and Lord Russel's dictum that the general meeting could have ratified the director's acts in that case. He concludes that Lord Russel's dictum was "unfortunate" and a minority action would have been possible since the breach of duty in *Regal* was self-serving and therefore not ratifiable.

The first objection to Dr Prentice's thesis is that in *Daniels v. Daniels* Templeman J. explicitly rejected plaintiff's counsel's submission that a minority shareholder has a right to sue for any and every breach of director's fiduciary duty.[150] To the extent that the "secret profits" obtained

---

145 K.W. Wedderburn, Note "Minority Shareholders and Directors' Duties" (1978) 41 *M.L.R.* 569 at p.570 following *Burland v. Earle* [1902] A.C.83,93 per Lord Davey.

146 A.J. Boyle, *supra* n.131 at p.6, see also Rider *supra* n.127, pp.281-5.

147 [1956] Ch.655.

148 D.D. Prentice, "Self-serving Negligence and the Rule in *Foss v. Harbottle" (1979)* 43 Conv. (N.S.) 47,51; for contrary views see Boyle, *supra* n.131 pp.6-7.

149 [1942] 1 All E.R. 378,399.

150 *Supra* n.136, pp.409-414. Instead Templeman accepted,without reservation the established "four exceptions" to the rule in *Foss v. Harbottle* (p.408).

in the *Regal* Case amounted to a breach of duty by the directors to the company, *Daniels v. Daniels* has no relevance to that case. Secondly, Templeman J. in *Daniels* appears to think that there is a distinction between the position of a director who is merely negligent or foolish that he makes a profit and that of one whose negligence or foolishness results into his making a profit at the expense of the company. He stated in this regard. "To put up with foolish directors is one thing; to put up with directors who are so foolish that they make a profit of GBP 115,000 and at the expense of the company is something entirely different".[151] If that distinction is accepted then it clearly distinguishes the fact situation in *Daniels v. Daniels* from that in the *Regal* case. It was not alleged in *Regal* that the directors' conduct, though beneficial to the directors harmed the company as was the case in *Daniels*. If follows that while the directors' conduct in *Regal* was in Lord Russel's view, ratifiable, the same could not be said of the directors' conduct in *Daniels* as alleged.

It is therefore possible to conclude that *Daniels v. Daniels* does not create an additional "exception" to the rule in *Foss v. Harbottle* in terms of the directors' negligence or breaches of fiduciary duty. Templeman's unreserved acceptance from counsel of the four established "exceptions" to *Foss v. Harbottle* and then his careful examination of the cases mainly relevant to the fraud on the minority or company exception clearly support the view that *Daniels v. Daniels* is carefully moulded within the fourth exception to the rule in *Foss v. Harbottle*.

**(c) The minority shareholder's action and the appointment of a receiver**

A decision of Templeman J. (as he then was) in chambers, appears, in addition to the indemnity order under the *Wallersteiner v. Moir* case[152] and the extended amplification of the "fraud on the minority" exception to *Foss v. Harbottle*, in *Daniels v. Daniels*[153] to have provided "a new remedial weapon to the shareholders' armament".[154] In that case,[155] during the course of proceedings against the shareholders in control of the Board of Directors, whose alleged misconduct included breach of trust and fiduciary duties respectively, the Chancery Court appointed a receiver on an *ex parte* application. This appointment was confirmed subsequently before all the parties. The purpose of the appointment was to remove control of the company from the hands of the board from whom it could suffer additional harm. Secondly, the aim was to enable the parties to the proceedings to get factual information about the past conduct and affairs of the company. It is apparent that Templeman J. indicated that "the Receiver had power, if he so wished, to conduct an investigation into the past affairs of the company."[156] In fact there was an accumulation of powers as the receiver's legal advisers kept going back to the court for directions.

As Professor Boyle has noted,[55] a "*Wallersteiner* order" (respecting indemnity for costs to a minority shareholder plaintiff) can be combined with an appointment of a receiver, He adds:[55]

> The interesting development does not appear to conflict with earlier authority. It assumes that, where a derivative action is properly brought by exception to the *Foss v. Harbottle* rule, one interlocutory remedy available to the court is the appointment of a receiver to safeguard the assets (and accounting records) of a company whose affairs it is alleged are continuing to be mismanaged. One of the great problems of minority shareholders is inequality of access to information in respect of the company's affairs. This can be a serious problem as inequality of

---

151 *ibid*, p.414.

152 *supra* n.109.

153 *supra* n.136.

154 A.J, Boyle, supra n.131, (1980) 1 *Co. Lawyer* 3,7, See also *Dipcharima v. Bornu Holding Co. Ltd.* 1989 NCLR 322, 325-326 (High Court of Nigeria).

155 In the Matter of *Company Developments Limited*, "Unreported (Chancery Division), 14 June, 1978.

156 Messrs. Coward Chance to Professor Boyle, letter: 18 July, 1979 p.2.

> financial resources. Without the difficulty and delay usually experienced in obtaining a Department of Trade inspection, the company's affairs may be put into the hands of a neutral professional man answerable to the Court. Clearly, such an application must be based on a fairly strong *prima facie* case of misconduct by the board of directors.

The scheme thus sanctioned by Templeman J. provides the minority shareholder in a derivative action with additional support in his corporate cause.

**(d) A statutory derivative action?**

There have been calls for a statutory derivative action in Britain, drawing "upon the Commonwealth experience of Statutory reform of the derivative action, as well as the rich experience of the uses and abuses of derivative suits which the American case law and reforming legislation provide.[157] This would be in addition to the Jenkins Committee proposals.[158] which, apart from being dated, are thought to be inadequate[58]. The latest effort towards introducing the derivative action in statutory form in Britain appears from the British Companies Act, 1985[159]. It is there provided:

> (1) Any member of a company may apply to the court by petition for an order under this section on the ground that the affairs of the company are being conducted in a manner which is unfairly prejudicial to the interests of some part of the members (including at least himself) or that any actual or proposed act or omission of the company (including an act or omission on its behalf) is or would be prejudicial.
>
> ....
>
> (3) If the court is satisfied that a petition under this section is well founded it may make such order as it thinks fit for giving relief in respect of the matters complained of.
>
> (4) Without prejudice to the generality of sub-section (3) above, an order under this section may:
>
> (a) regulate the conduct of the company's affairs in the future;
>
> (b) require the company to refrain form doing or continuing an act complained of by the petitioner or to do an act which the petitioner has complained it has omitted to do;
>
> (c) authorise civil proceedings to be brought in the name and on behalf of the company by such person or persons or on such terms as the court may direct.

This provision expressly reforms Section 210[160] of the Companies Act, 1948.[161] The introduction of a minority statutory action as an "appendage" to this provision is criticised in that though much more liberally expressed in comparison to the provision it replaces, it will not be as satisfactory, "as a general reform of the derivative action as a specific remedy for corporate abuse (as opposed to minority oppression)". Professor Boyle adds in this vein:[162]

> In large public companies there may well be serious abuses which do not on any realistic economic calculus, 'unfairly prejudice' any of the members - the market value of whose shares may well not be affected by the proceeds of a possible action against self-dealing directors.

Apart from that general objection, the section does not deal with the procedural aspects (including any incorporation of the right of indemnity and possibly the appointment of a receiver), relating

---

157 Boyle, *supra* n.131; See also A.J. Boyle, The Derivative Action in Company Law [1969] *J.B.L.* 120-127

158 *Report of the Company Law Committee* (1962) Cmnd 1749 para 212(e).

159 Ss 459-461.

160 identical to Companies Act, s.211 Uganda.

161 Companies Act, 1980 (UK), S.75(11).

162 Boyle, *supra* n.131 at p.8.

to the institution of a derivative action. Much more pertinent in this regard are the conditions under which a court would allow a derivative action; whether questions of ratification of the wrong complained of would be canvassed by the court and lastly whether in view of the *Wallersteiner* proceedings, it would be possible for an *ex parte* application to be made by the minority shareholder seeking leave to bring a derivative action. It may be contended though, that the wide discretion given to the court in section 461 may be sufficient to cover these matters. Many of these hypothetical questions relating to the introduction of a statutory derivative action in Britain seem to have found some answers in Canadian Legislation which attempted to introduce a statutory derivative action and thereby circumvent most of the procedural and substantive difficulties arising from the rule in *Foss v. Harbottle.*[163]

In British Columbia, a member or director, subject to four qualifications, may, with the leave of the Court, bring or defend an action in its name and on behalf of the company. The action may be brought to enforce a right, duty or obligation owed to the company that could be enforced by the company itself or to obtain damages for any breach of any such right, duty or obligation. The four qualifications are that (i) he has made reasonable efforts to cause the directors of the company to commence or diligently prosecute or defend the action; (ii) he is acting in good faith; (iii) it is *prima facie* in the interests of the company that the action be brought or defended; and (iv) in the case of a member, that he was a member of the company at the time of the transaction or other event giving rise to the cause of action.[164]

In the course of such proceedings, the court may give directions for the conduct of the action and order that the company pay the interim costs of the persons controlling the conduct of the action. Additionally, no action brought or defended under section 225[65] can be discontinued, settled or dismissed without the approval of the court. S.225(7), while providing that the possibility of ratification by the majority shareholders in general meeting, of the wrong complained of, is not a bar to the derivative action, nonetheless stipulates that "evidence of that approval or possible approval may be taken into account by the court in making an order under this section."

Under Section 99 of the Ontario Business Corporations Act, a shareholder, subject to the same four qualifications as those under section 225 of the British Columbia Act, may, with leave "maintain an action in a representative capacity for himself and all other shareholders of the corporation suing for and on behalf of the corporation to enforce any right, duty or obligation owed to the corporation.... or obtain damages for any breach of any such duty or obligation." The Court may also order interim costs to be paid to the plaintiff, and, upon final disposition, costs may be awarded and taxed as between a solicitor and his client. In addition, the court must approve any discontinuance, settlement or dismissal of the action for want of prosecution and may order that notice be sent to the shareholders or any class thereof if they may be substantially affected by the discontinuance, settlement or dismissal. The section does not allude to the effect of an actual or potential shareholders' ratification of the alleged misconduct.

The Canada Federal Act[165] provides that a "complainant" who is defined[166] to include "(a) a registered holder or beneficial owner of a former registered holder or beneficial owner of a security of a corporation or any of its affiliates, (b) a director or an officer or a former director or officer, (c) the Director or (d) any other person who, in the discretion of a court, is a proper person to make an application, may, subject to the same first three qualifications specified in the British Columbia

---

[163] See generally F. Iacobucci *et al, Canadian Business Corporations: An analysis of recent Legislative Developments* (Law Book Limited, Canada 1977) pp. 191-210, Beck, (1974) *Can Bar Rev.* pp.196-207.

[164] S.225 British Columbia *Companies Act.* 1979; see also S.99 *Ontario Business Corporation Act,* 1970 Cap.53. For a comparison with the United States in regard to contemporaneous ownership see P.P. Herbrect, "The Contemporaneous Ownership Rule in Shareholders' Derivative Suits" (1978) 25 *UCLA L.Rev.* 1041-66.

[165] *Canada Business Corporations Act,* 1974-1976, C.33, S.232,233 and 235.

[166] S.231 ibid.

and Ontario Acts but not the fourth with leave, "bring an action in the name and on behalf of a corporation or any of its subsidiaries or intervene in any action to which any such body corporate is a party, for the purpose of prosecuting, defending or discontinuing the action on behalf of the body corporate".

In regard to the derivative proceedings, the court may, "at any time make...... (a) an order authorising the complainant or any person to control the conduct of the action. (b) an order giving directions for the conduct of the action, (c) an order directing that any amount payable by a defendant in the action shall be paid in whole or in part, directly to former and present security shareholders of the corporation or its subsidiary instead of the corporation or its subsidiary (d) an order requiring the corporation or its subsidiary to pay reasonable legal fees incurred by the complainant in connection with the action."

The Federal Act also contains a provision to the effect of Section 225(7) of the British Columbia *Companies Act*[167] on the non-conclusiveness of shareholder approval. The major differences between the Federal and British Columbia provisions when compared to the Ontario Act are firstly that the former provisions make the derivative action available to a wider class of persons than just shareholders. Secondly, the action may be used to defend an action or bring one in the name of and on behalf of the company. Thirdly, the former provisions indicate that shareholder ratification of the wrong complained of is not conclusive of the merits of bringing the derivative action.

There are further features which distinguish the Federal provisions from those of the Ontario and British Columbia Acts. In regard to the former, the derivative action is available to "complainants" rather than just shareholders or directors, and is extended to subsidiaries of the corporation. In addition, the complainant, if a shareholder need not to have been a shareholder of the company at the time of the transaction or event militating the cause of action. The application for leave to institute a derivative action is available for purposes of institution, defending or intervening in any action to which the company is a party. Furthermore, the complainant is not required to give security for costs. Lastly, the court may order the amount recovered by way of damages to be paid directly to former or existing shareholders.

While in procedural terms, this Canadian legislation seriously attempts to circumvent *Foss v. Harbottle,* it is notable that it does not "provide the courts with directions as to the circumstances in which leave may be granted" to institute a derivative action,[168] and leaves a lot of discretion to the courts which may result into the courts making management decisions for the company contrary to the proscription in *Shuttleworth v. Cox Bros & Co. Maidenhead Ltd.*[169] At the other extreme, the courts could continue to work within the framework of the four exceptions to the rule in *Foss v. Harbottle,* thus effectually defeating the derivative action legislation. This danger is not merely conjectural. In *Goldex Mines v. Revill*[170] Haines J. expressed the view that section 99 of the Ontario *Business Corporations Act* should not be taken as exhaustive of the right to bring a derivative action. He stated:[171]

> It would seem more appropriate to apply the rule of statutory construction that common law rights are not held to have been taken away or affected by a statute unless it is so expressed in clear language or must follow by necessary implication.

[167] *ibid,* S.235(1).

[168] F. Iacobucci; *et al,* n.163, p.199.

[169] [1927] 2 K.B.9 at p.23. In certain circumstances, as in Templeman J.'s decision, *supra* n.155 this is not bad thing; now see too sub-s 75 4(a) British Companies Act, 1980.

[170] [1973] 10. R. 659.

[171] *ibid,* at p.680.

This approach was not approved by the Ontario Court of Appeal in *Farnham v. Fingold*[172] where Jessup J.A. held that section 99 had abrogated the common law right to bring a derivative action and was exhaustive of situations when such an action may be instituted. He stated:[173]

> The very broad language of S.99(1) embraces all causes of action under any statute or in law or in equity, that a shareholder may sue for or on behalf of a corporation. All forms of derivative actions.... come within it and therefore s-s (2) applies to all such situations.

If Jessup J.A.'s approach is to be followed, then allowance of a derivative action must be properly developed within the legislation providing for it. To that extent, recourse to the exceptions to the *Foss v. Harbottle* rule is proscribed. An express instances of this appears in S.225(7) of the British Columbia Companies Act and S.235(1) of the Federal Act relating to the non-conclusiveness of shareholder ratification of the wrong complained of, for purposes of the court giving leave for a derivative action to be brought.

It is lastly notable that the Canadian legislation relating to the derivative action is largely modelled on Rule 23(1) of the United States Federal Rules of Civil Procedure.[174] Furthermore, it is in many respects an improvement on similar efforts attempted elsewhere in the Commonwealth.[175] The attempts at serious legislative provision for corporate derivative action in the United Kingdom and Nigeria will, therefore, have to take account of those North American developments. It is conceded that the *Wallersteiner* indemnity provision for a derivative litigant and the appointment of a receiver in the unreported Chancery Court decision by Templeman J.(as he then was)[56] are indicators, albeit tentative, in that direction. However, as Professor Boyle has been at pains to point out,[176] judicial innovation in this area tends to be piecemeal and has sometimes produced "false starts". The solution would appear to be for the legislature to explicitly create the derivative action along the lines of United States, Canadian and Ghanaian relevant legislation, subject of course to refinements which take account of the shortcomings of those provisions.

**(e) The alternative remedy to winding up under Section 211**[77a]

Section 211 of the Companies Act,[177] arose out of the need to redress the imbalance between majority shareholder control and minority shareholders rights within the corporate structure.[178] This development was especially significant given the Courts' reluctance to interfere into the affairs of the company. Early this century Lord Davey had thus stated:[179]

---

[172] [1973] 2 O.R. 132 C.A.

[173] *ibid* p.135; see also *Goldex Mines Ltd. v. Revill* [1973] 30 R.869, 875-877 where Haines J. *(supra* n.171) was overruled.

[174] 23 U.S.C.A. Rule 23.1; See also P.P. Herbrect, *op.cit. supra* n.65

[175] S.210 *Ghana Companies Code, 1963*; see also Boyle *supra* n.58, (1969) *J.B.L.*120,123-127, comparing the Code with the then Ontario Bill, 125.

[176] Boyle, *supra* n.131.

[77a]See also Bakibinga, *Ogun State Univ. L.J. Vol.1 pp.1-22 (1990)*

[177] Companies Act identical to S.210 Companies Act, 1948 (UK). Now replaced by Companies Act 1980, S.75 (U.K.).

[178] It first appeared as S.9 of the 1947 English Companies Act, 10 & 11 Geo C.47. See also *British Columbia Companies Act*, 1960. C.67, S.185; *Ghana Companies Code*, S.218; *Malaysian Companies Act*. 1965, S.181; *N.Ireland Companies Act*, 1960, S.201(3); *New Zealand Companies Act*, S.209; *South Carolina Code* S.12-22, 23(a) (Supp.1960); *Uniform Companies Act of Australia*, S.186; for a useful analysis see A.B. Afterman, *Company Directors & Controllers* (Australia, 1970) Chap.4.

[179] *Burland v. Earle* [1902] A.C. 83, 93, following *Foss v. Harbottle*(1843) 2 Hare 461; and more recently *Howard Smith Ltd. v. Ampol Ltd.* [1974] A.C. 821, P.C. p.832: "There is no appeal on merits from management decisions to courts of law; nor will courts of law assume to act as a kind of supervisory board over decisions within powers of management, honestly arrived at".

> It is an elementary principle of the law relating to joint stock companies, that the court wili not interfere with the internal management of Companies acting within their powers and in fact has no jurisdiction to do so.

The resultant disregard of minority shareholder interests and rights was recognised by the Cohen Committee which proposed a legislative remedy for the minority shareholders[180]. The committee's recommendations subsequently became Section 210 of the British 1948 Act. The section essentially gives relief to a petitioner who is a member of the Company; and shows that (i) the Company's affairs are being conducted in a manner oppressive to some apart of the members (including himself); (ii) the facts of the situation would justify the winding-up of the company on the grounds that this would be just and equitable; (iii) to wind-up the company would unfairly prejudice the oppressed members. It is apparent in this regard that the petitioners may be majority shareholders, though lacking voting control.[181] Once the above allegations have been proved, "the court may, with a view to bringing to an end the matters complained of, make such order as it thinks fit".[182]

How effective then has Section 211 been? The first question in relation to the requirement that the petitioner must be a member of the company is whether a trustee in bankruptcy or personal representative of a bankrupt or deceased member would have *locus standi* under the section. In *Re Jermyn Street Turkish Baths Ltd.*[183], the petitioners were the personal representatives of a former shareholder in the company. Pennyquick J. held on the facts that the petitioners had in fact become registered as members and therefore their status was not in dispute. However, and by way of *obiter* the judge indicated that he would have held that even without registration, the petitioners were entitled to present the petition.[184] This view is criticised by Rajak[185] for being inconsistent with Section 28(2) of the Companies Act, which limits membership to "every other person [than subscribers to the memorandum] who agrees to become a member of a company and whose name is entered in its register of members". In addition, Rajak thinks that Section 353 (Section 343 Uganda Act) upon which Pennycuick J. relied is "procedural". He adds in this vein:

> whilst it is true that successfully to invoke subsection (6) the petitioner must feel aggrieved, he need only show that at the time the Company was stuck off it was carrying on business or in operation or otherwise that it would be just that the company be restored to the register.... any connection between the deregistered company and the petitioner is virtually irrelevant. With petitions under Section [211], however, the connection between the company and the petitioner is of the essence of the petition, both as regards the capacity of the petitioner and the effect on him of the company's behaviour.

Apart from this objection to Penncuick J., there has been judicial departure elsewhere in the Commonwealth from his view.[186] The Jenkins Committee,[187] was also doubtful whether the

---

180 *Report of the Committee on Company Law Amendment* (1945) Cmnd 6659 para 60

181 *Re: H.R.Harmer ltd.* [1959] 1.W.L.R. 62.

182 S.211(2), Companies Act (Uganda).

183 [1970] 1.W.L.R. 1194.

184 *ibid* p.1205, following S.353(6) Companies Act 1948 (Section 343 Uganda Act) which stipulates that "if a company or any member or creditor thereof feels aggrieved by (a) Company having been struck off the register [of Companies]..." he may petition for the restoration of the Company to the register. In *Re: Bayswater Trading Co. ltd.* [1970] 1.W.L.R.343, it was held that "member" in S.353(6) included representatives of the deceased member. See also *Politis v. Okudzeto* 1967(3) ALR Comm 178, 207

185 H. Rajak, "Oppression of Minority Shareholders" (1972) 35 *M.L.R.*156,158.

186 *Re Meyer Douglas Pty Ltd.* [1965] V.R. 638, 654-655.

187 *Report of the Company Law Committee* (Cmnd 1749) (1962).

88a *ibid*, para. 209.

category of persons who might present a petition under section 211 included personal representatives or trustees in bankruptcy[88a] and recommended that Section 211 be extended to include "legal personal representatives and others to whom shares are transmitted by process of law".[188]

The other difficulty about Section 211 is the requirement that a petitioner thereunder must show that he is being oppressed *qua* member. Although this is not explicitly stated, this requirement has wide acceptance.[189] In H. Rajak's view[190]

> [the] effect of interpreting section [211] subject to a requirement that oppression must be suffered *qua* member has been to limit the occasions on which the court has been required to consider whether 'the affairs of the company are being conducted in a manner oppressive to some part of the members'. The focus of the section has been shifted away from oppression towards a more manageable factual inquiry, undermining in the process the intention of the Cohen Committee that the new section should 'strengthen the minority shareholders of a small company'[191]

In *Re: Nakivubo Chemists (U) Ltd,*[191a], it was held that for a petitioner to succeed under Section 211 of the Companies Act, he must show not only that there has been oppression of the minority shareholders of a company but also that it has been the affairs of the company which have been conducted in an oppressive manner. The oppression must be to a person in his capacity as a shareholder and not in any other capacity. In this case, the removal of the petitioner form his post of Executive Director did not amount to oppression within the meaning of Section 211 of the Companies Act.

A further condition of Section 211(2)(b), viz., that the petitioner must show facts which would justify the winding up of the Company on the grounds that this would be just and equitable was recommended by the Jenkins Committee for repeal.[192] It is this additional technical condition which led to the failure of the petition in *Re: Bellador Silk Ltd.*[193] In that case, the petitioner under Section [211] failed to satisfy the just and equitable winding up requirement because in the light of evidence that the company may have been insolvent, he could not show that he had a tangible interest in the winding up.

Another difficulty about Section 211 was how to determine when the conduct pleaded by the petitioner was "oppressive". Lord Keith in *Elder v. Elder & Watson*[90] thought that oppressive conduct involved "an element of lack of probity and fair dealing"[194], while Lord Cooper in the same case suggested that it was conduct which amounted to "a visible departure from the standards of fair dealing and a violation of the conditions of fair play.[195] Viscount Simmonds, on the other

---

188 *ibid,* para 212(f):

189 *Elder v. Elder & Watson Ltd.* 1952 S.C. 49 at p.57; *Re: Lundie Brothers Ltd.* [1965] I.W.L.R. 1050, 1058; *Re: H.R. Harmer* [1959] 1.W.L.R. 62, 83. For Canada *Re: B.C. Aircraft Propeller &Engine Co. Ltd.* (1968) 66 D.L.R. (2d) 628, 639; Australia: *Re: Associated Tool Industries Ltd.* [1964] A.L.R. 73, 81 and *Re: Broadcasting Station* 2 G.B. [1964-65] N.S.W.R. 1648-1652; *Ebrahimi v. Westbourne Galleries Ltd.* [1972] 2 W.L.R. 1289 at pp.1293, 1303; Nigeria: *Ogunade v. Mobile Films* (W.A.) 2 F.R.C.R.101, 104.

190 *Supra* n.86 at p.160; see also Gower, *Company Law* (4th Ed. 1979) p.669

191 See *supra* n.180.

191a [1977] HCB 312 (Manyindo, J.).

192 *Supra* n.88, para 212(a): the Australian Provision (*supra* n.178) does not place this condition on the petition. See also *Re: Nakivubo Chemists supra.*

193 [1965] 1 All E.R. 669; see also the Ugandan case, *Mitha v. Mitha* [1967] E.A. 575 where a petition failed on this ground. See also *Cole v. Irving & Co. Ltd.* 1970 NCLR 472 where a S.[211] action was recommended in place of winding up petition. *Re: Italcomm (W.Nig.) Ltd.* 1972 NCLR 293.

194 *Supra* n.189 at p.60; see too the earlier remark by Lord Shaw in *Loch v. Blackwood* [1924] A.C. 783, *788.*

hand, six years later, adopted the dictionary meaning of "burdensome, harsh and wrongful".[196] The limited effect of such explanations of "oppressive" (conduct) has been recognised chiefly because of their generality.[197] Rajak appears to think that a meaningful appreciation of "oppressive" conduct is reached by drawing a connection between the conduct complained of and the valid exercise of power by the majority in general meeting. In his words: [198]

> The tension in the law is created, it is submitted, by the democratic process which *ex hypothesi* implies the existence of dissenting minority, whose reasons for dissent may be sensible and valid. The lot of the minority is not merely that others have expressed a different view but that it is required to embrace that view. Yet to allow otherwise constitutes the radical step of flouting the majority vote, made all the more grave by the fact that it is taken by a judiciary with a self-professed ignorance in matters of business. It can therefore be appreciated that very strong justification is necessary for oppression *de facto* to be declared to be oppression *dejure.* It is at that point that conduct becomes 'harsh', burdensome and wrongful' or contains 'an element of lack of probity and fair dealing' or constitutes 'a visible departure form the standards of fair play' or in short 'oppressive

It is that kind of problem, which, it is submitted, arose in the decision by Foster J. at first instance in *Clemens v. Clemens Bros. Ltd.*[199]. In that case, a minority shareholder successfully sued the company and its directors or prevent the majority shareholder from increasing the capital of the company by means of a scheme which would have increased the voting control of the directors as against the minority shareholder, plaintiff, whose "negative control" was thereby reduced. Although perfectly legitimate, the majority shareholder's exercise of her legal rights was judged to be subject to "equitable considerations".[200] Apart from the criticism that Foster J.'s application of the *dicta* in *Ebrahimi*[2] was "strictly obiter in relation to *Clemens*"[201], Foster J.'s decision appears to rest on the supposition that the aunt's conduct in Clemens was "oppressive". It has, however, been held that oppressive conduct is a ground for relief if it is sufficient to demonstrate absence of *bona fides.*[202] In this vein, Mr Joffe thus observed of Foster J.'s approach:[203]

> In view of Foster J.'s conviction that the aunt genuinely desired to bring about the proposed scheme, and the marked reluctance of the Courts, in the absence of

---

195 *ibid,* p.55.

196 *Scottish Co-operative Wholesale Society Ltd v. Meyer* [1958] 3 All E.R. 66, 71; [1959] A.C.324, 342; for another judicial attempt at defining "oppressive" see per Bowen C.J. in *Re Cumberland Holdings Ltd.* (1974-1976) A.C.L.R. 361, 376; "The word 'oppressive' in its context here means 'burdensome, harsh and wrongful'. it refers to action which unfairly and adversely affect one or more members in a proprietary sense in their capacity as members and is commonly found where there is shown some lack of probity in the conduct of the company's affairs.... The case where directors of a company are also directors of another company which is a subsidiary requires special mention. It is clear that unfair or unjust action (or, for that matter, inaction) taken in the interests of the parent and against the interests of the subsidiary and its other shareholders in relation to its trade and business operations may fall within this section..." See also *Ogunade v. Mobile Films (W.A.) Ltd., supra* n.189.

197 *Re: Broadcasting Station 2 G.B. Pty. Ltd.* [1964-65] N.S.W.R. 1648, 1662 per Jacobs J: "the further question arises of determining what conduct falls within the ambit of the word or words used, whether it be the word 'oppressive' as used in the section itself or the words used in the synonyms suggested in the cases to which I have referred. What is 'fair dealing' which a member is entitled to expect? When is conduct 'wrongful' or lacking in probity?"

198 Rajak, *supra* n.185 at pp.162-163.

199 [1976] 2 All E.R. 268.

200 Following Lord Wilberforce's dictum in *Ebrahimi v. Westbourne Galleries [1973] A.C.360*

201 Victor Joffe, Note (1977) 40 *M.L.R.*71,73.

202 *Shuttleworth v. Cox Bros. & Co. (Maidenhead) Ltd.* [1927] 2 K.B.9.

> mala fides, to grant relief in respect of conduct such as that complained of in this case, the reliance placed on this ground seems dubious.[204]

In any event, the *ratio decidendi* of *Clemens* is not clear.[205]

It may be chiefly the difficulty of establishing "oppressive" conduct under Section 211 which led to only three reported decisions in the United Kingdom succeeding in establishing "oppressive conduct"[206] In *S.C.W.S. v. Meyer*[206] the two petitioners were Managing Directors and minority shareholders of a subsidiary company formed by the co-operative society to enable it to expand into the rayon industry. Afterwards, the necessity to work through a separate company ceased and the society, through its nominee directors and otherwise employed a deliberate policy of running down the subsidiary's business with the result that its shares lost all value. The House of Lords, in confirming the decisions of the court of Sessions, upheld the petitioners' claim and the society was ordered to buy out the two minority shareholders. In *Re: H.R. Harmer Ltd.*[206] on the other hand, the founder of the company and his sons were life directors. Subsequently, the sons became majority shareholders, but their father the founder and his wife, had voting control. The father ran the business in total disregard of the wishes of his fellow shareholders and co-directors and the resolutions of the board. He claimed he was entitled to do this. Consequently, and as a result of his autocratic and unbusiness like behaviour, it became impossible for the company to be carried on successfully. Roxburgh J. held this to constitute oppressive conduct and was affirmed by the Court of Appeal.

In *Re: Jermyn Street Turkish Baths Ltd.*[207] the petitioners were the personal representatives of a deceased person, who, together with the first respondent were directors and equal shareholders of the company until the deceased's death. Afterwards the first respondent and two other directors (including her son) greatly improved the state of the company in terms of its assets over liabilities. In so doing, however, they committed a number of irregularities. The first was that a further 100 shares were issued to the respondent for the purpose of giving her a 75 per cent shareholding. Second, a resolution and bonuses to the directors was not ratified in general meeting, as was required and was therefore invalid. Third, an amount of GBP 2,936 owing by the company to the deceased's estate was cancelled from the books and lastly the company from 1954 onwards failed to give notice of meetings to the petitioners (adjudged by the court to be members of the company).

In drawing a connection between the above irregularities on the one hand, and the fact that excessive payments were made by the company by way of remuneration to the directors and management fees to a company in which the first respondent held 75 per cent of the shares and one other director had an interest, Pennycuick J. found that there was oppression.[207] The Court of Appeal disagreed with this reasoning[208] indicating that there was no link between the resolution

---

203 *supra* n.201.

204 See e.g. *Sidebottom v. Kershaw Leese & Co.* [1920] 1 Ch.154; *Greenhalgh v. Ardenne Dinemas Ltd.* [1951] 1 Ch.286.

205 See Joffe, *supra* n.201 at p.74; G.R. Sullivan, *"Protection of the Minority Shareholder: Another Advance"* (1977) Conv. (N.S.) 169, 178.

206 *S.C.W.S.Ltd. v. Meyer & Another, supra* n.97; *Re H.R. Harmer Ltd.* [1959] 1.W.L.R.62: *Re Jermyn Street Turkish Baths Ltd.* [1970] 1.W.L.R. 1194 was reversed on appeal: [1971] 1.W.L.R.1042. For comments on the *Meyer Case* see K.W. Wedderburn. [1958] *Camb L.J.1* 52; L.C.8. Gower (1958) 21 *M.L.R.*340: For comments on *Re: H.R.Harmer* see K.W. Wedderburn (1959) *Camb. L.J.* 37, P.Ford (1959) 22 *M.L.R.* 340: For a relatively detailed analysis of *Re: Jermyn Street Turkish Bath Ltd.* See Rajak, *supra* n.86, pp.163-166. *Cumberland Holdings Ltd. v. Washington H. Soul Pattinson & Co. Ltd.* (1977) 13 A.L.R.561: oppression was found by Bowen, C.J. in the New South Wales Supreme Court, but he was reversed by the Privy Council on appeal. See also (1976-1977) 2 A.C.L.R.307-319; see too in this regard, the Ugandan case, *Mitha v. Mitha* [1967] E.A.575: Russel J. held that the petitioners' complaint (under S.211 of the Companies Act, Cap.85 Uganda) that the principles of fair management were being deliberately and consistently violated did not constitute oppression. See further *Ogunade v. Mobile Films (W.A.) Ltd. supra* n.189.

207 [1970] 1.W.L.R.1194, 1207.

authorising the issue of shares (which did not amount to oppression), on the one hand, and on the other the authorization of excessive remuneration. In consequence the plea of oppression by the petitioners failed on appeal. The Appeal Court also found that the other irregularities did not amount to oppression and even if they did (as in the case of excessive remuneration), the petitioners could still not succeed under Section [211] as it could not be shown to be just and equitable to wind up the company.

In *Re: Westbourne Galleries Ltd.*[209] the petitioner, Nazar and Nazar's son were the sole shareholders and directors of the company. A resolution was passed, pursuant to section 184 of the 1948 (Section 185 Uganda Companies Act,) Companies Act and the Company's Articles, removing the petitioner from the Board of Directors. The court at first instance refused relief under Section [211]. The petitioner contended that he was oppressed in four instances. First, was his removal as a director. This could ground a winding up order (although not accepted by the Court of Appeal). However, if it constituted "oppression" this was oppression *qua* director rather than *qua* member. The second allegation was that Nazar sold carpets to the company at inflated prices. This was not proved; so was the third that the company was formed to subsidise Nazar's enterprises. The last allegation that Nazar failed to honour an agreement to sell the lease of certain premises owned by the company and which sale would have been in the company's interest was proved, but being an isolated incident was not sufficient to constitute oppression within Section [211].

Both *Re: Jermyn Street Turkish Baths Ltd.*[206] and *Westbourne Galleries*[209] buttressed the restrictive interpretation given by the Courts to section [211], which was most prominent in *Re: Five Minute Car Wash Service Ltd.*[210], where fifteen allegations of inefficiency and had management against a managing director, even if proved, were judged not to constitute "oppression". Thus Buckley J. stated:[211]

> The mere fact that a member of a company has lost confidence in the manner in which the company's affairs are conducted does not lead to the conclusion that he is oppressed: nor can resentment at being out-voted, nor mere dissatisfaction with or disapproval of the conduct of the company's affairs whether on grounds relating to policy or to inefficiency, however well founded.

However in *Re Nakivubo Chemists (U) Ltd.*[211a], a petition was brought under Section 211 of the Companies Act. The petitioner claimed that the affairs of the company had been carried out in an oppressive manner and that he had been oppressed by the majority namely Dr Rwanyarare and Rukuhikire and that Rwanyarare had acquired controlling shares by fraud leading to deterioration of relations between Rwanyarare and himself. It was held *inter alia* that the petitioner was and remained both a shareholder and a director in the company and it was illegal for Dr Rwanyarare to purport to take away the petitioner's shares and to remove him from his office of ordinary director for non-payment of Dr Rwanyarare's loan. Dr Rwanyarare's illegal act clearly amounted to oppression to the petitioner as a shareholder. The petitioner had also been oppressed by the majority in that he had not been allowed to attend any company meeting as shareholder since 1974 and had been excluded from all participation in the management of the company.

---

208 1971] 1.W.L.R.p.1058.

209 [1970] 1.W.L.R.1378. For comments thereon see H. Leigh, Note "Just & Equitable Winding up" (1972) 88 *Law.Q. Rev.* 268-472. M.Chesterman "The 'Just & Equitable' Winding Up of Small Companies" (1973) 36 *M.L.R.* 129-152; D.D. Prentice "Winding Up: the Parternship Analogy" (1973) 89 *Law.Q. Rev.*101-125; B.V. Slutsky, Note (1977) 11 *U.British Columbia L. Rev.* 326, 33033; See also *Ogunade v. Mobile Films* (W.A.) Ltd. supra n.189, on consistent pattern of oppression as prerequisite for grant of the remedy under S.[211].

210 [1966] 1.W.L.R. 745; see also *Ogunade v. Mobile Films (W.A.) Ltd. supra* n.189.

211 *ibid,* at p.751. See also the Ugandan case *Re Eryeza Bwambale & Co. Ltd.* [1969] E.A. 430 where it was held that outvoting minority shareholders is not evidence of oppression.

211a *supra* n.191a.

However, the court declined to order the winding up of the company as this would be prejudicial.

The resultant inert, ineffective or rusty nature of Section 211[212] is thus evident from the above brief review of its history and operation. The only aspect of it which has not been restrictive has been the requirement upon the petitioner to show that he will be "unfairly prejudiced" if a winding-up order were actually made.[213]

The way for reform of Section 210 of the British Act of 1948 was pointed out by the Jerkins Committee.[214]

## The Jenkins Committee recommendations

The committee firstly proposed that the reference to winding-up in Section [211(2)(b)] should be repealed.[215] Second, that the section should be amended to show that it covers isolated acts as well as course of conduct.[216] Third, the term oppression was regarded as too strong and it should be made clear that the section extended to cases where the affairs of the company are being conducted in a manner unfairly prejudicial to the interests of some or part of the members and not merely in an oppressive manner.[217] Fourth, personal representatives and others to whom shares were transmitted by process of law but who were not registered as members should be allowed to present a petition under the section.[218] Lastly, it was recommended that provision be made to enable the Court to restrain the commission or continuance of any act which would suffice to support a petition under the section and to confer upon the Court the express power to authorise the bringing of proceedings in the name of the company against any third party.[219]

## Section 459, 1985 Companies Act (Britain)

The above recommendations were accepted by the British Conservative Government and appeared in the lapsed Companies Bill of 1973.[220] They were also accepted by the Labour Administration and appeared again in the lapsed Companies Bill of 1978[221] before being enacted as Section 75 of the British Companies Act, 1980. (Ss.459-462 Companies Act 1985 U.K.)

Section 75 does not, however, go far enough in so far as a petitioner can only have *locus standi* in his capacity as a member and not in some other capacity. In the words of Mr Nigel Bastin:[222]

> This omission [to allow *locus standi* in some other capacity for a member] is to be regretted. Inevitably situations of oppression are more likely to occur in small private companies and in many such companies it is difficult to distinguish between the rights of a member as a shareholder and as a director...... to draft amendments to S.[211] in such a way as to exclude from its scope all oppressive or prejudicial conduct other than that directed towards members in their capacity as members is to disregard an important aspect of the problem and to overlook commercial reality in some cases.

---

212 Rajak, *supra* n.185, pp.165, 169; Prentice, *supra* n.209 at p.125; Slutsky, *supra* n.209 at p.327.

213 S.211(2) (b); Uniform Companies Act of Australia, S.186(2)(b); *Scottish Co-operative Society Case supra* [1959] A.C.324, at p.368; Afterman, *supra* n.178, pp.204-205, 219.

214 *supra* n.88.

215 *ibid* para. 212(a).

216 *ibid* para. 212(b).

217 *ibid* para. 212(c) and paras 203-204.

218 *ibid* para. 212(f).

219 *ibid* para 212(d), (e).

220 Clause 70.

221 Clause 65; see also Companies Bill (Bill 104), 1974, Clause 71.

222 N. Bastin, *"Minority Protection: A Need for Reform"* (1977) 127 New L.J.230, 232; see also Gower, *supra* n.190, p.669; For a review of S.75 see V. Joffe, *The Companies Act 1980: a Practical Guide* (1980) paras.12. 201 to 12.210.

Section 459 differs in some particulars from provisions elsewhere in the Commonwealth and South Carolina which had earlier amended or modified the equivalent of Section 211[223]. The Ghanaian, Malaysian and Singaporean provisions allow any member or *debenture-holder* to apply to the Court for an order that not only are the affairs of the company being conducted in a manager oppressive to one or more of the members or debentureholders, but also in relation to *the powers of the Directors being* so exercised. In addition, such exercise by the company or directors in disregard of the applicant(s)' interests as shareholder and debentureholders is also a ground for relief. In this regard those provisions are similar to Section 224(1)(a) of the British Columbia Companies Act[224] save that the latter provision only gives *locus standi* to a member of the company. The Ghanaian, Malaysian and Singaporean provisions also allow a shareholder or debentureholder to apply for relief on the ground:[225]

> that some act of the company has been done or is threatened or that some resolution of the members, holders of debentures or any class of them has been passed or is proposed which unfairly discriminates against or is otherwise prejudicial to one or more of the members or holders of debentures (including himself)

The British Columbia provision is slightly different, thus:[226]

> (b) that some of the company has been done, or is threatened, or that some resolution of the members or any class of members has been passed or is proposed, that is unfairly prejudicial to one or more of the members, including himself.

The Ghanaian, Malaysian and Singaporean provisions thus extend the grounds for relief by providing a remedy for "oppression" as well as for conduct which is in "disregard of the interests" of the shareholders and debentureholders. It is notable though that both the Malaysian and Singaporean Provisions as well as that in the British Columbia Act do not cover acts which affect the shareholder in his capacity as an officer or director as is the case with the Ghanaian,[227] South Carolina[228] and Federal Canadian[229] equivalent provisions. Presumably under the British Columbia Act, it would be up to the Court to decide whether a member who applies under the section in some other capacity has *locus standi.* It is thus provided:[230]

> For purposes of this section, a member includes
> (a) .....
> (b) any other person who, in the discretion of the Court, is a proper person to make an application under this section.

Unlike the British[231] and Northern Ireland Acts[232], the Ghanaian, Malaysian and Singaporean provisions do not give legal representatives *locus standi* to apply to Court for relief. Legal

---

223 See S.218 Ghana Companies Code, 1963; S.181 Malaysian Companies Act, 1965; S.181 Singaporean Companies Act, 1967. Emphasis Supplied.

224 R.S. Chap.59.

225 Ghana S.218(1)(b); Malaysia S.181(1)(b); Singapore S.181(1)(b).

226 S.224(1)(b) Companies Act.

227 S.218(1) (a) of the Ghana Code extends the remedy if the conduct is..... "in disregard of [their]..... interests as members, shareholders, officers, or debentureholders of the company..."

228 S.C.Code Ann S.12-22. 15(a)(4) (B) deals with conduct which is "oppressive or unfairly prejudicial either to the corporation or to any shareholder whether in his capacity as shareholder, director or officer of the corporation." See in this regard, A.B. Afterman, "Statutory Protection for Oppressed Shareholders: a Model for Reform", 55 *Virginia L. Rev.* 1043 (1969).

229 Under *Canada Business Corporation Act* S.234(2) a petition may be lodged in respect of conduct which "unfairly disregards the interests of any security holder, creditor or officer."

230 *supra* n.223 sub-section 224(6).

231 S. 459 Companies Act, 1985.

232 S.201(6) Companies Act, 1960.

representatives would presumably have *locus standi* under the British Columbia Act.[232] subject to the Court's discretion.

The discretion given to the Court as to the kind of order to give once a petition has been proved is largely the same under all the provisions we have discussed.[233] The provisions only differ in the detail of enumeration of the Court's action.

It is clear that the dormant nature of S.210 led to its reform in Britain and other Commonwealth Jurisdictions. In view of the fact that S.211 of the Uganda Companies Act, is in *pari materia* with S.210 it appears relevant to question whether that section should remain in the statute book on its unamended form.

# The "just and equitable" ground for winding up.[233a]

## Nature and rationale of the remedy

Section 222 (f) of the Companies Act, provides that " a company may be wound up by the Court if the Court is of opinion that it is just and equitable that the company should be wound up". A petition in this respect may be presented by the company, any creditor or member.[234] The petitioner may be a controlling shareholder or constituting the majority[235] or a holder of one of two substantially equal blocks.[236] A petitioning member must have a "tangible interest" in the winding up. This entails showing that the company is solvent and that there would be a surplus available for distribution among the shareholders on winding up.[237] This requirement was recommended for reversal by the Jerkins Committee in Britain.[238] Although the percentage of the petitioner's shareholding in the company and his motive are immaterial in determining his eligibility to bring the petition[239], these aspects may be considered in deciding whether or not an order should be made, since the remedy provided is essentially discretionary and has far reaching consequences. In this regard Lord Cross indicated in *Re: Westbourne Galleries Ltd.*[240] that the petitioner must "come to court with clean hands".

The justification for the "just and equitable" ground for winding up as a shareholder's remedy has thus been succinctly summarised by Chesterman:[241]

> The reason why (the section) has considerable practical importance as a shareholder's remedy is not that its use will inevitably bring the company into liquidation; indeed, liquidation is usually the last thing that the petitioner or anyone else, wants, because financially it spells disaster for all. It is instead the threat of liquidation that will often be effective in achieving recess for an aggrieved

---

233 e.g. S.461 Companies Act, 1985; S.224(2) British Columbia Companies Act; S.181(2), respectively of the Singaporean and Malaysian Companies Acts; S.218(2) Ghana Companies Code; S.234(3) Canada Business Corporations Act.

233a See generally M. Chesterman "The 'Just and Equitable' Winding Up of Small Companies" (1973) 36 *M.L.R.* 129-152. D.D.D Prentice, "Winding up: The Partnership Analogy" (1973) 89 *Law Q.Rev.*101-125; H. Leigh, Note, (1972) 88 *Law Q. Rev.*468-472; Akanki, "Judicial Discretion to Wind Up a Company", 1982 *Nig. C.L. Rev.* 110-120.

234 Companies Act, S.224

235 *Re: Consolidated South Rand Mines Deep Ltd. [1909] 1. Ch. 491*

236 *Re: Yenidje Tobacco Co. Ltd.* [1916] 2 Ch 426 C.A. *Re: Davis & Collett Ltd.* [1935] 1 Ch. 693; *Re Davis Investments (East Ham) Ltd.* [1961] 1 W.L.R. 1396; C.A. *Re: Lundie Brothers Ltd.* [1965] 1 W.L.R.1051

237 *Re: Rica Gold Washing Company Ltd.* (1879) 11 Ch.D. 36 C.A.; *Re: Othery Construction Ltd.* [1966] 1 W.L.R.514; *Cole v. R.C. Irving & Co. Ltd.* 1970 NCLR 472 (High Court of Lagos State), *Re: Italcomm (W.Nig.) Ltd.* 1972 NCLR 293 (High Court of Lagos State)

238 Cmnd 1749 (1962) Para.503(h)

239 *Brynston Finance Ltd. v. de Vries* (No.2) [1976] Ch.63 C.A.

240 [1973] A.C. 360, p.387

241 *supra* n.233a, pp.129-130. Referring to Companies Act, 1948 (Britain) S. 222(f) which is identical to S.222(f) of the Ugandan Act. See also *Re: Westbourne Galleries Ltd. ibid* [1972] 2 W.L.R. 1289, at *p.1303*

> member. He can stand beside the barrel of gunpowder with a lighted match in his hands, so to speak, demanding that he get what he wants - which in most cases in simply a good price for his shares - or else everyone, including himself, perishes swiftly and dramatically.

The effect of an order for winding up being made is that the warring parties would subsequently ask for the court to rescind it with a view to their reaching a settlement.[242]

## Scope of the remedy

Prior to the landmark decision of *Ebrahimi v. Westbourne Galleries Ltd.*[243], the law was that a quasi-partnership company (viz one which is in substance a partnership though operating in corporate form), should be wound up under Section 222(f), if the facts adduced before the court would satisfy the grounds for the dissolution of partnership under partnership law. The main shortcomings[244] of this approach were firstly that the inquiry as to whether a particular company in issue was "in substance a partnership" was difficult to fathom and largely depended on judicial intuition rather than any logic in determining the "essential" aspects of a partnership.[245] Secondly, the courts did not wholly consider the relevant partnership law relating to dissolution[246]. Consequently, "the common course, in English quasi-partnership cases at least, was simply to import various broad considerations of good faith, trust, and confidence which were said to underlay the dissolution of partnerships.[247] Thirdly, it was not clear what was meant by "partnership" in the context, quasi-partnership. The crucial issue here was whether the court should "apply the law, which governs the dissolution of 'partnerships in general' or the particular rules that would be appropriate for a partnership which in terms of its constitution resembles as closely as possible the particular company with which the company is dealing[248] Put differently, should the court in applying partnership law make relevant adjustments to take account of the particular provisions of the company's constitution or more specifically its articles?

The last controversial factor is graphically illustrated by two divergent decisions which pre-empted the controversy within the three judgments in *Ebrahimi v Westbourne Galleries Ltd.*[249] Thus, in *Re: Cuthbert Cooper & Sons Ltd.*[250] the court dismissed a petition to wind up a company which it treated as a quasi-partnership. This was because the conduct complained of in the petition accorded with the Company's Articles and was not shown to be *mala fide*. Furthermore, although such conduct indicated lack of mutual trust and confidence between the members of the company, it was not in the court's view adequate to justify the grant of a winding up order. Conversely, in *Re: Lundie Bros Ltd.*[251], a quasi-partnership company was wound up. This was despite the fact that two members having the casting vote at general meetings used the vote to pass an ordinary resolution which was valid and effective under section 184 of the Companies

---

242 See e.g. *Re: Lundie Bros Ltd. supra* n.236; *Re: Wondoflex Textiles Pty Ltd., infra* n.47.

243 *Symington v. Symington's Quarries* (1905) 8F 121, 130 per Lord Mclaren; *Re: Yenidije Tobacco Co. Ltd. supra* n.236; Chesterman, *supra* n.233a, p.131; *Re: Modern Retreading Co.Ltd.* [1962] E.A.57(1)

244 See generally Chesterman, *ibid.* pp. 131-135.

245 See e.g. *Re: Wondoflex Textiles Property Ltd.* (1951) *V.L.R.* 458, 465 (Supreme Court of Victoria); *Re: Fildes Bros Ltd.* (1970) 1 W.L.R. 592, 596-597 per Megarry J; *Re: Leadenhall General Hardware Stores Ltd.* Unrep. Feb.4 1971 (1971) 115 S.J. 202.

246 Partnership Act, 1890, Ss. 32-35; Partnership Law (Laws of Western Nigeria Cap.86), Ss. 33-36. See also Bakibinga, *Nigerian Law of Partnership*, Chap.5 Bakibinga, *Partnership Law in Uganda*, Chap.5

247 Chesterman, *supra* n.233a p.134. See further *Re Yenidje Tobacco Co. Ltd* supra n.236, p.430; *Re: Lundie Bros Ltd, supra* n.236. 1056; *Re: Westbourne Galleries Ltd.* [1970] 1 W.L.R.1378, 1384; *Re: Davis & Collet Ltd, supra* n.236 p.701; *Re: K/9 Meat Supplies (Guidford) Ltd.* [1966] 1 W.L.R.1112, p.1119.

248 Chesterman, *ibid*, p.135.

249 *supra* n.42 respectively at first instance, Court of Appeal and House of Lords.

250 [1937] Ch.392; Chesterman, *supra* n.233a.

251 *supra* n.236. *Re: Cuthbert Cooper* was not cited here.

Act, 1948[252] and the articles[253], by which the remaining member was removed from his post as a working director. Plowman J. based his decision on considerations as to the good faith expected between partners. He did not refer to the technical validity of the resolution.

In *Ebrahimi v. Westbourne Galleries*[254], Ebrahimi, the petitioner and Nazar one of the two individual respondents, were in business together as retailers in Persian Carpets. Nazar provided most of the capital. There was no written or oral agreement and Nazar thought of the arrangement as one whereby he merely employed Ebrahimi in his business. However, essentially a partnership was created by virtue of their working together in the business and sharing the profits.[255] Later, this arrangement was superseded by the incorporation of the respondent company, Westbourne Galleries Ltd. which took over the business. Under the articles, Nazar and Ebrahimi were each appointed a director and initially took 500 GBP1 shares. Soon after the incorporation, the third respondent, Nazar's son was made a director and each of the existing directors transferred 100 shares to him. Consequently, between them the Nazars had a majority of votes at the general meeting. Prior to the disputes, all three remained directors and the profits were for tax reasons distributed as directors' remuneration. Following misunderstandings between Ebrahimi and the two Nazars, the Nazars used their majority in general meeting to pass an ordinary resolution removing Ebrahimi form the Board of Directors. This step was effective by virtue of Section 184 of the Companies Act. 1948 and regulation 96 of Table A, which had been adopted by the Company[256]. Ebrahimi petitioned for relief under Section 210[257] or in the alternative, a winding up order under Section 222(f)[258] of the Companies Act, 1948.

The claim under Section 210 was dismissed. However, Plowman J. held that the company would be wound up under Section 222(f) following his decision in *Re Lundie Bros. Ltd.*[259] In essence, Plowman J. was insisting that "broad conceptions of the duties binding partners *inter se* should override strictly legal considerations arising from the Companies Act and the articles of the company. When it comes to deciding whether a quasi-partnership should be wound up under section (222)"[260].

On appeal, the Court of Appeal reversed both Plowman J.'s approach and the winding-up order. In his rationalisation of the Court's decision, Russel L.J. thus stated:[261]

> ...... in a case of quasi partnership company such as the present the exercise by a majority in general meeting of the power under the articles or the statute to remove a director from his office, and consequently to exclude him from a participation in the management and conduct of the business of the company does not form a ground for holding that it is just and equitable that the company he wound up unless it be shown that the power was not exercised *bona fide* in the interests of the company or that the grounds for exercising the power were such that no reasonable man could think that the removal was in the interest of the company.

The House of Lords in turn overruled the Court of Appeal and restored Plowman J.'s decision. In the leading Judgment of the Court, Lord Wilberforce indicated that the old conception of "quasi-partnerships" or "in substance partnerships" as pre-requisite for determining the remedy

---

252 Identical to Companies Act, S.185.

253 Equivalent to Companies Act, Table A. Art. 97.

254 *supra* n.240 [1970] 1 W.L.R. 1378 per Plowman J.

255 See Partnership Act Cap.86, S.3(1).

256 See *supra* notes 252 and 253.

257 identical to Companies Act, S.211. This aspect of the decision is considered *supra* Section c.

258 Companies Act S.222(f).

259 *supra* n.236.

260 Chesterman, *supra* n.233a, p.137.

261 [1971] Ch.799, 811 C.A. See also *Re Cuthbert Cooper & Sons Ltd, supra* n.251 per Simonds J.

under Section 222(f), was convenient but confusing[262] and should not be relied upon. In his view the function of Section 222(f) is to "enable the Court to subject the exercise of legal rights to equitable considerations"[263]. Although conceding that it is impossible and undesirable to define in advance all the circumstances in which legal rights should be thus subjected, Lord Wilberforce indicated that "typically", this may happen among small or private companies where one or more of the following elements can be found:[64]

(i) an association formed or continued on the basis of a personal relationship, involving mutual confidence - this element will often be found where a pre-existing partnership has been converted into a limited company;
(ii) an agreement, or understanding, that all, or some (for there may be 'sleeping' members), of the shareholders shall participate in the conduct of the business;
(iii) restriction upon the transfer of the member's interest in the company - so that if confidence is lost, or one member is removed from management, he cannot take out his stake and go elsewhere.

It is apparent that the remedy under Section 222(f) would be available irrespective of the absence of fraud or wrong doing.[264] The *Ebrahimi* case, while not preventing a company from dismissing a director and excluding him from participation in the management of its business, if this is done with respect to the types of company Lord Wilberforce had in mind as typical for purposes of Section 222(f), there would be risk of the company being wound up. It is also evident that for purposes of Section 222(f), the wrong complained of need not affect a member in his capacity as a member[265] In the *Ebrahimi* case, the petitioner's rights as a shareholder were unaffected by his dismissal as director. Yet the court held that he was entitled to a remedy. To this extent Section 222(f) may prove to be more useful to an aggrieved member than Section 211 of the Companies Act.

In *Suerre hang v. Buhemba Mines Ltd*[67a], it was held that each case where relief is sought on the ground that it is just and equitable that a company should be wound up depends on its own facts.

In spite of Lord Wilberforce's warning against enumerating all the circumstances under which Section 222(f) may be invoked, there are four broad situations where Section 222(f) may be resorted to. First, exclusion form participation contrary to some underlying obligation as illustrated by the *Ebrahimi* case itself[266] Second where it is shown that the petitioner has justifiably lost confidence in the ability of the existing company management to run its affairs in a proper way. Disagreement by the petitioner with management policy or displeasure at being outvoted are insufficient for this purpose[267] The loss of confidence must be based on the conduct of the directors or controllers affecting the company's business and should contain an element of lack of probity or impropriety[268]. In *Loch v. John Blackwood Ltd.*[70], the engineering business of John Blackwood, had, following his death been transferred to a company and run by one of his trustees, Mclaren for the benefit of the three beneficiaries of his estate, namely, Mclaren's wife, Mrs Lock and Rodger. Although profitable, the business was conducted in a way which was

---

262 [1972] 2 W.L.R. 1289 p. 1298. See also *Re: Modern Retreading Co. Ltd.* [1962] E.A.57.

263 *ibid* p.1297. "Legal rights"in this context means principally the Articles of Association. See also cases cited at note 245 *supra* and *Lewis v. Haas* (1970) S.L.T. (Notes) 67, *Mitha v. Mitha* [1967] E.A.575, 581 (High Court of Uganda), *Clemens v. Clemens Bros Ltd* [1976] 2 All E.R.268.

264 Gower, *op. cit.* p.66.

265 c.f. position under S.211 considered *supra*.

67a (1935) 20 EACA 28.

266 See further *Re: Davis and Collett Ltd. supra* n.236. Re: *Wondoflex Textiles Property Ltd.*, supra n.245, *Re: Lundie Bros Ltd., supra* n.236, *Re: A & B.C. Chewing Gum Ltd.* [1975] 1 W.L.R.579.

267 *Mith v. Mitha, supra* n.263, *Re: Eryeza Bwambale & Co. Ltd.* [1969] E.A.430 (High court of Uganda).

268 *Loch v. John Blackwood Ltd.* [1924] A.C.783 P.C. See also *Re: E.A. Tobacco Ltd.* (1921-52) 1TLR(2) 489; *Re: Teso Cotton Co. Ltd.* Companies Cause No.50 of 1960(U).

oppressive to the beneficiaries, with the exception of Mclaren's wife. Mrs Loch and Rodger petitioned for winding up on the just and equitable ground. The points raised in support of the petition were: (i) that the statutory conditions for holding general meetings were not observed; (ii) the balance sheets and profit and loss accounts were never submitted to the company and (iii) auditing as required by statute and the articles was not carried out. The Privy Council granted the petition. In contrast, in *Farmart Produce and Shipping Line Ltd.*[269], the grounds for the petition under Section 209(f) were that the Managing Director had, *inter alia,* (i) declined to produce accounts or summon any meetings of the company; (ii) kept "all the affairs of the company to himself alone". The court declined to grant the petition on the ground that the substratum of the company was not gone nor was there complete deadlock justifying such order. It is respectfully submitted that the court's decision failed to address the grounds amounting to loss of confidence by the petitioner in the management, itself sufficient to justify winding-up under Section 222(f). In *Cole v. R.C. Irving & Co. Ltd*[270], a petition was presented under section [222(f)] on the grounds *inter alia* of (i) improper or fraudulent allotment, issue, and transfer of shares (ii) certain acts by the company contravening its resolutions; (iii) financial rewards having been made to some members to the detriment of the petitioner. With respect to the first ground, Kazeem J. Held[271] that this was a matter between the petitioner and the other shareholders and not between him and the company. Consequently, it could not be determined on a petition for winding up. With regard to the last two grounds, though admitted by the second respondent, Kazeem J. held[272] that they could not justify the court's interference on the just and equitable ground, in the sense that since the acts were neither *ultra vires* or requiring special majority sanction they could be rectified by the company in general meeting. The line to be drawn between this case and *Loch v. John Blackwood Ltd.* is very tenuous, as arguably the grounds for complaint in the latter case could also have been rectified by the general meeting. The more acceptable rationalization of *Cole v. Irving & Co. Ltd* is that it was a case where the petitioner only held 4 out of the 100 shareholding of the company and it was inconceivable to talk of a "deadlock" between him and the other two shareholders, who between them constituted an unassailable majority. Nevertheless the issue as to whether the petitioner had justifiably lost confidence in the management of the company should have been addressed without sweeping it under the *Fos v. Harbottle* rule.

The third basis for grounding a petition under section 222(f) is where there is a deadlock usually in a company where the shares are equally divided between two members or two groups of members who are so irreconcilable that the company's business is effectively frustrated[273]. In *Re: Stevedoring (Nigeria) Co. Ltd.*[274], there was a period of disagreement between the six members-directors of a private company, leading to the petitioner being improperly removed from the board. A winding-up order was granted by the court. In *Re: Medipharm Publications (Nig) Ltd.*[275], the *Yenidje* decision[75] was applied in winding up a company on the ground of deadlock between the two directors.

---

269 [1971] 1 All N.L.R. 247 Supreme Court of Nigeria

270 (1970) NCLR 472 (High Court of Lagos State)

271 Following *Re: Bambi Restaurant Ltd.* [1965] 1.W.L.R.750

272 Supra n.270 at pp.482, following *Foss v. Harbottle, supra* and *Re: Longham Skating Rink Co.* (1877) 5 Ch.D.669

273 *Re: Yenidje Tobacco Co. Ltd. supra* n.38; Compare *Cole v. R.C.Irving & co. Ltd. supra* n.72 and *Re: Fermart Produce & Shipping Line Ltd., supra* n.71; *Re: Pool House Group (Nig.) Ltd.* Suit No. M/190/70 of 25/1/71 (Lagos High Court); *Re: Modern Retreading Co. Ltd., supra* n.243

274 (1962) L.H.C.R. 164 (High Court of Lagos)

275 (1971) 1 U.I.L.R. 421 (High Court of Lagos State)

276 (1882) 20 Ch.D.169. See also *Re: Bleroit Aircraft Co.* (1916) 32 T.L.R.253 *c.f. Re: Kitson & Co.* [1946] 1 All E.R. 435; *Re: W. Biney & Co.* CCHCJ 6/72/16; 1972 NCLR 282 (High Court of Lagos State)

The fourth possible ground for a Section 222(f) petition is where the substratum of the company has failed. Thus in *Re: German Date Coffee Co.*[276], the company was formed to work a German patent for making coffee from dates. It failed to get the patent. Upon petition by two members that it should be wound up on the just and equitable ground, it was held that since the substratum had failed it should be wound up. The invocation of Section 222(f) in these circumstances is simply an application of the *ultra-vires* doctrine. In *Re: Brinsmead and Sons*[277], the substratum principle was applied where the promotion of the company was found to be fraudulent and illegal from the outset.

## The effect of a S.222(f) Order

The logical result of an order Section 222 is that the company is wound-up, thereby ceasing to exist and the petitioner including all the other members are entitled to be paid their shares of the surplus assets.[278] Consequently, the remedy inherent in Section 222(f) is drastic especially when considered from the perspective of those members who are desirous of the company continuing in existence and is unsatisfactory redress for the petitioner. Previously the court could decline to issue winding-up Order where some alternative remedy was available to the petitioner.[279] Indeed, in *Cole v. R.C. Irving & Co. Ltd.*[280], Kazeem J. dismissed the action on the ground that the petitioner had acted unreasonably in petitioning for a winding-up on the just and equitable ground. He should, instead have proceeded under Section 201 of the Companies Act, [S.211 of the Uganda Act]. Nevertheless, the mere existence of an alternative remedy is not a ground for refusing a Section 222(f) order. Section 225(2)(b) of the Companies Act indicates that the order shall not be refused unless the court is of the opinion both that some other remedy is available and that the petitioner is acting unreasonably in seeking to have the company wound up instead of pursuing that other remedy as was the position in *Cole v. Irving & Co.* case[281]. The effect of this is that the winding-up remedy can be obtained very easily, thereby making "the threat of proceedings a more potent one"[282], though a clumsy method of ending oppression in view of its logical possibility. It is because of this that the Cohen Committee recommended[283] an alternative and less drastic remedy now laid down in Section 211 of the Companies Act[284].

# Misfeasance summons

Upon commencement of winding-up and irrespective of the type of liquidation[285], Section 328 lays down "a summary and effective a remedy for certain breaches of duty owed to the company.[286] By virtue thereof, any promoter, director, manager or officer of the company or the liquidator himself[287] who "has misapplied or retained or become liable or accountable for any money or

---

277 [1897] 1 Ch.406, C.A.

278 For more detail see *infra* Chap.18.

279 *Re: Cuthbert Cooper & Sons Ltd.* [1937] 1 Ch.392.

280 1970 NCLR 472 (High Court of Lagos State). c.f. *Obasi v. Pureway Corporation (Nig) Ltd* (1978) 4 F.R.C.R.214.

281 ibid. See also *Charles Forte Investment Ltd v. Amanda* [1964] 1 Ch.240, C.A. *Re: A & B.C. Chewing Gum ltd., supra* n.266.

282 Gower, *op.cit* p.664 referring to Chesterman's statement, *supra* text at n.241. See also *Re: Wondoflex Textiles Pty ltd. supra* n.245 and *Re Newman & Howard Ltd.* [1962] 1 Ch.257.

283 Cmnd. 6659, p.95 (1945).

284 See *supra* for a discussion thereof.

285 See *infra* Chap.18.

286 Gower, *op. cit.* p.657.

287 excluding a receiver and manager appointed by the debentureholders: *Re: B. Johnson & Co. (Builders) Ltd.* [1955] Ch.634 C.A. See also *Kirkel v. Adams* (1934) 1 EACA 26.

property of the company, or been guilty of any misfeasance or breach of trust in relation to the company", may on application by the official receiver, liquidator, creditor or contributory be examined as to his conduct and be compelled to repay or restore the money or property or part thereof with interest as the court thinks just or contribute such sum, as determined by the court, by way of compensation, in respect of the misapplication, retainer, misfeasance or breach of trust.[288]The provision has been interpreted to encompass breaches of fiduciary duties but excluding common law negligence.[289]

As a result of difficulties in proceeding against directors who are in control of the company, summons under section 328 is commonly used to enforce the directors' duties. It may also be possible for this purpose to resort to the more extensive remedy under Section 327 of the Companies Act, relating to fraudulent trading.[290]

# Investigations and inspections

## The appointment of inspectors

The court may[291] upon application, appoint one or more competent inspectors investigate the affairs of a company and to report thereon in a manner required by the Court. Such power is predicated upon the need to ensure a check on the powers of directors or majority shareholders who effectually control the company.[292]

With regard to a company having a share capital, the relevant application may be brought by members holding not less than one-tenth of the issued shares of any class,[293] while with respect to a company not having a share capital, the application may be made by not less than one-fifth of thenumber of persons on the company's register of members.[294]The application should be supported by such evidence as the court may require. The applicant may also be requested to provide security for the payment of the cost of investigation.

The court may also exercise his powers of appointment of inspectors for carrying out an investigation where the company has by special resolution or the court by order declared that its affairs should be investigated by an inspector appointed by the court.[295]

The minister can also exercise his powers under sections 165 and 166 where it appears from a report of the registrar that such is necessary for the inspection of any other company which is already pending or that there are circumstances indicating:[296]

(i) that the business of the company is being run fraudulently or for a fraudulent and unlawful purpose or in a manner oppressive of any of its members; or
(ii) that the persons concerned with the formation of the company or the management of its affairs have in connection therewith been guilty of fraud, misfeasance or other misconduct towards it or its members; or
(iii) that the members of the company have not been given all the information with respect to its affairs which they might reasonably expect.

---

288 S.328(1). See further *Re: Morecambe Bowling Ltd.* [1969] 1W.L.R. 133 where it is indicated that the respondents may claim indemnity or contribution *inter-se; Re: Modern Retreading Co. Ltd.* 1966(1) ALR Comm.494

289 *Re: B. Johnson & Co Ltd. supra* n.287.

290 See *supra* Chap.2 under *Lifting The Veil of Incorporation* and *infra* chap.18. See also *Ebrahim v. Tait* (1935) 2 EACA 51.

291 Companies Act, S.165.

292 See *Norwest Holst v. Secretary of State for Trade* [1978] 3 All E.R. 280 at pp.291-293 per Lord Denning; *Kasule Luyombo v. Ndikola Iga & others* [1977] HCB 328; *Re: Eryeza Bwambale & Co. Ltd* [1969] E.A.430 (per Goudie J.).

293 Companies Act, 165(1) (a).

294 *ibid* S,165(1)(b).

295 *ibid*, S.166(a). See also *Bozak (Nig) Ltd. v. Ziregbe (1978)* F.R.C.R.83; *Kasikwu Farms V.A.G. Bendel State* [1986] 1 N.W.L.R.695.

296 *ibid* S. 166(b).

297 ibid S.168(1).

Where an application is made under Ss.165 and 166 or there are circumstances which appear to the Court to warrant an investigation, the directors and officers of the company are required to supply to the Inspector upon request any document or information relating to the affairs of the company.[297], failure of which renders the relevant director or officer criminally liable.[298]

In *Norwest Holst v. Department of Trade*[299], the minister's power of appointment under Section 165(b) (ii) of the British Companies Act, 1948 which is in *pari materia* with Section 166 (b) (ii) (b) was challenged by the company on the ground that it was aware of no evidence which would justify such an appointment, and asked the minister to disclose his sources of information, which he declined to do. In upholding the decision of Foster J. at first instance, the Court of Appeal held that the power appointment was essentially administrative, not judicial in character and that the Minister had only to act in good faith. Furthermore, that the burden of showing that he had not acted in good faith lay "firmly and heavily" with the company. The minister was, moreover, not required by the rules of natural justice to give the company an opportunity of stating its case before the appointment: that opportunity could come later.

In *Kasule Luyombo v. Ndikola Iga & Others*[299a], it was held that in order to enable the registrar to complete investigations of a company's affairs under S.168, an application for the appointment of an inspector ought to be made under Section 165 of the Companies Act. In *Saint Benoist Plantations Ltd. v. Felix*[299b], it was indicated that the fact that a company has given some facilities for the private examination of its affairs does not preclude the court from ordering a formal investigation thereof. The court must be satisfied that the application is not malicious and that the applicant has "good reason" for requiring the investigation. *Prima facie* proof of misapplication of the company's funds or misconduct of a director may be "good reason".

## Powers of inspectors

Section 167 extends the investigatory powers to related companies to the one under investigation, while Section 168 gives the inspectors power to require the production of relevant books and papers, to examine on oath, and to certify to the court any person who refuses to answer their questions. In *Re: Pergamon Press Ltd,*[300] Lord Denning thus stated with respect to the powers of inspectors:[301]

> ......the inspectors are not a court of law. Their proceedings are not judicial proceedings. They are not even quasi judicial for they decide nothing. They only investigate and report. But this should not lead us to minimise the significance of their task.... they may ruin reputations or careers..... seeing that their work and their report may lead to such consequences, I am clearly of opinion that the inspectors must act fairly.

Nevertheless, such a duty does not extend to putting to a witness points critical of him which the inspectors intended to include in their report.[302] Consequently, within those limitations, the inspectors may make their own rules of procedure and having reached their conclusions should state their findings courageously, frankly and unreservedly. They should not be criticised for overlooking something. In this vein, Lord Denning thus stated:[6a]

---

298 *ibid* S.168(3).

299 *supra* n.292. See also J. Hull, "Department of Trade Investigations" *New Law J.*825, 826 (1979) and *Wiseman v. Borneman* [1969] 3 All E.R. 275 per Ormrod, L.J.

299a [1977] HCB 328 (High Court of Uganda: Ssekandi J.).

299b (1954) 21 EACA 105.

300 (1971) Ch.388.

301 *ibid* p.399. See also R.D. Fraser "Administrative Powers of Investigations Into Companies (1971) 34 *Mod. L.R.*260 and *Re: Grosvenor and West-end Railway Terminus Hotel Co. ltd.* (1897) 76 L.T 337.

302 *Maxwell v. Dept. of Trade and Industry* [1974] All E,R,122.

6a *ibid;* p.129.

> His task is burdensome and thankless as it is. It would be intolerable if he were to be liable to be pilloried afterwards for doing it. No one of standing would ever be found to undertake it. The public demands that so long as he acts honestly and does what is to he best of his ability, his report is not to be impugned in the courts of law.

All officers and agents of the company who are under investigation must refrain form interfering with the investigation, produce all books and documents required and give all such assistance in connection with the investigation which they are reasonably able to give.[303] However, legal practitioners are under no duty to disclose privileged communication made to them.[304] Bankers are also not obliged to disclose any information relating to the affairs of any of their customers other than the company.[305]

## The inspector's report

Upon direction by the Registrar, the inspectors may make interim reports to him for presentation to the court and on conclusion of the investigation they are required to make a final report to the court for presentation as aforesaid. Any such report may be written or printed in the manner required by the court.[306] The court may also cause the report to be printed and published and send a copy thereof to the registered office of the company and to the registrar; members of the company on payment of the prescribed fee or any body corporate affected by any investigation into the related companies[307] or which is a creditor of any of the companies under investigation[308].

Where the report discloses a criminal offence on the part of any person or company so investigated, the report shall be referred to the Attorney General and Director of Public Prosecutions who may direct the prosecution of such person.[309] Furthermore, in the case of a corporation which is liable to be wound up, if it appears to the Attorney General from the report that it is expedient to wind up such company in view of the circumstances enumerated in Section 166 (b)(i),(ii) relating to fraudulent or unlawful conduct of the company's business, the Attorney General may, in an appropriate case and unless the company is already being wound up, present a petition for it to be wound up on the just and equitable ground or present a petition for an order under Section 211 of the Act or under both of those sections[310]. If the report indicates that in the public interest proceedings ought to be brought by any affected company against any person in respect of any fraud, misfeasance or other misconduct relating to the promotion, formation of that company, management of its affairs or recovery of its property, the Attorney General may bring such proceedings in the name of the company and where such proceedings are commenced all officers and agents of the company are required to give him all the assistance in connection therewith[311].

A copy of the inspector's report which is authenticated by the seal of the company whose affairs they have investigated is admissible in any legal proceedings as evidence of the opinion of the inspectors in relation to any matter contained in the report.[312]

---

303 Companies Act, S.168(1).

304 *ibid* S.176(a).

305 *ibid* S.176(b).

306 *ibid* S.169(1). See also *Maxwell v. Dept. of Trade, supra* n.302

307 *ibid* S.169(2).

308 *ibid* S.169(2).

309 *ibid* S.170(1).

310 S.170. See also *Re: Travel & Holiday Clubs Ltd.* [1967] 1 W.L.R.711: [1967] 2 All E.R. 606; Re: *Pergamon Press Ltd. supra* n.300; *Re: SBA Properties Ltd.* [1967] 2 All E.R. 615.

311 *ibid* S.170(3). See also *SBA Properties Ltd.* [1967] 2 All E.R.615.

312 *ibid* S,172. See also *Re: A.B.C. Coupler & Engineering Co. Ltd.* [1962] 1 W.L.R.1236: *The Travel & Holiday Clubs Ltd.* [1967] 1 W.L.R.711; *Re: SBA Properties Ltd. Supra* n.310; *Re: Allied Produce Co Ltd.* [1967] 1 W.L.R.1469.

## Expenses of investigation

In a situation where an inspector has been appointed, the expenses of the investigation are defrayed in the first instance out of the appropriate consolidated Revenue Fund. However, the affected company or companies and any person found guilty or liable consequent upon the investigation may be required to make repayment of such expenses to the extent of sums or property recovered in the case of a company or liability in the case of any person or company, as the case may be.[313] It is also notable that members requesting an investigation may be required to give security for costs thereof.

## Investigation of company ownership

Under Sections 173 to 175 of the Companies Act, the registrar is empowered to appoint inspectors to investigate and report on the true ownership or control of any company. By Section 173 an inspector may be appointed to investigate and report on the membership of the company in order to determine who are financially interested in it or able to control or influence its policy. In the alternative, under Section 174, the registrar may require any person who has been interested in the securities under investigation or who has acted as advocate or agent of someone in relation to such securities to furnish the registrar with any information which such person may have about the security holders. Failure to provide such information attracts criminal liability and possible sanction under section 175. Under Section 175, where there is lack of co-operation on the part of any person in providing information relating to shareholding, the registrar may order that the affected shares shall be subject to restrictions which prevent rights in respect of them from being exercised or enjoyed until the holders have furnished full information.[314]

---

[313] *ibid* S.171

[314] As was the case in *Re: Ashbourne Investment Ltd.* [1978] 1 W.L.R.1346

# 16

# MEETING AND PROCEEDINGS

## Introduction

The Company's regulations normally empower the directors to manage its business[1]. However, ultimate control of the company lies with the general meeting[2]. The regulations require the convening each year of an annual general meeting and for extra-ordinary meetings to be convened when the need arises.[3]

A single member cannot generally constitute a meeting[4], save as may be directed by the Registrar in given circumstances[5], or where the quorum is realised at the beginning of the meeting but subsequently falls to one[6]. A meeting may be dispensed with "if all the individual shareholders, and not a majority only expressly assent to a transaction which is *intra vires* the company......."[7]

There are three kinds of general meetings at which all members are entitled to attend and vote, namely the statutory meeting,[8] the annual general meeting and extra-ordinary general meeting. Each will be considered, in turn.

## Statutory meeting

Every public company limited by shares or guarantee and having a share capital must hold a statutory meeting between at least one month and not more than thee months from the date of its entitlement to commence business.[9] At least fourteen days before the meeting, the directors must send a statutory report to every member; giving details of shares issued, whether they are paid up or not; cash received by the company, the nature of consideration for the issue of shares, abstract of the receipts of the company and of the payments made thereout; particulars of directors, managers, auditors and secretary of the company; particulars of any contract, the modification of which is to be submitted to the meeting for approval together with particulars of the modification or proposed modification[10].

The one month and three months indicated in Section 130(1) would on English authority refer to "calendar month"[11]. However, Nigerian authority appears to suggest that notice of one

---

1 Table A, Art.80. See also generally *supra* chap.11

2 *Barron v. Potter* [1914] 1 Ch.895. *Bamford v. Bamford*, (1970) Ch.212; [1969] 1 ALL E.R. and generally Chap. 11 *supra*

3 Table A Arts 47-49

4 *Sharp v. Dawes* [1876] 2 Q.B.D.26; *Daimler Co. v. Continental & Tyre Rubber Co.* [1916] 2 A.C.307.

5 Companies Act, S.131(2)

6 *Re: Hartley Baird Ltd.* [1955] Ch.143; [1954] 3 ALL E.R.695

7 *Okeowo v. Migliore* (1979) 11 S.C. 138, at p.192

8 This has been abolished in Britain. See Gower, *op.cit.* (4th Ed.) pp.301,527. N.B. absence of its discussion in Leigh, (3rd Ed.1983) *supra* Chap.14

9 Companies Act, S.130(1)

10 *ibid.* S.130 (2),(3)

11 *Dodds v. Walker* [1981] 2 ALL E.R. 609, at pp.610-611 per Lord Diplock. See also *Lester v. Garland* (1803-13) ALL E.R. Rep.436.

month must expire at the end of a current month i.e. at the end of the month following that in which it was given.[12]

The aim of the statutory meeting is to enable members to review the progress report from the directors and promoters.[13] The failure to hold the meeting is a ground for winding-up the company[14], although the court may, instead order that the meeting should be held with the defaulter paying the relevant costs.[15]

The statutory report is required to be certified by at least two directors, while the shares issued, the cash received in respect of such shares and the receipts and payments of the company on capital account must be certified by the auditors[16]. A copy of the statutory report must be sent to the registrar, in addition to those sent to members.[17] made available by the directors at the meeting.[18]

## Annual general meeting

A company is required[19] in each year[20] to hold an annual general meeting, specifying it as such in the notices calling it; and not more than fifteen months should elapse between one annual general meeting and the next. However, if the first annual meeting is held within eighteen months of the company's incorporation, it need not hold it in the year of its incorporation or the following year[21].

The annual meeting is normally called by the directors[22]. However, if the directors do not convene one, the registrar may on the application of a member direct the convening of one and give directions as to its conduct including a directive that one person may form a quorum[23].

Although the Companies Act does not exactly indicate the nature of the business to be transacted at the annual general meeting, the business invariably includes the appointment of auditors[24], fixing their remuneration, declaration of dividend, consideration of the accounts and balance sheets and reports of the directors and auditors, the election of new directors to replace those who are retiring and any special or other business[25].

Failure to hold an annual general meeting in the manner prescribed by Section 131 attracts criminal sanction[26].

The purpose of the annual general meeting has been aptly summarised by Professor Gower thus:[27]

> The annual general meeting is an important protection to members, for it is the one occasion when they can be sure of having an opportunity of meeting the directors and of questioning them on the accounts, on their report, and on the

[12] *Yaskey v. The Freetown City Council (1933) I W.A.C.A.* followed by *Oyekoya v. G.B. Ollivant (Nig) Ltd* [1969] 1 ALL N.L.R.80.

[13] Companies Act, S.130 (7).

[14] *Ibid*, S.222(b).

[15] *Re: Kent Outcrop Coal Co.* (1912) W.N.26.

[16] *Supra* n.13, s.130(4).

[17] *ibid* S.130 (5).

[18] *ibid.* S.130 (6).

[19] *ibid.* S.131(1).

[20] i.e. Calendar year and not every 12 months: *Gibson v.Barton* (1875) L.R.10 Q.B.329

[21] Companies Act, s.131 (1); Table A. Art.47.

[22] Table A. Art. 47.

[23] Companies Act, S.131(2),(3) See also *Re: El Sombrero* [1958] Ch.900.

[24] *ibid.* S.159.

[25] Table A. Art.52 *Kyaggwe Farmers Assoc. Ltd. v. Kafeero* [1975] HCB 97.

[26] S.131 (5).

[27] Gower, *op.cit. (4th Ed) p.528.*

> company's position and prospects. It is at this meeting that, normally, a proportion of the directors will retire and come up for re-election, and at which the members will be able to try to exercise their only real power over the board - that of dismissal. Moreover, it affords members an opportunity of moving resolutions on their own account. Most of these things could of course be done at an extra-ordinary meeting, but the members who want to raise these matters may not be able to insist upon the convening of an extra-ordinary meeting. The annual general meeting is valuable to them because the directors must hold it whether they want to or not.

## Extra-ordinary general meeting

The extra-ordinary general meeting is any general meeting other than the annual general meeting[28], and is usually convened by the directors at their discretion,[29] to deal with urgent matters which cannot wait until the next annual general meeting.

Furthermore, the directors must convene an extra-ordinary meeting, irrespective of any contrary provision in the company's articles, if holders of at least ten percent of the paid-up capital carrying voting rights requisition one. When the company has no share capital at least one-tenth of the members with voting rights may requisition the meeting[30]. The requisitionist must state the objects of the meeting, sign them and deposit them with the company's registered office[31]. If the directors do not convene the meeting within 21 days of deposit of the requisition, the requisitionist may themselves convene the meeting and recover reasonable expenses for so doing from the company which may in turn recover the same from the fees of the defaulting directors[32]. The main short coming of these provisions is "that in a company with a large and dispersed membership, it may be matter of considerable difficulty and expense to enlist the support of sufficient of his fellow - members to be able to make a valid requisition".[33]

Lastly, where it is impracticable to call a meeting or to conduct it in the manner prescribed by the Act or the articles, the court has residual power, on its own motion or upon application by a director or a member to order the holding of one in a manner directed by it including the direction that one person may constitute quorum for that purpose[34] . This will be done where lack of quorum is frustrating the company's business. The ancillary and consequential direction, will not be given with respect to matters which are exclusively scheduled for the meeting itself. Thus, in *Paul Iro v. Robert Park & Ors*[35], the first respondent who was a director and shareholder of a company applied under Section 135 for an order requiring the applicant to call, hold and conduct a meeting of the company and for ancillary and consequential directions enabling him to direct, manage and run the affairs of the company, to appoint additional directors and to appoint auditors. The trial court granted the order sought. However, on appeal, the Supreme Court held that although Section 135 authorises the court to order the holding of a meeting, it is only required to issue such ancillary and consequential directions as are aimed at enabling such a meeting to be held. Secondly, the consequential orders made by the trial court were *ultra vires*

---

28 Table A, Art.48.

29 ibid, Art.49.

30 Companies Act, S.132(1); Art.49.

31 *ibid* S.132(2).

32 *ibid.* S.132(3),(5).

33 Gower, *op.cit. supra* n.27, p.529.

34 Companies Act, S.137(1) See also *Re: El. Sombrero supra* n.23 and *Re H.R. Paul & Son Ltd.* (1974) 118 S.J. 166; see also *Re: Air Rep International Ltd* (1984) HCB63 (High Court of Uganda).

35 (1972) 1ALL N.L.R. (Pt.2.) 474 (Supreme Court of Nigeria).

it and therefore invalid in so far as they related to matter meant for the meeting to consider. Thirdly, the company should have been joined in the application.

The Nigerian Supreme Court decision, *Okeowo v. Migliore*[36] has also considered certain aspects of section 135 relating to the meaning of "impracticability" to hold a meeting, the jurisdiction of the court to order a meeting of the company where the application was in fact for a meeting of the board and whether unanimity of the company's members is a prerequisite for the court's exercise of its jurisdiction.

On the meaning of "impracticability", the Supreme Court indicated that the expression "impracticable" should be given a practical meaning i.e. the circumstances of a particular case should be examined to determine whether or not the meeting in issue can be conducted. The word is not synonymous with "impossible"[37] An example of impracticability is manifest from the facts of *Okeowo v. Migliore* [36]. There were five members - three Italians and two Nigerians. Between them they held about 46 percent of the total number of shares in the company. The ownership of the remaining 54 percent was disputed with the Nigerian shareholders challenging the claim of the Italian shareholders despite the latter being the administrators of the estate of the original holder and a court order in favour of the Italian shareholders. It was thus clear that the membership and directorate of the company was divided. The secretary was biased in favour of one fraction. The court concluded that it would not be easy to have a meeting of either the directors or the company to decide on the question of removal of the secretary or the issues affecting the general management of the company. Consequently, it ordered that a meeting of the company be held.

On the question of whether the court could order the holding of a meeting of the company when the application was for a meeting of the Board, the Supreme Court held[38] that this was permissable since a meeting convened as a meeting of directors is valid as a meeting of the company if all the members of the company are present.

With regard to the issue of unanimity of members as a prerequisite for a court order under section [135], Aniagolu J.S.C. indicated[39] that the Court's power under section [135]:

> ..............is not limited to where the directors and/or shareholders are in unanimous agreement but extends, in its wide scope, to a situation where there is a rift, such as in the instant case, among the directors and strenuous opposition by one faction of directors against the other...

# Notices of meetings

## Length of notice

The requisite notice of every general meeting must be sent to all members of the company, except where there is contrary provision in the articles.[40]

With respect to an annual general meeting, twenty one days written notice thereof must be given to the members[41]. These statutory provisions override anything in the articles providing for shorter notice. The "days" indicated refer to "clear" days i.e. exclusive both of the day of service and the day of the meeting[42]. However, a shorter notice may be given in respect of an

---

36 (1979) 11 S.C. 138

37 *ibid* p.187 per Idigbe, J.S.C. See also per Aniagolu, J.S.C. following Wynn-Perry, J in *Re: El. Sombrero, Supra* n.23 at p.904

38 Relying on *Palmer's Company Law* Paragraph 51-10, p.561.

39 *Supra* n.36, at p.164

40 *Smyth v. Darley* (1849) 2 H.L. Cas 789; *Onwuka v. Tayamani* (1965) L.C.R.62. *Young v. Ladies Imperial Club Ltd.* [1920] 2 K.B. 523.

41 Companies Act, S.133(1)

42 *Re: Hector Whaling* [1936] Ch.208 c.f. *Neil M'Leod & Sons Ltd., Petitioners,* 1967 S.C.16. See also Table A, Art.50.

annual general meeting if all members agree[43]. In respect of an extra-ordinary meeting shorter notice is permissable where holders of at least 95 percent in nominal value of the shares or in case of a company without share capital, 95 percent of total voting rights at that meeting of all the members agree[44].

It is also notable that decisions made informally i.e. without a meeting, but with the consent of all the members are valid as company decisions.[45]

## Service of notice

The procedure for service indicated in Table A to the Companies Act should be followed except where the company has contrary articles[46]. The relevant articles for this purpose in Table A are Articles 131 to 134. By Article 131, service of notice is affected either personally or through the post to the address of a member. Under Article 133, service may be affected upon the legal representative of a deceased member or trustee in bankruptcy of a bankrupt member at their addresses. Article 134 indicates that every member, legal representative of a deceased member or trustee in bankruptcy of a bankrupt member and auditor of the company are entitled to service or notice of the meetings of the company. Where there are joint holders of shares, notice may be given to the joint holder first named in the register of members in respect of the share (Art.132).

Failure to give notice to a person entitled to receive it renders any business transacted at the meeting void, unless otherwise provided by the articles[47]. For instance Article 51 in Table A says that the accidental omission to give notice or non-receipt of notice of a meeting by a person entitled to receive one does not invalidate the proceedings at that meeting. The article is, however, inapplicable where notice has not actually been sent to a member[48] or has been deliberately sent to a wrong address[49]. The omission to serve notice must be clearly accidental[50]. Otherwise the article is inapplicable. In *Ososanya v. J.A.O. Obadeyi*[51], the requisite notice was published in the Gazette as required by law. It was held that a member could not complain that he was unaware of the meeting taking place.

## Nature of notice

This is generally governed by the company's articles. Under Article 50 Table A, for instance, it is provided that the notice shall state the place, day and hour of the meeting and in the case of special business, the general nature of it. In addition, notice of the special business must also indicate the resolution to be passed. In *Baillie v. Oriental Telephone Electric Co. Ltd*[52], special resolutions were passed altering the articles of association in order to sanction the retention by directors of payments previously received in breach of trust. The notice convening the meeting at which the resolutions were passed did not give particulars of the amount of remuneration received by the directors. The plaintiff shareholder brought an action on behalf of himself and all other shareholders of the defendant company for a declaration that the resolutions were not binding on the ground of insufficient notice of the meeting at which they

---

43 Companies Act,S.133 (3) (a).

44 *ibid.* S.133(3)(b) See also s.141(2).

45 See *Parker & Cooper v. Reading* [1926] Ch.975; Re: Duomatic Ltd. [1969] 2 Ch.265; *Re: Bailey, Hay & Co. Ltd.* [1971] 1 W.L.R.1366; *Re: M.J. Shanley Contracting* (in Voluntary liquidation), (1979) 124 S.J.239; *Cane v. Jones* [1980] 1 W.L.R.1451. See also Table A, Part II, Art.5 read together with S.141(1), (2).

46 *ibid* S.127.

47 *Young v. Ladies Imperial Club Ltd.* [1920] 2 K.B.523; *Awoyemi v. Solomon* (1976) F.R.C.R.165; See also *Kyaggwe Farmers Assoc. Ltd. v. Kafeero* [1975] H.C.B.97 (High Court of Uganda).

48 *Onwuka v. Tayamani* 1968 (2) A.L.R. Comm. 313.

49 *Imonioro v. Seemuth Electro Engineering (Nig) Ltd.* Suit No. FRC/L/45/78 of 12/3/81 unreported.

50 *Musselwhite v. C.H. Musselwhite & Sons Ltd.* [1962] Ch. 134f *Re: West Canadian Collieries Ltd.* [1962] Ch 370.

51 1963(2) A.L.R.Comm.431.

52 [1915] 1.Ch.503 C.A. See also the Ugandan case, *Misango v. Musigire [1966]* E.A. 390.

were passed and for an injunction to restrain the company and directors from acting upon them. The action was upheld on appeal on the basis that the notice in issue did not give a sufficiently full and frank disclosure to the shareholders of the facts upon which they were asked to vote and the resolutions were not therefore, binding. Similarly, in *Kaye v. Croydon Tramways Co.*[53], provisional agreement was made between two companies for the sale of an undertaking of the one to the other. The purchasing company agreed to pay in addition to the sum payable to the selling company, a substantial sum to the directors of the selling company as compensation for loss of office and the agreement was made conditional upon its adoption by the shareholders of the selling company. The notice convening the meeting of shareholders to consider the agreement described it simply as an agreement for the sale of the undertaking. It did not mention the directors' remuneration. The selling company was governed by the Companies Clauses Act, 1845. It was held by the court of appeal that while the provision in favour of the directors did not render the agreement *ultra vires,* the notice by reason of its omission to refer to this provision did not fairly disclose the purpose for which the meeting was convened, and did not comply with Section 71 of the Companies Clauses Act, 1845. In *Tiessen v. Henderson*[54], it was indicated that the notice of an extraordinary meeting must disclose all facts necessary to enable the shareholder receiving it to determine in his own interest whether or not he ought to attend the meeting; and the preliminary interest of a director in the matter of a special resolution to be proposed at the meeting is a material fact for this purpose.

Notice of a special or extra-ordinary resolution must indicate the intention to propose it as such and the exact wording of the proposed special and extra-ordinary resolution must be shown in the notice[55]. The notice calling a meeting of a company with share capital must also state prominently that a member entitled to attend and vote is entitled to appoint a proxy and vote in his stead and that the proxy need not be a member.[56]

The notice of an annual general meeting must be accompanied by a balance sheet and auditors' report[57]. The balance sheet should have annexed to it the profit and loss account and group accounts.[58] These documents must be sent to each member at least 21 days before the meeting.[57]

## Special notice

Special notice is required to be given in respect of a meeting at which a resolution for the removal of a director[59], or the appointment of a director who is less than twenty one or over the age of seventy[60], or the appointment of a new auditor[61] is to be passed. Essentially, at least twenty-eight days notice must be given to the company of a meeting at which it is intended to move the relevant resolution. The company is in turn required to give notice of the resolution to its members at the same time and in the same manner as it gives notice of the meeting or alternatively advertise the notice not less than twenty-one days before the meeting[62]. The requirement of special notice, does not though override the requirement of numbers in Section 140 of the Companies Act [63].

---

53 [1898] 1 Ch.358 C.A. See also *Normandy v. Ind. Coope & Ltd. [1908] 1 Ch.84.*

54 [1899] 1 Ch.861. See also *Alexander v. Simpson* (2890) 43 Ch.D.

55 Companies Act, S.141. See also *Awoyemi v. Salomon* (1976) F.R.C.R.165; *Baillie v. Oriental Telephone Co. supra* n.52; *Maclonnel v. Prill(E) & Co.* [1916] 2 Ch.57.

56 *ibid.* S.136(2).

57 *ibid.* S.158.

58 *ibid,* S.156.

59 *ibid* S.185.

60 *ibid.* S.186.

61 *ibid.* S.160.

62 *ibid.* S.142.

63 *Pedley v. Inland Waterways Assocn. Ltd.* [1977] 1 ALL E.R. 209.

## Circulation of members' resolutions

Upon written requisition of members holding not less than one-twentieth of the total voting rights or 100 members holding shares on which there has been paid up an average of 2,000/= per member, the company must (i) give notice to all members of any resolution which requisitionists intend to move at the next annual general meeting; (ii) circulate to members any statement not exceeding one thousand words relating to any proposed resolution or business to be dealt with at that meeting[64]. The requisitions must sign and deposit the requisition at the registered office of the company at least six weeks before the meeting when it is notice of a resolution or one week in any other case[65], and also deposit or tender with the requisition a sum reasonably sufficient to meet the company's expenses.[66] The company is not obliged to circulate any statement which is essentially defamatory.[67]

## Proceeding at meetings

### Quorum

This is the minimum number of shareholders required to attend a meeting before business can be transacted.[68] Although the company's articles invariably regulate the quorum[68], where they are silent, the Companies Act provides[69]that in the case of a private company two members present in person and in the case of any other company three members personally present, constitute a quorum. However, the articles may prescribe that presence by proxy is adequate[70]. Although Table A Article 53 provides that"..... no business shall be transacted at any general meeting unless a quorum of members is present at the time when the meeting proceeds to business" it would appear that the requirement is satisfied if a quorum is present at the beginning of the meeting even if it does not subsist to the end[71] and more than one member remains throughout[72]. Exceptionally though, one member may constitute a quorum if he holds all the shares in his class[73] or where the registrar[74] or the court[75] declares that a quorum of one person is sufficient for a meeting.

The model articles further provide[76] that if within half and hour from the time appointed for the meeting a quorum is not present, the meeting if convened upon the requisition of members, shall be dissolved and that in every other case it shall stand adjourned to the same day in the next week at the same time and venue or as determined by the directors, when the members present shall form a quorum.

### Chairman

The articles usually stipulate who shall be the chairman at meetings. For instance, the model articles indicate[77] that the chairman of the board of directors, "if present and willing whom

64 *ibid*, S.140(1), (2)
65 *ibid*, S.140(4) (a)
66 *ibid*. S. 140(b)
67 *ibid*, S.140(5)
68 *ibid*, Table A. Art.53, Part II Art.4.
69 *ibid*, S.134
70 E.g. Table A Part II, Art.4 respecting a private company
71 *Re: Hartley Baird Ltd.* [1955] Ch.143; *Martins v. Ogungbadero & Ors.* 1967 NCLR 393 (High Court of LagosState)
72 *Martins v. Ogungbadero ibid. Sharp v. Dawes* (1876) 2 Q.B.D.26
73 *East v. Bennett Bros.* [1911] 1 Ch.162
74 Companies Act S.131(2)
75 *ibid*. S.135
76 *Table A*. Art.54

failing one of the directors, whom failing anyone selected by the members present, shall take the chair"[78]. Where the articles are silent as to who should be the chairmen, the members present may themselves nominate one.[79]

The chairman's duties are essentially to ensure proper and orderly conduct of the business at the meeting, regulate the proceedings and understand the sense of the meeting[80]. Article 60 in the model articles[81] gives the chairman a casting vote at the meeting.

## Resolutions

The Companies Act provides for three types of resolutions at meetings, namely, ordinary, extra-ordinary and special[82]. An ordinary resolution is passed by a simple majority of those voting. It is employed with respect to matters which do not require an extraordinary or special resolution under the articles or the Act. An extra-ordinary resolution is passed by a three-fourths majority at a general meeting of which notice specifying the intention to propose the resolution as an extraordinary resolution has been given[83]. Under the Companies Act an extraordinary resolution is required for specific matters relating to winding-up[84], although the articles may require one in other cases such as the modification of class rights at class meetings[85]. A special resolution is also passed by a three-fourths majority. However, 21 days' notice specifying the intention to propose the resolution as a special resolution has to be given[86]. A shorter notice may be given provided it is sanctioned by at least 95 percent of either holders in nominal value of the shares or holders of the total voting rights.[87] A special resolution is invariably required "before any important constitutional changes can be undertaken"[88] such as the alteration of the memorandum[89]or the articles[90], the reduction of capital with the court's consent[91]. The chairman's declaration that an extraordinary or special resolution has been carried is conclusive of the fact, unless a poll is demanded, without proof of the number or proportion of the votes recorded in favour of or against the resolution.[92]

Special and extraordinary resolutions are required to be registered with the Registrar of Companies.[93]

## Amendments to resolutions

The amendment to a resolution is proposed or moved, debated and then voted upon before considering the substantive resolution. Where the amendment is carried, the meeting then proceeds to consider the resolution as amended. Should the amendment be lost, the meeting considers the original resolution.

The general rule is that an amendment will only be allowed if it is within the ambit of the notice convening the meeting. In this vein it has been suggested that no amendment would be allowed to an extraordinary or special resolution because Section 141 of the Companies Act

77 *ibid,* Arts.55-56.
78 Gower, *op.cit.* p.543.
79 Companies Act, S.134(d).
80 See generally Gower, *op.cit.* pp.543-544; Orojo (2nd Ed. 1984), pp.446-447.
81 Table A.
82 These bear no relation to the distinction between ordinary and extraordinary meetings: Gower, *op.cit*, p.544.
83 Companies Act, S.141(1).
84 *ibid*, Ss.276, 301, 304, 336.
85 e.g. Table A. Art.4.
86 *ibid*, S.141(2). See also *Re: Moorgate Mercantile Holdings Ltd.* [1980] 1 ALL E.R.40.
87 *ibid.* S. 141(2) Proviso.
88 Gower, *op.cit.* p.544.
89 Companies Act, Ss.9,20(1),25.
90 *ibid.* S.13.
91 *ibid,* S.68. For other cases where a special resolution is required, see Ss.62,67,166,204,205,222,276,285.
92 *ibid.* S.141(3).

requires "notice specifying the intention to propose the resolution". Thus in *Maclonnell v. Prill(E) & Co.*[94] it was alleged that the notice convening the meeting did not firstly, specify the resolution and secondly, the intention to pass the resolution as an extra-ordinary resolution within section 69 of the British Companies Act, 1908. Sergeant J., upheld both objections and observed thus:[95]

> As regards the first objection, it is obvious that the notice signifies merely an intention to make the specific increase embodied in the resolution that was actually passed. It seems to me of great importance that shareholders should be protected in matters of this kind by specific notice of what is intended to be done.

This approach is premised on the idea that if the amendment goes beyond the notice convening the meeting, it is irregular because those members not attending the meeting might claim that they would have attended had they known of the nature of the amendment.[96] Nevertheless, Professor Gower submits that this is too strict an interpretation of (Section 141) and that amendments are allowed within certain narrow limits" and that it is advisable to frame the notice so that it indicates the possibility of amendments"[97].

## Voting

Except as may be provided by the company's regulations, in the first instance each member has one vote by a show of hands irrespective of the number of shares held by him and no proxies are allowed.[98]However, a poll may be demanded before or on the declaration of the result of a show of hands.[99] Nevertheless, the articles cannot exclude the right to demand a poll or require more than 5 voting members or members with at least one-tenth of total voting rights or members holding at least one-tenth of the total paid up capital to demand it.[100] Where a poll has been demanded voting may be either personally or by proxy[101]. Each share is entitled to one vote on a poll[102], while each 20 stock has one vote except where the articles otherwise provide.[103] Members are not obliged to exercise all their votes at once or in the same way.[104]

Where a poll has been demanded on the election of a chairman or the issue of adjournment it should be taken immediately. In any other case the chairman decides as to when it should be taken.[105] The poll is normally taken through members present or by proxy signing lists or slips which indicate whether they vote for or against and the number of votes polled by them.[106] The poll may be demanded by the chairman, at least three members present or proxy, any member(s) representing at least one-tenth of the total voting rights at the meeting or holding at least one-tench of the total paid up capital[107] In addition, a proxy is entitled to demand a poll.[108]

## Proxies

Any member of the company, entitled to attend and vote at a meeting of the company is entitled to appoint another person irrespective of whether the latter is a member as his proxy to attend

---

93 *ibid.* S.143. See also *Salgitter (W.A.) Ltd. v. Registrar of Companies* 1975 NCLR 149.

94 [1916] 2 Ch.57.

95 *ibid.* p.61.

96 Gower, *op.cit.* p.546.

97 *ibid.* p.545.

98 Companies Act, S.136(1) (c); Table A. Art 58 and 62. See also *Earnest v. Loma Gold Mines* [1897] Ch. 1C.A.

99 Table A. Art.58. See also *Curruth v. I.C.I.* [1937] A.C. 707, at pp.754-755 H.L. *Holmes v. Keyes* [1959] Ch.199.C.A.

100 Companies Act, S.137.

101 Table A; *ibid.*, Art.67.

102 Table A. Art. 62. See also S.134(e).

103 *ibid.* S.134(e).

104 *ibid.*, S.138.

105 e.g. Table A. Art.61.

106 Under Table A. Art.59 the chairman directs the mode of exercise of the poll.

107 *ibid.* Art.58.

and vote instead of himself and in respect of a member of a private company the proxy has the same right as the member to speak at the meeting.[109]The right to appoint a proxy only applies to Companies having a share capital, except where a company's articles provide otherwise[110]Furthermore unless there is contrary provision in the articles a member of a private company is not entitled to appoint more than one proxy to attend on the same occasion, nor is a proxy entitled to vote except on a poll[111]. Shareholders should be informed, in the notice convening the meeting of their right to appoint a proxy who need not be a member to attend and vote in their stead.[112] Where the proxies have been solicited at the company's expense, the invitation must be sent to all members entitled to attend and vote[113]. Provision in the articles to the effect that proxy instruments must be lodged more than 48 hours before a meeting or adjourned meeting is void[114]. Consequently, it is adequate for the relevant instrument to be received by the company at least 48 hours before the meeting. The proxy can be revoked expressly before it has been acted upon by the company or by the member attending and voting in person on a particular resolution[115], although the proxy can still vote on some other resolution not voted on by the member.[116]

## Company representative

A corporation, including a company as defined by the Companies Act, which is a member of another company may, by a resolution of its directors or other governing body authorise such person as it thinks fit to act as its representative at meetings and the representative may exercise the same powers on its behalf as it could itself exercise if it were an individual[117]. This is an instance where the representative of the company acts as its organ rather than mere agent.[118]

## Adjournment

An adjournment of a meeting may be necessary where thee is insufficient time for the conclusion of its business on the given day or because of lack of requisite quorum. The articles normally provide that in the latter case the meeting automatically stands adjourned to the sametime and place in the following week when the members present shall be quorum[119]. The adjourned meeting is taken to be a continuation of the original meeting, and consequently, no further notice is required except where the articles provide the contrary[120]. However, resolutions passed at an adjourned meeting shall be treated as having been passed on the date on which they were in fact passed and not on the date of the original meeting.[121] Furthermore, the regulations cannot prevent the lodging of further proxies up to 48 hours before the adjourned meeting.[122]

---

108 *ibid* S.137(2); Art.72.

109 *ibid* S. 136(1).

110 *ibid.* S.136 1 (a).

111 *ibid.* S. 136(1);(b),(c).

112 *ibid.* S. 136(2).

113 *ibid* S.136(4).

114 *ibid* S.136(3). See also Table A, Arts 67-73 for the form of the proxy instrument and the powers it confers. See too *Peel v. L. & N.W. Rly .Co.* [1907] 1 Ch. 5C.A. and Gower, *op.cit* pp.540-541.

115 *Cousins v. International Brick Co.* [1931] 2 Ch.90 C.A. See also Table A, Art.73.

116 *Anselt v. Butter Air Transport Ltd.* (no.2) 1958 75 W.N. P.S.W.) 306).

117 Companies Act, S.139. See also Table A. Art.74 and *Hillman V. Crystal Bowl Amusements Ltd.* [1973] a, W.L.R. 62 at p.165 per Russel L.J.

118 C.f. Chap.12 *Supra.*

119 e.g. Table A Art.54.

120 *Will v. Murray* (1850) 4 Exch.843 *N.B* Table A. Art.57 provides that notice of the adjourned meeting shall be given if the adjournment exceeds 30 days.

121 Companies Act, S.144.

122 *ibid* S.136(3).

### Minutes

Minutes of the all proceedings at the company's meetings are required to be recorded in books kept for that purpose[123]including loose-leaf books provided that sufficient precaution is taken against falsification[124]. Minutes signed by the chairman of the meeting or the next succeeding meeting shall be evidence of the proceedings[125] and the meeting is deemed to have been duly held, convened and regularly conducted[126]. The articles may provide that the minutes shall be conclusive evidence of the proceedings,[127] in the absence of fraud[128]. However, where the articles do not so provide, other evidence may be admitted[129].

The minutes are open to inspection by members only at the company's registered office[130].

## Class meetings

Apart from general meetings, of separate classes of members or debenture holders may be convened. The relevant rules in that regard depend on the articles interpreted relative to the general law. Although the Companies Act is generally silent about class meetings, certain provisions relating to proxies [131], representation of corporation[132], resolutions passed at an adjourned meeting[133] and voting on a poll[134] are expressly made applicable to meetings of any class of members[135]. It is also significant that the model articles indicate that [136] to any separate meeting of a class of shareholders the provisions of Table A relating to general meetings shall apply, provided that the quorum shall be two persons at least holding or representing by proxy one-third of the issued shares of the class. Furthermore, any holder of shares of the class present in person or by proxy may demand a poll.

## Privilege and the press

Company meetings are privileged with the result that statements made thereafter cannot be sued upon as defamation, except where they are malicious[137]. This notion stems from the fact that members and directors have a common interest in matters affecting the company and a duty to disclose information[138]. However, this common law privilege is not extensive to public broadcasts and media dissemination of company proceedings[139]. Consequently, a newspaper's usual defence against a libel case brought against it would be either justification or fair comment

---

123 *ibid* S.145(1). See also *Nasr v. Berini Beirut-Riyadh (Nig.) Bank Ltd.* 1968 NCLR 370 at p.385 (Supreme Court of Nigeria).

124 *ibid* S.393(2).

125 *ibid* S.145(2).

126 *ibid* S.145(3). See also *Tung. V. Nig. Carton & Packaging Manufacturing Co. Ltd.* Suit No. *FRC/L/M/ 82/78, Unreported.*

127 e.g. Table A. Art. 58.

128 *Kerr v. Mottram* [1940] Ch.657.

129 *Re: Fireproof Doors* [1916] 2 Ch.142.

130 S.146.

131 *ibid* S.136.

132 *ibid,* S.139.

133 *ibid* S.144.

134 *ibid* S.138.

135 *ibid.* S.136(5); S.139(1)(a); S.144(b); S.138.

136 Table A. Art.4.

137 *London-Griffiths v.Smith* [1951]1K.B. 295.

138 Gower, *op.cit.* p.552.

139 *Ponsford v. Financial Times* (1900) 16 T.L.R.

on a matter of public interest. In addition, there is statutory provision.[140] to the effect that publication of fair and accurate report of the proceedings at a general meeting of any company or association other than a private company is privileged and consequently not actionable except where malice is shown, in which case the publisher is required to publish a reasonable correction or explanation [141]. Where the subject matter of the meeting published is illegal or not of public interest or concern the publisher also loses his privilege[142] but may still rely on the common law right of privilege[143] as a defence.

---

[140] e.g. Defamation Law, Cap.17, Laws of Western Nigeria, 1959, Ss.16, 17, Sched. para 13

[141] *ibid*,S.16(2)

[142] *ibid*,S.16(3)

[143] *ibid*, S.16(4)

# 17
# RECONSTRUCTION AND AMALGAMATION OF COMPANIES

## Introduction

Broadly, a company may be reconstructed in five principal ways. First, by means of reduction of its capital[1] Second, through variation of class rights under the Memorandum and Articles of Association[1]. Third, by compromise and arrangement.[2] Fourth by way of take-over bid,[3] and finally, through reconstruction and amalgamation[4]. Since the first two modes have already been dealt with, attention in this chapter will centre on the last thee modes or reconstruction.

## Compromise and arrangement

### Schemes under Sections 207-208

It may be necessary to effect a compromise or an arrangement between a company and its creditors or any class of them or alternatively between a company and its members or any class of them[5]. Where the company is about to be or is in the course of being voluntarily wound up this may be done under Section 304 of the Companies Act. However, where the winding up is compulsory, the liquidator, may, with the court's sanction or that of a committee of inspection, make any compromise or arrangement with the creditors[6]. The procedure for a compromise or an arrangement, irrespective of whether or not the company is being wound-up is laid down in Section 207 of the Companies Act. The section applies to any compromise or arrangement between the company and its creditors of corporations or any class of them. An "arrangement" is defined[7] to include a reorganisation of share capital of the company by the consolidation of shares of different classes or by the division of shares of different classes or by the division of shares of different classes by those methods. Such arrangement also includes the exchange of debentures or other securities for shares in a new company[8], and any scheme which effects the contractual relationship between the company and its creditors or any class of them or between the company and its members or any class of them[9]. However, expropriation of shareholders' rights without compensation is not an arrangement.[10]

The phraseology of Section 207(1) assumes consent to the scheme of arrangement or compromise by the company as a legal personality separate from its members. Consequently, where the company does not assent to the scheme either through its board or by a requisite resolution passed in general meeting, the court will not sanction the scheme under section 207.[11]

---

1 See *supra* chap.9 and generally Chap.5.
2 Companies Act, Ss. 207-209 or 304.
3 *ibid,* S.210.
4 *ibid,* Ss.209, 285.
5 *ibid* S. 207(1).
6 *ibid* S. 244(1) (e).
7 *ibid* S.207(5)(b).
8 *Re: Empire Mining Co.* (1890) 44 Ch.40.
9 *Re: Savoy Hotel Ltd.* [1981] 3 All E.R. 646 *Lalji v. Ahmed* (1933) 15 L.R.K.16.
10 *Re: National Farmers Union Development Trust ltd.* [1972] 1 W.L.R.1548 at p.1555 per Brightman J.
11 *Re: Savoy Hotel Ltd., supra* n.10 interpreting Section 206 of the Companies Act, 1948 (U.K.) which is in pari *materia* with Section 207 of the Companies Act (Uganda).

Essentially, the procedure under sections 207 and 208 of the Companies Act is for a scheme of arrangement or compromise to be prepared by the company, its members, creditors or liquidator. An application is then made to the court by either of those persons for an order that a meeting of the company or class of members or creditors or class of creditors be summoned in a manner prescribed by the court. Where the order is granted, the meeting is held as directed by the court. Where the meeting is summoned, notice of it must be accompanied by a statement explaining the effect of the compromise or arrangement and indicating the material interests of the directors of the company and the effect thereon of the compromise or arrangement.[12] Similar particulars should be given in the case of a meeting summoned by means of an advertisement.[13] Should the compromise or arrangement affect the rights of debenture holders of the company, the relevant statement must give similar explanation relating to the trustees of any deed for securing the issue of debentures as in the case of the company's directors.[14]

The provisions of Sections 207 to 208 have been strictly interpreted. Consequently, it has been held that the order requested thereunder cannot be given by the court if those provisions have not been complied with[15] In *Re: Alabama, New, Orleans, Texas & Pacific Junction Railway Co.*[16], it was indicated[17] that the court should ensure that, the relevant statutory provisions have been carried out; the majority have acted *bona fide;* the minority is not overridden by the majority having interests of its own clashing with those of the minority whom they seek to coerce; the scheme is one as to which persons acting honestly, and viewing the scheme laid before them in the interests of these whom they represent, take a view which can be reasonably taken by businessmen. Furthermore the court will not sanction the scheme if it involves *ultra vires* transactions[18] or is contrary to the general law[19].

The next step is that at the meeting convened, the draft-scheme of compromise or arrangement must be approved, with amendments, where necessary by at least three-fourths of the creditors or class thereof or members or class thereof as the case may be and voting either in person or by proxy,[20]. Finally, an office copy of the court order must be filed with the companies registrar for registration.[21] The order will be ineffective except where it has been filed.[22]

## Schemes under Section 304

Section 304 of the Companies Act deals with any arrangement between the company and its creditors where the company is about to be, or is in the course of being wound-up. Subject to a right of appeal, such arrangement binds, (i) the company if sanctioned by an extraordinary resolution and (ii) the creditors if acceded to by three-fourths in number and value of the creditors. Any creditor or contributory who is not satisfied with the arrangement may appeal to the High Court within three weeks of completion thereof. The court may amend, vary or confirm the arrangement as deemed equitable.

---

12 Companies Act, S. 208(1)(a).
13 *ibid* S. 208(1)(b).
14 *ibid* S.208(2).
15 See *Re: Dorman Long & Co.* Ltd. [1934] Ch.635; *Rankin & Blackmore Ltd; Petitioners.* 1950 S.C. 218.
16 [1891] 1 Ch.213 C.A.
17 *ibid*, p.238.
18 *Re: Oceanic Steam Navigation Co. Ltd.* [1939], Ch.41.
19 *Re: St. James' Court Estate Ltd.* [1944] Ch.6.
20 Companies Act, S.207(2). See also *Re: Oceanic Steam Navigation Co. Ltd. supra* n.19.
21 *ibid*, S.207(3).
22 See also *Re: Hellenic & General Trust Ltd* [1975] 3 All E.R. 382.

This arrangement differs from schemes under section 207 in that in this case it can only be made between the company and its creditors and not with members. Additionally, the company must either be in the course of winding-up or about to be wound-up.

## Reconstruction and amalgamation

Reconstruction may be carried out to achieve better business efficiency or to eliminate competition in respect of sales, raw materials, markets or personnel or other reasons[23]. The reconstruction in this case is achieved by transferring the assets of the company to a new company owned by the same persons. This is done under an arrangement whereby he shareholders of the transferor company receive shares or other interests in the transferee company.[24] Essentially the process entails the amalgamation of two companies into one of them or a third formed for that purpose. For instance, where a company T. Ltd. consists of O,P and Q as shareholders and a scheme of reconstruction is arranged between T. Ltd. and a new company S. Ltd. the assets of T. Ltd will be transferred to S. Ltd, in return for the shares of S. Ltd. being allotted to O, P.Q. T. Ltd is then wound up. This amounts to a reconstruction. Alternatively, V. Ltd. may acquire the shares and assets of two companies, W. Ltd. and X. Ltd. Furthermore, if in the first example, instead of S. Ltd. acquiring the assets of T. Ltd, it only acquires its shares and keeps T. Ltd. alive as a subsidiary, this is regarded as an amalgamation.[25]

The reconstruction and amalgamation may be effected by means of three Procedures:[26]

### Arrangement under Sections 207-209

The Scheme already considered under Section 207 may be used to bring about an amalgamation or reconstruction of a company. Essentially, this would entail the formation of a new company, the transfer of the undertaking of the old company or companies to a new one or the distribution of part or all the shares of a new company to shareholders of the old company.[27] In line with Section 207, application has to be made to the court for the confirmation of the scheme. The court may make an order providing for any of the matters listed in Section 209(1). The relevant court order sanctioning or refusing the scheme must be delivered to the Registrar of Companies within seven days of its having been made.[28]

### Reconstruction under Section 285

The procedure here, which is relatively more straightforward than the one above, is for the company to resolve upon a voluntary winding-up and by special resolution to authorise the liquidator to sell to another company (usually formed for the purpose). In return, it receives in payment shares or other securities of that company for distribution among the members of the company in liquidation. This arrangement is binding on the members of the transferor or liquidated company[29]. However, any of the members who did not vote in favour of the special resolution may, within seven days after the passing of such resolution, express his dissent in writing to the liquidator and require him either to abstain form executing the resolution or to purchase his interest at a price to be determined by agreement or arbitration.[30]

---

23 Orojo, *op.cit.* (2nd Ed.) p.651.

24 See also *Re: Bendel Line Co. Ltd.* Suit No. FRC/W/20/78 of 2/2/79 Unreported.

25 This is in line with S.9(1) (g) of the Companies Act enabling a Company to alter the objects in its memorandum to enable it to amalgamate with any other company. See *supra* Chap.4.

26 See further Orojo, *supra* n.24 pp.652-655; Gower *op.cit.* pp.689-693.

27 See further section 209.

28 *ibid,* S.209(3).

29 *ibid,* S.285(2).

30 *ibid.* S.285(3).

The procedure under this section differs from that under Sections 207 to 209 in the following ways[31]. First, the transferor company must be put into liquidation following the normal procedure except that the consenting members receive shares in the acquiring company instead of cash. It is notable that there is no procedure similar to Section 209 for dispensing with formal assignments of property or of winding up. Second, there can be no variation of creditors' rights. Creditors can still prove in the liquidation of the old company and the liquidator has to ensure that claims are met to the extent of the company's assets. He cannot rely upon any indemnity given by the acquiring company.[32] Nevertheless, the sale of the undertaking is binding on creditors.[33] The effect of this is that the creditors have to look to the securities obtained in payment instead of the former assets of the company. However, since this may affect them adversely, especially where the securities consist of unlisted shares, it is provided under Section 285(5) that if an order is made within a year for the winding-up of the old company compulsorily or under supervision, the special resolution shall not be valid except where it has been confirmed by the court. Third, the extent to which there can be variation of the rights of members is also limited. Consequently, shares in the new company must be distributed among the members of the old company in strict accordance with their class rights on winding-up.[34]

As a result, it becomes difficult to apply the section unless all the shares in the old company have equal rights on winding-up or unless those with special rights expressly agree, or dissent and elect to be paid out[35] Fourth, shareholders may not against their will be forced to accept new shares. If they dissent, the liquidator has either to drop the scheme or pay them out according to their previous rights. Fifth, the scheme under Section 285 can be implemented without the need to apply to the court for confirmation. Consequently, it is the only mode of reconstruction which may be employed without involving an application to court for confirmation or affording dissentients a special statutory right to apply to the court.[36] Finally, it is only registered companies which can benefit form Section 285 in so far as it is expressly restricted to voluntary liquidation[37], whereas an unregistered company can only be wound up compulsorily.[38] It is also notable that the company to whom the undertaking is to be transferred need not be a company within the meaning of the Act, although the sale must be to a company and not an individual[39].

It is thus evident that Section 285 is narrower in its application than Sections 207-209. Nevertheless, the fact that the application to court is dispensed with, makes it cheaper and more convenient. It is specially useful in simple amalgmations of private companies when a new company can be formed to take over the undertakings of the various companies to be merged[40]. Its main disadvantage is that dissenting shareholders can insist on being paid out. This is possible even where the memorandum provides in the objects clause that the company may sell its business to another in consideration of the shares therein. It was formerly thought that this power enable the sale of shares to be effected without complying with the rights of dissentients under Section 285. However, this view was disallowed in *Bisgood v. Hendersons' Transvaal Estates*.[41] The controllers there attempted, by relying on the aforesaid authorisation in the memorandum to force members to accept shares with increased liability. It was held that while the sale of shares

[31] See Gower, *op.cit.*, p.689-691

[32] *Pulsford v. Davenish* [1903] 2 Ch.625.

[33] *Re: City & County Investment Co.* (1879) 13 Ch.D.475

[34] *Griffith v. Paget* No.1 (1877) 5 Ch.D. 894, No.2 (1877) 6 Ch.D.511.

[35] Gower, *op.cit.* p.690

[36] Except where they plead infringement of their rights: *Griffith v. Paget, supra* n.35; *Re: Consolidated South* Rand Mines Deep Ltd. [1909] 1 Ch.491

[37] S.285(1)

[38] *ibid*, S.363

[39] *ibid* S.285(1)

[40] Gower, *op.cit;* p.691

[41] [1908] 1 Ch.743 C.A.

might be *intra vires* and valid, if the transaction was intended as a sale and distribution, it could only be effected under the equivalent of Section 285.

This avenue for disregarding dissenting shareholders having been plugged, the companies tried to rely on the equivalent of sections 207-209 as a means of evading the shareholders' rights to dissent under Section 285. In such a situation guideline has been provided by Astbury J. in *Re: Anglo-Continental Supply Co.*[42] as to the position of the dissenters. First, if the scheme is really a simple sale under Section 285, it must be implemented under that section and the rights of dissentients cannot be evaded by resorting to a scheme under Section 207. Second, if the scheme cannot be carried out under Section 285, although it involves a sale for shares to be distributed, the court can sanction it under Section 207 and may, if it thinks fit, insist as a term of its approval that dissentients shall be protected in a similar manner to that provided for in section 285 as was the case here and in *Re: Sandwell Park Colliery Co.*[43] However, the court need not insist on this requirement.[44]

### Sale under power in the Memorandum

The Memorandum of Association sometimes gives power to the company to sell its undertaking, but unless such power is given the company cannot go ahead and sell the undertaking.[45] Where such a power exists, the reconstruction or amalgamation involves a simple sale of the undertaking of the company to a new company normally formed for the purpose. The members of the old company receive shares in the new company, while the old company is dissolved.

## Take-overs through acquisition of shares[46]

This is popularly known as a take-over bid. It differs form the previous methods in that the company being taken over does not itself participate in the operation. Essentially, one company or individual bidder makes an offer to the shareholders of another to buy their shares either for cash or for its own shares or debentures or for a mixture of both. The offer is usually expressed to be conditional on acceptance by a stated proportion of the shareholders (usually 90 percent) in such a way that those accepting become bound to sell but the offeror does not become bound to buy until the condition is fulfilled. Where, as a result, the acquiring company obtains a controlling interest in the taken-over company, the latter becomes a subsidiary of the former and a merger is thereby achieved. Where the consideration was shares in the acquiring company, the shareholders in the taken-over company will become shareholders in the acquiring company just as is the case under Sections 207 or 285.

The provision relevant to take-overs under the Companies Act, is to be found in Section 210. There, it is indicated[47] that if under a scheme or contract an offer by a company to acquire the shares or any class of shares of a registered company has been accepted within four months of the offer by the holders of at least 90 percent in value of the shares involved (other than shares already held), the acquiring company can within two months give notice to any non-accepting shareholder that it wishes to acquire his shares. The acquiring company is then entitled and bound to acquire his shares on the same terms unless the court, on application by the shareholder

---

42 [1922] 2 Ch.723.

43 [1914] 1 Ch.589.

44 *Sorbie v. Tea Corproation* [1904] 1 Ch.12 C.A.; *Re: Guardian Assurance Co.* [1917] 1 Ch. 431 C.A. See further Gower, *op.cit* pp.692-693.

45 *Ernest v. Nicholls* (1857) 6 H.L.C.401.

46 See also generally Gower, *op.cit.*, pp.693-699; Weinberg, *Take-overs and Mergers* [3rd Edn, 1971]; Davis, *The Regulation of Take-overs and Merger* [1976].

47 S.210(1).

within one month orders otherwise[48]. There is also provision for executing transfers on behalf of reluctant members.[49] Such a procedure will be available even though the acquiring company already owns more than 10 percent of the shares. However, in such a case the same terms of take-over must be offered to all the shareholders whose shares are involved,[50] and the offer must be accepted by three-fourths in number as well as 90 percent in value.[51] This may, however, give rise to difficulties[52]. As a result this provision was recommended for repeal in Britain.[53]

Dissenting minority whose shares are being acquired may appeal to the court firstly "to object to the terms where the acquiring company has given notice to acquire the minority's shares[54], and, secondly to settle the terms when the dissenter has served notice electing to be bought out."[55] The majority of cases [56] relating to the first ground of dissent indicate that the burden is on the applicants to prove the unfairness of the terms. Invariably this is a very heavy burden to discharge. Where an offer has been accepted by over 90 percent of the affected shareholders, in the words of Maugham J.[57]

> Prima facie the court ought to regard the scheme as a fair one in as much as it seems... impossible to suppose that the court, in the absence of very strong grounds, is to be entitled to set up its own view of the fairness of the scheme in opposition to so very large a majority of the shareholders who are concerned.

In *Re: Sussex Brick Co. Ltd*[57], the court declined to interfere even though it was apparent that "a better scheme might have been evolved" and indicated that such interference would only be justified where the offer was "obviously unfair patently unfair, unfair to the meanest intelligence."[58]

Evidence of lack of full disclosure to the dissenting shareholder is insufficient to amount to unfairness in this context[59]. The dissentients must indicate the grounds on which they rely in their application[60] and are not entitled to discovery in this regard.[61] Unfairness is moreover to be gauged relative to the general body of shareholders rather than the particular circumstances of the individual dissentient.[62]

Nevertheless, unfairness will be manifest and impeachable where it is shown that the shareholders who have approved a takeover scheme are not independent of the offeror. Thus in *Re: Bugle Press Ltd.*[63], the holders of 90 percent of the shares in a company formed another company which made an offer for the shares of the first company. The 90 percent shareholders then accepted the offer and the new company served notice on the holder of the other 10 percent

---

48 See e.g. *Re: Samuel Heap & Sons Ltd.* [1965] 1 W.L.R. 1455.

49 S. 210 (3),(4).

50 S.210(1) (a) Proviso.

51 *ibid.* S.210 (1) (b) Proviso.

52 See e.g. *Re: Simo Securities Trust Co.* [1971] 1 W.L.R.1455.

53 Report of the Company Law Committee (1962) para 288 (1749 Cmnd.)

54 S.210 (1).

55 *ibid.* S. 210(2). See also Gower, op. cit. p. 715.

56 *See Re: Hoare & Co. Ltd.* [1933] 150 L.T. 374; *Re: Evertite Locknuts Ltd.* [1945] Ch.220; *Re: Press Caps Ltd.* [1949] Ch.434 C.A.; *Re: Western Manufacturing (Reading) Ltd.* [1956] Ch.436; *Re: Trinidad Oil Co. Ltd.* The Times, April, 13, 1957; *Re: Sussex Brick Co. Ltd.* [1961] Ch.270, C.A.; *Re: Grierson* Oldham & Adams Ltd. [1968] Ch.17; *Re: Carlton Holdings Ltd.* [1971] W.L.R.918; *Re: Simo Securities Trust Ltd.* [1971] 1 W.L.R. 1455. See also Gower *ibid* pp.715-716.

57 *Re: Hoare & Co. Ltd.; ibid,* at p.375.

58 [1961] Ch. at p.292.

59 *Re: Evertite Locknuts Ltd.* supra n.57.

60 *Nidditch v.Calico Printers Association,* 1961 S.L.T. 282.

61 *Re: Press Caps Ltd.* [1948] 2 All E.R. 638.

62 *Re: Grierson, Oldham & Adams Ltd, supra* n.57.

of the shares indicating that it wished to buy his shares. It was held that in essence the new company was the same as the majority shareholders. Consequently, unless good reasons in the interest of the company were shown making the expropriation of the minority interest, tenable, the court would not sanction the compulsory purchase.

# 18
# LIQUIDATION

## Introduction

The law on the winding-up or liquidation of a company is an extension of the law of bankruptcy. However, special rules which are laid down in the Companies Act,[1] govern the winding up of companies.

Apart from the end of the company being brought about by the registrar striking it off the Register of Companies consequent upon its becoming defunct[2], or its being reorganised or amalgamated,[3] the usual way of terminating the life of a company is through winding-up. Winding-up may take three forms:[4] (i) by the High Court (ii) voluntarily by either the members or creditors of the company; (iii) subject to the supervision of the court.

## Bases for winding up by the court

A company may be wound up by the court in the following circumstances:[5]

(i) If the company has passed a special resolution for its winding up by the court.[6]

(ii) Where default is made in delivering the statutory report to the registrar or in holding a statutory meeting. This is only applicable to public companies[7], and can only he invoked by a shareholder.[8] The court has discretion to direct that a meeting he held or that the necessary report should be delivered, instead of issuing a winding-up order.[9] Where a contributory who petitions on this ground avers that the accounts and information about the company have not been supplied he is not required to prove that there is available surplus, following the winding up for distribution.[10]

(iii) If the company does not commence its business within a year from incorporation, or suspends its business for a whole year. A winding-up order will only be granted if there is not intention to carry on business. Consequently, the order will not be made if the company has been prevented by circumstances beyond its control from carrying business as for instance by legislative act or depression in trade or the omission is temporary and there is intention to carry on business following removal of the obstacles.[11] Additionally, where the company intends to carry on business both in Uganda and abroad, it will not be wound up on this ground if it carries on business abroad, but not in Uganda so long as it intends to do so as soon as practicable.[12]

1 Parts V, VI and IX.
2 Companies Act, S.343, considered *infra*.
3 See supra Chap.17.
4 Companies Act, 212(1).
5 Companies Act. S.222.
6 *ibid*, S.222(a).
7 *ibid*, S.130 (10).
8 *ibid*, S.224 (1)(b).
9 *ibid*, S.225(3).
10 A-*G for Lagos State v. Nigerian Oxygen & Allied Cases Ltd;* Suit No. ERC/L/M3/77 of 13/3/80, Unreported. Compare with *Re: Italcomm (W.Nig.) Ltd.* 1972 NCLR 293 (High Court of Lagos State).
11 *Re: Middlesborough Assembly Rooms Co.* (1880) 14 Ch.D. 104 C.A. *Re: Metropolitan Railway Warehousing Co.* (1867) 36 L.J. Ch. 827; Orojo *op.cit* (2nd Ed. 1984) p.528.
12 *Re: Capital Fire Insurance Association* (1882) 21 Ch.D.209; Orojo *ibid* p.529.

(iv) Where the number of members is reduced to below the legal minimum i.e. two in the case of a private company and 7 in the case of any other company. A contributory is expressly authorised to petition for winding up on this ground[13].

(v) Where the company is unable to pay its debts. This will be the case where the company has failed to satisfy an execution issued against it or to pay a debt of shs 1,000/= within three weeks of demand for payment.[14] Alternatively, a winding-up order will be issued where it is clear that the company cannot pay its debts considering its contingent and prospective liabilities.[15] In *Re: Medipharm Publications (Nig.) Ltd.*[16], a petition was lodged asking the court to wind-up the company. It was shown that the company was destitute, having a nominal capital of £100, which had since been expended. Additionally, it had no assets and could not meet its routine obligations. It had only about £3 in the bank and a cheque for £100 was dishonoured. Consequently, the winding-up order was granted. Furthermore, in *Bakare v. Bakado Line Ltd.*[17], during the cause of proceedings, it was established that the company's account showed a deficit of £5,000. Additionally, for several months no expenses could be paid and the company had done very little business following its incorporation. There were only two members with one share each. The company's bank overdraft facilities was on the personal security of one of them. They were, however, exhausted. An order for winding up was granted since the company could not pay its debts. However, the mere fact that for a period the company does not have sufficient money to pay its present debts, but demand for repayment thereof has not been made, does not constitute inability to discharge the debts[18].

The demand for repayment of the debts is therefore crucial in determining inability to pay the debts. No special form of words is required to constitute demand. In *Standard Bank (Nig.) v. B.G.C.Co. Nig. Ltd.*[19] a letter requesting the debtor to pay his debt was held to be valid demand. Nevertheless, a demand made by a company must be authenticated under Section 38 of the Companies Act by being signed by a director, secretary or other officer of the creditor company. A solicitor retained by the creditor company is not an officer of the company for this purpose.[20] In addition the demand must be properly served on the company. *In Re: W. Biney & Co. (Nig.) Ltd.*[21], the demand was sent to the company by post. It was held[22] that this was insufficient for purposes of Section 210(a) of the Act of 1968 which provides that a demand must be served on the debtor company by hand at its registered office.

A company will not be regarded as having neglected to pay its debt if it *bona fide* disputes the debt. In Re W. Biney & Co. (Nig.) Ltd.[21] the petitioner alleged that the company was unable to pay its debts by failing to pay his entitlements in lieu of notice which had been ordered to be paid by the court following an action. The company denied that it was indebted to the petitioner and filed evidence of solvency and its business activity indicating that it was not

---

13 Companies Act. S.224 (1)(a)(i)

14 *ibid.* S.223(a) (b): *Yinka FOlawiyo & Sons Ltd. v. T.A. Hammond Projects Ltd.* Suit No. AFRC/l/M62/76 and ERC/l/117/76 (Unreported. Orojo *op.cit.* p.529.

15 *ibid.* S.223(c). *Re Nanji & Sons Ltd.* (1934) 25 KLR 124

16 (1971) 1 U.I.L.R.421; 1970 NCLR 187.

17 High Court of Lagos Suit No. M/144/68 of 9/4/69 Unreported; Orojo, Supra n.11, pp.530-531.

18 *Re: Capital Annuities Ltd.* [1979] 3 All E.R.704

19 Suit No. FRC/L/M89/78 of 18/1/82. Unreported

20 *Nigerian Commercial & Industrial Enterprises ltd. v. Omagiago Builders Ltd. & Anors.* 1976 NCLR 399, 402-403 per Belgore J. (Federal Revenue Court). See also *In Re Lympne Investments Ltd.* [1972] 1 W.L.R. 523; *Lornho Export Ltd. v. Motorways (Nig). Ltd.* Suit No. FHC/L/M84/79 of 22/1/81. Unreported.

21 1972 NCLR 282 (High Court of Lagos State). See also *Re House of Garments Ltd.* Companies Cause No.2 of 1972 (Uganda)

22 *ibid*, pp.289-290 per Lambo, J.

insolvent. The court refused to grant a winding-up order on the ground that[23] this was not possible on a petition in respect of which a debt is *bona fide* disputed by the company. Instead, the petitioner must seek his remedy in an action, for until the issue of the company's liability is decided, it cannot be said that the company is indebted to the petitioner. Furthermore, in *Re: Paper Conversion Co. Ltd.*[24], the petitioner instituted an action against the company to recover a sum of money. While the action was pending, he petitioned for the winding-up of the company on the ground that it was unable to pay its debts. The amount claimed in the action included the debt alleged in the petition. The company applied to restrain further proceedings on the petition an supported the application by evidence which showed that the alleged debt was *bona fide* disputed and that its assets more than balanced its liabilities. The petitioner relied upon Section 213 of the Act of 1968 and averred that the petition took precedence over the pending action and that the action rather than the petition should be stayed. In granting the application, Savage J. adopted he reasoning in *Re: W. Biney (supra)* as to a disputed debt and added that[25] Section 213 is inapplicable where a creditor petitions for winding-up on the ground that a company is unable to pay its debts and alleges a debt which the company *bona fide* disputes. Consequently, Section 213 does not in such circumstances give the petition procedence over a pending action by the creditor to recover the debt.

The rationale behind the above two decisions is that "great damage might obviously be done to a solvent company by a winding-up petition presented by an unreasonable creditor whose debt the company are able and willing to pay if established but to whom they *bone fide* believe they are not indebted"[26]. In a similar vein, it has been observed in *National Bank of Nig. Ltd. v. The Blue 5 Co. Ltd*[27], that the machinery of a winding-up petition should not be converted into "an engine for debt collection in circumvention of the established legal procedure for instituting action in appropriate courts for the collection of debts." In *Re: Ranjan Nanji & Sons Ltd.*[27a], a petition was filed for winding up a company on the grounds that it was unable to pay its debts and that the winding up would be just and equitable. The petition was opposed by the company. However, it was held that by the company's admission that its resources amounted to shs 43/26, it could not pay its debts.

However, if the sum payable undoubtedly exceeds the statutory minimum of 1,000/= a dispute as to the exact amount is not an answer by the company, where it is generally insolvent.[28] Thus, in *Tandy v. Harmony House Furniture Co. Ltd.*[29], the sum of 20,000 naira was lent to the company by the appellant and another person. The company failed to repay the sum following demand by the creditors. Accordingly, they petitioned for the winding-up of the company by the appellant and another person. The company failed to repay the sum following demand by the creditors. Accordingly, they petitioned for the winding-up of the company on the ground that it was unable to pay its debts. While admitting owing the appellants money, the respondent indicated that there was a dispute as to the amount in that it would only admit 18,000 naira. The most up to date balance sheet of the company at the time, showed current liabilities, excluding the loan, of about 38,000 naira and current assets of 62,000 naira. It was held that although the company may own assets which if liquidated would be sufficient to discharge its debts, if, however, it has no

---

23 *ibid.* pp.288; 291-293 per Lambo J. See also *Re: Gold Hill Mines* (1883) 23 Ch.D. 210; *Re London & Paris Banking* Co. (1875) L.R. 19 Eq. 444. *Re: London Wharfing & Warehousing Co. Ltd.* (1865), 35 Beav. 37; 55 E.R.808.

24 1972 NCLR 391 (High Court of Lagos State).

25 *ibid* p.394. See also *Cadiz Waterworks v. Barnett* (1874), L.R. 19 Eq. 182; 31 L.T.640 S.213 of the Nigerian Act is similar to S.226 of the Companies Act (Uganda).

26 *ibid* p. 395, per Savage J. See also *Re: Tanganyika Produce Agency Ltd.* [1957] E.A.241.

27 Suit No. FRC/L/M56/74. Unreported. per Omo-Eboh J. See further *Re: Laceward Ltd.* [1981] 1 All E.R. 254, 256: *Mann v. Goldstein* [1968] 1 W.L.R.1091; See also *Saderet Nigeria Ltd. v. Maiden Electronics Works Ltd.* Suit No.ERC/L/M119/78 of 26/3/81.

27a 25 KLR 124 (1934).

28 *Re: Tweeds Garages Ltd. [1962] Ch.406.*

adequate assets to meet its current liabilities as in this instance, it is commercially insolvent and liable to be wound up. Furthermore, that once the court is satisfied that the company is insolvent, it would grant a winding-up to a petitioner who is owed money and would not hesitate to do so simply because there is a dispute as to the exact amount owed by the company. Similarly, in *National Bank of Nigeria Ltd. v. Sealion (Nig) Ltd.*[30], the petitioner petitioned for the winding-up of the respondent company on the ground that the respondent was indebted to her and was unable to pay the debt. The respondent's indebtedness which was proved at the hearing differed in amount from the indebtedness alleged in the petition. While striking out the petition for non-advertisement in line with the winding-up rules, the court nonetheless indicated[31] that a winding-up order may be granted notwithstanding the discrepancy between the amount of indebtness proved to have existed at the time when the petition was presented and the amount alleged in the petition.

A petition may be permitted by the court whose aim is to induce the payment of debts owed to the petitioner[32]. In addition, winding up proceedings may be stayed in accordance with the terms of settlement agreed between the creditor and the company sought to be wound up.[33] The rationale is that such settlement is "incompatible with the assertion that (the company) is unable to pay its debt".[34] However, the court will not give judgment in terms of the settlement precedent to stay of proceedings because it will not sanction or encourage threats of winding-up to force a company to pay a debt and will dismiss a petition presented apparently for a winding-up order but really to put pressure on the company.[35]

A company is also taken to be unable to pay its debts if execution or other process issued on a judgment decree or order of any court in favour of a creditor of the company is returned unsatisfied in whole or in part.[36] Nevertheless, in *Nigerian Commercial and Industrial Enterprises Ltd. v. Omagiafo Ltd. & Anors*[37], it was held that[38] the fact that the respondent disclosed that it had no property on which execution could be levied made it unnecessary for the petitioner to issue execution on the judgment and the fact that the respondent issued cheques which were dishonoured was sufficient to satisfy the court that the respondent was unable to pay its debts.

The "just and equitable" ground for winding up has already been considered.[39]

## Persons entitled to petition

### Company

A company may by special resolution resolve to be wound up[40] and may therefore present a petition to that effect.

---

29 [1964] 1 All N.L.R.31 Supreme Court of Nigeria.

30 1976 NCLR 415 (Federal Revenue Court).

31 *ibid,* p.419 per *Belgore* J. following *Re: Tweeds Garages Ltd. supra* n.28.

32 *Standard Bank of Nigeria Ltd. v. Communications Joint Services Ltd.* 1975(2) ALR. Comm. 336. See also *Re: St. Thomas Dock Co.* (1876) 2 Ch.d. 116 per Jessel M.R.

33 *National Bank of Nigeria Ltd. v. Kuta Shipping Co. Ltd.* (1978) 2 LRN 42 (FCA).

34 Orojo, *Supra* n.11 p.534.

35 *National Bank of Nigeria Ltd. Kuta Shipping Co. Ltd.*, 1975(2) A.L.R. Comm. 358; Orojo; *ibid.* p.567

36 Companies Act, S.223(b).

37 1976 NCLR 399 (F.R.C.).

38 *ibid* pp.403-404 per Belgore J. See also *Re: Flagstaff Silver Mining Co.* (1875), L.R.20 Eq. 268, 45 L.J. Ch. 136; *Re: Globe New Patent Iron & Steel Co.* (1875) L.R.20 Eq.337; 44 L.J.Ch.580.

39 See *supra* Chap.15.

40 Companies Act, S.222(a).

## Creditors

These usually initiate winding-up proceedings and may petition for winding-up at the discretion of the court. As we have seen above, if the ground for winding-up the company is its inability to discharge a debt and the debt is disputed on substantial grounds, the court will not issue a winding-up order. A contingent creditor (who is claiming unliquidated damages or who is entitled to future rents from the company or who holds a bill of exchange or debenture), may also petition but he must give security for costs and establish a *prima facie* case[41]. A holder of promissory notes from the company is a creditor who is entitled to petition[41a].

An assignee of a debt which is due from the company may also petition[42] provided the assignor has not himself presented a petition.[43]

In *Re: Air Safaris (Tim Air) Ltd*[43a], it was held that given that a director or a member may loan money to the company if it has power to borrow, there is no reason why he should not be considered a creditor, whether ordinary or secured, depending on the circumstances. Consequently he can prove in the liquidation of the company. The liquidator was wrong not to admit Mr Berry (a director and member's) claim.

## Contributory

This refers to a person who is liable to contribute to the assets of the company in the event of its being wound up[44]. It also includes present and some past members of the company[45] and the holder of fully paid shares[46]. A contributory must have been a shareholder for at least six months during the eighteen months before the commencement of the winding-up[47]. He should also show that there will be assets available for distribution among the shareholders and that he has interest in the winding-up.[48] However, if the company refuses to supply information to a contributory so that he cannot tell what the situation is, this will not be an obstacle and he can petition on the just and equitable ground[49]. In this regard it is significant that a company's articles cannot restrict the right of a contributory to petition for winding up.[50] Likewise, the fact that the petitioner is a minority shareholder will not preclude him from petitioning provided that he relies on any of the grounds stipulated under Section 222 and either of them is established.[51]

A contributory who is a bankrupt cannot petition, but his right to petition for winding-up can be exercised by his trustees in bankruptcy.[52]

## The official receiver

The official receiver who is the official receiver attached to court for bankruptcy purposes[53], may petition during a voluntary winding-up or winding-up under the court's supervision for a

---

41 *ibid.* S.224(1)(c); *Re: Olathe Silver Mining Co.* (1884) 27 Ch.D.278; *Re: Dunderland Iron Ore Co. Ltd.* [1909] 1 Ch.446.

41a *Re: Sejpal Ltd.* [1957] E.A.589 (Uganda).

42 *Re: Steel Wing Co.* [1921] 1 Ch.349.

43 *Re: Paris Skating Rink* (1877) 5 Ch.D.959.

43a [1969] E.A. (High Court of Tanzania).

44 Companies Act, S.214: See also *Re: Industrial and Commercial Bank* (1933) 10 N.L.R.85

45 *ibid* S.213.

46 *Re: National Savings Bank* (1866) L.R.1 Ch.App.547; *Re:Anglesea Colliery Co.* (1866) 1 Ch.App 555.

47 S.224(1)(a)(ii).

48 *Cole v. R.C. Irving & Co. Ltd.* 1970 NCLR 472 (High Court of Lagos State; Re: *Italcomm. (W.Nig.)Ltd.* 1972 NCLR 293 (High Ct. of Lagos State); *Re: Rica Gold Washing Co.* (1879). 11 Ch.D.36; *Re: Chesterfield Catering* [1976] 3 All E.R.294.

49 *Re: Newman and Howard Ltd.* [1962] Ch.257.

50 *Re: Peveril Gold Mines Ltd.* [1898] 1 Ch.122 C.A.

51 *Obasi v. Pureway Corpn. of Nig. Ltd.* Suit No. FRC/L/M10/78 of 18/9/78, Unreported. See also *Loch v. John Backwood Ltd.* [1924] A.C.783.

52 Companies Act, S.217; *Re: Wolverhampton Steel & Iron Co.* [1977] 1 W.L.R. 153.

53 *ibid*, S.233(1).

compulsory winding up. In such a case, the court must be satisfied that the voluntary winding-up or one under the court's supervision cannot be continued, having regard to the interests of the creditors or contributories[54]. In *Adebayo v. Official Receiver*[55], it was held that simply because a company was controlled by one shareholder, of whom a liquidator in voluntary liquidation could be considered a nominee did not mean that a voluntary winding-up could not be continued with regard to the interests of the creditors. Consequently, the lower court's order of compulsory winding-up was misconceived.

In having regard to the wishes of the creditors or contributories, the court may, in order to ascertain the relevant wishes, direct meetings to be called and in the case of creditors regard must be had to the value of each creditor's debt.[56] If the majority in value of the unsecured creditors oppose a petition and for some good reason in the absence of special circumstances, their wishes will prevail.[57]However, the court should not refuse a winding-up order merely because the assets of the company have been mortgaged to an amount equal or in excess of those assets.[58] Furthermore, where a voluntary winding-up is in process a compulsory order can be made provided it is not opposed by the majority of creditors or contributories. In this regard, the wishes of the majority will be conclusive as to the mode of winding-up to be adopted.[59]

### The Attorney General

The Attorney General may, present a petition for winding-up where an inspector's report has been submitted following investigation of the company under sections 165-166, 170. [60]

## Petition and procedure for winding-up

No attempt is made to treat the procedure in detail and only outstanding aspects are considered here. The reader is referred to the Companies Act.

The petition is presented before the High Court[61]Following presentation thereof an application can be made to the court for the appointment of a provisional liquidator before the winding-up order is made, if the company's assets are in jeopardy.[62]Usually, the official receiver is appointed in that case.[63] The provisional liquidator controls the assets of the company[64] and, after his appointment, no legal proceedings can be commenced or continued against the company without the court's leave.[65]

On hearing the petition, the court may dismiss it, adjourn the hearing conditionally or make an interim order or any other order it thinks fit.[66] Where a winding up order is made, the company is required to send a copy to the Registrar of Companies.[67]

---

54 *ibid,* S.224(2).

55 [1954] 1 W.L.R.681 P.C. Construing S.132(2) of the Companies Ordinance Cap.38 Laws of Nigeria (1948) in *pari materia* with Section 224(2) ibid.

56 Companies Act, S.340.

57 *Re: Vuma [1960]* 1 W.L.R.1283.

58 Companies Act, S.225.

59 *Re: Home Remedies Ltd.* [1943] Ch.1.

60 Section 224(1) (d).

61 *ibid* S. 224(1) read together with Section 218. See also *NBN v. Brothers (Nig.) Ltd.*1977(1) A.L.R. Comm.123

62 *Levy v. Napier 1962* S.C.468.

63 Companies Act, S.238(1).

64 *ibid,* S.242.

65 *ibid* S.231.

66 *ibid* S.225(1); *NBN V. Are Bros (Nig) Ltd.* supra n.61

67 *ibid.* S.230.

## Commencement of winding-up

Winding-up is deemed to start in the case of voluntary winding up when the relevant resolution is passed precedent to presentation of a petition.[68] In any other case it commences when the petition is presented but before the winding-up order is issued.[69]

Certain consequences flow from the commencement of winding up. First, the court may, pursuant to an application to that effect, restrain the proceedings against the company[70], although this is by no means automatic.[71] Second, any disposition of the company's property or transfer of shares is void unless the court otherwise directs.[72] Third, any attachment, sequestration, distress or execution lodged against the assets of the company is void.[73] However, this is subject to Sections 226 and 231 *(supra)* under which the court may grant leave for execution or other proceedings against the company.

## Consequences of a winding-up order

Following the issue of a winding up order, the following consequences arise. First, no legal proceedings can be instituted against the company without the court's leave.[74] However, a party who is sued by a company in liquidation may counterclaim[75] Second, where the liquidator has not been appointed, the official receiver becomes provisional liquidator[76] and may apply to court for the appointment of a special manager, if the nature of the company's business or interests of creditors or contributories require it.[77] Third, the directors' powers of management cease upon the appointment of the liquidator[78] although they may appeal in the company's name against the winding up order,[79] and retain residual authority to engage legal practitioners and to participate in interlocutory proceedings and the discharge of the provisional liquidator.[80] Fourth, the directors and company employees are dismissed,[81]though they may be re-employed by the liquidator.[82] Fifth, all the company's business letters, invoices and orders for goods must bear the statement that it is in liquidation.[83]

## Proceedings subsequent to issue of winding-up order

Persons who were directors or secretary of the company at the date of the issue of a winding up order are required to deliver a statement of affairs within 14 days, following the appointment of the provisional liquidator or after the winding up order to the official receiver, who then makes

---

68 *ibid* S.229(1).
69 *ibid* S,229(2).
70 *ibid.* S.226.
71 *Re: Bellaglade* [1977] 1 ALL E.R.319; *Re: Paper Conversion Co. Ltd.* 1972 NCLR 391 (High Court of Lagos State); *N.C.I.E.Ltd. v. T.A. Hammond Project Ltd.* 1977 1CCHCI 31.
72 Companies Act, S.277. See also *Re: Argentum Reductions* [1975] 1 ALL E.R. 608; *Re: Leslie Engineers Co. Ltd.* [1976] 2 ALL E.R.85; *Re: Clifton Place Garage Ltd.* [1970] Ch.447; *Re: Burton & Deakin Ltd.* (1977) 1ALL E.R.631.
73 *ibid.* S.228.
74 *ibid.* S.231.
75 *Langley Constructions (Brixham) Ltd. v. Weills* [1969] 1 W.L.R.503.
76 Companies Act S.238(1).
77 *ibid* S.261.
78 *Fowler v. Broads Patent Night Light Co.* [1983] 1 Ch.724.
79 *Re: Diamond Fuel Co.* (1879) 13 Ch.D.400 C.A., pp.404-5.
80 *Re: Union Accident Insurance Co. Ltd.* [1972] 1 W.L.R.503.
81 *Measures Ltd. V. Measures* [1910] 2 Ch.248, C.A.; *Chapman's Case* (1966) L.R.Eq.346
82 *Day v. Tait* (O.H.1900) 85 L.T.40.
83 Companies Act, S.333.

a report.[84] The statement must show particulars of assets, debts and liabilities of the company, details of creditors and their security.

The official receiver is required on receipt of the statement of the company's affairs, to submit a preliminary report[85] to the court showing the amount of capital issued, subscribed and paid up and estimated amount of assets and liabilities, the cause of the company's failure; whether further inquiry is required with regard to the promotion formation or failure or conduct of its business.[86] In such a case the official receiver should make a further report following which, if fraud is disclosed, the court may order a public inquiry pursuant to section 268 of the Companies Act[87]

The official receiver should also summon separate meetings of creditors and contributories and send them a summary of the statement of affairs, cause of failure of the company and any other observations[88]. The aim of the meetings is to decide on whether to make application to court for the appointment of a liquidator in the place of the official receiver. Where the meetings cannot agree, the court may decide.[89]

## Appointment of liquidator

The liquidator may be appointed by the court after the meetings of creditors and contributories. Where the two meetings do not agree on the appointment, the court decides. Where the court does not appoint a liquidator, the official receiver continues as liquidator.[90] Where a person other than the official receiver is appointed he must notify the Registrar of Companies of the appointment and give security in the manner prescribed by the court.[91] In a situation where more than one liquidator is appointed the court should indicate whether or not they are required to act jointly.[92]

## Committee of inspection

The committee is appointed by the court following decision of meetings of creditors and contributories.[93] It normally consists of creditors and contributories in agreed proportion.[94] However, where there is no agreement between the creditors and contributories as to its composition the court shall decide the difference and issue the relevant order.[95] The committee should meet at least once each month or as frequently as necessary.[96] If a committee is not appointed, the liquidator may apply to court for directions to perform any of the functions of the committee.[97]

84 *ibid* S.235(1) See also *In the matter of Pan African Pools (Nigeria Ltd.).* Suit No. M/101/66 of 11/4/69 H. Court of Lagos. Unreported *Attorney General v. Etukudo* (1967) N.M.L.R.292; (1967) F.N.I.R.138

85 *ibid* S.236(1).

86 *ibid* S.236(2).

87 *ibid* S.236(3).

88 *ibid* S.239(b).

89 *ibid* S.239 (b),(c).

90 *ibid* S.239)d), (e).

91 *ibid* S.240(a).

92 *ibid* S.241(4); See also *Re: Industrial and Commercial Bank* (1933) 10 N.L.R.85 (Divisional Court, Lagos).

93 *ibid* S.251.

94 *ibid,* S.252(1).

95 *ibid,* S.251(2).

96 *ibid* S.252(2).

97 *ibid* S.253.

# Company's property

## Reduction into possession or control

Following the issue of a winding up order or appointment of a provisional liquidator, the liquidator is required to have control of the company's property.[98] A winding up order does not automatically vest the company's property into the liquidator. The court has to make a vesting order relating to the property in favour of the liquidator upon his application.[99] The court may also order the transfer of the company's property in the custody of any shareholder, agent, officer or trustee of the company to the liquidator.[100]

The court is also empowered, after the winding up order has been made or the provisional liquidator has been appointed, to examine on oath, (i) any officer of the company; (ii) a person known or suspected to have in his possession any property of the company; (iii) a person who is supposed to be indebted to the company; (iv) any person whom the court deems capable of giving any information as to the promotion, formation, trade dealings, affairs or property of the company.[101] This is with a view to discovering up the company's property. In *Gerald Kostoris Ltd. v. Ali Mansour & Sons Ltd.*[102], the disputed property was mortgaged property on which the respondent was collecting rents. The property had previously been acquired compulsorily by the Government to which alone rent was thereafter payable. It was held that such property could not be said to be in possession of the respondent within the meaning of section 267. It has also been held that the examination under section 267 is not automatic.[103]

## Property of the company under execution or attachment

Execution or attachment levied by a creditor against the company's property will not bind the liquidator so as to enable the creditor to retain benefits accruing therefrom unless such has been completed before the commencement of the winding up.[104] The aim of this provision is "to ensure equity between unsecured creditors so that they rank *paripassu*"[105] The provision is inapplicable to distress by landlord.[106] The "benefit of the execution" and "benefit of the attachment" mean respectively the charge conferred on the creditor by the issue of execution[107] and the right to take necessary steps to complete attachment.[108] In addition, where any goods of the company are taken in execution and before they are sold or execution completed, notice is served on the sheriff that a provisional liquidator has been appointed or a winding-up order has been passed, the sheriff must hand over the goods to the liquidator. However, the sheriff's costs are a first charge on such property.[109] Where the sheriff has received money, he should retain it for fourteen days in case winding-up commences. In that case he should then hand over the money minus his costs to the liquidator.[110] The rights conferred by Section 321 may be set aside by the court in favour of relevant creditors.[111]

---

98 *ibid* S.242.
99 *ibid* S.243.
100 *ibid* S.256.
101 *ibid,* S.267, *Tejani v. Official Receiver* [1960] E.A.574 P.C.
102 High Court of Lagos Suit No. M/141/60 of 23/9/69 Unreported.
103 Re: *Bletchely Board* Co.[1974 1 ALL E.R. 1225 considering Companies Act, 1948 (UK) S.268 which is identical to S.267. See also *Re: Spiraflite Ltd.* [1979] 2 ALL E.R. 766; *Re: Castle New Homes Ltd.* [1979] All E.R.775.
104 Companies Act, S.320.
105 Orojo, *op cit* pp. 579.
106 *Re: Bellaglade* [1977] 1ALL E.R. 319.
107 *Re: Walkden Sheet Metal Co. Ltd.* [1960] Ch.170; *Re: Andrew, ex. p. Official Receiver* (Trusts) [1937] Ch.122.
108 *Re: Carribean Products (Yam Importers)* Ltd. [1966] Ch.331 C.A.
109 Companies Act, 321(1).
110 *ibid* S.321(2).
111 *ibid* S.321(3).

## Protection of the property

### (a) Fraudulent preferences

During the course of winding-up, the liquidator may be enabled to avoid certain payments and securities effected by the company before the onset of the winding-up. This has the effect of increasing the company's assets which are available to the creditors generally.

The rules of bankruptcy relating to fraudulent preferences apply to the winding-up of a company[112]. These are to the effect that any payment or disposition of property made to a creditor before the commencement of the winding-up will be invalid if the dominant intention of the debtor[113] in making it was to prefer the creditor or the guarantor of the debt over the other creditors. The effect of the preference would be to enable the creditors or guarantor to receive more than he would have got had he not been paid until the winding-up.[114] The onus of proof of intention to prefer is on the liquidator.[115] To constitute a "fraudulent preference", a payment or disposition must have been made by the director of the company, who at the time of such act know that the company is unable to pay its debts as they fall due and intend to pay one of its creditors in preference to the others.[116] Where the payment is made with some intention other than preference it will not be voidable. In *Re: G. Stanley & Co.*[117], the payment was made in order to mislead a creditor into advancing more money to the company. In *Re: F.L.E.Holding Ltd.*[118], the payment was intended to maintain good relations with a creditor, while in *Re: Eric Holmes (Property) Ltd.*[119], the payment was aimed at honouring a pre-existing legal obligation. However, the payment of money into a bank account arising from pressure in the ordinary course of business amounts to fraudulent preference.[120]

In *Highlands Commercial Union Ltd. v. Jamal*[21a], it was held that a payment being a disposition after the commencement of the winding up was void. In *John Lubega v. City Council of Kampala*[21b], the debt due by the garnisher to the company (in liquidation) was a part of the estate and effects of that company and in terms of section 228 of the Companies Act no execution against such debt could have been put in force after the winding up of the respondent.

Where a creditor is sued for the return of money or property alleged to have been received under a fraudulent preference, he may join a guarantor of the debt as a third party provided the claim avers that the payment was a preference of the guarantor,[121]. Should the claim be proved, the third party will be liable to indemnify the creditor against the judgment. The liquidator, however, has a right of direct action against the guarantor,[122] even though he was the person intended to be preferred. Nevertheless, irrespective of the fact that the guarantor may have simply mortgaged securities to the creditor he is personally liable on his guarantee if the payment made had the effect of preferring him.[123]

Any money recovered under a fraudulent preference is to be held for the benefit of the creditors generally and not for any particular class of them such as debenture holders.[124]

---

112 *ibid* S.316.

113 In the case of a company the intention is to be gathered from the acts of its directors. *Sharp v. Jackson* [1899] A.C. 419 *Official Receiver v. Sontag* (1938) 5 EACA 95

114 See also Leigh *op.cit* p.449. *Chand v. Liquidator, Exchange Bank (1950) 17 EACA*

115 *Sir William Henry Peat v. Gresham Trust Ltd.* [1934] A.C. 252.

116 *Re: F.P. and C.H. Mathews, Ltd.* [1982] Ch.257; [1982] 1All E.R. 338; [1982] 2 W.L.R.495.

117 [1925] Ch.148.

118 [1967] 3 All E.R.553.

119 [1965] Ch.1052.

120 *Re: M. Kushler, Ltd.* [1943] Ch.248.24.

21a[1957] E.A.641.

21b[1975] HCB101 C.A.

121 Companies Act, S.317(2).

122 *Re: Conley, Exparte Trustee v. Barclays Bank Ltd.* [1937] 4 All E.R.434, 317(2)

123 Companies Act S.317(2).

124 *Re: Yagerphone Co. Ltd.* [1937] 1 Ch.392.

**(b) Floating charges**[125]

A floating charge created within twelve months of the commencement of winding up, on the company's property is invalid, except where it is proved that the company was solvent immediately after its creation[126]. This restriction is very similar to the setting aside of fraudulent preferences.

**(c) Fraudulent trading**

If in the course of winding-up, it appears that any of the company's business has been carried on with intent to defraud creditors of for any fraudulent purpose, the court, may on an application order that any person knowing of this shall be personally responsible for the debts of the company without limitation of liability.[127] The expression "carrying of business" does not necessarily connote active carrying on trade. The realisation of assets obtained in the course of business and distribution thereof could constitute "carrying on business" since there is continuous course of active conduct[128]. "Defraud" and "fraudulent purpose" refer to actual dishonesty.[129] Consequently, an omission to give advice on the part of the erring person is not fraudulent.[130]

**(d) Misfeasance summons**[131]

Where, during the course of winding-up, it appears that any person has misapplied or retained any money or property of the company or has been guilty of any misfeasance or breach of trust, the court, may, upon application examine such person's conduct and order him to repay with interest or to contribute such sum as the court thinks just.[132]

**(e) Disclaimer**

Where any of the company's property consists of land burdened with onerous covenants; shares in companies; unprofitable contracts or property which is not easily saleable, the liquidator may, with the court's leave disclaim in writing the property within twelve months of commencement of winding up or within twelve months of his becoming aware of such property.[133] A person who is interested in the property can give a written notice to the liquidator requiring him to decide on a disclaimer.[134] A decision to disclaim must be made by the liquidator within twenty-eight days following receipt of the application.[135]Otherwise, he will not be entitled to disclaim. The court is also empowered to make any necessary vesting orders relating to the property sought to be disclaimed in favour of persons entitled thereto, provided that the interests of under lessees are unaffected.[136]

A person who is injured as a result of a disclaimer is deemed to be a creditor of the company with respect to the amount of injury and may prove the amount as a debt in the winding-up.[137] However, invariably the rights and liabilities of interested persons are respected and recognised.[138] The court may also, upon application rescind contract affected by the disclaimer and award damages which would be proved for in liquidation.[139]

---

[125] For a much more detailed treatment see *supra* chap.10.

[126] Companies Act, S.318.

[127] *ibid* S.327. See also *supra* Chap.2 under *"Lifting The Veil"*. See also *Ebrahim v. Tait* (1935) 2 E.A.C.A.51; *Tejani v. Official Receiver* [1960] E.A.574 C.A. [1962] E.A.574 P.C.

[128] *Re: Sarflax Ltd.* [1979] 1 All E.R. 529.

[129] *Re: Patrick & Lyon Ltd.* [1933] Ch.786.

[130] *Re: Maidstone Building Provisions Ltd.* [1971] 1 W.L.R.1085.

[131] For more detailed treatment see *supra* chap.15.

[132] Companies Act Section 328. See also *Re: Modern Retreading Co. Ltd.* 1966(1) ALR Comm.494

[133] *ibid* S.319(1). Such period can be extended by the court. See also *Re: A.B.C. Coupler & Engineering Co. Ltd. (no.3) [1970] 1W.L.R.702.*

[134] *ibid*, S. 319(4).

[135] *ibid.* The period of 28 days may be extended by the Court.

[136] *ibid* S.319(6). See also *Re: Katherine et Cie* [1932] 1Ch.70; *Warnford Investment Ltd. v. Duckworth* [1978] 2 W.L.R.741.

[137] *ibid* S.319(7).

[138] *ibid.* S.319(2).

[139] *ibid* S.319(5).

The provisions relating to disclaimer by the company are very similar to those relating to bankruptcy on disclaimer.[140]

## Contributories

Following the issue of a winding-up order, the liquidator is required to settle a list of contributories and to collect assets and discharge liabilities.[141]

A contributory has already been defined[142]. Every present and post member of the company is liable to contribute to the assets of the company to an amount sufficient to pay its debts and liabilities and costs of the winding-up[143].

There are two parts to the list of contributories. The "A list" consists of all present members or persons who are members at the commencement of the winding-up. The "B list" comprises persons who were members within one year before the commencement of the winding-up. The court may dispense with the list where it appears unnecessary to make calls or adjust the rights of contributories. In practice the B list is not prepared except where it is evident that the A list contributories are unable to meet their contributions.[144]

Persons on the A list are liable to the extent of the amount remaining unpaid on their shares.[145] The liability of persons on the B list is limited to the amount unpaid on the shares in respect of which they are liable as past members. A person on the B list is not liable to contribute for any debt or liability which was contracted by the company after he ceased to be member.[146] In addition such a person is not liable to contribute unless it appears to the court that the existing members cannot satisfy their statutory contributions.[45] The court may order a contributory on the list to pay up,[147] and also direct his arrest, seizure of his movable personal property where it is believed that he is about to leave Uganda, abscond, remove or cancel any of his property for purposes of a payment of calls.[148]

## Creditors

A creditor is a person who is entitled to claim against the company in respect of a debt. The expression includes a member to whom the company is indebted even if in his capacity as a member, as is the case with unclaimed dividends.[149] Nevertheless, such a debt which is owed *qua* member would be deferred to those of outside creditors.[150]

In the course of winding-up of a company, all debts payable on contingency and all claims against the company present or future, certain or contingent, ascertained or sounding only in damages are admissible to proof against the company.[151] Normally, where the company is solvent, where it is insolvent the procedure under Section 314 of the Companies Act (which applies bankruptcy rules in certain cases) must be applied with regard to the rights of creditors and debts provable. Consequently, all debts can be proved, including contingent claims.[152]

140 See Bankruptcy Act, Cap.71, S.57.
141 Companies Act.S.255.
142 *ibid* S.214. See *supra* under Persons Entitled to Petition.
143 *ibid* S.213.
144 *ibid* S.213(1) (c).
145 *ibid* S.213(1)(d).
146 *ibid* S.213(1) (b).
147 *ibid*,S.257.
148 *ibid*, S.269.
149 *Re: Compania de Electricidad de Buenos Aires* [1979] Ch.673.
150 Companies Act,S.213(1)(g).
151 *ibid*, S.313 *Re: Armstrong Whitworth Securities Co.* [1947] Ch.673.
152 See Bankruptcy Act, S.34.

A secured creditor may (i) realise his security and prove as unsecured for the balance;[153] (iii) surrender his security and prove as unsecured for the whole debt (iv) where fully secured rely entirely on the security and not prove at all.

### Priority of settlement of debts

The assets of the company should be applied in the following order in settling claims.[154] First, to meet the costs, charges and expenses of winding up including the liquidator's remuneration.[155] Second, to extinguish claims of preferred creditors. Third, to discharge the debts of ordinary creditors and finally to meet the claims of deferred creditors. The priority with regard to the payment of preferential creditors is determined as follows:[156] (i) local rates and charges and taxes due or deducted within one year of the date of winding up or commencement thereof,[157] (ii) wages or salaries of any clerk or servant for services rendered for the previous four months not exceeding shs 4,000/=[158]; (iii) wages of any workman or labourer not exceeding within two months of the relevant date[159]; (iv) all accrued holiday remuneration payable to a clerk, servant, workman or labourer on the termination of his employment before or by the effect of the winding-up; (v) all amounts due in respect of workman's compensation under the Workman's Compensation Act[160], except where the company is being wound up voluntarily for the purpose of reconstruction or amalgamation or has a contract with insurers for vesting or transferring rights of compensation to the workman; (vi) all outstanding contributions payable to the National Social Security Fund in respect of a worker.

## The liquidator

### Appointment and removal

Any person, except a body corporate[161], may be appointed a liquidator. Usually the appointee is an accountant of not less than five years standing.[162] A liquidator may resign or be removed by the court for cause shown and replaced.[163] The grounds for removal include personal unfitness[164], personal interest[165], prosecuting a claim where the majority of creditors are against such a course[166] or unwillingness to claim against directors with whom he was intimate.

### Remuneration

With regard to remuneration, a liquidator is paid a salary in an amount or by way of percentage or otherwise as the court directs. Where there are more than one liquidator, the remuneration is distributed among them in such proportions as directed by the court.[167]

---

153 *Alitalia Airlines Ltd v. Nigerian Industrial Development Bank Ltd.* [1967] F.N.L.R.134.

154 Companies act, S.315.

155 *ibid* S. 315(6), 306.

156 *ibid,* S.315(1).

157 *ibid* S.315(1)(a).

158 A Director may be regarded as a clerk or servant for this purpose: *Re Beeton & Co* [1913] 2 Ch.279.

159 "relevant date" is defined in S.315(8)(b).

160 Cap.197 Laws of Uganda, as amended from time to time.

161 *ibid S.330.*

162 *Re: Icknield* [1973] 2 All E.R. 168; *Re: Industrial & Commercial Bank* (1933) 10 N.L.R.85 (Div Court Lagos)

163 Companies Act, S.241(1).

164 *Re: The North Molton Mining Co. Ltd.* (1886) 54 L.T. 602 *Lysons v. Liquidator of the Miraflores Gold Syndicate Ltd.* (1895) 22 R. 605.

166 *Re: Tavistock Ironworks Co.* (1871) 24 L.T. 605.

167 Companies Act, S.241(2): *Re: Introductions* [1967] 3 All E.R.69.

## Duties

A liquidator is appointed, "for the purpose of conducting the proceedings in winding-up a company and performing such duties in reference thereto as the court may impose.[168] Accordingly the liquidator's duties include taking into his custody or control the company's property,[169], settling a list of contributories, collecting the company's assets, paying debts and distributing the surplus among the members according to their rights.[170] In this regard he will be personally liable if he distributes assets without providing for liabilities.[171] He is also required to have regard to the directions of creditors, contributories and the committee of inspection[172]. However, where there is conflict between the instructions of the committee of inspection and those given by the creditors or contributories at any general meeting, the latter shall prevail.[173] The liquidator is also obliged to summon meetings of creditors or contributories when directed by their resolution or by one-tenth in value of either as the case may be and may also summon a meeting on his own volition to ascertain the wishes of the contributories or creditors.[174] Furthermore, the liquidator must, keep proper books of account which subject to the court's control may be open to inspection by any creditor or contributory;[175] pay money received by him into the "Companies liquidation account" kept by the Registrar of Companies[176]; send accounts to the registrar at least twice a year for audit.[177] The liquidator, upon resignation or completion of his task must apply to the registrar for release.[178]

## Powers

The liquidator is empowered, with the sanction of either the court or the committee of inspection to [179]bring or defend any action or other legal proceeding in the name of the company[180] carry on the business of the company as far as may be necessary for the beneficial winding-up thereof[181], appoint a legal practitioner to assist him in the performance of his duties,[182] pay any classes of creditors in full; make any compromise or arrangement with creditors or persons claiming to be creditors or having or alleging themselves to have any claim against the company; compromise all calls and liabilities to calls, debts and liabilities and all claims between the company and a contributory and all questions relating to the assets or the winding up of the company; make calls.[183] The liquidator is also empowered without any sanction or leave to[184], sell the real and personal property and choses in action of the company by public auction or private contract with power to transfer the whole thereof to any person or company or to sell the same in parcels, do

---

168 *ibid.* S.237.

169 *ibid.* S.242.

170 *ibid* Ss.255,263.

171 *James Smith & Sons (Norwood) Ltd. v. Goodman* [1936] Ch.216 C.A.

172 Companies Act, Ss. 271(a), Proviso.245 *Balogun v. Agbaoye* (1977) F.R.C.R.122.

173 *ibid,* S.245(1).

174 *ibid* S.245(2).

175 *ibid* S.231.

176 ibid S.247(1). The Registrar, may upon application by the Committee of Inspection authorise the liquidator to maintain an account into which such sums received by him are paid, see also *Birchin Lane Nominee Ltd. v. Nicholson* [1969] 3 All E.R.1353.

177 *ibid* S.248.

178 *ibid* S.250.

179 *ibid* S.244(1).

180 See also *Economic Exports Ltd. v. Kasumu* 1966 NCLR 104 where it was held that a liquidator has a discretion whether to bring or defend an action on behalf of the company. See also *Agbaoye v. Chief Fed Land Officer* (1976) 2 F.R.C.R.33, 36.

181 In this regard he is deemed to be an agent of the company and is therefore not personally liable. *Stead Hasel & Co. v. Cooper* [1933] 1 K.B. 840. See also Re Peter & Co. Ltd. Companies Cause No.18 of 1960 (High Court of Uganda).

182 *Agbaoye v. Chief Fed. Land Officer, supra* n.81.

183 Companies Act *S.271(a),* 258.

184 *ibid* S.244(2).

all acts and to execute, in the name of the company, all deeds, receipts and other documents, and for that purpose to use when necessary, the company's seal; prove, rank and claim in bankruptcy, insolvency or sequestration of any contributory for any balance against his estate; draw, accept, make and indorse any bill or exchange or promissory note in the name and on behalf of the company; raise on the security of the assets of the company any requisite money, to take out letters of administration to the estate of any deceased contributory and to do in his official name any other act necessary for obtaining payment of any money due from a contributory or his estate which cannot be conveniently done in the name of the company; appoint an agent to do any business which the liquidator is unable to do himself to do all such other things as may be necessary for winding up the affairs of the company and distributing its assets. The powers given under section 244 are subject to control by the court and a creditor or contributory may apply to the court with regard to the exercise or proposed exercise of those powers.[185]

In *Re: Peter &Co. Ltd*[186], an agreement had been proposed under which a person would be authorised by the liquidator to take over and conduct the business of the company at his own risk for 3 years. Additionally, the unsecured creditors were to receive about 2-3 percent of their claims for each year. The liquidator sought court guidance as to whether this proposal was necessary for the beneficial winding up of the company within Section 193(3) of the Companies Ordinance (equivalent to Section 244 of the Companies Act). It was held that the carrying on of business for an indefinite period or with a view to the resuscitation of a company would not be for the winding up of the company and was outside the scope of the section.

The power to rectify the register of members under section 118 of the Companies Act can only be exercised with special leave of the court.[187]

## Liability and release

The liquidator is both an officer of the court and an agent of the company for purposes of winding-up the company. He thereby occupies a fiduciary position towards the company's creditors as a body but is not a trustee for individual creditors or contributories in the true sense of the term.[188] Consequently, he is not liable for negligence but only for fraud in his execution of duties[189], Nevertheless, where he misapplies the company's assets by admitting and paying an invalid claim without taking proper legal advice,[190] or paying members before creditors or creditors in the wrong order[191] or where he makes no provision for contingent claims of which he has been notified,[192] he will be personally liable to the creditors and misfeasance summons may be issued against him.[193]

The liquidator must exercise a high degree of care and diligence in his dealings if he is to escape liability. Thus in *Re: Home and Colonial Insurance Co. Ltd.*[194]; a liquidator paid a claim which he subsequently discovered to be invalid. It was held that he was negligent in not taking legal advice or applying for directions of the court, consequently he was liable to compensate the

185 *ibid* S.244(3). See also *Leon v. York-o-Matic Ltd.* [1966] 3 All E.R. 277

186 Supra n.181.

187 *ibid* S.271 proviso.

188 *c.f. I.R.C. v. Olive Mill Ltd.* [1963] 2 All E.R. 130; *Re: Oriental Inland Steam Co. Exparte Scinde Rail, co. (1874)*; 9Ch.App 557; *Re: General Rolling Stock Discount Co. Claim* (1872), 7Ch app.646; *Re: Paraguassu Steam Tramroad Co. Black &Co.'s Case* (1872) 8 ch.App. 254, 262; *Rudewa v. Commissioner of Stamp Duties* [1966] E.A.576.

189 *Knowles v. Scott* [1891] 1 Ch. 7171; *Re: Hill Waterfall Estate & Gold Mining Co.* [1896] 1 Ch.947

190 *Re: Windsor Steam Coal Co.* (1901) Ltd. [1929] 1 Ch. 151.

191 *Pulsford v. Davenish* [1903] 2 Ch.625.

192 *James Smith & Sons (Norwood) Ltd. v. Goodman* [1936] Ch.216 C.A.; Re: *Armstrong Whitworth Securities Co. Ltd.* [1947] Ch.673.

193 Companies Act S.328; *Re: Windsor Steam Coal, supra* N.190.

194 [1930] 1 Ch.102.

company. In addition, a liquidator litigates at his own risk and would be personally liable for the costs of the litigation and is not entitled to limit his responsibility to the assets of the company[195].

After the liquidator has distributed the final dividend and prepared a final return or has resigned or been removed from his office, he applies to the Registrar of Companies for a report on the accounts prepared by him and release[196].

The Registrar may grant or withhold the release subject to the liquidator's appeal to the High Court[3]. The release has the effect of discharging the liquidator from all liability in respect of his conduct in the winding-up.[197] However, such release may be revoked if it is found to have been obtained through fraud, suppression or concealment.[4]

### Control over the liquidator

For purposes of ensuring proper discharge of his duties, the liquidator is subjected to the control of the court[198], the directions of the creditors or contributories or the committee of inspection, the former of which prevail where there is a conflict.[199]

Finally, the court oversees through the Registrar of Companies, the conduct of the liquidator during the winding up of the company.[200]

## Completion of winding up by court

Where the winding-up of the company is not completed within a year the liquidator must send a statement at given intervals to the Registrar indicating the position of the liquidation.[201]

When the affairs of the company have been completely wound up, the court must on the application of the liquidator make an order dissolving the company[202].

Subsequently, the liquidator is required, within 14 days of the issue of the dissolution order to send a copy of thereof to the Registrar who notes down in his record the fact of dissolution. Alternatively the liquidator may apply to the registrar to dissolve the company by striking its name off the Register of Companies.[203] Following the release of the liquidator, the registrar then waits two years before striking it off.[204]

Following the dissolution, the property which was vested in the company or held on trust for its benefit immediately before the dissolution is deemed to vest in the state without further assurance as *bona vacantia*[205].

After the dissolution of the company, the court may, on the application of the liquidator or other interested person made within two years of dissolution make an order declaring the dissolution void.[206] The reason for the order may stem from the existence of unsatisfied claim by creditors[207] or the discovery of undistributed assets.[208] Such order should be filed with the Registrar for registration within seven days of the date of issue.[209]

195 *Re: Wilson Lovatt & Sons Ltd.* [1977] 1 All E.R.274.
196 Companies Act, S.250.
197 *ibid* S.250(3).
198 *ibid* S.245 (3) (5)
199 *ibid* S.245(1),(2).
200 *ibid* S.250.
201 *ibid* S.337(1).
202 *ibid* S.272(1)
203 *ibid* S.343(4).
204 *ibid* Ss.250,342.
205 *ibid* S.344.
206 *ibid* S.342(1).
207 *Re: Spottiswoods Dixon and Hunting Ltd.* [1912] 1 Ch.410.
208 *Champaany Jute Co. Ltd. Petitioners* 1924 S.C. 209.
209 Companies Act, S.342(2).

# Defunct companies

The Registrar of Companies is empowered to strike a company off the Register of Companies if he has reasonable cause to believe that it is not carrying on business or is not in operation.[210] Normally, the registrar writes a letter to the affected company to ascertain whether it is carrying on business or is in operation,[211] before going ahead to strike it off.[212] In both cases, notice of intention to strike and the striking off may be given in the Uganda Gazette[213]. The striking off, of the company, does not prevent the company from being wound up.[214] In such a case it must be restored to the register first.[21a] A restoration is possible within ten years from the publication of notice of striking off and may be effected upon application by the company, a member or a creditor[21a]. The application should be by means of petition[215] presented by a person entitled to apply.[216] Restoration validates retrospectively all acts done by the company or on its behalf between its dissolution and restoration[217].

In *Re: Jan Mohamed Kisii Cinema Ltd*[24a], it was held that a transferee of land belonging to a dissolved company was not a creditor of the company within Section 339(6) of the Companies Act of Kenya (equivalent to Section 343(6) of the Companies Act of Uganda) and could not, therefore apply for an order of restoration.

# Voluntary winding up

A company may be wound up voluntarily in the following instances:[218].

(i) When the period if any fixed for the duration of the company in its articles, expires or where the event occurs which the articles provide shall be a ground for dissolution and the company passes on ordinary resolution requiring the company to be wound up voluntarily.

(ii) If the company resolves by special resolution that it should be wound up voluntarily;

(iii) if the company resolves by extra-ordinary resolution that it cannot by reason of its liabilities continue its business and that it is advisable to wind up.

The passing of a resolution for winding up voluntarily is deemed to commence the winding up.[219]The effect, thereof is that the company must cease to carry on business except where it is necessary for its beneficial winding up.[220]

The procedure for voluntary winding-up depends on whether it is a member or creditors' voluntary winding-up.

## Members' voluntary winding-up

A principal characteristic of this mode of winding-up is that members appoint the liquidator and file a declaration of solvency viz. that the company will be able to pay its debts within

---

210 *ibid* S.343.

211 *ibid* S.343(1)-(3).

212 *ibid* S.343(5).

213 *ibid* S.343(2),(3),(5).

214 *ibid,* S.343(5) Proviso(b).

21a *ibid* S.343(6).

215 *Ezeoke v. The Registrar of Companies* (1971) I U.I.L.R.351.

216 *African Continental Bank v. The Registrar of Companies* (1974) 1 F.R.C.R.125. See also *Re: New Timbui Gold Mine Ltd.* [1961] Ch.329. A personal representative of a deceased Shareholder is also entitled to petition: *Re Bayswater Trading Co. Ltd.* [1970] 1 W.L.R. 343, *Re: Lukerere Coffee Factory Ltd.* C.C. No.3 of 1991(U).

217 *Re: Boxco Ltd.* [1970] Ch.442; *Tymans Ltd. v. Graven [1952] 2 Q.B. 100 C.A.*

24a [1971] E.A.268 (Kenya).

218 Companies Act, S.276.

219 *ibid* S.278.

twelve months of commencement of the winding-up. A notable feature is that there is no meeting of creditors or appointment of a committee of inspection.

Within five weeks before the passing of a winding-up resolution the directors of the company or a majority of them, if they are more than two in number, must make a statutory declaration that they have made full inquiry of the company's affairs and have formed the opinion that the company will be able to pay its debts within a period not exceeding twelve months from the commencement of the winding-up[221]. A director who makes a declaration in this context without reasonable grounds is criminally liable.[222]

The liquidator, appointed by the general meeting is not regarded as an officer of the court and his remuneration is fixed by that meeting.[223] Where the remuneration is not so fixed, it may be determined by the court.[224]The effect of appointing a liquidator is that all the powers of the directors cease except where they are allowed to continue with the permission of the general meeting or liquidator.[225] Notice of the liquidator's appointment must be published in the Gazette and also given to the Registrar of Companies within fourteen days of appointment.[226]The court has power to appoint a liquidator where none has been appointed and to remove a liquidator on cause shown and appoint another in his stead.[227] The general meeting has power to appoint another liquidator where the office of liquidator falls vacant.[228] The liquidator may resign his office without the necessity for a court order.[229]

Within three months after the end of the first and every succeeding year of liquidation, the liquidator must summon a general meeting an give an account of his acts and dealings and of the conduct of winding-up in the preceding year.[230]

Upon completion of the winding-up the liquidator must, after giving one month's notice, published in the Uganda Gazette and a newspaper printed in Uganda and circulating in the locality where the meeting is being called, summon a general meeting of the company. The purpose is for him to present an account of the winding-up and how property has been disposed of[231]. A copy of the account and return in respect of the meeting must be forwarded to the Registrar of Companies within a fortnight of the meeting.[232] The company is automatically dissolved three months after the registrar has registered the return, unless the court, upon application by an interested person, makes an order deferring the dissolution.[233]

Where the liquidator is of the view that the company will not be able to pay its debts in full within the period indicated in the declaration of solvency[234], he must summon a creditors' meeting and lay before it a statement of the assets and liabilities of the company[235]. From then on the winding-up proceeds as a creditors' voluntary winding-up and Section 297 and 298 replace Sections 287 and 288 as a source of procedure.[236]

---

220 *ibid*; S.279

221 *ibid*. S.281(1), (2);

222 *ibid*, S.281(3)

223 *ibid* S. 283(1)

224 *Ososanya v. J.A.O. Obadeyi Ltd.* 1968(2) A.L.R.Comm 431

225 Companies Act, S.283(2); *Re: Nyasaland Civil Servants Co-operative Soc. Ltd.* 1923-60 ALR Mal.9 (High Court of Nyasaland)

226 *ibid*. S.303(1)

227 *ibid* S.302

228 *ibid* S.284

229 See *Ososanya v. Obadeyi Ltd. Supra n.31*

230 Companies Act, S.287

231 *ibid* S.288(1),(2)

232 *ibid* S.288(3); See also *Re: Cornish Manures Ltd.* [1967] 1W.L.R. 807

233 ibid, S.288(4)

234 *ibid*. S. 288(4)

235 *ibid*, S.286

## Creditors' voluntary winding-up

A creditors' voluntary winding-up arises where no declaration of solvency has been filed with the registrar pursuant to Section 281 of the Companies Act.

In such a case the company is required to summon a meeting of its creditors fixed for the day or next day on which the resolution for voluntary winding-up is to be proposed. The notice of the meeting must be sent to the creditors and also advertised in the Uganda Gazette and a newspaper circulating in Uganda.[237] The meeting is presided over by a director appointed by the board.[238] The purpose of the meeting is to (i) receive a full statement by the directors of the position of the company's affairs together with a list of the company's creditors and the estimated amount of their claims[239]; appoint the liquidator;[240] appoint a committee of the inspection.[241]

The creditors and the company in general meeting at their respective meetings are required to appoint a liquidator. Where they clash over the nomination, the creditors' choice prevails subject to an order of court arising from an application by any director, member or creditor requesting that the nominee of the company be made liquidator or act jointly with the creditors' nominee or alternatively that a different person altogether should be appointed liquidator[242].

The remuneration of the liquidator may be fixed by the committee of inspection and in the absence of the committee the creditors may fix the remuneration[243]. Alternatively, such remuneration may be determined by the court depending on the circumstances of the case.[244]Upon appointment of a liquidator the powers of the directors cease, save where the committee of inspection or the creditors authorise their continuance.[245]Should the office of liquidator be vacated, it can be filled by the creditors, provided the former liquidator was not appointed by the court or at its direction[246]. A liquidator can be appointed by the court or removed for cause shown and replaced.[247]Such appointment must be published in the Uganda Gazette and notice to that effect delivered to the registrar.[248]

Creditors may at one of their meeting convened pursuant to Section 291 of the Companies Act appoint a committee of inspection consisting of not more than five (5) persons, to act with the liquidator[249].

Within three months after the end of the first and every succeeding year of liquidation, the liquidator is required to summon a general meeting of the company and a meeting of the creditors and lay before the meetings an account of acts and dealings and of the conduct of the winding-up[250]. Following completion of the winding-up the liquidator must give one month's notice in the Uganda Gazette and then call a final meeting of the company and the creditors and present his account.[251] Within one week of the meeting the liquidator must send a return of the meeting to the registrar.[252] The company is then regarded as dissolved automatically three months after registration by the registrar of the account and return relating to the winding-up and meetings

---

236 *ibid* S.289.
237 *ibid,* S.291(1),(2).
238 *ibid* S.291(3)(b),(4).
239 *ibid* S.291(3)(a).
240 *ibid.* S.292.
241 *ibid* S.293.
242 *ibid* S.292.
243 *ibid* S.294(1).
244 *Re Amalgamated Syndicates Ltd.* [1901] 2 Ch.181
245 Companies Act,S.294(2)
246 *ibid* S.295.
247 *ibid* S.302; See also *Re: Sir John Moore Gold Mining Co* (1879) 12 Ch.D. 325. *Re: Karamelli & Barrett Ltd.* [1917] 1Ch.203; *Re: Charterland & Barrett Ltd* (1909) 26 T.L.R.132
248 *ibid* S.303.
249 *ibid* S.293.
250 *ibid* S.297.
251 *ibid* s.298 (1),(2).

respectively, save where an application has been made by an interested person to the court seeking deferment of the dissolution date.[253] An order of deferment must be filed with the registrar within seven days of issue.[254]

## Consequences of voluntary winding-up

The following effects arise from any voluntary winding-up. First the company ceases to carry on business except as required for its beneficial winding-up from the commencement of the winding up.[255]From that date the company's documents must indicate that it is in liquidation. Second, any transfer of shares without the permission of the liquidator and any alteration in the status of the members of the company, following commencement of winding-up is void.[256]Third, on the appointment of the liquidator the powers of the directors cease except where they are allowed to continue by the members, creditors or committee of inspection as the case may be.[257] Fourth voluntary winding-up terminates contracts of employment, where the company is insolvent and the employees are entitled to claim damages for wrongful dismissal.[258]

The provisions by which actions and other proceedings against the company may be stayed in respect of a compulsory winding-up[259] do no apply to a voluntary winding-up, although the court has discretion to stay proceedings.[260]

## Application of assets

The order of disposing of the company's assets in a voluntary winding-up is the same as in a compulsory winding-up[261]. Following the satisfaction of liabilities of the company, the remaining assets should be distributed among the members, according to their rights and interests in the company, save where the articles provide otherwise. Such requirement cannot be superseded by the company contracting to effect a different arrangement.[262]

## Powers and duties of the liquidator

These are largely the same as those of the liquidator during a compulsory winding-up[263]. In *Rudewa Estates Ltd. v. Commissioner of Stamp Duties*[70], it was held that in the case of a solvent company in voluntary liquidation, there is no hindrance or limitation on the company's beneficial ownership of its assets, unless there is reason to doubt that the creditors will be paid in full.

## Application to court

The liquidator, any contributory or creditor may apply to court for the determination of any question arising from the winding-up, or to exercise any of the powers which the court could exercise if the company were being wound-up compulsorily by the court[264]. This enables the

---

252 *ibid*, S.298(3).

253 *ibid* S.299 (4).

254 *ibid* S.298(5).

255 *ibid* S.279.

256 *ibid* S.280.

257 *ibid* Ss.283, 294.

258 *Fowler v. Commercial Timber Co. Ltd.* [1930] 2 K.B.1 C.A; *Reigate v.Union Manufacturing Co. (Ramaabottom) Ltd.* [1918] 1 K.B.592

259 Companies Act, Ss.226, 227, 326.

260 *ibid* S.305, *See also Re: R-R Realisations Ltd. [1980] 1 All E.R. 1019*

261 See *ibid* Ss 315, 306.

262 *ibid* S.300. See also *British Eagle International Airline Ltd v. Compagnie Nationale Air France* [1975] 2 All E.R.390.

263 See *supra and ibid* Ss.244, 301, *Re: Britton & Millard Ltd* (1957) 107 L.J. 602; *Pulsford v. Devenish* [1903] 2 Ch.625; *Re: Windsor Steam Coal Co.* [1929] 1 Ch.151 *Rudewa Estates Ltd. v. Commissioner of Stamp Duties* [1966] E.A.576 (Court of Appeal for Eastern Africa (Tanzania); *Re: Peter & Co. Ltd.* Companies Cause No.18 of 1960 Unreported 3rd August, 1961 (High Court of Uganda).

264 *ibid* S.305. See further *Re: R-R Realisations Ltd* [1980] 1 All E.R.1019.

liquidator to seek the guidance of the court; for example where he thinks there has been a fraud he can obtain an order for a public or private examination.[265]

### Duty to report criminal offences

Where it appears to the liquidator during the course of a voluntary winding-up that any past or present officer or any member has committed a criminal offence he must report the matter to the Director of Public Prosecutions, who may apply to the court for an order conferring on him or any other person powers of investigating the company's affairs as they exist in the case of winding-up by the court.[266] However, the court is not by this provision entitled to order a public or private examination.[267]

### Compulsory winding-up following commencement of voluntary winding-up

Any creditor or contributory can apply for compulsory winding-up by the court, while the voluntary winding-up is continuing. However, an application by a contributory will not be granted by the court unless it is satisfied that the rights of the contributories will be prejudiced by the voluntary winding-up.[268] The court is also required to have regard to the wishes of all the creditors and will not issue an order if the majority of them oppose the application unless the applicant can show special circumstances.[269] Additionally, if the official receiver or other person presents a petition pursuant to Section 224, the court will not issue a winding-up order on such petition unless it is satisfied that the voluntary winding-up or winding-up subject to supervision cannot be continued with regard to the interests or the creditors or contributories.

Furthermore, instead of making a winding-up order, the court may order that the voluntary winding-up shall continue but subject to the supervision of the court.[270]

If the court makes an order for compulsory winding-up, such winding-up is deemed to commence from the date of passing the resolution for voluntary winding-up and in that regard, all proceedings taken in voluntary winding-up are deemed to have been validly taken unless the court, on proof of fraud or mistake thinks otherwise fit to direct.[271]

## Winding up subject to supervision of court

Upon petition, the court may order a voluntary winding-up to continue, subject to the court's supervision and in such case, the creditors contributories or others will be at liberty to apply to the court on such terms and conditions as the court thinks just.[272] Where the relevant application is not made by way of petition, it may be struck out.[273] The order sought is not automatically granted. Thus in *Re: Gresham Life Assurance Soc. (Nig) Ltd.*[274] the petitioning company was incorporated outside Nigeria and registered in Nigeria under Section 239 of the Companies Act[275]. The company carried on business in Nigeria through the agency of another insurance company at a place of business occupied by the latter company. Following the coming into force of the Companies Act, 1968, the petitioner informed the Registrar of Companies that it did not

265 Pursuant to Ss.267,268, *ibid.*
266 *ibid* S.329(2), (3).
267 *Re: Campbell Coverings Ltd.* (No.1) [1953] Ch.488 C.A.
268 Companies Act, S.307.
269 *Re: Home Remedies Ltd.* [1943] Ch.1 *Re: B. Karsberg Ltd.* [1950] 1 W.L.R.57, C.A.; *Re J.D.Swain Ltd.* [1965] 1W.L.R.909 C.A.
270 Companies Act. S.308.
271 *ibid* S.229(1).
272 *ibid* S.308.
273 *Ososanya v. J.A.O. Obadeyi Ltd.* 1968(2) A.L.R.Comm 431
274 1970 NCLR 78 (High Court of Lagos State), affd 1973 NCLR 215 (Supreme Court of Nigeria).
275 Cap. 37 Laws in Nigeria, 1958 (equivalent to Section 370 of the Companies Act (Uganda).

intend to carry on business in Nigeria and instituted proceedings for winding-up under supervision of the court. The petition was opposed on the ground that the petitioner company had not established place of business in Nigeria. Consequently, Section 369(3) of the Companies Act, 1968 of Nigeria[276] was inapplicable and was discretionary and the winding-up order should be refused. In up holding the objection *inter alia,* the court observed that the grounds for refusing an order of winding up under the supervision of the court, may in the case of an insurance company incorporated outside Nigeria and having no established place of business in Nigeria include the fact that a creditor and policy holder has a pending action against the company for breach of contract and the fact that the policy holders who wish to continue to pay premiums after the company goes into liquidation will not be able to pay them to an insurance company but only to the individual whom it is proposed to appoint as liquidator. The court also indicated[277] that a Nigerian court has no jurisdiction to entertain a winding-up by a company which has no established place of business in Nigeria and is not resident in Nigeria but merely transacts its business through an agent in Nigeria.

A petition for winding-up subject to supervision of the court is deemed to be a petition for compulsory winding-up for the purpose of giving jurisdiction to the court over actions.[278] Accordingly, Sections 227, and 228, of the Companies Act, will apply.[279]

Although the court may appoint an additional liquidator,[280] such liquidator has the same powers as in the case of a voluntary winding-up subject only to any restrictions contained in the relevant order.[281] Nevertheless, the sanction of the court or committee of inspection is required before the liquidator can bring or defend any action or other legal proceedings in the name and on behalf of the company.[282]

The significance of winding-up subject to supervision has been whittled down because under section 305 of the Companies Act the liquidator or any creditor or contributory may apply to the court to determine any question arising out of the winding-up or to exercise any powers which the court could exercise if the company were being wound up by the court. Nevertheless it is notable that under part X of the Companies Act, if a foreign company informs the Registrar of Companies that it does not intend to carry on business in Uganda, the registrar shall strike the Company off the register.[283]

---

276 Equivalent to Companies Act (Uganda), Ss.369, 370.

277 *ibid.* pp.224-225. See also The *Lalandia* [1932] All E.R. Rep.391; *In Re Lloyd Generale Italiano* (1885), 29 Ch.D.219.

278 Companies Act, S.309.

279 See also *ibid.* S.310.

280 *ibid* S.311(1).

281 *ibid* S.311(2).

282 *ibid* Ss.312(1)(d),(e),(f).

283 *ibid* S.377(1).

# INDEX


All entries are to page numbers.

ACCOUNTANT. *See* ACCOUNTS

ACCOUNTS, 139-148
- accountants' report in prospectus, 54-55
- articles of association and, 42
- audit and auditors. *See* AUDITORS
- balance sheet
  - auditor's report attached, 54,140
  - contents, 140
  - directors' report attached to,141
  - general meeting, laid before,140
  - group, 140, 141
  - purpose, 140, 141
- books,139
- companies liquidation account, 438
- duty
  - company's to keep, 139
  - directors' as to 139
- group
  - balance sheet, 140
  - consolidated, 140
  - contents, 140-141
  - form, 140-141
  - generally, 140-141
  - holding company, 140-141
  - profit and loss account, 140
  - purpose, 8, 140
  - subsidiary company 140-141
- See *also* AUDITORS

ACTIONS AND PROCEEDINGS. *See* COMPANY -legal proceedings

ADDRESS. *See* REGISTERED OFFICE

AGENT,
- broker as, 84
- company as shareholders, 154-159
- contracts by, 124-135
- crimes by 137-138
- directors as, 149-159
- liability of company for acts of, 124-136
  - contractual, 125-133
  - criminal, 137-138
  - tortious, 136-137
  - *ultra vires,* 29-38
  - promoter as, 19-20
  - torts, 136-137
  - *ultra vires,* 29-38
- promoter as, 19-20
- torts by 136-137
- *ultra vires* acts of 39-38
- See also DIRECTORS

ARTICLES OF ASSOCIATION (cont.)

ALIENS,
- mortgagees, as, 92

ALLOTMENT. *See* SHARES

AMALGAMATION. *See* REORGANISATION OF COMPANY.

ANNUAL, RETURNS, 77

APPLICATION,
- alteration of objects clause, for, 39-40
- appointment of inspector, for, 238-239
- dispense with "Limited", to, 28
- reduction of capital, for, 84-85
- restoration of name on register, 277
- shares, for. *See* SHARES.

ARRANGEMENT, SCHEME OF. *See* RE-ORGANISATION OF COMPANY

ARTICLES OF ASSOCIATION, 41-50
- alteration of, 47-50
  - company benefit test, 47-50
  - conversion of private into public company, 23
  - rectification, 50
  - restrictions upon, 57-50
  - special resolution for, 47
- compliance with Stock Exchange Regulations, 43
- contents of, 42-43
  - accounts, 43
- registration of, 42
- Stock Exchange Regulations and, 43
  - auditors, 42
  - borrowing, 92
  - commencement of business, 23
  - directors, 42
  - dividends, 89
  - indemnities, 90
  - interpretation clause, 42
  - meetings, 242-253
  - notices, 245-248
  - preliminary matters, 41, 42
  - reserve, 79
  - seal, 129, 132
  - secretary, 120-123
  - share capital, 79
  - winding-up, 130
- contract, as, 43-45
- distribution of, 42
- effect of, 45-47
- form of, 42
- interpretation of, 41, 42

memorandum, relation with, 41-42
notice of, 41
particulars of, 42-43
public document, as, 41
reduction of capital authorised by,84-85
persons ineligible as, 143
position of, 143-144
Table A, 42
Table C, 42
Table D, 42
transfer of shares, restrictions upon, 68
ASSETS. *See* WINDING-UP
ASSIGNMENT OF DEBTS, *See* CREDITORS
ASSOCIATION
articles of. *See* ARTICLES OF ASSOCIATION
memorandum of. *See* MEMORANDUM OF ASSOCIATION
ATTORNEY GENERAL,
approval of Registrar's winding-up petition by, 266
prosecution by, for misfeasance, 237-238, 271
AUDITORS,
appointment of 141-142
articles of association and, 43
breach of,
duty, 144-146
trust, 144-146
disclaimer of responsibility by, 145
duties of, 144-146
first, 141
negligence by, 145
qualifications of, 142-143
remuneration of, 142-143
report of
contents of, 141
inspection of, 141
liability for, 141
prospectus, in, 53
subsequent, 141-142
BUSINESS,
acquisition of existing name. *See* FORMATION
Commencement of. *See* ARTICLES, FLOTATIONS
BALANCE SHEET, *See* ACCOUNTS
BANKRUPTCY. *See* WINDING-UP
BILLS OF EXCHANGE
acceptance by company, 9, 29
authority to draw, 129
company not mentioned on, 9
endorsement by company, 129
Signature by company, 129
BOARD *See* DIRECTORS
BOND. *See* BORROWING
BOOKS. *See* ACCOUNTS
BORROWING,
articles of association and, 92
bond, by, 94-100
charge on uncalled capital, by 93
debentures, by, 94
directors, by, 32-34
mortgage, by, 94
protection of members, 85-86
protection of public,85-86
registration of order, 86
special resolution, by, 83
sub-division of shares, 83
power to borrow, 92
promissory note, by, 94
repayment of, 150
*ultra vires*. *See* ULTRA VIRES DOCTRINE
CALLS. *See* SHARES
CAPITAL
alteration of, 83-84
cancellation of unissued shares, 83
consolidation of shares,74, 83
conversion of shares into stock,74-75,83
increase, 83
reduction, 84-86
application for, 84
articles of association, authorization by, 84
confirming order, 84
consent of creditors, 85-86
court,by, 85
members' liability, 84-86
protection of creditors, 87-89
fixed, 94
floating, 95
circulating, 91
clause, alteration of, 39-40
equity share, 79-80
fixed, 90
issued, 78
loan capital. *See* DEBENTURES
nominal, 78
"no par value" share, 39
paid-up,78
payment of dividends out of, 144-147
required, 38
reserve, 79
statement in memorandum of association, 28
types, 78-79
uncalled, 79

CERTIFICATE,
registration of charges, of, 97-100
trading. *See* BORROWING
CHARGES,
debentures, securing, 93-94
defunct, 227
dissolution of, 276-277
advantages, 95
crystallisation, 95
definition, 94-96
priority, 94
mortgages. *See* MORTGAGES
register of, 97-100
*See also* DEBENTURES, MORTGAGES
CHEQUES. *See* BILLS OF EXCHANGE
MINISTER FOR TRADE
name of company powers in relation to, 28
COMMITTEE OF INSPECTION
voluntary winding-up, in, 277-280
winding-up by court, in, 276
COMMON SEAL. *See* SEAL
COMPANIES LIQUIDATION ACCOUNT. *See* WINDING-UP
COMPANY,
agent for shareholders, 154-159
bills of exchange, 129
co-operative society distinguished, 16-17
officers, acts of, 124-135
organs, act of, 124-135
tortious, 136-137
*ultra vires* acts, for, 29-37
"lifting veil", 8-15
domicile of, 13-15
duration, 7
expenses, 7-8
foreign. *See* FOREIGN COMPANY
formalities, 7-8
guarantee, limited by. *See* COMPANY LIMITED BY GUARANTEE
individual distinguished from 4-6
joint stock. *See* JOINT STOCK COMPANY.
land of, 6
legal proceedings,
generally, 6-7
misfeasance proceedings, 237-238, 171
oppression of minority, 224-232
representative action, 212-224
liability of, 6
contractual, 124-135
criminal, 137-138
limits, 135-136
*ultra vires* doctrine, 29-38
unlimited. *See* UNLIMITED COMPANY
unregistered. *See* UNREGISTERED COMPANY
winding-up petition by, 264
COMPANY LIMITED BY GUARANTEE,
articles of association of
contents of, 42-43
registration of, 42
Table C, 42
Table D, 42
liability of contributory in, 265
memorandum of association, 27-40
member, as, 65
nationality of, 13-15
organic theory of 136-137
organs of, 124-135
ownership, investigation of, 241
parent. *See* GROUP.
partnership distinguished, 16
personality of, 4-6, 135-138
property of, 6, 270-272
publicity, 7-8
registration, *See* REGISTRATION OF COMPANIES
reorganisation. *See* REORGANISATION OF COMPANIES.
residence, 13-15
"sham", 10
shares, limited by. *See* COMPANY LIMITED BY SHARES,
taxation of, 9
transfer of shares in, 7
seal, requirements of 129, 132
signature of, by director, 129
*ultra vires*. *See* ULTRA VIRES DOCTRINE.
COMPANY LIMITED BY SHARES
articles of association of, 65-69
memorandum of association of, 41-43
Table A, adoption of 42
CONTRACT,
articles of association as, 43-45
form of, 206
incorporation, prior to, 20-23

liability of company for agent's 124-125
rescission of, 20
subsidiary company, of, 9, 11-12
CONTRIBUTORIES,
arrest of, 272

attendance of, at hearing of winding-up
petition, 277
bankruptcy of, 265
calls on, 272
distribution among, 277
inspection of statement of affairs, 267
CONTROL. *See* SHAREHOLDERS
CO-OPERATIVE SOCIETY,
company, and, 16-17
CORPORATE PERSONALITY,
consequences of, 6-15
secured, 272
unsecured, 272
winding-up, in,
attendance at hearing of
petition, 266
notice of intention to appear,
266
petition by, 264-267
voluntary, 277-280
COURT,
alteration of objects clause by, 39-40
reduction of capital by, 84-86
winding-up by, 264-277
*See also* COMPANY - legal
proceedings.
CREDITORS,
application of company's assets to, 280
assignee, 264
attendance at hearing of winding-up
petition, 277
liability of, 265
lists of
A list, 272
B list, 272
meaning of, 265, 272
notice of intention to appear in
winding-up, 281
winding-up petition by, 264-267
CRIME,
agent of company. *See* AGENT.
liability for company for, 217-219
*ultra vires* doctrine and, 54-55
*See also* AGENT, COMPANY,
FORGERY.
DAMAGES,
deceit, for, 58-59, 63
experts, against, 63
consent to reduction of capital, 85-86
contingent, 264, 272
definition, 272
list of, 85-86
meeting of, 279-281
notice of intention to appear in
winding-up, 266
preferred, 272-273
proof of debts in winding-up, 272-273
prospective, 272
protection when capital reduced, 85-86
scheme of arrangement, in, 254-256
floating, 94-95
priority of, 94
chose in action, 94, 95
definition, 92-93
enforcement, 100-101
form
indorsed conditions, 93-94
holders, remedies of, 100-104
action, 100
proof in winding-up,420-422
receiver and manager, 101-103
sale, 93
valuation of security, 100
winding-up petition, 264-266
issue, 94-95
managers, 101-103
liability of promoter for, 63
misrepresentation, for, 58-59,63
non-compliance with prospectus
requirements, for, 62
DEBENTURES,
charges securing, 94-100
fixed, 94
registration of, 97-100
seal, under, 97
stock, 93
transfer of, 93-94
trust deed accompanying, 93
types
bearer, 94
registered, 94
receivers, 101-103
DEBTS, *See* BORROWING, CREDITORS,
WINDING-UP
DECEIT,
damages for, 58
DECLARATION OF COMPLIANCE,
definition, 24
DIRECTORS,
accounts, duty as to, 139
acts, validity of, 108
agents, as, 108

alternate, 107-108
appointment of, 107-108
first directors, 106
*Foss v. Harbottle,* rule in, 203-224
indemnification of, 111
joint and several liability of, 107
loans to 186
appointment of, 101-103
duties of. 101-103
remuneration of, 102
persons ineligible, 106-107
subsequent directors, 107
articles of association and, 107
borrowing powers of, 95
consent to act as, 107
contracts with company, 184-186
disqualification of, 1-7-108
duties, 141
books, as to, 141
care, of, 191-194
enforcement, 198-241
fiduciary, 149-184
company benefit, 159-166
conflict of interests, 174-184
disclosure of emoluments, 186-190
general, 174
*Foss v. Harbottle,* rule in and
exceptions to, 198-224
holding and subsidiary companies, in, 1 49-150
release from, 190-191
executive, 107-108
powers of...
general, 112-118
proceedings of, 118-119
prospectus particulars, 54
qualifications
age, 107
shares, 107
loss of office, compensation for, 176-178
managing, 119-120
meetings
chairmen, 118
deadlock, 190, 191
minutes, 118
notice, 380-384
quorum, 118
resolutions, 118
misfeasance, 379-380
number of, 106
particulars of, 108-109
position of, 105-106
powers of, 112
cessation, 118
delegation, 117
exercise, 118-119
effect of, 280
liability in, 271
refusal of share transfer by, 107
register of 8, 108-109
removal, 101-111
remuneration of, 111-112
disclosure of emoluments, 186-191
loss of office, compensation for, 186
report attached to balance-sheet, 139
resignation of, 109
retirement, 109
secretary as, 120
shareholding of, 8, 107-108
special, 175-176statutory report by, 141
trustees, as, 105-106
vacation of office, 109-111
winding-up, 267
DISSOLUTION. *See* WINDING-UP
DIVIDENDS
articles of association and, 89
declaration of, 89
definition of, 89
payments of
amount, 144-145
method, 145-146
preference shares, 129-133
DOCUMENTS, *See* ARTICLES OF ASSOCIATION, MEMORANDUM OF ASSOCIATION.
DOMICILE. *See* COMPANY
offers for sale, 51-52
placings, 55-56
share-hawking, 55
statement of particulars, 53-55
Stock Exchange and, 52-53
ENGLISH LAW,
common law, 1
equity 1,
reception of, 1
EXCHANGE CONTROL,
company borrowing and, 92
EXPROPRIATION,
company property, of. *See* COMPANY
members' property, of. *See* MEMBERS.
EXTRAORDINARY GENERAL MEETING. *See* MEETINGS

FLOTATIONS. 51-63
arrears. 80
cumulative. 78-79
non-cumulative. 80
participating. 80
reserve and capitalisation. 91
restrictions. 91
source of
capital. 89-91
profits not capital, 89-91

FORECLOSURE. *See* DEBENTURES
FORGERY,
share certificate, of, 132
share transfer, of, 72
FORMATION, 37-43
acquisitionof existing business, 23
formalities of, 24
form of company 23
incorporation, 24
particulars of company, 24
registration, 24-26
type of company, 23-24
commencement of business, 148
Commission
brokerage, 52
general, 52
sub-underwriting, 52
underwriting, 51-52
directors. liability of, 51, 61-62
meaning, 51
price. determination of, 52
prospectus, 52-55
public companies, 54-55
public issue, methods of
direct offers to public, 54-55
company property, of, 201, 212-224
members' property, of 212-224
representative action,
FOSS V. HARBOTTLE, RULE IN. *See* DIRECTORS
FRAUD ON MINORITY
alteration of articles, 47-50
lifting veil of 13-25
expropriation
documents for, 24
lifting veil of, 8-15
see also FORMATION.
FRAUDULENT PREFERENCE, 270-271
FRAUDULENT TRADING, 271
GOVERNMENT SECURITIES. *See* SECURITIES
GROUP,
accounts, *See* ACCOUNTS
holding company, *See* HOLDPING COMPANY
subsidiary company, *See* SUBSIDIARY COMPANY
GUARANTEE, COMPANY LIMITED BY. *See* COMPANY LIMITED BY GUARANTEE
HOLDING COMPANY,
accounts of, 140-141
what is, 8, 140
INCORPORATION,
consequences of, 6-8
effect of, 6-8, 23-26
INDIVIDUAL,
company and, 4-6
INFANTS,
members, as, 64
INJUNCTION,
name, to restrain use of, 45-46
INSPECTION AND INVESTIGATION, 238
application for, 238
appointment of inspectors, 238-239
expenses of, 241
grounds for, 238
investigation of company ownership, 241
powers of inspectors, 239-240
Registrar, at instance of, 238
related company, into, 9
report,240-241
statement of affairs, 238
INVESTIGATION. *See* INSPECTION AND INVESTIGATION
JUDGMENTS,
enforcement of, 72-73
LAND,
aliens and, 95
company holding, 6
mortgage of, 92, 94
power to hold, 6, 92, 94
LEGAL PROCEEDINGS. *See* COMPANY
LIEN, *See* SHARES
LIFTING VEIL OF INCORPORATION, 8-15
bill of exchange, company not mentioned in, 9
company agent for shareholders, 9
fraudulent trading, 9
holding companies, 9
investigation into related company, 9
number of members below minimum, 8-9
purpose, 8
reckless trading, 9

"sham" company, 10
subsidiary companies, 9, 11-12
taxation, 9
LIMITATION OF LIABILITY
effect of, 6, 38
statement in memorandum of association, 27, 28
"LIMITED", 28
LIMITED COMPANY,
formation, 23-26
guarantee, by, 6, 23
*See also* COMPANY LIMITED BY GUARANTEE
omission of "Limited" from name, 28
shares, by, 23
*See also* COMPANY LIMITED BY SHARES
LIQUIDATOR,
application of company assets by, 280
appointment of, 268, 273
control of, 276
costs and expenses of, 273
duties of, 273, 274
liability of, 275-276
list of contributories, 272
official Receiver as, 265
powers of, 274-275
property of company, administration of, 269
provisional liquidator, 267, 268, 269
release of, 275-276
removal of, 273
remuneration of, 273
resignation, 273
sale by, 274-275
voluntary winding-up, 277-280
LOAN CAPITAL. *See* DEBENTURES
purchase of company's own shares, for 88-89
*See also* BORROWING
MANAGER,
appointment, 101-103
duties, 101-103
receiver and, 101
remuneration, 164
MANAGING DIRECTOR. *See* DIRECTORS
MEETINGS,
agenda, 242, 246
annual general, 243-244
board, *See* DIRECTORS
Chairman, 248-249
Class, 252
creditors, 430-432
extraordinary general
convening, 244-245
expenses, 244
objects, 244
requisitioning, 244
voluntary winding-up, in, 277-280
general
powers, of, 243-244
supreme legislative authority, 106
minutes, 252
quorum, 248
resolutions
circulation, 248
extraordinary, 249
ordinary, 249
procedure, 249
special, 249
special notice, requiring, 247-248
show of hands, *See* VOTING
Statutory, 242
voting, 250
poll, 250
proxy, 250-251
MEETINGS
notice
form, 245
nature, 245
length 245
service, 246
poll. *See* VOTING
show of hands, 250
proceedings, 384-391
proxy. *See* VOTING.
MEMBERS,
annual returns, 77
becoming, 65-75
allotment, 55-57, 66
directors' qualification shares, 107
registration, 75-77
subscription, 55-57, 66
register of, 75-77
contents, 75-77
equitable interests, 124-126
generally, 75
inspection, 75
rectification, 76
requirement, 75
where kept, 75
scheme of arrangement
dissenting from, 256
generally, 254-258

voluntary winding-up by, 277-280
*See also* SHAREHOLDERS
MEMORANDUM OF ASSOCIATION,
articles of association, relation with, 41
capital, statement of, 38
transfer, 68
transmission,65, 73
companies as, 65
index of, 28, 75-77
infants as, 64
issue of shares, 64
liabililty of, 39
increase of, 39
reduced capital, on, 81-86
reservation of, 78
payment of shares by 66-68
personal representatives as, 65
property, expropriation of, 212-224
notice of, 42
objects clause, 29-37
particulars, 27-28
power to borrow, 31-32
public document, 42
registered office, 27-28
subscription to, 27, 42
variation of class rights, 82
MINORITY,
fraud on. *See* SHAREHOLDERS.
MINUTES, books of, 252 *See* also MEETINGS
MISFEASANCE,
generally 237-238
winding-up, 271
MISREPRESENTATION,
damages for, 58-59
MORTGAGES,
aliens, to, 92
contents of, 27
distribution of, 41
effect of, 43-45
limitation of liability, 38
name, 28
equitable, 72
legal, 72
NAME,
change of
company, by, 28
Registrar, direction by, 28

injunction to restrain use of, 28
"Limited", 28
publication of, 28
register, on
restoration of, 277
striking off, 277
restoration of, 277
restrictions on use of, 28
striking off, 277
NATIONALITY, *See* ALIENS, COMPANY, FOREIGN COMPANY.
NEGLIGENCE,
auditors, of, 144-146
debts, in paying, 262-267 *See also* TORTS.
NEGOTIABLE INSTRUMENTS. *See* BILLS OF EXCHANGE
NOTICE,
address of registered office, of, 27-28
chattels, of, 95-97
debentures secured by, 94
equitable, 72, 95-97
land, of, 92
legal, 72, 100
shares
alteration of objects clause, of, 39-40
articles of association, 41
meetings, of. *See* MEETINGS.
memorandum of association, 41
special, 247
winding-up order, 267
OBJECTS,
alteration of, 39-40
statement in memorandum, 28
*ultra vires* doctrine and, 29-30
*See also* MEMORANDUM OF ASSOCIATION
OFFER FOR SALE, *See* SHARES.
OFFICE. *See* REGISTERED OFFICE
OFFICERS,
Company's liability for acts of, 124-135
contractual, 125-133
criminal, 137-138
tortious, 136-137
*ultra vires*, 46-61 *See also* DIRECTORS, SECRETARY
OFFICIAL RECEIVER,
liquidator, as, 411
meeting of creditors and contributories, 272
notice of winding-up order, 265
winding-up petition by, 264
OPPRESSION OF MINORITY. *See* SHAREHOLDERS
ORDINARY RESOLUTIONS. *See* RESOLUTIONS
PARENT COMPANY. *See* GROUP.
PARTICULARS,
application, 52
articles of association, 41-43

company, 27-28
directors, 108-109, 184-191
memorandum, 27-18
statement of, 24, 53-55
PARTNERSHIP,
company and, 16-17
PERSONALITY. *See* CORPORATE PERSONALITY.
PERSONAL REPRESENTATIVES,
members, as, 65
rights
dividends, to receive 65
registration, 65
PROSPECTUS, 87-91
contents
accountant's report, 54
allotment particulars, 54-55
application particulars, 52
business record of company, 54
apply for, to, 65
transmission, on, 73
shares, to sell, 65
POLL. *See* MEETINGS.
PRIVATE COMPANY,
articles of association, 23
conversion into public company, 23
definition, 23
flotations, 23
formalities, 23-24
membership, 23
PROMISSORY NOTE. *See* BORROWING.
PROMOTERS, 19-20
contracts before incorporation, 20-23
damages, liability for, 19-20
deferred shares, 129
definition of, 19
fiduciary duty of, 19-20
founders' shares, 79
recovery of profits made by, 20
remuneration of, 20
rescission of contract made by, 20
suspension of, 106-107
directors and promoters, remedies against, 61-62
compensation, 62
damages for deceit, 96-97
damages for non-compliance with prospectus requirements, 62
experts, remedies against,
compensation, 61
consents, 53-55
debentures, 90
deferred shares, 4
directors' particulars, 54
exemption, 54
founders' shares, 54
minimum subscription, 54
number of shares, 54
opening subscription lists, 54
options, 54
reports to be annexed, 54
liability in respect of, 56-67
application without prospectus, 55
company, remedies against, 56-62
damages for misrepresentation, 56-57
rescission of contract, 59-60
PUBLIC COMPANY,
conversion from private company, 23
definition of, 23
flotations, 53-55
formalities, 23-24
membership of, 23
statutory meeting of, 242-243
PUBLIC CORPORATION,
company and, 17-18
PUBLIC DOCUMENTS, 27
PUBLIC ISSUES. *See* FLOTATIONS
QUORUM. *See* MEETINGS.
RATIFICATION,
illegal acts, 202
ordinary resolution, by, 202
*ultra vires* acts, of, 202
RECEIVER AND MANAGER,
debenture-holders, for, 101-103
RECEIVERS,
appointment
court, by, 163-164
debenture-holders, by, 162 -163
effect of, 164-165
notice of, 167 directors'
shareholdings, 175
persons eligible, 163
damages, 61
misstatements, 63-64
meaning, 52
public element, 52-54
purpose, 53
registration, 53-54
statement in lieu of, 24, 55
Stock Exchange Regulations, compliance with, 52-53
RECTIFICATION,
articles of association, of, 50
register of
charges, 97-100
members, 75-77

REGISTERED OFFICE. 28
address. 28
index of members. 123-126
books of account. 223-126
minutes books. 390
register of
charges. 157-162
directors and secretaries, 39, 175
members, 123-126
publication of, 103-104
duties
abstract of receipts and payments, 98
preferential payments, 97-98
statement of affairs, 103, 274,277
manager, and. *See* RECEIVER AND MANAGER
misfeasance proceedings, 237-238
remuneration, 103
RECONSTRUCTION. *See* REORGANISATION OF COMPANIES.
REGISTRATION OF CHARGES,
certificate of, 97
company's office, at, 97
non-registration, effect of, 99-100
rectification of register, 99
Registrar, with, 98-99
REGISTRATION OF COMPANIES,
foreign companies, 281
not formed under Act 281-282
restoration of name, 277
striking off defunct company, 277
REORGANISATION OF COMPANIES, 254-259
amalgamation, 256
arrangement, 254-255
compromise, 254-255
reconstruction, 256-258
sale
liquidator, by, 258
memorandum, under, 258
REGISTRAR OF COMPANIES,
inspection at instance of, 238
name of company, powers in relation to, 28
notice of alteration of objects clause to,objects, 39
striking defunct company off register, 277
winding-up petition by, 261
REGISTRATION OF BUSINESS,
formalities, 12-13
publicity, 12-13
inspection and investigation, of, 238-239
statutory, 238-239
RESCISSION,
contract, of, 20
misrepresentation in prospectus, for, 58-60
RESERVE,
articles of association and, 79
capital, 79
capitalization and, 91
RESIDENT. *See* FOREIGN COMPANY.
RESOLUTIONS,
extraordinary, 249
ordinary, 249
procedure
amendment, 249-250
registration, 250
voting, 250
special, 249 *See also* SPECIAL RESOLUTIONS.
special notice, requiring, 249
voluntary winding-up, in, 277-278
*See also* MEETINGS
scheme of arrangement, 254-256
take-over bids, 258-260
REPORT,
auditors' 141, 144
ROYAL BRITISH BANK v. TURQUAND, RULE IN, 124-135
*See also* ULTRA VIRES DOCTRINE
SALE,
debenture-holder's remedy, 101
liquidator, by, 256
memorandum, under, 258
SCHEME OF ARRANGEMENT. *See* RE-ORGANISATION OF COMPANIES
SEAL,
articles of association, 129, 132
SECRETARY.
articles of association, 120
director, as, 120
duties
books, as to, 194, 197
meetings, as to, 194, 197
returns, as to, 121
engagement of, 120
position of, 121-122
qualification of, 122
register, 107, 120
SHAREHOLDERS,
company as agent, 15
contributories,'as, 272
controlling
duties, enforcement of, 198-224

*Foss v. Harbottle*, rule and
exceptions, 201-224
individual action, 203-212
oppression, remedy for, 224-232
representative action, 212-224
winding-up petition, 232-237
infancy, 64-65
infringement of personal rights, 203-212
oppression of minority. *See* controlling.
SHARES,
allotment of, 55-57
irregular, 56-57
procedure for, 53-56
restrictions upon, 56
returns as to, 57-58
time for, 55-56
application for, 55
conditional, 55-56
form, 55
revocation, 56
calls
advance payment, 73
non-payment, 73-74
payment, 73-74
cancellation of unissued, 83
certificate, 67-68
company limited by. *See* COMPANY LIMITED BY SHARES.
consolidation of, 135
conversion into stock, 74-75
directors' qualification, 178
equity, 115-116
issue
discount, at, 66
premium, at, 66
price at, 66
lien on
enforcement of, 71
nature, 71
mortgage
equitable, 72
legal, 72
payment for, 66
preference, 80-82
price of issue, 66
sale of, 70-71
stocks, 74-75
sub-division, 83
transfer
capacity, to, 68
forgery, 72
form of, 69-90
generally, 68-73
procedure for, 70-71
refusal of, 68-69
restrictions upon, 68
right to, 68
transmission, 65, 73
warrant, 74
SIGNATURE,
bills of exchange, 129
statement of prospectus, of, 54
SPECIAL RESOLUTIONS,
articles, alteration of, 47-50
name, change of, 28
objects, alteration of, 39-40
reduction of capital, by, 84
shares, character of, 79
SPECIAL RESOLUTIONS
winding-up
court, by, 261
voluntary, 277
STATE MINISTER,
approval for mortgage of land, 92
STATEMENT,
affairs, of, *See* INSPECTION AND INVESTIGATION.
capital, of, *See* CAPITAL.
objects, of. *See* OBJECTS
prospectus, in lieu of. *See* STATEMENT IN LIEU OF PROSPECTUS
STATEMENT IN LIEU OF PROSPECTUS.
defective, 55, 63
failure to issue, 55
inaccurate, 55, 63
inspection of, 55
registration, 55
signature, 55
*See also* PROSPECTUS
STATEMENT OF AFFAIRS
contents, 267-268
delivery to Official Receiver, 267
deed, 93
trustee as director, 105-106
unit, 17
STOCK, *See* DEBENTURES, JOINT STOCK COMPANY, SHARES
SUBSCRIBERS,
memorandum, to, 27
who may be, 64-65
SUBSIDIARY COMPANY,
accounts of, 140-141
what is, 87-88
*See also* GROUP
TABLE A,
adoption of, 42
exclusion of, 42
TABLE C, 42

TABLE D, 42
TAKE-OVER BIDS. *See* REORGANISATION OF COMPANIES.
TAXATION,
income tax, 9
lifting corporate veil, 9
TORT,
liability of company for agent's 136-137
*ultra vires* doctrine and, 34
*See also* NEGLIGENCE
TRADING CERTIFICATE. *See* FLOTATIONS.
TRUST,
breach of, 174, 186-190, 194-197
sub-underwriting, 52
ULTRA VIRES DOCTRINE, 29-106
application to Uganda, 29
condonation, 202
form, 267-268
verification of, 268
UNIT TRUSTS, 17
UNLIMITED COMPANY,
articles of association contents of, 42
registration of, 24-26, 42
Table C, 42
controlling shareholders and, 202
crime and, 34
director's liability under, 300
effect, 35-36
meaning, 29-30
public documents and, 124-133
ratification of *ultra vires* acts, 202
reform
alteration of objects,by, 39
protection of third parties, by, 36-37
*Royal British Bank v. Turquand,* rule in, 124-133
scope, 29-36
tort and, 34
UNDERWRITING,
commission, 51-52
Table D, 42
definition, 38
formation, 38
memorandum of association, 39
VOLUNTARY WINDING-UP. *See* WINDING-UP.
VOTING. *See* MEETINGS.
WARRANTS. *See* SHARES
WINDING-UP,
accounts, 274
application of assets, 273, 280
contributories, 272
costs, 273
creditors, 272-273
expenses, 273
preferential payments, 273
secured creditors, 273
unsecured creditors, 273
commencement, 266
Companies Liquidation Account, 274
committee of inspection, 268-269
completion, 276-277
consequences, 267, 280
court, by,
appeal, 266
committee of inspection, 268, 279
company not carrying on business, 261
company unable to pay debts, 262
creditors' meeting, 279
grounds, 261-262
jurisdiction, 262
just and equitable, 232-238
liquidator, appointment of, 268
order, 267
persons who may petition, 264-266
powers, 274-275, 280
proceedings before hearing, 266
property of company, 267-272
provisional liquidator, 267
publicity, 267
reduction of membership below statutory minimum, 262
report by Official Receiver, 265-266
special resolution, 266
statement of affairs, 267-268
statutory meeting, default in holding, 262
statutory report, default in delivering, 262
stay of order, 266
voluntary winding-up started, after, 277
disclaimer, 271
dissolution of company, 276-277
fraudulent preference, 270-271
fraudulent trading,
just and equitable, 232-238
misfeasance, 237-238, 271
oppression, remedy for, 224-230
petition
Attorney-General, approval by, 266
company, by, 266
declaration of solvency, 266

contributory, by, 408-409
creditor, by, 407-408
debenture-holder, by, 407-408
dismissal, 410
hearing, 410
Official Receiver, 409-410
presentation, 410
Registrar, 410
shareholder, 408-409
voluntary, 428-435
committee of inspection, 430-431
creditors' 430-432
reckless trading, 14
dissolution, 428
effect, 432
liquidators, 433
meetings, 408,428,429
members', 413,428,429
member, by, 408-409
when appropriate, 428
WINDING-UP BY COURT. *See* WINDING-UP.
WINDING-UP UNDER SUPERVISION. *See* WINDING-UP.
returns, 422
supervision,under, 435-436
provisional liquidator, *See* court, by.
application to court, 433

www.ingramcontent.com/pod-product-compliance
Lightning Source LLC
LaVergne TN
LVHW080025210926
848481LV00011B/3102
* 9 7 8 9 9 7 0 0 2 2 4 4 1 *